Psychology and Law

A Publication of the European
Association of Psychology and Law

Psychology and Law

International Perspectives

Edited by

Friedrich Lösel
Doris Bender
Thomas Bliesener

Alliant International University
Los Angeles Campus Library
1000 South Fremont Ave., Unit 5
Alhambra, CA 91803

Walter de Gruyter · Berlin · New York 1992

Prof. Dr. *Friedrich Lösel*, Professor and Head of Department
Dipl.-Psych. *Doris Bender*, Research Scientist
Dr. *Thomas Bliesener*, Lecturer
Department of Psychology
University of Erlangen–Nürnberg
Bismarckstr. 1
8520 Erlangen
Germany

With 45 figures and 94 tables

⊗ Printed on acid-free paper which falls within the guidelines of the ANSI to ensure permanence and durability.

Library of Congress Cataloging-in-Publication Data

> Psychology and law : international perspectives / edited by Friedrich Lösel, Doris Bender, Thomas Bliesener.
>   p.   cm.
> "Selected contributions to the Second European Conference on Law and Psychology" – Acknowledgements.
> Includes bibliographical references (p.   ) and index.
> ISBN 3-11-013725-9 (acid-free paper)
> 1. Criminal psychology. 2. Law–Psychology. 3. Correctional psychology. 4. Police psychology. I. Lösel, Friedrich.
> II. Bender, Doris, 1956–   . III. Bliesener, Thomas.
> HV6080.P827 1992
> 364.3–dc20
>   92-30454
>   CIP

Die Deutsche Bibliothek – Cataloging-in-Publication Data

> **Psychology and law** : international perspectives / ed. by Friedrich Lösel ... – Berlin ; New York : de Gruyter, 1992
>   ISBN 3-11-013725-9
>   NE: Lösel, Friedrich [Hrsg.]

© Copyright 1992 by Walter de Gruyter & Co., D-1000 Berlin 30.
All rights reserved, including those of translation into foreign languages. No part of this book may be reproduced in any form – by photoprint, microfilm, or any other means nor transmitted nor translated into a machine language without written permission from the publisher.
Printing: WB-Druck GmbH & Co. Buchproduktions KG, Rieden am Forggensee. – Binding: Dieter Mikolai, Berlin. – Cover Design: Johannes Rother, Berlin. – Printed in Germany.

Acknowledgments

The present volume contains selected contributions to the Second European Conference on Law and Psychology. A great number of persons and institutions supported the conference and the publication of this volume. They all earn our sincere thanks. We wish to thank the German Research Association (Deutsche Forschungsgemeinschaft), the German Academic Exchange Service (Deutscher Akademischer Austauschdienst), and the University of Erlangen-Nürnberg for funding. The Social Sciences Research Center of the University kindly provided the facilities for the meeting. We are grateful for the welcome addresses given by the Minister of Justice of the Federal Republic of Germany, Hans Engelhard, and by the Prorector of the University of Erlangen-Nürnberg, Günter Buttler. We also wish to thank the members of the International Advisory Board (Hans Crombag, Graham Davies, David Farrington, Uberto Gatti, Elizabeth Loftus, John Monahan, Elisabeth Müller-Luckmann, Hans Thomae, Udo Undeutsch, John Yuille) and the members of the Program Committee (Günter Bierbrauer, Wilfried Hommers, Oskar Scholz, Willi Seitz, Max Steller, Egon Stephan, Hermann Wegener). Last, but not least, thanks to Jonathan Harrow for careful translations and "native speaker advice" and to Dirk Polzin, Waltraud Symanek, and Oliver Schultheiß for text processing and editorial assistance.

The Editors

International Perspectives on Psychology and Law: An Introduction

Friedrich Lösel, Doris Bender, and Thomas Bliesener

Background

Psychology in the field of law not only has a long-standing tradition but is also characterized by a recent upswing. Research in this area has significantly intensified during the past 15 years. Heightened interest can be demonstrated through, for example, numerous monographs and anthologies, relevant special issues of psychological journals, and new interdisciplinary periodicals. National psychological societies have instituted divisions for Psychology and Law, Legal Psychology, Criminological and Legal Psychology, and so forth. The International Association of Applied Psychology has created a division "Psychology and Law", and a European Association on this topic is currently being established. Course sequences and graduate programs of legal psychology have been or are being widely developed. In some countries, psychologists are already teaching as professors in law schools.

Some of the topics psychologists are currently working on are: causes of criminal behavior; decision-making behavior among judges; reliability of eyewitness testimony; factors that determine sentencing; interaction between citizens and police; problems of drunk driving; children as witnesses and victims in child abuse cases; tax evasion; decisions in divorce proceedings; varied effects of punishment and correctional treatment; the prediction of violence; internalization of legal norms; perception of justice; assumptions underlying specific laws or general concepts such as responsibility; deterrence; and so forth. Hence, the research covers criminal law as well as other fields of law.

Furthermore, an increase in international contacts is particularly significant. We do not just see the usual one-way-transfer of information from the United States to other countries, but also initiatives stemming from Europe (e.g., Chapman, Müller, & Blackman, 1984; Farrington, Hawkins, & Lloyd-Bostock, 1979; van Koppen, Hessing, van den Heuvel, 1988; Wegener, Lösel, & Haisch, 1989). In 1988 the First European Conference on Law and Psychology was held at Maastricht (Netherlands). The conference was so stimulating that participants were encouraged to view it as the first of many regular meetings. It was a pleasure for us to organize the Second European Conference on Law and Psychology at Nürnberg (Germany) in 1990. There was a very positive reaction to our invitation. One sign of this was that the number of contributions and participants has more than trebled since the first conference. The changes in the political situation permitted a number of colleagues from East Germany and the Eastern European countries to contribute. In addition, the increased participation of colleagues from Southern Europe demonstrated that mountain ranges, language, and other barriers are also not preventing European integration in the field of legal psychology. The participation of many scientists from the United States, Canada, and other non-European countries was in line with our intention of not only promoting psychology and law in Europe but also encouraging the exchange of ideas and information within the international scientific community. This is also one of the goals in establishing the European Association of Psychology and Law that was decided upon at the Nürnberg conference.

The conference was devoted to the entire field of psychology and law; however, the following topics were especially highlighted by keynote addresses and symposia: Psychological perspectives in criminological research; intervention against criminality; psychology and the police; witness testimony; juridical decision-making; children in the justice system; psychological aspects of civil law; legal psychology in Eastern and Southern Europe; and historical aspects of legal psychology. The present volume contains a selection of contributions to the conference. The criteria for this selection were not only quality but also representativeness for the main topics as well as cross-national variety. The volume is divided into nine parts.

Contents

Part I provides an introduction to the development of legal psychology and current research in the field. *Friedrich Lösel* reports a content analysis of articles in German-language journals dealing with topics in legal psychology and provides a sketch of major international trends. He systemizes the field in a model for a comprehensive legal psychology. In addition, problems and perspectives are outlined that address the situation within legal psychology, and its relation to law science and law practice. The next two articles deal with the contribution of psychological research and applied psychology to criminology and criminal justice. Both a leading law scientist and a leading psychologist summarize the results. The field of criminology was selected for several reasons: (a) There is a strong tradition of cooperation between law and psychology in this field. (b) In recent years, as both authors show, the field has seen a particularly intensive development in psychological research. (c) Recent legal psychology shows a trend toward concentrating on forensic assessment and behavior within the justice system. However, the importance of research on "input", that is, norm-related behavior is particularly revealed in the broad field of criminological psychology. In the first of the two articles, the law scientist *Günter Kaiser* provides an overview of the historical development and the current status of psychological contributions to criminology and criminal justice. He describes fruitful fields in basic and applied research and concludes that it really is possible to talk in terms of a newly established criminological psychology. Then *David Farrington* reviews the substantial empirical findings on the explanation, prediction, prevention, and treatment of offending from a psychological perspective. His article illustrates how important it is to link together research from the fields of personality psychology, developmental psychology, social psychology, biological psychology, psychological assessment, clinical psychology, and educational psychology. He completes his article by pointing out deficits and future trends in research.

Part II presents more specific, theoretical, and empirical contributions on the explanation of offending and the assessment of offenders. It reports various developments in recent criminal psychological research. Parallel to the consolidation of knowledge in learning and personality psychology on the conditions of persistent criminality (e.g., Eysenck

& Gudjonsson, 1989; Farrington, Ohlin, & Wilson, 1986), there is an increase in research on social psychological and situational factors of norm violation (e.g., Cornish & Clarke, 1986). Alongside the traditional focus on deficits and risk factors in delinquents, research is also addressing the other side of the coin, that is, why specific persons do not behave deviantly under riskful circumstances (e.g., Bliesener & Lösel, this volume; Werner, 1990). And, finally, attempts are being made from both a theoretical as well as a practical standpoint to delineate specific offender subgroups more precisely (e.g., Chaicken & Chaicken, 1984; Loeber, Stouthamer-Loeber, Van Kammen, & Farrington, 1991). In the first article, *Thomas Fabian* and *Michael Stadler* discuss the application of ideas from chaos theory to explain affective offenses. They apply their ideas to a case report. *Thomas Bliesener* and *Friedrich Lösel* investigate under which circumstances high-risk juveniles do not become delinquent. In a study of juveniles in social welfare institutions, they test the impact and interplay of protective factors in development. *Wilhelmina Wosinska* studies the effects of a declining living standard on Polish blue-collar workers and intellectuals. Her results show that both groups are affected differently by changes in the economic situation and react to these changes in different ways. *Graham Wagstaff* presents experimental studies on the conditions and correlates of norm-violating tailgaiting in road traffic. His results make clear how much subjects overestimate the safety of their distance. *Maria Pietras* studies the links between doing harm and breaking the law. The results of her interviews confirm that harm is often not intended but is nonetheless accepted as a necessary evil. *Serge Brochu, Lyne Desjardins, Alexandra Douyon,* and *Charles Forget* address a central problem of recent crime trends, drug usage among offenders. The data in their study confirm that a high percentage of offenders have used drugs in the year prior to their offense. *Eckhardt Littmann's* article deals with the use and outcome of psychological test instruments in forensic expert testimony. His study illustrates the contribution that standardized instruments can make to psychological and psychiatric expert testimony. Finally, *Lu Chan Ching-Chuen* presents the results of a study of sexual offenders. The profiles of the rape offenders and indecent assault offenders in her study show a high incidence of prior behavioral disorders in adolescence but not a high incidence of sexual disorders.

Part III contains articles on the treatment and prevention of offending. Fifteen years after Martinson's (1974) highly publicized conclusion that "nothing works", a fresh wind is blowing through the field of offender treatment. Recent results of evaluation studies and, in particular, of integrative meta-analyses indicate moderate but nonetheless consistent effects of specific forms of intervention (e.g., Andrews, Zinger, Hoge, Bonta, Gendreau, & Cullen, 1990; Lösel & Köferl, 1989). Without calling for an exaggerated treatment ideology, attitude and behavior modifications based on empirical psychology seem to be more effective than they have appeared to be for many years. Despite all kinds of problem, constructive approaches can also be seen in the area of early intervention and primary prevention (e.g., Lösel, 1987; Schweinhart & Weikart, 1987). In the first article in Part III, *Mark Lipsey* presents the most comprehensive meta-analysis to date on the effectiveness of treating delinquency. It also shows that although mean effect sizes are low, various treatment modalities clearly differ in their degree of effectiveness. *David Lane* addresses the problem of persistent criminality in youngsters and its treatment. He presents an intervention approach that is implemented not only within the framework of individual treatment but also as classroom and school programs. Preliminary evaluations are encouraging. *James McGuire* and *Philip Priestley* also address the "nothing works" doctrine. Their review of treatment show that specific ways of treating offenders can have highly promising outcomes. *Rudolf Egg* presents an evaluation study on drug therapy. His longitudinal comparison over three years confirms a lower recidivism rate among treated drug addicts than among therapy dropouts and those who refuse treatment. *Sheilagh Hodgins*'s article deals with the treatment of mentally ill offenders. In addition to problems in forensic expert testimony, she discusses the problems of competency to stand trial, reduced criminal responsibility, and the particular need for treatment in this population. *Dieter Dölling* describes the legal, criminological, and psychological problems in conceptualizing and evaluating general measures of prevention. Alongside the difficulties in interpreting criminal statistics kept by the police or surveys of undetected crime, he discusses fundamental problems and perspectives for a general theory of prevention.

Part IV deals with psychological research on the police. It is pleasing to see that this ethically, politically, and practically difficult field of research is well represented here. In many countries, psychology still tends to be underrepresented in the multidisciplinary research on police and policing. There are numerous topics for psychological research and application, for example, police-citizen interaction; behavior in extortion and hostage taking; determinants of the decision to arrest; de-escalation in political demonstrations; offense specialisation (modus operandi system); preventive patrol and other forms of situational crime prevention; communication behavior and problems in interviewing suspects, victims, and witnesses; credibility assessment; and the training of psychological skills and stress regulation (see Bull, Bustin, Evans, & Gahagan, 1984; Lösel & Mai, 1988; Yuille, 1986). There is also a variety of possible methodological approaches ranging from participant observation to theory-driven controlled field experiments. Articles relating to the police can be found not only in Part IV but also in the following sections. Part IV commences with *John Yuille*'s overview of topics and findings in psychological research on the police. From an Anglo-American perspective, John Yuille confirms that psychological findings are already widely applied in police work. However, he also notes that there are still numerous gaps between empirical findings in basic research and the application-oriented needs of police practice. *Stephen Moston* and *Geoffrey Stephenson* analyze police interviews with suspects. Their findings show that police interview behavior can be predicted partly by case characteristics. In serious cases and those with weak evidence, detectives favor information-gathering strategies; while, in less serious cases and those with strong evidence, more confrontational strategies are observed. *Aldert Vrij* and *Frans Winkel* present experiments on the impact of culturally determined speech and gestures in police-citizen interaction. Results suggest that white police officers evaluate black people's nonverbal behavior more negatively and, in particular, as being more suspicious. *Luise Greuel* investigates the competence of police officers to detect deceptive eyewitness statements, the kinds of fault they make in their credibility evaluation, and their ideas about cues associated with rape cases. Her findings show that police officers base their credibility judgment on valid as well as invalid cues to deception. Furthermore, there is a relationship between confidence in accuracy and beliefs about cues associated with lie detection. *Geoffrey Stephenson* and *Stephen Moston* study the effect of the right of silence on the prosecution and conviction of criminal suspects. Their findings show that the use of this right has no direct effect on the decision whether to press charges or to release the suspect. However, suspects who do not respond to allegations are more likely to be charged than those who have not used their right to silence. Subjects who have used their right to silence also are just as likely to be convicted in court as a group of control cases. *Frans Winkel* and *Leendert Koppelaar* report experiments with police officers conducting interviews with rape victims and suspects. Their findings suggest perceptual biases, with credibility depending on the self-presentation styles of victims and suspects as well as on situational characteristics. There seems to be a cognitive confirmation effect, depending on the police officers' prior expectations regarding the victims.

Part V contains articles on witness testimony. This is one of the "pillars" of legal psychology in which research is particularly lively. Eyewitness testimony reveals how fruitful basic and applied research in the field of law can be, and how both science and practice can profit equally (e.g., Loftus, 1979; Loftus & Ketcham, 1991). On the other hand, this research is also evaluated controversially. In the first article in Part V, *Graham Davies* discusses the controversy surrounding the generalization and reliability of studies on witness testimony. He considers that one possible way of resolving the dilemmas here is to replicate findings across a range of paradigms. *Willem Wagenaar* and *Nancy Veefkind* study how many members on a lineup provide the most reliable outcome for eyewitness identifications. On the basis of their results, it can be concluded that one-person lineups are to be avoided as they increase the likelihood of false identifications. Looking at the other end of the scale, there are no strong arguments in favor of lineups containing more than six persons. *Michael Stadler*, *Hans Schindler*, and *Thomas Fabian* investigate how far viewing photographs of suspected offenders in the interval between witnessing an offense and appearing in court influences eyewitnesses. Their findings indicate not only that persons can be identified better from a photographic presentation than from observation in a realistic setting but also that the probability of reliably identifying a person merely on the basis of a single observation in a short-time realistic setting is very low. The topic of how the contents of memory can be influenced by post-event information is also addressed by *Hunter Hoffman, Elizabeth Loftus, Christine Greenmun*, and *Richard Dashiell*. They present a review of results and methods on a theme that has been studied intensively by E. Loftus. In an experimental study using the "modified test" method, they specify those conditions under which memory of an event is particularly vulnerable or immune to the suggestive influences of misinformations. *Debra Bekerian, John Dennett, Kathleen Hill*, and *Rosalind Hitchcock* examine the effects of memory enhancement techniques, such as detailed image instructions, on recall for a highly enriched event. They find, for example, that imagery increases the absolute amount of correct as well as incorrect information recalled by a subject. In their study on eyewitness reliability, *Norine Jalbert* and *Jeanette Getting* focus on the possible main or interactive effects on subsequent identification tasks of the race and gender of subjects and stimulus persons. Their results lend support to the notion that cross-racial identifications are more difficult and, hence, perhaps less reliable than same-race identifications. Interindividual differences in the accuracy of eyewitness testimony observed in studies are also explained partially with biological variables (such as varying degrees of basal arousal). *Margarita Diges, Maria Rubio*, and *Maria Rodriguez* suspect that indvidual differences in memory performance might vary as a function of diurnal fluctuations in arousal. They show that mornings are better for short-term and verbatim memory as well as shallow processing of material, while the evening favors delayed and prose memory as well as deep processing. *Katharina Dahmen-Zimmer* and *Martina Kraus* point out that investigations of the occurrence of possible errors in witness memory have to consider not only the physiological limits of human visual perception but also the perceptual laws controlling event perception. The authors study whether and in which way eyewitness reports on an ambivalent social situation can be distorted by erroneous causal perceptions or conclusions. *María Alonso-Quecuty* draws a parallel between imagined memories and lies, as well as between perceived memories and truth. Her study on lie detection confirms former findings that the extent of false statements is greater than that of true ones, and that pauses are associated with lying, although this only applies to delayed statements.

Part VI is dedicated to children as witnesses and victims in the justice system, mainly to the problem of child abuse. In recent years, this field has become extraordinarily topical in many countries (e.g., Perry & Wrightsman, 1991; Spencer, Nicholson, Flin, & Bull, 1990). It is a field in demand of the practical assistance of psychologists. Psychology can and should contribute to dealing effectively with this problem while simultaneously selecting a path that increases the sensitivity to these problems without overdramatizing them. At the same time, the topic is an example of the importance of the international exchange of information in legal psychology. Regulations and psychological experiences differ greatly. For example, the many years of experience in Germany with witness testimony in children could make an important contribution here (see also Undeutsch, this volume). The articles in Part VI deal not only with the great variety of legal psychological approaches but also empirical research findings. *Debra Bekerian* and *John Dennett* discuss a general class of psychological assessment procedures that are used to determine the validity/reliability of evidence given by child witnesses, namely, analyses of the information contained in the child's account. *Herman Baartman* describes how society's and, more specifically, how scientific attitudes toward the credibility of children as witnesses and toward the sexual abuse of children have changed since the turn of the century. *Dennis Howitt* points out the kinds of errors that can occur in decisions of professional helpers to the well-intended protection of children, and illustrates this with a case study. The remaining articles in this part deal with legal procedures for children as witnesses in sexual abuse cases in different countries. *Max Steller* provides a brief introduction to the individual articles as organizer of a symposium at the Nürnberg conference. Considerung the different legal procedures he stresses that although there is no one and only adequate solution, all jurisdictions could benefit by reflecting on their weak points and adopting the positive aspects of other countries' procedures. *Rhona Flin* shows that the Scottish and English legal systems are entirely separate and have many distinct features. She sets out the major sources of stress in the pretrial, trial, and posttrial phase in the accusatorial system of the United Kingdom and proposes a model for reducing stress in British courts. *Renate Volbert* presents statistics on the frequencies of charges and convictions in cases of child sexual abuse in Germany. The figures reveal a decrease in the number of charges as well as a decrease in court proceedings and convictions up to 1987 followed by a slight increase up to 1989. The author complains about the lack of information on the frequency with which children testify in court, the types of event they testify about, and the frequency with which cases are dropped, dismissed, or lead

Introduction XIII

to acquittals or convictions. She presents the results of her study on these issues. *Toril Havik* describes and laments the discrepancy between official ideals and current practices in Norway when working with child witnesses in sexual abuse cases. She also analyzes the psychologist's job as an expert witness in the courts. *Marie O'Neill* reports the most recent changes in legislature on sexual offenses in Canada. She suggests that to ensure the success of the new legal procedures, psychosocial professions in this field should be encouraged to learn more about the mechanisms of law, and legal professions should try to understand the needs of children. *Tamar Morag's* article presents the progressive revision of the Israeli law of evidence from 1955, which introduced the youth interrogator who is allowed to substitute a child witness in court. The author suspects that this child protection measure might be responsible for relatively low conviction rates in Israel. A further change in laws on sexual abuse is reported by *Sandra McPherson* for the United States. The Child Abuse Prevention and Treatment Act of 1974 made provision for the appointment of a guardian ad litem (GAL) in every juvenile court case involving child abuse. The author discusses the cooperation with the professions involved in these cases before the court and sets out proposals for improvements.

Part VII deals with juridical procedures and decision making. This is one of the areas that has received a lot of attention in legal psychology over the last 20 years (e.g., Hans & Vidmar, 1986; Saks & Hastie, 1978). On the one hand, it concerns research into the numerous determinants of decisons that can lead to very different outcomes within the framework and bandwidths of legal regulations (and hence also lead to regional, ethnic, person-specific, and other inequalities). On the other hand, it involves more basic issues such as which forms of proceedings facilitate fact finding and which facilitate perceived justice (e.g., Thibaut & Walker, 1975). This area of research, which has already been marked out by H. Münsterberg (1908), has made advances by applying the methods of experimental social psychology. Nonetheless, deficits in closeness to reality and problems of external validity are also addressed. In the first article in Part VII, *Vladimir Konečni* and *Ebbe Ebbesen* discuss general methodological issues in research on legal decision-making and pay particular attention to the role of experimental simulation. They illustrate the problems involved with examples of jury selection and eyewitness testimony in the United States. They recommend the archival methodology. Although it is the most work-intensive, they consider it to be the best method for obtaining research findings with high external validity. In her study, *Margit Oswald* shows that judges' attitudes toward the general goals of punishment (utilitarian vs. retributional position) and their willingness to adopt the perspective of the victim or the offender play a major role in their judgment processes. By assessing individual goals of punishment, she is able to make predictions about punitiveness and inclinations to attribute guilt. *Ramón Arce, Jorge Sobral*, and *Francisca Fariña* also address judges' decision-making. They compare the sentencing behavior of mock juries that have been grouped together according to attribution profiles (internal vs. external) and ideological profiles (conservative vs. progressive). *Michael Bagby* and *Robert Nicholson* evaluate two scales for assessing fitness to stand trial. They conclude that the use of standardized psycholegal measures reduces the influence of nonlegal demographic variables in the determination of fitness. The contribution by *David Carson* addresses problems of the role of expert witnesses in the trial procedure. It focuses on the issue that the court has to decide and on the validity of expert evidence. From the perspective of a law scientist with sound knowledge of legal psychology, the author gives reasons for limiting the role of expert witnesses. However, the paper contains not only critical analyses but also concrete proposals to renegogiate the role of experts.

Part VIII deals with forensic psychology in civil law. Compared to criminal law, this field is underrepresented in psycholegal research. The articles collected here are correspondingly more heterogeneous than those in other parts. *Adelheid Kühne* reviews differences in the legal situation of children in Germany, Austria, Switzerland, England, and Spain from a psychological perspective. *Marie-Luise Kluck* describes the individual steps that are necessary in the diagnostic process of constructing an expert testimony in the area of family law. *Wilfried Hommers* studies the development of tort law competences in minors, namely, their capability of knowing right from wrong, and their understanding of the duty to make recompense. His results support the 7-year age limit imposed by the German civil code as well as its legal implications. *Dick Hessing, Henk Elffers*, and *Frank de Charro* discuss the problem of the legal regulation of organ donations. Their survey findings indicate upper limits in the willingness to donate organs in the population. The authors use these findings as a basis for plotting 12 possible legal systems for the donation of organs and computing the probabilities of the consequences of the individual systems with the inclusion of a decision-making option for relatives. Part VIII ends with an article from *Martin Usteri* and *Georges Baur* that presents an example of psychoanalytical approaches in legal psychology. They use examples from civil and criminal law to describe how unconscious impulses can have an effect in law. Unconscious phenomena are interpreted with the aid of elements (e.g., archetypes) and methods (e.g., amplificatory method) from Jungian psychology.

Part IX of this volume contains contributions on the development and history of legal psychology in different European countries. As the development of legal psychology in the international scientific community has been documented repeatedly, particularly for the Anglo-American field (e.g., Monahan & Loftus, 1982; Tapp, 1976), we wanted to present examples that provide information on other countries. On the one hand, we have selected examples from Southern and Eastern Europe, as, in previous years, "Europe" frequently ended at the Alps or the Iron Curtain for the majority of the scientific community. On the other hand, there are also two contributions from the German-speaking countries in which a long tradition of legal psychology does exist. *Udo Undeutsch* gives an overview of the development of forensic psychology in Germany since the beginning of the century. His historical review highlights the impact that advances in psychological research on eyewitness testimony and the assessment of cognitive and volitional capacity have had on legal thinking and proceedings. The development of legal psychology in Austria and Switzerland is portrayed by *Raimund Jakob*. His overview also gives an impression of some links between psychoanalysis and law in German-speaking countries. *Vicente Garrido* and *Santiago Redondo* discuss the development and current state of legal psychology in Spain. Their contribution emphasizes that Spanish legal psychology is, in many respects, still at an early stage of development. On the other hand, they show what important progress can be observed in research and practice over the last 10 years. The situation of law and psychology in Italy is depicted by *Giovanni Traverso* and *Paola Manna*. Their article analyzes developments in the field of forensic psychology over the last 30 years. It also

Introduction XV

gives an overview of recent theoretical issues, research, and practice in Italian criminal psychology. In the last contribution to this volume, *Jan Stanik* attempts to set in order both the terminology and subject matter of psychology as applied to the area of law in Poland. He discusses the different directions and spheres that have appeared in the application of psychology to law in his country.

General Trends

The nine parts demonstrate not only that traditional fields of legal psychology are alive and well but also that new areas are developing. Besides the specific topics addressed in the articles, they reveal some more general trends. These refer, for example, to:

Internationalization of perspectives. Particularly in a field with such strong cultural determination as the law, there is an urgent need for international exchange and a comparison of findings from more than one legal system. This concerns not only formal differences in procedure, such as the adversary or inquisitorial system, but also differences that are possibly more general, such as variations in legal socialization, the status of children, or attitudes toward punishment in one society (see, e.g., the factual functioning of Japanese law that is based partially on the German tradition). While both aspects can have a strong impact on respective findings, perspectives from different cultures can contribute to the generalization of findings and practical innovations.

Variety of research topics. As the editors of *Human Behavior and Law* have determined repeatedly (Roesch, 1990; Saks, 1986) and content analyses of other journals have also shown (Kagehiro & Laufer, 1992; Lösel, 1989), the majority of empirical research has been restricted to just a few areas such as eyewitness testimony, jury decision-making, criminal procedure, and mental health. Therefore, preserving those branches on which we have been sitting safely up to now as well as raising new thematic seedlings in the field of psychology and law is an important task.

Sensitivity for methodological problems. One of the main reasons for the recent success of research on psychology and law has been the rigorous application of trusted methods of basic research like the laboratory experiment. However, it has become increasingly evident that problems of sampling, instruments, and laboratory simulations have cast doubt on the external validity and generalization of many studies (King, 1986). Hence, a self-critical discussion on methods, studies that are close to law in practice, and a greater variety of methods in the sense of critical multiplism (Cook, 1985) are major developments.

Exchange between research and practice. As in other fields of applied psychology, research findings in psychology and law often contain rather indirect advice for practice. The latter is often restricted to a handed-down praxeology that is not supported by theory-driven, problem-oriented research (Lloyd-Bostock, 1988). Processing the variety of problems involved in the integration and transfer of detailed empirical findings to complex psychological technologies is necessary to have a practical impact (Monahan & Walker, 1985).

Relationship to law science. Psychologists have strengthened not only their research on legal topics but also their knowledge and understanding of the law and its procedures. Vice versa, legal science seems to be showing more of an open attitude toward psychological contributions and perspectives. However, "natural" conflicts remain (Carson, 1988; Melton, 1987). It is becoming increasingly clear, that a surface acceptance is not the ultimate goal. Difficulties should be dealt with in the most constructive way on both sides to improve our understanding of the law.

Coping with these problems is a major task for psychology and law in the 1990s. Although the present volume certainly contains no definite solutions, its contributions present a variety of steps and efforts that tackle these and other current issues.

References

Andrews, D.A., Zinger, I., Hoge, R.D., Bonta J., Gendreau, P., & Cullen, F.T. (1990). Does correctional treatment work? A clinically relevant and psychologically informed meta-analysis. *Criminology, 28,* 369-404.

Bull, R., Bustin, B., Evans, P., & Gahagan, D. (1984). *Psychology for police officers.* Chichester: Wiley.

Carson, D. (1988). Psychologists should be wary of involvement with lawyers. In P.J. van Koppen, D.J. Hessing, & G. van den Heuvel (Eds.), *Lawyers on psychology and psychologists on law* (pp. 28-34). Amsterdam: Swets & Zeitlinger.

Chaiken, M.R. & Chaiken, J.M. (1984). Offender types and public policy. *Crime and Delinquency, 30,* 195-226.

Chapman, A., Müller, D.J., & Blackman, D.E. (Eds.)(1984). Some applications of psychology to law (special issue). *International Review of Applied Psychology, 33 (1).*

Cook, T.D. (1985). Post-positivist critical multiplism. In L. Shotland, & M.M. Mark (Eds.), *Social science and social policy* (pp. 21-62). Beverly Hills, CA: Sage.

Cornish, D.B., & Clarke, R.V. (Eds.)(1986). *The reasoning criminal. Rational choice perspectives of offending.* New York: Springer.

Eysenck, H.J., & Gudjonsson, G.H. (1989). *The causes and cures of criminality.* New York: Plenum Press.

Farrington, D.P., Hawkins, K., & Lloyd-Bostock, S.M. (Eds.)(1979). *Psychology, law, and legal processes.* London: Macmillan.

Farrington, D.P., Ohlin, L.E., & Wilson, J.Q. (1986). *Understanding and controlling crime.* New York: Springer.

Hans, V.P., & Vidmar, N. (1986). *Judging the jury.* New York: Plenum.

Kagehiro, D.K., & Laufer, W.S. (1992). Preface. In D.K. Kagehiro, & W.S. Laufer (Eds.), *Handbook of psychology and law* (pp. XI-XIII). New York: Springer.

King, M. (1986). *Psychology in and out of court. A critical examination of legal psychology.* Oxford: Pergamon.

Lloyd-Bostock, S.M.A. (1988). *Law in practice.* London: The British Psychological Society and Routledge.

Loeber, R., Stouthamer-Loeber, M.S., Van Kammen, W., & Farrington, D.P. (1991). Initiation, escalation, and desistance in juvenile offending and their correlates. *Journal of Criminal Law and Criminology, 82,* 36-82.

Lösel, F. (1987). Psychological crime prevention: Concepts, evaluations, and perspectives. In K. Hurrelmann, F.X. Kaufmann, & F. Lösel (Eds.), *Social intervention: Potential and constraints* (pp. 290-313). Berlin, New York: de Gruyter.

Lösel, F. (1989). Zur neueren Entwicklung der Rechtspsychologie: Versuch einer Standortbestimmung.[On recent developments in legal psychology: Trying to determine where we are]. In W. Schönpflug (Ed.), *Bericht über den 36. Kongreß der Deutschen Gesellschaft für Psychologie in Berlin*, Vol. 2 (pp. 291-306). Göttingen: Hogrefe.

Lösel, F., & Köferl, P. (1989). Evaluation research on correctional treatment in West Germany: A meta-analysis. In H. Wegener, F. Lösel, & J. Haisch (Eds.), *Criminal behavior and the justice system* (pp. 334-355). New York: Springer.

Lösel, F., & Mai, K. (1988). Polizei [Police]. In D. Frey, C.G. Hoyos, & D. Stahlberg (Eds.), *Angewandte Psychologie* [Applied psychology](pp. 363-385). München: Psychologie Verlags Union.

Loftus, E.F. (1979). *Eyewitness testimony*. Cambridge, MA: Harvard University Press.

Loftus, E.F. & Ketcham, K. (1991). *Witness for defense: The accused, the eyewitness, and the expert who puts memory on trial*. New York: St Martin's Press.

Martinson, R. (1974). What works? Questions and answers about prison reform. *Public Interest, 10*, 22-54.

Melton, G. (1987). Bringing psychology to the legal system. Opportunities, obstacles, and efficacy. *American Psychologist, 42*, 488-495.

Monahan, J. & Loftus, E. (1982). The psychology of law. *Annual Review of Psychology, 33*, 441-475.

Monahan, J., & Walker, L. (1985). *Social science in law: Cases and materials*. Mineola, NY: The Foundation Press.

Münsterberg, H. (1908). *On the witness stand: Essays on psychology and crime*. New York: Clark, Boardman, Doubleday.

Perry, N.W., & Wrightsman, L.S. (1990). *When children take the stand*. Newbury Park, CA: Sage.

Roesch, R. (1990). From the editor. *Law and Human Behavior, 14*, 1-3.

Saks, M.J. (1986). The law does not live by eyewitness testimony alone. *Law and Human Behavior, 10*, 279-280.

Saks, M.J., & Hastie, R. (1978). *Social psychology in court*. New York: Van Nostrand.

Schweinhart, L.J., & Weikart, D.P. (1987). Evidence of problem prevention by early childhood education. In K. Hurrelmann, F.-X. Kaufmann, & F. Lösel (Eds.), *Social intervention: Potential and constraints* (pp. 87-101). Berlin, New York: de Gruyter.

Spencer, J., Nicholson, G., Flin, R., & Bull, R. (Eds.) (1990). *Children's evidence in legal proceedings*. Available from Cambridge University Law Faculty.

Tapp, J.L. (1976). Psychology and law: An overture. *Annual Review of Psychology, 27*, 359-404.

Thibaut, J., & Walker, L. (1975). *Procedural justice. A psychological analysis*. Hillsdale, NJ: Erlbaum.

Van Koppen, P.J., Hessing, D.J., & van den Heuvel, G. (Eds.)(1988). *Lawyers on psychology and psychologists on law*. Amsterdam: Swets & Zeitlinger.

Wegener, H., Lösel, F., & Haisch, J. (Eds.)(1989). *Criminal behavior and the justice system: Psychological perspectives*. New York: Springer.

Werner, E.E. (1990). Antecedents and consequences of deviant behavior. In K. Hurrelmann & F. Lösel (Eds.), *Health hazards in adolescence* (pp. 219-231). Berlin, New York: de Gruyter.

Yuille, J.C. (Ed.)(1986). *Police selection and training: The role of psychology*. Dordrecht: Nijhoff.

Contents

International Perspectives on Psychology and Law: An Introduction VII
F. Lösel, D. Bender, and T. Bliesener

Contributors XXV

Part I: General Perspectives

Psychology and Law: Overtures, Crescendos, and Reprises
F. Lösel 3

Psychological Contributions to Criminology: Perspectives of a Law Scientist
G. Kaiser 22

Psychological Contributions to the Explanation, Prevention, and Treatment of Offending
D. P. Farrington 35

Part II: Explanation of Offending and Assessment of Offenders

Applying Chaos Theory to Delinquent Behavior in Psychosocial Stress Situations
T. Fabian and M. Stadler 55

Resilience in Juveniles With High Risk of Delinquency
T. Bliesener and F. Lösel 62

Violation of Rules as a Reaction to Declining Living Standards Among Workers and Intellectuals
W. Wosinska 76

What Constitutes Reckless Driving? A Psychological Study of Motor Vehicle Following Distances
G. F. Wagstaff 86

Between Doing Harm and Breaking the Law: A Social-Psychological Perspective
M. Pietras 95

Drug Use Prevalence Among Offenders
S. Brochu, L. Desjardins, A. Douyon, and C. Forget 105

Using Psychological Tests in the Forensic Assessment of Offenders
E. Littmann 111

Profiles of Incarcerated Offenders Convicted of Rape and Indecent
Assault: An Exploratory Study
Lu Chan C.-C. 121

Part III: Treatment and Prevention of Offending

The Effect of Treatment on Juvenile Delinquents: Results from
Meta-Analysis
M. W. Lipsey 131

Intervention in Persistent Criminality in Children
D. A. Lane 144

Some Things Do Work: Psychological Interventions With Offenders
and the Effectiveness Debate
J. McGuire and P. Priestley 163

Therapy Versus Penalty: An Evaluation Study
R. Egg 175

The Treatment of Mentally Disordered Offenders in Canada
S. Hodgins 182

General Prevention: Criminological and Psychological Problems
D. Dölling 193

Part IV: Psychological Research on the Police

Psychologists and the Police
J. C. Yuille 205

Predictors of Suspect and Interviewer Behaviour During Police Questioning
S. J. Moston and G. M. Stephenson 212

Perceived Credibility of the Communicator: Studies of Perceptual Bias
in Police Officers Conducting Rape Interviews
F. W. Winkel and L. Koppelaar 219

Police Officers' Beliefs About Cues Associated With Deception in Rape Cases
L. Greuel 234

Police-Citizen Interaction and Nonverbal Communication: The Impact of
Culturally Determined Smiling and Gestures
A. Vrij and F. W. Winkel 240

The Effect of the Right to Silence on the Prosecution and Conviction
of Criminal Suspects
G. M. Stephenson and S. J. Moston 253

Part V: Research on Witness Testimony

Influencing Public Policy on Eyewitnessing: Problems and Possibilities
G. Davies 265

Comparison of One-Person and Many-Person Lineups: A Warning
Against Unsafe Practices
W. A. Wagenaar and N. Veefkind 275

The Influence of Eyewitness Observation and Photographic Presentation
on the Identification of Persons in Lineups
M. Stadler, H. Schindler, and T. Fabian 286

The Generation of Misinformation
H. G. Hoffman, E. F. Loftus, C. N. Greenmun, and R. L. Dashiell 292

Effects of Detailed Imagery on Simulated Witness Recall
D. A. Bekerian, J. L. Dennett, K. Hill, and R. Hitchcock 302

Racial and Gender Issues in Facial Recognition
N. L. Jalbert and J. Getting 309

Eyewitness Memory and Time of Day
M. Diges, M. E. Rubio, and M. C. Rodriguez 317

"Phenomenal Causality" in Eyewitness Report
K. Dahmen-Zimmer and M. Kraus 321

Deception Detection and Reality Monitoring: A New Answer to an
Old Question?
M. L. Alonso-Quecuty 328

Part VI: Children as Witnesses and Victims in the Justice System

The Truth in Content Analyses of a Child's Testimony
D. A. Bekerian and J. L. Dennett 335

The Credibility of Children as Witnesses and the Social Denial of the
Incestuous Abuse of Children
H. E. M. Baartman 345

Injustice to Children and Families in Child Abuse Cases
D. Howitt 352

Child Witnesses in Sexual Abuse Cases: Psychological Implications
of Legal Procedures
M. Steller 360

Child Witnesses in British Courts
R. H. Flin 365

Child Witnesses in Sexual Abuse Cases: The Juridical Situation in Germany
R. Volbert 374

Children's Evidence in Child Abuse Proceedings under the Israeli Legal
System: The Law of Evidence Revision
T. Morag 385

Official Ideals and Current Practice in Work With Child Witnesses in
Sexual Abuse Cases in Norway
T. Havik 393

Juridical Situation of Child Witnesses in Canada
M. J. O'Neill 399

Some Areas of Interface Between Psychology and the Guardian Ad Litem
Programs in Juvenile and Domestic Relations Settings
S. B. McPherson 404

Part VII: Juridical Procedures and Decision-Making

Methodological Issues in Research on Legal Decision-Making, With
Special Reference to Experimental Simulations
V. J. Konečni and E. B. Ebbesen 413

Justification and Goals of Punishment and the Attribution of Responsibility
in Judges
M. E. Oswald 424

Verdicts of Psychosocially Biased Juries
R. Arce, J. Sobral, and F. Fariña 435

Psychometric Evaluation of Two Scales Assessing Fitness to Stand Trial
R. M. Bagby and R. Nicholson 440

Beyond the Ultimate Issue
D. Carson 447

Part VIII: Forensic Psychology in Civil Law

The Child in the European Legal System
A. Kühne 467

Diagnostic Judgment on Parental Custody as a Decision-Making Process
M. L. Kluck 473

Fire-Setting: Age Trends and Psychometrical Diagnosis of Competency Criteria for Liability
W. Hommers 477

The Legislation of Organ Donation
D. J. Hessing, H. Elffers, and F. T. de Charro 491

Jung's Psychology Adopted in Law
M. Usteri and G. Baur 500

Part IX: History and Development of Legal Psychology in Different Countries

Highlights of the History of Forensic Psychology in Germany
U. Undeutsch 509

On the Development of Psychologically Oriented Legal Thinking in German Speaking Countries
R. Jakob 519

Psychology and Law in Spain
V. Garrido and S. Redondo 526

Law and Psychology in Italy
G. B. Traverso and P. Manna 535

Psychology and Law in Poland
J. M. Stanik 546

Subject Index 555

Contributors

Alonso-Quecuty, María L., Departamento de Psicologia Cognitiva, Social y Organizacional, Universidad de La Laguna, Tenerife, Canary Islands

Arce, Ramón, Facultade de Psicoloxia, Universitade de Santiago de Compostela, Campus Universitario, Santiago de Compostela, Spain

Baartman, Herman E.M., Faculty of Psychology and Pedagogics, Free University Amsterdam, Van der Boechorststraat 1, 1081 BT Amsterdam, The Netherlands

Bagby, R. Michael, Clarke Institute of Psychiatry, 250 College Street, Toronto, Ontario M5T 1R8, Canada

Baur, Georges, Juristische Abteilung der Universität Zürich, Rennweg 10, 8001 Zürich, Switzerland

Bekerian, Debra A., MRC Applied Psychology Unit, 15 Chaucer Road, Cambridge CB2 2EF, England

Bender, Doris, Institut für Psychologie, Universität Erlangen-Nürnberg, Bismarckstrasse 1, 8520 Erlangen, Germany

Bliesener, Thomas, Institut für Psychologie, Universität Erlangen-Nürnberg, Bismarckstrasse 1, 8520 Erlangen, Germany

Brochu, Serge, International Centre for Comparative Criminology, University of Montreal, P.O. Box 6128, Succ. A, Montréal, Québec H3C 3J7, Canada

Carson, David, Faculty of Law, University of Southampton, Highfield, Southampton SO9 5NH, England

Charro de, Frank T., Faculty of Law, Erasmus University Rotterdam, P.O.Box 1738, 3000 DR Rotterdam, The Netherlands

Dahmen-Zimmer, Katharina, Institut für Psychologie, Universität Regensburg, Universitätsstrasse 31, 8400 Regensburg, Germany

Dashiell, Richard L., Department of Psychology, University of Washington, 231 Guthrie Hall, Seattle, Washington 98195, USA

Davies, Graham M., Department of Psychology, University of Leicester, University Road, Leicester LE1 7RH, England

Dennett, John L., MRC Applied Psychology Unit, 15 Chaucer Road, Cambridge CB2 2EF, England

Desjardins, Lyne, International Centre for Comparative Criminology, University of Montreal, P.O. Box 6128, Succ. A, Montréal, Québec H3C 3J7, Canada

Diges, Margarita, Facultad de Psicologia, Universidad Autonoma de Madrid, Ciudad Universitaria de Canto Blanco, 28049 Madrid, Spain

Dölling, Dieter, Juristisches Seminar, Universität Heidelberg, Friedrich-Ebert-Anlage 6-10, 6900 Heidelberg, Germany

Douyon, Alexandra, International Centre for Comparative Criminology, University of Montreal, P.O. Box 6128, Succ. A, Montréal, Québec H3C 3J7, Canada

Ebbesen, Ebbe B., Department of Psychology, University of California, San Diego, C-009, La Jolla, California 92093, USA

Egg, Rudolf, Kriminologische Zentralstelle e.V., Adolfsallee 32, 6200 Wiesbaden, Germany

Elffers, Henk, Faculty of Law, Erasmus University Rotterdam, P.O.Box 1738, 3000 DR Rotterdam, The Netherlands

Fabian, Thomas, Bremer Institut für Gerichtspsychologie, Friedrich-Ebert-Strasse 116, 2800 Bremen 1, Germany

Fariña, Francisca, Facultade de Psicoloxia, Universitade de Santiago de Compostela, Campus Universitario, Santiago de Compostela, Spain

Farrington, David P., Institute of Criminology, Cambridge University, 7 West Road, Cambridge CB3 9DT, England

Flin, Rhona H., Robert Gordon Institute of Technology, Faculty of Management, Kepplestone House, Viewfield Road, Aberdeen AB9 2PW, Scotland

Forget, Charles, International Centre for Comparative Criminology, University of Montreal, P.O. Box 6128, Succ. A, Montréal, Québec H3C 3J7, Canada

Garrido, Vicente, Departamento de Teoria de la Educación, Facultad de Filosofía y Educación. Avda., Blasco Ibanez, 21, 46010 Valencia, Spain

Getting, Jeanette, Department of Psychology, Western Connecticut State University, 181 White Street, Danbury, CT 06810, USA

Greenmun, Christine N., Department of Psychology, University of Washington, 231 Guthrie Hall, Seattle, Washington 98195, USA

Greuel, Luise, Psychologisches Institut der Universität Bonn, Römerstrasse 164, 5300 Bonn 1, Germany

Havik, Toril, Center for Advanced Studies in Child Welfare, University of Bergen, Fr. Meltzersgt. 34, 5007 Bergen, Norway

Hessing, Dick J., Faculty of Law, Erasmus University Rotterdam, P.O.Box 1738, 3000 DR Rotterdam, The Netherlands

Hill, Kathleen, Cambridge University, 7 West Road, Cambridge CB3 9DT, England

Hitchcock, Rosalind, Cambridge University, 7 West Road, Cambridge CB3 9DT, England

Hodgins, Sheilagh, Institute Philippe Pinel De Montréal, 10 905 est, Boulevard Henri-Bourassa, Montréal, Québec H1C 1H1, Canada

Hoffman, Hunter G., Department of Psychology, University of Washington, 231 Guthrie Hall, Seattle, Washington 98195, USA

Hommers, Wilfried, Institut für Psychologie, Universität Würzburg, Domerschulstrasse 13, 8700 Würzburg, Germany

Howitt, Dennis, Department of Social Sciences, Loughborough University, Loughborough, Leicestershire LE11 3TU, England

Jakob, Raimund, Lehrkanzel für Rechtsphilosophie, Universität Salzburg, Franziskanergasse 2, 5020 Salzburg, Austria

Jalbert, Norine L., Department of Psychology, Western Connecticut State University, 181 White Street, Danbury, CT 06810, USA

Kaiser, Günther, Max-Planck-Institut für ausländisches und internationales Strafrecht, Günterstalstrasse 73, 7800 Freiburg i.Br., Germany
Kluck, Marie-Luise, Sanddornweg 50, 4330 Mülheim an der Ruhr 13, Germany
Konečni, Vladimir J., Department of Psychology, University of California, San Diego, C-009, La Jolla, California 92093, USA
Koppelaar, Leendert, Vrije Universiteit, Sociale Psychologie, De Boelelaan 1081, 1081 HV Amsterdam, The Netherlands
Kraus, Martina, Institut für Psychologie, Universität Regensburg, Universitätsstrasse 31, 8400 Regensburg, Germany
Kühne, Adelheid, Universität Hannover, Bismarckstrasse 2, 3000 Hannover 1, Germany
Lane, David A., Professional Development Foundation, Studio 21, Limehouse Cut, Morris Road, London E14 6NT, England
Lipsey, Mark W., Psychology Department, Claremont Graduate School, 241 E. Eleventh St., Claremont, California 9177, USA
Littmann, Eckhard, Zentrum für Nervenheilkunde, Medizinische Fakultät (Charité) der Humboldt-Universität zu Berlin, Abt. f. Forensische Psychiatrie und Psychologie, Schumannstrasse 20/21, O-1040 Berlin, Germany
Lösel, Friedrich, Institut für Psychologie, Universität Erlangen-Nürnberg, Bismarckstrasse 1, 8520 Erlangen, Germany
Loftus, Elizabeth F., Department of Psychology, University of Washington, 231 Guthrie Hall, Seattle, Washington 98195, USA
Lu Chan, Ching-Chuen, Correctional Services Department, Headquarters, 24/F Wanchai Tower I, 12 Harbour Road, Wanchai, Hong Kong
Manna, Paola, Dipartimento Di Scienze Medico-Legali, Policlinico "Le Scotte", University of Siena, 53100 Siena, Italy
McGuire, James, Department of Clinical Psychology, University of Liverpool, P.O.Box 147, Ashton Street, Liverpool L69 3BX, England
McPherson, Sandra B., University Mednet, 3609 Park East Suite 305, Beachwood, Ohio 44122, USA
Morag, Tamar, National Council for the Child, Center for the Child and the Law, 20A, Radak St., Jerusalem 92186, Israel
Moston, Stephen J., Faculty of Social Sciences, Psychology Department, Deakin University, Geelong, Victoria, Australia 3217
O'Neill, Marie J., Family & Community Services, City Center, Hindmarsh Square, Adelaide SA 5000, Australia
Nicholson, Robert, University of Tulsa, Tulsa, Oklahoma 74100, USA
Oswald, Margit, Kriminologisches Forschungsinstitut Niedersachsen e.V., Leisewitzstrasse 41, 3000 Hannover, Germany
Pietras, Maria, Department of Social Psychology of Education, University of Silesia, Ul.Tyszki 53, 40-126 Katowice, Poland
Priestley, Philip, Peace Close, West Horrington, Wells, Somerset BA5 2ED, England
Rodriguez, Maria C., Facultad de Psicologia, Universidad Autonoma de Madrid, Ciudad Universitaria de Canto Blanco, 28049 Madrid, Spain

Rubio, Maria E., Facultad de Psicologia, Universidad Autonoma de Madrid, Ciudad Universitaria de Canto Blanco, 28049 Madrid, Spain

Schindler, Hans, Institut für Kognitionspsychologie, Universität Bremen, Postfach 330440, 2800 Bremen 33, Germany

Sobral, Jorge, Facultade de Psicoloxia, Universitade de Santiago de Compostela, Campus Universitario, Santiago de Compostela, Spain

Stadler, Michael, Institut für Kognitionspsychologie, Universität Bremen, Postfach 330440, 2800 Bremen 33, Germany

Stanik, Jan M., Silesian University, Ul. Tyszki 53, 40-126 Katowice, Poland

Steller, Max, Institut für Forensische Psychiatrie, Freie Universität Berlin, Limonenstrasse 27, 1000 Berlin 45, Germany

Stephenson, Geoffrey M., Institute of Social and Applied Psychology, University of Kent, Canterbury, Kent, CT2 7LZ, England

Traverso, Giovanni B., Dipartimento Di Scienze Medico-Legali, Policlinico "Le Scotte", University of Siena, 53100 Siena, Italy

Undeutsch, Udo, Psychologisches Institut, Universität zu Köln, Herbert-Lewin-Strasse 2, 5000 Köln, Germany

Usteri, Martin, Juristische Abteilung der Universität Zürich, Rennweg 10, 8001 Zürich, Switzerland

Veefkind, Nancy, Faculty of Social Sciences, Unit of Experimental and Theoretical Psychology, Leiden University, P.O.Box 9555, 2300 RB Leiden, The Netherlands

Volbert, Renate, Institut für Forensische Psychiatrie der FU Berlin, Limonenstrasse 27, 1000 Berlin 45, Germany

Vrij, Aldert, Vrije Universiteit, De Boelelaan 1081, 1081 HV Amsterdam, The Netherlands

Wagenaar, Willem A., Faculty of Social Sciences, Unit of Experimental and Theoretical Psychology, Leiden University, P.O.Box 9555, 2300 RB Leiden, The Netherlands

Wagstaff, Graham F., Department of Psychology, University of Liverpool, Eleanor Rathbone Building, PO.BOX 147, Liverpool L69 3BX, England

Winkel, Frans W., Vrije Universiteit, Sociale Psychologie, De Boelelaan 1081, 1081 HV Amsterdam, The Netherlands

Wosinska, Wilhelmina, Department of Social Psychology of Education, University of Silesia, Ul. Tyszki 53, 40-126 Katowice, Poland

Yuille, John C., Department of Psychology, University of British Columbia, 2136 West Mall, 2 Vancouver, B.C. V6T 1Y7, Canada

Part I
General Perspectives

Psychology and Law: Overtures, Crescendos, and Reprises

Friedrich Lösel

About 15 years ago, Tapp (1976) published an article in the *Annual Review of Psychology* entitled "Psychology and Law: An Overture." This programmatic formulation is somewhat misleading insofar as it neglects the long tradition in the research and practice of legal psychology, exemplified since the beginning of this century by the work of pioneers like H. Gross (1898), W. Stern (1903), A. Binet (1905), C.G. Jung (1905), M. Wertheimer (1906), O. Lipmann (1906), H. Münsterberg (1908), K. Marbe (1913), and others. And, even more recently, there have been various activities in legal psychology, particularly in the fields of forensic and criminal psychology (e.g., Toch, 1961; Undeutsch, 1967; see also Kaiser, this volume; Undeutsch, this volume). Hence, the overture should be understood less as a beginning and more as a revival, or to retain the musical metaphor, as a reprise. Nonetheless, Tapp's formulation is appropriate insofar as it was followed by a strong expansion of legal psychology, which Monahan and Loftus (1982) have already referred to as a "crescendo" in their article in the *Annual Review of Psychology*.

Some Data on Recent Legal Psychology

The recent international "flourishing" of forensic psychology, criminal psychology, legal psychology, or psychology and law is widely confirmed. It is revealed in the great number of monographs and edited books (e.g., Bartol, 1983; Farrington, Hawkins, & Lloyd-Bostock, 1979; Kagehiro & Laufer, 1992; Lipsitt & Sales, 1980; Lloyd-Bostock, 1988; Monahan & Walker, 1985; Müller, Blackman, & Chapman, 1984; Scheirer & Hammonds, 1983; Tapp & Levine, 1978; van Koppen, Hessing, & van den Heuvel, 1988; Wegener, Lösel, & Haisch, 1989; Weiner & Hess, 1987). Relevant journals have been established (e.g., Law and Human Behavior; Behavioral Science and the Law; Law and Psychology Review; Mental Health and Criminal Behaviour; Expert Evidence), and other journals have published special issues on the subject (e.g., Applied Social Psychology Review; Journal of Personality and Social Psychology; Journal of Social Issues; International Review of Applied Psychology). Psychological associations have set up relevant divisions, for example, in Great Britain in 1979, the USA in 1981, and in Germany in 1984. Particularly in the United States, but also in other countries, graduate courses or postgraduate programs in legal psychology have been established (Freeman & Roesch, 1992; Grisso, Sales, & Bayless, 1982). International conferences have been held, for example, at Oxford, Swansea, Braunschweig, Maastricht, Nürnberg, Maratea, and Amsterdam. In some countries, even law faculties have dedicated chairs to legal psychology (Crombag, 1989; Melton, Monahan, & Saks, 1987).

Signs of an activation or reactivation of research in legal psychology are also recognizable in Germany. Roughly 15 years after the publication of Undeutsch's (1967) handbook on forensic psychology, there has been an increase in the number of German language monographs and edited books on psychology and law (e.g., Amelang, 1986; Dettenborn, Fröhlich, & Szewczyk, 1984; Egg, 1991; Hommers, 1991; Kette, 1987; Kühne, 1988; Lösel, 1983; Schneider, 1981; Seitz, 1983; Wegener, 1981). The legal psychology division of the German Psychological Association has organized some of the above-mentioned and other conferences at Würzburg, Wiesbaden, and Berlin. Nearly 20 percent of the psychological departments at universities offer regular courses in legal psychology (e.g., in Berlin, Bremen, Braunschweig, Erlangen-Nürnberg, Freiburg, Hannover, Kiel, Köln, Mainz, Osnabrück, and Würzburg). There is a postgraduate program in criminology at the University of Hamburg. University programs for the whole field of psychology and law are being developed (see Hommers, Bierbrauer, Lösel, Rolinski, Scholz, & Steller, 1991; Lösel, 1992). In nonuniversity research institutes, such as the Max Planck Institute for Foreign and International Criminal Law (Freiburg) the Niedersachsen Criminological Research Institute (Hannover), or the Central Criminological Office (Wiesbaden), psychologists are playing an important role. While psychology in the field of law has long stood in the background compared to sociology (Kaiser, 1988; Kury, 1983; Lösel, 1983), Berckhauer (1988) has determined in his bibliography on criminology that psychologically oriented contributions are gaining ground in recent times.

Such indicators of a certain flourishing of legal psychology can also be confirmed in a more systematic analysis of selected German-language journals. In a small study, we have analyzed for the years 1950 to 1989 a total of 33 journals in which psychologists publish their articles and in which articles on legal psychology could be anticipated.* A total of 569 articles were found that dealt with topics of legal psychology in the broadest sense (and were written by a psychologist or psychologically oriented author of related sciences). Each article was assigned to the categories "empirical" or "nonempirical." Empirical articles reported studies on samples of persons; nonempirical articles covered, for example, theoretical papers, reviews, discussions on special problems, or (mostly "qualitative") single-case studies.

The average number of journal articles per year is shown in Figure 1. It can first be seen that there is a marked, long-term increase in the number of articles on legal psychology. We cannot say whether this is larger than that in other areas of psychology because of a lack of suitable comparative data. However, the increase is certainly related to the general expansion in psychology at German universities during the 1960s and 1970s (see Heckhausen, 1983). Second, it is notable that the ratio of empirical to nonempirical articles has risen. While, for example, the quotient for the interval 1950-1954 was 0.28, it reached 0.58 in 1970-1974 and 0.94 in 1985-1989.

The third conspicuous feature in Figure 1 is a particularly steep rise in the early 1970s. This corresponds with the general expansion of psychology and criminology in German universities at this time. Since the second half of the 1970s there has been a general stagnation in manpower. Therefore, the smaller increase in later years should not be underestimated.

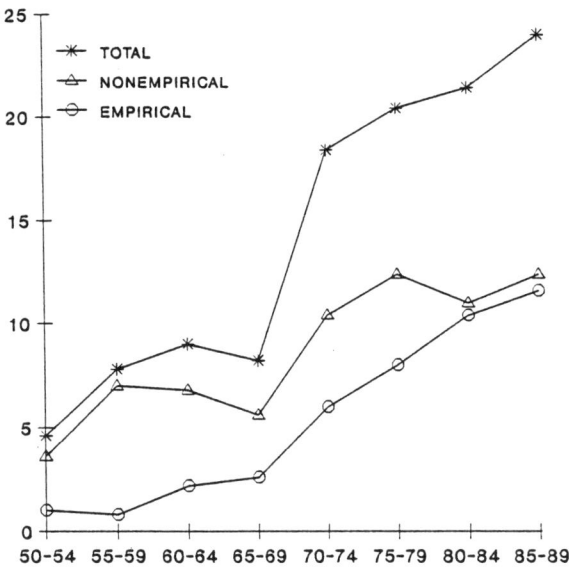

Figure 1: Mean Annual Number of Articles on Legal Psychology in German-Language Journals.

Alongside the general trends mentioned above, our literature analysis also shows changes in subject areas. We have categorized the articles according to six content fields:

1. *Conditions of criminality*. For example, explanations, correlates, predictions, epidemiology, and prevention of criminality.

2. *Forensic-psychological diagnosis*. For example, expert testimonies on credibility, criminal responsibility, or developmental problems.

3. *Other behavior within the justice system*; insofar as this is not assessed under (2) and (4). For example, the psychology of the courts, behavior of judges, decision making, sentencing.

4. *Incarceration and resocialization*. For example, prison problems, treatment of criminals, probation, or education measures.

5. *General problems of legal psychology*. For example, methods, professional structure, the relation between theory and practice, and professional policies.

6. *Remainder*. For example, the history of legal psychology, special crime problems, or the role of the media.

Our results are presented in Figure 2. Now as before, the majority of articles concern incarceration and resocialization (4). Articles on the explanation, prediction, and so forth of crime (1), that made a major contribution to the increase in the 1970s, have become less common. A subject reorientation in some productive authors or the end of relevant special research programs could be partially responsible for this drop. Instead, articles on problems of forensic-psychological assessment (particularly on witness testimony) have increased in the 1980s. At the same time, there is a small increase in psychological articles on other behavior within the justice system (3). As some of the articles on both forensic-psychological diagnosis and incarceration/ rehabilitation also refer to the behavior of the institutions of social control, the impression is confirmed that the actual functioning of the legal system has become more often a subject of psychology (law in practice vs. law in books).

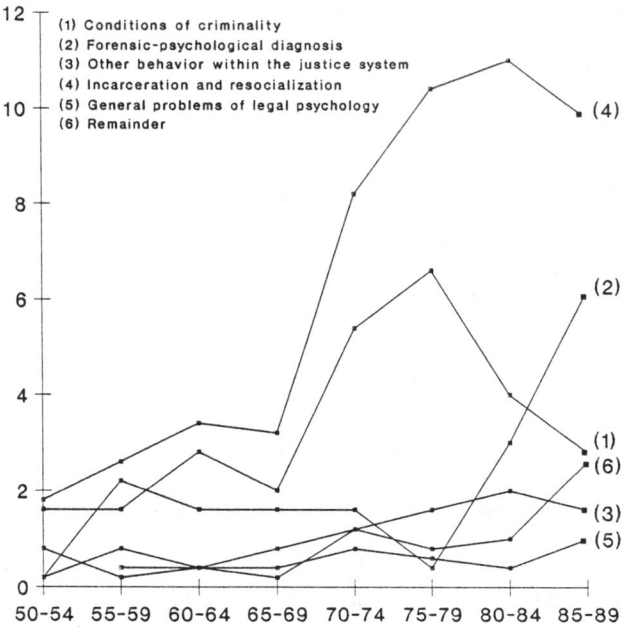

Figure 2: Mean Annual Number of Articles on Legal Psychology in German-Language Journals According to Content.

On the Characteristics of Recent Developments

Some authors imply that the quantitative increase and the broadening in topics indicate a qualitative transition in legal psychology. This argument particularly stresses developments in the United States. Thus, for example, we find in the book from Kette (1987) formulations such as: "The entire forensic literature in Europe lacks an underlying theoretical concept" (p. 8; translated). Apart from the fact that there are deficits in theory in many studies all over the world, such sweeping statements neither do justice to the whole field at present nor to the traditions going back to W. Stern, H. Münsterberg, M. Wertheimer, A. Binet, K. Marbe, and the like. As fruitful as the importation and reimportation of Anglo-American approaches was and is, fact should not be mixed with fiction, and dramatic changes should not be claimed by neglecting older developments. Despite the recognizable flourishing of legal psychology, it is necessary to be skeptical about quasi-imperialist metaphors according to which, for example, "we have gone far beyond the boundaries of forensic and criminal psychology because of the breadth of new research questions" (Kette, 1987, p. 7; translated). Such a boundary is neither established convincingly nor has it probably ever existed.

The terms "forensic psychology" and "criminal psychology" are in no way applied in a unified and strict sense (Lösel, 1980/88). Attempts to give boundaries to legal psychology are mostly more or less artificial (e.g., Sporer, 1985). In broad terms, forensic psychology is understood as the application of psychological theories, methods, and findings to the administration of justice. In Germany, much attention has been focused on the practice of expert testimony (see Arntzen, 1983; Undeutsch, 1967). The scientific principles used here have their origins in different areas of psychology depending on whether they have to deal with punishment, families, administration, road traffic, labor law, and so forth. Forensic psychology also considers problems in incarceration, predicting crime, and court procedures. Here, as in expert testimony in criminal law, it overlaps with criminal psychology, that is, the application of psychological theories, methods, and findings to problems of crime (or, in broader terms, of social deviance). This context includes research on the explanation of crimes, on the behavior of the police and the courts, on general and special prevention, on crime-related attitudes in the population, on the relation between the criminal and the victim, on offender treatment, and so forth (Lösel, 1983; Schneider, 1981; Seitz, 1983). The increasingly used (and reused) term of "legal psychology" or "psychology and law" in recent years should comprehensively cover all applications of psychological theories, methods, and findings to the legal system. On the one hand, this investigates the validity of the psychological assumptions underlying material law, on the other hand, it studies the formal and informal processes in the actual functioning of the legal system (Konečni & Ebbesen, 1982; Monahan & Loftus, 1982). Up to now, most research is in the field of criminal law; however, compared to criminal psychology, there is less emphasis on the conditions of deviant behavior, while compared to forensic psychology, it goes beyond the dominant task of diagnosis.

How far one wishes to determine "new horizons" or a "decisive progress" in recent legal psychology, probably depends on the degree of differentiation that is seen in earlier developments. The situation is similar to that satirized by Graumann (1988) for the "boom," "decisive progress," or "new orientation" of research on social cognition: "It would appear that only the historian or the researcher with a good long-term memory has the advantage of knowing that all these imperialisms only have a relatively short life precisely because of their totalitarian demands" (p. 86; translated). A sober evaluation of recent legal psychology that is oriented more toward long-term changes nonetheless does not imply that no essential developments can be determined. Among others, the following trends can be emphasized:

Increased psychological research "on" law

The research in forensic psychology was mostly concerned with how legal goals could better be attained with psychological means. This psychology *in* law (Haney, 1980; Lösel, 1980/88) or psychotechnical orientation of legal psychology (Loh, 1980) has clearly been expanded toward a greater autonomy of research. Research relates, for example, more toward the discrepancy between legal schemes and psychological findings or between the psychological principles and the effects of law. Both developments are contrasted (rather fuzzily) as "psychology *and* law" and "psychology *of* law" with "psychology *in* law" (Bartol, 1983; Haney, 1980; Sporer, 1985). These are no longer aimed at being mainly scientific aids but represent relatively autonomous, problem-oriented research on law. The concern is not only to optimize legal procedures but to develop a more general understanding of law (e.g., van Koppen & Hessing, 1988). It is asked, for example, how judges' information processing and decision making can be explained (e.g., Hans & Vidmar, 1986; Oswald, this volume); which factors influence role perceptions and behavior in prison personnel (e.g., Lösel & Bliesener, 1989; Lösel, Bliesener, & Molitor, 1988); or how legal and extralegal variables determine police-citizen interactions (e.g, Lundman, 1980; part IV, this volume). Such a more autonomous and partially critical position can already be recognized in the early days of forensic psychology, for example, in that W. Stern (1903) - to some extent unfairly - relativized the evidential value of statements by witnesses, or Marbe (1913) asked whether the punishment of corporations would be psychologically meaningful. The increase in research *on* law also does not mean that its usefulness for the law becomes secondary. Then, on the one hand, externally valid research that is actually acknowledged by justice can only be engaged in for a longer period of time if it is useful *in* law (see Lloyd-Bostock, 1988). On the other hand, the autonomous, problem-oriented research in legal psychology is often transformed into technologies. For example, psychological measures of crime prevention or police training are developed and evaluated (see Lösel, 1987a; Lösel & Mai, 1988).

Increased empirical-experimental orientation

The empirical orientation has already been mentioned above (see Figure 1). As in basic research, there is an increase in the attempts to use experiments in the study of questions of legal psychology. Loh (1984) even talks about an "experimental attack". Examples of this are the social-psychological experiments on legal proceedings (e.g., Hans & Vidmar, 1986; Thibaut & Walker, 1975; part VII, this volume) or perception and memory research on eyewitness testimony (e.g., Loftus, 1979; Wells & Loftus, 1984; part V, this volume). The most important arguments for and against an experimental psychology of testimony are discussed in Köhnken and Wegener (1985). However, the more recent "experimental attack" does not represent a new direction insofar as it readopts traditions of earlier research (e.g., Stern, 1903). It also should not become a one-sided methodological orientation (Davies, this volume), which would be questionable in view of the general methodological discussion in psychology or the critics of experiments in legal psychology (e.g., Bray & Kerr, 1982; King, 1986). The main aim is that the experimental ideal of control should be directed more strongly toward applied problems. From this perspective, quasi-experimental research is of particular importance in modern legal psychology. Thus, for example, the social-therapeutic prison is one of the few domains in Germany in which "reforms as experiments" (Campbell, 1969) were actually conceived and evaluated (see Lösel, Köferl, & Weber, 1987).

Stronger theoretical orientation of research

Although research was in no way as atheoretical as it has sometimes been claimed, even in the diagnostic areas of forensic psychology, theory-guided research has increased in recent legal psychology. Theories of information processing, attribution theories, decision-making theories, and so forth, play a particularly important role (see Kette, 1987; Wegener et al., 1989). Examples for this are the decision-making research on behavior in the justice system (Cornish & Clarke, 1986; Konečni & Ebbesen, 1982), the research on person identification (Clifford & Bull, 1978; Davies, Ellis, & Shepherd, 1981), or the analyses of correlates of credibility (Köhnken, 1990; Steller, 1987); see also parts IV, V, VI, and VII (this volume). For some problems, such as criminal responsibility, the overstressing of cognitive theories is nevertheless questionable (Thomae, 1988). As welcome as the increased theoretical guidance in research is, it must not be overlooked that the concept of a one-stage derivation of problem solutions from tested theoretical principles is far too simplified (see Lösel, 1987b). Moreover, deficits can result if researchers in legal psychology are more interested in testing their special theories in an exchangeable practical field and less in problem-related research on the respective topic. For example, Monahan and Loftus (1982) have shown that the social-psychological research on judges' decisions has predominantly studied juries. In actual legal practise in the USA, the jury decision is nevertheless a comparatively infrequent event: In 97 percent of cases, a solution is found through plea bargaining. However, among 400 articles on plea bargaining, Monahan and Loftus did not find one in a psychological journal.

Increased research on behavior within the legal system

This trend can also be recognized in Figure 2. However, our analysis of the literature did not reveal such a strong expansion in Germany as can be seen in the United States. There, a large proportion of studies deal with decision making and sentencing processes in juries and judges (see Roesch, 1990). It has been shown (e.g., Hagan, 1989; Hans & Vidmar, 1986; Schünemann & Bandilla, 1989) that decisions can be influenced by not only characteristics of the object of judgement (e.g., severity of offense, prior convictions, socioeconomic status of the offender) but also the judgment situation or procedures (e.g., perseverance following the inspection of criminal records, primacy and recency effects in the presentation of information, inoculation through prior counterarguments) as well as characteristics of the judge (e.g., causal attributions, attitudes to crime policy, professional socialization of judges). Another example is research on the police (see Lösel & Mai, 1988; Lundman, 1980; Sykes & Brent, 1983; see also part IV, this volume). The following have been among the characteristics that mostly Anglo-American studies have shown to be related to decisions: features of the problem (e.g., legal severity of an offense); of the accused (e.g., ethnic group); the situation (e.g., presence of third persons); police organization (e.g., efficiency criteria); and police officers (e.g., perceived stress). By expanding its study of behavior within the legal system, psychology has followed a trend that is more advanced in sociology. The institutions of social control have long been a central research topic of sociology, particularly in the labeling perspective or "critical criminology" (for an overview, see Sack, 1978). An increased research in the functioning of legal institutions is visible in all disciplines that are dealing with the law (see, e.g., Kaiser, Kury, & Albrecht, 1988). Furthermore, even within legal psychology, it is necessary to defend against all too stereotyped judgments of previous research. For example, Marbe (1913) had already addressed behavior in the legal system by asking why certain whole-number punishments (e.g., three years incarceration) occurred much more frequently than legally completely admissable intermediate values (e.g., 2;8 years). And already in 1938, Gaudet had addressed the problem of individual differences in the sentencing tendencies of judges.

Increased exchange of knowledge between research and practice

Research on witness testimony has become very frequent in Anglo-American psychology and law (e.g., Saks, 1986). As Figure 2 shows, this trend is somewhat delayed in Germany. While forensic expert testimonies have frequently been used in German courts since the 1950s (see Arntzen, 1983; Undeutsch, this volume), an increase in methodologically controlled research in this field only came later (e.g., Köhnken, 1990). The boom in research on witness testimony is closely linked to basic research in general psychology and has accumulated substantial knowledge (e.g., Loftus, 1979; part V, this volume). In recent years, there has been criticism that although a great variety of falsifying influences in the phases of perception, memory, and recall have been studied in laboratory routines, it is very difficult to integrate these findings into legal practice and there is uncertainty about how they generalize to real life (e.g., King, 1986; Konečni & Ebbesen, this volume). However, there are also more attempts to improve the transfer from basic research to technologies that can be handled by practice. Examples are case-oriented demonstrations of eyewitness expertise (e.g., Loftus & Ketcham, 1991) or the cognitive interview (Geiselman, Fisher, MacKinnon, & Holland, 1986). A more two-sided example of the exchange with practice stems from the increased social awareness of child abuse. In the United States as well as other countries, this has led to a high practical demand (see Spencer, Nicholson, Flin, & Bull, 1990; part VI, this volume), that includes some rather problematic aberrations, e.g., in disputed divorce cases. Here, the German tradition in the field of juvenile witnesses to sexual offenses can be of use (e.g., Arntzen, 1983; Undeutsch, 1967; see also Undeutsch, this volume). In close exchange between research and practice, attempts have been made to systematically test those credibility criteria developed from experience in expert testimony (e.g., Littmann & Szewczyk, 1983; Steller & Köhnken, 1989).

Increased research outside the area of criminal law

Most research in legal psychology is addressed to topics of criminal law. However, not only in forensic-psychological practice but also in research, there has been a marked increase in activities in other areas of law (see Kagehiro & Laufer, 1992). Guided by theories, psychologists are dealing with, for example, social cognition and tort law (Wiener & Small, 1992), reparations (Hommers, 1986), the honesty of tax payers (Hessing, Elffers, & Weigel, 1988), or the best interest of child in family law (Fthenakis, 1988). This trend can also be linked to early lines of development as Marbe (1913) had already introduced questions of civil law into forensic psychology.

According to the latter and other trends, a systematization of legal psychology will be proposed in the following (see Figure 3). Instead of using metaphors like "psychology *in* law" or "psychology *of* law," and so forth, I will proceed from an explicit concept of the application of psychology (see Brocke, 1980; Lösel, 1987b). According to this, applied psychology is problem-oriented research that can involve explanatory, predictive, or intervention problems. These types of problem form the columns of the model in Figure 3. The explanatory, predictive, or intervention problems refer to three main fields (see the rows in Figure 3): (1) the psychological assumptions and conditions that underlie the norms of law (e.g., the control characteristics of criminal responsibility); (2) the behavior of the citizen toward legal norms (e.g., a criminal act); and (3) the application of legal norms within the framework of the legal system (e.g., sentencing and punishment). The same problem structure is used for each different domain of law, for example, in criminal law, family law, traffic law, and so forth (the third dimension in Figure 3). Individual examples of research are entered into the cells of this cube. This involves, on the one hand, examples from criminal law (white fields); on the other hand, those from various other domains of law (dotted fields).

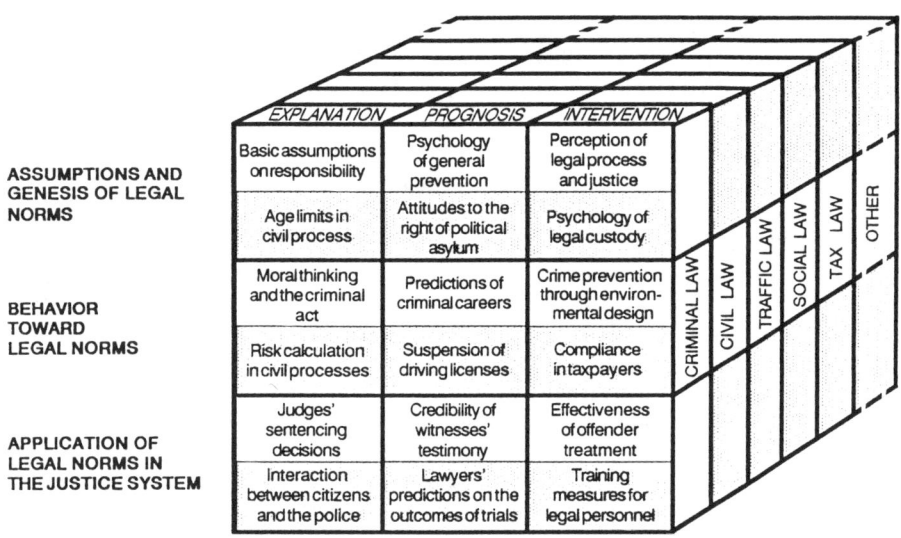

Figure 3: Systematization of Legal Psychology (Forensic Psychology, Criminal Psychology) With Research Examples.

Like any model, the one presented here is highly simplified. Among others, it does not take into account that many problems in the application of legal psychology simultaneously require research on the explanation, prediction, and change of phenomena (complex application problems). Further differentiations can also be made, for example, by separating the psychological assumptions in legal norms from the process of the genesis of norms on the first level, or separating psychological aspects of the application of legal norms (police, courts, etc.) from their consequences (e.g., resocialization, stigmatization) on the third level. Such differentiations nonetheless vary in meaningfulness depending on the specific field of law.

Problems and Perspectives

Despite the generally encouraging development of recent legal psychology, a number of problems still remain. I shall briefly sketch some of these in the following and attempt to point out perspectives. These involve (a) the internal situation of legal psychology; (b) its position within psychology; and (c) its relation to legal science and practice.

Within legal psychology

Within legal psychology, there has existed up to the present a great imbalance in the intensity with which various topics have been treated. While, for example, the causes of criminality or eyewitness testimony have been researched particularly intensively, other areas have received little empirical attention (e.g., legal socialization, custody law, questions in civil law). Therefore, the previously empty or scarcely filled cells in Figure 3 should be "filled" with research.

When some authors plausibly argue against the dominance of criminal law in legal psychology (e.g., Bierbrauer, 1989), this does not suggest that one wants to cut down the strongest branch on which one is sitting. Developments within legal psychology must take the form of a diversification of topics and not a substitution. If, as Figure 2 suggests, increased research on behavior in the legal system is made at the expense of that on criminal behavior, this looks like retreating from the challenge of a difficult social problem. In other countries, however, research on the processes within the legal system is simultaneously being accompanied by a strengthening of crime- and criminal-related research, particularly in the form of longitudinal studies on criminal careers and studies on the situational conditions of criminal acts (Cornish & Clarke, 1986; Farrington, Ohlin, & Wilson, 1986; see also Farrington, this volume; Kaiser, this volume).

When choosing the content of research, more attention should also be paid to multinational approaches. Although many psychologists tend to consider the cultural dependence of their findings only incidentally, they nevertheless base their assumptions more or less implicitly on general theories. This is particularly problematic in the domain of legal psychology, as its object is culture-specific. Although it can be assumed that the processes of perception, memory, motivation, and so forth that are relevant to witness testimony and other areas of legal psychology are relatively universal. The content characteristics of these processes and the related social interactions nonetheless depend on the specific legal system or the cultural context. Thus it is, for example, very questionable to what extent findings from the context of the Anglo-American adversary system can be transferred to the continental European context of the inquisitorial system. The same applies to research on the determinants of police decisions. The German police, for example, have much more restricted discretionary powers as their American collegues. Some authors (e.g., van Koppen & Hessing, 1988) discuss the problem but argue that research should be mainly restricted to each specific legal system. On the other side, they call adequately for a theoretically sound basis of psycholegal research (which should stop at national borders?). I think that more multinational research or cross-cultural comparisons are an important way to improve theory as well as practice in legal psychology.

The deficit regarding cultural framing conditions is at the same time one aspect of the more general question of the external validity of research in psychology and law. To some extent, there are considerable problems here. For example, research on judgment formation and sentencing often uses simulated court processes with "mock juries" (experimentally composed courts) or "shadow juries" (subjects who make decisions after observing real court cases). In many studies, the material is fictitious or reduced to a minimum of information. To some extent, it is only presented in a written form and the highly important dynamics of interaction before the court remain excluded. All too often, the subjects are college students or law freshmen with little professional experience. In the research on sentencing response modi are frequently used that would not be possible in court practice (e.g., rating scales). These and other problems (see Bray & Kerr, 1982) correspond to the general criticism of experimental social psychology. However, because of the relation to practice, they are particularly important in legal psychology. Recent research (e.g., Oswald & Langer, 1990; Schünemann & Bandilla, 1989) already places much more emphasis on criteria of external validity. In some research questions, alternative methodological solutions are nonetheless very difficult, for example, when phenomena in the legal system are not directly accessible, when factors such as the seriousness of the crime have to be held constant in the interests of internal validity, and so forth.

This is not the place to discuss the hierarchical relation between internal and external validity (Cook & Campell, 1979). Nevertheless, according to general pro and contra discussions on the generalizability of the findings of legal psychology, this problem should be approached much more intensively in empirical work (Davies, this volume; Konečni & Ebbesen, this volume). One important approach is to systematically test research in legal psychology according to single dimensions. Haisch (1989), for example, proposes the type of subject, the experimental material, and the setting as possible categories. More far-reaching approaches could refer to, for example, the comprehensive categories of construct validity and external validity in Cook and Campell (1979), the concept of critical multiplism (Cook, 1985), the principles of symmetry (Lösel & Wittmann, 1989), and the hierarchical UTO concept of the generalizability of units (U), treatments (T), and observing options (O) in Cronbach et al. (1980).

That a testing of the generalizability is thoroughly possible in the practice of research in legal psychology is shown, for example, in a study of Konečni and Ebbesen (1979). They used the following methods to study the sentencing behavior of judges: interviews on important determinants of decisions; structured questionnaires with items such as seriousness of the crime, previous convictions, and family status; rating scales on reasons for imposing milder or heavier sentences; simulation studies with fictitious cases and set decision alternatives; judgment of the decision-making behavior by observers in court; and analyses of court records on previous cases. The results showed only a partial agreement between the different approaches. Relatively consistent - and thus tentatively generalizable - were the results on the impact of crime seriousness, the probation officers prediction, and the record of previous convictions.

Within psychology

Despite its growing development legal psychology does not belong to the big fields of applied psychology. In Germany about 5-10 percent of psychologists work at least part-time in this field. In the Professional Unit of German Psychologists (Berufsverband Deutscher Psychologen) approximately 10 percent of the members are organized in the division of forensic and criminal psychology. There are deficits in training and further education, however, attempts are being made to solve these problems (see Hommers et al., 1991; Lösel, 1992). A more basic problem is the position of legal psychology within psychology as a science. Therefore I will concentrate on this topic.

Figure 3 shows that the topics of legal psychology are very heterogeneous: The only thing they have in common is that they refer to the law and legal system in some way. Depending on the topic, there are sometimes much closer relations to other areas of psychology than to other areas of legal psychology: for example, between research on juridical decision-making and general and social psychology; between prison research and clinical and organizational psychology; between eyewitness testimony research and general psychology and assessment; and between child custody research and developmental or educational psychology. To some extent, and this is in my opinion positive, interdisciplinary relations are also stronger than intradisciplinary ones, such as, for example, the relations to criminology, sociology, or psychiatry. In the sense of multidimensional scaling, the maximum differences within legal psychology are probably larger than the minimum distances to other areas, that is, there is no separable type. Legal psychology continually requires the problem-related integration of findings from all disciplines of basic psychological research (Lösel, 1987b). A close connection to basic research disciplines at the same time increases research competence and the rapid transfer of new findings.

All this, and, in any case, the inflation in applied psychological disciplines (when what is really meant is fields of problem-oriented research), are opposed to legal psychology as a clearly separate subdiscipline. Therefore, the legal psychology division of the German Psychological Association does not aim too much at defining and defending professional territories but at promoting legal psychology in its centripetal as well as centrifugal aspects. However, problems with regard to professional structure should not be ignored. Carrying out substantial research requires highly qualified scientists who are able to work in one field over a longer period of time. Young researchers must at least have the chance of making a successful career within their chosen specialization. In German legal psychology, this is no problem up to the Ph.D. level. Even the job opportunities outside the universities are comparatively good. However, the situation regarding university careers is more difficult, and not just because of the momentarily low turnover in professors. Compared to the obligatory applied fields of clinical, educational, and organizational psychology legal psychology in Germany is a small academic discipline. As mentioned, less than 20 percent of German universities have an elaborated curriculum and conduct examinations on forensic psychology, criminal psychology, or legal psychology. There are no chairs specifically designated to legal psychology. Research and teaching in this field is normally done by professors who are engaged in other psychological subdisciplines as well. In criminology where a number of psychologists are engaged in research, nonlawyers are passed over for higher positions. The retention or creation of real perspectives for highly qualified young researchers in the field of legal psychology is just as important for the stabilization of the international upward trend as the training of graduate psychologists.

Compared to the much bigger and more specialized psychology in the United States, it is necessary not to neglect those research specializations that do not fit exactly into the obligatory teaching "slots" (see Heckhausen, 1983). Legal psychology can help in this; on the one hand, in that it places emphasis on the broad inter- and intradisciplinary demands in its field. Some apparently "general" psychology is de facto narrower than this. On the other hand, legal psychology should be better institutionalized. This is greatly aided by the foundation of special divisions in psychological associations. It is not necessary to offer legal psychological courses in all universities but to develop existing or new centers at universities. This does not mean that a great number of chairs for legal psychology need to be created. A more realistic path, particularly for the smaller states and universities, would be to pay attention to an applied connection with legal psychology when chairs become vacant in basic research departments or "large" applied departments (e.g., general psychology, social psychology, clinical psychology - each linked to legal psychology). Such a model would not only be economic and flexible but it would also simultaneously ensure the necessarily close contacts between legal psychology and the current state of basic research.

Relation to legal science and practice

The long-term development of legal psychology finally depends on its relationship to legal science and, above all, legal practice. This relationship is naturally not without conflict (see Carson, 1988; King, 1986; Lloyd-Bostock, 1981; Melton, 1987). The situation differs from country to country. For example, the United States seem to be more open to the inclusion of legal psychology in law schools and have even established appropriate chairs. In Germany, there is a long tradition of practical collaboration. However, in academic training, law remains cool toward the social sciences. Social scientists are only called to be professors in law schools in a negligible number of "progressive" universities. Even if we disregard differences due to culture and tradition, there are many reasons why problems arise when law and psychology meet. These include the following areas of tension:

Psychological versus legal terminology. Naturally there are language barriers between the disciplines that make an understanding difficult. For example, the language of the social sciences is often criticized by jurists as being too full of foreign words and hard to comprehend. Ironically, such statements are made by jurists whose "legal language" is in no way less hard to understand. As in any meeting between two cultures, it holds that one's own familiar peculiarities are less conspicuous than those of the other. However, problems also arise with terms that are hard to "translate" even when one knows what they mean. Thus legal terms such as "criminal energy" or "responsibility" have no correspondence in psychological theories. Additional constructs must be introduced that, in turn, are unfamiliar to the jurists.

Empirical versus normative approach. The normative approach of law requires prescriptions that can be problematic from an empirical perspective. This applies, for example, for the effects of punishment or the setting of fixed age limits that may not correspond to individual development. There is also a juxtaposition of different normative goals (e.g., in criminal law: guilt compensation, special prevention, protection of the public, general prevention). In contrast, most psychological research is interested in specific goal categories that are as empirically accessible as possible. Here one could extend the application of, for example, concepts of multiattributive utility theory (e.g., Hammond, McClelland, & Mumpower, 1980) in legal psychology.

Pluralism in psychology versus the goal of uniformity in law. For the psychologist, the multiplicity of theories and perspectives in the discipline is a matter of course. It corresponds to the complexity of the objects of research and can, in a genetic sense, contribute to the evolution of suitable models. Although law science also contains different concepts of many legal problems, the intrinsic goal is uniformity and the avoidance of inequality. This should be achieved through precise laws, commentaries, and the judgments of the highest courts. In contrast, for many jurists, the multitude of standpoints in psychology often appears too noncommitted or contradictory.

Probabilistic psychological findings versus legal demands for certainty. Even when psychological statements are empirically well-grounded, they are probabilistic hypotheses with a great deal of uncertainty. For case-related decisions in legal practice, high demands are placed on the probability or certainty of a statement, for example, when releasing dangerous criminals from prison, in the credibility of witnesses, or in certifying commitment. Jurists are sometimes less sensitive to the probabilistic character of their own statements. Legal psychology should not only improve the probability of its statements through better research but also make jurists more aware of the basic problems of prediction and the flexibility of human behavior.

New psychological findings versus long-term establishment in law. It often takes a long time for new scientific findings to be implemented in legal practice. This easily can lead to impatience among psychologists. However, this delay has a positive side as well: Longer experience with a legal practice is necessary to implement, differentiate, and optimize it suitably. The all too short-term application of scarcely consolidated findings can contribute not only to questionable fashions in legal policy but also to the opposite of what has been intended (e.g., the pessimistic discussions on offender treatment; for recent meta-evaluations, see Lipsey, this volume; Lösel & Köferl, 1989; McGuire, this volume).

Empirical experimentation versus principles of equal treatment and fixed jurisdiction. Many questions in legal psychology require flexible model programs. Because of the equal treatment and fixed jurisdiction in the justice system, desired field experiments often cannot be carried out (e.g., in the adjudication of punishment, in the reaction to child abuse). Without doubt, it is difficult to find an acceptable compromise here. Some objections to close-to-practice experiments nevertheless only serve an unspecific defensive attitude that wants to avoid "unrest" in the institution.

Research autonomy versus officially commissioned research. Social science research in the legal system is increasingly also initiated and carried out by the state (e.g., in Germany by the Federal Criminal Police Office, in Great Britain by the Home Office, and in the Netherlands by the Ministry of Justice). Some authors (e.g., Brusten, 1986) object that this leads to "uncritical" research that encourages state control. There is also the risk that independent research will be excluded from studying legal topics. It is important to remain sensitive to this problem. However, it should not be distorted. In my opinion, the findings of "state research" have up to now scarcely been any different from those produced by researchers at universities. However, sensitivity is also required in the other direction: "Independent" researchers should show as much consideration as possible for legal practice in their research questions and methodologies. They should be self-critical in evaluating the meaning of their findings and not just use legal practice as "suppliers of data" for their own research (and careers).

In both law and psychology, there has been an increase in sensitivity for these and other problems. There is growing understanding for the possibilities, peculiarities, and idiosyncracies of the other side. At the same time, this field of tension between the disciplines should not just be regarded as negative. It contains reciprocal stimulations to thought and does not lead to an infertile pseudo-harmony. Thus it is important for legal psychology to retain a relative autonomy. It should not - as was previously the case - see itself as merely a scientific aid or a praxeology whose topics are defined by lawyers. This may not be the best way to influence law (e.g. Carson, 1988; Lloyd-Bostock, 1988) and has at times led to legal psychology being less visible and articulate than sociology (e.g., Kaiser, 1988).

In sum, recent legal psychology seems to be one of those fields in which psychology's relationship to neighboring disciplines, which Kornadt (1985), for example, has judged to be most deficient, has developed relatively successfully. Despite numerous problems, there is little evidence that the overtures, crescendos, and reprises will be leading up to any finale in the near future.

Endnote

* The present data are an update of a previous analysis for the years 1950-1987 (Lösel, 1989). I wish to thank Sabine Just, Thomas Meyer, and Cornelia Pfaff for their assistance. This study was not designed to be representative but served more illustrative purposes. The 33 journals are: Diagnostika, Dynamische Psychiatrie, Familiendynamik, Forensia, Integrative Therapie, Jahrbuch der Psychoanalyse, Kölner Zeitschrift für Soziologie und Sozialpsychologie, Kriminologisches Journal, Mitteilungen der DGVT, Monatsschrift für Kriminologie und Strafrechtsreform, Partnerberatung, Praxis der Kinderpsychologie und Kinderpsychiatrie, Psyche, Psychologische Beiträge, Psychologische Forschung, Schule und Psychologie/Psychologie in Erziehung und Unterricht, Psychologische Rundschau, Psychologie und Praxis/Zeitschrift für Arbeits- und Organisationspsychologie, Zeitschrift für Entwicklungspsychologie und Pädagogische Psychologie, Zeitschrift für diagnostische Psychologie und Persönlichkeitsforschung/Schweizer Zeitschrift für Psychologie, Soziale Welt, Zeitschrift für Differentielle und Diagnostische Psychologie, Zeitschrift für experimentelle und angewandte Psychologie, Zeitschrift für klinische Psychologie, Jahrbuch für Psychologie, Psychotherapie und medizinische Anthropologie, Zeitschrift für klinische Psychologie, Psychopathologie und Psychotherapie, Zeitschrift für Psychologie, Zeitschrift für Psychotherapie und medizinische Psychologie, Psychotherapie und medizinische Psychologie, Zeitschrift für Sozialpsychologie, Zeitschrift für Strafvollzug und Straffälligenhilfe, Zeitschrift für Verkehrssicherheit. If the two raters were unable to agree on the classification, a decision was made in discussions with myself. This was necessary in about one-quarter of the cases. The fact that many journals were first published after 1950, were absorbed into other journals, or were not published in individual years did not require special attention in the present study, as we were only concerned with absolute numbers or averages per year (not per journal).

References

Amelang, M. (1986). *Sozial abweichendes Verhalten*. Berlin: Springer.
Arntzen, F. (1983). *Psychologie der Zeugenaussage*. Systematik der Glaubwürdigkeitsmerkmale. München: Beck.
Bartol, C.R. (1983). *Psychology and the American Law*. Belmont, CA: Wadsworth.
Berckhauer, F. (1988). Kriminologische Auswahlbibliographie. In G. Kaiser, H. Kury, & H.J. Albrecht (Eds.). *Kriminologische Forschung in den 80er Jahren, Vol. 1* (pp. 281-343). Freiburg i.Br.: Max-Planck-Institut für ausländisches und internationales Strafrecht.
Bierbrauer, G. (1989). Rechtspsychologie ohne Recht. Rezension von G. Kette: Rechtspsychologie. *Zeitschrift für Sozialpsychologie, 20*, 254-258.
Binet, A. (1905). La science du témoigne. *Année Psychologique, 1*, 128-138.

Bray, R.M., & Kerr, N.L. (1982). Methodological considerations in the study of the psychology of the courtroom. In R.M. Bray, & N.L. Kerr (Eds.), *The psychology of the courtroom* (pp. 287-323). New York: Academic Press.

Brocke, B. (1980). Wissenschaftstheoretische Grundlagen der Angewandten Psychologie. *Zeitschrift für Sozialpsychologie, 11*, 207-244.

Brusten, M. (1986). Kriminologische Forschung unter staatlicher Regie? Probleme und Konsequenzen des Einflusses staatlicher Behörden auf die Struktur und Entwicklung der Kriminologie. In M. Brusten, J.M. Häußling, & P. Malinowski (Eds.), *Kriminologie im Spannungsfeld von Kriminalpolitik und Kriminalpraxis* (pp.25-38). Stuttgart: Enke.

Campbell, D.T. (1969). Reforms as experiments. *American Psychologist, 24*, 409-429.

Carson, D. (1988). Psychologists should be wary of involvement with lawyers. In: P.J. van Koppen, D.J. Hessing, & G. van den Heuvel (Eds.), *Lawyers on psychology and psychologists on law* (pp. 28-34). Amsterdam: Swets & Zeitlinger.

Clifford, B., & Bull, R. (1978). *The psychology of person identification*. London: Routledge & Kegan Paul.

Cook, T.D. (1985). Post-positivist critical multiplism. In L. Shotland, & M.M. Mark (Eds.), *Social science and social policy* (pp. 21-62). Beverly Hills, CA: Sage.

Cook, T.D., & Campell, D.T. (1979). *Quasi-experimentation: Design and analysis issues for field settings*. Chicago: Rand McNally.

Cornish, D.B., & Clarke, R.V. (Eds.) (1986). *The reasoning criminal. Rational choice perspectives of offending*. New York: Springer.

Crombag, H. (1989). When law and psychology meet. In H. Wegener, F. Lösel, & J. Haisch (Eds.), *Criminal behavior and the justice system: Psychological perspectives* (pp. 1-13). New York: Springer.

Cronbach, L.J., Ambron, S.R., Dornbusch, S.M., Hess, R.D., Hornik, R.C. Phillips, D.C., Walker, D.F., & Weiner, S.S. (1980). *Toward reform of program evaluation*. San Francisco: Jossey Bass.

Davies, G.M., Ellis, H.D., & Shepherd, J.W. (Eds.) (1981). *Perceiving and remembering faces*. London: Academic Press.

Dettenborn, H., Fröhlich, H. H., & Szewczyk, H. (1984). *Forensische Psychologie*. Berlin: VEB Deutscher Verlag der Wissenschaften.

Egg, R. (Ed.) (1991). *Brennpunkte der Rechtspsychologie. Polizei, Justiz, Drogen*. Bonn: Forum-Verlag.

Farrington, D.P., Hawkins, K., & Lloyd-Bostock, S.M. (Eds.) (1979). *Psychology, law, and legal processes*. London: Macmillan.

Farrington, D.P., Ohlin, L.E., & Wilson, J.Q. (1986). *Understanding and controlling crime: Toward a new research strategy*. New York: Springer.

Fthenakis, W.E. (1988). Der Einfluß psychologischer Erkenntnisse auf die neuere Ehe- und Familienrechtsreform. In F. Lösel, & H. Skowronek (Eds.), *Beiträge der Psychologie zu politischen Planungs- und Entscheidungsprozessen* (pp. 354-362). Weinheim: Deutscher Studien Verlag.

Freeman, R.J., & Roesch, R. (1992). Psycholegal education: Training for forum and function. In D.K. Kagehiro, & W.S. Laufer (Eds.), *Handbook of psychology and law* (pp. 567-576). New York: Springer.

Gaudet, F.J. (1938). *Individual differences in the sentencing tendencies of judges*. Archives of Psychology, Vol. 230. New York: Columbia University.

Geiselman, R.E., Fisher, R.P., MacKinnon, D.P., & Holland, H.L. (1986). Enhancement of eyewitness memory with the cognitive interview. *American Journal of Psychology, 99*, 385-401.

Graumann, C.F. (1988). Der Kognitivismus in der Sozialpsychologie - die Kehrseite der "Wende". *Psychologsiche Rundschau, 39*, 83-90.

Grisso, T., Sales, B.D., & Bayless, S. (1982). Law-related courses and programs in graduate psychology departments. *American Psychologist, 37*, 267-278.

Gross, H. (1898). *Kriminalpsychologie*. Graz: Leuschner & Lubensky.

Hagan, J. (1989). Strafzumessungsforschung in Nordamerika. In C. Pfeiffer, & M. Oswald (Eds.), *Strafzumessung* (pp. 147-180). Stuttgart: Enke.

Haisch, J. (1989). Introduction to part II. In H. Wegener, F. Lösel, & J. Haisch (Eds.), *Criminal behavior and the justice system: Psychological perspectives* (pp. 129-135). New York: Springer.

Hammond, K.R., McClelland, G.H., & Mumpower, J. (1980). *Human judgment and decision making. Theories, methods, and procedures.* New York: Praeger.

Haney, C. (1980). Psychology and legal change: On the limits of factual jurisprudence. *Law and Human Behavior, 4*, 147-199.

Hans, V.P., & Vidmar, N. (1986). *Judging the jury.* New York: Plenum.

Heckhausen, H. (1983). Zur Lage der Psychologie. *Psychologische Rundschau, 34*, 1-20.

Hessing, D.J., Elffers, H., & Weigel, R.H. (1988). Exploring the limits of self-reports and reasoned action: An investigation of the psychology of tax evasion behavior. *Journal of Personality and Social Psychology, 54*, 405-413.

Hommers, W. (1986). *Die Entwicklungspsychologie der Delikts- und Geschäftsfähigkeit.* Göttingen: Hogrefe.

Hommers, W. (Ed.) (1991). *Perspektiven der Rechtspsychologie.* Göttingen: Hogrefe.

Hommers, W., Bierbrauer, G., Lösel, F., Rolinski, K., Scholz, O.B., & Steller, M. (1991). Ausbildung und Weiterbildung in Rechtspsychologie. *Mitteilungsblatt der Fachgruppe Rechtspsychologie in der Deutschen Gesellschaft für Psychologie, 1*, 8-20.

Jung, C.G. (1905). Die psychologische Diagnose des Tatbestands. *Schweizerische Zeitschrift für Strafrecht, 18*, 368-408.

Kaiser, G. (1988). *Kriminologie,* 2nd ed. Heidelberg: C.F. Müller.

Kaiser, G., Kury, H., & Albrecht, H.-J. (Eds.) (1988). Kriminologische Forschung in den 80er Jahren, 3 Vols. Freiburg i.Br.: Max-Planck-Institut für ausländisches und internationales Strafrecht.

Kagehiro, D.K., & Laufer, W.S. (Eds.) (1992). *Handbook of psychology and law.* New York: Springer.

Kette, G. (1987). *Rechtspsychologie.* Wien: Springer.

King, M. (1986). *Psychology in and out of court. A critical examination of legal psychology.* Oxford: Pergamon.

Köhnken. G. (1990). *Glaubwürdigkeit.* München: Psychologie Verlags Union.

Köhnken, G., & Wegener, H. (1985). Zum Stellenwert des Experiments in der forensischen Aussagepsychologie. *Zeitschrift für Experimentelle und Angewandte Psychologie, 32*, 104-119.

Konečni, V.J., & Ebbesen, E.B. (1979). External validity of research in legal psychology. *Law and Human Behavior, 3*, 39-70.

Konečni, V.J., & Ebbesen, E.B. (Eds.) (1982). *The criminal justice system. A social psychological analysis.* San Francisco: Freeman.

Kornadt, H.-J. (1985). Zur Lage der Psychologie. *Psychologische Rundschau, 36*, 1-15.

Kühne, A. (1988). *Psychologie im Rechtswesen.* Weinheim: Deutscher Studien Verlag.

Kury, H. (1983). Psychologie im Bereich der Kriminologie. Chancen und Probleme. *Psychologische Rundschau, 34*, 1-14.

Lipmann, O. (1906). Die Wirkung von Suggestivfragen. *Zeitschrift für Pädagogische Psychologie, 8*, 89-96.

Lipsitt, P., & Sales, B. (Eds.) (1980). *New directions in psycholegal research.* New York: Van Nostrand.

Littmann, E., & Szewczyk, H. (1983). Zu einigen Kriterien und Ergebnissen forensisch-psychologischer Glaubwürdigkeitsbegutachtung von sexuell mißbrauchten Kindern und Jugendlichen. *Forensia, 4*, 55-72.

Lösel, F. (1980/1988). Forensische Psychologie und Kriminalpsychologie [Rechtspsychologie]. In R. Asanger, & G. Wenninger (Eds.). *Handwörterbuch der Psychologie,* 1st ed. [4th ed.] (pp. 143-149) [pp. 644-653]. München: Psychologie Verlags Union.

Lösel, F. (Ed.) (1983). *Kriminalpsychologie. Grundlagen und Anwendungsbereiche.* Weinheim: Beltz.

Lösel, F. (1987a). Psychological crime prevention: Concepts, evaluations, and perspectives. In K. Hurrelmann, F.-X. Kaufmann, & F. Lösel (Eds.), *Social intervention: Potential and constraints* (pp. 289-313). Berlin: de Gruyter.

Lösel, F. (1987b). Konzeptuelle Probleme und Heuristiken der Angewandten Sozialpsychologie. In J. Schultz-Gambard (Ed.), *Angewandte Sozialpsychologie* (pp. 29-42). München: Psychologie Verlags Union.

Lösel, F. (1989). Zur neueren Entwicklung der Rechtspsychologie: Versuch einer Standortbestimmung. In W. Schönpflug (Ed.), *Bericht über den 36. Kongreß der Deutschen Gesellschaft für Psychologie in Berlin 1988, Vol. 2* (pp. 291-306). Göttingen: Hogrefe.

Lösel, F. (1992 in press). Aus- und Weiterbildung in Forensischer, Kriminal- und Rechtspsychologie. In J.-M. Jehle (Ed.) *Kriminologische Aus- und Fortbildung.* Wiesbaden: Kriminologische Zentralstelle.

Lösel, F., & Bliesener, T. (1989). Psychology in prison: Role assessment and testing of an organizational model. In H. Wegener, F. Lösel, & J. Haisch (Eds.), *Criminal behavior and the justice system: Psychological perspectives* (pp. 419-439). New York: Springer.

Lösel, F., Bliesener, T., & Molitor, A. (1988). Social psychology in the criminal justice system: A study on role perceptions and stereotypes of prison personnel. In P.J. van Koppen, D.J. Hessing, & G. van den Heuvel (Eds.), *Lawyers on psychology and psychologists on law* (pp. 167-184). Amsterdam: Swets & Zeitlinger.

Lösel, F., & Köferl, P. (1989). Evaluation research on correctional treatment in West Germany: A meta-analysis. In H. Wegener, F. Lösel, & J. Haisch (Eds.), *Criminal behavior and the justice system: Psychological perspectives* (pp. 334-355). New York: Springer.

Lösel, F., Köferl, P., & Weber, F. (1987). *Meta-Evaluation der Sozialtherapie*. Stuttgart: Enke.

Lösel, F., & Mai, K. (1988). Polizei. In D. Frey, C. Graf Hoyos, & D. Stahlberg (Eds.), *Angewandte Psychologie* (pp. 363-385). München: Psychologie Verlags Union.

Lösel, F., & Wittmann, W.W. (1989). The relationship of treatment integrity and intensity to outcome criteria. In R.F. Conner, & M. Hendricks (Eds.), *International innovations in evaluation methodology. New directions for program evaluation, Vol. 42* (pp. 97-107). San Francisco: Jossey-Bass.

Lloyd-Bostock, S. (Ed.) (1981). *Psychology in legal contexts: Applications and limitations*. London: Macmillan.

Lloyd-Bostock, S. (1988). *Law in practice*. London: The British Psychological Society and Routledge.

Loftus, E.F. (1979). *Eyewitness testimony*. Cambridge, MA: Harvard University Press.

Loftus, E., & Ketcham, K. (1991). *Witness for the defense: The accused, the eyewitness, and the expert who puts memory on trial*. New York: St. Martin's Press.

Loh, W.D. (1980). Perspectives on psychology and law. *Journal of Applied Social Psychology, 11*, 314-355.

Loh, W.D. (1984): *Social research in the judicial process. Cases, readings, and text*. New York: Russel Sage.

Lundman, R.J. (1980). *Police and policing*. New York: Holt, Rinehart & Winston.

Marbe, K. (1913). *Grundzüge der Forensischen Psychologie*. München: Beck.

Melton, G. (1987). Bringing psychology to the legal system. Opportunities, obstacles, and efficacy. *American Psychologists, 42*, 488-495.

Melton, G.B., Monahan, J., & Saks, M.J. (1987). Psychologists as law professors. *American Psychologist, 42*, 502-509.

Monahan, J., & Loftus, E. (1982). The psychology of law. *Annual Review of Psychology, 33*, 441-475.

Monahan, J., & Walker, L. (1985). *Social science in law: Cases and materials*. Mineola, NY: The Foundation Press.

Müller, D.J., Blackman, D.E., & Chapman, A.J. (Eds.) (1984). *Perspectives in psychology and law*. Chichester: Wiley.

Münsterberg, H. (1908). *On the witness stand: Essays on psychology and crime*. New York: Clark, Boardman, Doubleday.

Oswald, M., & Langer, M. (1990) Versuche eines integrierten Modells zur Strafzumessungsforschung. Richterliche Urteilsprozesse und ihre Kontextbedingungen. In C. Pfeiffer, & M. Oswald (Eds.), *Strafzumessung* (pp. 197-228). Stuttgart: Enke.

Roesch, R. (1990). From the editor. *Law and Human Behavior, 14*, 1-3.

Sack, F. (1978). Probleme der Kriminalsoziologie. In R. König (Ed.). *Handbuch der empirischen Sozialforschung, Vol. 12, Wahlverhalten, Vorurteile, Kriminalität*, 2nd ed. (pp. 192-492). Stuttgart: Enke.

Saks, M.J. (1986). The law does not live by eyewitness testimony alone. *Law and Human Behavior, 10*, 279-280.

Scheirer, C., & Hammonds, B. (Eds.) (1983). *Psychology and law*. Washington, DC: American Psychological Association.

Schneider, H.-J. (Ed.) (1981). *Die Psychologie des 20. Jahrhunderts, Vol. 14, Auswirkungen auf die Kriminologie*. München: Kindler.

Schünemann, B., & Bandilla, W. (1989). Perseverance in courtroom decisions. In H. Wegener, F. Lösel, & J. Haisch (Eds.), *Criminal behavior and the justice system: Psychological perspectives* (pp. 181-192). New York: Springer.

Seitz, W. (Ed.) (1983). *Kriminal- und Rechtspsychologie*. München: Urban & Schwarzenberg.

Spencer, J., Nicholson, G., Flin, R., & Bull, R. (Eds.) (1990). *Children's evidence in legal proceedings*. Available from Cambridge University Law Faculty.

Sporer, S. (1985). Rechtspsychologie versus forensische Psychologie. In F. Hehl, V. Ebel, & W. Ruch (Eds.), *Diagnostik und Evaluation bei betrieblichen, politischen und juristischen Entscheidungen* (pp. 403-412). Bonn: Deutscher Psychologen Verlag.

Steller, M. (1987). *Psychophysiologische Aussagebeurteilung*. Göttingen: Hogrefe.

Steller, M., & Köhnken, G. (1989) Criteria-based statement analysis. In D. Raskin (Ed.), *Psychological methods in criminal investigation and evidence* (pp. 217-245). New York: Springer.

Stern, W. (Ed.) (1903). *Beiträge zur Psychologie der Aussage, 1. Heft*. Leipzig: Barth.

Sykes, R.E., & Brent, E.E. (1983). *Policing. A social behaviorist perspective*. New Brunswick, NJ: Rutgers University Press.

Tapp, J.L. (1976). Psychology and law: An overture. *Annual Review of Psychology*, 27, 359-404.

Tapp, J.L., & Levine, F. (Eds.) (1978). *Law, justice, and the individual in society: Psychological and legal issues*. New York: Holt, Rinehart & Winston.

Thibaut, J., & Walker, L. (1975). *Procedural justice. A psychological analysis*. Hillsdale, NJ: Erlbaum.

Thomae, H. (1988). Ein Beitrag der Psychologie zu politischen Entscheidungsprozessen im geschichtlichen Rückblick: Das Beispiel der Schuldfähigkeit im Strafrecht. In F. Lösel, & H. Skowronek (Eds.), *Beiträge der Psychologie zu politischen Planungs- und Entscheidungsprozessen* (pp. 27-35). Weinheim: Deutscher Studien Verlag.

Toch, H. (Ed.) (1961). *Legal and criminal psychology*. New York: Holt, Rinehart & Winston.

Undeutsch, U. (Ed.) (1967). *Handbuch der Psychologie, Vol. 11, Forensische Psychologie*. Göttingen: Hogrefe.

Van Koppen, P.J., & Hessing, D.J. (1988). Legal psychology or law and psychology? In P.J. van Koppen, D.J. Hessing, & G. van den Heuvel (Eds.), *Lawyers on psychology and psychologists on law* (pp. 1-8). Lisse: Swets & Zeitlinger.

Van Koppen, P.J., Hessing, D.J., & van den Heuvel, G. (Eds.) (1988). *Lawyers on psychology and psychologists on law*. Amsterdam: Swets & Zeitlinger.

Wegener, H. (1981). *Einführung in die Forensische Psychologie*. Darmstadt: Wissenschaftliche Buchgesellschaft.

Wegener, H., Lösel, F., & Haisch, J. (Eds.) (1989). *Criminal behavior and the justice system: Psychological perspectives*. New York: Springer.

Weiner, I.B., & Hess, A.K. (Eds.) (1987). *Handbook of forensic psychology*. New York: Wiley.

Wertheimer, M. (1906). Experimentelle Untersuchungen zur Tatbestandsdiagnostik. *Archiv für die gesamte Psychologie*, 6, 59-131.

Wells, G.L., & Loftus, E.F. (Eds.) (1984). *Eyewitness testimony: Psychological perspectives*. New York: Cambridge University Press.

Wiener, R.L., & Small, M.A. (1992) Social cognition and tort law: The roles of basic science and social engineering. In D.K. Kagehiro, & W.S. Laufer (Eds.), *Handbook of psychology and law* (pp. 435-454). New York: Springer.

Psychological Contributions to Criminology: Perspectives of a Law Scientist

Günther Kaiser

Among the manifold relations existing between law and psychology the *points of contact with the criminal law* and the empirical assessment of the latter form, as is well known, merely a subset of the overall subject complex, as "legal" or "forensic psychology" reaches far beyond this point. The broad range of topics covered by the program of the present conference on law and psychology is in itself a clear indication of this fact. Nonetheless, it cannot be overlooked that traditionally - but also within the scope of modern research endeavors - psychological factors related to crime, the investigation and determination of crime, as well as the treatment of criminals still represent *primary points* of interest (e.g., Kette, 1987; Wegener, Köhnken, & Steller, 1988). The reason for this, which has also fostered the development of criminology as an independent discipline, ultimately lies in the fact that criminal law - and the rebellion against the order it maintains - occupies the public mind to a much greater degree than all other legal subsystems.

So far, one aspect has not yet been touched, which, as of recently, has become a focal point of research interest - that is, *criminal law as a manifestation of state authority*. But even if one considered the problem requiring explanation not to lie in the committed crime - as is the case with abolitionism and critical criminology - but in criminal law and criminal justice (Blad, Mastrigt, & Uildriks, 1987; Sack, 1990), and reinterpreted the criminal offense in a decriminalizing fashion as a nuisance or as a personal existential crisis, this would not render psychological analysis and technologies obsolete, but, on the contrary, all the more necessary. Especially in such a case, the processes of establishing political consensus and deriving laws would require psychological investigation and analysis (see Lösel & Skowronek, 1988), since functional equivalents to criminal law and punishment would remain hardly less worth investigating due to their intensity of encroachment and the threat they pose to the basic rights of the individual citizen. The processes in penal legislation and the analysis of the criminal law in research and teaching also draw upon empirical psychological knowledge or in themselves become the object of dedicated psychological analysis.

The abundance of conventional points of contact with the criminal law or, more carefully expressed, references to criminal law, becomes apparent in dealing with problems reaching from "criminal psychology" (Groß, 1898; Hauptmann, 1989; Lösel, 1983; Muench, 1799; Schaumann, 1792; Seitz, 1983) on one hand, to "psychology of punitive society" (Hochheimer, 1969; Naegeli, 1969) and associated institutions in the light of attribution theory on the other hand. These problem domains are often interrelated. The activities of the psychological expert, the investigation of psychological structures of police action, criminal-judicial decisions and judicial behavior, as well as the psychology of sentencing are embedded in this context.

"The need for psychological insights in assessing crime" - such is the meaning of a manuscript dating from 1791 (von Eckartshausen, 1791; Kürzinger, 1986) - has been emphasized in the literature of the German-speaking countries for nearly 200 years. This demand and the underlying insight thus date back to a period in which psychology had not yet evolved as an independent discipline in the encyclopedia of sciences. The driving force behind this demand was a feeling of unease toward a concept that regarded a purely juridical assessment as an exhaustive approach to crime and dealing with the criminal (see also Lieber, 1845). Therefore, *enlightened doubt marks the beginning* of the path that led to the lingual merging of the terms psychology and crime to form the term "criminal psychology". This term was the response to a period that had just witnessed its last burnings of witches and had abolished torture; it would be more correct to say: that had rejected torture as an instrument suitable for extracting the truth in criminal proceedings. But even in recent times (1987), the Council of Europe has seen cause to adopt a convention for the prevention of torture and to appoint a responsible supervisory commission[1]. This demonstrates that the ideals of the age of enlightenment have yet to become reality. Hence, the historical development and the evolution of crime-psychological perspectives are among the programmatic topics of this conference.

Already at the onset of criminal psychology, interest was focused on the causes of crime, the uncertainties of eyewitness testimony, and criticism aimed at the conventional manner of practicing the criminal law; this is reflected especially by complaints against the criminal judge and his or her incapability of pronouncing a just verdict (Schneider, 1971). Upholding the ideals of enlightenment, there is a demand for more knowledge and education for the professional in criminal law, a stronger position of empirical science, and more rationality - in other words: more humanitarianism and justice.

If there has been a growing perception since World War II, and especially in the last decade, that psychology should contribute to criminal law and also to enhancing criminological analysis, this demonstrates not only the *renewal of a centuries-old demand,* but is also an indication of insufficient cooperation in the past, despite isolated attempts that appeared promising. Therefore, the reasons given are not entirely new in asserting that traditional disciplines - on the basis of their original self-definition - have to a certain extent consumed their innovative potential (Katz & Burchardt, 1971), and that, furthermore, the conviction of the need for cooperation is supposed to reflect merely the current mood, which enjoys widespread acceptance, maintaining that a more concentrated and prosperous exchange of ideas between the disciplines is taking place. Nonetheless, the *rise of forensic-psychological research* since the 1970s cannot be overlooked, especially in view of the impressive growth of the associated (scientific) community. If one can currently speak of a "craving for psychology", and if it is furthermore true that society is "currently measured exclusively in terms of psychological categories", so that the "victorious advance of psychological explanation patterns" becomes universally visible (Keupp et al., 1989), then these developments must also manifest themselves in criminology and criminal justice.

But just at the time when modern psychology is stepping forward at full pace to apply its questioning, methods, and techniques to crime, criminal law, and criminal justice,

---

[1] European Convention for the Prevention of Torture or Inhumane and Degrading Treatment or Punishment, November 26, 1987, printed in EuGRZ 16 (1989), p. 502.

an *increasing number of objections* is being encountered in the attempt to provide a rationalized scientific basis for the practice of criminal law. Indeed, there had already been oppositional attitudes in the penal-judicial field two decades ago, insofar as the current development period of criminal law had been characterized ominously as the subjugation of criminal law under psychology (Bockelmann, 1968). However, nowadays there is less concern by professionals in criminal law about being interdicted than about the issue whether scientific rationalization of (state) criminal justice is at all desirable (e.g., Beste, 1989; Kreißl, 1989) and if the conventional assumption that more research and more knowledge also lead to more humane social conditions is not possibly incorrect or even detrimental, since this assumption underrates the fundamental differences between theory and practice and thus ignores the complex problem of application. In the penal-forensic sector, the technology orientation of the empirical sciences is considered not only as dangerous as far as the exertion of power by the state is concerned but - with respect to criminology - even as incorrect and inadmissible on scientific grounds (Sack, 1989).

I do not fail to recognize the misgivings that arise when science includes application, innovation, and modification among its objectives (e.g., Beck & Bonß, 1989; Mummendey, 1988), thus modifying the outlook of the scientist. Still, I feel that *criticism* launched against this point is *ultimately unjustified*. Such critique is based on a restricted notion of science that excludes technology-oriented research (Irle, 1978; Lösel, 1986), rejects scientific guidance in the realm of practice, and assigns to the latter the role of acquiring eclectically connected knowledge (see Keupp et al., 1989). Also, application-oriented scientists participate in discussing the issue of power in the field of criminal justice to a lesser extent than is claimed by critics of the practical orientation of science. But even the critics want to exert their influence in the debate on the issue of power, at least insofar as they would like to have their analyses interpreted as a "challenge" to the state criminal law and thus as an appeal for modifications. But they have yet to disclose how this should come about, or more specifically, how such a process should be defined. Moreover, such a view reflects role diffusion and identity problems of the critics, as well as a disturbed relationship to practice, rather than adversities in the development of criminology. Suspicions raised about the applied social sciences being corruptly instrumentalized are justified under totalitarian conditions sooner than anywhere else. In such a case, even the basic sciences are not excluded from corruption, as has been demonstrated recently. This, on the other hand, does not imply the absence of tensions between empirical scientists, the police, criminal justice, or those responsible for enforcing punishments (Kury, 1983). Also, conflicts breaking out can be handled only with difficulty, if the "ethos of science" is not to be encroached upon and professional standards are to be retained. As psychological investigation in the criminological-forensic field primarily means implementation and utilization, that is to say, application, only systematically conducted technology research and critical cooperation, but not refusal and long-term confrontation, will lead onward.

In this respect the positions adopted by legal, criminological, or forensic psychology in the international literature hardly seem to show any differences. Psychology is always looked upon as a pacesetter and motor of the scientific rationalization of criminological and forensic practice. There are indeed sufficient grounds for this, which can be ascribed to the methodological know-how, the procedural techniques, and also to the long-established research ethics within psychology. Psychological contributions to criminology promise to be especially valuable in these fields.

Which in fact are the *psychological contributions* that have become an integral part of the criminological reservoir of knowledge? Do such "hard" facts based on a genuinely psychological contribution actually exist, or do psychological insights primarily serve as a means of self-reflection and self-monitoring of criminological knowledge? Does the psychological contribution mainly lie in the influence it has had on general views and the school of thought in criminology and perhaps also in criminal justice?

Such questions concerning impact research cannot be answered as unequivocally and clearly as we may wish. Still, we can conclude that - under the aspects of *research methodology* and *research ethics,* as well as *theory orientation* and *scope of application* including the theory-practice relationship - psychological research has left a lasting impression on criminology and criminal law. This, of course, has resulted largely from the fact that psychologists have become thematically involved in criminological problems and professionally engaged in the application of the criminal law to the field of social control, and also from their participation as partners in criminological research and as forensic experts. This enhanced degree of availability and, consequently, intensified participation naturally has its effects on the structure of the applied research instruments, on acceptance, and on the pattern of thinking in criminology. Thus, psychologically trained research workers in criminological research institutions, without exception, determine the empirical know-how in the Federal Republic of Germany and predominate in number (Kury, 1988).

One only has to call to mind the more recent research on treatment and prevention, and also the media analysis all the way up to meta-evaluation (Lösel, Selg, Schneider, & Müller-Luckmann, 1990; Ronge, 1989). It was only by adopting and applying such methods that criminology gradually gained a status corresponding to that of a scientific discipline. This development is not in contradiction to the fact that we have thus far not heard of any similarly distressing effects of cognitive advances in psychology on the penal-judicial field - as, for example, has occurred in biology and medicine, where "breakthrough points" into criminal law have existed for quite some time.

Therefore, present-day *criminology exhibits a distinctly empirical orientation* that occasionally has been questioned and criticized as a manifestation of extreme empiricism (Sack, 1990). Since counterbalancing the more speculative elements of criminological thinking is effectively expounded in theory and literature by the critical criminology movement, empirical research objectives and scopes of application are unobjectionable, as they are incorporated into a critical context. This struggle of opposing forces raises the expectation of a prosperous future development of criminological knowledge. Its existence is therefore highly desirable, and should actually have to be established if it did not already exist.

If, by broad international consensus, criminology is regarded as the reality-based science of criminal law, that is, it deals with rule making, rule breaking, and rule enforcement, it becomes clear that the psychological contributions also cover an equally *broad spectrum* - beginning, for example, with the rule-obedient behavior of the citizen (Tyler, 1990) and ending with political decision-making processes (Lösel, & Skowronek, 1988), or vice versa, if one proceeds from the formation and establishment of rules. Accordingly, crime-psychological texts used in teaching and textbooks reproduce a corresponding structure;

thus, psychological perspectives in explaining delinquency, for example, are generally found at the beginning, sometimes integrating the particularities of mental disorder and crime, and subsequently the psychology of the course of criminal prosecution up to the topics of the psychology of correction and psychological intervention (Hollin, 1989; Lösel, 1983), are covered. In such a context, the terminologically more restricted branch of forensic psychology consequently forms only a part of the entire field, since it defines itself as psychology in the courtroom, and in doing so takes an active and qualified stand in the identification of the suspect, the evidence, the procedure of taking evidence, and in assessing the psychological peculiarities of the delinquent and potential treatment.

Whereas the psychology of testimony has become firmly established in the framework of criminal law practice[2], it is mainly the methods for conceptualizing the investigations and the research techniques stemming from psychology that have successfully found their way into criminological research and determine everyday practice in this field. Psychology has its special achievements first and foremost in the domain of methodological problems and techniques. Psychology is superior to other neighbouring branches of science in regard to diagnostic *"techniques and methods"* in self-monitoring the validity of its findings (Kornadt, 1988). Thus, its repertoire includes assessment and validation technologies such as standardized tests or technologies of intervention, for example, forms of therapy that can at least be partly validated.

There are mainly two research paths with predominantly psychological origins, or at least developed toward maturity mainly by psychology that have - if I am not mistaken - found an impressive echo at the present time - namely, evaluation research and *cohort studies*. Both methods have attracted a significant research potential, have brought about advances in knowledge, and can be expected to lead to further innovations[3]. The objections repeatedly raised against this point (Bettmer, Kreissl, & Voß, 1989), however, remain unsubstantiated. The above considerations continue to remain valid, even if the possible implications on crime policy toward chronic or intensive offenders are taken seriously. The feared connection with selective incapacitation is in no case a necessary result.

The situation is different, however, in *evaluation research* and with the problems of *meta-analysis*. The accelerated increase of empirical research in the forensic-criminological field has led to a high number of individual results that can hardly be surveyed comprehensively. These differ quite a bit as to theoretical basis, method, and actual result. Comprehensive evaluations and assessments, that is, meta-evaluations, thus turn out to be correspondingly controversial. Even though "reviewers" strive to achieve a high level of objectivity, implicit selection, subjective priority assignments, and differences in emphasis imposed on the research material remain unavoidable (Lösel, 1986). Such problems are aggravating on scientific grounds - as far as the question of substantiated knowledge is concerned - and from the point of view of practice. Therefore, the qualitative and quantitative methods of integration and comprehensive assessment of individual findings, especially methods of meta-analysis, have become one of the most important areas of interest in evaluation research (e.g., Lösel, Köferl, & Weber, 1987).

---

[2] See, e.g., Decision of the Federal Administrative Court (BVerwGE) 25, 318, as early as 1966.

[3] See in this context the recent extensive project involving a longitudinal interdisciplinary study of the American National Institute of Justice, NJI-Reports No. 220, 1990.

Mainstream psychology is closely bound to a scientific ethos with its research centered around an *experimental, laboratory-based methodology*. Although there are limitations and criticisms to such a methodology, it also has its undoubted strengths. One such strength is that it allows any given topic to be examined in depth in a highly controlled manner. While this can lead to a greater understanding, it also sets the problem of whether the laboratory setting has produced artificial results. At worst this may mean that the experimental results are meaningless, or, alternatively, that they are in some way distorted. This empirical matter is highlighted by the debate on the applicability of laboratory research to witness memory. Moreover, the focus on a single factor or variable in an experimental study, controlling for other influences, may well act to magnify or diminish the effect of the variable of interest. Thus, jury studies in the laboratory may demonstrate the influence of different types of evidence, but in the courtroom, this effect does not appear to be of the same magnitude. The single variable in the laboratory loses some of its power when other variables are also present and exerting their influence. To design experiments that are meaningful in that they include all the relevant variables and so point to interactive effects while remaining manageable is a perennial difficulty in any experimental science (Hollin, 1989).

Nonetheless, empirical research generally makes experimental possibilities with extensive methodological checks necessary. In the field of criminology, juridical-ethical factors are, however, often opposed to such objectives. As far as barriers cannot be removed by the already highly sophisticated *research ethics* of psychologists for comprehensive information[4], flexible possibilities offered by quasi-experiments, by corresponding time series, and by the controlled analysis of individual cases that fulfil the scientific demands imposed in the research method will have to act as substitute solutions (Lösel, 1986). The most urgent problems among the many ethical issues are those of deceit, of consent, and the maintenance of secrecy of research data (Kaiser, 1990a; Kette, 1987). This can also be inferred by criminology from psychological research experience and discussions.

Psychological explanations of delinquent behavior provide the basis of crime-psychological practice. They often flow inconspicuously into many other activities of criminal justice and political policies on crime. The basically neglected explanation of delinquent behavior is an urgent issue, especially in view of treatment and prevention concepts (Lösel, 1983). But in terms of both a relationship between the various areas of research and in generating theories, psychology has occasionally tended to maintain a piecemeal-isolationist stance. There is little or no attempt to draw together the various aspects of psychological inquiry, such as say on the police, the courts, and the offender, in a unified way so as to make sense of the overall picture. Psychological theories of criminal behavior can therefore be criticized for concentrating too much on the individual offender to the neglect of the context of the crime. In short, psychology has in the main been about crime; what is lacking is a psychology of and for crime (Hollin, 1989).

In criminology there exists a striking multitude of theories and speculative hypotheses, and, on the other hand, a multitude of results on single variables. Even if given explanations compete with each other only partially, the question of assessment criteria and comparison of theories arises, especially in view of the fact that comparatively rigid hypothesis tests

---

[4] For a detailed discussion of this topic see Montada (1990).

are rare and yield partly unsatisfactory results (Lösel, 1983). Furthermore, common approaches such as learning theory turn out to be irrelevant in practical applications (Keupp et al., 1989; Kornadt, 1988; Lösel et al., 1990), so that the partly contradictory implications of different scientific theories have to be adapted to the practical issue at hand. Current concepts such as that of life-style remain more or less descriptive and limited in their significance (Kaiser, 1990b). In comparison to crime-sociological approaches, crime-psychological explanations are derived to a somewhat greater extent from general behavior theories. They mostly center on the analysis of the individual personality and its interactions in smaller groups. However, historical and social aspects of crime are given less attention, as would be expected. This is not an indication of a categorical "blindness" in generating psychological theories, but rather reflects the long established division of labor between the disciplines (Lösel, 1985a).

As is well known, Eysenck's *theory of variable conditionability*, also regarded as a control theory, has gained widespread importance in the present. Indeed, a number of empirical research results confirming the proposed relationships tend to support Eysenck's theory. Nonetheless, the basic premises and results of the investigations are "far from being consistent in the sense that officially registered persons generally show higher average measurement values than those free of penalties"; on the whole the findings are inconclusive (Amelang, 1986). In addition, the conceptual inclusion of the social environment as to the type and effects of conditioning is lacking (Ortmann, 1987). In particular, it still has to be clarified why sociopathic personalities show normal behavior in most areas of daily life and why crime clearly decreases with increasing age (Lösel, 1985b).

Furthermore, the *theory of moral development* according to Kohlberg (1981), which assumes the development of moral judgement to take place in six stages has also gained criminological relevance (Kohlberg, 1981). In the light of this concept, it is assumed that significant differences exist between the moral orientations of persons exhibiting a high level of delinquency and nondelinquents. Kohlberg's theory also leads to the assumption that the development of higher levels of moral reasoning generally protects a person against offending. This is understandable in itself, however, not too far removed from tautology. Still, the relationship between the development of morals and rule-conform behavior is not too close and even tends to be partly contradictory (Lösel, 1985b). Law-breakers are apparently less concerned about solving moral problems or conflicts than about achieving their aims as quickly and unobstructedly as possible. Moral judgment is at the most a necessary, but by itself not a sufficient condition for nondelinquent behavior, as Kohlberg's followers themselves admit.

In order to overcome the clearly visible, current stagnation in theory development in criminology, retrospective contemplation and concentration on the four most important theory traditions can be of help. Apart from anomie theory and labeling theory, these include the *learning and control theories*, as is well known. It is here that possibilities for advancement appear to exist, especially if institutional and victimological aspects can be absorbed integratively. The control theories based on the concept of informal social control want to again start out at the point where Hobbes' "Leviathan" posed the initial question as to the origin of social order, that is, to explain why humans develop obedience toward societal norms. This problem has recently been the subject of a study coming from the psychological community and has been answered empirically in the sense of procedural justice achieved by acceptance, legitimacy, and fairness (Kaufmann, 1990; Tyler, 1990). On the basis of the social-psychological realization that aggression and misconduct belong to the basic attributes of mankind, proponents of this approach do not seek primarily to know why human beings behave detrimentally to society, but investigate all the more how rule-conform behavior is learned.

In this context, control theory, which, as is well known, belongs to the so-called *social bond theories*, has gained wide recognition as a theoretically significant contribution. The number of four relevant levels or bond components as defined, for example, in the version of Hirschi appears very low, of course. The qualities of the bond relationships, especially the bond patterns, are only assessed very roughly. Also, the bonds can be best understood if one considers the conditions under which they were formed. But control theory gives little insight into the dynamics and intensity of bond relationships, that is, into the development of bonds or the origination of bondlessness. In this respect the theory still has to be expanded. The socialization concept proves helpful in defining bond formation and thus in explaining the nature of bonds or the absence of bonds (Hirschi & Godfredson, 1988) since it emphasizes the relationship with a generalized theory of social learning and moves the development of bonds into the center of interest. Accordingly, younger and older people, for example, have different socialization experiences. These lead to differences in the strengths of bonds toward the prevailing social order. Bonds based on trust, however, represent inner control mechanisms or safeguards against deviations. Once they have been established bond patterns remain quite stable over time. The more stable the bonds of the individual toward societal rules, the greater the intensity with which the conscience rejects deviant behavior, and the more probable the preventive effect toward offending becomes. Older bond patterns can, however, change as a result of more recent life circumstances, new relationships, and also therapy. Furthermore, excessive demands and stress situations imposed on the individual, as well as cultural conflicts can weaken bonds (Mawson, 1987). The strength of bonds therefore does not remain invariant, but is influenced by later experiences with fellow humans, and also by success or failure at school and in one's profession and by family unity and family crises. Thus, psychological and psychoanalytic approaches (e.g., Jacobsen & Edelstein, 1989) have provided a significant contribution to expanding and advancing the theories of learning and control, and to enhancing their explanatory potential.

This also applies to *psychological analyses of socialization and standards of value in cross-cultural comparisons* (Trommsdorff, 1989). According to the latter, experimental evidence clearly contradicts Inglehart's premise (1977) of a universal acceptance of postmaterial values in highly industrialized societies. Whereas change in all socialization contexts is promoted in individual-oriented cultures, primary socialization in the family retains quite a strong functional stability in group-oriented cultures with a high level of control and emotional bonds. Correspondingly, the effectiveness of sanctions must be exceptionally high in a culture in which emotionally positive social relationships gain central importance: Without this emotionally based social orientation, which forms tight bonds to one's own group (the family, the company, among others), an individual feels lost (Trommsdorff, 1989).

The third larger complex of psychological influence on criminological thinking deals with - apart from the aspects of methodology and theory development - the implementation of scientific knowledge in practice, that is to say, *applications and technology orientation*.

Independent of how one differentiates between basic science on one hand and applied science, or considers such a differentiation permissible or misconstrued (Kornadt, 1988), the existence of differences in distance of perspective in the application of empirical and scientific findings cannot be denied. As criminology considered itself an application-oriented discipline from the very first, even though this view may nowadays be strictly contradicted by critical sociologists and accused of coming close to sacrilege, it is understandable that the influence of applied psychology in the field of criminal justice is especially intense and productive (Kette, 1987). Thus, psychological contributions to the problem areas of prognostic planning and decision-making are in demand and play an important role (see Lösel & Skowronek, 1988). As of recently, this trend is also reflected by the psychological expertise produced in the framework of the so-called Commission for the Prevention of and Intervention Against Criminal Acts of Violence (Lösel et al., 1990).

The discussion on the scope of application in psychology represents an important contribution to criminology, insofar as problem and technology orientations are being reflected increasingly and the problems of implementation are being outlined clearly. They also preserve criminology from an unreflected, naive application mentality according, for example, to the formula "better knowledge - better actions - better life". Today, there is a greater tendency to emphasize the *discontinuity* of problem complexes facing science, technology, and technical practice (Drerup, 1987), that is, to stress the *"rationality gap"* between theory and practice (Beck & Bonß, 1989). On the other hand, there is a call for a "reflective scientific rationalization". Nonetheless, practice is also granted an independent reflective knowledge base of its own. At any rate it has been recognized correctly that objectives and thought patterns of science and practice differ: discursive learning on one side, strategic learning on the other.

Furthermore, psychological research results can make an instrumental as well as a conceptual *utilization* possible (Lösel & Skowronek, 1988). These are complemented by the mere symbolic-legitimatory utilization. The network of relationships between theory and practice is, at any rate, more complex than indicated by either the scientific rationalization of social fields of action or the scientific "control of the controllers" which, in turn, cannot do without further control measures.

Despite the criticism, which, in any case is, presented mainly by rival fractions within critical criminological sociology, research on prediction, prevention, and intervention belongs to the especially significant problem areas of psychological investigation in regard to criminology. Although the target accuracy of the predictive techniques could not be increased appreciably, at least the different risk factors and their conditions could be outlined (Farrington & Tarling, 1985; Gabor, 1989). This holds for the behavior of both the offender and the victim. The high error rate and the implications on criminal policy admittedly remain aggravating. The consequences of predictions on abuse and risks, especially of faulty predictions, underline the problem (Monahan, 1981). On the other hand, I do not see how one can achieve a greater degree of rationality and humaneness than by scientific rationalization. History since at least the time of the Amsterdam penitentiaries in the 16th century shows that it was the experience gained in the experimental exploration of alternatives, i.e. the attempt to venture on new paths, that ultimately promoted the process of humanitarian progress and thus contributes to "civilizing state power" (Elias, 1976).

In view of the above considerations we may, *in concluding*, raise the following questions: (a) What has psychology contributes to the understanding of crime and crime control? (b) How useful is this contribution? (c) Furthermore, are there any weaknesses, or even gaps, in the messages given? The overwhelming impression gained from reviewing the literature is that *psychological research into crime and criminal justice have achieved most* in precisely the areas in which mainstream psychology is the strongest: that is, particularly in the development of research techniques, furthermore in the study of the individual, and to a lesser extent the social group, in terms of motivation, behavior, perception, psychopathology, personality, and group dynamics. Psychology is at its best in studying the individual offender, in the development of empirically based offender taxonomies, and in studies of witness memory, jury deliberation, and interpersonal skills training for police or correction officers (Hollin, 1989). The same holds for psychological approaches to understanding serious crime.

On the other hand, one cannot fail to acknowledge that investigations of the processes of criminal policy involved in decision-making and deriving laws, as well as the *study of crime victims* have *not yet gained* the *recognition* within psychology that they deserve. These sets of problems would be potential and meriting areas of research. Furthermore, it appears that empirical research on penalty assessment has to date not yet made full use of its psychological potential, despite highly promising isolated efforts (Pfeiffer & Oswald, 1989). Besides that, the absence of a basic theoretical concept, and especially the fact that this lack is not subject to criticism, are viewed as an aggravating state of affairs by the entire forensic literature (Kette, 1987). Therefore, there is the demand for a *reflection of the position* of forensic psychology in order to counteract unreflected pragmatism. However, it remains doubtful whether this will lead to more than just a reflective-individualized form of interconnecting various systems of knowledge.

Yet, on the whole - after a period of eventful development - one can now speak of a *newly established criminological psychology* that is in keeping with a great and long tradition and lives up especially to modern expectations. A mere 80 years after the pioneering studies of William Stern and Hugo Münsterberg, one notes that legal psychology exists as an independent theoretical and applied discipline (Kette, 1987). An impressive amount of knowledge has been accumulated in this field. It is superior to nonprofessional knowledge in that it is based on systematic observation, on careful analysis of contexts, and on efforts aimed at comprehensive theoretical interpretation (Kornadt, 1988). It provides background knowledge as well as technologies. The development of criminological psychology has in this respect generated a wealth of knowledge that will serve to deepen and expand the empirical data base of criminology and to scientifically reinforce its scope of application. In psychology, as in sociology, merely a small share of research efforts focus on criminological problems. Yet, in contrast to sociology, problem localization in psychology differs in that the crime-psychological contributions are firmly embedded in the encompassing and institutionalized context of reflection in applied research and are critically developed from here.

References

Amelang, M. (1986). *Sozial abweichendes Verhalten*. Berlin: Springer.
Beck, U., & Bonß, W. (Eds.)(1989). *Weder Sozialtechnologie noch Aufklärung? Analysen zur Verwendung sozialwissenschaftlichen Wissens*. Frankfurt: Suhrkamp.
Beste, H. (1989). Zur Rolle der Sozialwissenschaften im Strafrecht. Kritische Anmerkungen zum Verhältnis von Soziologie, Strafrechtwissenschaft und Kriminalpolitik. *KritV, 2*, 149-178.
Bettmer, F., Kreissl, R., & Voß, M. (1988). Die Kohortenforschung als symbolische Ordnungsmacht. Zur Neuordnung von Kriminalität zwischen Diversion und "selective-incapacitation". *Kriminologisches Journal, 20*, 191-212
Blad, J., Mastrigt, H., & Uildriks, N. (Eds.)(1987). *The criminal justice system as a social problem: An abolitionist perspective*. Rotterdam: Liber Amicorum Louk Hulsman.
Bockelmann, P. (1968). Bemerkungen über das Verhältnis des Strafrechts zur Moral und zur Psychologie. In G. Radbruch (Ed.), *Volume in memory* (pp. 252-259). Göttingen: Vandenhoeck & Ruprecht.
Drerup, H. (1987). *Wissenschaftliche Erkenntnis und gesellschaftliche Praxis. Anwendungsprobleme der Erziehungswissenschaft in unterschiedlichen Praxisfeldern*. Weinheim: Beltz.
Eckartshausen, K. von (1791). *Ueber die Nothwendigkeit physiologischer Kenntnisse bey Beurtheilung der Verbrechen*. München.
Elias, N. (1976). *Über den Prozeß der Zivilisation*, 2 Vols. Frankfurt/M.: Suhrkamp
Farrington, D., & Tarling, E. (Eds.) (1985). *Prediction in criminology*. New York: University of New York Press.
Gabor, T. (1989). The prediction of criminal behaviour. Statistical approaches. *British Journal of Criminology 29*, 93.
Groß, H. (1898). *Criminalpsychologie*. Graz: Leuschner & Lubensky's.
Hauptmann, W. (1989). *Psychologie für Juristen, Kriminologie für Psychologen. Einführung in die Sozialpsychologie des Strafrechts*. München: Oldenburg.
Hirschi, T., & Godfredson, M. (Eds.) (1988). *Understanding crime. Current theory and research*. Beverly Hills, CA: Sage.
Hochheimer, W. (1969). Zur Psychologie von strafender Gesellschaft. *Kriminologisches Journal, 2*, 27-49.
Hollin, C. (1989). *Psychology and crime. An introduction to criminological psychology*. London: Routledge.
Inglehart, R. (1977). *The silent revolution*. Princeton: University Press.
Irle, M. (Ed.) (1978). Einführung. In *Kursus der Sozialpsychologie, Part III: Angewandte sozialpsychologische Forschung und ethische Probleme der Anwendung*, (pp. 472-482). Darmstadt: Luchterhand.
Jacobsen, T., & Edelstein, W. (1989). Internal models of attachement as related to cognitive development in middle childhood and adolescence. Unpublished manuscript, Berlin.
Kaiser, G. (1990a). *Normative Voraussetzungen und ethische Implikationen sozialwissenschaftlicher Forschungen unter besonderer Berücksichtigung der Kriminologie. Volume in honour of D. Goldschmidt*. Berlin: Max-Planck-Institut für Bildungsforschung.
Kaiser, G. (1990b). "Lebensstil". Entwicklung und kriminologische Bedeutung eines Konzepts. In *Festschrift für H. Göppinger*. Berlin: Springer
Katz, M., & Burchardt, J.D. (1971). Psychology and the legal enterprise. *University of Kansas Law Review 19*, 197-210.
Kaufmann, A. (1990). Richtiges Recht - eine Skizze. *Universitas, 2*, 150-161.
Kette, G. (1987). *Rechtspsychologie*. Wien: Springer.
Keupp, H., Straus, F., & Gmür, W. (1989). Verwissenschaftlichung und Professionalisierung. Zum Verhältnis von technokratischer und reflexiver Verwendung am Beispiel psychosozialer Praxis. In U. Beck, & W. Bonß (Eds.), *Weder Sozialtechnologie noch Aufklärung? Analysen zur Verwendung sozialwissenschaftlichen Wissens* (pp. 149-195). Frankfurt/M.: Suhrkamp.
Kohlberg, L. (1981). *The philosophy of moral development*. San Francisco: Harper & Row.
Kornadt, H.-J. (1988). Möglichkeiten und Probleme der Anwendung und politischen Umsetzung psychologischer Forschungsergebnisse. In F.Lösel, & H. Skowronek (Eds.), *Beiträge der Psychologie zu politischen Planungs- und Entscheidungsprozessen* (pp. 8-26). Weinheim: Beltz.

Kreißl, R. (1989). Soziologie und soziale Kontrolle. Mögliche Folgen einer Verwissenschaftlichung des Kriminaljustizsystems. In U. Beck, & W. Bonß (Eds.), *Weder Sozialtechnologie noch Aufklärung? Analysen zur Verwendung sozialwissenschaftlichen Wissens* (pp. 420-456). Frankfurt: Suhrkamp.

Kürzinger, J. (1986). Karl von Eckartshausen (1752-1803) und die Anfänge der Kriminalpsychologie in Deutschland. In: *Festschrift für W. Middendorf* (pp. 177-192). Bielefeld: Gieseking.

Kury, H. (1983). Psychologie im Bereich der Kriminologie: Chancen und Probleme. *Psychologische Rundschau, 34,* 72-85.

Kury, H. (1988). Rechtswesen. Einführung. In F. Lösel, & H. Skowronek (Eds.), *Beiträge der Psychologie zu politischen Planungs- und Entscheidungsprozessen* (pp. 332-338). Weinheim: Beltz.

Lieber, F. (1845). *Bruchstücke über Gegenstände der Strafkunde, besonders über das Eremitensystem.* Hamburg.

Lösel, F. (1983). *Kriminalpsychologie. Grundlagen und Anwendungsbereiche* (pp. 15, 18). Weinheim: Beltz.

Lösel, F. (1985a). Kriminalitätstheorien, psychologische. In G. Kaiser, F. Sack, & H. Schellhoss (Eds.), *Kleines Kriminologisches Wörterbuch* (pp. 219-229). Heidelberg: Müller.

Lösel, F. (1985b). Täterpersönlichkeit. In G. Kaiser, F. Sack, & H. Schellhoss (Eds.), *Kleines Kriminologisches Wörterbuch* (pp. 177, 471-477). Heidelberg: Müller.

Lösel, F. (1986). Kriminologische Wissenschaft und Praxis: Probleme und Chancen aus empirisch-sozialwissenschaftlicher Sicht. In J.M. Jehle, & R. Egg (Eds.), *Anwendungsbezogene Kriminologie zwischen Grundlagenforschung und Praxis* (pp. 71-85). Wiesbaden: Kriminologische Zentralstelle.

Lösel, F., Köferl, P., & Weber, F. (1987). *Meta-Evaluation der Sozialtherapie.* Stuttgart: Enke.

Lösel, F., & Skowronek, H. (Eds.) (1988). *Beiträge der Psychologie zu politischen Planungs- und Entscheidungsprozessen.* Weinheim: Beltz.

Lösel, F., Selg, H., Schneider, U., & Müller-Luckmann, E. (1990). Ursachen, Prävention und Kontrolle von Gewalt aus psychologischer Sicht. Gutachten der Unterkommission I. In H.-D. Schwind, J. Baumann, F. Lösel, H. Remschmidt, R. Eckert, H.-J. Kerner, A. Stümper, R. Wassermann, H. Otto, & W. Rudolf (Eds.), *Ursachen, Prävention und Kontrolle von Gewalt, Vol. II* (pp. 1-56). Berlin: Duncker & Humblot.

Mawson, A.R. (1987). *Transient criminality. A model of stress-induced crime.* New York: Praeger.

Monahan, J. (1981). *Predicting violent behaviour. An assessment of clinical techniques.* Beverly Hills, CA: Sage.

Montada, L. (1990). *Ethical issues in communicating with participants.* Paper presented at the Workshop of the European Science Foundation on Ethical and Legal Issues in Longitudinal Research, Copenhagen/Denmark, June 7-9, 1990.

Muench, J.G. (1799). *Über den Einfluß der Criminalpsychologie auf ein System des Criminal-Rechts, auf menschliche Gesetze und Cultur der Verbrecher.* Nürnberg: Steinische Buchhandlung.

Mummendey, H.D. (1988). Zur Kritik der Anwendungsorientierung der Psychologie. In F. Lösel, & H. Skowronek (Eds.), *Beiträge der Psychologie zu politischen Planungs- und Entscheidungsprozessen* (pp. 36-43). Weinheim: Beltz.

Naegeli, E. (1969). Die Gesellschaft und ihre Kriminellen - Ausstoßung des Sündenbocks. In W. Bitter (Ed.), *Verbrechen - Schuld oder Schicksal* (pp. 40-72). Stuttgart: Klett.

Ortmann, R. (1987). *Resozialisierung im Strafvollzug. Ergebnisse einer vergleichenden Längsschnittstudie, ihre theoretische Erklärung und ihre kriminalpolitischen Schlußfolgerungen.* Freiburg: Max-Planck-Institut für Ausländisches und Internationales Strafrecht.

Pfeiffer, C., & Oswald, M. (1989). *Strafzumessung. Empirische Forschung und Strafrechtsdogmatik im Dialog.* Stuttgart: Enke.

Ronge, V. (1989). Verwendung sozialwissenschaftlicher Ergebnisse in institutionalisierten Kontexten. In U. Beck, & W. Bonß (Eds.), *Weder Sozialtechnologie noch Aufklärung? Analysen zur Verwendung sozialwissenschaftlichen Wissens* (pp. 323-354). Frankfurt/M: Suhrkamp.

Sack, F. (1989). Kriminologie und Geschichtswissenschaft: Wege der Reflexion einer Disziplin. In J. Savelsberg (Ed.), *Zukunftsperspektiven der Kriminologie in der Bundesrepublik Deutschland. Materialien zu einem DFG-Kolloquium* (pp. 28-32, 71-141). Stuttgart: Enke.

Sack, F. (1990). Das Elend der Kriminologie und Überlegungen zu seiner Überwindung. Ein erweitertes Vorwort. In: Ph. Robert (Ed.), *Strafe, Strafrecht, Kriminologie, eine soziologische Kritik* (pp. 16-55). Frankfurt: Campus.

Schaumann, J.G. (1792). *Ideen einer Kriminalpsychologie*. Halle.

Schneider, H.J. (1971). Psychologie des Verbrechens (Kriminalpsychologie). In *Handwörterbuch Kriminologie*, Vol. 2 (pp. 415-458). Berlin: de Gruyter.

Seitz, W. (1983). *Kriminal- und Rechtspsychologie*. München: Urban & Schwarzenberg.

Trommsdorff, G. (1989). Sozialisation und Werthaltungen im Kulturvergleich. In G. Trommsdorff (Ed.), *Sozialisation im Kulturvergleich* (pp. 97-121). Stuttgart: Enke.

Tyler, T.R. (1990). *Why people obey the law*. New York: Yale University Press.

Wegener, H., Köhnken, G., & Steller, M. (1988). Recht. In: D. Frey, C. Graf Hoyos, & D. Stahlberg (Eds.), *Angewandte Psychologie* (pp. 342-362). München: Psychologie Verlags-Union.

Psychological Contributions to the Explanation, Prevention and Treatment of Offending

David P. Farrington

Introduction

Psychology and crime

The distinctive contributions of psychologists to the explanation, prevention, and treatment of offending follow from their commitment to the scientific study of human behavior (e.g., Farrington, 1984). Lawyers and sociologists are less interested in the scientific method, with its emphasis on quantitative data, falsifiable theories, controlled experiments, systematic observation, valid and reliable measures, replications of empirical results, and so on.

Psychologists view offending as a type of behavior, similar in many respects to other types of antisocial or deviant behavior. Hence, the theories, methods, and knowledge of other types of antisocial behavior can be applied to the study of crime. The focus is on the types of offenses that dominate the official criminal statistics in Western countries, principally theft, burglary, robbery, violence, vandalism and drug abuse. Most research has concentrated on offending by males, since this is more frequent and serious than offending by females (e.g., Farrington, 1987).

Psychologists believe that, like other types of behavior, criminal behavior results from the interaction between the person (with a certain degree of criminal potential or antisocial tendency) and the environment (which provides criminal opportunities). Given the same environment, some people will be more likely to commit offenses than others, and conversely the same person will be more likely to commit offenses in some environments than in others.

In comparison with sociologists, psychologists emphasize the importance of individual difference factors, and especially the consistency of criminal propensity across situations and its continuity over time. Psychologists also argue that officially recorded offenders and non-offenders (or, in self-report studies, more and less serious offenders) are significantly different in numerous respects - before, during, and after their offending careers.

Psychologists have made many contributions to the explanation, prevention, and treatment of offending, and it is only possible to mention a small number of these, without a great deal of detail, in this paper. Wilson and Herrnstein (1985) and Hollin (1989), among others, have provided more extensive reviews. I will focus especially on knowledge gained in the Cambridge Study in Delinquent Development, which is a prospective longitudinal survey of over 400 London males from age 8 to age 32 (e.g., Farrington & West, 1990). However, similar results have been obtained in similar studies elsewhere in England (e.g., Kolvin et al., 1988), in the United States (e.g., McCord, 1979; Robins, 1979), in the Scandinavian countries (e.g., Pulkkinen, 1988; Wikstrom, 1987), and in New Zealand (e.g., Moffitt & Silva, 1988a).

This paper will begin by reviewing the natural history of offending and will then outline some key findings on individual difference factors (intelligence and personality) and family, peer, school, and situational influences on offending. It will then continue by mentioning some prevention and treatment programs focusing on these influences. Psychologists have also made important contributions to knowledge about genetic (e.g., Mednick, Gabrielli & Hutchings, 1983; Rowe, 1987), biochemical (e.g., Magnusson, 1988; Olweus, 1987), and psychophysiological factors (e.g., Raine, 1988; Venables, 1987) in offending. These studies will not be reviewed here, partly because of lack of space and partly in view of uncertainty about their implications for prevention and treatment.

Natural history of offending

Developmental research shows that the prevalence of most types of offending increases with age to a peak in the teenage years, and then decreases in the twenties and thirties. This pattern is seen in cross-sectional and longitudinal research with self-reports and official records of offending. For example, in the London longitudinal survey of over 400 males, the prevalence of convictions increased to a peak at age 17 and then declined (Farrington, 1990a). Self-reports showed that burglary, shoplifting, theft of and from vehicles, and vandalism all decreased from the teens to the twenties, but the same pattern was not seen for theft from work, fraud, or drug abuse (Farrington, 1989).

Many theories have been proposed to explain why offending peaks in the teenage years (see Farrington, 1986a). For example, offending has been linked to testosterone levels in males, which increase during adolescence and early adulthood and decrease thereafter, and to changes in physical abilities or opportunities for crime. The most popular explanation focuses on social influence. From birth, children are under the influence of their parents, who generally discourage offending. However, during their teenage years, juveniles gradually break away from the control of their parents and become influenced by their peers, who may encourage offending in many cases. After age 20, offending declines again as peer influence gives way to a new set of family influences hostile to offending, originating in spouses and cohabitees.

While the absolute prevalence of offending varies with age, there is also considerable continuity in offending over time. In the London longitudinal survey, nearly three-quarters of those convicted as juveniles (age 10-16) were reconvicted between ages 17 and 24, and nearly half of the juvenile offenders were reconvicted between ages 25 and 32 (Farrington & West, 1990). The males first convicted at the earliest ages tended to become the most persistent offenders, in committing large numbers of offenses at high rates over long time periods.

This continuity over time does not merely reflect continuity in police reaction to crime. Farrington (1989) showed that, for 10 specified offenses, the significant continuity between offending in one age range and offending in a later age range held for both self-reports and official convictions. Therefore, it might be concluded that the relative ordering of individuals on some underlying construct such as criminal tendency stays tolerable constant over time, even though the behavioral manifestations of this construct may change.

Explanations

Intelligence and cognitive factors

Loeber and Dishion (1983) and Loeber and Stouthamer-Loeber (1987) extensively reviewed the predictors of male offending. They concluded that poor parental child management techniques, offending by parents and siblings, low intelligence and educational attainment, and separation from parents were all important predictors. Longitudinal (and indeed cross-sectional) surveys have consistently demonstrated that children with low intelligence are disproportionally likely to become offenders.

In the London longitudinal survey, West and Farrington (1973) found that one-third of the boys scoring 90 or less on a non-verbal intelligence test (Raven's Progressive Matrices) at age 8-10 were convicted as juveniles, twice as many as among the remainder. Non-verbal intelligence was highly correlated with verbal intelligence (vocabulary, word comprehension, verbal reasoning) and with school attainment, and all of these measures predicted juvenile convictions to much the same extent. Low non-verbal intelligence was especially characteristic of the juvenile recidivists (who had an average IQ of 89) and those first convicted at the earliest ages (10-13). Furthermore, low non-verbal intelligence predicted juvenile self-reported offending to almost exactly the same degree as juvenile convictions, and measures of intelligence predicted measures of offending independently of other variables such as family income and family size. Similar results have been obtained in other projects (e.g., Wilson & Herrnstein, 1985).

The key explanatory factor underlying the link between intelligence and offending is probably the ability to manipulate abstract concepts. People who are poor at this tend to do badly in intelligence tests such as the Matrices and in school attainment, and they also tend to commit offenses, mainly because of their poor ability to foresee the consequences of their offending and to appreciate the feelings of victims (i.e., their low empathy). Certain family backgrounds are less conducive than others to the development of abstract reasoning. For example, lower class, poorer parents tend to live for the present and to have little thought for the future, and tend to talk in terms of the concrete rather than the abstract. A lack of concern for the future is also linked to the concept of impulsivity, which will be discussed in the next section.

Modern research is studying not just intelligence but also detailed patterns of cognitive and neuropsychological deficit. For example, in a New Zealand longitudinal study of over 1.000 children from birth to age 15, Moffitt and Silva (1988b) found that self-reported offending was related to verbal, memory and visual-motor integration deficits, independently of low social class and family adversity. Neuropsychological research might lead to important advances in knowledge about the link between brain functioning and delinquency. For example, the "executive functions" of the brain, located in the frontal lobes, include sustaining attention and concentration, abstract reasoning and concept formation, anticipation and planning, self-monitoring of behavior, and inhibition of inappropriate or impulsive behavior (Moffitt, 1990). Deficits in these executive functions are conducive to low measured intelligence and to offending.

Personality and impulsivity

It is plausible to suggest that there is an "antisocial personality" that arises in childhood and persists into adulthood, with numerous different behavioral manifestations, including offending. This idea has been popularized by Robins (1979), and is embodied in the DSM-III-R diagnosis of antisocial personality disorder (American Psychiatric Association, 1987). The antisocial male adult generally fails to maintain close personal relationships with anyone else, performs poorly in his jobs, is involved in crime, fails to support himself and his dependents without outside aid, and tends to change his plans impulsively and to lose his temper in response to minor frustrations. As a child, he tended to be restless, impulsive, and lacking in guilt, performed badly in school, truanted, ran away from home, was cruel to animals or people, and committed delinquent acts.

A similar pattern was seen in the London longitudinal survey (Farrington, 1991a). The typical offender - a male property offender - tended to be born in a low income, large sized family and to have criminal parents. When he was young, his parents supervised him rather poorly, used harsh or erratic child-rearing techniques, and were likely to be in conflict and to separate. At school, he tended to have low intelligence and attainment, was troublesome, hyperactive and impulsive, and often truanted. He tended to associate with friends who were also delinquents.

After leaving school, the offender tended to have a low status job record punctuated by periods of unemployment. His deviant behavior tended to be versatile rather than specialized. He not only committed property offenses such as theft and burglary but also engaged in violence, vandalism, drug use, excessive drinking, reckless driving, and sexual promiscuity. His likelihood of offending reached a peak during his teenage years and then declined in his twenties, when he was likely to get married or cohabit with a woman.

By the time he was in his thirties, the offender was likely to be separated or divorced from his wife and separated from his children. He tended to be unemployed or to have a low paid job, to move house frequently, and to live in rented rather than owner-occupied accommodation. His life was still characterized by more evenings out, more heavy drinking and drunk driving, more violence, and more drug-taking than his contemporaries. Hence, the typical offender tended to provide the same kind of deprived and disrupted family background for his own children that he himself experienced, thus perpetuating from one generation to the next an antisocial personality syndrome of which offending was only one element.

Psychologists have demonstrated a clear link between the constellation of personality factors variously termed "hyperactivity-impulsivity-attention deficit" or HIA (Loeber, 1987) and offending. For example, in the London longitudinal survey, Farrington, Loeber and Van Kammen (1990b) showed that HIA at age 8-10 significantly predicted juvenile convictions independently of conduct disorder at age 8-10. They therefore concluded that the linkage between impulsivity and offending held independently of the continuity in antisocial behavior. In this survey, the rating of "daring" or risk-taking at age 8-10 by parents and peers significantly predicted convictions up to age 32 independently of all other variables (Farrington, 1990b).

Family influences

Loeber and Stouthamer-Loeber (1986) completed an exhaustive review of family factors as correlates and predictors of juvenile conduct problems and delinquency. They found that poor parental supervision or monitoring, erratic or harsh parental discipline, marital disharmony, parental rejection of the child, and low parental involvement with the child (as well as antisocial parents and large family size) were all important predictors of offending.

In the London longitudinal survey, West and Farrington (1973) found that harsh or erratic parental discipline, cruel, passive or neglecting parental attitude, poor supervision, and parental conflict, all measured at age 8, all predicted later juvenile convictions. Furthermore, poor parental child rearing behavior (a combination of discipline, attitude and conflict) and poor parental supervision both predicted juvenile self-reported as well as official offending (Farrington, 1979), and poor parental child-rearing behavior predicted offending independently of other factors such as low family income and low intelligence. Harsh parental discipline and attitude at age 8 also significantly predicted later violent as opposed to non-violent offenders (Farrington, 1978), although more recent research showed that it was equally predictive of violent and non-violent but frequent offenders (Farrington, 1991b). Poor parental child rearing behavior was related to early rather than later offending (Farrington, 1986b), and was not characteristic of those first convicted as adults (West & Farrington, 1977).

Psychologists have also shown that broken homes and early separations predict offending. West and Farrington (1973) found that both permanent and temporary (more than one month) separations before age 10 predicted official offending, providing that they were not caused by death or hospitalization, and similar results were obtained by Wadsworth (1979). Furthermore, such separations were related to self-reported as well as to official offending (Farrington, 1979). However, homes broken at an early age were not unusually criminogenic. Separations predicted convictions up to age 32 independently of all other variables (Farrington, 1990b).

Criminal, antisocial and alcoholic parents also tend to have criminal sons, as Robins (1979) found. In the London longitudinal survey, the concentration of offending in a small number of families was remarkable. West and Farrington (1977) discovered that less than 5 % of the families were responsible for about half of the criminal convictions of all family members (fathers, mothers, sons, and daughters). West and Farrington (1973) showed that having convicted mothers, fathers, and brothers by a boy's tenth birthday significantly predicted his own later convictions. Furthermore, convicted parents and delinquent siblings were related to self-reported as well as to official offending (Farrington, 1979). Unlike most early precursors, convicted parents were related less to offending of early onset (age 10-13) than to later offending (Farrington, 1986b). Also, convicted parents predicted which juvenile offenders went on to become adult criminals and which recidivists at age 19 continued offending (West & Farrington, 1977), and they predicted convictions up to age 32 independently of all other variables (Farrington, 1990b).

These results are concordant with the psychological theory that offending occurs when the normal social learning process, based on rewards and punishments from parents, is disrupted by erratic discipline, poor supervision, parental disharmony and unsuitable (antisocial or criminal) parental models (e.g., Trasler, 1962). However, some part of the link between criminal parents and delinquent sons may reflect genetic influences.

Peer influences

The reviews by Zimring (1981) and Reiss (1988) show that delinquent acts tend to be committed in small groups (of two or three people, usually) rather than alone. In the London longitudinal survey, most officially recorded juvenile and young adult offenses were committed with others, but the incidence of co-offending declined steadily with age from 10 onwards. Burglary, robbery and theft from vehicles were particularly likely to involve co-offenders, who tended to be similar in age and sex to the study males and lived close to the males' homes and to the locations of the offenses. The study males were most likely to offend with brothers when they had brothers who were similar in age to them (Reiss & Farrington, 1991).

The major problem of interpretation is whether young people are more likely to commit offenses while they are in groups than while they are alone, or whether the high prevalence of co-offending merely reflects the fact that, whenever young people go out, they tend to go out in groups. Do peers tend to encourage and facilitate offending, or is it just that most kinds of activities out of the home (both delinquent and non-delinquent) tend to be done in groups? Another possibility is that the commission of offenses encourages association with other delinquents, perhaps because "birds of a feather flock together" or because of the stigmatizing and isolating effects of court appearances and institutionalization. It is surprisingly difficult to decide among these various possibilities, although most researchers argue that peer influence is an important factor.

There is clearly a close relationship between the delinquent activities of a young person and those of his friends. Both in the United States (Hirschi, 1969) and in the United Kingdom (West & Farrington, 1973), it has been found that a boy's reports of his own offending are significantly correlated with his reports of his friends' delinquency. In the American National Youth Survey of Elliott, Huizinga, and Ageton (1985), having delinquent peers was the best independent predictor of self-reported offending in a multivariate analysis.

In the London longitudinal survey, association with delinquent friends was not measured until age 14, and so this was not investigated as a precursor of offending (which began at age 10). However, it was a significant independent predictor of convictions at the young adult ages (Farrington, 1986b). Also, the recidivists at age 19 who ceased offending differed from those who persisted, in that the desisters were more likely to have stopped going round in a group of male friends. Furthermore, spontaneous comments by the youth indicated that withdrawal from the delinquent peer group was seen as an important influence on ceasing to offend (West & Farrington, 1977). Therefore, continuing to associate with delinquent friends may be a key factor in determining whether juvenile delinquents persist in offending as young adults or desist.

Delinquent peers are likely to be most influential where they have high status within the peer group and are popular. However, studies both in the United States (Roff & Wirt, 1984) and in the United Kingdom (West & Farrington, 1973) show that delinquents are usually unpopular with their peers. It seems paradoxical for offending to be a group phenomenon facilitated by peer influence, and yet for offenders to be largely rejected by other adolescents (Parker & Asher, 1987). However, it may be that offenders are popular in offending groups and unpopular in non-offending groups. More worrying is the suggestion that some people act as "recruiters", constantly dragging more people into the net of offending (Reiss, 1988).

School influences

It is clear that the prevalence of offending varies dramatically between different secondary schools, as Power, Alderson, Phillipson, Shoenberg, and Morris (1967) showed more than 20 years ago in London. However, what is far less clear is how much of this variation should be attributed to differences in school climates and practices, and how much to differences in the composition of the student body.

In the London longitudinal survey, Farrington (1972) investigated the effects of secondary schools on offending by following boys from their primary schools to their secondary schools. The best primary school predictor of offending in this study was the rating of troublesomeness at age 8-10 by peers and teachers. The secondary schools differed dramatically in their official offending rates, from one school with 21 appearances per 100 boys per year to another where the corresponding figure was only 0.3. However, it was very noticeable that the most troublesome boys tended to go to the high delinquency schools, while the least troublesome boys tended to go to the low delinquency schools. Furthermore, it was clear that most of the variation between schools in their delinquency rates could be explained by differences in their intakes of troublesome boys. The secondary schools themselves had only a very small effect on the boys' offending.

The most famous study of school effects on offending was also carried out in London, by Rutter, Maughan, Mortimore, and Ouston (1979). They studied 12 comprehensive schools, and again found big differences in official delinquency rates between them. High delinquency rate schools tended to have high truancy rates, low ability pupils, and low social class parents. However, the differences between the schools in delinquency rates could not be entirely explained by differences in the social class and verbal reasoning scores of the pupils at intake (age 11). Therefore, they must have been caused by some aspect of the schools themselves or by other, unmeasured factors.

In trying to discover which aspects of schools might be encouraging or inhibiting offending, Rutter et al. (1979) developed a measure of "school process" based on school structure, organization and functioning. This was related to school misbehavior, academic achievement and truancy independently of intake factors. However, it was not significantly related to delinquency independently of intake factors. The main school factors that were related to delinquency were a high amount of punishment and a low amount of praise given by teachers in class. Unfortunately, it is difficult to know whether much punishment and little praise are causes or consequences of antisocial school behavior, which in turn is probably linked to offending outside school.

Situational influences

While most psychologists have aimed to explain the development of offending people, some have tried to explain the occurrence of offending events. As already mentioned, offenders are predominantly versatile rather than specialized. The typical offender who commits violence, vandalism or drug abuse also tends to commit theft or burglary. For example, in the London longitudinal survey, Farrington (1991b) reported that only 7 out of 50 convicted violent offenders had no convictions for non-violent offenses. Hence, in studying offenders, it seems unnecessary to develop a different theory for each different type of offense. In contrast, in trying to explain why offenses occur, the situations are so diverse and specific to particular crimes that it probably is necessary to have different explanations for different types of offenses.

The most popular theory of offending events suggests that they occur in response to specific opportunities, when their expected benefits (e.g., stolen property, peer approval) outweigh their expected costs (e.g., legal punishment, parental disapproval). For example, Clarke and Cornish (1985) outlined a theory of residential burglary which included such influencing factors as whether a house was occupied, whether it looked affluent, whether there were bushes to hide behind, whether there were nosy neighbors, whether the house had a burglar alarm and whether it contained a dog. Several other psychologists have also proposed that offending involves a rational decision in which expected benefits are weighed against expected costs (e.g., Wilson & Herrnstein, 1985).

In the London longitudinal study, the most common reasons given for offending were rational ones, suggesting that most property crimes were committed because the offenders wanted the items stolen (West & Farrington, 1977). Also, a number of cross-sectional surveys have shown that low estimates of the risk of being caught were correlated with high rates of self-reported offending (e.g., Erickson, Gibbs, & Jensen, 1977), although the direction of causal influence is not clear in this kind of research. Farrington and Knight (1980) carried out a number of studies, using experimental, survey, and observational methods, that suggested that stealing involved risky decision-making. Hence, it is plausible to suggest that opportunities for crime, the immediate costs and benefits of crime, and the probabilities of these outcomes, all influence whether people offend in any situation.

Prevention and Treatment

Effectiveness of interventions

Interest in rehabilitative treatment for offenders declined in the mid-1970's, as the influential reviews by Martinson (1974) in the United States and Brody (1976) in the United Kingdom suggested that existing treatment techniques had no differential effects on the recidivism of detected offenders. This conclusion was substantially confirmed by a U.S. National Academy of Sciences panel in an impressive, methodologically sophisticated review (Sechrest, White & Brown, 1979). However, for a number of reasons, it should not be concluded that "nothing works", nor even that everything works equally well.

Many psychologists have never given up hope that offenders can be changed. Indeed, recent literature reviews provide hope that offending *can* be reduced through rehabilitative treatment (e.g., Gendreau & Ross, 1987; Kazdin, 1987; Thornton, 1987). However, bearing in mind the difficulty of changing people once their offending is in full flow, the best chance of a long-term decrease in offending may lie in prevention rather than treatment.

Methods of preventing or treating offending should be based on theories about causes. In this section, prevention and treatment applications will be drawn from some of the causes of offending listed above. (For a more detailed review, see Farrington et al., 1990a). The applications reviewed here are those for which there is some empirical justification, especially in randomized experiments. The effect of any intervention on offending can be demonstrated most convincingly in such experiments (Farrington, 1983; Farrington, Ohlin, & Wilson 1986). As already mentioned, one of the distinctive features of psychologists is their commitment to randomized experiments.

Skills training

Psychologists have aimed to change impulsivity and other personality characteristics of offenders using the set of techniques variously termed "cognitive-behavioral interpersonal social skills training" (e.g., Michelson, 1987). For example, the methods used by Ross to treat juvenile delinquents (e.g., Ross, Fabiano, & Ewles, 1988; Ross & Ross, 1988) are solidly based on some of the known individual characteristics of delinquents: their impulsivity, poor abstract reasoning, egocentricity, and poor interpersonal problem-solving skills.

Ross argued that delinquents can be taught the cognitive skills in which they are deficient, and that this can lead to a decrease in their offending. His reviews of delinquency rehabilitation programs (e.g., Gendreau & Ross, 1979, 1987) show that those which have been successful in reducing offending have generally tried to change the offender's thinking. Ross carried out his own "Reasoning and Rehabilitation" program in Canada, and found (in a randomized experiment) that it led to a significant decrease in reoffending for a small sample in a 9-month follow-up period. His training was carried out by probation officers, but he believes that it could be administered by parents or teachers.

Ross' program aimed to modify the impulsive, egocentric thinking of delinquents, to teach them to stop and think before acting, to consider the consequences of their behavior, to conceptualize alternative ways of solving interpersonal problems, and to consider the impact of their behavior on other people, especially their victims. It included social skills training, lateral thinking (to teach creative problem solving), critical thinking (to teach logical reasoning), value education (to teach values and concern for others), assertiveness training (to teach non-aggressive, socially appropriate ways to obtain desired outcomes), negotiation skills training, interpersonal cognitive problem-solving (to teach thinking skills for solving interpersonal problems), social perspective training (to teach how to recognize and understand other people's feelings), role-playing and modelling (demonstration and practice of effective and acceptable interpersonal behavior).

Parent training

If poor parental supervision and erratic child rearing behavior are causes of offending, it seems likely that parent training might succeed in reducing offending. The behavioral parent training developed by Patterson (1982) is one of the most hopeful approaches. His careful observations of parent-child interaction - again, a distinctive method used by psychologists - showed that parents of antisocial children were deficient in their methods of child rearing. These parents failed to tell their children how they were expected to behave, failed to monitor the behavior to ensure that it was desirable, and failed to enforce rules promptly and unambiguously with appropriate rewards and penalties. The parents of antisocial children used more punishment (such as scolding, shouting or threatening), but failed to make it contingent on the child's behavior.

Patterson attempted to train these parents in effective child rearing methods, namely noticing what a child is doing, monitoring behavior over long periods, clearly stating house rules, making rewards and punishments contingent on behavior, and negotiating disagreements so that conflicts and crises did not escalate. His treatment was shown to be effective in reducing child stealing over short periods in small-scale studies.

Peer programs

If having delinquent friends causes offending, then any program which reduces their effect or increases the influence of prosocial friends should have a reductive effect on offending. Feldman, Caplinger, and Wodarski (1983) carried out an experimental test of this prediction in St. Louis. Over 400 boys who were referred because of antisocial behavior were randomly assigned to two kinds of activity groups, each comprising about 10-12 adolescents. The groups consisted either totally of referred (antisocial) youth or of one or two referred youth and about 10 non-referred (prosocial) peers. On the basis of systematic observation, self-reports by the youth, and ratings by the group leaders, the researchers found that the antisocial behavior of the referred youth in groups with prosocial peers decreased relative to that of the referred youth in antisocial groups.

Several studies show that school students can be taught to resist peer influences encouraging smoking, drinking and marijuana use. For example, Telch et al. (1982) employed older high school students to teach younger ones to develop counter-arguing skills to resist peer pressure to smoke, using modelling and guided practice. This approach was successful in decreasing smoking by the younger students, and similar results were reported by Botvin and Eng (1982). Murray et al. (1984) used same-aged leaders to teach students how to resist peer pressures to begin smoking, and Evans et al. (1981) used films. These techniques, designed to counter antisocial peer pressures, could help to decrease offending.

School programs

If low intelligence and school problems are causes of offending, then any program that leads to an increase in school success should lead to a decrease in offending. One of the most successful delinquency prevention programs was the Perry pre-school project carried out in Michigan by Schweinhart and Weikart (1980). This was essentially a "Head Start" program targeted on disadvantaged black children, who were allocated (approximately at random) to experimental and control groups. The experimental children attended a daily pre-school program, backed up by weekly home visits, usually lasting two years (covering ages 3-4). The aim of the program was to provide intellectual stimulation, to increase cognitive abilities, and to increase later school achievement.

More than 120 children in the two groups were followed up to age 15, using teacher ratings, parent and youth interviews, and school records. As demonstrated in several other Head Start projects, the experimental group showed gains in intelligence that were rather short-lived. However, they were significantly better in elementary school motivation, school achievement at age 14, teacher ratings of classroom behavior at 6 to 9, and self-reports of offending at 15. Furthermore, a later follow-up of this sample by Berrueta-Clement et al. (1984) showed that, at age 19, the experimental group was more likely to be employed, more likely to have graduated from high school, more likely to have received college or vocational training, and less likely to have been arrested. Hence, this pre-school intellectual enrichment program led to decreases in school failure and to decreases in offending.

Several researchers have suggested that, if school failure is linked to offending, sending troublesome children to alternative schools where failure experiences are minimized might lead to a decrease in their offending. Gold and Mann (1984) studied three alternative schools in Detroit for disruptive and delinquent juveniles, which aimed to increase their success experiences through individualized curricula and grades based on a student's own progress (i.e., not in relation to other students). They found that students allocated to the alternative schools showed less disruptive behavior than controls allocated to regular high schools. Similary, Gottfredson (1987) evaluated several alternative school projects and found that some led to decreases in offending. Therefore, there is some evidence that changes in school organization can decrease offending. (For an extensive review of schooling and delinquency, see Hawkins & Lishner, 1987.)

Hawkins et al. (1991) carried out a theoretically-based program intended to decrease aggressive behavior, delinquency and drug abuse, and increase prosocial behavior, by promoting social bonding. About 500 first grade children (aged 6) in 21 classes in 8 Seattle schools were randomly assigned to be in experimental or control classes. The children in the experimental classes received special treatment at home and school which was designed to increase their attachment to their parents and their bonding to the school. Their parents were trained to notice and reinforce socially desirable behavior in a program called "Catch 'em being good". Their teachers were trained in classroom management, for example to provide clear instructions and expectations to children, to reward children for participation in desired behavior, and to teach children prosocial methods of solving problems.

In an evaluation of this program 18 months later, when the children were in different classes, Hawkins et al. (1991) found that the boys who received the experimental program were significantly less aggressive than the control boys, according to teacher ratings. This difference was particularly marked for white boys rather than black boys. The experimental girls were not significantly less aggressive, but they were less self-destructive, anxious and depressed.

Situational crime prevention

A number of crime prevention methods have been based on situational influences on crime. These methods are typically aimed at specific types of offenses and are designed to change the environment to decrease criminal opportunities (e.g., Clarke, 1983). They include increasing surveillance (e.g., by installing closed-circuit television cameras in subway stations), hardening targets (e.g., by replacing aluminum coin boxes by steel ones in public telephone kiosks), and managing the environment (e.g., by paying wages by check rather than by cash). These techniques have been shown to be effective in reducing crime in experimental and time series studies.

The major difficulty with this approach is displacement. If some people have criminal propensities, and if one outlet for these is blocked, they will seek other outlets: other types of crimes, other methods of committing crimes, other targets, and so on. Also, as Clarke (1983) pointed out, situational approaches provoke fears of "big brother" forms of state control and of a "fortress society" in which frightened citizens scuttle from their fortified house, in their fortified car, to their fortified workplace, avoiding contact with other citizens. Nevertheless, situational crime prevention is clearly an important approach, developed by psychologists, which holds out the promise of decreasing offending.

As mentioned earlier, situational approaches are often linked to a rational decision-making theory of crime (e.g., Cornish & Clarke, 1986). If offending involves a rational decision in which the costs are weighed against the benefits, it might be deterred by increasing the costs of offending or by increasing the probability of costs. Indeed, experimental and quasi-experimental research on drunken driving (e.g., Ross, Campbell, & Glass, 1970), driving with worn tires (e.g., Buikhuisen, 1974), and domestic violence (e.g., Sherman & Berk, 1984) suggests that adults can be deterred in this way. However, the attempt to deter juveniles in the "Scared Straight" program, by having adult prisoners tell them about the horrors of imprisonment, was not successful (e.g. Finckenauer, 1982; Lewis, 1983). Given the "macho" orientation of many young offenders, it may be that these warnings made offending seem more risky and hence more attractive.

Conclusion

Key issues

This short paper has reviewed a few of the important contributions that psychologists have made to the explanation, prevention, and treatment of offending. It is now vital to plan for the further advances in knowledge that will be needed to ensure that crime is a less harmful social problem in the next century than it is at present (see also Farrington, 1988a).

Most prior explanatory research provides information about the correlates of offending in full flow in the teenage years. However, it does not yield knowledge about why offending begins, why it continues or escalates, why it diversifies into different types, and why it diminishes or ceases. Future explanatory research should focus on the causes of onset, continuation, and desistance - which would be of more relevance to prevention and treatment - rather than on the causes of offending (i.e., why some people are worse offenders than others).

If only because these processes happen at different ages, the causes of onset, continuation, and desistance are likely to differ. For example, parental child-rearing techniques may influence onset, peers may influence continuation, and settling down in a steady job and getting married may influence desistance. In the London longitudinal survey, Farrington and Hawkins (1991) indeed found that child-rearing predicted early onset but not desistance, while school achievement predicted desistance but not early onset.

Future explanatory research needs a developmental focus. While we know a great deal about offending in the teenage years, we know less about antisocial behavior in the pre-teenage years and less still about factors in infancy that influence later offending. Also, few studies have tried to document the changes in adulthood that coincide with the decline in offending. It is important to establish developmental sequences. For example, impulsivity at age 2-5 may lead to conduct disorder at age 6-10, which may lead to shoplifting at age 12-15, burglary at age 16-19, violence in the 20s, and drunken driving and spouse assault in the 30s. Knowledge about such developmental sequences would help in determining when and how it was best to intervene to try to disrupt them.

Most prior studies essentially compare offending *between individuals* - that is, most research shows that offenders differ from non-offenders in intelligence, parental child-rearing techniques, peer delinquency, school failure, and so on. Unfortunately, between-individual comparisons do not permit unambiguous conclusions about causal influences with high internal validity, especially when predictor variables are highly intercorrelated. More convincing conclusions could be drawn from *within-individual* comparisons, such as by showing that an individual's offending decreased after his or her school performance improved (e.g., Farrington, 1988b). Also, within-individual comparisons are more relevant to prevention and treatment, which require changes within individuals.

While psychologists have studied biological, individual, family, peer, school, and situational factors, they have tended to neglect community influences. However, it is clear that crime rates are much greater in some areas (e.g., in inner cities) than in others, and it has been argued that these differences hold independently of immigration into and emigration out of these areas (e.g., Shaw & McKay, 1969). It may be that a complete explanation of offending requires some consideration of community influences, and that offending might be decreased by changing communities (e.g., Hope & Shaw, 1988).

Future research needs

Much of our firm knowledge about the development of offending has been obtained in longitudinal surveys. Similarly, much of our firm knowledge about the effectiveness of prevention and treatment has been obtained in randomized experiments. These considerations led Farrington et al. (1986) to recommend a new generation of longitudinal-experimental studies, combining the two methods. They suggested that four cohorts of children be followed up, from birth to age 6, from 6 to 12, from 12 to 18, and from 18 to 24, with experimental interventions included in each age range.

Recently, these proposals have been greatly extended and elaborated by Tonry, Ohlin and Farrington (1991). Their aim is still to advance knowledge about the development of offending and about the effectiveness of methods of preventing and treating offending. They proposed that 7 cohorts should each be followed up for 8 years, starting prenatally and at ages 3, 6, 9, 12, 15, and 18. Each multiple-cohort study should be carried out in a large city, and individuals and communities should be followed up within that city. If these kinds of studies were undertaken, they would lead to significant advances in knowledge about explanation, prevention, and treatment.

References

American Psychiatric Association (1987). *Diagnostic and Statistical Manual of Mental Disorders,* 3rd rev. ed., Washington, DC: Author.

Berrueta-Clement, J.R., Schweinhart, L.J., Barnett, W.S., Epstein, A.S., & Weikart, D.P. (1984). *Changed lives.* Ypsilanti, MI: High/Scope.

Botvin, G.J., & Eng, A. (1982). The efficacy of a multicomponent approach to the prevention of cigarette smoking. *Preventive Medicine, 11*, 199-211.

Brody, S.R. (1976). *The effectiveness of sentencing.* London: Her Majesty's Stationery Office.

Buikhuisen, W. (1974). General deterrence: Research and theory. *Abstracts in Criminology and Penology, 14*, 285-298.

Clarke, R.V. (1983). Situational crime prevention: Its theoretical basis and practical scope. In M. Tonry, & N. Morris (Eds.), *Crime and justice, Vol. 4* (pp. 225-256). Chicago: University of Chicago Press.

Clarke, R.V., & Cornish, D.B. (1985). Modelling offenders' decisions: A framework for research and policy. In M. Tonry, & N. Morris (Eds.), *Crime and justice, Vol. 6 (pp.* 147-185). Chicago: University of Chicago Press.

Cornish, D.B., & Clarke, R.V. (Eds.) (1986). *The reasoning criminal.* New York: Springer.

Elliott, D.S., Huizinga, D., & Ageton, S.S. (1985). *Explaining delinquency and drug use.* Beverly Hills, CA: Sage.

Erickson, M., Gibbs, J.P., & Jensen, G.F. (1977). The deterrence doctrine and the perceived certainty of legal punishment. *American Sociological Review, 42*, 305-317.

Evans, R.I., Rozelle, R.M., Maxwell, S.E., Raines, B.E., Dill, C.A., Guthrie, T.J., Henderson, A.H., & Hill, P.C. (1981). Social modelling films to deter smoking in adolescents: Results of a three-year field investigation. *Journal of Applied Psychology, 66*, 399-414.

Farrington, D.P. (1972). Delinquency begins at home. *New Society, 21*, 495-497.

Farrington, D.P. (1978). The family backgrounds of aggressive youths. In L. Hersov, M. Berger, & D. Shaffer (Eds.), *Aggression and antisocial behavior in childhood and adolescence* (pp. 73-93). Oxford: Pergamon.

Farrington, D.P. (1979). Environmental stress, delinquent behavior, and convictions. In I.G. Sarason, & C.D. Spielberger (Eds.), *Stress and anxiety, Vol. 6* (pp. 93-107). Washington, DC: Hemisphere.

Farrington, D.P. (1983). Randomized experiments on crime and justice. In M. Tonry, & N. Morris (Eds.), *Crime and justice, Vol. 4* (pp. 257-308). Chicago: University of Chicago Press.

Farrington, D.P. (1984). Delinquent and criminal behavior. In A. Gale, & A.J. Chapman (Eds.), *Psychology and social problems* (pp. 55-77). Chichester: Wiley.

Farrington, D.P. (1986a). Age and crime. In M. Tonry, & N. Morris (Eds.), *Crime and justice, Vol. 7* (pp. 189-250). Chicago: University of Chicago Press.

Farrington, D.P. (1986b). Stepping stones to adult criminal careers. In D. Olweus, J. Block, & M.R. Yarrow (Eds.), *Development of antisocial and prosocial behavior* (pp. 359-384). New York: Academic Press.

Farrington, D.P. (1987). Epidemiology. In H.C. Quay (Ed.), *Handbook of juvenile delinquency* (pp. 33-61). New York: Wiley.

Farrington, D.P. (1988a). Advancing knowledge about delinquency and crime: The need for a coordinated program of longitudinal research. *Behavioral Sciences and the Law, 6*, 307-331.

Farrington, D.P. (1988b). Studying changes within individuals: The causes of offending. In M. Rutter (Ed.), *Studies of psychosocial risk* (pp. 158-183). Cambridge: Cambridge University Press.

Farrington, D.P. (1989). Self-reported and official offending from adolescence to adulthood. In M.W. Klein (Ed.), *Cross-national research in self-reported crime and delinquency* (pp. 399-423). Dordrecht: Kluwer.

Farrington, D.P. (1990a). Age, period, cohort, and offending. In D.M. Gottfredson, & R.V. Clarke (Eds.), *Policy and theory in criminal justice: Contributions in honor of Leslie T. Wilkins* (pp. 51-75). Aldershot: Gower.

Farrington, D.P. (1990b). Implications of criminal career research for the prevention of offending. *Journal of Adolescence, 13*, 93-113.

Farrington, D.P. (1991a). Antisocial personality from childhood to adulthood. *The Psychologist, 4*, 389-394.

Farrington, D.P. (1991b). Childhood aggression and adult violence: Early precursors and later life outcomes. In D.J. Pepler, & K.H. Rubin (Eds.), *The development of childhood aggression* (pp. 5-29). Hillsdale, NJ: Lawrence Erlbaum.

Farrington, D.P., & Hawkins, J.D. (1991). Predicting participation, early onset, and later persistence in officially recorded offending. *Criminal Behavior and Mental Health, 1*, 1-33.

Farrington, D.P., & Knight, B.J. (1980). Four studies of stealing as a risky decision. In P.D. Lipsitt, & B.D. Sales (Eds.), *New directions in psycholegal research* (pp. 26-50). New York: Van Nostrand Reinhold.

Farrington, D.P., Loeber, R., Elliott, D.S., Hawkins, J.D., Kandel, D.B., Klein, M.W., McCord, J., Rowe, D.C., & Tremblay, R.E. (1990a). Advancing knowledge about the onset of delinquency and crime. In B.B. Lahey, & A.E. Kazdin (Eds.), *Advances in clinical child psychology, Vol. 13* (pp. 283-342). New York: Plenum.

Farrington, D.P., Loeber, R., & Van Kammen, W.B. (1990b). Long-term criminal outcomes of hyperactivity-impulsivity-attention deficit and conduct problems in childhood. In L.N. Robins, & M. Rutter (Eds.), *Straight and devious pathways from childhood to adulthood* (pp. 62-81). Cambridge: Cambridge University Press.

Farrington, D.P., Ohlin, L.E., & Wilson, J.Q. (1986). *Understanding and controlling crime.* New York: Springer.

Farrington, D.P., & West, D.J. (1990). The Cambridge study in delinquent development: A long-term follow-up of 411 London males. In H.J. Kerner, & G. Kaiser (Eds.), *Criminality: Personality, behavior, and life history* (pp. 115-138). Berlin: Springer.

Feldman, R.A., Caplinger, T.E., & Wodarski, J.S. (1983). *The St. Louis conundrum.* Englewood Cliffs, NJ: Prentice-Hall.

Finckenauer, J.O. (1982). *Scared straight.* Englewood Cliffs, NJ: Prentice-Hall.

Gendreau, P., & Ross, R.R. (1979). Effective correctional treatment: Bibliotherapy for cynics. *Crime and Delinquency, 25*, 463-489.

Gendreau, P., & Ross, R.R. (1987). Revivification of rehabilitation: Evidence from the 1980s. *Justice Quarterly, 4*, 349-407.

Gold, M., & Mann, D.W. (1984). *Expelled to a friendlier place.* Ann Arbor, MI: University of Michigan Press.

Gottfredson, D.C. (1987). Examining the potential of delinquency prevention through alternative education. *Today's Delinquent, 6*, 87-100.

Hawkins, J.D., & Lishner, D.M. (1987). Schooling and delinquency. In E.H. Johnson (Ed.), *Handbook on crime and delinquency prevention* (pp. 179-221). Westport, CT: Greenwood Press.

Hawkins, J.D., Von Cleve, E., & Catalano, R.F. (1991). Reducing early childhood aggression: Results of a primary prevention program. *Journal of the American Academy of Child and Adolescent Psychiatry, 30*, 208-217.

Hirschi, T. (1969). *Causes of delinquency.* Berkeley, CA: University of California Press.

Hollin, C.R. (1989). *Psychology and crime.* London: Routledge.

Hope, T., & Shaw, M. (Eds.) (1988). *Communities and crime reduction.* London: Her Majesty's Stationery Office.

Kazdin, A.E. (1987). Treatment of antisocial behavior in children: Current status and future directions. *Psychological Bulletin, 102*, 187-203.

Kolvin, I., Miller, F.J.W., Fleeting, M., & Kolvin, P.A. (1988). Social and parenting factors affecting criminal-offense rates: Findings from the Newcastle Thousand Family Study (1947-1980). *British Journal of Psychiatry, 152*, 80-90.

Lewis, R.V. (1983). Scared straight - California style. *Criminal Justice and Behavior, 10*, 209-226.

Loeber, R. (1987). Behavioral precursors and accelerators of delinquency. In W. Buikhuisen, & S.A. Mednick (Eds.), *Explaining criminal behavior* (pp. 51-67). Leiden: Brill.

Loeber, R., & Dishion, T. (1983). Early predictors of male delinquency: A review. *Psychological Bulletin, 94*, 68-99.

Loeber, R., & Stouthamer-Loeber, M. (1986). Family factors as correlates and predictors of juvenile conduct problems and delinquency. In M. Tonry, & N. Morris (Eds.), *Crime and justice, Vol. 7* (pp. 29-149). Chicago: University of Chicago Press.

Loeber, R., & Stouthamer-Loeber, M. (1987). Prediction. In H.C. Quay (Ed.), *Handbook of juvenile delinquency* (pp. 325-382). New York: Wiley.

Magnusson, D. (1988). *Individual development from an interactional perspective.* Hillsdale, NJ: Erlbaum.

Martinson, R.M. (1974). What works? Questions and answers about prison reform. *The Public Interest, 35,* 22-54.

McCord, J. (1979). Some child-rearing antecedents of criminal behavior in adult men. *Journal of Personality and Social Psychology, 37,* 1477-1486.

Mednick, S.A., Gabrielli, W.F., & Hutchings, B. (1983). Genetic influences on criminal behavior: Evidence from an adoption cohort. In K.T. Van Dusen, & S.A. Mednick (Eds.), *Prospective studies of crime and delinquency* (pp. 39-56). Boston: Kluwer-Nijhoff.

Michelson, L. (1987). Cognitive-behavioral strategies in the prevention and treatment of antisocial disorders in children and adolescents. In J.D. Burchard, & S.N. Burchard (Eds.), *Prevention of delinquent behavior* (pp. 275-310). Beverly Hills, CA: Sage.

Moffitt, T.E. (1990). The neuropsychology of juvenile delinquency: A critical review. In M. Tonry, & N. Morris (Eds.), *Crime and Justice, Vol. 12* (pp. 99-169). Chicago: University of Chicago Press.

Moffitt, T.E., & Silva, P.A. (1988a). IQ and delinquency: A direct test of the differential detection hypothesis. *Journal of Abnormal Psychology, 97,* 330-333.

Moffitt, T.E., & Silva, P.A. (1988b). Neuropsychological deficit and self-reported delinquency in an unselected birth cohort. *Journal of the American Academy of Child and Adolescent Psychiatry, 27,* 233-240.

Murray, D.M., Luepker, R.V., Johnson, C.A., & Mittelmark, M.B. (1984). The prevention of cigarette smoking in children: A comparison of four strategies. *Journal of Applied Social Psychology, 14,* 274-288.

Olweus, D. (1987). Testosterone and adrenaline: Aggressive antisocial behavior in normal adolescent males. In S.A. Mednick, T.E. Moffitt, & S.A. Stack (Eds.), *The causes of crime: New biological approaches* (pp. 263-282). Cambridge: Cambridge University Press.

Parker, J.G., & Asher, S.R. (1987). Peer relations and later personal adjustment: Are low accepted children at risk? *Psychological Bulletin, 102,* 357-389.

Patterson, G.R. (1982). *Coercive family process.* Eugene, OR: Castalia.

Power, M.J., Alderson, M.R., Phillipson, C.M., Shoenberg, E., & Morris, J.N. (1967). Delinquent schools? *New Society, 10,* 542-543.

Pulkkinen, L. (1988). Delinquent development: Theoretical and empirical considerations. In M. Rutter (Ed.), *Studies of psychosocial risk* (pp. 184-199). Cambridge: Cambridge University Press.

Raine, A. (1988). Antisocial behavior and social psychophysiology. In H.L. Wagner (Ed.), *Social psychophysiology and emotion* (pp. 231-250). Chichester: Wiley.

Reiss, A.J. (1988). Co-offending and criminal careers. In M. Tonry, & N. Morris (Eds.), *Crime and justice, Vol. 10* (pp. 117-170). Chicago: University of Chicago Press.

Reiss, A.J., & Farrington, D.P. (1991). Co-offending behavior: Results from a prospective longitudinal survey of London males. *Journal of Criminal Law and Criminology, 82,* 360-395.

Robins, L.N. (1979). Sturdy childhood predictors of adult outcomes: Replications from longitudinal studies. In J.E. Barrett, R.M. Rose, & G.L. Klerman (Eds.), *Stress and mental disorder* (pp. 219-235). New York: Raven Press.

Roff, J.D., & Wirt, R.D. (1984). Childhood aggression and social adjustment as antecedents of delinquency. *Journal of Abnormal Child Psychology, 12,* 111-126.

Ross, H.L., Campbell, D.T., & Glass, G.V. (1970). Determining the social effects of a legal reform: The British breathalyzer crackdown of 1967. *American Behavioral Scientist, 13,* 493-509.

Ross, R.R., Fabiano, E.A., & Ewles, C.D. (1988). Reasoning and rehabilitation. *International Journal of Offender Therapy and Comparative Criminology, 32,* 29-35.

Ross, R.R., & Ross, B.D. (1988). Delinquency prevention through cognitive training. *New Education, 10,* 70-75.

Rowe, D.C. (1987). Resolving the person-situation debate: Invitation to an interdisciplinary dialogue. *American Psychologist, 42,* 218-227.

Rutter, M., Maughan, B., Mortimore, P., & Ouston, J. (1979). *Fifteen thousand hours.* London: Open Books.

Schweinhart, L.J., & Weikart, D.P. (1980). *Young children grow up.* Ypsilanti, MI: High/Scope.

Sechrest, L., White, S.O., & Brown, E.D. (1979). *The rehabilitation of criminal offenders: Problems and prospects.* Washington, DC: National Academy of Sciences.

Shaw, C.R., & McKay, H.D. (1969). *Juvenile delinquency and urban areas,* rev. ed. Chicago: University of Chicago Press.

Sherman, L.W., & Berk, R.A. (1984). The specific deterrent effects of arrest for domestic assault. *American Sociological Review, 49,* 261-272.

Telch, M.J., Killen, J.D., McAlister, A.L., Perry, C.L., & Maccoby, N. (1982). Long-term follow-up of a pilot project on smoking prevention with adolescents. *Journal of Behavioral Medicine, 5,* 1-8.

Thornton, D.M. (1987). Treatment effects on recidivism: A reappraisal of the "Nothing Works" doctrine. In B.J. McGurk, D.M. Thornton, & M. Williams (Eds.), *Applying psychology to imprisonment* (pp. 181-189). London: Her Majesty's Stationery Office.

Tonry, M., Ohlin, L.E., & Farrington, D.P. (1991). *Human development and criminal behavior.* New York: Springer.

Trasler, G.B. (1962). *The explanation of criminality.* London: Routledge and Kegan Paul.

Venables, P.H. (1987). Autonomic nervous system factors in criminal behavior. In S.A. Mednick, T.E. Moffitt, & S.A. Stack (Eds.), *The causes of crime: New biological approaches* (pp. 110-136). Cambridge: Cambridge University Press.

Wadsworth, M. (1979). *Roots of delinquency.* London: Martin Robertson.

West, D.J., & Farrington, D.P. (1973). *Who becomes delinquent?* London: Heinemann.

West, D.J., & Farrington, D.P. (1977). *The delinquent way of life.* London: Heinemann.

Wikstrom, P.O. (1987). *Patterns of crime in a birth cohort.* Stockholm: University of Stockholm, Department of Sociology.

Wilson, J.Q., & Herrnstein, R.J. (1985). *Crime and human nature.* New York: Simon and Schuster.

Zimring, F.E. (1981). Kids, groups and crime: Some implications of a well-known secret. *Journal of Criminal Law and Criminology, 72,* 867-885.

Part II
Explanation of Offending and Assessment of Offenders

Applying Chaos Theory to Delinquent Behavior in Psychosocial Stress Situations

Thomas Fabian and Michael Stadler

Introduction

The assessment of so-called "crimes of passion" has always posed a problem in criminal law practice - especially the question of diminished culpability: On one hand, many offenders do not show pronounced psychopathology - they almost seem "normal". On the other hand, their offense behavior seems incomprehensible. It was this contradiction that opened the door into penal courts for psychologists in the 1950s (Fabian & Stadler, 1987). Two features in particular typically characterize crimes of passion and unerringly call forth the interest of the mass media: Often the deed can be put down to a trifling, seemingly coincidental cause, and the intensity of the deed - the reaction - is often apparently disproportionately strong ("overflowing reaction").

In the following, an attempt will be made to explain these two aspects with the help of chaos theory (cause of the deed) and stress theory (intensity of the reaction). Maybe chaos theory offers not only a new way of understanding, but also new ways for psychologically evaluating crimes of passion.

Forensic psychology as well as forensic psychiatry have developed detailed criteria lists for the assessment of crimes of passion. So far, however, a theoretical explanation going further than description has not been put forth. Especially the criterion "inconstancy of behavior style" (Thomae & Schmidt, 1967) or "strangeness to the personality" (Bochnik, Legewie, Otto, & Wüster, 1965) are superficial terms without explanative content. The same can be said for the criterion "incoherence of behavior" (Mende, 1986), which actually obstructs the access to an explanation of the deed.

In the history of psychology, it can be seen repeatedly how the emergence of new paradigms in the natural sciences has also led to new theoretical approaches in psychology. The youngest example is synergetics, which have been applied successfully in the context of psychological research (Haken & Stadler, 1990). While the theory of self-organization explains how instable states develop into stable states, chaos theory explains how stable states can "tilt" and lead to turbulence, which cannot be forecast in detail.

The transfer of terminology from the natural sciences to the social sciences brings with it the danger of mistaking semantic innovation for progress of knowledge. Therefore the concepts of natural science - especially the terminology and results of mathematical models - cannot be transferred directly but must be filled with psychological content. If concepts from the natural sciences are used by psychologists as new working hypotheses to approach their subject, then this can further the future development of psychological theories.

The Theoretical Approach of Chaos Research

Chaos theory (see Crutchfield, Farmer, Packard, & Shaw, 1989; Gleick, 1987; Haken, 1981; Steward, 1990) does not explain connections of effects with a classical causal model in the sense of *causa aequate effectum*. Nonetheless, effects in a chaotic system are not random but lawful. We will apply this central statement of chaos theory to an explanation of crimes of passion.

Chaotic systems are characterized by a sensitive dependency on initial conditions, which cannot be determined exactly. Therefore the development - although it is lawful - cannot be predicted. Minimal causes can lead to large effects (the so-called "butterfly effect"). As the effects are not incidental, one speaks of a "deterministic chaos". Chaotic behavior exists only in nonlinear systems. Human behavior can be seen as nonlinear.

Stable systems can founder through in their initial conditions. Important for this is especially the fact that several minimal changes in the system conditions, which by themselves are insignificant, can - when added up - lead to a toppling of the system. An extreme weakening can lead the system to a bifurcation point at which further development can turn into an unexpected direction. This direction is, however, not at all incidental or arbitrary, it depends on the concrete initial and marginal conditions of the system.

If the system is in an unstable state, its behavior tends toward attractors that were previously ineffective because of the prior stability of the system. Rapid changes can be explained only if it is known what caused the prior stability of the system. From a psychological viewpoint, attractors can be described as valences in the life space as proposed in the book of Lewin (1935).

Different situations or intrapsychic events that are experienced as highly threatening can be bifurcation points for human beings at which the possibility to foresee further behavior no longer exists. Such bifurcation points can, for example, be critical life events or an injury to the ego. In such situations, previous coping mechanisms may cease to function and reactions can be exhibited that are not directly deducible from prior behavior.

This could explain why discussion on crimes of passion has long focussed on the "strangeness of the deed to the personality". Rasch (1980, 1986) and Mende (1986) are right when they emphasize that "strangeness to the personality" is an unsuitable criterion. There is no such thing as behavior that is "strange to the personality", but only behavior that is not predictable but nonetheless based on existing behavior repertoires. Behavior repertoires, however, contain not only behavior controlled by cognition but also phylogenetically inherited behaviors, such as stress reactions.

Stress defence

The basic approach of stress research is physiological stress theory (Selye, 1946, 1956). Selye called the whole of physiological reactions to stress-producing stimuli a "general adaption syndrome". The organism responds to a noxious stimulus with an "alarm reaction", which is characterized by a "shock phase" and the following "counter-shock phase". While, during the shock phase, the direct effects of the stressor are felt, the counter-shock phase is often characterized by an overflowing mobilization of energy toward the stressor. If the organism stays under the influence of a strong stressor for a prolonged amount of time, the counter shock phase does not turn into the "resistance phase", but the organism enters into the "phase of exhaustion" and the symptoms of the shock phase appear once again.

Animals show three patterns of defence in case of threats: pretending to be dead, flight, or attack. Human beings show similar behaviors in reaction to stressors, such as apathy, avoidance, or aggression.

Psychological stress theory has concerned itself mainly with the mediative effects of psychological processes in stress events. It is, however, also based on the assumption that the threatening meaning of a stimulus can be grasped without the conscious recognition of its detailed structural quality ("subception" model) (see Lazarus & Riess, 1960). A central role in psychological stress theory, however, is assigned to the cognitive processes of stress regulation. The most prominent model in this context is surely the model proposed by the Berkeley group around Lazarus (1966), in which processes of stress appraisal and coping with stress are described. The coping mechanisms are differentiated in direct action and intrapsychic processes (Lazarus & Averill, 1972).

Crimes of passion from the perspective of chaos in connection with stress theory

Many crimes of passion take place in dissolving partnerships. When relationships have been stable over a period of often many years, the announcement of the intention to leave the partnership by one partner - in the case of later crimes of passion these are mostly announced by the woman - leads to an instability of the system. Only in a very small fraction of separations does the deserted partner kill - and in those few cases, not immediately after the first announcement of the intention to leave but more often weeks or even months later. This period of time is called in forensic practice the "preceding history of the deed". The exact date and time of the deed often appears to be sudden, unexpected, and triggered by a minimal stimulus. Such a minimal stimulus can be, for example, the rejection of physical approaches, which may have happened repeatedly before but did not lead to a strong aggressive reaction on the side of the partner who was pushed away. Or they can be verbal remarks that in the sense of a code word, start a chain of reactions (Ritzel, 1980). In the literature on crimes of passion one finds many descriptions of how "trivial stimuli" (Mende, 1986) lead to killings.

From the perspective of chaos theory, however, these stimuli may by themselves be of little importance, but, in the context of changes in the marginal conditions, they can by summation become a lawful trigger for the killing reaction. The intensity of the reaction - in the literature often described as "primitive reaction" (Kretschmer, 1971) - can be explained insofar as the offender, due to the instability finds himself or herself at a bifurcation point. At this point, there is no possibility to predict his or her further behavior, which is nonetheless lawful according to chaos theory. Because of the experienced threats of the situation, behavior tends to be attracted towards response patterns that are not controlled on a cognitive level, such as phylogenetically inherited stress reactions. In a certain, not predictable combination of stimuli, the cognitive coping mechanisms of the person fail to function and he or she reacts with aggressive actions. From the point of view of problem-solving research, we can talk about a "primitive termination reaction" (Dörner, Reither, & Stäudel, 1983).

Besides crimes of passion in the context of partnership separations, there is another typical constellation in which maltreated women kill their partners. These cases are especially interesting from the perspective of chaos theory, since there is often no extended past history in the exact sense. The killing occurs so to speak "on the spur of the moment". In the following we will present a case study as an example for this, taken from the case material of the research project on affect diagnostics performed by Steller and Eiselt (1986) and shortened for this presentation.

Case study

The female offender (A) had been married to her husband (B) for 12 years prior to the deed. She had been together with him for two years before the marriage. One year before the marriage their son was born. A had pressed for the marriage, since she worshipped B and saw him as the ideal partner for a happy family life. But soon she was disappointed by the marriage, since B repeatedly committed criminal offenses, worked irregularly, and consumed a considerable amount of alcohol. He went on extended drinking tours two or three times per week. When B was drunk he was very aggressive. He treated A in a way that can be called sadistic. Already in the third year of their marriage, he beat up A so strongly that she finally became unconscious. In the further course of their marriage, B began to threaten her with a knife and once injured her hand with it. In such situations he often threatened her: "I'll kill you, I'll stab you."

A held a regular job and was esteemed as a reliable and diligent worker. When B maltreated her, she tried to soften him with calming and soothing behavior. Several times she had to leave the apartment in order to escape from B. On these occasions she also took with her the daughter born in the fifth year of the marriage, whom she used to put to bed fully dressed and ready for flight. The firstborn son had been staying with A's mother since right after his birth. While the son had been repeatedly kicked by B, she had succeeded in protecting the younger daughter. In spite of all this, A never gave much thought to the possibility of divorce, because she continued to hope for a harmonious marriage and to long for a change in B's behavior. B promised again and again to start working regularly and to quit drinking. A complete marital breakdown and alienation between A and B was averted by their fulfilling sexual relationship during the times when B was sober. When A thought about a divorce she used to come to the conclusion that this would mean a social decline for her, that B would still not leave her alone, and that she did not want the children to loose their father. Therefore she tried to keep up the appearance of a harmonious marriage. When she had been beaten by B she went for a demonstrative walk with him arm in arm. She pretended that B held a regular job and covered bruises and grazes with make-up or sunglasses. In everyday life A behaved in a markedly reserved, sensible, and conformist manner. She usually took the blame for marital fights. Her rare defence reactions were limited to verbal statements such as "You're crazy!" A tried repeatedly to hide B's knife, but he got himself a new one immediately.

On the evening before the deed, B hit the eight-year-old daughter while inebriated. The girl fled to her mother and cried for help. A pleaded with him and asked him to hit her instead. B did this, but continued to hit the girl in-between. After A had brought the girl to bed, B dumped the contents of the ashtray on the floor and forced her to pick up the cigarette stubs. On the following morning A drove B and the girl to her parents-in-law and went to work. B soon left the house and visited several bars. Around five o'clock in the afternoon he went back and started a fight with his father, who in the course of the fight injured him with scratches. When A came back around six o'clock and heard about the fight she immediately wanted to drive home with her family. B forced her, however, to visit several more bars with him beforehand. Shortly before eight o'clock B agreed to drive home. During the drive he got to talk about the fight with his father and remarked, that he would have stabbed him a long time ago if he had not been his father.

After arriving in the appartment, A took a short break in the living room. She was exhausted, since she had hardly slept the night before because she was distressed about B's treatment of the daughter, and also because she had worked all day and had been forced against her will to go on the drinking tour with B. Furthermore, she was in the premenstrual phase and as always in this phase felt more nervous and fearful than usual. B sat down across from her, took out his knife and put it on the table. A left the room and went into the kitchen to prepare herself a sandwich. There she heard how B told her to again accompany him to a bar. A answered him that she would not do that and took hold of the breadknife, which she then laid down on the kitchen table. Suddenly B stood next to her and shouted at her: "What, you're not doing what I'm telling you? - Then I'll kill you today and stab you!" At that moment A felt the edge of his knife on her neck. She turned around and said: "I think you're mad. Take your knife away!" Although she was scared, at that moment, A did not think of a disaster. Not until B approached her threatening her with the knife did she feel fear of death. She tried to fence B off and pushed him against the kitchen table, which shook so that the knife fell down from the table and onto the floor. B then cornered A in such a way that she could not escape, A pushed him again back in the direction of the table, so that the table was also moved. Visibly in rage, B again approached A and tried to grab her. With this he slid on the floor and fell down backwards. A reached for him and tried to keep him from falling because she was afraid B would blame her for his fall. They both went down. A sat half kneeling next to him and he lay with his upper body upright in her arm. When in this position B also threatened to kill her, A happened to see the breadknife on the floor. She lifted it up with her right hand and at around eight thirty she stabbed B repeatedly with the knife, which penetrated his thorax nine times. Afterwards she sat for a while in the kitchen and said to B: "I loved you. It was all your fault." Then she took her daughter and left the house. The next day, when she went to see a lawyer, she was still frightened her husband would come and harm her.

With this case, it can be demonstrated from the perspective of chaos theory, how the development of the deed was lawful, but not predictable. The stability in the relationship between A and B was based mainly on the fact that A continued to treat B softly and that a separation was out of the question for her. The system of interaction and communication was balanced insofar as A reacted to the aggressive behavior of B with nothing but flight, avoidance, or denial.

The maltreatment of the daughter changed the initial conditions of the system. Within A, this activated a functional area - from an ethological perspective it would be called "brood care" - which phylogenetically can be maintained in the face of danger only by attack. Thereby the threshold was lowered for a deeper lying attractor. Attack behavior as an attractor had furthermore come to attention and was also strengthened by the fact that in the fight with the father it had become obvious that B could be wounded. As attack became an attractor alongside avoidance behavior, a bifurcation became possible. At the same time, there was a change in the inner system conditions for A, which led to a further instability of the system. Her inner initial conditions were changed by the premenstrual phase as well as by the exhaustion due to sleeplessness and stress. These changes in the initial conditions were prerequisite for the possibility of a bifurcation.

Within the immediate situation of the deed, B's threats led to a fear of death on A's side. Due to the changes in the initial conditions, we can assume that there were now two equally strong attractors to her behavior - flight and attack. She was, so to say, on a "razor's edge". With one small change of marginal conditions - the close positioning of the bread knife that had fallen off the table - A's behavior "slid" into the attack attractor and she killed B.

The example shows that single changes in initial conditions by themselves did not lead to the inversion of A's behavior tendencies. Some of these changes had occurred before. A was in a premenstrual phase every month, she had surely been physically exhausted before, and she had experienced B's threats repeatedly over the last years. Also, the breadknife must have been within reach often enough. Not until several changes in initial and marginal conditions came into being at the same time did the killing of B happen.

From the perspective on chaos theory we do not have to assume an increasing build-up of emotion that, at a certain level, has to vent itself, but that it is the combination of several different conditions that leads to a crime of passion.

Some authors in forensic literature have used the criteria "gaps in the memory" as an indicator for the dimming of consciousness (Mende, 1986; Thomae & Schmidt, 1967), but Rasch (1980) and Ritzel (1980) have pointed out that this is only due to the state after the actual act of killing. A stress theoretical explanation for this phenomenon would be that the organism has not reached the phase of resistance after the aggressive act in the counter-shock phase, but that the symptoms of the shock phase have reappeared.

From a psychological point of view, the stability of the relationship between A and B was based on several barriers on A's side for seeking help or terminating the battering relationship. There were environmental reasons like the fear of social decline. But more importantly, there were typical psychological reasons like sex-role stereotypes and expectations, the "battering cycle" in which B promises to stop drinking and abusing, as well as the so-called "traumatic bond" between the battered woman and batterer, which can be compared with hostage-captor relationships (Ewing, 1987).

Now, if A was not able to leave B, why had she not killed him before? The research on battered women who kill, shows that they suffered more serious physical injuries, were more often threatened with death, their children were more often abused, and there was more often a presence of weapons than in the cases of battered women who did not kill the batterers (Ewing, 1987). Again, from the point of view of chaos theory, we would argue that the reason why A did not kill B before was that one condition is not enough to make a battered women kill the batterer.

Prospect

Within the context of our perspective on crimes of passion, the question arises as to whether we have to assume a physiological dimming of consciousness, or whether we can say that the aggressive act in these cases is a psychologically lawful act that is not controlled on a cognitive level.

Maybe the application of a chaos theory perspective does not give us any new psychological insight into delinquent behavior, but, as a metatheory, it may help - as we have tried to show - to organize our knowledge from different research areas in a systematic way that then may give us a better understanding of the dynamics of, for example, crimes of passion. At least the perspective of chaos theory will make us realize that human behavior is not based on chance but that there is a lawfulness even if it is not predictable.

References

Bochnik, H.J., Legewie, H., Otto, P., & Wüster, G. (1965). *Tat, Täter, Zurechnungsfähigkeit*. Stuttgart: Enke.

Crutchfield, J.P., Farmer, J.D., Packard, N.H., & Shaw, R.S. (1989). Chaos. In H. Jürgens (Ed.), *Chaos und Fraktale* (pp. 8-20). Heidelberg: Spektrum der Wissenschaft.

Dörner, D., Reither, F., & Stäudel, T. (1983). Emotion und problemlösendes Denken. In H. Mandl & G.L. Huber (Eds.), *Emotion und Kognition* (pp. 61-84). München: Urban & Schwarzenberg.

Ewing, C.P. (1987). *Battered women who kill*. Lexington, MA: Lexington.
Fabian, T., & Stadler, S. (1987). Die psychologische Begutachtung der Schuldfähigkeit - Entwicklung, Meinungen, Perspektiven. In H. Kury (Ed.), *Ausgewählte Fragen und Probleme forensischer Begutachtung* (pp. 117-179). Köln: Heymanns.
Gleick, J. (1987). *Chaos - Making a new science*. New York: Viking.
Haken, H. (1981). *Erfolgsgeheimnisse der Natur*. Stuttgart: Deutsche Verlags-Anstalt.
Haken, H., & Stadler, M. (1990). *Synergetics of cognition*. Berlin: Springer.
Kretschmer, E. (1971). *Medizinische Psychologie*, 13th ed. Stuttgart: Thieme. (Original work published 1922)
Lazarus, R.S. (1966). *Psychological stress and the coping process*. New York: McGraw Hill.
Lazarus, R.S., & Averill, J.R. (1972). Emotion and cognition. With special reference to anxiety. In C.D. Spielberger (Ed.), *Current trends in theory and research, Vol.* 2 (pp. 241-283). New York: Academic Press.
Lazarus, R.S., & Riess, B.F. (1960). Clinical psychology and the research problems of stress and adaption. In A. Riess & B.F. Riess (Eds.), *Progress in clinical psychology, Vol. 4* (pp. 54-67). New York: Grune & Stratton.
Lewin, K. (1935). *A dynamic theory of personality*. New York: McGraw Hill.
Mende, W. (1986). Die affektiven Störungen. In U. Venzlaff (Ed.), *Psychiatrische Begutachtung* (pp. 317-325). Stuttgart: Fischer.
Rasch, W. (1980). Die psychologisch-psychiatrische Beurteilung von Affektdelikten. *Neue Juristische Wochenschrift, 33*, 1309-1315.
Rasch, W. (1986). *Forensische Psychiatrie*. Stuttgart: Kohlhammer.
Ritzel, G. (1980). Forensisch-psychiatrische Begutachtung der Affekttat. *Münchener Medizinische Wochenschrift, 122*, 623-627.
Selye, H. (1946). The general adaption syndrome and the diseases of adaption. *Journal of Clinical Endocrinology, 6*, 117-230.
Selye, H. (1956). *The stress of life*. New York: McGraw Hill.
Steller, M., & Eiselt, W. (1986). *Entwicklung und Evaluation eines Beurteilungssystems für Affektmerkmale*. Kiel: Christian-Albrechts-Universität, Institut für Psychologie.
Steward, I. (1990). *Does god play dice? The new mathematics of chaos*. London: Penguin.
Thomae, H., & Schmidt, H.D. (1967). Psychologische Aspekte der Schuldfähigkeit. In U. Undeutsch (Ed.), *Forensische Psychologie* (pp. 326-396). Göttingen: Hogrefe.

Resilience in Juveniles With High Risk of Delinquency[1]

Thomas Bliesener and Friedrich Lösel

Introduction

Etiological research on the development of delinquency and antisocial behavior in previous years has predominantly been oriented toward deficit models and has produced a great number of risk factors for problem behavior. Since Glueck and Glueck (1950), various longitudinal and cross-sectional studies have shown repeatedly that conditions within the multiproblem milieu such as parental criminality, neglect, passive or rejecting childrearing attitudes, erratic or harsh discipline, conflicts, large families, and socioeconomic disadvantage correlate with the incidence and manifestation of delinquent careers (Farrington, Ohlin, & Wilson, 1986; Loeber & Stouthamer-Loeber, 1986). Long-term longitudinal studies have also confirmed the substantial predictive power of these risk variables (e.g., Farrington, 1989; Farrington, Gallagher, Morley, Ledger, & West, 1986). Nonetheless, a large proportion of the variance of disorders still remains unexplained, particularly when base rates are considered. In many cases, delinquency is only a transitional phenomenon of (male) adolescence. The precision with which long-term criminal careers can be predicted on the basis of risk factors is thus generally limited (Blumstein, Cohen, & Farrington, 1988; Gottfredson & Hirschi, 1986).

Part of the error variance in these typical prognoses is contributed by those individuals whose development is relatively free of disorder despite risky life conditions. Indeed, in recent years, there has been an increased interest in the study of precisely these individuals. The headings "stress resistance," "invulnerability," or "ego resilience," have been used to study those conditions and competences that permit the individual to cope with the stressors and deprivations that represent a threat to development. This approach places a much stronger emphasis on the flexibility of human development. On the one hand, it serves to increase the proportion of variance explained in the etiology; on the other hand, it can contribute to the destigmatization of risk groups and provide indications on the design of prevention in natural settings (Cowen & Work, 1988; Lösel, 1987).

Terms such as "invulnerability" or "resilience" are nonetheless often misunderstood as expressing an absolute, permanent, and eventually even genetically determined resistance to stress. What is meant, however, is a relatively stable ability to cope with stressful life conditions and events in which not only genetic dispositions play a role but also, above all, protective factors from complex disposition-environment interactions. Compared

---

[1] The research was carried out in project A2 of the Research Center "Prevention and Intervention in Childhood and Adolescence" (Sonderforschungsbereich 227) of the University of Bielefeld. The project is funded by a grant from the German Research Council (Deutsche Forschungsgemeinschaft).

to risk factors, little research has been performed on protective factors. Well-known longitudinal studies, such as the study on the Great Depression (Elder, 1974); the Menninger Coping Project (Murphy & Moriarty, 1976); the Berkeley Ego-Resilience Study (Block & Block, 1980); the New York Longitudinal Study (Thomas & Chess, 1984); or the Study of Adult Development at Harvard Medical School (Felsman & Vaillant, 1987), have nonetheless provided indications on significant factors (for a summary, see Köferl, 1989). On the basis of the previous findings, Rutter (1985) considers the following personal and social factors to be among those that are significant: (a) the way in which persons deal with stressors, and, above all, how far they act and do not just react; (b) cognitions of self-efficacy and self-esteem as prerequisites for this willingness to act; (c) stable emotional relationships to and positive experiences with other persons; (d) temperament factors that favor successful coping and positive relationships to others; and (e) parental modeling and childrearing behavior that guides the child's responses to life events. Garmezy (1983, 1985), Remschmidt (1986, 1989), or Felsman and Vaillant (1987) similarly describe some personal (competences) and social (environmental conditions) factors that are significant for resilience. Compared to the models of coping processes that refer to single, critical life events and research on adults, this nonetheless remains a field in which little research has been performed. In addition, previous resilience research has revealed a great number of problems and deficits:

1. The relevant constructs are derived from different theoretical contexts or levels of analysis and are in no way consistently confirmed empirically.

2. An adequate conceptual differentiation of risk conditions and protective factors has yet to be achieved.

3. Some of the studies are directed toward coping with single, critical life events in middle-class families in which the developmental setting is otherwise intact (see also Ulich, 1988). However, it is known from several studies that a certain cumulation of stressful living conditions or critical life events is a prerequisite of any marked increase in the risk of emotional and behavioral disorders (e.g., Thomas & Chess, 1984).

4. Studies with cumulative risk loads in the sense of a particularly significant, psychopathological, multiproblem milieu have mostly been carried out within specific cultural contexts (e.g., Werner & Smith, 1982), and it is questionable how far they can be generalized to, for example, Western industrialized countries.

5. The criteria of psychological disorder or health are hard to compare in the available data.

6. To some extent, it cannot be ruled out that, although the resilient children and adolescents have remained free of deviance in the externally more noticeable and easier to diagnose externalizing symptoms, they may possibly have developed disorders in the area of internalizing symptoms.

7. The quantitative significance of the mechanisms and factors mentioned in the prevention of psychological disorders can hardly be estimated at present.

8. Age- and gender-specific variations in resilience have hardly been taken into account so far (Rutter, 1989).

9. Most of the studies come from the Anglo-American countries. There are only a few studies from the European countries (Ulich, 1988).

Concept of the Bielefeld Study

Against the background of the above-mentioned state of research, we carried out our study on resilience. Some of the goals of the assessment are:

1. to study the concept of resilience in individuals with serious, cumulative stressful life events and circumstances (multiproblem milieu);
2. to simultaneously test the major factors that are assumed to be conditions or correlates of resilience in the literature;
3. to evaluate the consistence of the results across different methodological approaches and operational definitions of resilience in order to avoid artifacts;
4. to work out any eventual differential patterns or configurations of protective factors; and finally
5. to test the temporal stability of the findings across the entire period of adolescence.

In order to provide a stronger theoretical integration of the conditions or correlates of resilience mentioned in the literature, we chose to base our study of relevant constructs on Mischel's social cognitive learning theory (1973, 1981). Accordingly, some major personal resources for resilience could be expected in the following areas: (a) behavior construction competences (e.g., intelligence, temperament); (b) coding strategies and personal constructs (e.g., coping styles, constructs of social resources); (c) behavior- and stimulus-related expectations and evaluations (e.g., self-efficacy, learned helplessness); and (d) self-regulating systems (e.g., self-esteem, achievement motivation).

We included factors of temperament although these are not treated by Mischel. According to recent findings in personality psychology, temperament factors appear to have more significance than has sometimes been assumed in cognitive theories (see Lerner, Palermo, Spiro, & Nesselroade, 1982; Strelau, 1984; Thomas & Chess, 1984). With their emphasis on the "how" of behaviors, temperament variables can be subsumed under the behavior construction competences.

In a similar way, social resources can also be integrated into Mischel's approach. We have included characteristics of social support and of social climate. As resilience is a result of the individual processing of the environment, we understand these characteristics as personal constructs of phenomenal, social resources.

In our studies, we proceeded by differentiating adolescents with high, cumulative risk loads in childhood into groups that either show emotional and behavioral disorders in the sense of deficit models ("deviants") or have managed to develop in relative mental health or without mental disturbances in the sense of resource models ("resilients"). The theoretical relationship between the constructs of risk factors, protective factors, and mental health is illustrated in Figure 1.

We selected the age group of 14- to 17-year-olds as our target population for the first study for several reasons: (a) because they can well be subject to a long-term accumulation of risk factors, (b) this is a particularly sensitive period for the stabilization of disorders, and (c) further assessments with highly comparable instruments are possible.

In several pilot studies involving circa 750 students of both sexes and 30 teachers, we particularly tested instruments for assessing the risk load and the symptoms of mental health or disorder. These assessments were also intended to provide standardized scores for the level of stress. These findings are reported in Lösel, Bliesener, and Köferl (1989, 1990). In the main study, we investigated groups from residential homes for children and adolescents. This target population is particularly relevant for the concept of resilience insofar as the adolescents often come from a multiproblem milieu and thus a higher level of risk can be anticipated. The present paper reports on some of the findings from our first assessment of this group (see also Lösel et al., 1990).

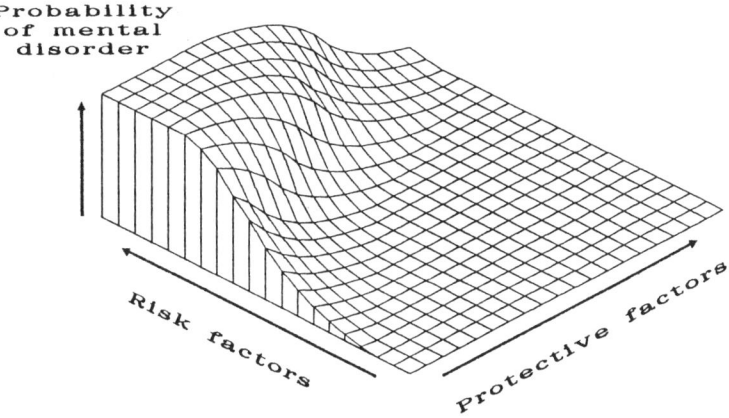

Figure 1: Hypothetical Model on the Relation Between Risk Factors, Protective Factors, and the Amount of Mental Disorder.

Method

Sample

We contacted 60 residential homes for children and adolescents in North-West Germany. In order, as far as possible, to assess the forms of resilience that actually arose in everyday life, and not just those that are defined artificially, we chose a naturalistic approach for the selection of the sample. The managers, social workers, or care givers in the residential homes were given a detailed explanation of the concept of invulnerability/resilience. If they considered that suitable adolescents were present in their residential home, these cases were discussed in detail in a kind of case conference. In this way, we were able to obtain 66 adolescents aged between 14 and 17 for the sample of resilients from a total of 27 residential homes. As a control group, we recruited a sample of 80 adolescents from the same residential homes who, according to the diagnosis of the staff, had developed marked emotional and behavioral disorders while exposed to a comparable risk load.

The average age of the group of resilients was 15;5 years, that of the deviants was 15;7. The gender distribution was approximately 3:2 (male:female) in both groups. These naturalistically diagnosed groups were specified more precisely with objective instruments during the course of the further assessment (see the section below entitled Differentiation of Groups.

Instruments

The adolescents and the staff were subjected to an exhaustive interview and written surveys using a range of instruments. Both the interview and the tests and questionnaires were used to assess four complexes of characteristics in the adolescents: (a) biographical risk load; (b) emotional and behavioral disorders; (c) personal resources; and (d) social resources.

a) Biographical risk load and risk conditions. The biographical risk due to deprived living conditions and life events was assessed through semistructured interviews with the adolescents that, if necessary, were supplemented with reports from the staff. The selection of the characteristics was oriented toward the risk or stress factors discussed in the literature (see Honig, 1986; Rutter, 1983; Werner & Smith, 1982). From the items tested in the pilot study, we collected data on 47 single items concerning events involving loss and separation, change of home and school, financial difficulties, and time spent in hospital. These biographical stress characteristics were assessed quasi-longitudinally across the entire life period.

A written survey also assessed the adolescents' experiences of extreme parental childrearing behavior, experiences of deprivation, and drug and alcohol usage in the family (24 items). All items were selected from a larger pool by six experts and rated on 3-point scales according to their significance as risk factors. The items were added together to form a risk index.

b) Emotional and behavioral disorders. For a detailed assessment of the second criterion for resilience - mental health - we translated and adapted the various versions of the Child Behavior Checklist (CBCL; Achenbach & Edelbrock, 1983, 1986; Achenbach, Verhulst, Baron, & Althaus, 1987). The CBCL is an internationally tested instrument for estimating the behavioral development of the child from the perspective of its parents. Various observer-specific parallel forms are available: The behavior and emotions of the adolescents can be rated from the perspective of teachers (Teacher's Report Form - TRF), as self-reports (Youth Self Report - YSR), and from the perspective of a neutral observer (Direct Observation Form - DOF). The CBCL forms assess emotional, motivational, cognitive, and psychosomatic information. Alongside a total problem score, the information on behavioral disorders can also be differentiated according to narrow-band syndromes (e.g., anxious, depressive, nervous and hyperactive, delinquent, aggressive) and broad-band syndromes (internalizing vs. externalizing). The narrow-band syndromes correspond to DSM-III criteria and are presented as age- and gender-specific behavior profiles. The pilot study findings on the methodological validity of the CBCL adaptations were generally satisfactory (see Bliesener & Lösel, 1993; Lösel et al., 1991).

c) Personal resources. To estimate differences in *intelligence,* we selected a short form of the Prüfsystem für Schul- und Bildungsberatung (PSB; Horn, 1969). This is a vocational aptitude test assessing the factors verbal intelligence, reasoning, and technical ability. *Temperament* was assessed by the Dimensions of Temperament Survey (DOTS; Lerner et al., 1982). This instrument contains dimensions on approach-avoidance tendencies in minor, everyday hassles; on rigidity versus flexibility in behavioral expectations toward oneself and others; on general emotional state; and on task orientation among adolescents.

We translated the DOTS ourselves. It is available in parallel forms for both self-reports and ratings by an adult observer.

The adolescents' *coping styles* were assessed with Seiffge-Krenke's (1984) modified form of Westbrook's (1979) Coping Questionnaire. The instrument consists of 20 items on various coping strategies with particular emphasis on the factors (a) active coping with problems through the use of social resources, (b) economic coping with problems, and (c) fatalistic, problem-avoiding behavior. As the construct of resilience addresses relatively permanent strategies, we did not perform a differentiation according to situations.

On the basis of the Self-Descriptive Questionnaire of Marsh and O'Neill (1984) and the scales of Jerusalem and Schwarzer (1986), we developed an instrument to assess *self-directed regulations*. The instrument contains the dimensions self-efficacy, helplessness, and self-esteem. In addition, we applied the achievement motivation scale of the Mehrdimensionaler Persönlichkeitstest für Jugendliche (Schmidt, 1981), a personality test for adolescents.

d) Social resources. To include perceptions of *social support* received from third persons, we developed a questionnaire to assess social support (FESU; see Bliesener, 1988; Lösel et al., 1989). This instrument presents 10 different situations dealing with different types of social support (e.g., emotional, material, and informative support). For each situation, the adolescent gives an unstructured response stating which persons help them in this situation, how frequently they receive this help, and how they evaluate it. These reports are used to form indices of network size, frequency of support, and satisfaction with support. In addition, the persons named and the reports on the frequency of support across the individual situations are used to calculate an index of the situational variability (see Bliesener, 1988). This index expresses how far the adolescent differentiates between various supporters and support situations or whether his or her cognitive scheme of helpers is unstructured (see Bieri, Atkins, Briar, Leaman, Miller & Tripodi, 1966, pp. 184ff; Kelly, 1955, pp. 312f).

To assess the *social climate* in the immediate setting of the adolescents, we used a selection of family climate scales (FCS) from Schneewind, Beckmann, and Hecht-Jackl's (1985) Familien-Diagnostischen-Test-System, a test battery for family diagnosis. This instrument has been developed on the basis of the Family Environment Scales constructed by Moos (1974; Moos & Moos, 1981). As our study was being conducted in residential homes, we modified some of the terms used in the FCS items.

Differentiation of groups

The objective criterion of risk load confirmed the validity of the naturalistic diagnoses from the home staff. Our total risk index produced a mean of 29.04 ($SD=14.94$) in the resilients (R) and a mean of 27.40 ($SD=14.32$) in the deviants (D). Both groups thus showed a comparable risk load with the anticipated high level of risk that lay roughly on the 90th percentile of the "standard sample" ($N=641$) in the pilot study. The naturalistic diagnoses on the second criteria of resilience, the emotional and behavioral disorders, were also validated by quantitative data. Table 1 presents the group differences on the broad-band scales of the TRF and the YSR. In both forms of the CBCL, the deviants exhibited markedly higher syndrome scores in the externalizing field. In contrast, the differences in the internalizing syndrome were weaker and only above random in the TRF.

Table 1: Comparison of Resilient (R) and Deviant (D) Adolescents in the Naturalistic Groupings on the Broad-Band Scores of TRF and YSR.

		R		D			
		M	SD	M	SD	t	p
TRF	Externalising syndrome	26.02	15.06	42.71	19.63	5.40	.001
	Internalising syndrome	12.89	8.09	15.80	7.91	2.05	.05
YSR	Externalising syndrome	15.06	7.64	20.41	11.06	3.27	.001
	Internalising syndrome	18.23	9.93	22.05	12.29	1.95	.06

In line with our intention of testing the consistency across different operationalizations of resilience, we applied a multiple gating procedure (Loeber, Dishion, & Patterson, 1984). This contained three, increasingly stricter definitions of the resilient and deviant groups:

1. In Step 1, we compared the naturalistically diagnosed groups ($N_R=66$, $N_D=80$).

2. Step 2 excluded all members of the group of resilients whose scores lay above the 95th percentile on one or more narrow-band syndrome scales in the TRF version of the CBCL completed by the home staff. Among the deviants, all cases were dropped that did not lie above the 95th percentile on at least one narrow-band syndrome scale. This criterion excluded subjects who had originally been labeled resilient but showed, for example, marked anxiety or withdrawal symptoms ($N_R=39$, $N_D=46$).

3. In Step 3, the self-reports in the YSR form of the CBCL were used to exclude resilient and deviant adolescents who had rated themselves as either deviant or resilient respectively. This procedure applied the same criteria as those used in Step 2 ($N_R=21$, $N_D=26$).

Results and Discussion

The means for the variables of personal and social protective factors were compared on the three levels of group definition. These results are presented in Tables 2 and 3. In view of the increasingly smaller sample size and multiple testing, one should nonetheless not place too much confidence in significance tests. In our opinion, the relative consistency of the pattern of results across the different types of group formation is particularly meaningful. For this reason and also for reasons of transparency, the distribution scores are not presented in the tables. Instead, we report the direction of the differences and Cohen's (1977) r_m coefficient as a measure of effect size. The anticipated direction in each case is also presented in the tables (except when the previous assumptions about relations are either unclear or probably nonlinear).

Table 2: Comparison of the Personal Resources in the Various Defined Groups (r_m: Effect Size).

	Expected direction	Naturalistic group diagnosis 66/88			Naturalistic group, validated by TRF 39/46			Naturalistic group, validated by TRF and YSR 21/26		
		Empirical direction			Empirical direction			Empirical direction		
	R D	R D	r_m	p	R D	r_m	p	R D	r_m	p
Intelligence										
Verbal	>	>	.13	(*)	>	.21	*	>	.17	
Reasoning	>	>	.11	(*)	>	.21	*	>	.19	(*)
Technical/perceptual	>	>	.16	*	>	.26	**	>	.37	**
Temperament										
Approach orientation	>	>	.06		>	.12		>	.26	*
Flexibility	>	>	.05		>	.05		>	.37	**
Quality of mood	>	<	.00		<	.10		<	.17	
Task orientation	>	<	.02		<	.08		>	.14	
Rhythmicity	?	>	.07		<	.05		>	.09	
Coping styles										
Active problem solving	>	>	.08		>	.16	(*)	>	.26	*
Economic handling	>	>	.07		>	.04		<	.08	
Problem avoiding/fatalism	<	<	.09		<	.11		<	.31	*
Self-directed regulations										
Self efficacy	>	>	.09		>	.15	(*)	>	.22	(*)
Helplessness	<	<	.09		<	.25	*	<	.45	**
Achievement	>	>	.13	*	>	.16	(*)	>	.21	(*)
Self esteem	>	>	.10		>	.20	*	>	.33	*
Mean effect size r_m (corrected)			.08			.14			.22	

(*) p(t) < .10   * p(t) < .05   ** p(t) < .01

Table 3: Comparison of the Social Resources in the Various Defined Groups (r_n: Effect Size).

	Naturalistic group diagnosis 66/88				Naturalistic group, validated by TRF 39/46			Naturalistic group, validated by TRF and YSR 21/26	
	Expected direction R D	Empirical direction R D	r_n	p	Empirical direction R D	r_n	p	Empirical direction R D	r_n	p
Social support										
Frequency	∨	∨	.11	*	∨	.16	(*)	∨	.11	
Netsize	∨	∨	.19	*	∨	.27	**	∨	.21	(*)
Satisfaction	∨	∨	.16	*	∨	.22	*	∨	.28	*
Complexity	∨	∨	.07		∨	.13		∨	.12	
Social climate										
Cohesion	∨	∨	.10		∨	.11		∨	.21	(*)
Openness/frankness	∨	∨	.22	**	∨	.23	*	∨	.32	*
Tendency for conflict	∧	∧	.14	(*)	∧	.19	*	∧	.25	*
Autonomy	∨	∨	.16	*	∨	.27	**	∨	.41	**
Achievement orientation	∨	∨	.04		∨	.04		∧	.10	
Planning of leisure time	∨	∨	.09		∨	.08		∧	.04	
Religious orientation	?	∨	.15		∨	.12		∧	.05	
Organisation	∨	∨	.10		∨	.08		∨	.16	
Control	?	∨	.04		∧	.04		∧	.11	
Mean effect size r_n (corrected)			.13			.16			.18	

(*) p(t) < .10   * p(t) < .05   ** p(t) < .01

As expected, a series of variables that are assumed to represent protective factors with regard to stressors differentiated between the two groups. The extent of this difference could not be explained by "fishing for significance" alone. All 28 significant differences took the expected direction. When all the group differences were included, 38 out of 42 comparisons showed the expected direction in the personal protective factors and 32 from 33 in the social protective factors (a total of 93%). The effect sizes were low to moderate.

The course of the increasingly strict group definitions showed a clear trend in the personal protective factors. The mean of the r_m coefficients corrected for direction increased across the three group definitions from .08 to .22. In the same way, the number of significant differences also increased here despite the decreasing group sizes. Resilient adolescents proved to be more intelligent than deviants facing the same risk. The variable of verbal intelligence, which is more closely related to education, played a less important role in this than the reasoning component. Resilients tended to cope with problems more actively than passively and fatalistically. In their self-related cognitions, they experienced themselves as being less helpless and they had a more positive self-evaluation. In the domain of temperament, they proved to be more strongly approach-oriented and flexible. These findings show a high level of agreement with the assumptions reported in the literature on the construct of resilience.

The differences in the characteristics also showed the expected directions in the protective factors from the social domain. Unlike the findings on the personal protective factors, the effect sizes increased with the strictness of the group definitions. However, the increase was not as high as in the personal resources. The resilients consistently reported a larger network of social support. In addition, they were more satisfied with the support that they received. In the scales on childrearing climate, the resilients particularly reported a childrearing climate that was more strongly oriented toward autonomy, more open, and less conflict-laden.

When judging the social protective factors, it nevertheless has to be considered that the social characteristics of a long-term residential home situation are probably harder to differentiate, as the framing conditions appear to be homogeneous and some constellations of social support are possibly the same for both resilients and deviants.

Alongside the bivariate differences in characteristics in the domain of the personal and social resources of the two groups, we were particularly interested in possible synergetic effects and interactions among the protective factors. The importance of configurations or characteristic patterns has also been supported by, for example, the findings of the Swedish research program on individual development and adjustment (Magnusson & Bergman, 1988). Even if studies of the "person-as-a-whole" (Magnusson & Bergman, 1988, p. 1) can only be meant in an ideal way, the perspective of the person (instead of the variables) as the unit of analysis is particularly meaningful in resilience research, because many protective factors only attain their function within specific configurations of characteristics (see Rutter, 1985). To detect the possible presence of specific configurations of characteristics, we applied the explorative technique of HYPAG/SEARCH (Härtner, Matthes, & Wottawa, 1980; Wottawa, 1984) to the analysis of multidimensional contingency tables.

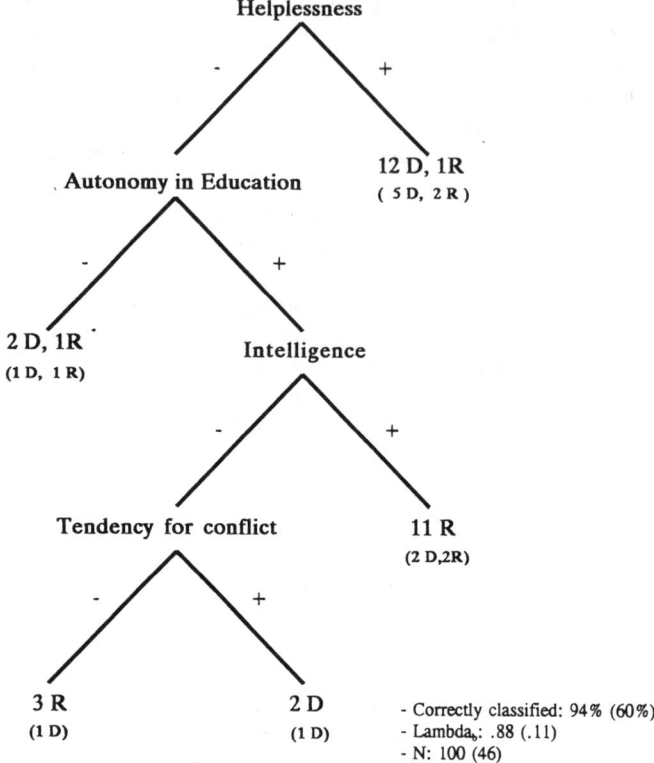

Figure 2: HYPAG/DISC-Structure for Selected Protective Factors to Discriminate Resilient (R) and Deviant (D) Adolescents in the Naturalistic Groupings. Results of the Cross Validation in Parenthesis.

With the help of the subprogram DISC, we attempted to describe the group variable through the most simple possible combination of median-dichotomized characteristics of the protetive factors. An analysis of the groups on the third level of group definition resulted in a combination of the two personal factors "learned helplessness" and "intelligence" (arithmetic mean of the three PSB scales) and the two characteristics of the social climate "conflict tendency" and "autonomy" (see Figure 2). This model correctly classified 94% of the cases. This corresponds to a relative improvement compared to the base rate of $\lambda_b = .88$. However, in a cross classification, the model only achieved 60% correct predictions ($\lambda_b = .11$). In addition, some other combinations of variables also showed a similarly good description of the group variable (see Wottawa, 1987). A simple sum index calculated from the four dummy characteristics of the HYPAG model also already showed a predictive precision of 83% ($\lambda_b = .62$). Other combinations of characteristics attained similar scores.

In view of the loss of information and testing power because of the dichotomization of the independent variables (Cohen, 1983), the group discrimination performed by the HYPAG model and the sum index can be regarded as being thoroughly satisfactory. The comparison of the two methods, the unsatisfactory cross-validation, and the equivalence of various other descriptive models nonetheless casts doubt on the existence of interactive-synergetic effects among the protective factors. The effectiveness of the simple sum indices points more toward a simple additive relation of the protective factors.

One major limitation of the findings reported here has to be emphasized: As yet, we are only dealing with cross-sectional data. In a second assessment, which is being performed at the present time, the adolescents are being surveyed once more after an interval of circa two years. This study should particularly provide information on the temporal stability of the differential findings.

References

Achenbach, T.M., & Edelbrock, C. (1983). *Manual for the Child Behavior Checklist and Revised Child Behavior Profile.* Burlington: University of Vermont, Department of Psychiatry.

Achenbach, T.M., & Edelbrock, C. (1986). *Manual for the Teacher's Report Form and teacher version of the Child Behavior Profile.* Burlington: University of Vermont, Department of Psychiatry.

Achenbach, T.M., Verhulst, F.C., Baron, G.D., & Althaus, M. (1987). A comparison of syndromes derived from the Child Behavior Checklist for American and Dutch boys aged 6 - 11 and 12 - 16. *Journal of Child Psychology and Psychiatry, 28,* 427-453.

Bieri, J., Atkins, A.L., Briar, S., Leaman, R.L., Miller, H., & Tripodi, T. (1966). *Clinical and social judgement: The discrimination of behavioral information.* New York: Wiley.

Bliesener, T. (1988). *Stressresistenz und die kognitive Konstruktion sozialer Ressourcen.* Dissertation, University of Bielefeld.

Bliesener, T., & Lösel, F. (1993). Verhaltensbeobachtung psychischer Auffälligkeiten in der Schule: Eine Studie zur Adaption und Validierung der Direct Observation Form der Child Behavior Checklist. *Diagnostica, 37,* (in press).

Block, J.H., & Block, J. (1980). The role of ego-control and ego-resiliency in the organization of behavior. In W.A. Collins (Ed.), *The Minnesota symposia on child psychology,* Vol. 13, (pp. 39-101). Hillsdale: Erlbaum.

Blumstein, A., Cohen, J., & Farrington, D.P. (1988). Criminal career research: It,s value for criminology. *Criminology, 26,* 1-35.

Cohen, J. (1977). *Statistical power analysis for the behavioral science,* 2nd ed. New York: Academic Press.

Cohen, J. (1983). The costs of dichotomization. *Applied Psychological Measurement, 7,* 249-253.

Cowen, E.L., & Work, W.C. (1988). Invulnerable children, psychological wellness, and primary prevention. *American Journal of Community Psychology, 16,* 591-607.

Elder, G.H. (1974). *Children of the Great Depression: Social change in life experience.* Chicago: University of Chicago Press.

Farrington, D.P. (1989). Later adult life outcomes of offenders and non-offenders. In M. Brambring, F. Lösel, & H. Skowronek (Eds.), *Children at risk: Assessment and longitudinal research* (pp. 220-244). Berlin: de Gruyter.

Farrington, D.P., Gallagher, B., Morley, L., Ledger, R.J., & West, D.J. (1986). *Cambridge study in delinquent development: Long-term follow-up. Second annual report to the Home Office.* Cambridge: Institute of Criminology.

Farrington, D.P., Ohlin, L.E., & Wilson, J.Q. (1986). *Understanding and controlling crime.* New York: Springer.

Felsman, K.H., & Vaillant, G.E. (1987). Resilient children as adults: A 40-year study. In E.J. Anthony, & B.J. Cohler (Eds.), *The invulnerable child* (pp. 289-314). London: Guilford Press.

Garmezy, N. (1983). Stressors of childhood. In N. Garmezy, & M. Rutter (Eds.), *Stress, coping, and development in children* (pp. 43-84). New York: McGraw-Hill.

Garmezy, N. (1985). Stress resistant children: The search for protective factors. In J. E. Stevenson (Ed.), *Recent research in developmental psychopathology. Journal of Child Psychology and Psychiatry. Book Supplement No. 4* (pp.213-233). Oxford: Pergamon Press.

Glueck, S., & Glueck, E. (1950). *Unraveling juvenile delinquency.* Cambridge: Harvard University Press.
Gottfredson, M., & Hirschi, T. (1986). The true value of lambda would appear to be zero: An essay on career criminals, criminal careers, selective incapacitation, cohort studies, and related topics. *Criminology, 24,* 213-234.
Härtner, R., Matthes, K., & Wottawa, H. (1980). Computergestützte Hypothesenagglutination zur Erfassung komplexer Zusammenhänge. *EDV in Medizin und Biologie, 11,* 53-59.
Honig, A.S. (1986). Risk factors in infancy. In A. S. Honig (Ed.), *Risk factors in infancy* (pp. 1-8). New York: Gordon, & Breach.
Horn, W. (1969). *Prüfsystem für Schul- und Bildungsberatung P-S-B.* Göttingen: Hogrefe.
Jerusalem, M., & Schwarzer, R. (1986). "Selbstwirksamkeit" und "Hilflosigkeit" (Skalenbeschreibungen). In R. Schwarzer (Ed.), *Skalen zur Befindlichkeit und Persönlichkeit.* Research Report No. 5 (pp. 15-42). Free University of Berlin, Department of Psychology.
Kelly, G.A. (1955). *The psychology of personal constructs,* Vol. 1. New York: Norton.
Köferl, P. (1989). *Invulnerabilität und Stressresistenz: Theoretische und empirische Befunde zur effektiven Bewältigung von psychosozialen Stressoren.* Dissertation, University of Bielefeld.
Lerner, R.M., Palermo, M., Spiro, A., & Nesselroade, J.R. (1982). Assessing the dimensions of temperamental individuality across the lifespan: The Dimensions of Temperament Survey (DOTS). *Child Development, 53,* 149-159.
Loeber, R., Dishion, T.J., & Patterson, G.R. (1984). Multiple gating: A multistage assessment procedure for identifying youths at risk for delinquency. *Journal of Research in Crime and Delinquency, 21,* 7-32.
Loeber, R., & Stouthamer-Loeber, M. (1986). Family factors as correlates and predictors of juvenile conduct problems and delinquency. In M. Tonry, & N. Morris (Eds.), *Crime and justice, Vol. 7, An annual review of research* (pp. 29-150). Chicago: University of Chicago Press.
Lösel, F. (1978). Konfigurationen elterlicher Erziehung und Dissozialität. In K. Schneewind, & H. Lukesch (Eds.), *Familiäre Sozialisation* (pp. 233-245). Stuttgart: Klett-Cotta.
Lösel, F. (1987). Psychological crime prevention: Concepts, evaluations, and perspectives. In K. Hurrelmann, F.-X. Kauffmann, & F. Lösel (Eds.) *Social intervention: Potential and constraints* (pp. 289-313). Berlin: de Gruyter.
Lösel, F., Bliesener, T., & Köferl, P. (1989). On the concept of "invulnerability": Evaluations and first results of the Bielefeld Project. In M. Brambring, F. Lösel, & H. Skowronek (Eds.), *Children at risk: Assessment and longitudinal research* (pp.187-221). Berlin: De Gruyter.
Lösel, F., Bliesener, T., & Köferl, P. (1990). Psychische Gesundheit trotz Risikobelastung in der Kindheit: Untersuchungen zur "Invulnerabilität". In I. Seiffge-Krenke (Ed.), *Jahrbuch der Medizinischen Psychologie, Bd. IV, Krankheitsverarbeitung von Kindern und Jugendlichen* (pp. 103-123). Berlin: Springer.
Lösel, F., Bliesener, T., & Köferl, P. (1991). Erlebens- und Verhaltensprobleme bei Jugendlichen: Deutsche Adaption und kulturvergleichende Überprüfung der Youth Self-Report Form der Child Behavior Checklist. *Zeitschrift für Klinische Psychologie, 20,* 22-51.
Magnusson, D., & Bergman, L.R. (1988). *Longitudinal studies: Individual and variable based approaches to research on early risk factors.* Reports from the Department of Psychology, No. 674, University of Stockholm.
Marsh, H.W., & O'Neill, R. (1984). Self Description Questionnaire III: The construct validity of multidimensional self-concept ratings by late adolescents. *Journal of Educational Measurement, 21,* 153-174.
Mischel, W. (1973). Towards a cognitive social learning reconceptualization of personality. *Psychological Review, 80,* 252-283.
Mischel, W. (1981). A cognitive social learning approach to assessment. In T. Merluzzi, C. Glass, & M. Genest (Eds.), *Cognitive assessment* (pp. 479-502). New York: The Guilford Press.
Moos, R.H. (1974). *Family Environment Scale (FES).* Palo Alto: Stanford University, Social Ecology Laboratory.
Moos, R.H., & Moos, B.S. (1981). *Family Environment Scale (Manual).* Palo Alto: Consulting Psychologists Press.
Murphy, L.B., & Moriarty, A.E. (1976). *Vulnerability, coping, and growth.* New Haven: Yale University Press.

Remschmidt, H. (1986). Was wird aus kinderpsychiatrischen Patienten? Methodische Überlegungen und Ergebnisse. In M.H. Schmidt, & S. Drömann (Eds.), *Langzeitverlauf kinder- und jugendpsychiatrischer Erkrankungen*, (pp. 1-14). Stuttgart: Enke.

Remschmidt, H. (1989). Epidemiology and classification of psychiatric disorders in childhood and adolescence. In M. Brambring, F. Lösel, & H. Skowronek (Eds.), *Children at risk: Assessment, longitudinal research, and intervention* (pp. 3-23). Berlin: de Gruyter.

Rutter, M. (1983). Stress, coping, and development: Some issues and some questions. In N. Garmezy, & M. Rutter (Eds.), *Stress, coping, and development in children* (pp. 1-41). New York: McGraw-Hill.

Rutter, M. (1985). Resilience in the face of adversity. Protective factors and resistance to psychiatric disorder. *British Journal of Psychiatry, 147*, 598-611.

Rutter, M. (1989). Pathways from childhood to adult life. *Journal of Child Psychology and Psychiatry, 30*, 23-51.

Schmidt, H. (1981). *Mehrdimensionaler Persönlichkeitstest für Jugendliche (MPT-J)*. Braunschweig: Westermann.

Schneewind, K.A., Beckmann, M., & Hecht-Jackl, A. (1985). *Das Familienklima-Testsystem*, Research Report No. 8.1. University of Munich, Department of Psychology.

Seiffge-Krenke, I. (1984). *Problembewältigung im Jugendalter* (Habilitationsschrift). University of Giessen, Department of Psychology.

Strelau, J. (1984). *Das Temperament in der psychischen Entwicklung*. Berlin: Volk und Wissen.

Thomas, A., & Chess, S. (1984). Genesis and evolution of behavioral disorders: From infancy to early adult life. *American Journal of Psychiatry, 141*, 1-9.

Ulich, M. (1988). Risiko- und Schutzfaktoren in der Entwicklung von Kindern und Jugendlichen. *Zeitschrift für Entwicklungspsychologie und Pädagogische Psychologie, 20*, 146-166.

Werner, E.E., & Smith, R.S. (1982). *Vulnerable but invincible*. New York: McGraw-Hill.

Westbrook, M. T. (1979). A classification of coping behavior based on multidimensional scaling of similarity ratings. *Journal of Clinical Psychology, 35*, 407-410.

Wottawa, H. (1984). HYPAG : Ein neuer Ansatz zur Datenanalyse in der Marktforschung. *Planung und Analyse, 11*, 15-21.

Wottawa, H. (1987). Hypotheses agglutination (HYPAG): A method for configuration-based analysis of multivariate data. *Methodika, 1*, 68-92.

Violation of Rules as a Reaction to Declining Living Standards Among Workers and Intellectuals

Wilhelmina Wosinska

Introduction

Human nature is so perverse that socioeconomic well-being becomes one of the most important goals of people's activity. This desire is often so strong that people are ready to violate moral and legal rules in order to satisfy it. How they do this, depends on the specific sociopolitical, economic, and legal system existing in a society. Changes in the society lead to changes in the strategies oriented toward regaining socioeconomic well-being. Simultaneously, the ways in which rules are violated change. Particularly distinctive transformations can be expected when sociopolitical changes are rapid and people do not have well-determined adaptive strategies at their disposal. This is the recent situation in Polish society, where commodity shortages have been replaced by a drastic shortage of money.

When faced with severe economic shortages - as Wosinski (1985) has shown - people mainly develop the strategy of making use of an intermediary to improve their standard of living[1]. In practical terms, this means buying goods that are relatively cheap but difficult to obtain on the market. In Poland, the role of intermediary was performed by, for example, shop assistants, truck drivers delivering commodities to shops, bosses of flat cooperatives, or coal miners who possessed coupons allowing the purchase of scarce goods in special shops. As money is not a high-value commodity in this situation, people made use of exchange services. For example, physicians offered prescriptions and access to scarce medical equipment to shop assistants in return for meat or clothes. As a result, the hierarchy of social prestige becomes mixed up.

The most commonly violated rule in a situation of economic commodity shortage is the rule of just distribution.

To protect this rule, controllers were appointed. However, the actual possibilities of controlling these violations or preventing them were very slight, as controllers were not paid well enough to ensure their honesty. Hence, whole hierarchies of controllers would have to be established, which - as confirmed long ago by Katz and Kahn (1966) - does not prevent activities that violate the law.

The question addressed in this chapter is how do people change their behavior when the economic commodity shortage situation transforms into a shortage of money? The rapid decline in financial resources is defined as economic deprivation (Komarowsky, 1971), which is experienced as a critical life event. It may also be regarded as a situation of economic decline as it is accompanied by an observable drop in the standard of living.

---

[1] This term is a simplification of the problem. However, a detailed discussion of this goes beyond the concerns of the present chapter.

In such situations, people develop different adaptive strategies (Liker & Elder, 1983) as mechanisms for regaining control in the face of economic decline. One possible adaptive strategy is to increase one's readiness to violate moral and legal rules in order to maintain a reasonable standard of living.

The goal of the present research program was to answer the following questions:

1. How is the present economic situation in Polish society evaluated, and what strategies are used to maintain a reasonable standard of living?

2. What kinds of rule do people violate in order to maintain a reasonable standard of living?

3. Do groups separated on the basis of life-style and social prestige differ in the types of adaptive strategy they use and the ways in which they violate rules?

The last question is of particular interest in view of the continued economic and legal destabilization in Poland. This destabilization gives rise not only to the expectation of suffering material loss but also to loss of prestige. Hence, it can result in a differentiation of adaptive strategies used to cope with economic decline.

Procedure

Subjects were 47 workers (W: coal miners working underground) and 41 intellectuals (I: academic teachers from different secondary schools in an industrial region of Poland [Silesia]). All subjects were men with families (consisting of a wife and at least one child) aged between 29 and 45. The survey consisted of interviews carried out in June 1990. Statistical analyses were performed with χ^2 and z tests.

Results

How is the present economic situation evaluated and what strategies are applied to maintain a reasonable standard of living?

As many as 67.3% of the workers and 50.0% of the intellectuals (see Table 1) reported that they thought the economic situation was deteriorating. At the same time, 14.3% of workers and 21.7% of intellectuals thought that it was improving. Decline manifested itself as a decrease in real income, a lowering of the level of consumption, and the use of all available financial resources to pay for the basic needs of everyday life. Improvements in the economic situation predominantly manifested themselves in an increase in the quality of life, mostly due to easy access to commodities on the market despite very high prices. Some subjects (W: 10.2%; I:15.3%) stated that there was no change in the economic situation, while others (W: 8.2%; I: 13.0%) gave inconsistent answers: They felt that they had higher incomes (salaries are paid in millions!) while being simultaneously less able to satisfy their needs. The comparison groups did not differ statistically in their evaluations of their economic situation, $\chi^2=2.97$, n.s.

Table 1: The Present Economic Situation Compared to the Past.

Evaluation	Workers	Intellectuals
Better	14.3	21.7
The same	10.2	15.3
Worse	67.3	50.0
Inconsistent answer	8.2	13.0

It should be noted that intellectuals referred mostly to the 1980s when evaluating their present economic situation (see Table 2), while workers referred just as much to the 1980s as to earlier periods, $\chi^2=3.84, p \leq .05; z=2.26, p \leq .05$. The main pre-1980s reference period for workers was the 1970s, the period when they were the group receiving most favorable treatment from the government. This is probably why a slightly larger (though not statistically significant) proportion of workers experienced a deterioration in the economic situation compared to intellectuals, for many years a traditionally inferior social class in Poland.

Table 2: Reference Periods Used for Evaluating the Present Economic Situation.

Reference period	Workers	Intellectuals
Pre-1980s	49	25 *
1980s	51	75

* $p \leq .05$

Reference groups for our subjects proved to be very differentiated: the average family; "similar others" with contrasting status (e.g., our teachers referred to technicians employed in industry, while our coal miners referred to textile workers); "similar others" without contrasting status (teachers with other teachers, workers with other workers); and "others" (workers with physicians, intellectuals with workers). In addition, reference was made to a group called "people who gain benefits very easily" (merchants, dealers, and small-scale businessmen who gain great wealth by exploiting temporary situations; see Table 3).

The only significant difference involved this latter reference group (W: 8.3%; I: 29.3%; $z=2.56, p \leq .01$). More often, references to so-called "crafty" people by intellectuals probably reflect their helplessness and some kind of envy, as intellectuals are neither able nor willing to participate in such activities, preferring to defend their professional dignity. (In fact, some academic teachers have left their jobs, though this was not reported among our subjects).

Table 3: Reference Groups Used for Evaluating the Present Economic Situation.

Reference group	Workers	Intellectuals
Similar others		
a) Without contrasting status	33.3	26.8
b) With contrasting status	6.3	2.4
Dissimilar others	4.2	9.8
The average family	33.3	26.8
Informal contact persons (neighbors, friends, etc.)	14.6	4.9
People who gain benefits very easily	8.3	29.4 **

** $p \leq .01$

Apart from these detailed differences, there were no significant general differences between workers and intellectuals, $\chi^2 = 11.1$, n.s. The lack of stable reference groups that are specific to particular socioeconomic groups may well be an indication of value uncertainty and a mixing up of prestige within a society. Two general spheres of life were experienced as having deteriorated: everyday life resources (W: 45.8%; I: 52.0%) and culture, health, and recreation (W: 45.8%; I: 52.0%; see Table 4). Within these general categories, no significant differences could be found between groups, $\chi^2 = 2.21$, n.s.

Table 4: Dimensions of Life Experienced as Deteriorated.

Dimension	Workers	Intellectuals
Everyday life resources	38.5	25.4
Culture, health, and recreation	45.8	52.0
Feeling of security	1.2	1.3
No dimension	4.8	12.0
All dimensions are limited	2.4	9.3
Others	7.3	0.0 *

* $p \leq .05$

Nonetheless, more detailed analysis (see Table 5) allowed us to state that, compared to workers, intellectuals more frequently viewed limited access to culture (mainly referring to the opportunities to buy books), $z = 2.80$, $p \leq .01$, and a general lack of financial resources, $z = 2.42$, $p \leq .05$, as being most painful. Workers, in contrast, were more concerned about restrictions to their social life, $z = 2.34$, $p \leq .05$. For example, they complained that receptions were no longer being organized like they used to be, or there was not enough money to go out and have a drink when one wanted to.

Table 5: Statistically Significant Differences in Deterioration of Dimensions of Life.

Type of Dimension	Workers	Intellectuals
Financial resources	1.7	13.5 *
Access to culture	5.1	23.1 **
Social life	10.0	0.0 *

* $p \leq .05$ ** $p \leq .01$

What steps are taken to maintain a reasonable standard of living? The most common response in both groups was to take on an additional job (mostly part-time) and economize in housekeeping. It should be noted that the latter behavior has no tradition in Polish society, as, under the earlier conditions of commodity shortage, every single zloty would be spent on any commodity available, even it was not required at the time, which is why people in Poland have two or three refrigerators, washing machines, vacuum cleaners, and so forth, purchased during the earlier 1980s.

Table 6: Actions Performed by Subjects Themselves and Attributed to Others in Order to Maintain a Reasonable Standard of Living (W = Workers, I = Intellectuals).

Activity	Subjects themselves		Other	
	W	I	W	I
Real actions				
Additional job	38.8	52.6	34.6	42.2
Financial support from the family	3.0	20.3 **	11.5	9.9
Better housekeeping	19.4	10.2	10.3	5.7
semilegal trading	1.5	1.7	38.5	24.5 *
Postulated actions	9.0	0.0 *	0.0	0.0
No actions				
No additional job	10.4	8.4	5.1	11.1
Doing nothing	17.9	6.8	0.0	0.0
Psychological actions	0.0	0.0	0.0	4.4
I don't know	0.0	0.0	0.0	2.2

* $p \leq .05$ ** $p \leq .01$

The next most important activity aimed toward maintaining a reasonable standard of living was to obtain financial support from the family (parents, relatives living abroad, etc.). This occurred more frequently among intellectuals than workers, $z=3.09, p \leq .01$. Engaging in semilegal trading was reported very rarely (W: 1.5%; I: 1.8%). However, this was reported to be a very common activity when subjects were asked how other persons cope with economic decline, and was reported significantly more frequently by workers (W:

38.5%; I: 24.5%; $z=1.96$, $p \leq .05$). As Table 6 shows, some people stated that they did nothing in the above situation ("I'm just waiting . . .") or acted on a psychological level ("I may only claim"). No general differences were found either between groups or within the subjects' own perspectives, $\chi^2=3.78$, n.s.

Table 7: Do People Violate Rules to Maintain a Reasonable Standard of Living (W = Workers, I = Intellectuals)?

	\multicolumn{6}{c}{Who violates rules}
	Generalized "others"		Own working environment		Subject himself	
	W	I	W	I	W	I
Yes	93.3	95.1	60.0 *	23.8	28.6	48.3 *
No	6.7	4.9	40.0	76.2	71.4	51.7 *

* $p \leq .05$

What rules are violated to maintain a reasonable standard of living and how are they violated?

The issue here is whether people are prepared to violate moral and legal rules when engaging in different activities aimed at maintaining a reasonable standard of living. Subjects were asked this question from three different perspectives: Do (a) "generalized others," (b) people within the subject's working environment, and (c) the subject himself violate rules? Results are shown in Table 7. The pattern found among the workers is easy to understand: As many as 93.9% of workers perceived generalized others as rule violators. They perceived their own working environment more defensively (60.0% yes), while only 28.8% perceived themselves in the role of a violater of rules.

It is interesting that the same pattern did not appear among intellectuals: As many as 48.3% stated that they were prepared - in special circumstances - to violate rules personally. As one intellectual stated, I was taking care of a group of scientists from abroad. In the end, they wanted to hand me 10 DM. I refused of course, as it seemed like they were giving alms to a beggar. But if it had been 100 DM and I had been faced at the time with an important expense, things might have been different; perhaps I would have taken it. I don't know exactly, but who knows? This statement was classified as a "Yes," because it admitted a readiness to violate rules.

How does rule violation manifest itself?

As Table 8 shows, the most frequent violation indicated by both groups is of interpersonal norms (W: 38.8%; I: 37.8%). The symptoms are predominantly moral violations (using others to one's own advantage, deceiving others, etc.). Other violations were thefts and burglaries (W: 28.6%; I: 24.3%), offenses against the law at work (W: 12.2%; I: 18.9%; e.g,. thefts, avoiding work, doing private jobs in company time, poor work, bribery). Additional mention was made of tax evasion and smuggling. Hence, only the first category refers to moral rules in the strict sense; the others are more sociolegal. No significant differences could be found between workers and intellectuals within the general categories, $\chi^2=0.82$, n.s.

Table 8: Manifestations of Rule Violation.

Type of manifestation	Workers	Intellectuals
Violation of rules by individuals or groups		
Violation of interpersonal norms	38.8	37.8
Thefts, burglaries	8.6	24.3
Offence against the law in enterprises	12.2	18.9
Taxes evasion	16.3	2.7 *
Smuggling	2.1	13.5 *
Violations by the governmentor state	2.0	2.8

* $p \leq .05$

Only the destabilization of sociolegal order was perceived as an important cause of rule violation (W: 25.0%; I: 17.2%; see Table 9). Subjects claimed that there was a lack of detailed legislation pertaining to different domains of social life as well as a lack of clarity and much inconsequence in existing legislation. Intellectuals (44.8%) more than workers (15.0%) stated that the decline in the economic standard of living leads to violation, $z=2.19$, $p \leq .05$. The other causes of rule violation mentioned were: lowering of moral standards, the threat to social security, and the specificity of human nature ("people always violate rules"). Group comparisons did not produce any significant differences, $\chi^2=5.22$, n.s.

Table 9: Causes of Rule Violation.

Type of causes	Workers	Intellectuals
Destabilization of sociolegal order	25.0	17.2
Deterioration of the economic standard of living	15.0	44.8 *
Lowering of moral standard	10.0	13.8
Threat to social security	20.0	3.5
Specificity of human nature	25.0	13.8
Specificity of the former political system	0.0	6.9
Others	5.0	0.0

* $p \leq .05$

Subjects' perceptions regarding the consequences of rule violation generally addressed the moral decline of society: increasing egocentrism, downfall of the value system, increasing willingness to take advantage of others, and loss of social ties (W: 40.9%; I: 54.9%).

Other consequences mentioned were: the disorganization of sociopolitical, economic, and legal order (W: 37.9%; I: 31.4%), that is, a rise in crime, strikes, and emigration as well as decreasing production. The next more general category was closely linked to the latter kind of consequence: decline of professional morality (W: 12.1%; I: 2.0%), that is, loss of work motivation, work prestige, and so forth. This type of consequence was mentioned significantly less often by intellectuals than workers, $z=2.05$, $p \leq .05$, implying that intellectuals experience more prestige from their job than workers do. Subjects also reported some positive consequences of rule violation, namely, individual economic advantages (W: 9.1%; I: 2.0%). This marginal response frequency seems a bit sophistic, as people naturally violate rules for economic gain. However, when asked to verbalize the consequences of this process, this category was regarded as secondary; moral decline and legal disorganization prevailed in subjects' minds.

Table 10: Consequences of Rule Violation.

Type of consequences	Workers	Intellectuals
Moral decline of the society:		
Lowering of interpersonal morality	40.9	54.9
Decline of professional morality	12.1	1.9 *
Desorganization of sociopolitical, economic, and legal order	37.9	31.4
Individual economic advantages	9.1	3.0
I don't know	0.0	9.8 **

* $p \leq .05$ ** $p \leq .01$

The last category of responses concerned what should be done to prevent or limit rule violation. As many as 93.8% of the workers and 83.7% of the intellectuals stressed the need to improve legal regulations. The data reveal that three types of legal regulation need to be reformed:

1. Those connected with work (W: 54.5%; I: 40.8%). The main issue here was how to specify the relationship between quality of work (amount of effort, level of education, skills, etc.) and pay.

2. Macrolevel regulations dealing with widescale economic reforms (W: 25.7%; I: 24.7%), for example, clear rules against industrial pollution.

3. Microlevel regulations with a direct impact on people's behavior (W: 13.6%; I: 8.2%). The basic issue here was how to stop the spread of opportunism ("so that an opportunistic person wouldn't be called a man of initiative"). Otherwise, to make rapid financial gains due to changes in regulations is condoned officially, as demonstrated by the annulment of import duties on alcohol at the end of 1989/beginning of 1990. It is interesting to note that some subjects thought that this annulment was an intentional act by "the rest of the old Polish authorities," enabling former privileged persons to grow rich. At the same time, opportunistic persons also grew rich. There were no significant differences between groups regarding these two aspects, $\chi^2=2.30$, n.s.

Table 11: Suggestions for the Prevention of Rule Violations.

Type of postulates	Workers	Intellectuals
Improving legal regulations		
Improving microlevel legal regulations	13.6	8.2
Improving macrolevel legal regulations	25.7	34.7
Improving legal regulations referring to work	54.5	40.8
Education	3.1	16.3
I don't know	3.1	0.0 **

** $p \leq .01$

Some subjects, particularly intellectuals, suggested education as a remedy for rule violation (W: 3.0%; I: 16.3%), creating an attitude change from having to being. This difference was significant between groups, $z=2.50$, $p \leq .05$. In comparison with the frequency of reports on legal regulations, the proportion of answers suggesting this way of improving the situation seems rather vacuous.

Conclusions and Comments

Many people perceive the deterioration in the economic situation as an important cause of an increasing readiness to violate rules. These are mainly those rules whose violation permits an improvement in the economic situation of some people, namely, theft, burglaries, tax evasions, smuggling, avoiding work in factories, and so forth. These are the rules that are under loosened legal control before considering economic destabilization. In addition, the fact that moral rules are violated in such a situation results from the moral decay of the society confronted with economic decline.

As a consequence of rule violations aimed toward maintaining a reasonable standard of living, there is a continuous downhill slope of social demoralization as well as a disorganization of legal order. In improving legislation (formulating new laws, making existing laws clearer and more consequent), people perceive a basic opportunity to limit and prevent the violation of rules in a situation of economic destabilization.

Contrary to the rather "peaceful" strategies of making use of intermediaries (typical for situations in which there is a commodity shortage), shortages of money evoke active destruction that is prejudicial to individuals, institutions, and the whole of society.

The broad outline of the perception of the general economic situation and the most painfully deteriorating spheres of life within this situation prove to be similar in groups of workers and intellectuals. This is probably because economic decline was a sudden and relatively recent occurrence in Poland (the rapid changes occurred in the winter of 1989 to 1990), and no single group has as yet been able to create specific adaptive strategies adjusted to their own life-style. A lack of differentiation in the reactions to the money shortage may, in its basic patterns, have another cause; namely, the decomposition of life-styles that has been a continuing process in Poland for many years (Kaczmarek, 1986) as a result of the favored treatment of workers. And if we are interested in any differences between workers and intellectuals, it can be noticed that there are some indications that intellectuals are more deeply attached to their work and feel that their profession has a higher prestige, but simultaneously suffer from feelings of inferiority due to the one-sidedness of their skills and abilities. It is not only that intellectuals are often convinced that they should not act in order to preserve their dignity but also that they are simultaneously aware that they are unable to do anything else. Some kind of helplessness plays a role here, no doubt reinforced by many years of underpayment to this social group.

References

Kaczmarek, G. (1986). Zroznicowanie spoleczne a styl zycia. Bydgoskie Towarzystwo Naukowe. *Prace Wydzialu Nauk Humanistyczych.*
Katz, D., & Kahn, R.L. (1966). *The social psychology of organizations.* New York: Wiley.
Komarowsky, M. (1971). *The unemployed man and his family.* New York: Wiley.
Liker, J.K., & Elder, G.H. Jr. (1983). Economic hardship and material relations in the 1930s. *American Sociological Review, 4,* 343-359.
Wosinski, M. (1985). A model of consumer behaviour in the situation of shortages. In K.G. Grunert, & F. Olander (Eds.), *Understanding economic behaviour* (pp. 369-390). Dordrecht: Kluwer Academic Press.

What Constitutes Reckless Driving? A Psychological Study of Motor Vehicle Following Distances

Graham F. Wagstaff [1]

The Tailgating Phenomenon

Studies in both Britain and the USA estimate that rear-end shunt incidents (incidents in which vehicles collide with those in front) account for 12.13 % of all vehicle involvement in road traffic incidents. Rear-end shunt incidents are the second most common kind of road accidents, second only to accidents at road junctions, and a study published in 1980 by Bedfordshire County Council indicated that the rear-end shunt was the most frequent cause of personal road accident injury (Colbourn, Brown, & Coperman, 1978; Postans & Wilson, 1983). Significantly the consensus of opinion seems to be that such accidents result primarily from a failure by drivers to leave an adequate headway, or distance between themselves and the vehicle in front; a phenomenon known as 'tailgating'.

The results of tailgating can be catastrophic. For example, in an incident on the M25 near Godalming, Surrey, on 11th December 1984, a motorist in the early morning darkness ran into a wall of fog and braked suddenly, a vehicle ran into the back of him, then another and so on. The domino effect lasted *six* minutes. By the end eleven people had died in only 37*m* of motorway; some burned to death inside flaming vehicles. One witness referred to the incident as 'a scene from hell itself' (Autoexpress Magazine, 14th November 1989).

According to the Transport and Road Research Laboratory (1975) the recommended 'safe' time gap that drivers should maintain between their vehicle and the one in front is 2*s*, or approximately 1*yd* per *mph* (57*cm* per *km/h)*, and this interval is now specified in literature from the Police and the Department of Transport (HMSO, 1985, 1988, 1989). It should be noted that according to the estimates and formulae provided by these authorities, even a 2*s* gap would not be enough to prevent an average driver, driving at 40*mph* (64*km/h*) or over, from colliding with a stationary vehicle, or one that stops with zero deceleration distance; nevertheless, it has been argued that in most circumstances in good driving conditions, a 2*s* interval should provide a reasonable safety margin. In bad driving conditions, such as wet and fog, however, the gap should be extended.

On the basis of results from experimental studies, some investigators have concluded that drivers do attempt to maintain a minimum headway of 2*s* (Colbourn et al., 1978; Rockwell, 1972). However, these conclusions may be misleading. Most importantly, they are based on average estimates from small numbers of subjects ($N < 20$) and thus may disguise the between driver variance which may be significant in everyday situations; also, they ignore the fact that headway varies according to driving conditions and driver intentions and instructions. For example, according to Rockwell (1972), when drivers

---

[1] The author would like to thank Darice Broomfield, Louise Howard, Keith Morgan, Dr. Joana Wagstaff and Louise Whittaker for their help in data collection and collation.

are instructed to follow 'so as not to lose the lead car' the headway adopted can be as much as 6*s*; but when asked to 'follow at a minimum safe distance', or follow and prepare to pass, the headway can drop to 1*s* or less. In addition, other research indicates that a major predictor of average headway is traffic flow density; the more dense the traffic, the smaller the headway (Lines, 1981).

The fact is, large scale observational studies of motorists in real-life everyday motoring situations seem to contradict any generalized view that drivers attempt to maintain a minimum headway of 2*s*; a large number of motorists clearly do *not* maintain a minimum headway of 2*s*; for instance, Sumner and Baguley (1978) reported that 31% of vehicles on two motorway sites followed with gaps of less than 2*s*, and 15% with gaps of less than 1*s*; and Lines (1981) reported that on the M1 motorway, when speed restriction signals had been set to 50*mph* (81*km/h*) there were periods in which over 50% of motorists were inside the 2*s* interval and 30% maintained gaps of less than 1*s*. In another study of over 2,000 tailgating incidents on the M1, Postans and Wilson (1983) reported 23% of them involved a headway gap of less than 0.5*s*, with an overall mean of 0.65*s*. It should be noted that 0.65*s* is actually less than the commonly specified reaction/thinking time of 9.7*s*, that is the time taken to react to a stimulus such as brake lights, before braking can begin (see, for example, HMSO, 1985); and some even consider the 0.7*s* estimate to be too low. For example, according to Johansson and Kumar (1971) the median reaction time to an unexpected demand is more like 0.9*s* with 25% of subjects exceeding 1.2*s*, and a few over 2*s*. In practice then, it could be argued that in an alert state, and in good driving conditions, with a vehicle in good condition, any driver maintaining a following distance of less than 2*s* could be taking some risk; anyone following with a gap of less than 2*s* could be taking a very serious risk, and virtually anyone maintaining a following distance of less than 0.7*s* is almost *bound* to collide with the vehicle in front should it brake suddenly; indeed, such drivers are likely to collide before they have even touched their brakes!

Tailgating and the Law

Given the serious consequences of tailgating one would expect that the English law would deem such behaviour an offence. Nevertheless, conversations between the author and police officers indicate that prosecution in tailgating incidents is often difficult. One difficulty is that, following multiple shunt incidents, participants will frequently claim they were keeping a safe distance but they were shunted by the vehicle behind them into the vehicle in front. However, perhaps a more significant problem concerns the actual operation of English law in such cases. The two criminal offenses which would seem most relevant to tailgating are those of reckless driving, and careless driving. Section 2 of the 1972 Road Traffic Acts states that 'a person who drives a motor vehicle on a road recklessly shall be guilty of an offence; but it has been left to the courts to decide what constitutes reckless driving. In the classic case of *R. v. Lawrence* (1982) the Lords agreed that the *actus reus* of reckless driving is driving in a manner that crates an obvious and serious risk of causing physical injury to any other road user or substantial damage to property', and the *mens rea* of the offence is 'driving in such a manner without giving any thought to the risk'. Importantly, it is for the jury to decide whether the defendant was driving in such a way as to create an appropriate risk, and in doing this 'they may apply the standard of the ordinary prudent motorist as represented by themselves'. However, although the jury are entitled to infer on the basis of this that the appropriate *mens rea* was present, they must take note of any explanation the defendant may give as to his state of mind which may displace such an inference. Basically this means an accused cannot be convicted of recklessness if he/she had actually considered whether there was a risk and decided (albeit unreasonable) that there was not (Cross, Jones, & Card, 1988, p. 502). If reckless driving is not proved, the jury or magistrates may find the accused guilty of the lesser charge of careless driving. According to the 1972 Road Traffic Acts s.3, concerning careless driving, if any person drives a motor vehicle on a road without due care and attention, or without reasonable consideration for other persons using the road, he/she is guilty of an offence. The standard of what is due care and attention is again that which a prudent driver would have exercised in the circumstances, but in the case of careless driving there is no need to establish whether the failure to exercise due care and attention was deliberate, or due to an error of judgment, or any other cause (*Simpson v. Peat*, 1952).

The case for a judgment of both reckless and careless driving thus rests very heavily on the 'standard of the ordinary prudent motorist'. But this invites two obvious questions with regard to tailgating; namely, what *is* the standard of the ordinary prudent motorist regarding safe and risky following distance, and how satisfactory is this standard? It was to these questions that the following research was addressed.

The Preliminary Study

It was import ant for the present project that a reasonably large subject sample should be tested, and that they could not be forewarned of any testing (problems of small sample sizes and possible demand characteristics may have been evident in some earlier studies; (see, for example, Colbourn et al., 1978). In addition there were safety and financial constraints. These considerations ruled out the use of real-life driving situations, and driving simulators. The basic measure chosen instead was a static roadside headway estimate. Subjects were shown a car and asked to stand behind this car at their normal following distance which was then recorded. Although one cannot assume that this estimate will necessarily reflect accurately a driver's actual following distance in a real-life dynamic, driving situation, it should be noted, nevertheless, that roadside witnesses may be called to give crucial evidence of inter vehicle gaps in legal situations (see, for example, *DPP v. Parker)*, and, according to Rockwell (1972) drivers are very good at estimating velocities without the aid of a speedometer. Consequently, the static measure should be capable of providing some useful data on relative headway estimates, and correlates of such estimates.

To determine the viability of such a method, a preliminary study was first conducted. This study was carried out by Darice Broomfield (1990) as part of her undergraduate thesis. Forty subjects from various occupations participated; their mean age was 32 (range 18-57). All were drivers. A car was parked approximately 1*m* from the kerb of a two-lane road and subjects were asked to estimate, by standing at the appropriate spot, the distance they would drive behind the car at 30*mph* (48*km/h*) and 50*mph* (81*km/h*). This distance was then measured by the experimenter. All subjects were then given a questionnaire which required them to answer questions about various aspects of driving. Included were scales of aggressiveness and cautiousness.

The recommended distances to maintain a 2s gap are 27m and 46m for 30 and 50mph (48 and 81km/h) respectively. When asked to estimate headway at 30mph (48km/h) the mean response was 9.15m (range 4.00-43.60m; SD=7.02); this is appreciably less than the recommended distance of 27m. Indeed, all but one subject indicted less than the recommended distance, and 75% situated themselves at less than 10m from the target vehicle. The figure of 9.15m is equivalent to approximately a 0.7s gap in a dynamic situation.

When asked to estimate the headway at 50mph (81km/h) the mean response was 19.42m (range 5-120m; SD=22.01); again much less than the recommended distance of approximately 46m. All but one subject indicated less than the recommended distance, and 83% situated themselves at less than 20m from the target vehicle. The figure of 19.42m is equivalent to approximately a 0.9s gap in a dynamic situation.

The correlation between the 30mph (48km/h) and 50mph (81km/h) headway estimates was significant (0.93; $p<0.001$) and a number of significant correlations between the headway estimates and questionnaire responses were found. In each of the following cases the first and second correlations are for 30 and 50mph (48 and 81km/h) respectively. In particular, longer headways were indicated by drivers with more years driving experience (0.41, 0.46, $p<0.01$; mean driving experience was 11.90 years, SD=7.84); and drivers who had been in serious motor accidents (0.43, 0.36, $p<0.02$); though only five subjects had been involved in serious accidents. Longer headway estimates also correlated significantly with the degree of agreement (5 point Likert scale, strongly agree 5 - strongly disagree 1) with the statement 'Driving too close to the vehicle in front is a major cause of road accidents' (0.32, 0.32, $p<0.05$; mean response 3.40, SD=0.59). Although no subject actually disagreed with the statement, two subjects were 'neutral'. The correlation between age per se and headway estimates was not significant; and neither were the correlations between headway estimates and the scales of aggressiveness and cautiousness. Further partial correlation analyses revealed that, with the effect of years of driving experience partialled out, the correlation between headway estimates and serious motor accidents (accidents in which personal injuries requiring medical attention were incurred) remained acceptably statistically significant; the resulting correlations were 0.39 ($p<0.05$) and 0.31 ($p<0.06$) for the 30 and 50mph cases respectively. On the whole these results would appear to supply some external validity for the headway estimate measure as well as providing useful information in their own right.

Another part of the study involved estimating headways by reference to a series of specially prepared photographs showing a view through the windscreen of one car toward one ahead. These estimates correlated very significantly with the real-life static estimates (0.68, 0.49; $p<0.001$), though subjects tended to select photographs in which the gaps depicted were greater than those selected in the real-life static estimates (the means were 16.35 m, SD=8.26, and 32.10 m, SD=17,59 for the 30 and 50mph conditions respectively); this suggests that headway estimates from photographs provide a very *conservative* estimate of real-life static responses. It is therefore interesting to note that when subjects were given photographs of, and verbally told, the actual recommended distances, by no means all were convinced such headways would make driving safer. When asked the question

'Do you think that if drivers followed these recommended distances, it would make driving: very safe, safe, no effect, dangerous or very dangerous' the mean response was only 2.60 ($SD=0.84$; very safe, 5 - very dangerous, 1); five subjects (approximately 13%) stated that keeping to the recommended distances would make driving *more* dangerous, and a further 10 subjects (25 %) said it would have 'no effect' on driving safety.

It is also of relevance to note that before being told the recommended headway distance, subjects were asked if they knew what the recommended distance were. Not a singly subject replied 'yes'.

The Main Study

Having developed the headway estimate measure and determined some of its correlates, a further study using a larger sample was conducted to explore some additional variables.

Whereas in the pilot study subjects were interviewed in a variety of situations, the main study was conducted at an M62 motorway service station. The subjects were 139 visitors to the service station. A vehicle was placed on a two lane stretch of road by the service station and subjects were asked the following (item 1): 'Assuming driving conditions are good, please indicate the distance at which you would normally drive behind this car at 50*mph*, by standing in the appropriate position. Remember this is the distance at which you would follow the vehicle at 50*mph*.' Subjects then placed themselves at the appropriate distance. Having measured the distance the experimenter then asked a series of set items from a questionnaire.

When asked to estimate their headway at 50*mph* (81*km/h*) the mean response was 15.84*m* (range 6-37 m; $SD=6.51$). All subjects indicated less than the recommended distance (46 m) and 63% situated themselves less than 15*m* from the target vehicle. Males and females did not differ significantly. The figure of 15.84*m* is equivalent to approximately a 0.7s gap in a dynamic situation. The difference between this mean estimate and that found in the first study is not statistically significant ($p>0.10$).

When asked (item 2) 'Would you consider this distance (their selected distance) a safe following distance?', the mean response on a five point rating scale (definitely yes, 5 - definitely no, 1) was 3.79 ($SD=0.76$). Although the majority (85%) thought their selected gap was *not* safe.

When asked (item 3) 'Would you consider this distance to be dangerously close?' the mean response on a five point rating scale (definitely yes, 1 - definitely no, 5) was 3.91 ($SD=0.56$). The majority disagreed that their distance was dangerously close (91%), but 7% *were* prepared to say that their selected gap was 'dangerously close'.

The next question (item 4) was: 'If you were travelling at 50*mph*, and the car in front, at this distance, braked suddenly and came to an emergency stop, do you think you could stop without colliding with it?' The mean response on a five point rating scale (definitely yes, 5 - definitely no, 1) was 3.87 ($SD=0.73$). The majority of subjects (88%) thought they could stop, though 10% thought they could not, at their selected distance.

The next question (item 5) was: 'If you were travelling at 50*mph*, and the car in front of you, at this distance, hit a stationary vehicle and virtually stopped dead (like it had hit a solid wall), do you think you could stop without colliding with it? The mean response on a five point rating scale (definitely yes, 5 - definitely no, 1) was 2.89 ($SD=1.89$).

In this case just over half of the subjects (53%) considered they would *not* be able to stop, and 37% thought they would be able to stop. In fact, at the distances they had specified, *none* of them would have been able to stop.

Subjects were then asked (item 6): 'Please tell me what you think the distance is between here and the car in front' (that is, their estimate of their selected headway). The mean response was 23.54m (SD=17.90); this is significantly greater ($p<0.001$) than their actual selected distance of 15.83m (SD=6.51), but still much less than the recommended distance of 46m. In fact, although 59% of subjects overestimated their actual selected headway distance, only 7% of subjects thought they had exceeded 46m.

The next question was (item 7): 'If the car in front of you were standing still, and you were driving at 50mph, how long would it take you to get to the spot where it is now standing *(in seconds)*?' the mean response was 3.26s (range 0.1-30s, SD=4.10); 35% of subjects chose the 2s response and 36% exceeded it; however, the mean selected headway for those who chose 2s was virtually identical to the mean of the sample as a whole (15.63, SD=6.67).

The next part of the study involved taking the subject to the actual recommended distance (46m) and asking (item 8): 'How far do you think this is from the car in front of you?' The mean response was 85.37m (SD=95.66; range 13.70-804 m); approximately 63% of subjects exceeded the correct response of 46m, and 29% of subjects considered the distance to be in excess of 90m. Subjects thus tended to overestimate the specified distance.

Subjects were then asked (item 9): 'How many *car lengths* is there between you and the car in front: that is, what is the distance in *car lengths*: one length, five lengths, etc.?' The mean response to this item was 11.69 (SD=4.72). An average British car is assumed to be approximately 4.6m in length, so 10 cars should more or less represent the actual distance of 46m; 11.69 cars is about 54m and 90m is about 19.5 car lengths. Twenty-eight percent of subjects reported 10±1 car lengths, 47% exceeded this, but only 7% exceeded 19.5 car lengths (approximately 90m). Thus subjects tended to be more accurate when estimating the specified distance in car lengths; nevertheless, the range was from 5 to 40 car lengths! It should be noted that at no time during the last items were subjects actually told they were at the recommended distance.

Further analyses involved correlating all the variables with the original static headway estimates (item 1). Only two correlations were significant: first, the longer the static headway selected (item 1), the longer the distance subjects estimated it to be (item 6) (0.36; $p<0.001$). Second, the shorter the static headway selected (item 1), the longer people judged the actual recommended 46m distance (item 8) to be (- 0.22; $p<0.02$), or, in other words, the shorter the headway subjects select, the more they overestimate a standard distance.

Finally, subjects were asked 'Do you think that following too closely behind another vehicle is against the law?' Fifty-two percent replied 'Yes', 29% replied 'No', and the remainder, 19%, could not decide.

The Time Study

The recommendation of a 2s following interval between cars invites a further obvious question: how well are people able to estimate a 2s time interval? To determine this 30 subjects of varying occupations were approached. Subjects were first asked the following: 'According to the Police, drivers should maintain a certain time gap between their own vehicle and the vehicle in front. Do you know what the recommended time gap is?' Only five subjects (17%) said they did know the recommended time gap: of these, two, correctly, said it was 2s, two said it was 3 to 4s, and the other said 10s! Subjects were then provided with a Casio lap recorder, and asked to estimate 2s by pressing the recorder button every 2s. All subjects were given a series of practice trials, the final estimate being based on a mean of five experimental trials. The overall mean was 2.05s (range 1.11-4.52s; $SD=0.64$), but eight (2%) of the subjects estimated 2s at less than 1.7s. Finally, subjects were asked: 'Can you tell me of a technique for maintaining a two second gap between vehicles?' Subjects were scored correct if they reported a feasible technique: for example, timing vehicles between fixed points. Only nine subjects (30%) were able to report such a technique. There were no sex differences on any of these variables.

A additional feature of this study involved teaching those whose majority of responses were below a mean of 2s, to count 2s by the device of covertly saying 'one second second, two second second'. The device was effective in raising the estimate in all cases (the mean for those concerned rose from 1.64, $SD=0.23$, to 2.17, $SD=0.30$, $N=14$).

Implications

As pointed out earlier it cannot be assumed that headway estimates arrived at in a static situation will necessarily accurately reflect the headway a driver might maintain in a real-life dynamic situation. But even allowing for the fact that there are bound to be problems in generalizing from static estimates to real-life driving behaviour, it perhaps bodes ill for real-life driving behaviour that more than 60% of subjects in the main study positioned themselves at less than 15m from the target vehicle for 50mph (81km/h); 15m would be the recommended gap for about 16mph (26km/h)! Moreover, these headway estimates were *not* significantly correlated with views about safe headway intervals; most people thought their selected interval was 'safe', and that they could avoid colliding with the car in front, regardless of the size of gap they had selected. This is well illustrated by the fact that although five subjects in the main study situated themselves a mere 6.10m from the rear of the target vehicle for a speed of 50mph (80.5km/h) that is a gap of 0.3s, *all* five considered this 'safe'.

There were even a few people who apparently believed that maintaining wider inter-vehicle intervals would make driving *more* dangerous.

When all the data are taken together they suggest that although their estimates differ widely, the general tendency is for people to *underestimate* the actual headway necessary to avoid most rear-shunt accidents, yet *overestimate* their selected headway distance when asked to verbally estimate it in standard units of length (though even these verbal estimates indicate distance well short of those headway intervals recommended by the authorities). The tendency to overestimate distance when making a verbal judgment also applies to estimates of a standard distance, though estimates in terms of car lengths tend to be better than estimates in terms of meters, feet or yards. This tendency to overestimate an actual specified distance is most apparent in those who are more likely to select shorter headways.

The implications of these results for the offenses of recklessness and careless driving in tailgating incidents would appear to be clear. The standard of the ordinary prudent motorist seems to be a variable and very inaccurate one which is likely to favour those accused of recklessness and careless driving offenses. For, not only is there widespread ignorance and uncertainty about what constitutes an obvious and serious risk in terms of headway distances (it was remarkable how many subjects in their incidental comments said they thought a safe headway was the same distance for all speeds), but also, many seem to underestimate what is a safe headway, yet overestimate the distance actually adopted.

A very good illustration of the problems involved is provided by the case of *DPP. v. Parker* (1989). In this case the defendant was accused of careless driving when his Volkswagen car collided with the rear of a Ford car which had stopped in a line of traffic. Because of rain the road was wet and slippery. According to the reported facts, the defendant had been driving at a speed of between 30 and 40*mph* (48-64*km/h*), approximately two car lengths behind the car into which he ran. There was no denial that he had, in fact, run into the Ford in front of him. However, justices concluded that 'since a reasonable and prudent driver could have been involved in such an accident, the case against the defendant was not proved beyond reasonable doubt'. The justices also dismissed an appeal by the prosecutor that the defendant was guilty by reason of the uncontroverted evidence of him having run into the back of the vehicle in front. Reasons given by the justices for dismissing the evidence against the defendant included 'the road conditions were wet and slippery', and 'a number of other vehicles were involved in similar minor accidents'. The significance of this decision is perhaps made more pertinent when it is realized that, on the defendant's admission, he was driving about two car lengths behind a vehicle at 30 to 40*mph* (48-64*km/h*). At 30*mph* (48*km/h*) this represents a gap of 0.68*s*, and at 40*mph* (64*km/h*) a gap of 0.59*s*. If the average reaction time or 'thinking time' response is accepted as 0.7-0.9*s*, then the defendant was almost bound to collide with the car in front; and in the wet, it was a virtual certainty. It should be noted that the Police recommend the 2*s* gap is *doubled* in the wet. So were the justices correct in finding the defendant not guilty? According to the data presented here, perhaps they were; the 'average prudent motorist' might very well drive at this dangerously close distance behind the vehicle in front, and not recognize the risk.

As things stand at present in Britain, it is little wonder that the offenses of reckless driving and careless driving for tailgating incidents appear very difficult to establish (no previous case was referred to in *DPP. v. Parker)*. Moreover, things are likely to remain so unless a fairly extensive educational program is administered to provide drivers, jurors and jurists with the appropriate knowledge necessary to understand what constitutes a 'safe headway', and how a safe headway is to be calculated and maintained.

For the moment, however, when nearly a third of the sample tested stated they did not think driving too close to the vehicle in front was against the law, for most practical purposes, according to English law, they were probably right.

References

Broomfield, D. (1990). *The psychology of driving: Why do drivers drive too close?* University of Liverpool, unpublished manuscript.
Colbourn, C.J., Brown, I.D., & Copeman, A.K. (1978). Drivers' judgments of safe distances in vehicle following. *Human Factors, 20,* 1-11.
Cross, R., Jones, P.A., & Card, R. (1988). *Introduction to criminal law.* London: Butterworths.
DPP. v. Parker, RTR, 413 (1989).
HMSO (1985). *Road craft: The police driver's manual.* London: Her Majesty's Stationery Office.
HMSO (1988). *The highway code.* London: Her Majesty's Stationery Office.
HMSO (1989). *Driving: The department of transport manual.* London: Her Majesty's Stationery Office.
Johansson, G., & Rumar, K. (1971). Drivers' brake reaction times. *Human Factors, 13,* 23-27.
Lines, C.J. (1981). The effect of motorway signals on traffic behaviour. *Transport and Road Research Laboratory, Suppl.* Report 707.
Postans, R.L., & Wilson, W.T. (1983). Close-following on the motorway. *Ergonomics, 26,* 317-327.
R. v. Lawrence, 1 All ER, 974 (1982).
Rockwell, T. (1972). Skills, judgment, and information acquisition in driving. In T.W. Forbes (Ed.), *Human factors in highway trafic safety research* (pp. 348-379). New York: Wiley Interscience.
Simpson v. Peat, 1 All ER, 447 (1952).
Sumner, R., & Baguley, C. (1978). Close-following behaviour at two sites on rural lane motorways. *Transport and Road Research Laboratory,* Report 859, Crowthorne, Berks.
Transport and Road Research Laboratory (1975). The minimum braking distance obtained with some cars and heavy vehicles. *TRRL,* Leaflet LF 537.

Between Doing Harm and Breaking the Law: A Social-Psychological Perspective

Maria Pietras

Introduction

In daily life, one may observe many cases of persons harming each other, caused by breaking a great variety of social and interpersonal norms. As is clear from research by social psychologists, such examples of injustice may occur in every kind of interpersonal relation (Deutsch, 1985; Mikula, 1986; Walster, Walster, & Berscheid, 1978). Many examples of harm-doing behaviour have - or might have - their epilogue in court (e.g., physical aggression, insulting, adultery in marriage). On the other hand, doing harm to somebody does not necessarily mean breaking the law and it is not always followed by somebody's personal feeling of being harmed (e.g., tax evasion). This point is illustrated on Figure 1 that shows relations between these two kinds of behaviour.

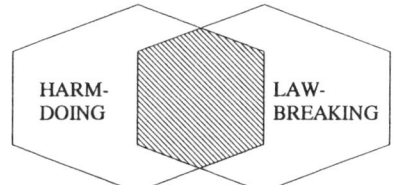

Figure 1: Relations Between Harm-Doing and Law Breaking.

Both breaking the law and doing harm are examples of "wrong", unfair or deviant behaviour, consisting in a violation of the social norms transmitted in socialization that result in a certain level of moral development in an individual. One may expect, then, that psychological mechanisms of doing harm and breaking law are similar and, hence, we may use psychological knowledge concerning the harm-doer to understand the psychological portrait of the delinquent, at least in cases when another human being is a victim of criminality.

Some elements of this portrait are better known from psychological research on breaking law and doing harm. This mainly concerns justifications - their functions in deviant behaviour and classifications (see Matza, 1964; Scott & Lyman, 1968; Sykes & Matza, 1957). Little is known, however, about other cognitive and emotional processes of the perpetrator.

The main goal of this research was to describe how people experience the situation of doing harm, that is, how do they perceive intentionality of harming; what kinds of emotions are evoked in this situation; what do they think about the situation; what are their attributions of responsibility and formulated justifications; and how do they perceive victim's reactions to injustice and the end of the event?

The influence of some factors on the harm-doer's experience was also examined, such as: level of aggression, neuroticism, criminal record[1], belief in just world, conditions of socialization, self-esteem, attitude towards victim and drug addiction.

Method

Individual interviews were administered to 711 people at different age, education and job. They were asked to recall and describe a situation from their life in which another person had felt harmed because of their specific behaviour. In the context of this situation, they were asked some questions concerning intentionality of harming, emotions, reflections, attributions of responsibility, formulated justifications, perception of victim's reaction and the end of the episode.

Results

Who is the victim? Most often members of family are the objects of our harm-doing behaviour (more than 40% of the participants recalled examples of harm done to members of the family; see Table 1). Such episodes were significantly more often described by neurotics and teenagers with a criminal record. Strangers were hardly ever mentioned as victims of harm-doing behaviour.

Table 1: Who is the Victim?

Category of victim	% of subjects	Groups of subjects significantly more often describing the category ($p<0,05$)	
Family	40.7	Neurotics	$z=4.65$
		Teenagers with criminal records	$z=3.98$
Colleague, acquaintance	30.4	Orphans	$z=2.63$
Sweetheart	13.4	Drug addicts	$z=1.97$
		Low level of aggression	$z=3.20$
Friend	6.6		
Boss	4.7		
Stranger	4.2		

This obviously does not mean that we do not harm strangers. For example, many cases of crime behaviour concern a victim unknown to offender. It rather may suggest that we hardly think about an unknown victim of our inappropriate behaviour within the category of harmed person.

---

[1] This group of subjects consisted of teenagers living in residential care. They were being compared with a group of teenagers growing up in the family.

Table 2: What is Harm?

Category of harm	% of subjects	Groups of subjects signif. more often describing the category	
Insult, offence	34.9		
Unfulfilment of a duty, expectations	16.8	Drug addicts, Low level of aggression	z=2.7 z=2.1
Break off relation, breach	9.2	Neurotics	z=2.59
Lie, cheating, betrayal	8.1		
Breaking one's promise	7.9		
Disrespect, disregard	6.4		
Undeserved accusation	6.3	Neurotics	z=2.02
Physical aggression	5.8	Not using drugs	z=3.29
Unsuccessful joke	2.3		
Stealing, not returning something	0.8		
Other	3.2		

What is the harm? The list of episodes described by subjects as harm done to another person is very long (see Table 2). Most often different forms of verbal harming were reported, such as insult, offence (35% of the subjects).

Also such examples of behaviour as not fulfilling a duty or somebody's expectations (17%), breaking one's promise (8%), lie, betrayal (8%) and breaking off relations, breach (9,2%), were often mentioned as causing harm to another person.

Teenagers in residential care did not differ in this respect from the contemporary group. It is interesting that no member of this group recalled stealing as an example of their harm-doing behaviour (although such behaviour had very often been the reason why they had been placed in residential care).

Table 3: Intentionality and Forseeability of Harm.

Intentionality and forseeability of harm	% of subjects	Groups of subjects signif. more often choosing the category	
I didn't want, didn't know	36.0	Indifferent attitude, Positive attitude towards victim	z=3.94 z=2.90
I didn't want, knew	40.9		
I wanted, knew	23.0	Criminal record High level of aggression, Negative attitudes, Orphans, Non-neurotics	z=2.77 z=2.04 z=4.22 z=4.05 z=2.83

Intentionality and predictability of harming. Our subjects were asked to classify behaviour described by them as harm done to another person to one of the following categories:
  1. I didn't want to harm, and I didn't foresee that my behaviour might harm him/her.

2. I didn't want to harm, but I knew that my behaviour would harm him/her.[2]
3. I wanted to harm, and I knew that behaving in such a way would achieve this.

The results of this classification are illustrated in Table 3. Intentional harming was more seldom recalled by interviewees, probably because it is most immoral behaviour, and defence mechanisms cause some difficulties in remembering and talking about it (e.g., among neurotics, who are known to use strong defence mechanisms, such behaviour was described significantly more rarely than among nonneurotics).

Young persons in residential care, orphans, people with a high level of aggression and negative attitudes towards victims were more inclined to present stories of intentional harming. One should be careful, however, with inferring from this conclusion that teenagers with criminal records or orphans more often harm others intentionally. Perhaps they only do not have such a strong resistance to talking about it.

Table 4: Moral Dilemmas of Harm-Doer.

Moral dilemmas	% of Subjects	Groups of subjects signif. more often choosing the category	
Yes	47.8	Not believing in just world,	$z=2.53$
		Middle level of self-esteem	$z=2.35$
No	52.2	Believing in just world,	$z=2.53$
		Orphans,	$z=4.28$
		High level of self-esteem	$z=2.35$

Moral dilemmas. Almost the same proportions of harm-doers experience (47%) and do not experience (52.2%) any moral conflicts and dilemmas before action. Only belief in a just world and self-esteem were found as possible factors influencing the experience of such dilemmas: Respondents with high levels of self-esteem and those who believe that the world is just more rarely have such moral conflicts before harming (see Table 4). Belief that the world is just may work in this case as a kind of justification for immoral behaviour.

Who is to blame? People tend rather to perceive their own responsibility (42.5% of respondents) or at least joint responsibility (27.4%) for the harming event (see Table 5). It is possible that the instruction the subjects: "Recall a situation in which somebody felt harmed *because* of your behaviour" - biased recall towards such events in which responsibility of the respondent was more visible.

---

[2] In this case harm is only a side effect of behaviour, directed towards other goals (e.g., a thief stealing somebody's car is directed towards profit; harming the owner is not the main goal of this activity).

Table 5: Harm-Doer's Attributions of Responsibility.

Attribution of responsibility	% of subjects	Groups of subjects signif. more often choosing the category	
Harm-doer only	42.5	Not believing in just world,	z=1.90
Partly harm-doer	27.4	High level of aggression,	z=3.15
		Negative attitude	z=3.94
Others only	30.2	Drug addicts,	z=2.00
- victims only	(16.5)	Neurotics,	z=2.08
		High level of self-esteem	z=4.19

Drug addicts, neurotics and subjects with high levels of self-esteem more often than contemporary groups showed tendency to blame for the harm others, including victim oneself. No differences between teenagers with a criminal record and contemporary group were obtained in respect of attribution of responsibility.

Table 6: Justification Formulated by Harm-Doer.

Category of justification	% of subjects	Groups of subjects signif. more often reporting the category	
Lack of justification	23.4	Orphans,	z=2.77
		Drug addicts	z=2.84
Situational excuses	14.6	Positive attitudes	z=3.99
Personal features, mood of victimizer	11.0	Neurotics,	z=2.02
		High level of aggression	z=2.34
Feeling of right	8.6	High level of self-esteem	z=2.04
Profits for victimizer	7.9	Neurotics	z=2.83
Depreciation of victim	6.3	Negative attitudes	z=2.78
Superior right, value	5.3	Neurotics	z=2.02
Self-promotion	5.2	High level of aggression	z=2.36
Revenge	4.9	Negative attitude	z=3.07
No choice	3.2		
Profits for victim	2.8		
Minimizing of harm	2.5	Drug addicts	z=2.15
Outside authority	2.4		
Others	2.6		

Justifications for doing harm. Justifications produced by people breaking some moral norms (e.g., delinquents) are discussed in the literature as a very important element of decision-making processes as well as evaluative processes after harm (or crime) has been done. They are named in different ways, for example, rationalizations, neutralizations, excuses, explanations or defence attributions.

We found that about one-quarter of subjects did not formulate such justifications before action (see Table 6). Mainly people who did not want to harm and did not expect such a consequence of their behaviour did not "produce" justifications before acting.

Most frequently, perpetrators point out some features of the situation (14.6%) as well as their personal features, mood (11.0%) or profits from the unfair behaviour to justify the action. Appealing to the perpetrator's "feeling of right" (8.6%) and depreciation of the victim (6.3%) were also rather popular kinds of justification.

Table 7: Emotions Experienced by the Harm-Doer.

Category of emotions	% of subjects		Groups of subjects signif. more often reporting the category	
	Before action	After action		
Distress, shame, annoyance	27.0	55.3	Positive attitude,	$z=2.58$
			Middle level of self-esteem,	$z=3.48$
			Not believing in just world,	$z=1.90$
			Children having family	$z=2.58$
Anxiety, hesitation	11.5	3.7	Non-neurotics,	$z=2.59$
			Not using drugs	$z=3.70$
Tension, nervousness	13.9	5.2	Low level of aggression	$z=2.75$
Anger, irritation	16.7	7.1	High level of aggression	$z=2.34$
Fear	6.1	2.7	Neurotics	$z=3.04$
Helplesness	3.5	1.2	Positive attitude	$z=2.58$
Sympathy (pity) for victim	1.4	11.1		
Enjoyment, satisfaction	11.0	13.5	Negative attitude	$z=3.25$
Indifference	11.1	6.1	Orphans,	$z=1.80$
			High level of self-esteem	$z=2.20$
Don't remember	5.9	1.9	Drug addicts	$z=3.45$
Others	3.4	2.4		

Depreciation of victim seems to be very a efficient way of justifying inappropriate behaviour: 60% of victimizers did not change this kind of justification after the harm was done, whereas such a change took place among 60% of subjects referring to outside factors or features of the situation. Additionally, the former did not experience such negative emotions as shame, annoyance or tension after perception of victim's reaction to the harm. No differences between teenagers in residential care and the comparison group were found in respect of the justifications used by the harm-doer.

What does the harm-doer feel? A great spectrum of emotions evoked in unjust situations and experienced by the harm-doer before action was found in the study. The main groups are showed in Table 7.

More than one-quarter of the victimizers felt annoyance, shame or distress before acting against another person. Many perpetrators experienced anxiety and hesitation (11.5%) or tension and nervousness (13.9%) before harming. The occurrence of such emotions may suggest for the perpetrator. On the other hand, some of the subjects, mainly having negative attitudes towards the victim, reported experience of positive emotions (e.g., enjoyment, satisfaction) when harming (11.0%). A great number of victimizers (16.7%) were irritated and angry with the victim before acting against him/her.

No difference were found between teenagers with a criminal record and the comparison group regarding emotions experienced when harming. Emotions change with the development of the situation of harming. When reactions of the victim are observed, harm-doers experience more often such emotions as shame, distress and sympathy for the victim, and less often emotions such as anger, anxiety or tension (see Table 7).

Table 8: Reactions of Victims as Perceived by Harm-Doers.

Reactions of victims	% of subjects	Groups of subjects signif. more often reporting the category	
Annoyance, sorrow, tears	28.4	Positive attitude,	z=3.28
		Middle level of self-esteem	z=2.25
Resentment, attack on victimizer	22.4		
Silence, withdrawal	11.4	Neurotics	z=2.08
Persuasion, explanation	9.0	Criminal record,	z=2.08
		Neurotics	z=2.58
Tension, nervousness	7.0	Drug addicts	z=2.14
Lack of reaction	6.5		
Surprise, astonishment	5.9	Positive attitude	z=2.58
Irony	5.9	Negative attitude	z=1.99
Justifying victimizer, self-blame	5.8	Neurotics	z=2.04
Looking for support from others	5.2		
Don't know	2.3		
Others	0.7		

What are victims' reactions in the harm-doers' perception? More than one-quarter of investigated harm-doers described victims' annoyance, sorrow or tears as reactions to the harming behaviour. About one-quarter of victims expressed resentment and attacked the victimizer (see Table 8). It happened also that victims were eager to understand the offender and to explain to them the problem (5.8%). Some of them even showed willigness to blame themselves for the harm.

Teenagers in residential care more often perceived victims' tendency to defend themselves not by attacking the victimizer but rather by using explanations and persuasion. Probably this result has a connection with data showing that teenagers with criminal records very often reported examples of harming behaviour concerning their parents and other members of family.

Table 9: Reflections of Harm-Doer.

Category of reflections	% of Subjects	Groups of subjects signif. more often reporting the category	
Negative evaluation of behaviour and victimizer	30.9	Not using drugs,	z=2.89
		Children having familiy,	z=1.94
		Not believing in just world	z=2.06
Negative evaluation of victim	13.9	Negative attitude,	z=4.05
		Criminal record,	z=2.01
		Neurotics,	z=2.59
		Believing in just world	z=2.60
Justifying behaviour	13.0	High level of self-esteem,	z=3.74
		Believing in just world	z=2.19
Revindication of justice	11.7	High level of aggression,	z=2.45
		Positive attitude	z=2.39
Being doubtful towards the behaviour	11.0	Neurotics	z=2.34
Concerning feelings, evaluations by victim	10.3	Positive attitude	z=2.38
General reflections	5.8		
Concerning consequences of the behaviour	5.2	Positive attitude	z=2.58
Lack of reflections	4.3	Orphans	z=2.81
Desire that the situation is finished	4.6	Drug addicts	z=2.90
Don't remember	3.4		
Positive evaluation of victimizer	3.1	Neurotics	z=2.02
Others	1.2		

What does harm-doer think? Reflections formulated by the harm-doers concern behaviour itself, victim, victimizer, revindication of justice and later consequences of the behaviour. Most common among the victimizers are negative evaluations concerning harming behaviour and the perpetrator oneself (one-third of the respondents) or at least some doubts concerning equity of the behaviour (11.0%).

More than one-fifth of the perpetrators focused on victims' feelings, evaluations of the victimizer ("What does he/she think about me now?") and on demands for justice. Aforementioned groups of harm-doers as well as those who expressed desire for the situation to be finished (4.6%) constitute about 64% of perpetrators experiencing the situation as unpleasant and uncomfortable.

However, there are also victimizers who point out the restitute of their behaviour (13.0%), evaluate themselves positively (3.0%) and perceive the victim in a negative way (13.9%). The latter were found more often among teenagers in residential care (see Table 9).

The end of the event. As reported by about 40% of the investigated victimizers, they try to restore justice by offering an apology to the victim or changing their behaviour in the next relation with the harmed person. Very often, other factors, such as time or the intervention of other people influence the positive end of the episode (22.4%). So many positive endings to the harming episodes are caused probably by the fact that mainly members of the family, friends and colleagues were the objects of harm.

Table 10: The End of the Episode.

The end of the episode	% of subjects	Groups of subjects signif. more often reporting the category	
Apology, excuses	37.0	Not using drugs,	$z=3.48$
		Positive attitude	$z=3.49$
Outside factor resolves the problem	22.4	Orphans	$z=2.58$
Break off relation	16.3	Negative attitude	$z=2.18$
Victim resolves the problem	10.3	Neurotics	$z=2.59$
Harm-doer changes behaviour	5.3	Indifferent and positive attitude	$z=2.02$
Situation is not finished	5.5		
Punishment for victimizer	2.8		
Others	0.8		

Sometimes the victims themselves tend to restore a positive relationship with the perpetrator (10.0%; see Table 10). In many cases, however, the harming episode finds its epilogue in breaking off relations between victim and offender (16.3%). No differences were found between teenagers in residential care and those living in families in respect to the end of the harming situation.

Conclusion

The reason for presenting research on doing harm at a conference on law and psychology is based on an assumption that many cases of delinquency are followed by somebody's feeling of being harmed. In other words, breaking the law may be usually defined as doing harm to somebody.

As this research makes clear, when people harm they experience a great spectrum of emotions, formulate different justifications and reflections and in a specific way, they perceive responsibility for the harm and victim's reactions. They also differ according to intentionality and foreseeability of the harm. The main impression is that people do not want to harm, even if they are aware of such result of their behaviour (80.0% of subjects). For most of them the situation of doing harm is unpleasant and uncomfortable, and it generates many negative emotions and evaluations (especially after the victim's reactions are perceived) and stimulates attempts to restore justice (apology, excuse).

It was also found that young people with a criminal record do not differ very much from the contemporary group in their experience of unjust interpersonal situations (more differences were obtained to other factors, such as attitude towards victim, neuroticism, level of aggression, belief in just world, self-esteem etc.). Teenagers in residential care were able to feel shame or annoyance or apologize to the victim. The main problem is, however, that all those feelings, evaluations and positive tendencies to recompense harm are evoked in a situation, that is *defined* by the perpetrator as *harming* another person. Therefore, two questions should be raised when transferring these results to the field of criminology.

First, how can we make the delinquent perceive the situation of breaking law as harmful? Second, is it naive to claim that making offenders think about harmful consequences of their criminal behaviour is likely to reduce their offending behaviour? I am not able to answer these questions on the basis of the present results. However, some examples of studies dealing with closly related questions can be found in the literature. First, Howard (1979; see Launay, 1987), who has collectes cases of would-be-victims who have successfully deterred their offenders' attack in face-to-face confrontation. Drawing on these cases, Howard advices the potential victim as to which type of behaviour makes it psychologically difficult for the offender to behave violently. The main idea is to impress on the assailant that the would-be-victim is a worthy human being, who suffers from the behaviour of the offender.

Another study, in which the British "Victim and Offender in Conciliation" scheme was used, shows positive influence of victim-offender meetings on the offenders' perception of the situation and their tendency to restory justice (Launay, 1987).

The aforementioned studies show indirectly the importance of the perpetrator's experience of the deviant interpersonal situation. The research presented in this paper may serve to promote a better understanding of the nature of this experience.

References

Deutsch, M. (1985). *Distributive justice: A social-psychological perspective.* New Haven: Yale University Press.
Howard, W.B. (1979). Some psychological strategies for dealing with the violence criminal. *The Police Chief, May,* 71-77.
Launay, G. (1987). Victim-offender conciliation. In B. J. McGurk, D. M. Thornton, & M.Williams (Eds.), *Applying psychology to imprisonment. Theory and practice.* London: Her Majesty's Stationary Office.
Matza, D. (1964). *Delinquency and drift.* New York: Wiley.
Mikula, G. (1986). The experience of injustice: Toward a better understanding of its phenomenology. In H. Bierhoff, R.L. Cohen, & J. Greenberg (Eds.), *Justice in interpersonal relations.* New York: Plenum Press.
Scott, M.B., & Lyman, S.M. (1968). Accounts. *American Sociological Review, 33,* 46-62.
Sykes, G.M., & Matza D. (1957). Techniques of neutralization: A theory of delinquency. *American Sociological Review, 22,* 664-670.
Walster, E., Walster, G.W., & Berscheid, E. (1978). *Equity: Theory and research.* Boston: Allyn and Bacon.

Drug Use Prevalence Among Offenders

Serge Brochu, Lyne Desjardins, Alexandra Douyon and Charles Forget

Introduction

According to many authors, (Bergeret, 1981; Cardinal, 1988; Chami, 1987; Cloutier, 1987; Valeur, 1988) substance abuse has always existed and always will. However, the abuse can take many forms and attract different types of people.

Since 1960, it is possible to note many changes in the type and style of drug use and abuse. Drug abuse was originally restricted to some specific groups, whereas today, the phenomenon is observed in every strata of society. Drug users in the 60's were looking for the effects while the new consumers try to reach new sensations and do not always care about the quality of the substance.

In the same vein, drug use is now associated with criminal behavior and the judicial system is more and more concerned about this phenomenon. The United States has put a Drug Use Forecasting system in more than 20 large cities throughout the country. Canada has launched a major action program against drugs. More specifically, the Canadian correctional service has set up an important steering committee on the control of drug users and abusers among prison inmates. The underlying hypothesis is that drug use and, more importantly, drug abuse could precipitate recidivism. In North America, drug use among offenders is considered a question of major importance.

Drug use among offenders

Innes (1988) recently reported that 35% of U.S. state penitentiary inmates were under the influence of a drug while committing the crime of which they were accused. Almost 80% of inmates report having used illegal drugs at least once in their life, and 52% admitted having used hard drugs. Half of the inmates who report using drugs, start using it around the age of 15. About 13% of inmates could be classified as drug dependents who are committing crimes in order to get their drug.

The U.S. Drug Use Forecasting System affords a great deal of interesting information concerning drug use among arrestees. In the city of New York, in 1984, 56% of arrestees tested positive for opiates, cocaine, PCP, or methadone. Two years later this percentage rose to 80%. This situation was due, in large part, to cocaine abuse (Wish, 1987). We must remember, however, that the City of New York is unique and that other American cities do not have the same drug problem. But generally, it is possible to say that between 44% and 87% of women arrested in large American cities test positive to at least one substance, while the percentage is between 50% and 85% for men (Wish & O'Neil, 1989). This indicates a rising trend in drug use among offenders.

In Canada, Lightfoot, Kalin, Laverty, and MacLean (1985) interviewed 275 volunteer male prisoners in Ontario penitenciaries. According to their results, 80% of inmates report having used at least one type of drug in the six months prior to being arrested. Moreover, 79% of inmates declared having used alcohol or illegal drugs on the day they committed the crime for which they were incarcerated. The Drug Abuse Screening Test (DAST) revealed that 68% of inmates were at least moderately dependent on illegal drugs. For their part, Berzins and Colette-Carrière (1979) revealed that for 58% of the 91 women incarcerated in an Ontario penitentiary, alcohol or drug use played an important part in the commission of the crime of which they were accused.

In Quebec, there are only very few studies on the prevalence of drug use among offenders. A study by the Department of the Solicitor General of Canada (1988), mainly interested in the prevalence of mental problems among penitentiary inmates, gives some indication of drug use and abuse among federal inmates. This study, based on the Diagnostic Interview Schedule, revealed that 49% of inmates were drug abusers, if not drug dependent. No comprehensive study on the prevalence of drug use among Québec female offenders has yet been done, but according to Langelier-Biron and Savard (1986) it appears that drug dependency carries the risk that a woman will be involved in criminal activities. The same is true for adolescent drug users, according to Le Blanc (1986).

It is very important to obtain a clear image of the prevalence of drug use among various categories of offenders in order to control the situation and, if necessary, develop some specialized addiction services designed for this population.

Method

This paper reports aggregate data from three simultaneous studies conducted at the Addiction Unit of the International Center for Comparative Criminology (Brochu & Douyon, 1990; Desjardins, Brochu, & Biron, 1991; Forget, 1991). The aim of this paper is to present data on the prevalence of drug use by offenders. More specifically, this paper will address drug consumption by adult offenders (male and female) and by young offenders (male and female).

Data were collected through a structured interview adapted from that of Lightfoot et al. (1985). In addition, adults were asked to answer to the Drug Abuse Screening Test (DAST) (Skinner, 1982). The DAST is designed to give a quick portrait of problematic drug use. This questionnaire is based on 20 items and can be answered in about five minutes.

A total of 453 offenders were interviewed in order to obtain information about their drug use and the level of their drug dependency. Of this total, the sample includes 224 adult offenders (130 men and 94 women) and 229 young offenders (175 boys and 54 girls). For the sake of clarity young male offenders will be called "boys" while young female offenders will be called "girls". The sample was drawn from three adult prisons, two offender half-way houses and five young offender readaptation centres of the province of Québec. The overall participation rate is 82% (453/550).

The average age for male adults was 29.9 ($SD=9.7$) while it was about the same for the women: 30.4 ($SD=7.6$). The situation was clearly different for the young offenders, where the average age for boys was 15.7 ($SD=1.3$) and for girls was 15,5 ($SD=1.4$).

Results

The data analyses will proceed in three parts. First, results concerning drug use during the 12 months prior to the incarceration[1] will be presented. This will be followed by the results of drug use during the 30 days before the incarceration.[2] Finally, the drug dependency level of the adults will be reported.

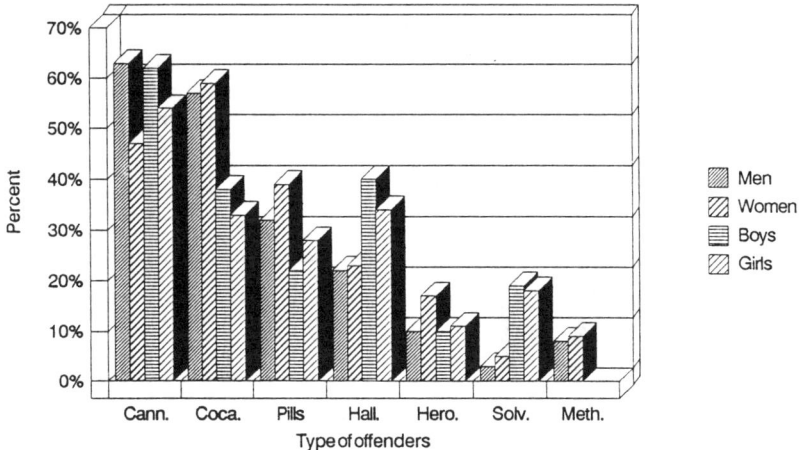

Figure 1: Drug Used in a 12 Months Period.

Drug use during a 12 months period

Offenders were asked to report their drug use during a 12 months period. Figure 1 shows that cannabis is the most popular drug for every group except for women. More specifically 47% of the women, 54% of the girls, 63% of the men and 63% of the boys used cannabis during the 12 months period. Cocaine follows in popularity, but its price contributes to the fact that more adults (57% of men and 59% of women) use it than adolescents (38% of boys and 33% of girls). Prescribed drugs have been used without medical supervision by about one third of the adult sample (32% of men and 39% of women), and by one quarter of the adolescents (22% of males and 27% of females). We note in general, that females use slightly more pills than males. These data are in line with the Canadian national census which constantly reports this type of difference between males and females (Eliany, 1989 and Lapierre, 1988). During this same period (12 months), hallucinogens were more popular among young offenders (39% of boys and 33% of girls) than among adult offenders (22% of males and 23% of females).

The other drugs were not very popular among the subjects who constituted our sample since they were used by less than 20% of them. However, it is important to note that

---

[1] Young offenders were not incarcerated but placed in a halfway house from where they were able to go outside. We then asked them to report on this drug use in the last 12 months.

[2] Young offenders were asked to report on their drug use in the last 30 days.

solvents were used, in the 12 months period, by a majority of young offenders. The low cost and availability of substance could partly explain the reason why this drug attracts a majority of adolescents.

Drug use during 30 days

Figure 2 presents the results concerning drug use by offenders during a 30 days period. A first observation is the fact that the percentage of young people reporting the use of drugs considerably decreased when compared with the 12 month period. This difference is less apparent for the adults, and can be explained by the different pattern of use among adults and adolescents. Adult users tend to be regular users while the young offenders tend to be experimental users.

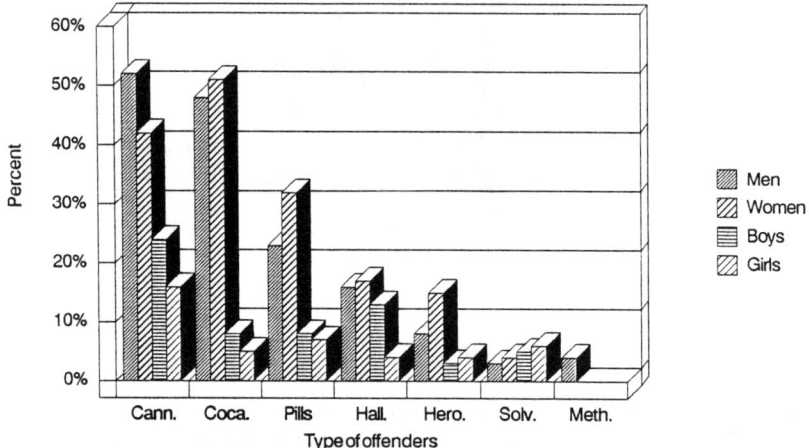

Figure 2: Drug Used in a 30 Days Period.

Cannabis is still the most popular drug for every group except for women (with 52% of men, 42% of women, 24% of boys and 17% of girls having reported using it in the 30 days period). In fact, more women reported a preference for cocaine over any other drug, and lead the way with 51% of users, while the men report 48% of users. Only a few young offenders report using cocaine during this time frame (9% of males and 6% of females). Here again, more women than men reported having used pills during the 30 days prior to their incarceration (32% of females and 23% of males). But this time, the results are not backed up by young offenders, since only 9% of males and 8% of females reported having done so during the last 30 days. The other substances were reported to be used by less than 22% of the sample. Some people could find in these results arguments in favor of the hypothesis that drug use could cause delinquency. However, young offender were asked to report on the age of their first crime and on the age of their first use of drugs. Results indicate that, on average, initiation to crime is around 10 years old, while initiation to drugs will follow three years later. These results confirm the ones reported by Le Blanc (1986). Nontheless, many offenders develop symptoms of drug abuse.

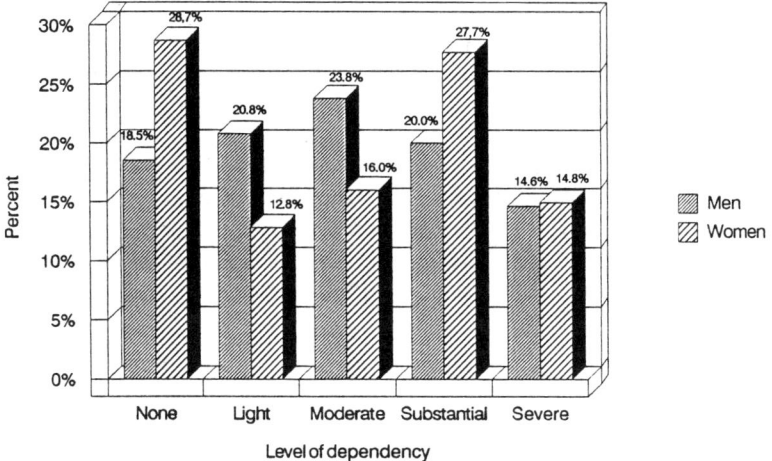

Figure 3: Level of Drug Dependence.

Level of drug abuse

The level of drug abuse was obtained through the Drug Abuse Screening Test (DAST). The results of the DAST were compiled using Skinner's norms (Skinner, 1982). It is important to remember that only adult offenders were asked to answer this questionnaire. Figure 6 indicates that 58.4% of male offenders and 58.6% of female offenders experienced at least a moderate level of drug abuse. This is slightly more than the results reported by the Solicitor General of Canada (1988). Considering these data, it is possible to affirm that the drug/crime connection is certainly not artificial. In order to get a better understanding of the nature of this relationship, adult offenders were asked to report on the role played by the drug on the crime they were accused of. Twenty six percent of men and 41% of women thought that drugs gave them the courage to commit the crime; 24% of male and 16% of female answered that drugs did not affect them in any way; 24% of men and 26% of women said that drugs calmed them; 18% of male and 29% of female reported having become more aggressive because of drugs; and 16% of men and 26% of women were made nervous (the total is not equal to 100% because some subjects attributed more than one role to the drug).

Discussion

Drug use among offender populations is certainly not a marginal phenomenon. It is estimated that about half of the offenders would have used one type of psychoactive substance during the 12 months prior to their incarceration. Cannabis is the substance most commonly used, followed by cocaine for adults. Adolescents appears to be experimental users while adults seems to be more regular users and abusers.

These data do not mean that drug use cause crime, but it could sometimes facilitate criminal activities for people already engaged in a criminal career. For this reason, it is important to intervene. Drug intervention should therefore be undertaken through primary and secondary prevention for adolescents and through secondary and tertiary prevention for adults. For the time being no coordinated efforts have been made to combat drug abuse among offender populations in Québec. The Correctional Service of Canada has named an important steering committee to make recommendations about drug intervention aimed at adult inmates in federal prisons. These recommendations will deal with the three levels of prevention (primary, secondary and tertiary). This is a very good initiative, but the question arises whether adult offenders are the best target for these coordinated efforts, and if we should not also direct some energy to prevent young drug users from becoming adult drug abusers.

References

Bergeret, J. (1981). Les jeunes, la drogue...et les autres, *Bulletin des Stupéfiants, XXXIII*, 1-15.
Berzins, L.; Collette-Carrière, R. (1979). La femme en prison: U inconvénient social. *Santé Mentale au Québec, 4*: 87-103.
Brochu, S., & Douyon, A.(1990). *La consommation de psychotropes chez les jeunes de 13 à 18 ans en centre réadaptation.* Montréal: Association des Intervenants en Toxicomanie du Québec.
Cardinal, N. (1988). Dimensions culturelle et historique de l'usage des psychotropes, In P. Brisson (ed.), *L'usage des drogues et la toxicomanie* (pp. 21-36). Chicoutimi: Gaetan Morin.
Chami, M. (1987). *Toxicomanie et interventions sociales.* Paris: ESF.
Cloutier, R. (1982). *Psychologie de l'adolescence.* Chicoutimi: Gaetan Morin.
Desjardins, L., Brochu, S. & Biron, L. (1991). *Étude épidémiologique sur la consommation de psychotropes chez les contrevenantes.* Montréal: Centre International de Crimininologie Comparée.
Eliany, M. (1989). *Licit and illicit drugs in Canada.* Ottawa: Health and Welfare Canada.
Forget, C. (1991). *La consommation de psychotropes chez les détenus du centre de détention de Montréal.* Mémoire de maîtrise inédit: École de criminologie, Université de Montréal.
Innes, C.A. (1988). Drug use and crime. *National Institute of Justice.* U.S. Department of Justice, Washington.
Langelier-Biron, L., & Savard, C. (1986). *Les femmes auteures de délits graves.* Ottawa: Solliciteur général du Canada, no 1986-16.
Lapierre, L. (1988). La consommation de psychotropes au Québec et au Canada: Profil statistique. *In* P. Brisson (Ed.), *L'usage des drogues et la toxicomanie* (pp. 91-102). Chicoutimi: Gaétan Morin.
Le Blanc, M. (1986). *Drogue et délinquance chez les adolescents et les pupilles du tribunal de Montréal: Épidémiologie et esquisse d'une politique sociale.* Montréal: CICC.
Lightfoot, L., Kalin, R., Laverty, S.G., & MacLean, A. (1985). *Phase III of a four phase proposal to develop and evaluate offenders alcohol and drug abusers treatment programs.* Ottawa: Correctional Service of Canada.
Skinner, H.A. (1982). *Drug Abuse Screening Test (D.A.S.T.).* Toronto: Addiction Research Foundation.
Soliciteur Général du Canada (1988). *Étude de faisabilité d'unité de traitement psychiatrique en milieu pénitentiaire et communautaire.* Mémoire du Comité Régional de Gestion. Ottawa: Soliciteur Général du Canada.
Valeur, M. (1988). Jeunesse, toxicomanie et délinquance: de la prise de risques au fléau social, In P. Brisson (Ed.), *L'usage des drogues et la toxicomanie* (pp. 297-310). Chicoutimi: Gaetan Morin.
Wish, E. (1987). *Drug use forecasting: New York 1984 to 1986.* Washington: National Institute of Justice.
Wish, E., & O'Neil, J.A. (1989). *Drug use forecasting (DUF) research update.* Washington: National Institute of Justice.

Using Psychological Tests in the Forensic Assessment of Offenders

Eckhard Littmann

Introduction

The inclusion of psychological tests in the process of forensic appraisement has, in the past, been somewhat controversial (Littmann, 1985; Wegener & Steller, 1986). However, more and more specialists in the field are coming to the conclusion that any forensic evaluation that has not been compiled on the basis of psychometrically founded procedures must be held to be inadequate and deficient, though it should be added that the primary roles in the process played by forensic exploration and observation remains in no way disputed. Wegener and Steller (1986) have demanded an enhancement of empirical research activity to improve the psychodiagnostic procedures to be used within the forensic context. A withdrawal of psychodiagnostics from the process of psychological-psychiatric expert testimony would reduce the rationality, transparency, validity, and objectivity of forensic diagnoses. The availability of a standardized psychometric testing system makes diagnosing objectively, comparable, and quantifiable. Tests can provide important psychological information about the motivations, relationships of offenders with their environment, and socio-dynamic factors along with their subsequent effect upon the criminal act itself.

The drawbacks and limitations of the test methods are as follows:

1. Most of the tests that psychologists have at their disposal are based on concepts of clinical psychology that are mostly not designed to address specific legal questions. Tests that are tailored to the needs of forensic appraisal, are sadly few in number (Littmann, 1985; Seitz, 1983). The objective of forensic assessment is not, however, to compile a broad and comprehensive personality profile of the client - psychodiagnostics is instead always a case-specific problem-solving process in which the goal is to assign the individual case to a diagnostic category (see Wegener & Steller, 1986).

2. The diagnoses concentrate rather simplistically on habitual personality traits and peculiarities and neglect the fact that the offender's motivation and decision to commit a criminal act are very often determined by the actual circumstances accompanying the act at the given point in time and by temporary psychological factors related to the criminal act. However, factors such as these mostly fall outside the bounds of established testing procedures.

3. Traditional testing procedures fail to achieve the unity between regnosis, diagnosis, and prognosis that a reliable forensic appraisal requires. Drawing conclusions about the personality profiles of clients at the time the offense was committed from the test results at the time of examination is something of a gray area, since dramatic changes in the offender's life situation (mainly imprisonment on remand) or even just the pressure of the situation of being examined and appraised can significantly influence these findings.

Our own written survey of 100 clients (see Littmann, 1988) both before and after they were examined by experts has suggested that, on the side of the (especially) nonvoluntary clients, specific attitudes, expectations, and behaviour styles (e.g., fear, distrust, anger, latent and manifest aggression, tendencies to simulate or dissimulate) can be considered to have such a strong impact that they invalidate the outcome of test-psychological examination.

Some findings

In our department of forensic psychiatry and psychology at the Berlin Charité University-Hospital, we have been using and testing various standardized psychometric intelligence and personality tests for appraisements of young and adult offenders since about 1970. In our practice, we employ projective tests mainly on a case-to-case basis. In such cases, we are using mostly the Picture-Frustrations-Test, Rorschach Test, and Thematic Apperception Test (Jähnig & Littmann, 1985), all in psychometrically based test-modifications.

The following findings were obtained from a randomly selected sample of accused persons referred for psychological-psychiatric assessment during the last five years ($N=573$ cases).

Intelligence diagnostics

In terms of IQ-distribution, the overall sample falls slightly, though significantly, below the population average in two tests used routinely: the Raven Progressive Matrices and the Mehrfach-Wahl-Wortschatztest (Form B) (Lehrl, 1977).

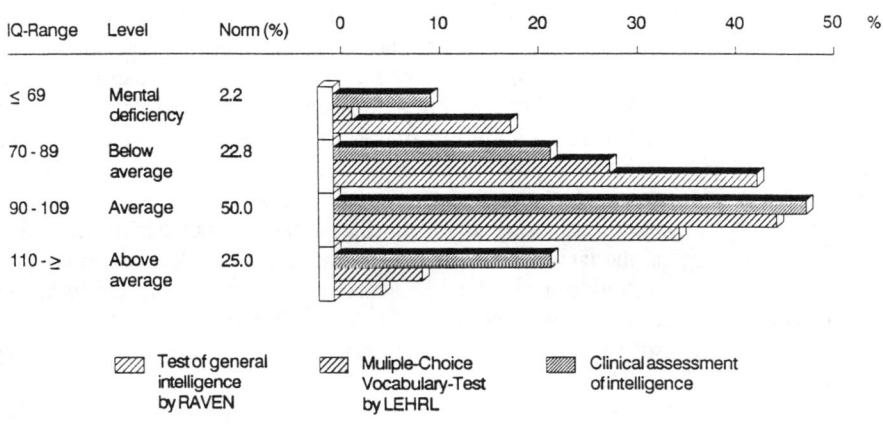

Figure 1: Results of Diagnostic of Intelligence in Total Sample of Offenders.

Noticeable (see Figure 1) is a higher proportion of cases of mental deficiency among the sample, with low intelligence being relatively common among offenders referred for psychiatric assessment. Restricted mental capability is more noticeable where performance is dependent on educational and environmental factors (crystallized intelligence according to Cattell) while actual cognitive capabilities, intellectual potential (fluid intelligence), remain closer to the norm. These aspects are revealed by the vocabulary test and the Raven Progressive Matrices respectively.

The expert's subjective clinical evaluation of intelligence level, however, frequently results in a diagnosis of feeble-mindedness. It may well be the case that the reason for this lies in the fact that the tests do not differentiate sufficiently between levels of intelligence at the lower end of the intelligence scale or are even wholly inapplicable to cases of backwardness. Also, the tests are unable to assess life-practical skills, social intelligence, and competency - aspects that are actually very much more important for the final forensic expert decision on legal responsibility.

Personality diagnostics

In a study, we have analyzed the usefulness of a routinely advanced test program consisting of the following personality questionnaires: Freiburger Persönlichkeitsinventar (FPI), developed by Fahrenberg, Selg, and Hampel (1978) ($N=573$), Mini-Mult, a short form of MMPI (Kincannon, 1969) ($N=230$) and the Gießen-Test (Beckmann & Richter, 1972) ($N=130$). The 29 scales of these three inventories indicate factor loadings (principal component factor analysis with Varimax rotation) on four second-factor dimensions (Littmann, 1985, 1988). Compared to the norm values of standardization samples, the overall group of appraised offenders displayed the following peculiarities to a statistically significant degree (see also Table 1):

1. Greater affective excitability and irritability, higher likelihood of becoming depressive and being intolerant in situations of conflict or frustration (Factor 1: Emotional Lability or "neuroticism").

2. Disturbed psychosocial interaction (Factor 2), with high introversion and inhibition, restricted social contact, and reduced social adaptability.

3. Frequent complaints of vegetative and functional disorders and physical and/or psychological symptoms (Factor 3).

4. Pronounced personality defects with features such as weak temperament, lack of social ties, paranoia, stubborness, and a marked tendency to oppose behavioral norms (Factor 4).

The distinctions from the norm profiles were very clear. However, it must be added that the proportion of offenders with mental problems and disturbances in a sample of evaluation clients is higher than that of random samples of culprits, judging from most previous surveys reported in the literature (Arnold, 1980; Steller & Hunze, 1984). While sharing a markedly higher emotional lability (see Steller & Hunze, 1984), those seen for psychiatric evaluation differ from those unappraised in terms of more pronounced tendencies toward introversion (neurotic disorders according to Eysenck), with their test mean profiles being strikingly analogous to those of clinical random samples of neurotic patients (Jähnig & Littmann, 1985). The borderline between the evaluation clients and neurotics can be divided from scales scores of Factor 4 (see above); these being best revealed by the Mini-Mult.

Table 1: Comparison of Appraised Offenders, Controls, and Neurotics on Three Personality Questionnaires.

	Group comparisons		Discriminability of the method		
	Appraised offenders compared with controls	Appraised offenders compared with neurotics	Percentage of statistical significant differing questionnaire-scales between the subgroups		
Personality Questionnaires	...scores significant higher (+) or lower (-) on... (MANOVA, t-test; $p < 0.05$)		Appraised offenders vs. controls	Appraised offenders vs. neurotics	Across all sub-groups of offenders
Freiburg-Personality Inventory by Fahrenberg et al. (1978)	Nervousness(+) Depressivity(+) Excitibility(+) Inhibitivity(+) Neuroticism(+) Sociability(-) Placidity(-) Extraversion(-) Masculinity(-)	Placidity(+), Nervousness(-)	75.0	16.7	39.0
Mini-Mult (MMPI short form) by Kinncannon (1968)	Lie(+) Validity(+) Hypochondriasis(+) Depression(+) Hysteria(+) Psychopathia(+) Paranoia(+) Psychoasthenia(+) Schizophrenia(+) Hypomania(+)	Validity(+) Psychopathia(+) Paranoia(+) Psychoasthenia(+) Schizophrenia(+) Hypomania(+)	90.9	50.0	33.0
Gießen-Test by Beckmann and Richter (1972)	Social resonance(-) Dominance(-) Self-control(-) Depressive mood(+) Social insensivity(+) Social impotence(+)	Social resonance(-) Self-control(-) Social insensitivity(-)	100.0	50.0	11.5

Summarizing, Table 1 shows the validity of gradations (discriminability) between overall appraised offenders, normals (standardization sample), neurotics (from the literature), and various subgroups of appraised offenders for the three inventories we checked. Altogether, in terms of discriminability, the best two are the FPI and the Mini-Mult. The deviations of mean personality profiles of evaluation clients from those of normal controls on most questionnaire scales (see Table 1) are also to be found as a basic tendency in the comparison of various subgroups, though with corresponding variability. A calculation of MANOVA indicated quite a few significantly differing effects on questionnaire scale scores, for example, both on such single variables (in terms of range order of their efficiency) as age of evaluation clients, duration of imprisonment on remand, and offense type, as well as interaction effects between them:

1. Youth (versus adults) scored higher on the extraversion scales (sociability, dominance, masculinity, extraversion, according to FPI), while elderly individuals scored higher on neuroticism scales (nervousness, depression, inhibition, emotional lability, according to FPI) and those of our Factor 4 (personality defect, see above).

Using Psychological Tests in the Forensic Assessment 115

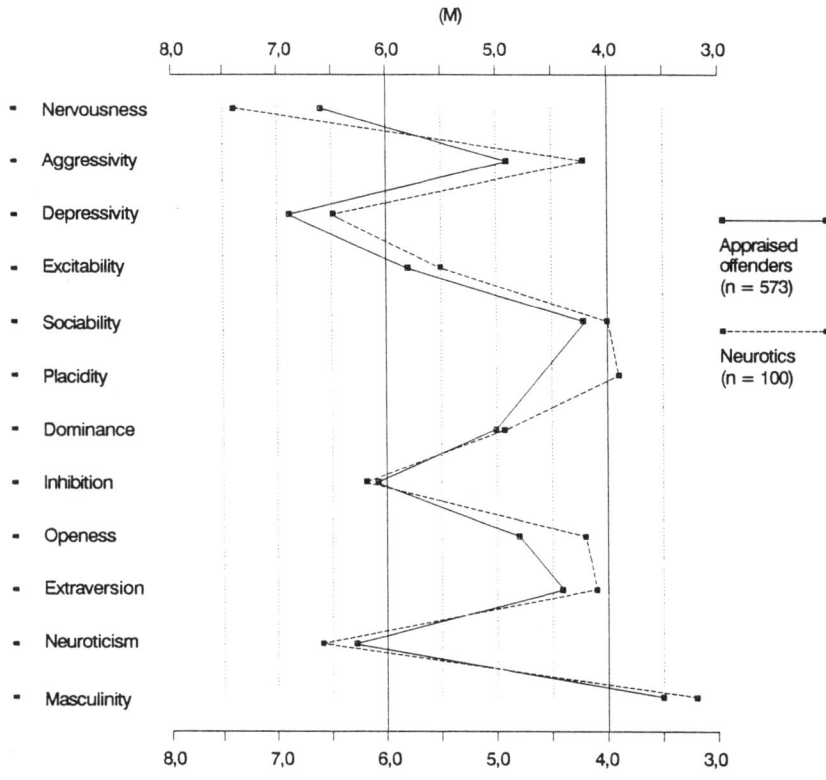

Figure 2: Mean Test Profile of the Freiburger Persönlichkeitsinventar (FPI).

2. In the total sample of evaluated clients, with increasing duration of imprisonment on remand (especially shorter vs. longer than 6 months) we obtained a significant rise in mean values on the scales intended to measure emotional lability, nervousness, aggressiveness, social isolation, resignation, and retreat from other detainees.

3. Like other researchers (e.g., Arnold, 1980; Holcomb & Adams, 1985), our findings suggest that appraised homicides taken as a whole form the offense type exhibiting the greatest deviations on personality profiles from the norm. The Mini-Mult profile makes this clear (see Figure 3):

In accordance with other surveys (Holcomb & Adams, 1985; Steigleder, 1968), lines can be drawn between uncontrollable impulses (e.g., affect), sexual drive, and rationale as the (mainly) dominant motive for murders. A relationship was presupposed between various aspects of personality and the act itself, whereby the criminogenic significance of determining factors outside the offender's control decrease in the following order: uncontrollable impulses, sexual drive, rationale. The Mini-Mult on impulse and conflict homicides reveals a typical "neurotic test profile", the sort of people who are easily hurt and offended. This type seems prone to loss of control particularly in unusual conflict situations. The rational type, on the other hand, is shown by the mean test profile to have (to a statistically significant degree) more marked aggressive tendencies linked to a carrying out of the criminal act subsequent to more long-term planning and much deliberation and calculation (80% murders with robbery). Their profiles corresponds to those of persons with abnormal cum psychopathic behavioral patterns. Seventy percent of them were polymorphous second offenders. Deformations of personality and maldevelopments of an antisocial nature obviously play a greater role in this field of criminogenesis than act-situational influences. Sexually motivated homicides (not illustrated in Figure 3) fall between the mean profiles of the two other groups: Test-diagnostically, they are characterized primarily by social problems, such as social inhibition, greater introversion, and poor social adaptability.

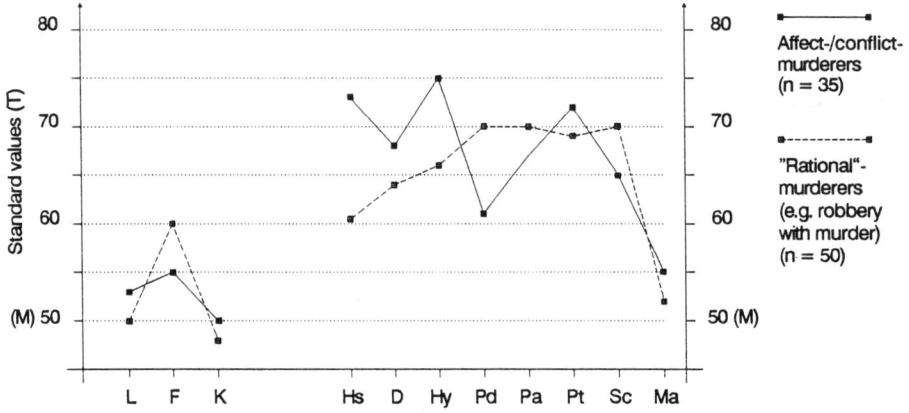

Figure 3: Mini-Mult-Test-Profiles of 2 Subtypes (Motives) of Homicides.

All in all, these findings support the requirement to calculate and develop, in future, special and different group norms for use in single case assessment of evaluation clients, as a supplement to standardization norm values.

The "Personality questionnaire relevant to the prison situation" developed by Seitz (1983) is intended for use on appraisement cases being held in prison, such cases accounting for about 75% of our evaluation clients. This inventory covers various dimensions of prisoner's self-image and their social attitudes toward fellow detainees (see Figure 4).

The inclusion of this inventory (revised form: see Littmann, 1989) has increased the accuracy of the conclusions that can be drawn on the personality of evaluation clients at the time the act was committed, in that it enables the expert to gain additional information about the potential extent of personality changes brought about by the special conditions of being in prison on remand (e.g., increased emotional lability, aggressiveness). The rationale for such comments relates to the (intraindividual) statistical comparison of personality features specific to individual traits and the detention situation, and the subsequent effects of those in individual cases. A cluster analysis (Littmann, 1989) indicated that five cluster groups exist, two of which are depicted in Figure 4:

1. In Group V, virtually all scale values are above average, which points to those individuals having pronounced difficulties in social adjustment, above all in the sense of insecurity in social contact with, and isolation from other detainees. The offense type of sexual

child molesters (with a higher proportion of cases with diminished responsibility, appraised by expert opinion) made up the bulk of this cluster. Additional comparison with their test values in more trait-oriented testing systems (FPI and Mini-Mult) performed on those higher-grade psychological maldevelopment cases gives further pointers toward a higher degree of increasing neuroticism (which is related obviously to their imprisonment) than is found for members of other cluster groups.

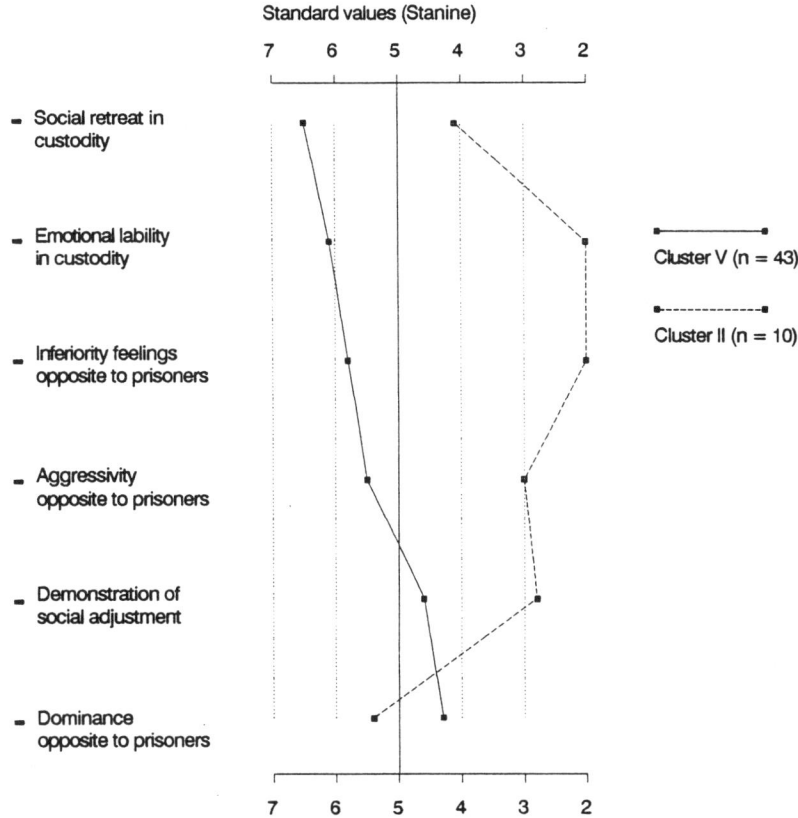

Figure 4: Mean Test Profiles (Two Cluster Groups) pf the Personality Questionnaire Relevant to the Prison Situation.

2. On the other hand, the mean profile of Group II with below average scores on all scales leads us to refer to the cluster as "normopaths". Having said that, those individuals show up also in other inventories (FPI, Mini-Mult) as having distinct tendencies toward lying and disclaiming their legal responsibility and are not motivated to give honest answers to questions (that was mainly evaluation clients whose crimes were committed under the influence of alcohol) - a factor which is always a problem when interpreting tests during forensic appraisement. Members of forensic populations may have strong internal or external motivations to either claim or deny psychological traits and symptoms, and, therefore, an important contribution of clinical-forensic psychologists is the psychometric assessment

of malingering (simulation, exaggeration) or dissimulation. There is little empirical research on this, especially in such individuals undergoing evaluation for sanity or legal responsibility at the time of the crime (see Grossmann & Wasyliw, 1988).

We have analyzed (Littmann, 1991) the various validity scale scores and indexes of Mini-Mult and FPI questionnaires ($N=260$ evaluation clients) for both the overall sample and various criterion groups. Mean T-scores on the scales intended to be primarily sensitive to malingering (F scale, cut-off $T>70$; F-K index $> +12$, row values, Mini-Mult) are only slightly increased - the tendency to exaggerate "psychological abnormality' is weak. The percentages of such psychometrically defined malingering were low: 4% (F-K) to 8% (F). Inversely, a slightly higher percentage was obtained on the minimization indexes L (Lie scale) and openness as a measure of unsophisticated, respectively K as a measure of sophisticated attempts to "fake good", that is, to deny symptoms and psychological disturbances. The range of clearly minimized Mini-Mult and FPI-validity scale profile was from 13% (low openness), 15% (F-K index <-12), to 17% (L). Therefore, the majority (80%) of evaluation clients had valid Mini-Mult profiles. Generally, we cannot support the hypothesis that a psychiatric evaluation sample would show significantly more evidence of malingering or minimization than normal controls or clinical samples. Although we did not have exact criteria for this independent of the test findings, it was interesting that, tendencially, the highest percentages of exaggeration scores were obtained in the following subgroups: adult second offenders, offense type of sexual violence, long duration of imprisonment on remand (corresponding with higher severity of charge), cases with below average IQ, and individuals considered by experts as having diminished responsibility due to a grave and abnormal personality maldevelopment. Inversely, slight correlations were obtained between minimization scores and such features as first guilt, juvenile offender, weak severity of charge, and nonimprisonment. On the other hand, this finding seems to indicate that the validity of so-called "validity scales" remains unclear and dubious.

All in all, according to our practical experiences, the empirical results strongly suggest that personality tests can be of assistance in quantifying traits and behavioral defects that are predominantly habitual cum independent of the time the act was committed. Such tests have, consequently, a definite role to play only in what Maisch (1983) referred to as "graduated diagnostics". However, our results, in accordance with the findings of previous studies (e.g., Arnold, 1980), have suggested generally more evidence on psychometrically measured "psychopathology" than indicated by the forensic expert evaluation, which was reported to the court. The contribution that traditional personality tests can make to forensic "effect diagnostics" is, however, considerably smaller, as this is a question and decision of grading the level of evaluation clients' legal responsibility as either undiminished, diminished, or as completely nonaccountable according to the penal code.

Figure 5 depicts the Mini-Mult mean profiles of three groups of evaluation clients categorized on the basis of the final experts' appraisements on legal responsibility. In this pilot study (Littmann, Friemert, & Szewczyk, 1989), psychiatric experts had no knowledge on individuals' test results at the time the expertise was formulated. First, it can be seen that the Mini-Mult made it possible to draw a line between those evaluation clients with clinically assessed psychosocial maldevelopments and those without. Secondly, it was also possible to differentiate to a statistically significant degree between the profiles of the two groups with maldevelopments, both in terms of quantity and quality of profile differencies. The group with diminished responsibility due to a "grave and abnormal development of their personality equating to illness" (according to section 16,1 of penal code of the former GDR (comparable to "serious other mental abnormity" in sections 20/21 of the penal code of the FRG), is striking for its very distinctly pronounced profile deviations from the norm, indicating a higher psychological maladjustment with particularly high T means on the Mini-Mult character-scales (Factor 4: personality defects, see above). The sample of fully responsible clients with psychosocial maldevelopments displays a more complaints, functional symptoms, and disorders. But it should be added that the ability of this and other personality tests to distinguish between groups is of little use and of smaller value when it comes down to assessments on an individual level of single-case evaluation.

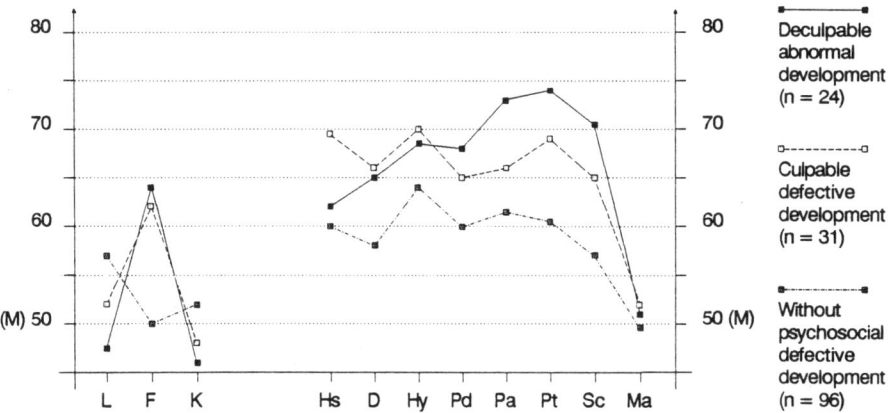

Figure 5: Mean Test Profiles of Offenders With Differing Defective Development.

In any case, for their full value to be realized, psychological tests must be employed in conjunction with case records, the exploration of the personality and the accused offense, as well as results of the numerous other neuropsychiatric tools at the forensic expert's disposal. Future empirical research needs to assess to what extent the examiners employed the psychological results of test application in making their expert determination.

References

Arnold, L.S. (1980). MMPI profiles of men referred for pretrial psychiatric assessment as a function of offense type. *Journal of Clinical Psychology, 36,* 410-417.

Beckmann D., & Richter, H.S. (1972). *Gießen-Test* (Handbuch). Bern: Huber.

Fahrenberg, J., Selg, H., & Hampel R. (1978). *Das Freiburger Persönlichkeitsinventar* (Handbuch), 3rd ed. Göttingen: Hogrefe.

Grossmann, L.S., & Wasyliw, O.N. (1988). A psychometric study of stereotypes: Assessment of malingering in a criminal forensic group. *Journal of Personality Assessment, 52,* 3, 549-563.

Holcomb, W.R., & Adams, N.A. (1985). The development and cross-validation of a MMPI typology of murderers. *Journal of Personality Assessment, 49,* 240-244.

Jähnig, H.U., & Littmann, E. (1985). *Kriminalpsychologie und Kriminalpsychopathologie.* Jena: Fischer.

Kincannon, J.C. (1968). The prediction of the scale scores of the standard MMPI with 71 items. *Journal of Consulting and Clinical Psychology, 32*, 3-10.

Lehrl, S. (1977). *Mehrfach-Wahl-Wortschatztest (MWT/B.)*. Erlangen: Straube.

Littmann, E. (1985). Zum Stellenwert der Psychodiagnostik im Rahmen forensisch-psychologischer und psychiatrischer Begutachtungen. *Kriminal.Forensische Wissenschaften, 57*, 90-104.

Littmann, E. (1988). Die forensisch-psychologisch-psychiatrische Begutachtung im Erleben zu Begutachtender. Daten einer Befragung. *Psychiatrie, Neurologie und Medizinische Psychologie, 40*, 655-664.

Littmann, E. (1989). 'Inhaftierungsadäquate' Persönlichkeitsdiagnostik mit dem (revidierten) PFI von Seitz im Rahmen forensisch-psychologisch-psychiatrischer Begutachtungen. *Psychiatrie, Neurologie und Medizinische Psychologie, 41*, 280-287.

Littmann, E. (1991). *Zur Psychometrie von simulations- und dissimulationsverdächtigen Fehleinstellungen im Rahmen der forensischen Begutachtungstätigkeit*. Unpublished paper presented at the 6. Forensische Herbsttagung der AGFP. University of Munich.

Littmann, E., Friemert K., & Szewczyk, H. (1989). Psychosoziale Fehlentwicklung und strafrechtliche Verantwortlichkeit - Ergebnisse psychopathometrischer Untersuchungen. *Psychiatrie, Neurologie und Medizinische Psychologie, 41*, 269-279.

Maisch, H. (1983). Diagnostische Urteilsbildung zur Einschätzung von Schweregraden psychischer Störungen und ihrer Auswirkungen für forensische Zwecke. *Monatsschrift für Kriminologie und Strafrechtsreform, 66*, 343-354.

Seitz, W. (1983). Zur Struktur und Erfassung der Persönlichkeit von Inhaftierten - Am Beispiel eines inhaftierungsadäquaten Persönlichkeitsfragebogens. *Zeitschrift für Differentielle und Diagnostische Psychologie, 4*, 261-281.

Steigleder, E. (1968). *Mörder und Totschläger*. Stuttgart: Enke.

Steller, M., & Hunze, D. (1984). Zur Selbstbeschreibung von Delinquenten im Freiburger Persönlichkeitsinventar (FPI) - Eine Sekundäranalyse empirischer Untersuchungen. *Zeitschrift für Differentielle und Diagnostische Psychologie, 5*, 87-109.

Wegener, H.W., & Steller, M. (1986). Psychologische Diagnostik vor Gericht - Methodische und ethische Probleme forensisch-psychologischer Diagnostik. *Zeitschrift für Differentielle und Diagnostische Psychologie, 7*, 103-126.

Profiles of Incarcerated Offenders Convicted of Rape and Indecent Assault: An Exploratory Study

Lu Chan Ching-Chuen

Introduction

During the past decade, an increase in clinical and research literature on the sexual offender has significantly advanced our understanding of the characteristics of the offender as well as on those circumstances related to the offender. However, locally, such data-based literature of offenders convicted of sexual offences is scarce. The psychological unit of the Correctional Services Department has for the past years endeavoured to collect relevant data on those incarcerated sexual offenders with a view to formulating profiles for eventual classification and treatment purposes. The preliminary observations made in the present paper are therefore mainly derived from data collected at the unit.

Broadly speaking, sexual offences refer to offences involving nonconsensual or coercive sexual acts, that is, rape, indecent assault, incest, and so forth, or offences of a sexual nature but involving no physical contacts, that is, indecent exposure; as well as those sexual behaviours considered to be against the moral code, that is, homosexual acts. In the local penal code, there are over 10 offences covered under such a category. Since sexual offending is not a unitary category either in terms of forms, motives or clinical problems, no one model can adequately explain the phenomenon. The bulk of the data thus far accumulated has been predominantly descriptive, portraying sex offenders sampled from diverse correctional and psychiatric facilities and generally including information on characteristics related to offenders themselves as well as the nature and process of the offence and the victim. Although studies on offence characteristics have differed in methods of data collection and analysis and samples might not be completely comparable, the following findings regarding sexual offenders have been described repeatedly: a history of delinquency preceding the first sexual offence (Awad, Saunders, & Levene, 1984; Becker, Cunningham-Rathner, & Kaplan, 1987; Fehrenbach, Smith, Monatersky, & Deisher, 1986; Saunders, Award, & White, 1986); a history of severe family problems including separations from parents and placement away from home (Awad et al., 1984; Becker et al., 1987); experience of sexual abuse, neglect or physical abuse (Awad et al., 1984; Fehrenbach et al., 1986; Saunders et al., 1986); Social awkwardness or isolation (Awad et al., 1984; Markey, 1950; Saunders et al., 1986; Waggoner & Body, 1941); academic or behavioural problems at school (Awad et al., 1984; Fehrenbach, Smith, Monatersky, & Deisher, 1986; Markey, 1950; Saunders et al., 1986); and psychopathology, including primarily neurotic, conduct and personality disorders (Brancale, Ellis, & Doorbar, 1952; Kavoussi, Kaplan, & Becker, 1988; Maclay, 1960; Shoor, Speed, & Bartelt, 1965). Though the above-mentioned studies generally covered a diverse group of sexual offenders, the two groups most frequently referred to are rape offenders and child molesters. Comparative studies involving the rape offender and other types of offence, that is, indecent exposure, incest and so forth, are rare.

Amongst those incarcerated sexual offenders who are under the custody of the Correctional Services Department, those convicted of offences of rape and indecent assault account for more than 65% of the group. The present paper, therefore, will limit itself to describing and comparing the characteristics of those convicted of these offences. Since adequate description of offender characteristics is an essential primary step for later investigation, the paper aims at identifying and comparing their common attributes with regards to their demographic/family and other psychosocial backgrounds.

Method

Subjects and setting. Offenders admitted to the Correctional Services Department would routinely be assessed by the clinical psychologists for formulating a treatment and management plan. In order to standardize the assessment and recording procedures, a Sexual Offender Assessment Checklist was devised to serve as a guideline for the interview in mid-1989. Subjects included in the study were male offenders convicted of rape and indecent assault who were assessed by the psychologists for the above-mentioned purpose. From 41 subjects, 24 were convicted of indecent assault and the remaining 17 were rape offenders. The mean age for the whole group was 24.90 ($SD=8.79$).

Procedures. All subjects were interviewed by the psychologists using the Sexual Offender Assessment Checklist. The checklist covered the following information: variables related to family pathology, that is, intactness and emotional stability of the family, history of criminality amongst family members, history of violence/sexual deviation in the family, history of abuse and neglect; childhood behavioural adjustment; education and employment history; social adjustment; delinquency and criminal history; psychosexual adjustment; and information relating to the offences. Unless otherwise noted, the findings presented in the following sections were compiled from the Sexual Offender Assessment Checklist of the 41 male offenders. In addition, the interviewers also reviewed pertinent documents regarding the offender, that is, penal records, criminal records as well as Police Brief Facts of Case.

Results

The two groups were compared with χ^2 statistics for all items included in the questionnaire. In view of the limited sample in the study, this comparison was conducted mainly for exploratory purposes, rather than hypothesis testing at this stage of our study.

Indications of family pathology. Although there were no statistically significant findings on variables related to family pathology in the present sample, there were indications that the two groups differed in terms of their siblings' criminal history, emotional stability at home as well as history of childhood neglect. The rape offender group were found to have higher incidences of the above-mentioned factors.

Table 1: Frequency of Sexual Offenders Reported to Have Siblings With a Criminal History, Emotional Instability at Home and History of Childhood Neglect.

Sexual offender	Siblings with criminal history		Instability at home		History of childhood neglect	
	n	%	n	%	n	%
Rape offender (n=17)	4	23.5	8	47.1	8	47.1
Indecent assault offender (n=24)	1	4.1	5	20.8	6	25.0

Note. No significant findings were noted in respect of other variables included in this category, i.e., parents' mental and criminal history, child abuse, violence/sexual deviation in the family.

No significant findings were noted in respect of other variables included in this category, that is, parents' mental and criminal history, childhood abuse, violence/sexual deviation in the family.

Childhood behavioural adjustment. More than one third of both groups reported moderate to severe behavioural problems at school, that is, attendance or discipline problem. However, no significant difference was detected between the groups. Behavioural problems at school were reported by 46.3% (n=10) of the rape offenders and 37.5% (n=9) of the indecent assault offenders. There were no significant differences on other variables measuring early childhood behaviour problems, that is, excessive lying and stealing, discipline problems and so forth.

Education and employment data. About 85% of both groups had received at least primary education. With respect to their employment stability, although about one-third (37.5%) of the indecent assault group were found to be sporadic in their employment, they were generally more stable at work when compared with the rape group (64.7%).

Table 2: Social Adjustment of Sexual Offenders.

	Socially withdrawn during adolescence		Socially withdrawn in adulthood		Withdrawn in premorbid social adjustment	
	n	%	n	%	n	%
Rape offender (n=17)	6	35.2	3	17.6	8	47.0
Indecent assault offender (n=24)	8	33.3	11	45.0	12	50.0

Social adjustment. About one-third of both groups were assessed to be antisocial and socially withdrawn as adolescents, though indecent assault offenders inclined to be socially more maladjusted even in adulthood. About one-half of the sexual offender sample were assessed to be withdrawn and antisocial in their premorbid personal relations. Statistically there was no significant difference between the two groups.

Delinquency and criminal history. There are significant differences amongst these two groups in terms of their subcultural orientations ($x^2=5.79, p<.05$). The rape offenders were found to be more subculturally oriented than the indecent assault group. With regard to other variables related to their criminal development, half of the sexual offender group had a record of prior conviction; 16.6% of the indecent assault group and 17.6% of the rape group had been convicted of sexual offences in their prior convictions. At the same time, about one-quarter of the sexual offender group were charged with other non-sexual offences at the time of their admission to the Correctional Services Department.

Table 3: Incidences of Subcultural Affiliations and Past Convictions in Sexual Offenders.

	Subcultural affiliation		Past convictions		Prior sexual offence conviction		Other non-sexual offence convictions at the time of admission to CSD	
	n	%	n	%	n	%	n	%
Rape offender (n=17)	13	76.5	7	41.2	3	17.6	4	23.5
Indecent assault offender (n=24)	8	33.3	12	50.0	4	16.6	8	33.3

$x^2 = 5.79, p < .05$

Psychosexual adjustment. Although no significant differences were found between the two groups, there were indications that the indecent assault group was more heterosexually maladjusted than the rape offenders. While about one-half of both groups were found to be sexually inadequate, indecent assault offenders were again found to be more maladaptive in this respect than the rape group. About one-quarter of the sample were assessed to have abnormal sexual practices at different developmental stages, and about the same proportion were found to have had problematic early sexual experiences. At the same time, no major deviation was found in the areas of attitude towards sex, gender role identification and behaviour, sexual dysfunction and sexually transmitted disease.

Information relating to the offence. Enquiries were made on the nature and process of the offences, that is, behaviour at time of offence including method of approaching the victim and sexual acts involving the victim as well as victim characteristics. Over one-half of the victims in both groups were strangers to the offender. The data we collected on the nature and process of the offence was inadequate for a meaningful analysis, as the subjects were generally reluctant to discuss the details of the offence or admit the offence. Offences were denied by 33.3% of the indecent assault group and 47% of the rape group. While 59% of the rape offenders were assessed to have prior planning before committing the offence, only 30% of the indecent assault group was assessed to have planned the offence.

Table 4: Psychosexual Adjustment of Offenders.

	Heterosexually maladjusted		Sexually inadequate		Problematic early sexual experiences		Abnormal sexual practices at different development stages	
	n	%	n	%	n	%	n	%
Rape offender (n=17)	4	23.5	8	47.1	4	23.5	4	23.5
Indecent assault offender (n=24)	10	42.0	16	66.7	8	33.3	5	20.8

Clinical evaluation of the offenders. At the end of the interview, the interviewing psychologists were asked to evaluate whether sexual deviance/psychological problems could be identified in the offenders in relation to their offences. Only two subjects (one in each group) were assessed to be sexually deviant. The indecent assault group were found to have more psychological problems with respect to their social competence, sexual adjustment and problems of impulse control then the rape offender group. For the rape offender group, the commission of the offence was seen more as a by-product of their subcultural orientation and general criminality.

Table 5: Psychological Evaluation of Offenders.

	No psycho-pathology detected		Psychological problem		Sexual deviation		By-product of general criminality	
	n	%	n	%	n	%	n	%
Rape offender (n=17)	1	5.8	6	35.3	1	5.8	9	53.0
Indecent assault offender (n=24)	5	21.0	13	54.2	1	4.1	5	21.0

Discussion

Being an exploratory study based on a relatively small sample, the findings observed so far are meant to be used for generating further hypotheses on the subject. Though no significant differences were observed amongst the two groups except in the areas of subcultural affiliations and orientation, there appear to be slightly different profiles for the rape and the indecent assault groups in terms of their family environment, social adjustment and psychosexual development and adjustment. Common to both groups of offenders, about one-third of them were noted to have problems of childhood behavioural maladjustment and a history of past convictions. It should, however, be noted that history of prior convictions may be a characteristics common to all "incarcerated offenders" and not only to the sexual offender, as those without prior conviction are less likely to be sentenced to a custodial sentence. Another point worth highlighting is the relatively low incidences of sexual disorder (as defined in the DSM III - R) identified amongst the present sample. The finding is therefore contrary to the commonly held myth that sexual offender are sexual deviants.

Comparatively speaking, the rape offender group has a slightly higher incidence of emotional instability in their family as well as incidence of childhood neglect then the indecent assault group. Though about one-third of the rape group were assessed to be socially maladjusted in their adolescence, as adults, they were generally more socially adjusted, and particularly, in their heterosexual adjustment, than the indecent assault group. The most distinctive feature of the rape group is their subcultural orientation and the relative importance that such characteristics may have contributed to their offences. Contrary to common belief that sexual offenders are impulsive individuals, 59% of the rape group were found to have prior planning before committing the offence. The indecent assault group, on the other hand, were found to be socially more isolated and withdrawn and heterosexually more maladjusted. They are, however, slightly more stable at work and were less subculturally oriented. Psychological problems, that is, social incompetence, sexual adjustment, and problems of impulse control, were found to be more prevalent in the indecent assault group, and such problems were considered to be contributive to their offences.

Emerging from all the variables examined in the study, the relationship between subcultural affiliation/criminality and sexual offending as well as the relationship between social adjustment/psychosexual adjustment and sexual offending would warrant further examination. Though we have not included a control group of non-sexual offenders in our study, it appears from the present data that the rape group shared more commonalities with the offender populations in that there are higher incidences of family pathology; incidences of subcultural orientation; a history of unstable employment; history of offending; and a higher level of premeditation in carrying out the offence. Similar observations are also found in other studies on rapists and child molesters (Gebhard, Gagnon, Pomeroy, & Christenson, 1965). As a result, their involvement in sex offending may be symptomatic of a more generalized pattern of antisocial behaviour as suggested in other studies (Davis & Leitenberg, 1987; Hall & Proctor, 1987). Sexual offending of the indecent assault group, however, appears to stem more from problems of social and heterosexual maladjustment as well as from psychological problems relating to social competence and impulse control. Though there are still controversies over the problem of social skill deficits in relation to sexual crime, the present data suggests that further studies are required on a larger sample of indecent assault offenders before conclusions can be reached.

References

Awad, G., Saunders, E., & Levene, J. (1984). A clinical study of male adolescent sexual offender. *International Journal of Offender Therapy and Comparative Criminology, 28,* 105-116.

Becker, J.V., Cunningham-Rathner, J., & Kaplan, M.S. (1987). Adolescent sexual offenders: Demographics, criminal and sexual histories, and recommendations for reducing future offences. *Journal of Interpersonal Violence, 1,* 431-445.

Brancale, R., Ellis, A., & Doorbar, R.R. (1952). Psychiatric and psychological investigation of convicted sex offenders: A summary report. *American Journal of Psychiatry, 109,* 17-21.

Davis, G.E., & Leitenberg, H. (1987). Adolescent sex offenders. *Psychological Bulletin, 101,* 417-427.

Fehrenbach, P.A., Smith, W., Monatersky, C., & Deisher, R.W. (1986). Sexual offenders: Offender and offence characteristics. *American Journal of Orthopsychiatry, 56,* 225-233.

Gebhard, P.H., Gagnon, J.H., Pomeroy, W.B., & Christenson, C.V. (1965). *Sex offenders: An analysis of types.* New York: Harper & Row.

Hall, G.N., & Proctor, W.C. (1987). Criminological predictors of recidivism in a sexual offender population. *Journal of Consulting and Clinical Psychology, 1,* 111-112.

Kavoussi, R.J., Kaplan, M., & Becker, J.V. (1988). Psychiatric diagnosis in adolescent sex offenders. *Journal of the Academy of Child and Adolescent Psychiatry, 27,* 241-243.

Maclay, D.T. (1960). Boys who commit sexual misdemeanours. *British Medical Journal, 1,* 186-190.

Markey, O.B. (1950). A study of aggressive sexual misbehaviour in adolescents brought to juvenile court. *American Journal of Orthopsychiatry, 20,* 719-731.

Saunders, E., Awad, G., & White, G. (1986). Male adolescent sexual offenders: The offender and the offence. *Canadian Journal of Psychiatry, 31,* 542-549.

Shoor, M., Speed, M.H., & Bartelt, C. (1965). Syndrome of the adolescent child molester. *American Journal of Psychiatry, 122,* 738-789.

Waggoner, R.W., & Boyd, R.J. (1941). Juvenile aberrant sexual behavior. *American Journal of Orthopsychiatry, 11,* 275-291.

Part III
Treatment and Prevention of Offending

The Effect of Treatment on Juvenile Delinquents: Results from Meta-Analysis

Mark W. Lipsey

Introduction

There are many reasons to be interested in the prevention of juvenile delinquency. Delinquency reduction may be part of crime control strategy that recognizes that juveniles are responsible for a large proportion of certain types of offenses (e.g., property crimes). Also, those juveniles who persist in their criminality past adolescence have potentially long careers, making prevention at an early point an attractive strategy. Moreover, most societies feel some special responsibility to provide assistance to youth during their formative years so that they are more likely to mature into productive, responsible citizens.

Up until the mid 1980s, however, the prevailing opinion among delinquency researchers was that rehabilitative treatment of juvenile delinquents was not effective. A large body of research on a diverse range of treatments had been reviewed from multiple perspectives with discouraging results (e.g., Greenberg, 1977; Lipton, Martinson, & Wilks, 1975; Lundman, McFarlane, & Scarpitti, 1976; Romig, 1978; Sechrest, White, & Brown, 1979; Wright & Dixon, 1977). Despite a few counterclaims (e.g., Gendreau & Ross, 1979; Palmer, 1975, 1983), the established view was that, in Martinson's (1974) words, "nothing works" in criminal rehabilitation.

In recent years a new wind has been blowing in rehabilitation research and the dismal "nothing works" conclusion has been vigorously challenged. One line of attack has been to assert the political and philosophical theory that supports a rehabilitation ethic in contrast to more punitive alternatives (Cullen & Gilbert, 1982). Another approach has been to draw attention to selected research that documents successful treatment thus showing that rehabilitation can work if it is done correctly (e.g., Gendreau & Ross, 1987).

A third approach, and that taken in this paper, is to re-examine the full corpus of delinquency treatment research literature on the premise that the interpretations drawn from previous reviews were flawed and resulted in erroneous conclusions. This approach is motivated, in part, by the development of the new techniques for synthesizing and integrating research results that are known collectively as meta-analysis. These techniques approach research synthesis as a systematic process of sampling, quantifying, aggregating, and analyzing research results to elucidate the details of the evidence that supports the reviewer's interpretative judgment about the nature of the findings in the domain of interest (Glass, McGaw, & Smith, 1981).

From the meta-analysis perspective, the major shortcoming of traditional literature reviewing practices for interpreting treatment effectiveness research is their emphasis on statistical significance. In such reviews, studies that yield statistically significant differences between treatment and control groups are considered to demonstrate treatment effects. Those that do not yield significance are taken to show that there were no treatment effects or, in the hands of a more careful reviewer, are judged inconclusive. The body of research is then assessed according to the frequency of significant effects. If a high proportion of studies show such effects, the treatment at issue is judged generally effective; if not, serious doubts are raised.

The problem with this reasoning is that statistical significance as an index of research outcome confounds two different matters. The statistical significance of a difference between a treatment and a control group is a function of the actual effectiveness of the treatment in the sample under study *and* the size of the sample. Studies with small samples can fail to yield statistical significance even when the treatment under examination has large effects. Statistical power analysis reveals that to reliably attain statistical significance in studies of treatment with genuine, but numerically modest effects, sample sizes of up to 1000 in each research condition may be required (Lipsey, 1990). Since research on the effectiveness of delinquency treatment rarely attains such sample sizes (indeed, averages about 50 per experimental group), statistical significance testing is a poor indicator of whether treatment effects are present.

Meta-analysis approaches this situation by examining each research study in terms of the magnitude of the difference between the treatment and the control group means, standardized to produce a common metric for different measures. While this standardized mean difference, known as the effect size, is subject to sampling error, its value does not depend upon sample size directly. The variability in effect sizes due to sampling error is managed by aggregating effect sizes across studies to produce distributions that represent the combined samples of all the studies at issue. A meta-analysis of 100 studies averaging 100 subjects each, for example, yields an effect size distribution based on 10,000 subjects - a sufficient number to make sampling error relatively negligible in the estimation of the overall mean treatment effect.

A number of meta-analytic investigations of delinquency treatment have been conducted in recent years. Garrett (1984, 1985) analyzed the results of 111 studies of treatment with adjudicated delinquents in residential facilities. A meta-analysis by Gottschalk, Davidson, Gensheimer, and Mayer (1987) included 90 studies of adjudicated delinquents in both community and residential settings. More recently, Whitehead and Lab (1989) reported a meta-analysis of 50 published treatment studies that used control groups and dichotomous recidivism measures. Andrews et al. (1990) reanalyzed the Whitehead and Lab results, augmented by additional studies, distinguishing between treatment approaches they judged clinically appropriate and those that were inappropriate for the clientele treated.

These various meta-analysts have drawn diverse conclusions from their work, ranging from negative (Whitehead & Lab, 1989) through inconclusive (Gottschalk et al., 1987) to positive (Andrews et al., 1990; Garrett, 1985). Despite the differing interpretations, however, these investigations all reported positive mean effects sizes of about the same order of magnitude - approximately a one-fourth standard deviation decrease in delinquency for treatment groups compared to controls.

While it is encouraging to find some convergence in the empirical results of these various meta-analyses, they are more notable for their differences than their similarities. Each has been circumscribed in the volume of research literature examined and the range of study characteristics coded for analysis. Moreover, these efforts have employed diverse effects size indices and statistical models for analyzing those indices.

The meta-analysis summarized here was designed to improve on previous work by broadening the coverage of the available research literature, coding sufficient detail from eligible studies to support probing analysis of the correlates of treatment effects, and applying state of the art statistical models to the resulting data. The two matters of primary importance in this regard are the magnitude of the treatment effects found in available studies and the source of variation in those effects.

The Delinquency Meta-Analysis

The body of research that comprises the current database includes over 400 control/comparison group delinquency treatment studies, published and unpublished, with at least one delinquency outcome measure for which an effect size or direction of effect can be determined. The effect size (ES) for a selected "best" delinquency measure (police arrest recidivism or the nearest analog) was coded for each study in addition to 156 variables describing details of the methods, treatment, treatment circumstances, and study context.

The dependent variables for this meta-analysis were the main delinquency outcome effect size, available for virtually all of the studies, and the effect sizes for any nondelinquency outcome variables that happened to be available in a particular study (e.g., attitude, self esteem, school performance, etc.). Nondelinquency outcome measures were categorized as psychological (including atttitude and personality variables), interpersonal adjustment, school participation (e.g., attendance, dropout), academic performance (e.g., grades, achievement scores), or vocational accomplishment (e.g., employment, wages). If a study reported more than one nondelinquency outcome measure for the same category, those effect sizes were averaged. Each study thus could, at most, contribute one delinquency effect size and one effect size for each of the nondelinquency categories.

Independent variables, i.e., variables describing study characteristics, were classified into the following clusters:

Method
Experimental groups, sample size, sampling (Samples)
Initial equivalence of experimental groups (Equivalence)
Subject attrition after assignment to groups (Attrition)
Nature of the control condition (Control)
Characteristics of the delinquency outcome measures (Measures)
Information about the effect size statistics (ES Info)

Treatment
Characteristics of the subjects receiving treatment (Subjects)
Amount or intensity of treatment (Dosage)
Nature of the treatment and treatment circumstances (Treatment)
Level of theoretical development, sponsorship, etc. (TContext)

The Overall Effects of Delinquency Treatment

The first question that was asked in this meta-analysis was whether there was evidence of positive effects of treatment on delinquency when the results of all the available studies were aggregated. One approach to this question is to examine the direction of the differences between treatment group outcomes and control group outcomes, irrespective of statistical significance. If there were no treatment effects, we would expect a 50-50 split, with half the studies showing results that favored the treatment group, half favoring the control group. Panel A in Table 1 shows that, instead, nearly two-thirds of the studies show a direction of difference favoring the treatment group. A binomial test reveals that it is unlikely that such a large departure from 50-50 would result from sampling error.

Table 1: The Overall Effect of Delinquency Treatment.

A.	Direction of difference on outcome delinquency measure between treatment and control group (N=443)			
			N	%
	Favors treatment		285	64.3
	Favors control		131	29.6
	Favors neither		27	6.1
	Binomial test (by z approximation) that population proportions are 50/50: z=7.32, p< .001			
B.	Mean effect size for difference between treatment and control group on delinquency outcome measure (N=397)			
	Mean N-adjusted ES		.17	
	Weighted mean ES		.10	
	p= .01 confidence interval for weighted mean ES: .083 to .123			
C.	Conversion of weighted mean Es into equivalent recidivism rate differential			
	Estimated control group recidivism		.50	
	Estimated treatment group recidivism		.45	
	Difference		.05	(5/50=10% reduction)

Notes: Coded ES is the difference between the treatment group mean and the control group mean divided by the pooled standard deviation; the N-adjusted ES is the coded ES multiplied by Hedges' small sample correction; the weighted mean ES is the mean of the N-adjusted ES with each weighted by the inverse of its variance to adjust for the unequal sample sizes upon which the ESs are based.

Estimated control group recidivism is the recidivism rate from those studies in which dichotomous recidivism rates were used as the delinquency outcome measure (N=208); estimated treatment group recidivism is the recidivism required to result in an ES= .10 difference between treatment and control group.

For those studies that report sufficient statistical information about their treatment-control group comparisons, it is also possible to examine the mean standardized effect size (i.e., the difference between the treatment mean and the control mean divided by the pooled standard deviation). This effect size (ES) index yields information about the magnitude of treatment effect (in standard deviation units) as well as the direction (positive ES favors treatment; negative favors control).

Panel B of Table 1 presents the mean effect size for the difference between treatment and control groups on delinquency outcome for the 397 studies with sufficient statistical information to permit effect size to be estimated. The weighted mean effect size, which adjusts for differing sample sizes and is therefore the best summary statistic, was one-tenth of a standard deviation. Though numerically modest, this value does demonstrate a statistically significant overall positive effect for delinquency treatment.

When the weighted mean delinquency effect size is translated into the equivalent reduction in recidivism rate (Panel C, Table 1), we find that it represents a five percentage point decrement. A five percentage point decrement from the 50% recidivism of the typical control group corresponds to an overall 10% decrease in recidivism with treatment. While a 10% reduction in delinquency is not spectacular, neither is it obviously negligible. We must conclude, therefore, that, on average, treatment is associated with a modest improvement in delinquent behavior.

Table 2: Statistical Tests for Effect Size Means and Homogeneity.

A.	**N-adjusted effect sizes for all studies**		
	Inverse-variance weighted ES mean	.103	(N=397)
	.01 confidence interval for mean	.083 to .123	
	Inverse-variance weighted ES variance	.089	
	Homogeneity test statistic	H=1319.00	df=237
	Chi-square .01 critical value	273.78	
B.	**N-adjusted effect sizes for studies with random assignment**		
	Inverse-variance weighted ES mean	.110	(N=294)
	.01 confidence interval for mean	.086 to .134	
	Inverse-variance weighted ES variance	.080	
	Homogeneity test statistic	H=904.14	df=293
	Chi-square .01 critical value	351.46	
C.	**N-adjusted effect sizes for studies with random assignment and no appreciable attrition from experimental groups**		
	Inverse-variance weighted ES mean	.140	(N=78)
	.01 confidence interval for mean	.094 to .186	
	Inverse-variance weighted ES variance	.090	
	Homogeneity test statistic	H=281.08	df=77
	Chi-square .01 critical value	107.98	

One might wonder if the positive mean effect size found in this collection of studies is biased by inclusion of research of lower quality design, e.g., studies in which assignment of subjects to treatment and control conditions was not random. To check on this matter, mean effect sizes were also computed for two subsets of studies. First, an examination was made of only those studies with random assignment. Second, an even more restrictive analysis was made of the subsets of studies with random assignment *and* no appreciable attrition from experimental groups prior to outcome measurement. As Table 2 shows in Panels B and C, the resulting mean effect sizes were actually larger than those computed on all the studies in the collection (Panel A). The overall positive effect size, therefore, cannot be dismissed as a distortion stemming from poorly controlled studies.

Variability in Study Results

It is important to consider the variance of study effects as well as the mean. A great deal of variability among those effects indicates that some studies yielded larger effects than others and we might well wonder why. One approach to explaining the variability in effect sizes is to determine which study characteristics are most highly correlated with them.

Table 3: Summary Table for Stepwise Hierarchical Inverse-Variance Weighted Multiple Regression Using Clusters to Predict Effect Size on the Primary Delinquency Measure.

Step	Variable cluster	Cumulative multiple R	Cumulative R^2	R^2 change	Change as proportion of total R^2
	METHOD			.25	.53
1	Samples	.20	.04	.04*	.09
2	Equivalence	.31	.10	.06*	.12
3	Attrition	.36	.13	.03*	.07
4	Control	.40	.16	.03	.06
5	Measures	.44	.20	.04*	.08
6	ES Info	.46	.21	.01	.03
7	Meth x meth	.50	.25	.04*	.09
	TREATMENT			.22	.47
8	Subjects	.51	.26	.01	.02
9	Dosage	.53	.29	.03*	.07
10	Treatment	.63	.40	.11*	.24
11	Tcontext	.65	.42	.02*	.04
12	Tx x meth	.68	.46	.04*	.09
13	Tx x Tx	.68	.47	.01	.02

* $p < .05$
The multiple regression model accounted for 65% of "explainable" variance (i.e., variance other than sampling error).

A homogenity test (Hedges, 1982) on the distribution of delinquency effect sizes revealed far more variability than could be attributed to sampling error (Table 2). Indeed, there was approximately three and a half times as much variability among the delinquency effect sizes as expected. The interesting question, then, was whether any of the independent variables (study characteristics) coded in the study were associated with these large differences in delinquency outcome.

Because of the number of study characteristics coded in this meta-analysis, multiple regression was used to examine independent variable, dependent variable relationships. Study characteristics were categorized as indicated earlier and stepped clusterwise into a hierarchical multiple regression analysis. Method variables were entered first on the grounds that any effect size variance correlated with different study methods should first be accounted for before examining more substantive factors. After that, various clusters of subject and treatment variables were entered in a sequence that permitted variability related to subject differences and treatment dosage to be accounted for before considering the specific treatment modality.

For purposes of this summary, the details of the regression analysis results are not important. What we can note is that, overall, the regression model accounted for about 50% of the total variance in the delinquency effect sizes or, alternatively, 65% of the variance that remained after sampling error was subtracted. Indeed, when the reliability of typical delinquency measures was also taken into account, the regression analysis came close to accounting for all the remaining variance. The set of predictor variables available for this analysis, therefore, is sufficient to very nearly give a complete accounting of the variance in the delinquency effect size.

The regression results for each cluster of predictors are shown in Table 3. About 53% of the variance in delinquency effects that was associated with those predictors was attributable to differences in study method. What we learn from this, therefore, is that to a considerable extent the effects found in a delinquency intervention study are a function of the research methods used and not the nature of the intervention being studied. The methodological category playing the largest role in this finding was that representing the initial equivalence of treatment and control groups (Equivalence). Not surprising, when there were important differences between comparison groups before treatment, there tended to be delinquency differences after treatment. For the interested reader, Table 4 provides a brief summary of the main effect relationships found for each cluster of predictor variables.

With the method variables stepped into the regression analysis, it became possible to next step in the substantive treatment variables and examine their influence on delinquency effects with method differences statistically controlled. Table 3 shows that the characteristics of the subjects treated (Subjects) had little relationship to the magnitude of the delinquency effect. Amount of treatment (Dosage) played a somewhat larger, but still modest role, with more treatment associated with larger effects.

The largest factor related to effect size differences was the nature of the treatment itself. Table 5 presents the mean effect sizes (with method variance partialled out) for the different categories of treatment modality. The major division was between treatments administered to juveniles who were under the authority of the juvenile justice system and those who were not. Within each of these broad divisions, effects for various treatment approaches were broken out by category.

Table 4: General Nature of the Multiple Regression Results for Each Major Variable Cluster.

Cluster	R^2 change	
METHOD		
Samples	.04	Studies with larger sample sizes were associated with smaller effect sizes.
Equivalence	.06	Specific dimensions of initial nonequivalence between treatment and control groups (e.g., sex, delinquency type) were associated with larger or smaller effect sizes. Overall method of subject assignment (e.g., random vs. nonrandom), however, was not associated with effect size.
Attrition	.03	Greater attrition from either treatment or control group was associated with smaller effect sizes.
Control	.03	Control groups receiving some contact, e.g., "treatment as usual" in the juvenile justice system, were associated with smaller effect sizes than "no treatment" controls except for probation treatment as usual.
Measures	.04	Large number of delinquency outcome measures, long spans of time covered in those measures, and weak reliability and validity were associated with smaller effect sizes.
ES info	.01	Less explicit reporting of statistical results was associated with larger effect sizes as was more explicit reporting of general methodological procedures.
TREATMENT		
Subjects	.01	Juveniles with more indication of delinquency (higher "risk") were associated with larger effect sizes.
Dosage	.03	Longer duration treatment and that judged to provide larger amounts of meaningful contact were associated with larger effect sizes.
Treatment	.11	A) Treatment provided by the researcher or situations where the researcher was influential in the treatment setting were associated with larger effect sizes. B) Treatment in public facilities, custodial institutions, and the juvenile justice system were associated with smaller effect sizes. C) Behaviorally-oriented, skill-oriented, and multi-modal treatment were associated with larger effect sizes than other treatment approaches.
Tcontext	.02	Treatment judged to have a more sociological and less psychological orientation was associated with larger effect sizes.

Determining the correct treatment category from the often limited information provided in study reports is quite approximate at best. The most appropriate interpretation of the results in Table 5, therefore, is based on the overall patterning rather than on the specific effect sizes for individual treatment categories. From that perspective what appears is a rough ordering of treatment modality from those that are most behaviorally specific and structured to those that are more psychological and diffuse. Thus, in general, we find larger effects for skill-oriented, behavioral, and multi-modal (generally including skill-oriented or behavioral components) treatment than for traditional counseling, casework, and the like.

Table 5 also reveals the importance of the variability in study effects found in this meta-analysis. Whereas the overall mean effect size was only about one-tenth of a standard deviation, the more successful treatment approaches resulted in effects two or three times that magnitude. Viewed as a recidivism decrement, these values translate into 20-30% reductions from the control group level - a substantial effect by almost any reckoning.

Table 5: Treatment Predictor Variables and the Estimated Mean Effect Size Associated with Each after Methodological Variance is Partialled Out.

Treatment modality	ES	Equivalent recidivism change from 50% control
JUVENILE JUSTICE		
Employment (4)	.37	-.18
Multimodal (12)	.25	-.12
Behavioral (8)	.25	-.12
Institutional-other (9)	.20	-.10
Skill oriented (15)	.20	-.10
Community residential (12)	.16	-.08
Any other JJ (5)	.14	-.07
Prob/parole release (16)	.11	-.05
Prob/parole reduce caseload (11)	.08	-.04
Prob/parole restitution (13)	.08	-.04
Individual counseling (20)	.08	-.04
Group counseling (39)	.07	-.03
Prob/parole other enhance (7)	.07	-.03
Family counseling (6)	.02	-.01
Vocational (9)	-.18	+.09
Deterrence (9)	-.24	+.12
NON JUVENILE JUSTICE		
Skill oriented (17)	.32	-.16
Multimodal/broker (29)	.21	-.10
Behavioral (31)	.20	-.10
Group counseling (17)	.18	-.09
Casework (7)	.16	-.08
Other counseling (5)	.06	-.03
School class/tutor (14)	.00	-.00
Individual counseling (24)	-.01	+.00
Any other non JJ (3)	-.01	+.00
Employment/vocational (22)	-.02	+.01

Note: The number of studies in each category is reported in parentheses.

Effects for Other Outcome Variables

Intervention may result in a variety of changes among those subjects or clients treated. It can also fail to have impact on some variables while affecting others. We might ask, for example, if change in delinquent behavior was regularly accompanied by change in, say, psychological adjustment. It is commonly assumed that delinquency treatment works by first influencing such psychological variables as self-esteem, attitudes toward authority, and self-control which then, in turn, lead to a reduction in delinquent behavior. If this assumption is true, studies that show larger delinquency effects should also show larger effects on psychological variables.

As noted earlier, the effect size dependent variables in this meta-analysis were classified into seven groups: delinquency, psychological measures, interpersonal adjustment, school participation, academic performance, vocational accomplishment, and all others. Each study in the meta-analysis could contribute one effect size for each category, but not more (multiples were averaged). Table 6 reports the mean effect size for the outcomes in each of these categories. All of these means were positive and, with the exception of the miscellaneous category ("all others"), they were as large as, or larger than the mean delinquency effect size.

Table 6: Mean Effect Sizes for Other Categories of Outcome Issues Compared with Mean Effect Size for Delinquency Outcome.

Outcome category	Weighted mean ES	Standard deviation
Delinquency	.10	.30
Psychological measures	.27	.55
Interpersonal adjustment	.12	.32
School participation	.11	.36
Academic performance	.14	.38
Vocational accomplishment	.10	.28
All other	.08	.29

The separation and unitary coding of the various outcome categories made it possible to analyze the across-study correlations among them. Since delinquent behavior was the major target for change in these research studies, we ask what other kinds of change also occurred in a group of juveniles when their delinquency was reduced. The results should provide some insight into the dynamics of the change process.

Table 7, Panel A, presents the across-study correlations between the effect sizes for delinquency and those for each of the other categories of outcome variables. Since not all studies measured and reported outcome variables in some of these categories, there was a different number of studies involved in each of these correlations. What is most striking about the results is the wide range of values among the correlations - from a high of .57 with school participation to a low of .09 with academic performance.

Recall (from Table 6) that the mean effect size in all these outcome categories was as large as (or larger than) that for delinquency. We know, therefore, that there were effects on all these dimensions. What Table 7, Panel A, shows is that these changes are not all facets of a more global overall change involving the delinquent behavior of the group of youth receiving treatment. A study that shows a large effect on the delinquency of the subjects involved does not necessarily also show a large effect on psychological measures or academic performance. It appears that there is some independence among these constructs; they are not linked such that change on one would necessarily be accompanied by change on the other.

The linkages we do find (the larger correlations in Table 7, Panel A) connect the delinquency effect sizes with school participation effect sizes and, to a lesser extent, with vocational accomplishment and interpersonal adjustment. It appears from this pattern that increased school attendance was more closely associated with the constructive effects of intervention on delinquents than was the widely assumed improvement in psychological adjustment. Indeed, change in psychological factors showed almost no correlation with change in delinquent behavior. Moreover, there was no significant correlation with changes in academic performance either. Apparently the important issue is whether or not the juveniles attend school, not how well they do academically.

Table 7: Across-Study Correlations Among the Different Categories of Outcome Variables.

A. Across-study correlations between effect sizes on delinquency outcome and effect sizes on other outcomes

Outcome category	Weighted correlation with delinquency ES (N)		
Psychological measures	.12	(80)	n.s.
Interpersonal adjustment	.25	(54)	$p < .10$
School participation	.57	(84)	$p < .01$
Academic performance	.09	(40)	n.s.
Vocational accomplishment	.30	(40)	$p < .05$

B. Across-study correlations between effect sizes on school outcome and effect sizes on other outcomes

Outcome category	Weighted correlation with school ES (N)		
Psychological measures	.66	(37)	$p < .01$
Interpersonal adjustment	.67	(31)	$p < .01$
Academic performance	.36	(36)	$p < .05$
Vocational accomplishment	.31	(29)	$p < .10$

C. Across-study correlations between effect sizes on vocational outcome and effect sizes on other outcomes

Outcome category	Weighted correlation with vocational ES (n)		
Psychological measures	.03	(17)	n.s.
Interpersonal adjustment	.30	(14)	n.s.
School participation	.31	(29)	$p < .10$
Academic performance	.40	(7)	n.s.

Given that increased school participation seems to be linked with reduced delinquency, we might go one step further and inquire into the correlates of school participation. For this purpose we are restricted to a still smaller subset of the studies in the meta-analysis, those that measured both school participation and some other type of nondelinquency outcome. Panel B in Table 6 reports the across-study correlations between school participation effect sizes and each of the other categories. The results are rather striking.

Whereas few of these outcome variables showed much direct correlation with change in delinquency, they all showed some correlation with school participation. In particular, the correlations of school participation with psychological outcomes and interpersonal adjustment were substantial. So, while change in psychological variables and interpersonal adjustment for a sample of juveniles does not seem to be closely linked to change in their delinquency, it does seem to be closely linked to change in their school participation which, in turn, is linked to change in delinquency.

What is suggested by these results is a pattern of direct and indirect connections between change in delinquency and change in the other factors that researchers have often presumed would also be affected by successful intervention. Moreover, we might assume that change in overt behavior is mediated by changes by psychological factors and adjustment, i.e., that the latter are likely to change first and lead to behavior change rather than the other way around (as assumption that might seem reasonable to all but die-hard behaviorists). On that basis we can assign a causal order to the relationships found among the various outcome effects.

In particular, the pattern of across-study correlations of effect sizes for different outcome variables suggests that positive changes in psychological factors and/or improved interpersonal adjustment for a sample of delinquents lead to increased school participation. Academic performance does not necessarily improve, but the treated juveniles, as a group, show better attendance or are less likely to drop out. Increased school participation in turn, leads to a reduction in delinquency. It should be noted that the delinquency intervention literature often discusses the presumed relationship between schooling and delinquency (e.g., Rutter et al., 1979), so the above scenario is consistent with what many researchers already find plausible.

Conclusion

The meta-analysis results summarized here support a different interpretation of the body of research on delinquency treatment than that conveyed by traditional research reviews. Quantitative aggregation and statistical analysis of study effect sizes revealed that the overall mean was positive and statistically significant. While that mean itself was numerically modest, it was not trivial and, more importantly, only summarized the central tendency of widely varying study effects, some quite substantial. Much of this variability in study effects was attributable to methodological differences among the studies. Beyond that, however, the most important factor was the type of treatment modality used. Those treatments that were more behaviorally specific and structured generally produced larger effects than traditional counseling and casework approaches. The effect sizes for these more successful treatments were not so modest, representing reductions of 20% or more in the recidivism of treated juveniles compared to control juveniles.

In addition, treatment showed positive effects on psychological, interpersonal, school participation, academic, and vocational outcomes. Such changes, however, were not correlated across studies in such a way to indicate that all these dimensions were uniformly improved by treatment. Rather, it appears that reduced delinquency in a sample of juveniles is most regularly accompanied by increased school participation. School participation, in turn, is most regularly associated with positive effects on psychological and interpersonal variables.

The meta-analytic work summarized in this paper confirms and extends the pattern of results found in prior meta-analyses. All show positive mean treatment effects, disproving the "nothing works" interpretation of the research literature. More important, perhaps, is the evidence of substantial variability in those effects from study to study. Researchers in delinquency and rehabilitation should put arguments about whether delinquency treatment works to rest and move on to the more interesting and challenging questions of what works best, when, and why.

References

Andrews, D.A., Zinger, I., Hoge, R.D., Bonta, J., Gendreau, P., & Cullen, F.T. (1990). Does correctional treatment work? A clinically-relevant and psychologically informed meta-analysis. *Criminology*, 28, 369-404.

Cullen, F.T., & Gilbert, K.E. (1982). *Reaffirming rehabilitation.* Cincinnati, Ohio: Anderson.

Garrett, C.J. (1984). Meta-analysis of the effects of institutional and community residential treatment on adjudicated delinquents. Unpublished doctoral dissertation, University of Colorado.

Garrett, C.J. (1985). Effects of residential treatment on adjudicated delinquents: A meta-analysis. *Journal of Research in Crime and Delinquency*, 22, 287-308.

Gendreau, P., & Ross, B. (1979). Effective correctional treatment: Bibliotherapy for cynics. *Crime and Delinquency*, 25, 463-489.

Gendreau, P., & Ross, R.R. (1987). Revivification of rehabilitation: Evidence from the 1980s. *Justice Quarterly*, 4, 349-407.

Glass, G.V., McGaw, B., & Smith, M.L. (1981). *Meta-analysis in social research.* Newbury Park, CA: Sage.

Gottschalk, R., Davidson, W.S., Gensheimer, L.K., & Mayer, J. (1987). Community-based interventions. In H.C. Quay (Ed.), *Handbook of juvenile delinquency* (pp. 266-289). New York: John Wiley.

Greenberg, D.F. (1977). The correctional effects of corrections: A survey of evaluations. In D.A. Greenberg (Ed.), *Corrections and punishment* (pp. 111-148). Newbury Park, CA: Sage.

Hedges, L.V. (1982). Estimation of effect size from a series of independent experiments. *Psychological Bulletin*, 92, 490-499.

Lipsey, M.W. (1990). *Design sensitivity: Statistical power for experimental research.* Newbury Park, CA: Sage.

Lipton, D., Martinson, R., & Wilks, J. (1975). *The effectiveness of correctional treatment: A survey of treatment evaluation studies.* New York: Praeger.

Lundman, R.J., McFarlane, P.T., & Scarpitti, F.R. (1976). Delinquency prevention: A description and assessment of projects reported in the professional literature. *Crime and Delinquency*, 22, 297-308.

Martinson, R. (1974). What works? Questions and answers about prison reform. *Public Interest*, 10, 22-54.

Palmer, T. (1975). Martinson revisited. *Journal of Research in Crime and Delinquency*, 12, 133-152.

Palmer, T. (1983). The effectiveness issue today: An overview. *Federal Probation*, 47, 3-10.

Romig, D. (1978). *Justice for our children.* Lexington, MA: Lexington Books.

Rutter, M., Maughan, B., Mortimore, P., & Ouston, J. (1979). *Fifteen thousand hours.* London: Open Books.

Sechrest, L.B., White, S.O., & Brown, E.D. (1979). *The rehabilitation of criminal offenders: Problems and prospects.* Washington, D.C.: National Academy of Sciences.

Whitehead, J.T., & Lab, S.P. (1989). A meta-analysis of juvenile correctional treatment. *Journal of Research in Crime and Delinquency*, 26, 276-295.

Wright, W.E., & Dixon, M.C. (1977). Community prevention and treatment of juvenile delinquency: A review of evaluation studies. *Journal of Research in Crime and Delinquency*, 14, 35-67.

Intervention in Persistent Criminality in Children

David A. Lane

Introduction

This paper presents the results of a fifteen year study of children who became involved in persistent criminality. It traces the careers of a group of children from the age of ten to twenty years. Data from public records, school, social, and psychological reports from the age of five years are traced. Several hundred children were involved in the initial data collection, but this paper concentrates on the outcome for children involved in delinquency and comparisons with control groups.

The data on, social, educational, and individual differences were analyzed to establish factors which were predictive of later criminality and type of offence together with responsiveness to therapeutic interventions.

An account of a therapeutic program involving the children's schools is reported, and outcome data analyzed. The data indicate that a controlled program, which includes specific interventions by the child's school, can significantly influence future patterns of offending behaviour.

The demand for action

There have been increasing demands over the years for special provision or intervention schemes for children and youths at risk of delinquency. These demands were paralleled by demands for action on school disruption (Tattum, 1988), truancy (Reid, 1988), and more recently, bullying (Lane, 1988) in part because of the link between these various activities. However, by the late 1960's those demands became increasingly vocal. Three factors received particular attention in the UK, the raising of the school leaving age, the move to comprehensive education, and a public perception of increasing violence and drug use, were each seen as cause and effect of a decline in values.

Two contradictory themes emerged as a response to these demands. The first, looked to schools to help with the problems of children in need. The second theme looked to special off-site units in which difficult pupils could be based either long term or with the intention of a return to school. Within these two themes a variety of programs appeared which tried to prevent, reduce or divert children from involvement in disruption, truancy and delinquency. Some programs clearly had as their aim diversion from court process and were aimed at delinquents. In practice substantial overlap between schemes existed. Thus, truancy programs were justified and funded as intermediate treatment packages to reduce the prospects of criminal activity.

The outcome literature in these areas has continued to produce variable results although positive short-time findings are increasingly reported. Difficulties in demonstrating long-term gains consistently remain (Hersov, Berger & Schaffer, 1978; Mayer, Gensheimer, Davidson,

& Gottschalk, 1986; Topping, 1983). As Gensheimer, Mayer, Davidson and Gottschalk (1986) point out the use of diversion programs does not produce evidence of strong effects positive or negative. This failure reflects the more general weakness of the general child psychotherapy literature (Callias, 1992; Kazdin, 1988).

The Impossible Child Series

As part of a general trend to increased provision in the 1970's, the Islington Education Guidance Center was established. I was appointed in 1974 to provide a service to work with children seen as to difficult to retain in school, most of whom were involved in delinquent activity (80 % in our first survey). The area covered was an area of high unemployment (1:5). In the top ten areas of the country for incidence of deprivation, and in the top three for crime rates. Inner London in general is a multicultural area (160 plus languages are spoken) and schools were encouraged to use that diversity creatively.

We set out not to remove children, but rather to persuade schools to work with their difficult pupils. It was not a popular idea, but it increasingly became a model for programs elsewhere and was seen as effective (HMI, 1980; Lane, 1978, 1990; Topping, 1983). The main thrust of the work was change within schools, however, the strong research orientation also led to the development of programs aimed at reducing delinquent activity.

Our approach was pragmatic (maybe simplistic), we asked key questions.
- Who are these children at risk of delinquency, how do they come to be defined.
- What factors predict outcome.
- How do we design interventions to take account of these factors.
- If we design such interventions, can we run them and how effective are they.
- If we can do it, can others replicate it.

To us these seemed like the right type of questions to ask. This was it must be remembered the early 1970's, and we did not have the benefit (?) of meta-analysis of studies. Thus we started not with a commitment to a particular theoretical position. We were not testing the effectiveness of psycho-dynamic or behavioural approaches. We were not evaluating a particular demonstration project. We were making it up as we went along based on careful evaluation of the answers to the basic questions. It was the perception of many that we were working behaviourally. That was largely true, not out of a commitment to a model but because the ideas worked. But many other ideas were also featured in the program, and others were tried and abandoned .... all on pragmatic grounds.

This paper outlines some of the problems we encountered and the conclusions we reached (Data is reported elsewhere, Lane, 1978, 1983, 1990).

Problem 1. Who defines whom?

A child is referred by a parent, teacher, or some other agent. The question of how the referral happens, the label used and the point at which this label is removed, is not a neutral issue. A number of factors will influence referral decisions. These include resource differences between areas, attitudes of teachers towards their role, and the attitudes of support services (Fitzherbert, 1977), attribution processes (Green, 1980), and discretionary judgements (Lane, 1985, 1989). A child may be labelled and remain labelled when no objective data for the continuation of the difficulty any longer existed (Lane, 1976).

In view of this how do you select children for intervention and how will you be able to measure effectiveness. For some of the pupils referred, it was non problematic. They were seen as so bad, nobody would want them. For other pupils referral was very much a reflection of widely varied tolerance levels of individual practitioners. Pupils found themselves in an intervention project because a powerful figure with a low threshold forced his (usually) opinion on less powerful program providers. That threshold greatly influenced referral for Court processing (Lane, 1990). These issues have been widely covered in the literature (Adams, 1986; Clarizio, 1968; Cunningham & Davis, 1985; Galloway, Ball, Bloomfield, & Seyd, 1982; Lane & Miller, 1990; Scheff, 1966; Scheff & Sundstorm, 1970; Ullmann & Krasner, 1975; Warnock, 1978).

The process by which definitions emerged was one of negotiation between the parties involved. In order to deal with power inequalities, an 'open file' system was instituted, borrowed from earlier work (1973) which two of the staff (David Lane and Fiona Green) had originated elsewhere (see Lane & Green, 1990). The idea of a social exchange was introduced to the process by which a definition was negotiated. Therefore, any investigation became a social exchange in which each party negotiated definitions and knew where they stood. The negotiation of problem definitions became our starting point for work with the child.

Problem 2. What factors should we investigate?

There is a vast literature devoted to explanations of why individuals develop behaviour disorders. The literature on aggression and anti-social behaviour (conduct disorders/delinquency) is very extensive. Some ideas will be outlined to illustrate that breath.

Delinquent neighborhoods. The assumption that delinquent behaviour relates to the existence of poverty and neighborhoods or delinquent sub-cultures which generate anti-social behaviour is one of the earliest of cultural theories (Burt, 1925; Cloward & Ohlin, 1961; Cohen, 1955; Merton, 1951; Shaw & McKay, 1942; Thrasher, 1964). In a major report based on ten years of accumulated research, Brown & Madge (1982) concluded that all the evidence suggested that cultural values are not important for the development and transmission of deprivation. They also quote West's (1979) research for the same project as concluding that the role of delinquent sub-cultures can be largely discounted. This confirms Robbins (1966) earlier challenge to cultural theories. However, research into, bullying behaviour has pointed to the role of peer groups and power/affiliation issues (Askew, 1988; Roland, 1988).

Delinquent families and socialization. Alternative theories are those which see anti-social behaviour as arising from patterns within families. Research from pioneering studies such as that of the Gluecks' (1950), through to a review by Argyle (1964) reflected these early theories. Recently, Ellis (1988) has reviewed over five hundred studies internationally which look at demographic correlates of criminal behavior. It is argued that there is a universal sense of what constitutes criminal behaviour and this is based on the role of the victim. For crimes involving a victim seven universal demographic correlates are presented - intactness of parent's sexual/marital bond, family size, race, social status, urban/rural residency, age and sex. The difficulties with this area are illustrated by the fact that even with the comprehensive coverage of the literature undertaken by Ellis, major studies which present a contrary view, such as those of Stott, Marston & Neill (1975) are not mentioned.

Delinquent schools. During the 1960's there was an increasing emphasis on the role of the school in promoting anti-social behaviour or low expectations in pupils (Hargreaves, 1967; Musgrove, 1964; Partridge, 1966; Willmott, 1958). Power and his associates (Power, Aldeson, Phillipseon, Shoenburgh & Morris, 1969) pointed to differences between schools in fostering delinquent attitudes. The role of the school has recently received far more attention. The work of Reynolds (1982), Rutter, Maighan, Mortimore and Ouston (1979), and Mortimore, Sammons, Stoll, Lewis and Ecob (1988) has been very important in refocusing the debate on the role of the school. The studies by Galloway and his associates (Galloway et al., 1982) are highly relevant in their concentration on disruptive behaviour and delinquency, is a complex one worthy of attention but much of the data is difficult to interpret. It does appear, as a Home Office research review indicates, that some practices in schools influence the progression from minor misbehaviour to delinquency (Graham, 1988).

Thus it is not just the school attended which matters by patterns of interaction within it. Understanding those patterns may be very useful in explaining the persistent of problems related to delinquency.

Discrimination and language. Discrimination in society is clear and obvious and whole groups can receive adverse treatment (Brown and Madge, 1982). However, the possibility of selective labelling of children from different ethnic minorities, and the consequent placement of them in special education, has concentrated attention. A number of suggestions that black children were overrepresented in units for disruptive children did raise questions about differences between groups in levels of difficulty (West, Davies & Varlaan, 1986). Selective Labeling of Black children for prosecution has also been raised and the evidence lends some support to this effect (Lane, 1985). That language can have a powerful effect on how children are seen and labelled in schools was clearly established by Eggleston, Dunn and Ajjali (1985).

The labelling the child. As Becker (1963) pointed out, "Social groups create deviance by making the rules whose infraction constitutes deviance and by applying those rules to particular people and labelling them as outsiders." A detailed study of life in school provided evidence of the effect of such processes (Hargreaves, Hester & Mellor, 1975). The function served by placing the child in an out group may have to be considered as Galloway et al. (1982) have already referred to some possibilities including the issue of removing evidence of tension within the school.

Social learning explanations aggression and anti-social behaviour. There are numerous experimental studies supporting the value of learning principles applied to behaviour problems (Ullmann & Krasner, 1975). It is not as simple as it appears. Recent research in animal conditioning and learning theory indicates that "conditioning is neither a simple nor well understood process" (Dickinson, 1987), and may have to allow for the observation that inappropriate behaviours and beliefs may arise through conditioning experience. For example, the experience of the individual might be one of severe punishment or punishment based on the adults' shifting moods rather than on consistent objective principles related to the child's behaviour. The result is that the individual learns that people are sources of punishment, to be avoided, rather than sources of reinforcement to be sought.

Genetic, individual difference and congenital explanations. Although the learning principles discussed above are well established, it is necessary to explain why some individuals respond more readily than others to some learning situations. There does appear to be some evidence to support the idea that individuals vary constitutionally in responsiveness to conditioning.

Theories of causation include the concept of 'minor physical abnormalities'. High rates of "MPA's" have been found in various groups of children presenting behaviour problems, and these features are usually evident from birth (Quinn & Rapaport, 1974).

More sophisticated studies, based on brain wave activity, have shown that delinquents in general do not differ from non-delinquents but certain groups who often commit offenses do differ on such measures (Michaels, 1955; Volavka, 1987). The personality models of both (Cattell & Cattell, 1969; Eysenck & Eysenck, 1975) provide a framework to consider this issue. The prediction they make is that behaviour problems are more likely in extraverted, emotionally unstable children who are also toughminded. A large number of studies have been undertaken to test this prediction. The results have not always been consistent but do show some correlation at the extreme but not for mild disorders (Eysenck & Gudjonsson, 1989; Rutter & Madge, 1976). The argument that there might be constitutional 'personality' differences has been extended to the possibility of congenital involvement (Stott et al., 1975).

Problem 3. What should we take into account?

There are clearly a range of potential explanations. At the individual level, gender differences and the role of arousal and personality need to be considered. Health and possibly the occurrence of minor physical abnormalities will also have to be included. A link between social class, higher levels of problems and health difficulties would be of interest. Cultural factors are likely to prove more difficult but the existence of problems within the family at some level has to be examined, and several aspects of the role of the school are worthy of further examination. More difficult will be consideration of the way labels and beliefs impact on the child. The child's own view of these factors cannot be ignored.

Discovering factors that make it more likely that children will have difficulties is not an easy task. Unfortunately, it is made still more difficult since factors which lead to problems may not be the same as those which maintain them (Yule, 1978). It is not just the existence of problems that we have to explore but also factors which relate to remission from them.

Our own research over many years sought to discover key factors in relation to our group of children. The studies were based on samples of children from rural and urban schools and we examined personality data, indications of multiple stress and consistency in behaviour across ages. The total sample of children was around three thousand but these were subdivided into smaller groups for various studies. Of particular interest were findings for a group of 100 children who were persistently presenting behaviour problems in school, and had resisted therapy attempts. Data on this group were available from records from the age of five and in follow up data on delinquency up to the age of 20. However, data on other samples of children confirmed the basic findings. A number of conclusions were drawn (Findings are reported in Lane, 1974, 1978, 1983, 1990).

What factors correlate with the occurrence of difficulties? Three propositions were given particular attention:

That personality features made conduct difficulties more likely to occur. It was argued that conditionability (high extraversion) influenced the likelihood of conduct difficulties developing. Furthermore, high drive levels (high neuroticism) were also implicated. Psychoticism was also seen as a crucial component.

The data, in relation to general conduct disorder in school, supported the position for E & P, but not N. However, when translated into a prediction for criminality, only P emerged.

Conditionability (in so far as it is reflected in E) is therefore seen to play a role, but the nature of its influence in respect of particular patterns of behaviour needed further clarification.

Our later studies did provided such clarification, in that it formed part of a factor associated with hyperactive/destructible behaviour (inconsequence on BSAG). It was not linked with norm violating or peer maladaptive behaviour. It was also linked more strongly with hostility to adults in the long term, rather than short term, suggesting that hostility emerges as an outcome of the pattern of difficulties over time.

In relation to the occurrence of disorder, P is found to be associated with general conduct and criminality. E is found to be related to general conduct disorder, but it is probably through its association with specific hyperactive types of behaviour that its effect is greatest.

That those suffering multiple stresses are more likely to develop conduct disorders. This position was strongly supported. Across a wide range of measures, it was found that the level of disorder related to the level of adversity in the child's background. However, the absence of positive compensating features was also found to be important.

That the occurrence of behaviour difficulties at one stage are predictive of difficulties at a later stage. Again this position was strongly supported. Behaviour measures at five years of age and through to the end of school career showed a consistent pattern. Even a broadly drawn category of conduct disorder was predictive of later delinquency.

To sum up, it is apparent that all three theoretical positions receive some support, and play a role in the occurrence of conduct difficulties.

What factors correlate with remission from difficulties? Although valid, these arguments take us so far. A more subtle examination is necessary. The study of the group of children presenting severe conduct disorders provided some of the answers. A factor analysis of the range of possible features of influence was undertaken. Two general factors were apparent, dominated by variables indicating behavioural features. That two such features should emerge serves to emphasize that a general category of 'conduct disorder' is too imprecise. The first factor contained a variety of behavioural variables including the continuity of negative behaviour rating by teachers from the first to the final years of secondary school. Certain children were seen not only as badly behaved but as 'bad' people, who are themselves at loggerheads with adults and peers. This raises important questions as to the sources of support available to such pupils. Their subsequent delinquent career extends their conflict with others, from a period stretching in some cases from five to twenty years of age.

The second main factor suggests that certain children are temperamentally (extravertly) inclined to consistent difficulties of conduct marked by inconsequential (impulsive) behaviours. Such children and such behaviours cannot be lumped together in a general anti authority grouping even though they may come eventually to be in direct conflict with adults. Thus, the behaviour itself, in relation to specific items rather than generalised categories, must be the focus of attention. The results also raised the distinction between a rating as improved (remission) and behavioural evidence of change. The two might not be the same thing.

Beyond the focus on the behavioural itself, other features emerge. The most important of these corresponds, in part, to the concept of 'fortuitous events' influencing outcome. It is apparent that pupils showing less teacher related change long term are also the subject of negative life experiences, both as individuals and in terms of their school careers.

A subsequent analysis looked at the children included in the factor analysis and examined aspects of case study material. The detailed material from the case study data pointed to a range of factors of importance. The view held by the child and key others, particularly teachers, had a major impact. The beliefs about change generated (or failed to generate) change. The extent to which professionals, teachers and social workers, for example, were able to assist children and parents to act effectively on their environment significantly affected outcomes. Some children generated particular stress at sensitive points 'sore spots' in the system. These included areas where philosophical conflicts existed between staff. The children exhibited a wide range of behaviours and an equally wide range of techniques were used to work with the pupils. This perhaps indicates that individual analysis is necessary. A packaged set of approaches is unlikely to meet the complexity of the each situation.

The personality feature of Psychoticism also appears and suggests a pattern in which the high P child is more likely to be the recipient of punishing, rather than reinforcing life events (in part independently of the behaviour). Therefore, we must look not simply at the child's behaviour, but also to the events experienced, for an explanation of remission.

Two further elements of interest are the absence of positive family and other features and a preponderance of negative features, which appear also to play a role in the initial occurrence of problems. Thus, the child who starts life in a difficult situation is more likely to develop behaviour problems, but it is to subsequent events that one must look for evidence of maintaining factors.

What then is the pattern of remission? It is apparent that the process of remission involves more than a change in behaviour. To some extent, it appears that the behaviour of the child and a rating as improved are independent variables. In reality the belief system of the key change agents (primarily teachers) is part of the overall pattern. If they do not believe in the possibility of change, they will not see it even when the behavioural evidence exists. As argued elsewhere, perhaps we can only see what we believe (Lane, 1989). The relationship between final ratings, life events and personality features points to some children being less likely than others to be given whatever help is available.

A general factor of 'behaviour towards others' appears to suggest that certain behaviours, namely those directed towards adults or peers, are more strongly featured, positively or negatively, in a rating of change by teachers than more impulsive behaviours.

Understanding remission requires a detailed knowledge of the behaviour itself and the way it is viewed by key agents. It requires also a consideration of the events that happen in the life of the child. Knowing that the child has suffered multiple adversities tends to strengthen any prediction of later difficulties, as does the absence of positive compensating features. However, remission relates very strongly to the subsequent events in the child's life, rather than to the general presence or absence of adversity. The expectation remains that those suffering greater adversity will develop more problems of conduct over a longer time scale, but it is only a partial explanation.

Certain patterns of conduct, namely impulsive behaviours (inconsequence) are seen to be related to general impulsivity or personality (extraversion). It seems that the extravert child who develops or shows conduct difficulties of an impulse type will be less likely to change and will also develop further difficulties in time, in response to the actions of others (hostility).

Understanding remission, therefore, involves all three of the explanatory propositions originally stated. They are not mutually exclusive but interact in defined ways. As to which explanations carriers the strongest prediction, it appears to be 'behaviour predicting subsequent behaviour of a similar type'. The strength of the other factors discovered does nevertheless underline the need to take account of their role. It is apparent that simply changing behaviour is not enough; one must act also to change the way the child is viewed, and to deal with the significant negative life events the child experiences. To this extent, professional attempts to promote remission require a multimodel input, focusing on the behaviour and the significant agents and events in the child's life. An effective short-term therapeutic intervention would need to be supported by longer term action in the child's community. The primary focus would seem to be the school.

Problem 4. What must we do to achieve change?

We must: Act to change the behaviour itself, a task made particularly difficult by the low levels of conditionability of the pupil.
- Act to change the action of the school itself towards the child.
- Assist the child through individual crisis periods, rather than rejecting him (or her) because of their difficult nature.
- The child most difficult to like is also the most in need of support.

Such action must involve the school in providing ongoing support, and also the range of other agencies and professionals involved at different stages in the life of the child and family.

The traditionally established variables of multiple adversity draw attention one again to the need for support for families at risk. However, there has also been a traditional tendency to place all behavioural disorder at the door of the poor family. Such a position is not tenable for these pupils. The school itself, in the way children are labelled and the response offered, is part of the situation of concern. Ongoing action within the community of the child, and principally the school, is needed.

CONTEXT-FOCUSED ANALYSIS: Summary of steps

PHASE ONE: Definiton

1. Obtain statement of the problem from those involved.
2. Clarify initial objectives of those involved.
3. On the basis of initial information received consider roles.

Theme: A process of awareness aimed at achieving a shared concern.

PHASE TWO: Exploration

4. Hypotheses of cause are generated.
5. Observation technologies are chosen.
6. Data is collected to test the hypotheses.

Theme: The process is one of increasingly refined observations.

PHASE THREE: Formulation

7. The adequacy of the hypotheses are checked.
8. A formulation and intervention hypotheses are established.
9. Discussion with participants and redefinition of objectives takes place.

Theme: The process is one of testing the hypotheses until an adequate explanation is available.

PHASE FOUR: Intervention

10. The procedures to be used are specified.
11. An intervention contract is established.
12. The agreed programme is enacted and monitored.

Theme: The process is one of structured practice.

PHASE FIVE: Evaluation

13. Outcomes achieved are evaluated.
14. Any gains made are maintained, the programme optimised and new objectives which arise are tackled.
15 Re-evaluate, re-think and review outcome and ideas.

Theme: The process is one of monitored achievement...
WITHIN A SUPPORTIVE ENVIRONMENT.

A Research Model of Intervention

The research does point to the need for a more systematic approach to the design of intervention. If work with children is going to impact on later delinquency it must involve the child's school. This is not an easy task, but it does point to the need to include five key elements in any model of the change process which we use. These are issues of particular relevance for persistently delinquent children (see box).

How is the behaviour to be defined? The definition phase. It is clear that the behaviour of the child must be carefully defined in the context in which it occurs. That change in behaviour may not be recognized raises important questions about the objectives of those involved. A variety of people are making the decisions, including the child. Each person able to influence the outcome may have to be included in the definition of the problem. Discrepancies between their views may be the appropriate point to start a change process. Given this interactive labelling process, any approach may require a social exchange of meaning/value. A contract for change may be necessary to enhance that process. The role each party is to play in the change process may have to be defined as part of the contract. A definition phase based on social exchange concepts would represent the obvious starting point for a change process.

For most of our children involved in delinquent behaviour the process of interaction with figures of authority has involved a battle. This is particularly the case in respect of the school. They are the people who write reports for Court which impact on the likelihood of a custodial sentence (Lane, 1990). If they are to become active partners in a change process they must become actively involved in defining their behaviour as changeworthy. Thus teachers/ social workers were taught how to negotiate definitions of behaviour to be changed and the children were taught similar skills. They were encouraged to reach "shared concerns". This is in marked contrast to the majority of behavioural interventions in school setting in which teachers/psychologists define the behaviour and set the parameters for change.

What factors must be taken into account? The exploration phase. The data suggests the existence of constitutional and historical factors which have shaped the behaviour of the child. These predisposing factors are part of the child's past. There is little to be gained by considering them unless they impact on the present - and there is a suggestion that they might. For example, if there has been a history of problems between a child and a teacher, the beliefs that they hold, based on that history, influence the present. Knowing the history can help to construct a framework for change. The child's personal style of action (personality) will influence preferred behavioural styles for responding to events. Knowing those patterns has the potential to improve program design. Individual differences will, therefore, have to be taken into account in any change program.

The patterns of support within the school and the community/family were found to be implicated, so may have to be included. So some predisposing events will need to be explored. If their impact in the present can be demonstrated. It was, however, current events, that were found to alter the balance for the child, the reinforcement available for change, and the beliefs of the participants. The data indicated that the day to day learning experiences of the child in school were important and could be altered, resulting in powerful beneficial effect. Events which precipitate and maintain current behaviours must feature strongly in any analysis. Although group comparisons have been drawn, the particular combinations of events for each child, happening day by day, will be unique.

Global change packages are unlikely to be helpful. What is needed is a careful formulation of the key factors for each child.

What is it like for me? A personal formulation phase. Each child's teacher's, school's, family's unique view of the events which matter must be understood. This must be backed by careful experimental data collected in the context in which the problem is defined. Thus for each event, a formulation which explains what factors control the occurrence of the behaviour in context must be provided. If what is happening is understood, changing what is happening becomes possible.

What must we do to change? A planned intervention phase. If it is to take account of key factors and potentially involve several change agents, the change process is going to be complex. Without a step by step plan, the process is going to become muddled. No one will be accountable, and the child will loose. Each person's responsibility for the change will have to be determined. The detail of what they are expected to do will have to be known. The outcome (performance) against which success is going to be measured must be specified. In this way the complexity might be successfully managed. However, the data suggests that long term change might have to be managed, in addition to short term interventions. An evaluation and follow up process, to ensure that gains are not lost and new problems are tackled, will have to be included (managed partnerships).

What must we do to ensure continued success? An evaluation phase. We know that long term outcome depends on the events that happen subsequently to the child. We also know that change in behaviour may not be related to an evaluation of change by key agents. An agreed basis must be established to measure change for each program. Once a predetermined performance target has been reached, the new situation must be addressed. It was established that, faced with success, new demands may emerge which are difficult for the child to manage. A long term support strategy may be needed, until the child has developed the skills to meet new challenges, and not just solve the existing difficulties. A careful evaluation and follow up process is required.

An example of the process. The study took place under the auspices of the Islington Educational Guidance Center, based on joint work between the school and center staff.

John is the youngest of five children. His father was in regular work but had always been aggressive towards the children according to the mother's and child's accounts. She used to intervene to prevent the children being hit, but gave up after receiving beatings herself. She reported that the father had a poor relationship with all the children. Attempts over the years to involve the family in Family Therapy failed. The older brother had been suspended from school for bullying and was increasingly involved with the Police. John spent several months in hospital in his early years, for a series of operations to correct birth defects. He remembered that period clearly, and his feelings of fear. Difficulties with language development added to his problems. Speech therapy over several years, two years in a specialist unit for language difficulties and, later, a period in a unit for the 'emotionally disturbed', preceded his transfer to mainstream secondary education. At this time, he was still a non-reader and had poorly developed social skills, although his speech had improved. He developed a severe stutter at the age of twelve when he was becoming increasingly involved in violence and vandalism and, subsequently, football hooliganism.

The school he attended made extensive use of the cane as a punishment, in spite of the fact that, as the Deputy Head said, 'You might as well cane the wall as some of these children for all the good it does'.

In terms of the research findings reported previously. This is an example of a child with multiple problems. However, there were also several positive compensatory features. John had established a very good relationship with the special needs teacher in the school, who made a determined and successful attempt to teach him to read. A number of other teachers felt there were positive aspects in his behaviour, although they neither accepted nor tolerated his bullying.

Several teachers wanted him further beaten, suspended, prosecuted or 'xxxed'. His mother, although powerless against the father, did provide a compassionate model and he felt loved by her.

The school decided to make a referral for Child Guidance but that broke down (Psychotherapy is often sought - 'perhaps he needs individual help', - but is rarely useful for a toughminded, extravert pupil, who has learned a pattern of violent response and has been consistently reinforced for using it.) They than made a referral to the Islington Center. A complex analysis and intervention followed in brief, it identified certain key elements:

- Both his father and some male teachers provided models of aggressive behaviour. John disliked them but saw them as powerful models.
- He valued the compassion he was shown but saw it as weakness.
- He greatly valued being in school, at least that part of it which gave him some sense of success. He feared the prospect of further suspension.
- His speech difficulty and lack of social skills prevented his expressing/asserting himself effectively. When confronted, he found that hitting out worked: children did not tease you if you terrorized them, and being unpredictable made teachers uncer
  tain about confronting you. Violence worked; reason did not.
- The school did not have a consistent policy, and conflicts were apparent between staff dealing with these issues and this pupil.

One particular aspect of the case will be considered. Point 4th above looked at the problem of hitting out as a result of stress. The way the hypotheses were tested in this area provides an example of the process.

Three situations of violence were identified for consideration:
- Bullying other children
- Attacks on certain teachers
- Fights in other contexts.

The initial hypotheses linked the idea of stress to violence as follows:

When faced with a confrontation situation, John's level of stress is increased. As a result, his speech difficulty becomes worse, he has difficulty expressing himself, and he hits out - which reduces his anxiety.

The various components in this sequence can be tested. The situation in which confrontations occur can be listed, the levels of stress he feels can be established on a scale on which he rates the level (say 1 - 10). Speech fluency could be checked, and the occasions on which he hits out could be recorded. Specific 'Attribution' or 'ABC' techniques could be used to provide a fine-grain analysis of the contexts in which violent or non-violent outcomes were observed.

This process of observation led to the realization that there were in fact at least four different patterns.
- *Cognitive justification.* In some settings when faced with stress, John became angry, told himself that it was wrong that he was treated that way and chose to hit out.
- *Stress Management/Skills deficit.* In some settings he would become anxious, be unable to talk his way out because of his stutter, and hit others in frustration.
- *Just World.* In some settings where he saw some one acting unjustly he would 'punish' the offender by hitting them. This was cold, calculated violence.

- *Sheer pleasure.* Certain settings, mostly involving football, were ones in which he sought out fights, for the pleasure involved. This was entertainment, not stress.

Given these very different patterns, the hypothesis that stress leads to violence cannot be sustained. It might do, but the circumstances in which it did were very specific.

Alternative hypotheses were needed to cover the varied situations. The case study describes one of these patterns to devise a formulation and intervention, but it would not cover other settings which give rise to the violence. Hence the intervention had to include issues to do with the 'Just World', and direct control was needed in other contexts.

A program was introduced to teach John mechanisms to deal with stress situations and to develop his social skills. A review of the models in his environment took place, to help him to identify power as legitimate assertion rather than aggression. A contracted set of relationships was established with teachers, so that events were rendered predictable, with defined consequences. It was made clear that any incident of bullying would be followed by a suspension, but that the issue of provocation by others would also be tackled, that is, he saw it as fair. Over a nine month period, the program took effect with only two incidents being reported. No violence was reported in his final year at school. He left without qualifications but did eventually obtain work.

The one area not covered in the original program was 'sheer pleasure', and it is not surprising, therefore, that no change occurred in that area. In fact, two years later, he was involved in an incident with others (his old football gang) but, following further discussions with him and a period of probation and good social work support, stayed out of further trouble. Five years on he was working, developing on ongoing relationship and feeling positive about himself.

Problem 5: How do we evaluate the success of the programs, and can others do it?

There are at least three types of outcome data which are of interest:
- Data agreed on the basis of the dialogue between child and referring agent.. the *noteworthy difficulty* that comes to be seen as no longer noteworthy.
- The *experimental data* of interest to a world outside of the child's immediate concern.
- A *public agenda* based on reports which have real consequences for the child's life but over which there is no direct control.

We can look at all three types.

The noteworthy difficulty. Some three thousand cases studies were reduced to a sample of 300. For each of these a shared agreement is reached. A program is agreed. An evaluation is undertaken for each objective.

We can thereby explore the variations in patterns of improvement. If we take various samples from within the group, we find very high levels of improvement. That is the objectives are reached. But is that good, bad or only to be expected? For the child and teacher concerned, this is the key data. The noteworthy difficulties are no longer a concern. Two aspects of this will be considered here, prior to a more detailed forthcoming study.

How many objectives might be tackled? The programs for 100 pupils were examined and a mean number of objectives established. A figure of 7.8 was obtained. There were, therefore, approximately eight objectives in each program and a range of techniques were used. The top ten program components for this sample group were:

Contract: 98 %, report system/tokens: 90 %, parental involvement: 85 %, specific targeting of school reports: 75 %, specific targeting of behaviours: 75 %, help with work difficulties: 70 %, social/cognitive skills training: 60 %, specific time limit 'what by when': 35 %, additional monitoring systems (additional to contract/report system): 25 %, counselling/psychotherapy: 10 %.

How much did they improve? In the original data one of the criteria for success was judged to be the attitude of the school to the need for continuing involvement. It was found that the decision by the school that they no longer needed support for the child was a crucial one.

Based on this criteria over 95 % were judged sufficiently improved by their school for program termination. For a specific group who had additional intervention programs based on a partial withdrawal to the Islington Center, the rate drops to 90 %.

Is that good or bad? It is certainly above the rate of spontaneous remission established in the earlier data (Lane, 1983), but how does it compare? It is only by the asking the question 'how does it compare?', that the figures become meaningful, yet that question is meaningless to the individual at the center of the program. Thus we have to obtain some experimental comparisons to satisfy an agenda different from that of the child involved.

But for the teachers and pupils involved it is this judgement, the end of noteworthy difficulties that matters.

Experimental data. Establishing a direct comparison group is difficult and does present some political difficulties. However, the ILEA did monitor outcome data for different types of support service over the years. We have some difficulty with the data for they only included in the figures for Islington those pupils who we took off-site, when the whole thrust of our work was to keep pupils on site. They include for us, therefore, only the most difficult of our pupils. They also include pupils with long term truancy problems, although they formed part of a separate component of our work.

Nevertheless it does provide some level of comparison.
The Inner London Education Authority, in its monitoring of the school support program, produced figures on rates of return to school.

The rates of return to school reported by ILEA for On and Off Site Units (RS744/80) ranged from 25 % for Off-site Units, 54 % for Guidance Centers (such as Islington) to 75 % for On-site Units.

The figure for Islington using the artificial restriction referred to above produces a finding of 79 %, for our sample. This includes pupils involved in long term truancy. Excluding that group, and only counting the standard population of the units, that is those referred for behaviour problems produces a figure of 87 % in one test period. This as we point out is at the bottom end of our calculation.

The figures sound good and are higher than those reported above. Of course, all the units were admitting different children and attempting different things, so is a comparison realistic?

A more effective comparison can be made between pupils who received an intervention in one of the various facilities and those who received no specific additional programs. Any statistical difference between the groups can provide a base line for judging the relevance of any of the improvement rates.

For our research we followed a sample of 114 pupils involved in programs (but not at the Islington Center) compared with untreated controls based on a three year follow up. No statistically significant difference was found between them. That is, treated groups showed no significant improvement over the untreated groups. Splitting the groups into children primarily referred for anxiety or for conduct disorders did produce some positive trends for both treatment groups. The improvement rates for the anxiety group were 65 %, untreated, and 80 % treated. For the conduct group the figures were 31 % untreated and 52 % treated. (The figures failed to reach significance.)

This provides a possible base line to consider the figures above.

The problem is that the groups who formed the data base for the ILEA study were varied. They certainly found that those most likely to improve were, girls, younger pupils, and those with anxiety problems of recent origin. They clearly do not fit our criteria for the Impossible Child. We are therefore comparing our pupils against a less difficult group.

An alternative comparison is to take two groups of pupils matched prior to admission and then involved in different intervention programs. This was attempted for our follow-up study. Two groups of fifty pupils attending other provision or the Islington Center were matched by BSAG patterns, age, sex and school. Two years after completion of programs provided at Islington or other provision, a comparison was made of those who were re-referred for further intervention or suspension from school. The alternative program pupils were re-referred in 66 % of cases and the Islington pupils in 25 % of cases, a significant difference.

It appeared that the rates of return, and long-term outcome were significantly better than a base line based on spontaneous remission or other comparison groups/interventions. But does that really answer the question?

Indeed the findings are sufficiently encouraging for the question to immediately be raised of whether or not others would obtain equally effective results. Several replications on a small scale basis are underway, and practitioners in various parts of the UK who have set up similar programs are contributing to a data base. Only one study has been reported so far, based on an application of the approach to a support team in a part of London as deprived as that in which the original study was completed. The Tower Hamlets Support Team have reported outcome data on their work which indicates an equally impressive level of success (Coulby & Harper, 1983). Preliminary reports from others participants are promising. It does appear that the approach is effective when transferred to other settings and practitioners.

The public agenda. The issue of statistics is of more than ideal concern, since, as the data in the first part of this study indicated, a measure of behaviour change did not correlate with a rating of change - the label involved something more. The label is the part that has consequences for the child's life. The issue of shared concern is critical here, for if we can come to share the concern we can also come to share a view about what constitutes evidence of change. The consequences for some children of a failure to achieve a shared view are substantial... i.e., suspension, negative court reports, possible imprisonment.

The issue of the public agenda is a very real one. In an earlier paper I had referred to the problem facing pupils in relation to reports made by teachers to courts and the very damming effect such reports could have on outcome (Lane, 1985). A recent major study of decision making in the courts has pointed to this problem. The authors argue that reports from teachers have a major influence on the decisions reached. Yet these reports are often inaccurate, contain unsubstantiated allegations, and as we have shown may not reflect the child's attempts at change (Parker, Summer, & Jarvis, 1989).

The patterns of offending for the pupils were studied over a ten year period. Control groups of pupils involved with various other programs and no programs at all were included. Offending during different age periods was also traced. One study traced the cumulative patterns on convictions from ten to twenty years of age. Effective intervention had a significant impact and reduced patterns of offending. (Full details will appear in a subsequent report.) A chart is included here (see Figure 1).

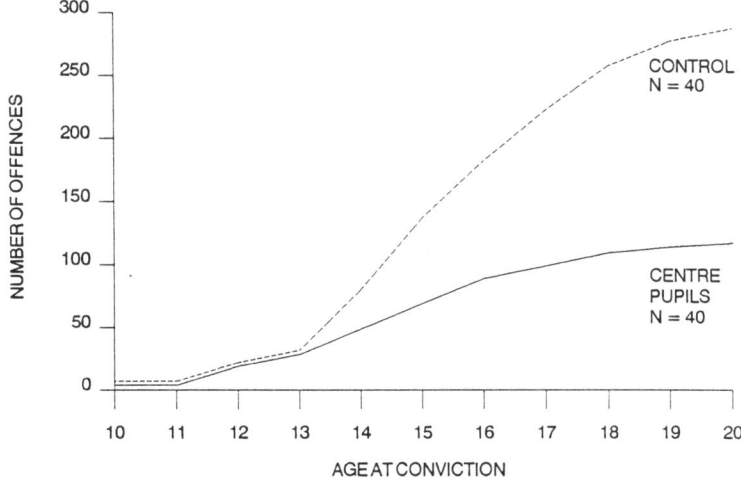

Figure 1: Number of Offences in Relation to Age at Conviction in Centre Pupils amd Controls.

The findings above are promising but such comparisons are difficult to make and the subject therefore requires a detailed report of its own. A further report is planned. However, the findings above remain; programs for change are viable even with groups of pupils written off as impossible.

Conclusion

A research based approach to dealing with behaviour problems and any extension to applications for dealing with delinquency is viable but must include the vital role of the school context. The approach described here has been used for individual, class and whole school approaches (Lane & Tattum, 1987).

Certain principles need to be applied, however, if the process by which an individual achieves or fails to achieve perceived objectives is to be made explicit. It is argued that:

- Problems may be multifaceted, they exist in a context, and they are amenable to understanding only in so far as that context is understood.
- A framework of formal analysis is necessary for understanding without preconceptions or 'explanatory fictions' in order that the unstated may be revealed and unused skills recognized.
- Understanding is not enough; it needs to be followed by agreement on objectives and intervention.
- Planned action must follow understanding, for without action there is no significant learning.
- Schools are dynamic, needs and resources change, consequently programs introduced to work with children must be evaluated and objectives periodically challenged and, if necessary, altered.

The delinquent child provides a challenge to the school. If the school can respond to that challenge and recognize it as part of its own construction and reconstruction, then more positive behaviour will be promoted.

References

Adams, F. (1986). *Special education.* Councils and Education Press. Longman Group.
Argyle, M. (1964). *Psychology and social problems.* London: Methuen.
Askew, S. (1988). Aggressive behaviour in boys: To what extent is it institutionalised? In D.P. Tattum, & D.A. Lane (Eds.), *Bullying in schools.* Stoke on Trent: Trentham Books.
Becker, H.S. (1963). *Outsiders: Studies in the sociology of deviance.* Glencoe: The Free Press.
Brown, M., & Madge, N. (1982). *Despite the welfare state.* London: Heinemann.
Burt, C. (1925). *The sub-normal school-child: 1. The young delinquent.* University of London: London Press.
Callias, M. (1992). Evaluations of interventions with children and adolescents. In D.A. Lane, & A. Miller (Eds.), *Handbook of child and adolescent therapy.* Milton Keynes: Open University Press.
Cattell, R.B., & Cattell, M.D.L. (1969). *Handbook for the high school personality Questionnaire.* IPAT Illinois.
Clarizo, H. (1968). Stability of deviant behaviour through time. *Mental Hygiene, 52,* 288-293.
Cloward, R.A., & Ohlin, L.E. (1961). *Delinquency and opportunity.* London: Routledge and Kegan Paul.
Cohen, A.K. (1955). *Delinquent boys: The culture of the gang.* New York: The Free Press.
Coulby, D., & Harper, T. (1983). *D.O.5. Schools Support Unit. Evaluation: Phase 2.* London: ILEA. (Published by Croom Helm, London)
Cunningham, C., & Davis, H. (1985). *Working with parents: Frameworks for collaboration.* Milton Keynes: Open University Press.
Dickinson, A. (1987). Animal conditioning and learning theory. In. H.J. Eysenck, & I. Martin (Eds.), *Theoretical foundation of behaviour therapy.* New York: Pergamon.
Eggleston, S.J., Dunn, D.K., & Ajjali, M. (1985). *The educational and vocational experiences of 15-18 year old young people of ethnic minority groups.* University of Keele: Department of Education.
Ellis, L. (1988). The victimful victimless crime distinction, and seven universal demographic correlates of victimful behaviour. *Personality and Individual Differences, 9,* 525-548.
Eysenck, H.J., & Eysenck, S.B.G. (1975). *The Eysenck Personality Questionnaire.* London: Hodder & Stoughton.
Eysenck, H.J., & Gudjonsson, G.H. (1989). *The causes and cures of criminality.* London: Plenum Press.
Fitzherbert, K. (1977). *Child care services and the teacher.* London: Temple Smith.
Galloway, D., Ball, T., Bloomfield, D., & Seyd, R. (1982). *Schools and disruptive pupils.* London: Longman.

Gensheimer, L.K., Mayer, J.P., Davidson, W.S., & Gottschalk, R. (1986). Diverting youth from the juvenile justice system. In S.J. Apter, & A.P.Goldstein (Eds.), *Youth violence*. New York: Pergamon Press.
Glueck, S., & Glueck, E. (1950). *Unraveling juvenile delinquency*. New York: Commonwealth Find.
Graham, J. (1988). *Disruptive behaviour and delinquency*. London: HMSO.
Green, F. (1980). *Becoming a truant*. Cranfield: Masters Thesis.
Hargreaves, D.H. (1967). *Social relations in a secondary school*. London: Routledge & Kegan Paul.
Hargreaves, D.H., Hester, S.K., & Mellor, F.J. (1975). *Deviance in classrooms*. London: Routledge & Kegan Paul.
Hersov, L., Berger, M., & Schaffer, D. (1978). *Aggression and antisocial behaviour in childhood and adolescence*. New York: Pergamon.
H.M.I. (1990). *Report on ILEA*. London: HMI.
Kazdin, A.E. (1988). *Child psychotherapy - developing and identifying effective treatments*. Oxford: Pergamon Press.
Lane, D.A. (1974). *The behavioural analysis of complex cases*. Conference Paper, IEGC, Islington.
Lane, D.A. (1976). *Persistent failure and potential success*. Research Monograph, IEGC, Islington.
Lane, D.A. (1978). *The impossible child*. Vols. 1 & 2. London: ILEA.
Lane, D.A. (1983). *Whatever happened to the impossible child?* London: ILEA.
Lane, D.A. (1988). Violent histories: bullying and criminality. In D.P.Tattum, & D.A. Lane (Eds.), *Bullying in schools*. Stoke on Trent: Trentham Books.
Lane, D.A. (1989). *Attributions, beliefs and constructs in counselling psychology*. Leicester: British Psychological Society.
Lane, D.A. (1990). *The impossible child*. Stoke on Trent: Trentham Books.
Lane, D.A., & Green, F. (1990). Partnerships with pupils. In M. Shearer, I. Gersch, & L. Fry (Eds.), *Meeting disruptive behaviour*. London: Macmillian.
Lane, D.A., & Miller, A. (1990). *Handbook of child and adolescent therapy*. Milton Keynes: Open University Press.
Lane, D.A., & Tattum, D.P. (1987). *Supporting the child in school*. London: Professional Development Foundation.
Mayer, J.P., Gensheimer, L.K., Davidson, W.S., & Gottschalk, R. (1986). Social learning treatment within juvenile justice. In S.J. Apter, & A.P. Goldstein (Eds.), *Youth violence*. New York: Pergamon Press.
Merton, R.K. (1951). *Social theory and social structure*. Glencoe, Ill.: Free Press.
Michaels, J.J. (1965). *Disorders of character*. Illinois: Thomas.
Mortimore, P., Sammons, P., Stoll, L., Lewis, D., & Ecob, R. (1988). *School matters: The junior years*. London: Open Books.
Musgrove, F. (1964). *Youth and the social order*. New York: Routledge & Kegan Paul.
Parker, H., Summer, M., & Jarvis, G. (1989). *Unmasking the magistrates*. Milton Keynes: Open University Press.
Partridge, J. (1966). *Life in a secondary modern school*. Harmondsworth: Penguin Books.
Power, M.S., Alderson, M.R., Phillipson, C.M., Shoenburg, E., & Morris, J.N. (1969). *Delinquent schools in crime, deviance and social sickness*. London: New Society Publications.
Quinn, P.O., & Rapaport, J.L. (1974). Minor physical anomalies and neurologic status in hyperactive boys. *Pediatrics, 53*, 742-747.
Reid, K. (1988). Bullying and persistent school absenteism. In D.P. Tattum, & D.A. Lane (Eds.) *Bullying in schools*. Stoke on Trent: Trentham.
Reynolds, D. (1982). 'A state of ignorance'. *Education for Development, 7*, 4-35.
Robbins, L.N. (1966). *Deviant children grown up*. Baltimore: Williams & Williams.
Roland, E. (1988). Bullying: The scandinavian research tradition. In D.P. Tattum, & D.A. Lane (Eds.), *Bullying in schools*. Stoke on Trent: Trentham.
Rutter, M., & Madge,N. (1976). *Cycles of disadvantage*. London: Heinemann.
Rutter, M., Maighan, B., Mortimore, P., & Ouston, J. (1979). *Fifteen thousand hours*. London: Open Books.

Scheff, T.J. (1966). *Being mentally ill: A sociological theory.* Chicago: Aldine.

Scheff, T.J., & Sundstorm, E. (1970). The stability of deviant behaviour over time: A reassessment. *Journal of Health and Social Behaviour, 11,* 37-43.

Shaw, C.R., & McKay, H.D. (1942). *Juvenile delinquency and urban areas.* Chicago: University of Chicago Press.

Stott, D.H., Marston, M.C., & Neill, S.J. (1975). *Taxonomy of behaviour disturbance.* London: London University Press.

Tattum, D.P. (1988). Violence and aggression in schools. In D.P. Tattum, & D.A. Lane (Eds.), *Bullying in schools.* Stoke on Trent: Trentham.

Tattum, D.P., & Lane, D.A. (1988). *Bullying in schools.* Stoke on Trent: Trentham.

Topping, K.J. (1983). *Educational systems for disruptive adolescents.* London: Croom Helm.

Trasher, G.B. (1964). Socialisation, a new approach. *Cambridge Opinion, 38,* 17-22.

Ullmann, L.P., & Krasner, L. (1975). *A psychological approach to abnormal behaviour.* New Jersey: Prentice Hall.

Volavka, J. (1987). Electroencephalogram among criminals. In S.A. Mednick, T.E. Moffit, & S.A. Stack (Eds.), *The causes of crime.* Cambridge: Cambridge University Press.

Warnock Report (1978). *Special educational needs. Report of the Committee of Enquiry into the Educational Needs of Children and Young People.* London: HMSO.

West, A., Davies, J., & Varlaam, A. (1986). The management of behaviour problems: A local authority response. In D.P. Tattum (Ed.), *Management of disruptive pupil behaviour in schools.* New York: John Wiley & Sons.

West, D.J. (1979). The distribution of young adult delinquency and other social problems in relation to early social deprivation and family background. In M. Brown, & N. Madge (Eds.), *Despite the welfare state: Studies in deprivation and disadvantage.* London: Heinemann Educational Books.

Willmott, P. (1958). *Adolescent boys in east london.* London. Routledge & Kegan Paul.

Yule, W. (1978). Behavioural treatment of children and adolescents with conduct disorders. In L. Hersov, M. Berger, & D. Shaffer (Eds.), *Aggression and anti-social behaviour in childhood and adolescence.* New York: Pergamon Press.

Some Things Do Work: Psychological Interventions With Offenders and the Effectiveness Debate

James McGuire and Philip Priestley

Introduction

Our starting point is this paper is the stark and widely-accepted statement that "Nothing works" as a means of treating offenders and of reducing rates of criminal recidivism. This conclusion emerged from systematic reviews of the penological treatment literature, conducted during the 1970s in response to the fundamental question: "What works?". In fact the question was asked, and attempts made to answer it, almost simultaneously by researchers and evaluators on both sides of the Atlantic; most notably by Martinson (1974; Lipton, Martinson, & Wilks, 1975) in the United States and by Brody (1976) in the United Kingdom. These authors and others embarked on the not inconsiderable task of surveying the sizeable quantities of work that had been done, and subjecting it to close methodological scrutiny. What they saw left them uniformly unimpressed. They found little of quality in the bulk of the research that had been undertaken. Flaws of sampling and design were common to many published studies; properly controlled experiments were rare; in many cases it simply was not possible to grasp exactly what had been the nature of the supposed intervention. Their disappointing conclusions, especially in the USA, were the subject of much controversy and heated public debate. They were also subsequently to have a pervasive influence on the mood of criminology and penology, and to lower the expectations of criminal justice policymakers; with repercussions that can still be felt today. Said Martinson (1974):

> It may be ... that there is a more radical flaw in our present strategies - that education at its best, or that psychotherapy at its best, cannot overcome, or even appreciably reduce, the powerful tendency for offenders to continue in criminal behaviour.

This viewpoint was echoed with corresponding resignation by Brody (1976):

> Reviewers of research into the effectiveness of different sentences or ways of treating or training offenders have unanimously agreed that the results so far offered little hope that a reliable and simple remedy for recidivism can be easily found ... studies which have produced positive results have been isolated, inconsistent in their evidence, and open to so much methodological criticism that they must remain unconvincing.

The notion that 'nothing' or 'almost nothing' works is a potentially very persuasive one and it has acquired the status almost of a doctrine (or at the very least became a deep-rooted assumption) undermining the very idea of 'rehabilitation'. It accords well with a cynical and dismissive orientation towards 'optimism' which is thoroughly entrenched in our culture. It fits neatly into a hard-headed view of the (admittedly pronounced) tendencies towards inertia and resistance to change often manifested by human beings. It was not long before the Martinson and Brody reviews were adopted virtually as key texts, signposting the way to a re-evaluation of whether any effort to change offenders' behaviour was worth making. As Bottoms and McWilliams (1979) remarked,

> ... all those who have responsibly reviewed the relevant literature ... have reached the same broad conclusion - that dramatic reformative results are hard to discover and are usually absent.

The goals and priorities of probation work, which represented the only form of contact with offenders that held out any real prospect of altering their behaviour, were substantially re-ordered by these authors. In case you should think that such views no longer hold sway in current thinking on this issue, consider the following more recent statements by other influential commentators like Smith and Blagg (1989):

> The work of Robert Martinson and his colleagues ... suggested, on the basis of a large-scale review of experimental evaluations of 'correctional treatment', that there were no grounds for preferring any one approach to any other: all produced equally bad results.

Or by Davies (1990):

> In the hey-day of therapeutic social work, some people no doubt presumed that probation officers could 'change behaviour' by techniques of social engineering, but two decades of disappointing research results in criminology and social work have made such claims of dubious legitimacy.

Such assertions have had far-reaching effects across the whole spectrum of activities in criminology and criminal justice. They affect the basic attitudes and practices of those who work face-to-face with offenders. They probably place tacit limitations on the availability of research funds for, say, intervention or comparative outcome studies. And they inform the thinking of those whose job it is to formulate policy, to make new laws particularly regarding the disposal and sentencing of offenders. An acceptance of negative conclusions concerning the possibility of behaviour change or of rehabilitation can thus have an extensive impact on how offenders are dealt with and what opportunities are offered them. The dangers of this situation are still more fully appreciated when we realize that the conclusions on which it rests are in themselves erroneous and misleading.

Criticism of the 'Nothing Works' Doctrine

Following on the work of Martinson, Brody and their associates by a gap of a few years, a variety of other workers re-assessed their arguments and reached conclusions quite opposite to theirs. For example Blackburn (1980) examined a series of studies carried out during the second half of the 1970s. He subjected them to a set of fairly rigorous methodological tests proposed by Logan (1972), in which studies were required to satisfy specified criteria as regards use of control groups, replicability of treatments, minimum two-year follow-up periods, and so on. Blackburn unearthed only five pieces of work which met these criteria in full. However, all five produced outcomes in which significant reductions in recidivism were obtained amongst treated as compared with untreated groups.

This is a far cry from the view that 'nothing works' and that criminal behaviour is not susceptible to change.

Similarly, Gendreau and Ross (1979) compiled a 'bibliotherapy for cynics', in the form of an edited volume of articles reporting positive findings in offender treatment. McGuire and Priestley (1985) assembled a sizeable list of studies in which promising outcomes had been obtained; and sought to challenge the (by then, widespread and firmly established) view that nothing constructive could be done to alter patterns of offence behaviour.

Equally damaging for the 'nothing works' position was a paper by Thornton (1987) in which he re-investigated a selection of the studies used by Martinson and his colleagues to derive their original (1974) conclusions. Contrary to what had been claimed by Lipton et al. (1975), a number of these projects had in fact described positive outcomes. Indeed, focussing on those studies which employed controlled experimental designs, a figure approaching 50 % of the studies had demonstrated a positive advantage for therapeutic intervention. In the remainder of the studies, no differences were detectable and in one, therapy yielded a net disadvantage. But as Thornton pointed out in the wake of this re-analysis, while many questions could still be asked about the exact nature of the gains secured, the one conclusion that was not permissible was that 'nothing works'.

But in any case, in parallel to these diverse criticisms and insistent raking over of the coals of the controversy, Martinson had himself acknowledged his own errors and had recanted the views he first expressed in 1974. On the basis of a fresh look at the empirical evidence, in 1979 he referred to his initial conclusion thus:

> On the basis of the evidence in our current study, I withdraw this conclusion. I have often said that treatment added to the networks of criminal justice is 'impotent', and I withdraw this characterization as well. I protested at the slogan used by the media to sum up what I said - 'nothing works'. The press has no time for scientific quibbling and got to the heart of the matter better than I did. But for all of that, the conclusion is not correct.

Yet despite this reversal, and the accumulation of further data some of which will be discussed below, the 'nothing works' principle continues to be the unspoken starting-point of much thinking on how we should set out to deal with offenders.

Positive Outcomes

In practice, there are numerous examples of research studies in which positive effects, in the form of reductions in re-offending rates, have been exhibited. It is true that not all of them have stood the test of replication with different subject samples, or that the methods utilized within them have proven adaptable to altered circumstances. This applies, for example, to the social casework study of Shaw (1974) in which significant reductions in recidivism were reported; which then failed to appear when the project was repeated in another prison setting (Fowles, 1978). In another vein, the work of Shore and Massimo (1979) using vocationally-oriented therapy can be faulted for small sample sizes, but the follow-up period of no less than fifteen years remains impressive nevertheless.

A particularly striking set of results was obtained recently from a study by Ross, Fabiano and Ewles (1988). These workers compared re-offence rates in three groups of high-risk offenders placed on probation. One group received 'regular' probation supervision; the second probation plus a 'life skills training' input; and the third was given both of these ingredients plus a course of cognitive training. A nine-month follow-up showed significant between-group differences; the respective recidivism figures for the three groups being 69.5 % (for the regular probation group), 47.5 % (probation plus life skills) and 18.1 % (probation, life skills and cognitive training). These are highly significant findings in every sense of the word, the more so because they illustrate the importance of applying a form of treatment in addition to the standard administration of a sentence or other type of post-adjudicative procedure.

Of course, the difficulty is that it is almost always possible to adduce some objection to a positive research finding. Quasi-experiments in real-world settings can seldom if ever have the elegance of laboratory research. But equally, a failure to recapture the same success rate on replication should not entail the dismissal of the original positive results. What is required is a close perusal of what it was that worked, why it has not done so a second time, and what can be learnt from undertaking the work yet again and examining another pattern of findings.

If a serial citation of successful outcomes remains insufficient proof that 'some things do work', let us turn instead to the findings of reviews that have employed the statistical technique of meta-analysis. A number of such papers have been published on the criminal justice field. They include such studies as those of Garrett (1985) which integrated findings from 111 studies involving a total of 13.055 subjects; more than eight thousand of them 'experimentals' and the remainder 'controls'. Although only a sub-set of the studies used recidivism as an outcome measure, the meta-analytic findings, while modest, were positive for this measure. On other measures results were considerably stronger.

A series of meta-analyses of delinquency outcome studies has been conducted by Davidson and his colleagues (Davidson, Gottschalk, Gensheimer, & Mayer, 1984; Gottschalk, Davidson, Gensheimer, & Mayer, 1987). These encompassed 90 research studies but in contrast to the Garrett review focussed not on institutional but on community-based programs for delinquents. Unfortunately, conflicting findings were obtained by the authors when their data were analyzed using different statistical methods, and their conclusions, though tentatively positive regarding recidivism, must be interpreted with caution. Far clearer, quite unambivalent and surely convincing findings have been reported at this conference from the meta-analysis by Lipsey (1990); and we hope that these will once and for all lay the suggestion that 'nothing works' to rest.

In the study by Garrett (1985) outlined above, treatment gains were particularly marked with interventions based on cognitive-behavioural therapies. This finding is congruent with a more recent meta-analytic report by Izzo and Ross (1990) which found a sharp contrast in overall effectiveness between programs with and without a 'cognitive' component. Izzo and Ross analyzed a batch of 46 studies and classified them according to their usage (or not) of procedures such as negotiation training; problem-solving; or cognitive-behaviour modification. Programs which did include these components showed a clear superiority in terms of outcome over those which did not. Taken in combination with Garrett's results and with those of Ross et al. (1988), these are powerful indicators of the potential efficacy of a package based upon the development of cognitive-behavioural problem-solving skills.

By and large, such findings surely take us a long way from the 'two decades of disappointing research results' alluded to by Davies (1990). They point instead to an affirmation of the possibility that offenders can be induced to change. Certainly, there are numerous questions that we still need to ask, and many refinements in treatment and training programs (as well as in research methodology) that still should be made. Nevertheless we are in possession of considerable evidence that 'some things work' of a more than just rudimentary kind; and we have at least some preliminary conceptions of what they are. We are surely in a position to reject the 'nothing works' view and endorse instead the declaration of Gendreau and Ross (1987):

> In summary, it is downright ridiculous to say 'Nothing works'. This review attests that much is going on to indicate that offender rehabilitation has been, can be, and will be achieved. The principles underlying effective rehabilitation generalize across far too many intervention strategies and offender samples to be dismissed as trivial.

What Does Work?

In attempting to narrow down the possibilities and obtain a sharper focus on what is most likely to be effective, we want to make some specific suggestions which derive from our own research with offenders in prisons and on probation in the United Kingdom. We undertook a study in which specially trained prison and probation staff were assigned to run courses for groups of offenders. For the prisoners, the courses were mounted in the period immediately prior to their release; for the probationers, they constituted an 'alternative to custody' package which they attended on a daily basis in a training center. The courses were intended to address a cluster of 'survival' and 'interpersonal' problems identified by prisoners in a survey; and included such difficulties as finding work or accommodation, managing money, securing rights, dealing with officialdom, and handling personal encounters. Our courses then, were designed to help the offenders deal more satisfactorily with these issues in their everyday lives.

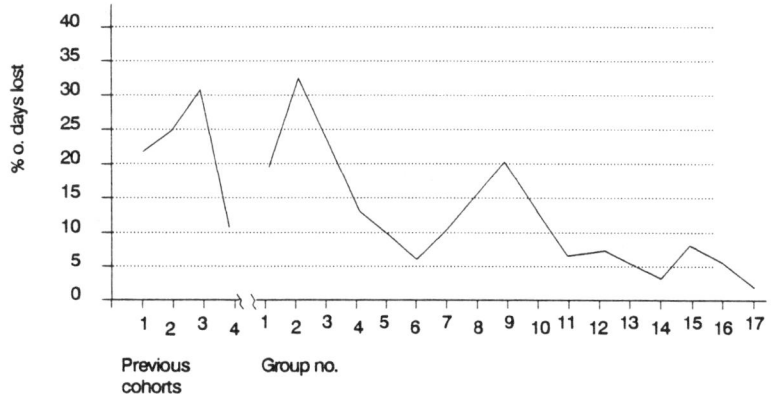

Figure 1: Unexplained Absence.

Our results implied that overall, the courses were extremely valuable in enabling offenders to achieve this goal. Their self-reports, the corroborative reports of probation officers, and subsequent work records all showed significant improvement as compared with control groups. Even the attendance at the Day Center, which at the outset of our research was very poor, increased dramatically over the 17 successive groups which we ran; as can be seen in Figure 1.

We could show a variety of results like that but we want instead to turn your attention to another final outcome of the study - the recidivism rates of our experimental and control groups. This is shown in Table 1 for the two prisons which took part in the study.

Table 1: Percentage Reconviction Rates.

Prison	Course members	Unsuccessful applicants	Non-applicants
Ashwell	23.0 (87)	31.4 (35)	26.3 (99)
Ranby	42.1 (114)	30.6 (36)	45.9 (98)

As can be seen, there is a small difference between treatments and controls but it did not reach statistical significance. The same finding emerges if you look at 24-month re-offence rates for our prison groups; these are depicted in Figure 2.

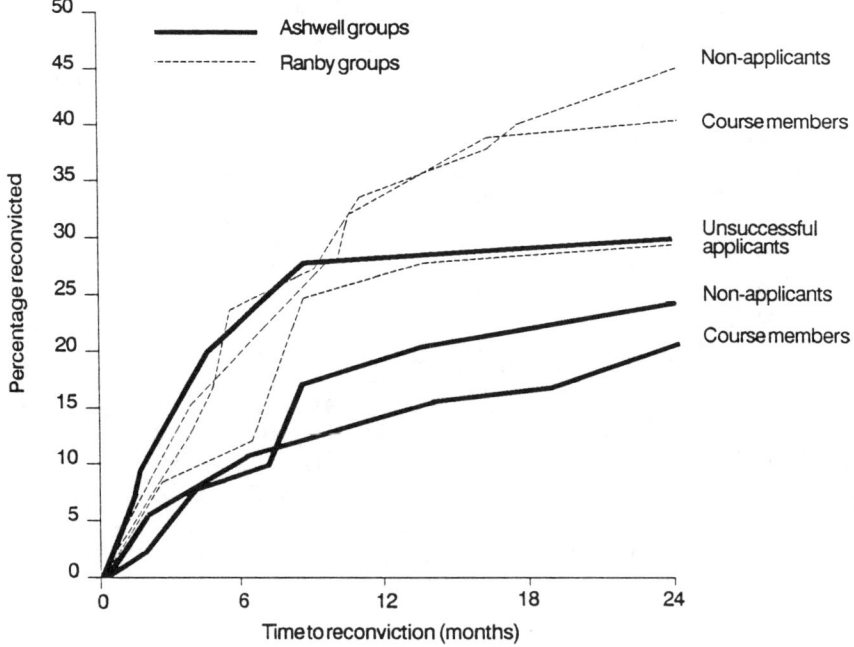

Figure 2: Percentage of Group Reconvicted Over Time.

For the probation groups, the difference was slightly larger but it too failed to reach statistical significance. In general, this is exactly the kind of finding which has been so common in criminology and on which the conclusions of the 'nothing works' school are based. Though our offenders were - on every index we could gather - happier by virtue of having been on the project, they were as likely to commit offences at the end as they had been at the beginning.

Except for one other finding we obtained: concerning violence. Some of the prison courses focussed upon this as the group members were personally concerned about it. When we examined their criminal records afterwards, we found they were significantly less likely to be re-convicted of a violent offence, as delineated in Figure 3.

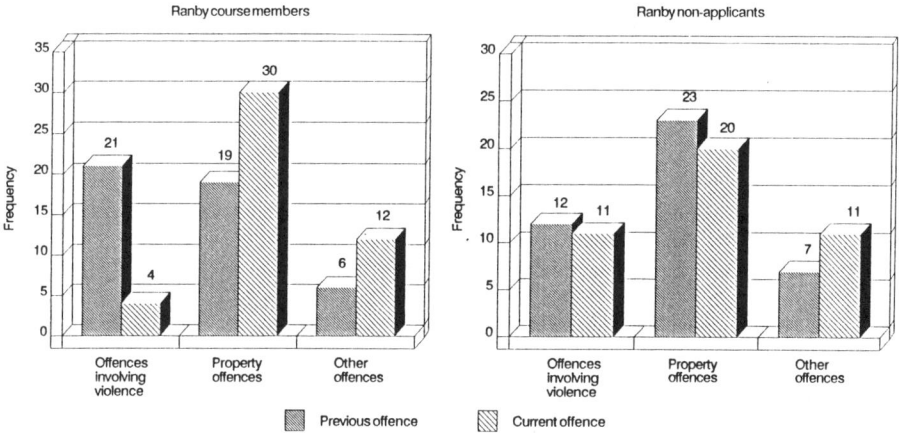

Note: Previous offences were those committed prior to the study. Current offences were those committed after release.

Figure 3: Comparison of Previous Offences with Current Offences for Men at Ranby who where Reconvicted.

What does this apparently odd pattern of findings suggest? For us, it points to a very simple and straightforward possibility concerning the reduction of offence-proneness. If you wish to change a particular aspect of someone's behaviour, you need to focus on that target behaviour and attempt to alter it directly. We know from the training literature how important this is but we rarely seem to apply it when contemplating offending behaviour. Because we had an implicit theory - that crime (and the sociology textbooks support this) is correlated with unemployment, housing problems, personal inadequacies and the like, we envisaged that solving those problems would automatically solve the offending problem too. On the contrary, the lesson from this research seems clear: if you want to change offending behaviour, you must concentrate on it and on delivering strategies which the individual can use to make such change more likely.

Results of Offence-Focussed Work

When we return to the research literature and interrogate it in terms of the question: 'What are the outcomes of studies in which aspects of offence behaviour have been targets?', we find a veritable plethora of positive and encouraging results. They cover a broad span in respect of target behaviours; which may include resisting group pressure, negotiating conflicts within families, handling encounters with the police, or securing self-control of angry and aggressive behaviour. All of these are features of behaviour known to be closely linked with criminal acts of various sorts. They also differ widely in terms of the type of treatment or training used: for example social skills training, relaxation, systematic desensitization, contingency contracts, stimulus satiation, role-reversal, cognitive-behavioural programs, stress inoculation, and moral education, have all elicited changes in constituents associated with an overall target of offending behaviour. The research methodologies include experimental group-comparisons and single-case designs; the subjects range from juvenile first-offenders to adults with lengthy criminal records.

(1) Positive results using social skills training and allied methods have been reported by Chandler (1973), Klein, Alexander, and Parsons (1977), Rice and Chaplin (1979) and Sarason (1978). Chandler for example used a series of role-reversal exercises with groups of young offenders whom he had shown to be 'ego-centric'. The role-reversal procedure greatly enhanced their perspective-taking skills in inter-personal situations; but in addition, their recidivism at 18-month follow up was significantly lower than that of a matched control group. For these juveniles, 'ego-centrism' as a frame of mind was associated with offence behaviour.

More dramatically still, Klein et al. (1977) undertook a controlled study of the effect of behavioural family therapy with the families of young delinquents. Poor parent-child communication and high levels of inter-generational conflict are features frequently conjoined with delinquency-proneness. The intervention consisted of a family-based 'negotiation skills' package, which had highly significant effects not only on the frequency of disruption in the families, but also on the recidivism rates of their teenage members. Other groups of families on comparison programs of psychodynamic and client-centered therapies showed no such change.

(2) A large number of studies have demonstrated the capacity of social skills training techniques for modification of specific offence-related behaviours. For instance, assertion training has been used to reduce frequencies of aggressive outbursts and explosive rages (Foy et al., 1975; Frederiksen et al., 1976; Rahaim et al., 1980; Rimm et al, 1974). SST has also been effective as a method of helping sex offenders learn more appropriate means of handling encounters with the opposite sex (e.g., Crawford & Allen, 1979; Daniel, 1987a). Needless to say, this is only one dimension of sex offender treatment, and we would not venture to suggest that this alone will prevent re-offending. However, it is likely to prove an essential component of any comprehensive program designed to lower sexual dangerousness.

(3) Relaxation and desensitization methods, drawn from the traditional behaviour-therapy manuals, have proven valuable in helping individuals control a variety of target behaviours linked to offensiveness. A number of single-case studies have shown their efficacy with individuals convicted of sexual exhibitionism (Bond & Hutchinson, 1960; Wickramasekera, 1968) and of chronic stealing (Marzagao, 1972). In some of these cases, the offending behaviour was closely associated with high and uncontrolled levels of anxiety which precipitated it. In others, a hierarchy of situations was devised in which offenders felt progressively greater compulsion to expose themselves.

But it is in the areas of alcohol abuse and aggressiveness that these methods show their massive potential. Given that studies have shown desensitization can be a suitable treatment for alcohol problems (which, it need hardly be added, are a precursor of many types of offence), it is puzzling that there are so few attempts to explore this avenue more systematically (Hedberg & Campbell, 1974; Lanyon et al., 1972). In relation to violence, positive outcomes for reduction have been obtained in several studies dealing with general aggressiveness; racial tension and hostility; and aggression at the wheel of a car (Evans & Hearn, 1973; Hazaleus & Deffenbacher, 1986; O'Donnell & Worrall, 1973; Rimm, de Groot, Boord, Heiman, & Dillow, 1971).

(4) The cognitive-behavioural approaches are now firmly fixed in the treatment repertoires of many clinical psychologists and have been applied to a considerable assortment of problems. Their principal application with offenders to date has been in the area of anger and aggression control. The pioneering work of Novaco (1975, 1977, 1980) showed that individuals could learn tactics for controlling severe and highly damaging outburst of anger. Other researchers following in his wake have extended his methods and target groups to include abusive and assaultive parents (Denicola & Sandler, 1980; Nomellini & Katz, 1983); adolescent psychiatric patients (Feindler et al., 1986; Kolko et al., 1981); prisoners (McDougall, Barnett, Ashurst, & Willis, 1987); and forensic patients (Stermac, 1987). There are now well-researched anger management packages for young offenders using combinations of skills-training and stress-inoculation techniques (Feindler & Ecton, 1986; Goldstein et al., 1989).

(5) Finally, a tantalizing diversity of approaches has been shown, in a range of recent studies, to hold out further potential for development in offence-focussed work. They include stimulus satiation, which reduced the arsonistic tendencies of a young firesetter (Daniel, 1987b); covert sensitization, which had a beneficial effect in decreasing sexual fantasy in a man convicted of sexual molestation of children (Harbert et al., 1974); and the use of a structured role-reversal procedure to modify anti-social attitudes in young offenders with convictions for football violence (McDougall, Thomas, & Wilson, 1987). Opening up a quite separate vista of possibilities, a number of studies have shown how specially constructed moral dilemmas can increase the moral reasoning and developmental levels of pre-delinquents (Arbuthnot & Gordon, 1986; Gibbs et al., 1984; Rosenkoetter et al., 1980). Quite clearly, there is no shortage of ideas on which to build!

But Have We Learned Anything?

It is our hope that the above discussion will have sealed the fate of the ill-founded belief that 'nothing works'. We hope in addition that it may have highlighted the importance of a focus on the offence in any attempt to reduce rates of criminal recidivism; and may have drawn attention to some directions in which the search for effectiveness might proceed. Yet paradoxically, in spite of the breadth of the possibilities now available, the process of dealing with offenders in most countries still resides in a comparative 'treatment' vacuum. Sentencing rarely addresses the root causes of offence behaviour or prescribes, in conjunction with offenders, how they might be given assistance towards behaviour change.

In the United Kingdom, we are poised to embrace a new set of criminal justice measures which sees punishment as the central mechanism for bringing about change in offenders. The possibility of engaging in work on offence behaviour is allowed; but on a more or less coercive principle, which is likely to detract from the chances of success of whatever methods are actually employed. Denunciation of and retribution for the crime are still seen as the prime objectives of a criminal justice policy; and rehabilitation of the offender still comes a poor third or fourth place in the British government's proclaimed agenda of goals (Home Office, 1990). We wonder whether this is the position in other European countries. Is there any criminal justice system which has addressed the fact that existing dimensions of sentencing practice, and methods of changing offenders, are orthogonal to each other? Have we made any real progress towards placing our responses to crime on a rational and scientific foundation?

References

Arbuthnot, J., & Gordon, D.A. (1986). Behavioural and cognitive effects of a moral reasoning development intervention for high-risk behavior-disordered adolescents. *Journal of Consulting and Clinical Psychology, 54*, 208-216.

Blackburn, R. (1980). *Still not working? A look at some recent outcomes in offender rehabilitation.* Paper presented at the Scottish Branch of the British Psychological Society conference on 'Deviance', University of Stirling.

Bond, I.K., & Hutchinson, H.C. (1960). Application of reciprocal inhibition therapy to exhibitionism. *Canadian Medical Association Journal, 83*, 23-25.

Bottoms, A.E., & McWilliams, W. (1979). A non-treatment paradigm for probation practice. *British Journal of Social Work, 9*, 159-202.

Brody, S. (1976). *The effectiveness of sentencing.* London: HMSO.

Chandler, M.J. (1973). Egocentrism and anti-social behaviour: The assessment and training of social perspective-taking skills. *Developmental Psychology, 9*, 326-332.

Crawford, D.A., & Allen, J.V. (1979). A social skills training programme with sex offenders. In M. Cook, & G. Wilson (Eds.), *Love and attraction.* Oxford: Pergamon.

Daniel, C.J. (1987a). Shame aversion therapy and social skills training with an indecent exposer. In B.J. McGurk, D.M. Thornton, & M. Williams (Eds.), *Applying psychology to imprisonment: Theory & practice.* London: HMSO.

Daniel, C.J. (1987b). A stimulus satiation treatment programme with a young male firesetter. In: B.J. McGurk, D.M. Thornton, & M. Williams (Eds.), *Applying psychology to imprisonment: Theory & practice.* London: HMSO.

Davidson, W.S., Gottschalk, L., Gensheimer, L., & Mayer, J. (1984). *Interventions with juvenile delinquents: A meta-analysis of treatment efficacy.* Washington, D.C.: National Institute of Juvenile Justice and Delinquency Prevention.

Davies, M. (1990). Balance between court and client. *Community Care, 25 January*, 16-17.

Denicola, J., & Sandler, J. (1980). Training abusive parents in child management and self-control skills. *Behavior Therapy, 11*, 263-270.

Evans, D.R., & Hearn, M.T. (1973). Anger and systematic desensitization: A follow-up. *Psychological Reports, 32*, 569-570.

Feindler, E.L., & Ecton, R.B. (1986). *Adolescent anger control: Cognitive-behavioral techniques.* Oxford: Pergamon Press.

Feindler, E.L., Ecton, R.B., Kingsley, D., & Dubey, D.R. (1986). Group anger-control training for institutionalized psychiatric male adolescents. *Behavior Therapy, 17*, 109-123.

Fowles, A.J. (1978). *Prison welfare: An account of an experiment at Liverpool.* Home Office Research Study No. 45. London: HMSO.

Foy, D.W., Eisler, R.M., & Pinkston, S. (1975). Modeled assertion in a case of explosive rages. *Journal of Behavior Therapy and Experimental Psychiatry, 6*, 135-138.

Frederiksen, L.W., Jenkins, J.O., Foy, D.W., & Eisler, R.M. (1976). Social skills training to modify abusive verbal outbursts in adults. *Journal of Applied Behavior Analysis, 9*, 117-125.

Garrett, C.J. (1985). Effects of residential treatment on adjudicated delinquents: A meta-analysis. *Journal of Research in Crime and Delinquency, 22,* 287-308.

Gendreau, P., & Ross, R.R. (1979). Effective correlation treatment: Bibliotherapy for cynics. In R.R. Ross, & P. Gendreau (Eds.), *Effective correctional treatment.* Toronto: Butterworths.

Gendreau, P., & Ross, R.R. (1987). Revivification of rehabilitation: Evidence from the 1980s. *Justice Quarterly, 4,* 349-407.

Gibbs, J.C., Arnold, K.D., Ahlborn, H.H., & Cheesman, F.L. (1984). Facilitation of sociomoral reasoning in delinquents. *Journal of Consulting and Clinical Psychology, 52,* 37-45.

Goldstein, A.P., Glick, B., Irwin, M.J., Pask-McCartney, C., & Rubama, I. (1989). *Reducing delinquency: Intervention in the community.* Oxford: Pergamon.

Gottschalk, R., Davidson, W.S., Mayer, J., & Gensheimer, L.H. (1987). Behavioral approaches with juvenile offenders: A meta-analysis of long-term treatment efficacy. In E.K. Morris, & C.J. Braukmann (Eds.), *Behavioral approaches to crime and delinquency.* New York: Plenum.

Harbert, T.L., Barlow, D.H., Hersen, M., & Austin, J.B. (1974). Measurement and modification of incestuous behavior: A case study. *Psychological Reports, 34,* 79-86.

Hazaleus, S.L., & Deffenbacher, J.L. (1986). Relaxation and cognitive treatments of anger. *Journal of Consulting and Clinical Psychology, 54,* 222-226.

Hedberg, A.G., & Campbell, L. (1974). A comparison of four behavioural treatments of alcoholism. *Journal of Behavior Therapy and Experimental Psychiatry, 5,* 251-256.

Home Office (1990). *Crime, justice and protecting the public.* Gmn 965. London: HMSO.

Izzo, R.L., & Ross, R.R. (1990). Meta-analysis of rehabilitation programmes for juvenile delinquents. *Criminal Justice and Behaviour, 17* 134-142.

Klein, N.C., Alexander, J.F., & Parsons, B.V. (1977). Impact of family systems intervention on recidivism and sibling delinquency: A model of primary prevention and program evaluation. *Journal of Consulting and Clinical Psychology, 45,* 469-474.

Kolko, D.J., Dorsett, P.G., & Milan, M.A. (1981). A total-assessment approach to the evaluation of social skills training: The effectiveness of an anger control program for adolescent psychiatric patients. *Behavioral Assessment, 3,* 383-402.

Lanyon, R.I., Primo, R.V., Terrell, F., & Wener, A. (1972). An aversion-desensitization treatment for alcoholism. *Journal of Consulting and Clinical Psychology, 38,* 394-398.

Lipton, D., Martinson, R., & Wilks, J. (1975). *The effectiveness of correctional treatment: A survey of treatment evaluation studies.* New York: Praeger.

Lipsey, M.W. (1990). *The effects of treatment on juvenile delinquents: Results from meta-analysis.* Paper presented at the 2nd European Conference on Law and Psychology, Universität Erlangen-Nürnberg, Germany.

Logan, C.H. (1972). Evaluation research in crime and delinquency: A reappraisal. *Journal of Criminal Law, Criminology and Police Science, 63,* 378-387.

Martinson, R. (1974). What works? Questions and answers about prison reform. *The Public Interest, 10,* 22-54.

Martinson, R. (1979). New findings, new views: A note of caution regarding sentencing reform. *Hofstra Law Review, 7,* 243-258.

Marzagao, L.R. (1972). Systematic desensitization treatment of kleptomania. *Journal of Behavior Therapy and Experimental Psychiatry, 3,* 327-328.

McDougall, C., Barnett, R.M., Ashurst, B., & Willis, B. (1987). Cognitive control of anger. In: B.J. McGurk, D.M. Thornton, & M. Williams (Eds.), *Applying psychology to imprisonment: Theory & practice.* London: HMSO.

McDougall, C., Thomas, M., & Wilson, J. (1987). Attitude change and the violent football supporter. In: B.J. McGurk, D.M. Thornton, & M. Williams (Eds.), *Applying psychology to imprisonment: Theory & practice.* London: HMSO.

McGuire, J., & Priestley, P. (1985). *Offending behaviour: Skills and stratagems for going straight.* London: Batsford.

Nomellini, S., & Katz, R.C. (1983). Effects of anger control training on abusive parents. *Cognitive Research and Therapy, 7,* 57-68.

Novaco, R.W. (1975). *Anger control: The development and evaluation of an experimental treatment.* Lexington, Mass.: D.C. Heath & Co.

Novaco, R.W. (1977). A stress inoculation approach to anger management in the training of law enforcement officers. *American Journal of Community Psychology, 5,* 327-346.

Novaco, R.W. (1980). Training of probation counselors for anger problems. *Journal of Counseling Psychology, 27,* 385-390.

O'Donnell, C.R., & Worell, L. (1973). Motor and cognitive relaxation in the desensitization of anger. *Behavior Research and Therapy, 11,* 473-481.

Priestley, P., McGuire, J., Flegg, D., Hemsley, V., Welham, D., & Barnitt, R. (1984). *Social skills in prison and the community: Problem-solving for offenders.* London: Routledge.

Rahaim, S., Lefebvre, C., & Jenkins, J.O. (1980). The effects of social skills training on behavioral and cognitive components of anger management. *Journal of Behavior Therapy and Experimental Psychiatry, 11,* 3-8.

Rice, M.E., & Chaplin, T.C. (1979). Social skills training for hospitalised male arsonists. *Journal of Behaviour Therapy and Experimental Psychiatry, 10,* 105-108.

Rimm, D.C., de Groot, J.C., Boord, P., Heiman, J., & Dillow, P.V. (1971). Systematic desensitization of an anger response. *Behaviour Research and Therapy, 9,* 273-280.

Rimm, D.C., Hill, G.A., Brown, N.N., & Stuart, J.E. (1974). Group-assertive training in treatment of expression of inappropriate anger. *Psychological Reports, 34,* 791-798.

Rosenkoetter, L.I., Landman, S., & Mazak, S.G. (1980). The use of moral discussion as an intervention with delinquents. *Psychological Reports, 16,* 91-94.

Ross, R.R., Fabiano, E.A., & Ewles, C.D. (1988). Reasoning and rehabilitation. *International Journal of Offender Therapy and Comparative Criminology, 20,* 165-173.

Sarason, I.G. (1978). A cognitive social learning approach to juvenile delinquency. In R.D. Hare, & D. Schalling (Eds.), *Psychopathic behavior: Approaches to research.* New York: Wiley.

Shaw, M. (1974). *Social work in prison: An experiment in the use of extended contact with offenders.* Home Office Research Study No. 22. London: HMSO.

Shore, M.F., & Massimo, J.L. (1979). Fifteen years after treatment: A follow-up study of comprehensive vocationally-oriented psychotherapy. *American Journal of Orthopsychiatry, 49,* 240-245.

Smith, D., & Blagg, H. (1989). *Crime, penal policy and social work.* London: Longman.

Stermac, L.E. (1987). Anger control treatment for forensic patients. *Journal of Interpersonal Violence, 1,* 446-457.

Thornton, D.M. (1987). Treatment effects on recidivism: A reappraisal of the 'Nothing Works' doctrine. In B.J. McGurk, D.M. Thornton, & M. Williams (Eds.), *Applying psychology to imprisonment: Theory & practice.* London: HMSO.

Wickramasekera, I. (1968). The application of learning theory to the treatment of a case of sexual exhibitionism. *Psychotherapy: Theory, Research, and Practice, 5,* 108-112.

Therapy Versus Penalty: An Evaluation Study

Rudolf Egg

Introduction

This report deals with drug addiction, a central and quite difficult area of deviance. Currently, different strategies and campaigns are being launched all over the world in attempts to cope with this problem. These various forms of drug policy can be divided roughly into three different groups (Kreuzer, 1987, pp. 98-103).

1. *The repressive or punitive approach.* This approach comprises the threat and application of control measures and punitive measures by police and justice. By establishing and carrying out respective prohibitions of drug use, drug dealing, drug production, and so forth, the aim is to prevent or at least limit the spread and consumption of illegal drugs.

2. *The liberal or permissive approach.* To a certain degree, this approach favors the opposite path, that is, the decriminalization or legalization of drug usage. Even though this can be based on different arguments, supporters of this approach generally intend to partially or totally tolerate minor drug usage in order to prevent worse, that is, especially the international drug market.

3. *The therapeutic approach.* Beyond the question of the liability to punishment for drug usage, this approach stresses treatment measures and offers assistance to drug users as well as their partners and relatives. Measures applied in this context are aimed toward rehabilitation and therapy or also prevention and counseling.

None of these three approaches in drug policy are applied in a pure version. Usually, we find mixed forms that stress different aspects (see Heckmann 1987, p. 257). This is also the case in the Federal Republic of Germany, where the last reform of the Narcotic Drugs Act (Betäubungsmittelgesetz) in 1982 set a new accentuation for national drug policy (see Körner, 1990).

On the one hand, the possibilities of punishing drug offenders (especially drug dealers) were reestablished and made more severe (hereby stressing the repressive approach). On the other hand, there was also a minimal extension of the liberal approach providing the possibility to refrain from penalty in cases in which illicit drugs are only used for private consumption.

Of special importance, however, is the implementation of several new laws for drug addicted offenders. The intent of these regulations is to enable a greater number of persons to undergo therapy.

Such therapies have been possible before; either (a) in the case of suspension of sentence or suspension of the remaining sentence (probation or parole), or (b) in the case of a special "mandatory treatment" based on a judicial directive (Maßregelvollzug).

As both regulations are only applicable for a respectively limited number of persons, new judicial ways for a referral to therapy were provided. Although therapy should not replace penalty, a pronounced sentence should not stand in the way of therapy.

The Deferment Regulation

The focus of the new judicial regulation is the so-called *deferment of execution of sentence*. In the following, this will be called the deferment regulation. This enables the law enforcement authority to defer a prison sentence in favor of therapy. Prerequisite is that the term of imprisonment does not exceed two years and that the offense committed was based on a drug addiction, no matter what offense it was.

The deferment actually means that the convicted person will be released from prison in order to participate in the program of a therapeutic community. The time spent in therapy will be - at least partially - credited to the penalty. The last third of the prison sentence will be suspended on probation - provided therapy was successful.

Although no special prognosis of success is necessary for the granting of this deferment, the formal setting of the therapy, that is, start, course, financing, and so forth, must be ensured. In cases in which the convicted person breaks off therapy or is released prematurely, deferment is revoked if treatment is not continued in another institution. This revocation means a return to prison. Another deferment, that is, a second therapy attempt, is also possible afterwards. Often drug addicts need several therapy attempts before a lasting treatment can be carried out.

This deferment regulation - sometimes called "therapy instead of penalty" - requires the cooperation of very different persons and institutions. A special problem here is the cooperation between the representatives of justice and the therapy representatives (see Hellebrand, 1990, pp. 120-123).

In view of this complex situation, it is not surprising that these regulations have been the subject of numerous controversial discussions since their introduction. The fundamental rejection of any form of legally induced or controlled treatment is referred to; more often, however, special questions concerning the execution of deferment and therapy are criticized (see for a summary, Böllinger, 1987, pp. 145-150; Kreuzer cited in Kreuzer & Wille, 1988, pp. 109-118; Roloff, 1985; Scheerer, 1982).

By way of contrast to these manifold critical statements, the empirical-scientific analysis of the deferment regulation has remained limited to only very few aspects that have not provided enough data for a comprehensive evaluation. Official federal government statistics certify that the application of deferment has increased substantially since 1982 and recently involved about 1,600 persons per year. In many cases, however, therapy was broken off and the decision revoked. A recently published study carried out in two therapy institutions shows, however, that persons who went into therapy by means of a legal provision more often complete treatment than so-called voluntary clients (see Vollmer & Ellgring, 1988).

The KrimZ Research Project

The research project of the Central Institute of Criminology (KrimZ) in Wiesbaden, a documentation and research institution of the Federal Republic and the Federal States, is investigating questions concerning the practical application of the deferment regulation. The following data sources are being evaluated in several stages (see Egg, in press):

1. Entries in the Federal Central Criminal Register, which contains all imposed fines and prison sentences as well as (in cases of prison sentences) indications on the execution of sentence and settlement.

2. Criminal files kept by the public prosecution.

3. Replies to a written survey of more than 100 therapy institutions throughout the Federal Republic of Germany (see Egg & Kurze, 1989).

4. Written and verbal interviews with judges and public prosecutors from four different federal states.

This paper is limited to some results from the first two data sources.

The investigation started with the total population of those persons who in one special year - 1984 - were sentenced to prison and then, by means of a deferment, could claim "therapy instead of penalty." This was a total of 862 persons, 721 (83.6%) males and 141 (16.4%) females. At the time of the verdict, the average age of the convicts was 26.6 years ($s=3.98$) and ranged from 15 to 46 years. Convictions concerned "pure" drug offenses (possession, dealing, burglary, production of illegal drugs) in 68%, drug offenses and other offenses (theft, forgery, fraud, etc.) in 17%, and exclusively other offenses in 15%.

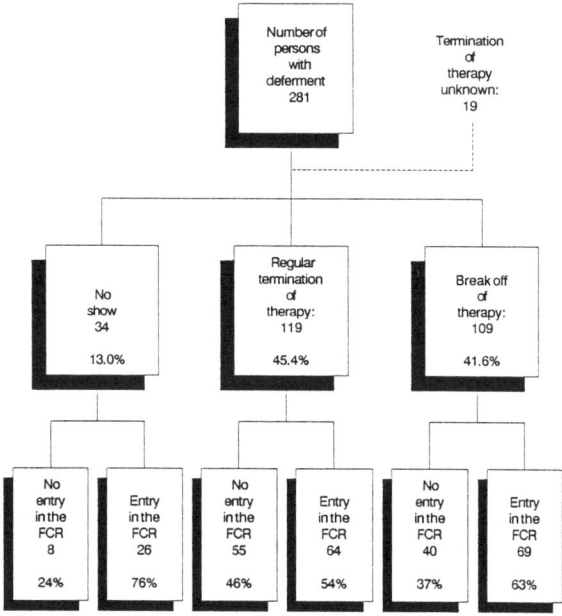

Figure 1: Termination of Therapy (1st Therapy) and Entry in the Federal Central Criminal Register (FCR).

Prison sentences varied between 2 months and just under 5 years, with an average penalty of between 15 and 18 months (according to age group and gender).

For a random sample of about 300 persons we examined the entries in the Federal Central Criminal Register at the beginning of 1990 in order to (a) follow the settlement of the verdicts from 1984, and (b) register possible new entries (recidivism).

Information about therapy course obtained from criminal files is presented in Figure 1.

About 45% of the persons with a deferment terminated their therapy on a regular basis, that is, at the time scheduled. The remaining persons were either released early or dropped out of treatment themselves (41.6%) or did not even start the therapy available to them (13%). In these two groups deferment was generally revoked; the convicts had to go back to prison. About 30% of them, not presented in Figure 1, later received a second deferment and started a second therapy. In these cases there were also numerous dropouts and revocations, so that altogether about 50% of the entire group achieved a regular therapy end. To simplify matters, only the first therapy will be considered in the following.

The recidivism in our sample is recorded by new entries in the Criminal Register. The relevant follow-up interval in this investigation was fixed at a maximum of 3 years since the beginning of the therapy. For the total sample, there were new convictions in about 60% of cases (172 out of 281). This is a relatively high percentage, which demonstrates the problematic nature, that is, the high incrimination, of this group.

A comparison between the different groups shows a slightly lesser recidivism rate in the therapy group. This difference becomes larger when we also look at the number and severeness of the new entries (see Table 1).

Table 1: Therapy Termination and Number of New Entries in the Criminal Register (follow up interval: 3 years after therapy start).

	No entry	1 entry	2 entries	3 entries	4 or 5 entries
Scheduled/successful termination of therapy (N=119)	46%	32%	13%	6%	3%
Break off/disciplinary release from therapy (N=109)	37%	33%	21%	7%	2%
No show to therapy (N=34)	24%	32%	26%	15%	3%

While about one-third of all persons received a new entry, the portion of those who received two or more entries in the Criminal Register was clearly higher in the two groups without (a terminated) therapy than in the therapy group, 44% and 30% compared to 22%.

By the way, only about 40% of the offenses that led to this first entry were drug offenses, the remaining 60% were thefts and offenses against property, but also traffic offenses. In this context no essential differences could be found between the various groups (with and without therapy termination). This is a further indication that the group we investigated was more highly incriminated - even outside the area of "pure" drug offenses.

What are the penalties for these new convictions? To answer this question, one must look at the first entry in the Criminal Register (see Figure 2).

Fines and sentences suspended on probation dominated in the group with regular therapy termination. In the dropout group more than one-half of all new first entries referred to sentences without probation, that is, quite severe sanctions.

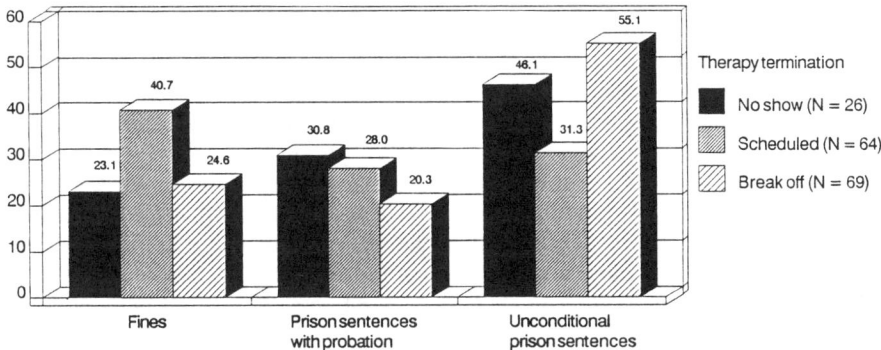

Figure 2: Type of Sanction (1st entry) and Type of Therapy Termination.

This figure is confirmed if we take into consideration all new entries in the Criminal Register and if we differentiate according to the kind of the respective severest sanction (see Table 2).

Table 2: Therapy Termination and Severest Sanctioning in the Follow up Interval.

	No entry	Fine	Prison sentence with probation	Unconditional prison sentence
Scheduled/successful termination of therapy (N=119)	46%	15%	16%	23%
Break off/disciplinary release from therapy (N=109)	37%	10%	16%	38%
No show to therapy (N=34)	24%	6%	26%	44%

Only half of those who underwent a complete treatment program, by means of a referral from prison to therapy, remained unpunished in the first three years after the start of therapy. However, the remaining half was also less often convicted to severe sentences compared to the other two groups (break offs, refusals). No comparable trend could be seen for the length of the prison sentences, at least not when all offenses were considered. The average sanction of all prison sentences and prison sentences for juveniles (median) amounted to about 12 months, ranging from 1 month to 7 years.

In contrast, another difference in favor of the therapy group could be seen for penalties imposed for theft: While fines or sentences suspended on probation were mostly imposed on the therapy group, the opposite was true for the two comparison groups: Here unconditional prison sentences were dominant. However, this was not found in cases of new convictions because of violations against the Narcotic Drugs Act (drug offenses). This indicated that the dropout and no show group demonstrated more deviant behavior than the therapy group, especially in the area of general criminality.

Conclusion

The main results of the parts of the investigation presented here are that the sample of people who received the chance to be referred from prison to therapy can be subdivided into three groups: a therapy group (regular therapy termination, 45.4%), therapy dropouts (41.6%); and a group who never start/refuse therapy (no show, 13.0%).

After an investigation interval of 3 years (after the start of the therapy), a relatively high proportion of newly committed offenses and convictions is found in the criminal register for all three groups. A comparative analysis of different criteria for recidivism shows, in some aspects, more favorable results for the therapy group.

Undergoing a therapy in the context of these legal possibilities does not guarantee a future life free of offenses, but, in many cases, it seems to offer more favorable chances for a new start than an unfinished therapy or no therapy at all.

These results are comparable to data on the legally conducted or induced treatment of criminal offenders collected in other areas (see Lösel et al., 1987). The results of these efforts are not characterized by "nothing works" as sometimes claimed, but they also do not give reason for an exaggerated optimism regarding the long-term effects of such therapy facilities.

In further steps we will analyze the results in more detail and, for example, investigate whether any differences can be found between various subgroups (e.g., age, gender) of all different therapy forms.

Should the trends presented here be confirmed, this could be valuable evidence that the so-called deferment regulation really provides many drug addicts with an opportunity to develop a way of life free of drugs and without offenses.

Even in the most favorable case, this form of therapy referral, however, cannot be considered as the royal road of treating drug addicts. One must bear in mind that a referral always requires long-term prison sentence. We still do not know how to help all those for whom these regulations are not apt - maybe because they do not want to be confronted with a therapy initiated and designed in such a way. This issue requires not only more fantasy and insight on the part of the jurisdiction and the administration of justice but also more flexibility and creativity in drug therapy itself.

References

Böllinger, L. (1987). *Drogenrecht, Drogentherapie*, 2nd ed. (Materialien zur Sozialarbeit und Sozialpolitik, Bd. 12). Frankfurt am Main: Fachhochschule.

Egg. R. (in press). Criminal law and the therapy of drug addicts. In G. Bühringer & J.J. Platt (Eds.), *Drug addiction and AIDS research: American and German perspectives*. Malabar, FL: R.E. Krieger.

Egg, R., & Kurze M. (1989). *Drogentherapie in staatlich anerkannten Einrichtungen - Ergebnisse einer Umfrage*. Wiesbaden: Kriminologische Zentralstelle.

Heckmann, W. (1987). Drogenpolitik in der Bundesrepublik aus therapeutischer Sicht. *Bewährungshilfe, 34*, 254-263.

Hellebrand, J. (1990). *Drogen und Justiz - Überlegungen zur Einbindung der Justiz in eine fortschrittliche Drogenpolitik*. Bonn: Forum.

Körner, H.H. (1990). *Betäubungsmittelgesetz*, 3rd ed. Munich: Beck.

Kreuzer, A. (1987). *Jugend - Drogen - Kriminalität*, 3rd ed. Neuwied: Luchterhand.

Kreuzer, A., & Wille, R. (1988). Drogen-Kriminologie und Therapie. Heidelberg: R.v. Decker & C.F. Müller.
Lösel, F., Köferl, P., & Weber, F. (1987). *Meta-Evaluation der Sozialtherapie*. Stuttgart: Enke.
Roloff, J. (1985). Das Betäubungsmittelgesetz: Strafe, Ausgrenzung und Verwahrung dominieren (Drogen) Sozialarbeit. *Kriminalpädagogische Praxis, 3,* 28-32.
Scheerer, S. (1982). Freiheit und Kontrolle im neuen Betäubungsmittelgesetz. *Kritische Justiz, 15,* 229-247.
Vollmer, H.C., & Ellgring, H. (1988). Die Vorhersage der vorzeitigen Therapiebeendigung bei Drogenabhängigen. *Suchtgefahren, 37,* 273-284.

The Treatment of Mentally Disordered Offenders in Canada

Sheilagh Hodgins

Introduction

The purpose of this chapter is to provide an overview of the evaluation and treatment of mentally disordered offenders in Canada today, and the role played by psychologists in this complicated interface between the criminal justice and mental health systems. What do we mean by the term "mentally disordered offenders"? What consitutes "treatment" for these persons? Where are they treated? What are the goals and objectives of treatment programmes? Each of these questions will be the subject of a separate section of this chapter. The concluding section will identify some continuing problems and policy concerns that merit attention.

Mentally Disordered Offenders

The term mentally disordered offender is generally used to refer to the following categories of persons: (1) persons charged with a criminal offense who are referred for an evaluation of their present mental state and/or their mental state at the time of the alleged crime; (2) criminal defendants who are declared unfit to stand trial because of mental disorder; (3) defendants adjudged not guilty by reason of insanity (NGRI); (4) inmates of penal institutions who are diagnosed as suffering from major mental disorders.

It is important to note that many persons are admitted to psychiatric wards following the commission of illegal acts. Except in the case of serious crimes, police in Canada have discretionary power with respect to individuals suspected of committing a crime and whom they judge to be behaving "abnormally". The police may request that they be admitted to a hospital for treatment rather than formally charging them. Studies (Lagos, Perlmutter, & Saexinger, 1977; Psychiatric News, 1984; Skodol & Karasu, 1978; Tardiff & Sweillam, 1980) have demonstrated that up to 37% of persons admitted to psychiatric wards were physically aggressive in the preceeding days. Other investigations (Cyr, Hodgins, & Elysée, 1985; Hodgins, 1983, 1987a) have shown that many persons are admitted to psychiatric wards following the commission of illegal acts for which they are never charged.

In this chapter the treatment of individuals diagnosed as presenting an antisocial personality disorder (who, in the past, have been labelled as psychopaths or sociopaths) is not discussed. In Canada, although persons with this diagnosis are sometimes found NGRI, this is not very common (Hodgins, Webster, Paquet, & Zellerer, 1989). It has been estimated that about 22% of penitentiary inmates present antisocial personality disorders (Wong, 1984). However, these persons generally do not qualify for mental health care. Psychologists have been at the forefront in demonstrating that such individuals present a stable set of psychological and behavioural characteristics, and that they commit more crimes and more crimes of violence than do other criminals (Hare & McPherson, 1984; Wong, 1984).[1] As well, psychologists have documented the management problems such cases present within the criminal justice system and the ineffectiveness of attempts to treat them (Harris, Rice, & Cormier, 1989; Ogloff, Wong, & Greenwood, 1986). There are currently no programmes that aim to alter the psychological and behavioural characteristics associated with the criminal lifestyles of persons diagnosed as having antisocial personality disorders.

We also exclude sex offenders from the discussion. Research has clearly shown that this group of offenders do not suffer from major mental disorders and that they respond to specific, behaviourally oriented treatment programmes (see Quinsey 1984, 1986; Furby, Weinrott, & Blackshaw, 1989). Such programmes are provided within the penitentiaries and prisons during the last months of the sentence, and also in the community, often under court order. Psychologists dominate this area of research and are responsible for the design, management, and evaluation of the treatment programmes.

Pre Trial Evaluations

About one-half of persons accused of a criminal offense are evaluated before their trial by a psychiatrist or a multidisciplinary mental health team to determine if they are fit to stand trial (Ministère de la Justice du Québec, 1983; Webster, Menzies, & Jackson, 1982)[2]. These evaluations aim to determine if the individual understands the charges against him/her, understands the possible consequences, is able to instruct counsel, and can comprehend what occurs in the courtroom. In most cases such an evaluation is carried out in less than an hour. However, in more difficult cases the accused may be transferred to a psychiatric ward for up to 60 days. If the accused is transferred to a hospital, the primary role of the mental health professionals during this period is to answer the specific question posed by the criminal court. They do, as well, treat the acute episode of schizophrenia, depression or mania. In most cases, the court follows the recommendations of the mental health professionals. While psychologists do not on their own submit reports to the courts on the issue of fitness, they have been instrumental in developing structured assessment procedures (see for example Roesch, Webster, & Eaves, 1984), evaluating their efficacy (Webster, Menzies, & Jackson, 1982), and in examining the factors which determine fitness (Bagby, 1990; Rogers, Gillis, McMain, & Dickens, 1988).

---

[1] In Canada a penitentiary houses individuals who receive sentences of two years or longer. A prison houses persons who receive sentences of two years or less and a jail houses persons prior to their trial.

[2] It is important to note that many persons held in jails may suffer from a major mental disorder, but still be mentally fit to proceed to trial.

Unfit to Stand Trial

Very few persons are judged to be unable to stand trial. On March 1st, 1989, 128 persons were being treated on psychiatric wards in Canada because they had been judged by the criminal court unfit to stand trial (Hodgins, Webster, & Paquet, 1990). In an investigation of all persons being held as unfit to stand trial between March 1st, 1988 and February 28th, 1990, we have found that 86% of these persons are men, aged, on average, 37 years old. Before the judgment, 87% of them were unemployed. Most (85%) had previously been hospitalized on a psychiatric ward, 62% of them involuntarily. Almost half (49%) had been previously convicted of a criminal offense. At the time of being found unfit, 30% were accused only of minor offenses, while almost all the others were charged with violent offenses. Seventy percent were diagnosed as schizophrenic, eight percent intellectually handicapped, seven percent delusional disorder, seven percent other psychoses, and five percent affective disorders. These persons were held in hospital, on average for 15 months with the goal of making them fit to stand trial.

Once judged unfit, if not already hospitalized the individual is transferred to a psychiatric ward. It is usually assumed by the in-patient treatment team that eliminating, or at least ameliorating, the mental disorder will make the patient mentally fit. Consequently, treatment with various medications is typically used, just as for any other person suffering from an acute episode of a similar mental disorder.

In recent years there has been a development toward more specific treatments for those found unfit to stand trial. Mowbray (1979) has argued that these patients receive better care when they are treated in specialized units. A programme developed, managed and evaluated by psychologists is run at the Metropolitan Toronto Forensic Services (Webster, Jenson, Stermac, Gardner, & Slomen, 1985). The programme is designed to educate patients about basic legal and psychiatric issues that could be relevant to both their present circumstances and their future. This course is offered to patients once the acute phase of their disorder is passed. It involves a series of eight classes which focus on various fitness issues, courtroom procedures, theories and treatments of mental disorders, strategies for surviving outside the hospital, and for locating and using various support services in the community.

The trend in treatments offered to persons who have been found unfit to stand trial, both in Canada other common law countries (see for example, Mowbray, 1979; Pendleton, 1980), is clearly towards more specific services offered within specialized facilities. These programmes are usually developed, directed and evaluated by psychologists. While the initial phase of treatment is designed to reduce the symptoms of an acute mental disorder, and is similar to treatment provided to non-offender patients, the subsequent phases of treatment are specifically designed to address the legal issue of fitness. These treatment programmes are important insofar as they render individuals fit, return them without too much delay to face the pending criminal proceedings, and thereby allow them to benefit from the presumption of innocence until proven guilty.

During the period of time that the individual is mentally unfit to proceed to trial a board, composed principally of lawyers and psychiatrists, is responsible for them. When the treatment team convinces this board that the person is fit, the individual returns to court. In almost all cases the judge accepts the treatment team's and the board's recommendation.

Once the individual is judged mentally fit, either a trial date is set or, as often occurs in the case of minor offenses, the charges are dropped (Hodgins, 1983).

Not Guilty by Reason of Insanity

If, at the pre-trial stage, the accused is mentally fit to proceed, an evaluation may be requested by the court to determine if, at the time of the alleged offense the accused was "insane". According to the *Criminal Code* "a person is insane when he is in a state of natural imbecility or has a disease of the mind to the extent that renders him incapable of appreciating the nature and quality of an act or omission or of knowing that an act or omission is wrong". This is essentially a modified version of the old McNaughton criteria (for a further discussion see Martin, 1981). Psychiatrists, not psychologists, are used by the courts to conduct the "insanity" evaluations.

On March 1st 1989 there were 991 persons being held in Canada because they had been found NGRI. Again, 90% were men, aged, on average, 39 years. Previous to the alleged crime, 79% of them were unemployed, 77% had been hospitalized on a psychiatric ward, 41% involuntarily, and 37% had been convicted of a criminal offense. One third of these persons were alleged to have committed a homicide, another 17% an attempted homicide, and 29% an assault. Only nine percent had been charged with minor offenses. Sixty-three percent were diagnosed schizophrenic, nine percent as suffering from major affective disorders, seven percent delusional disorder, five percent other psychoses and four percent were evaluated as having an intellectual handicap (Hodgins et al., 1990).

Once found NGRI the individual is sent to a psychiatric ward for treatment for an indeterminate period under the reponsability of a board composed principally of lawyers and psychiatrists. This board advises "... whether ... that person has recovered and, if so, whether in its opinion it is in the interest of the public and of that person for the lieutenant-governor to order that he be discharged absolutely or subject to conditions as the lieutenant-governor may prescribe." This section of the Criminal Code thus explicitly defines one goal of treatment as curing or ameliorating the mental disorder and, implicitly, adds the goal of eliminating or reducing the person's dangerousness to society.

There are few treatment programmes specifically designed for persons found NGRI. The initial phase of treatment almost always involves medications to reduce the acute symptoms of the mental disorder. Since most of these patients may previously have been hospitalized and treated during the evaluation period and/or after findings of unfitness to stand trial, the continuing mental disorder may not now be acute. In addition to medications, few other treatments are offered (Quinsey, 1981). In a recent review of medium and maximum security units for psychiatric patients in Ontario, Rice (1984) stated that:

> Programming at most units was relatively unstructured. Few specific problem-oriented programmes are in place. While hospitals have some form of a level (or privilege) system for managing patients, few of these were "behavioural" in the sense that they targetted specific problem behaviours, and few other programs have been designed to reduce specific "dangerous" behaviours (p.11)

A similar conclusion can be drawn about treatment programmes for NGRI patients in Alberta (De St. Croix, Dry, & Webster, 1985).

Recently, specific anger control programmes have been identified for use with certain types of mentally disordered offenders (for example, arsonists and paranoid patients). One programme designed to improve the social skills of arsonists has been described in detail and has also been evaluated (Harris & Rice, 1984; Rice & Chaplin, 1979). Arsonists are generally shy and unassertive men who tend to set fires when angry about some interpersonal situation. The programme teaches them alternate strategies for coping with anger in these and similar situations. While this programme has been shown to be effective in teaching appropriate responses to anger within the institutional setting (in a pilot project involving 10 subjects), it is not known if the persons who had successfully completed the programme continued to make effective use of what they had learned following their release.

At the Institut Philippe Pinel de Montréal a psychiatric hospital with physical security around the exterieur, several programmes have been established in an attempt to lower rehospitalization and recidivism rates, and to help patients live more autonomous lives once they return to the community (the conceptual basis for these programmes is presented in Hodgins & Gaston, 1987a,b). Specific training programmes aim to teach patients how to take their medications and evaluate side effects (Laliberté, 1990), basic life skills, (Lebourhis, 1990; Poulin, 1990), and social skills (Garceau, 1990; Tremblay, 1990). The impact of these programmes is presently being evaluated. As well, psychotherapy is offered to the very small number of patients likely to benefit from it.

The above types of programmes, it must be noted, are rare. Usually, once medications have been employed to treat the acute phase of the mental disorder, further therapy typically involves adjusting medication dosages to prevent a recurrence of an acute episode. The difficulties which led the individual to commit a criminal act may not have been identified or treated; indeed, they may not even be very amenable to available mental health interventions. Rather, the traditional psychiatric approach appears to assume that the criminal act was the result of the mental disorder and, consequently, that recovery from the disorder, per se, should eliminate the criminal behaviour. To date there is no empirical evidence to support this assumption.

Once the acute phase of the mental disorder has adequately been treated, both treatment staff and the patients favour discharge. The staff because, from their point of view, the in-hospital phase of treatment has been completed and continued hospitalization is no longer necessary for further treatment and care. As far as the patients are concerned, they understandably prefer release from the facility and return to the community. However, these patients cannot in fact be released until the advisory board can be convinced that the patients are no longer a danger to the community. Predictably, therefore, some patients are held in forensic hospitals long after they have recovered from their mental disorders and inpatient care is no longer indicated.

Just as in the case of non-offenders suffering from similar major mental disorders, most persons who have been found NGRI require a structured programme of carefully graduated release from the hospital and continued outpatient care and follow-up in order to prevent relapse (see Hodgins, 1988a). Although the quantity and quality of such aftercare varies, it would not be inaccurate to suggest that, in most instances, it is totally inadequate. In addition, many of these patients require some form of supervised living arrangements because they lack the skills necessary to survive in the community. Or, in many cases, they may simply have no where to go. Upon leaving the safe and secure environment provided by the hospital, these persons must confront the terrible stigma of being mentally disordered *and* criminal.

One interesting attempt to structure aftercare services for mentally disordered offenders (Goldmeier, Sauer, & White, 1977) has been made in Edmonton, Alberta. Patients are gradually transferred from hospital to a specialized half-way house. Some of the residents are employed, some participate in sheltered workshops, and some take educational and vocational courses. Professionals from the forensic hospital continue to follow patients during their stay at the half-way house and provide consultation to house staff. Half-way house residents are rehospitalized for short periods if staff judge that they have relapsed and are dangerous or that their mental state has deteriorated to a degree that inpatient care and treatment is needed (De St.Croix et al., 1985).

To sum up, treatment for persons found NGRI is often limited to medications which reduce or eliminate the symptoms of an acute episode of a major mental disorder. To the extent that this intervention produces recovery from the mental disorder and a state of "non-dangerousness" the goals of the treatment, as laid out by the Criminal Code, have been fulfilled. Treatment for persons suffering from major mental disorders is becoming more and more structured targetting specific behavioural difficulties. While medications continue to be the treatment of choice to eliminate positive symptoms, the other aspects of the disorder are more effectively treated with behavioural strategies. Treatments for persons judged NGRI are following this trend. There appears to be growing awareness of the necessity for long term community care. In a nine year follow-up study it has been found that 61% of these patients were rehospitalized (Hodgins, 1987a) and 36% were convicted of crimes (Hodgins, 1987b).

Mentally Disordered Inmates

Currently, there are about 13,000 persons, mainly men, incarcerated in Canadian penitentiaries. Recently, we investigated (Hodgins & Côté, 1990) a representative sample of 650 male penitentiary inmates using the Diagnostic Interview Schedule (Robins, Helzer, Croughan, & Ratcliff, 1981). This instrument has been designed specifically for epidemiological studies and estimates the prevalence of mental disorders as defined by the DSM-III (American Psychiatric Association, 1983). It has been shown to be both reliable and valid (Helzer et al., 1985, Helzer, Spitznagel, & McEvoy, 1987; Robins et al., 1981), and has been used to establish prevalence rates for the general population.

It was found that 23% of the inmates had experienced at least one episode of schizophrenia, major depression or bipolar disorder; 17.5% of them in the 12 months preceeding the assessment; 15.7% in the six months preceeding the assessment. In 75% of the cases the major mental disorder was present before the incarceration. Fifty-two percent of these inmates reported never having received any treatment. These findings have been replicated in other regions of Canada. As well, in the U.S. investigations of representative samples of jail inmates (Abram, 1989) and prison inmates (Collins & Schlenger, 1983; Daniel, Robins, Reed, & Wilfley, 1988; Neighbors et al., 1987) have all found prevalence rates for the major disorders to exceed those for the non-criminal population. All of these investigations have used standardized, reliable and valid diagnostic instruments. In our study, we also found many of these inmates met the DSM-III criteria for alcohol abuse and/or dependence and drug abuse and/or dependence (Côté & Hodgins, 1990).

Inmates suffering from various mental disorders are, as far as is possible, treated within penal institutions where they are housed. Most often treatment is limited to medications (see, for example, Béliveau & Laflamme-Cusson, 1984; Hodgins, Cyr, Paquet, & Lamy, 1988; Wolwertz & Laflamme-Cusson, 1985). Sometimes the symptoms of the disorder are so severe that transfer to a hospital setting is necessary. Treatment in the hospital setting will rely heavily on medications, will also utilize other available programmes such as group therapy, occupational therapy, and recreational therapy as indicated. Treatment in the hospital setting may not last longer than a couple of months, after which time the patient will be returned to the correctional facility.

As noted above, only the most severe cases who cannot be treated in the prison or penitentiary setting are transferred to a psychiatric hospital. When such persons return to the penal institution they still require mental health care, as do those others who were not seriously enough disturbed to require transfer to the hospital. Many of these mentally disordered inmates present a dilemma for the mental health professionals. Their first responsibility is towards the patients. However, the patients´ needs for care and treatment may well conflict with certain security or custodial requirements. This conflict (for a discussion see Steadman, Morrissey, & Robbins, 1985) is most evident in the case of prisoners for whom the prison environment may well be one factor, among many, contributing to the exacerbation of the mental disorder. In such cases the mental health professionals are obliged to treat the symptoms but may simply have to ignore the causes.

To reiterate, only the most severely and acutely disordered prison and penitentiary inmates receive mental health treatment, and this too tends to be limited to short term interventions to ameliorate the symptoms of an acute episode.

Conclusions

Many persons suffering from major mental disorders enter the Canadian criminal justice system. It has been proposed (see for example, Menzies & Webster, 1989) that these disordered persons commit minor crimes due to inadequate community mental health care. There are however, few, if any, data to support the proposition (see for example Hodgins, Cyr & Gaston, 1991). Rather, a great deal of evidence suggests that individuals who suffer from major mental disorders are at increased risk to commit violent offenses (Hodgins, in press). Psychologists are now leading the field in conducting research to further clarify the links between the major mental disorders and crime, to identify the type of patient who is at risk for violent behaviour, and to understand the factors which determine the violent behaviour (for a review see Hodgins, 1992). Psychologists are also playing leading roles in experimental programs designed to identify the mentally disordered person at the moment of arrest and provide appropriate care.

While psychologists are not often recognized by the Canadian criminal court as evaluators of either fitness to stand trial or the state of mind of an accused at the time of crime, they are actively involved as members of multidisciplinary assessment teams. However, the principal contribution of psychologists has been, and continues to be, the design of structured assessment procedures which are systematically evaluated and improved as a result of the evaluation. Research by psychologists has demonstrated the importance of using such structured and specific evaluations by showing the extent to which unstructured, clinical assessments may be highly influenced by sociodemographic variables (see for example Rogers et al., 1988).

The treatment programs for accused who have been judged unfit to proceed to trial are becoming more structured, systematic and specific. They are designed essentially to teach the accused the information necessary to be judged fit to proceed to trial. These learning based programs, designed, managed and evaluated by psychologists are almost always, coupled with a psychopharmacological intervention. The problem is however, that once this individual returns to the community care is inadequate and he or she is quickly rehospitalized or rearrested (for a vivid description of this vicious cycle see McMain, Webster, & Menzies, 1989). The provincial governments who are responsible for health care do not provide sufficient community care. While it is still an empirical question, all findings to date suggest that more adequate and appropriate community care would at least reduce rehospitalization rates (Hodgins, 1987a, 1988a).

Similarly, treatment programmes for persons judged not guilty by reason of insanity are also becoming more specific for the behavioural difficulties presented by these persons. While neuroleptic medication is necessary to eliminate the positive symptoms of the disorders, learning how to take these medications, learning basic life skills and social skills, learning how to resolve interpersonal conflicts without resorting to physical violence are equally important. Psychologists design, manage, and evaluate these programmes.

Psychologists are also actively involved in evaluating the effectiveness of community treatment programmes and in designing what are thought to be better programmes. For example, in British Columbia a special programme has been set up to care for persons who have a history of being either in hospital or in jail or prison (Corrado, Doherty, & Glackman, 1989). The programme aims to more effectively use the available ressources to help these individuals remain in the community.

Psychologists' research has identified the problem of the huge numbers of mentally disordered inmates within the penitentiary system. This research has also shown that less than half of these persons were receiving any treatment. Not only do many of these persons receive no care while in a penitentiary, once returned to the community the mental health system, already overburdened with non criminal patients, rejects them and again, a vicious cycle is established.

As has been previously noted (see Hodgins, 1988b) the distinctiveness of the Canadian system for mentally disordered offenders, is the integration of research into planning and modification of treatment services. Psychologists are largely responsible for these significant advances in knowledge and improvement in the quality of care.

References

Abram, K.M. (1989). The effect of co-occurring disorders on criminal careers: Interaction of antisocial personality, alcoholism, and drug disorders. *International Journal of Law and Psychiatry, 12*, 133-148.

American Psychiatric Association. (1983). *DSM-III: Manuel diagnostique et statistique des troubles mentaux.* New York: Masson.

Bagby, R.M. (1990). *Psychometric evaluation of two scales assessing fitness to stand trial.* Paper presented at the 2nd European Conference on Law and Psychology, Nurnberg.

Béliveau, L., & Laflamme-Cusson, R. S. (1984). L'organisation au Québec des soins psychiatriques pour les détenus. *Revue Internationale de Criminologie et de Police Technique, 37,* 71-81.

Collins, J.J., & Schlenger, W.E. (1983). *The prevalence of psychiatric disorder among admissions to prison.* Paper presented at the American Society of Criminology, Denver.

Corrado, R.R., Doherty, D., & Glackman, W. (1989). A demonstration program for chronic recidivists of criminal justice, health, and social service agencies. *International Journal of Law and Psychiatry, 12,* 211-229.

Côté, G., & Hodgins, S. (1990). Co-occurring mental disorders among criminal offenders. *Bulletin of the American Academy of Psychiatry and the Law, 18,* 271-281.

Cyr, M., Hodgins, S., & Elysée, R. (1985). Etude de relance auprès d'hommes traités en milieu psychiatrique sécuritaire: I. Description des antécédents et du séjour-cible. *Cahier de Recherche de l'Institut Philippe Pinel de Montréal, 11.*

Daniel, A.E., Robins, A.J., Reid, J.C., & Wilfley, D.E. (1988). Lifetime and six-month prevalence of psychiatric disorders among sentenced female offenders. *Bulletin of the American Academy of Psychiatry and the Law, 16,* 333-342.

De St. Croix, S., Dry, R., & Webster, C.D. (1985). Patients on warrant of the Lieutenant-Governor in Alberta: A statistical summary with comments on treatment and release procedure. (Unpublished manuscript)

Furby, L., Weinrott, M.R., & Blackshaw, L. (1989). Sex offender recidivism: A review. *Psychological Bulletin, 105,* 3-30.

Garceau, L. (1990). *The implementation of a social skills program in a psychodynamically oriented hospital.* Paper presented at the XVIth International Congress on Law and Mental Health, Toronto.

Goldmeier, J., Sauer, R.H., & White, V. (1977). A halfway house for mentally ill offenders. *American Journal of Psychiatry, 134,* 45-59.

Hare, R.D., & McPherson, L. (1984). Violent and aggressive behaviour by criminal psychopaths. *International Journal of Law and Psychiatry, 7,* 35-50.

Harris, G., & Rice, M.E. (1984). Mentally disordered firesetters: Psychodynamic versus empirical approaches. *International Journal of Law and Psychiatry, 7,* 19-34.

Harris, G.T., Rice, M.E., & Cormier, C.A. (1989). *Violent recidivism among psychopaths and nonpsychopaths treated in a therapeutic community.* Penetanguishene Mental Health Centre Research Report, Vol. VI.

Helzer, J.E., Robins, L.N., McEvoy, L.T., Spitznagel, E.L., Stoltzman, R.K., Farmer, A., & Brockington, I.F. (1985). A comparison of clinical and Diagnostic Interview Schedule diagnoses: Physician reexamination of lay-interviewed cases in the general population. *Archives of General Psychiatry, 42,* 657-666.

Helzer, J.E., Spitznagel, E.L., & McEvoy, L. (1987). The predictive validity of lay Diagnostic Interview Schedule diagnoses in the general population: A comparison with physician examiners. *Archives of General Psychiatry, 44,* 1069-1077.

Hodgins, S. (1983). A follow-up study of persons found incompetent to stand trial and/or not guilty by reason of insanity in Québec. *International Journal of Law and Psychiatry, 6,* 399-411.

Hodgins, S. (1987a). Etude des rechutes constatées dans une cohorte de personnes jugées inaptes à subir leur procès ou acquittées pour cause d'aliénation mentale. *Revue Canadienne des Sciences du Comportement, 19,* 441-453.

Hodgins, S. (1987b). Men found unfit to stand trial and/or not guilty by reason of insanity: Recidivism. *Canadian Journal of Criminology, 29,* 51-70.

Hodgins, S. (1988a). An aftercare programme for mentally disordered offenders. In F. Koenraadt & M. Zeegers (Eds.), *Trends in law and mental health* (pp. 223-235). Arnhem, The Netherlands: Gouda Quint BV.

Hodgins, S. (1988b). The organization of forensic services in Canada. *International Journal of Law and Psychiatry, 11,* 329-339.

Hodgins, S. (1992). *Mental disorder and crime.* Newbury Park, CA: Sage.

Hodgins, S. (in press). Mental disorder, intellectual deficiency, and crime: Evidence from a birth cohort. *Archives of General Psychiatry*.

Hodgins, S. & Côté, G. (1990). The prevalence of mental disorders among penitentiary inmates. *Canada's Mental Health, 38,* 1-5.

Hodgins, S., Cyr, M., & Gaston, L. (in press). A study of criminal justice system contacts of former inpatients. *Canadian Journal of Community Mental Health, 10,* 83-91.

Hodgins, S., Cyr, M., Paquet, J., & Lamy, P. (1988). Etude de relance auprès des détenus fédéraux traités en milieu psychiatrique: Description des antécédents du séjour, des rechutes et des récidives. *Criminologie, 21,* 27-62.

Hodgins, S., & Gaston, L. (1987a). Les programmes communautaires pour patients chroniques: L'élaboration d'un cadre conceptuel. *Santé Mentale au Canada, 35,* 7-10.

Hodgins, S., & Gaston, L. (1987b). Composantes d'efficacité des programmes de traitement communautaires destinées aux personnes souffrant de désordres mentaux. *Santé Mentale au Québec, 12,* 124-134.

Hodgins, S., Webster, C., & Paquet, J. (1990). *Annual report year-2 Canadian database: Patients held on Lieutenant-Governors' Warrants*. Department of Justice, Ottawa, Canada.

Hodgins, S., Webster, C., Paquet, J., & Zellerer, E. (1989). *Annual report year-1 Canadian data base: Patients held on Lieutenant-Governor's Warrants*. Department of Justice, Ottawa, Canada.

Lagos, J.M., Perlmutter, K., & Saexinger, H. (1977). Fear of the mentally ill: Empirical support for the common man's response. *American Journal of Psychiatry, 134,* 1134-1137.

Laliberté, L. (1990). *A nursing self care program within a maximum security hospital*. Paper presentend at the XVIth International Congress on Law and Mental Health, Toronto.

Lebourhis, G. (1990). *Development of a life skill's activity program in a maximum security hospital*. Paper presented at the XVIth International Congress on Law and Mental Health, Toronto.

Martin, G.A. (1981). Mental disorder and criminal responsibility in Canadian law. In S.J. Hucker, C.D. Webster, & M.H. Ben-Aron (Eds.), *Mental disorder and criminal responsibility* (pp. 15-31). Toronto: Butterworths.

McMain, S., Webster, C.D., & Menzies, R.J. (1989). The post-assessment careers of mentally disordered offenders. *International Journal of Law and Psychiatry, 12,* 189-203.

Menzies, R. & Webster, C.D. (1989). Mental disorder and violent crime. In N.A. Weiner & M.E. Wolfgang (Eds), *Pathways to criminal violence* (pp. 109-136). Sage: Newbury Park, California.

Mowbray, C.T. (1979). A study of patients released as incompetent to stand trial. *Social Psychiatry, 14,* 31-39.

Neighbors, H.W., Williams, D.H., Gunnings, T.S., Lipscomb, W.D., Broman, C., & Lepkowski, J. (1987). *The prevalence of mental disorder in Michigan prisons*. Final report submitted to the Michigan Department of Corrections, MI.

Ogloff, J.R.P., Wong, S., & Greenwood, A. (1986). *The efficacy of treating adult psychopaths in a therapeutic community programme within a correctional setting: Some preliminary data*. Paper presented at the fourty-seventh annual conference of the Canadian Psychological Association, Toronto.

Pendleton, L. (1980). Treatment of persons found incompetent to stand trial. *American Journal of Psychiatry, 137,* 1098-1100.

Poulin, C. (1990). *Developing measures to be used by ward staff to assess life skills*. Paper presented at the XVIth International Congress on Law and Mental Health, Toronto.

Psychiatric News (1984). *Incidence of violent patient admissions apparently stabilisized at 37 percent*. Washington, D.C., June 15th.

Quinsey, V.L. (1981). The long-term management of the mentally abnormal offender. In S.J. Hucker, C.D. Webster, & M.H. Ben-Aron (Eds.), *Mental disorder and criminal responsibility*, (pp. 137-155). Toronto: Butterworths.

Quinsey, V.L. (1984). Sexual aggression: Studies of offenders against women. In D.N. Weisstub (Ed.), *Law and mental health: International perspectives*, Vol. 1 (pp. 84-121). New York: Pergamon Press.

Quinsey, V.L. (1986). Men who have sex with children. In D.N. Weisstub (Ed.), *Law mental health: International perspectives*, Vol. 2 (pp. 140-172). New York: Pergamon Press.

Rice, M.E. (1984). Medium and maximum security units for psychiatric patients in Ontario. Paper presented at the Secure Treatment Unit Conference, Penetanguishene, Ontario.

Rice, M.E., & Chaplin, T.C. (1979). Social skills training for hospitalized male arsonists. *Journal of Behavior Therapy & Experimental Psychiatry, 10*, 105-108.

Robins, L.N., Helzer, J.E., Croughan, J., & Ratcliff, K.S. (1981). National Institute of Mental Health Diagnostic Interview Schedule: It's history, characteristics, and validity. *Archives of General Psychiatry, 38*, 381-389.

Roesch, R., Webster, C.D., & Eaves, D. (1984). *The fitness interview test: A method for examining fitness to stand trial.* Center of Criminology of University of Toronto and Criminology Research Center of Simon Fraser University.

Rogers, R., Gillis, J.R., McMain, S., & Dickens, S.E. (1988). Fitness evaluations: A retrospective study of clinical, criminal, and sociodemographic characteristics. *Canadian Journal of Behavioural Science, 20*, 192-200.

Skodol, A.E., & Karasu, T.B. (1978). Emergency psychiatry and the assaultive patient. *American Journal of Psychiatry, 135*, 202-205.

Steadman, H.J., Morrissey, J.P., & Robbins, P.C. (1985). Reevaluating the custody-therapy conflict paradigm in correctional mental health settings. *Criminology, 23*, 165-179.

Tardiff, K., & Sweillam, A. (1980). Assault, suicide, and mental illness. *Archives of General Psychiatry, 37*, 164-169.

Tremblay, L. (1990). *Measuring social skills of patients with major mental disorders.* Paper presented at the XVIth International Congress on Law and Mental Health, Toronto.

Webster, C.D., Jenson, F.A.S., Stermac, L., Gardner, K., & Slomen, D. (1985). Psychoeducational assessment programmes for forensic psychiatric patients. *Canadian Psychology/ Psychologie Canadienne, 26*, 50-53.

Webster, C.D., Menzies, R.J., & Jackson, M.A. (1982). *Clinical assessments before trial.* Toronto: Butterworths.

Wolwertz, J. & Laflamme-Cusson, S. (1985). Les soins psychiatriques au jour le jour chez les prévenus du centre Parthenais. *Revue Internationale de Criminologie et de Police Technique, 3*, 315-323.

Wong, S. (1984). *The criminal and institutional behaviours of psychopaths.* (Programs Branch User Report). Ministry of the Solicitor General of Canada.

General Prevention: Criminological and Psychological Problems

Dieter Dölling

Introduction

General prevention is at present one of the preferred topics in criminological research. Two of the reasons for this are a certain disillusionment about the possibilities of special prevention and the great importance increasingly attached to economic theories in the debate on criminological theory (see Kaiser, 1988, pp. 199, 208-209). These facts drew attention to general preventive penal theory.

In this context, general prevention is identified partially with deterrence. The hypothesis of deterrence says that the potential perpetrator is deterred from committing the crime for fear of the punishment threatening the criminal action. In addition to this, the theory of general prevention comprises yet another element: the stabilization of the population's legal loyalty. Sanctioning rule violations aims at strengthening the population's conviction that the legal rule must always be adhered to and that any violation is condemnable (see Maurach & Zipf, 1987, pp. 65, 81-82, on elements of the penal theory of general prevention). In the jurisdiction and literature of the Federal Republic of Germany, deterrence is described as negative general prevention and encouragement of legal loyalty as positive general prevention (see Jescheck, 1988, pp. 60-61).

Criminological research on general prevention to date reveals a considerable discrepancy. A very large number of studies have yielded but few validated results. In the following, an attempt is made to outline the state of research and to discuss the reasons for the not very encouraging outcome. As shall be revealed in the following, the reasons comprise both methodological problems in empirical research and difficulties in the appropriate theoretical approach to the social and psychological relations included in the theory of general prevention.

In line with the development of empirical research, studies based on criminal statistics are discussed first followed by surveys. Finally, a few considerations regarding the theory of general prevention and the possibilities of subjecting it to empirical analysis are presented.

Studies Using Criminal Statistics

In criminal statistics studies, official data concerning the practice of prosecution and punishment - for instance, clearance rates or data on types and severity of penalties imposed by the courts - are correlated to officially registered criminality. This method is used to obtain information on the relations between probability of punishment or severity of punishment and the extent of criminality. The studies partly compare regions with different laws or different criminal prosecution practices, and partly analyze crime rates in one region before and after an amendment of a law or a change in prosecution practice.

Regional comparisons mainly have revealed a negative relationship between sanction probability - which is, for instance, expressed by clearance rates, arrest rates or prisoner rates - and the extent of criminality (see Avio & Clark, 1978; Tittle, 1969). Severity of punishment proved for the most part to be irrelevant or of less importance than probability of sanctions. Time-series analyses conducted over long periods, which, for instance, correlated the arrest rate in one year with the criminality rate in the following year, yielded different results (see Greenberg, Kessler, & Logan, 1979; Phillips & Votey, 1972).

Studies dealing with the impact of amendmends to laws or specific changes in the prosecution or sanction practice in one region revealed mostly that laws introducing a sanction for a certain behavior and that an increase of the intensity of prosecution had a reducing influence on such behavior (see Gallagher, 1978; Killias, 1985). Increases in severity of punishment mostly proved to be insignificant (see Chauncey, 1975; Schwartz, 1968; but also Beha II, 1977).

Numerous methodological objections are brought forward against criminal statistics studies (see Nagin, 1978, p. 95-98). The measurement of the dependent variable "criminality" by means of the official criminal statistics is problematic because undetected crimes are not considered. The direction of correlations between criminal prosecution and criminality rate is doubtful. Besides an impact of criminal prosecution on the extent of criminality a reverse influence might also be possible: Increasing criminality can result in a decrease in the intensity of criminal prosecution because of an overstressed prosecution apparatus. In addition to this, the correlation between criminal prosecution and criminality can be influenced by various other variables such as, the "moral climate" predominating in a society.

Finally the criminal statistics approach does not completely register the elements of the causal chain postulated by the theory of general prevention. According to this theory, the penal system induces perceptions of the penalties for specific criminal acts among the population. These perceptions cause people to refrain from criminal acts or strengthen the population's legal loyalty. These psychological links of the general preventive causal chain are not examined in the approach by criminal statistics. This approach only deals with the beginning and the end point of the causal chain, that is, the penal system and the criminal acts. This can adversely affect the results of studies using official data. The fact that clearance rates differ in two regions might not even be noticed by the public. Therefore a crime preventive impact of the intensity of criminal prosecution cannot be inferred without reservations from differently high criminality rates in the two regions.

Against this background, it is not astonishing that criminological research has attached increasing importance to the psychological aspects of general prevention. The main method applied is interviewing. Hence the following deals with survey research on general prevention.

Interview Studies

Different approaches have been used in survey studies. In some, interviewed persons are asked to estimate whether another person would commit a criminal offense under specific circumstances. In this method, both probability of sanction and severity of sanction vary under the given circumstances. Most surveys, however, focus on the behavior of the respondents themselves. In part, perceptions of the probability of a punishment and the severity of punishment are related to self-reported prior delinquency, partly correlations between punishment perception and behaviour readiness, that is, the self-assessed probability to commit the crime in the future are analyzed. Finally, panel studies have been conducted in which at a certain time subjects are asked to estimate the punishment and at a later time the criminal offenses committed by the subjects between the first and the second wave are asked for.

Concerning surveys to investigate the behavior of third persons as a rule probability of punishment and severity of punishment proved to be significant (see Breland, 1975; Rettig & Rawson, 1963; Sinha, 1968). The persons interviewed thought that perpetration of a criminal offense by another person was less probable when there was a higher risk of detection and more severe punishments. But these data do not provide any direct information on how the interviewed persons themselves would decide given a different risk of detection and a different severity of punishment. Assumptions on the crime preventive impact of sanctions on the behavior of other persons are registered. These assumption express everyday theories of the respondents.The relations of such assumptions of the interviewed persons to their own behavior have not been clarified. Moreover, these interviews postulate a specific probability of punishment, and a specific severity of punishment and in this way the subjects are made aware of these facts. It is doubtful whether and with which intensity the interviewed persons would think of such circumstances under real-life conditions.

Most surveys on self-reported delinquency in the past have yielded significant but not very strong negative correlations between the perceived detection probability and the criminal offenses reported. Those persons who estimated a higher risk of detection reported less criminal offenses (see, e.g., Diekmann, 1980; Jensen, 1969; Silberman, 1976; Williams III, 1985). The severity of punishment turned out to be only partly important.

Apart from the general problems of surveys on self-reported delinquency, it can also be argued that this method of interviewing cannot establish precisely the direction of the relationship between the present perception of the risk of detection and self-reported criminal offenses in the past. Possibly it is not the assumed risk of detection that influences delinquency but delinquency influences the estimated detection probability. Those persons who commit many offenses and are not detected will estimate a low risk of detection.

In order to avoid this objection, perceptions of the punishment variables can be correlated to the self-estimated probability to commit crimes in the future instead of to the self-reported delinquency in the past. Most surveys using this approach showed a negative relationship between punishment perceptions and readiness to criminal behavior (see Albrecht, 1980; Anderson, Harris, & Miller, 1983; Stewart & Hemsley, 1979; Tittle, 1976). However, the relationship between self-estimated perpetration probability and actual behavior is not clear. Consequently, investigations should be carried out to examine more closely whether those persons who assess their perpetration probability higher actually do commit crime more frequently.

A clear determination of the direction of correlations between sanction perceptions and delinquency is possible by the panel studies. They partly reported a weak relationship between the perceived detection risk and delinquency and partly no relationship at all (see Bishop, 1984; Minor & Harry, 1982; Saltzman, Paternoster, Waldo, & Chiricos, 1982; Schumann, Berlitz, Guth, & Kaulitzki, 1987). When other factors that possibly support conformity are used in the survey apart from the sanction variables, and multivariate evaluation procedures are applied in order to investigate the specific contribution of the punishment variables on conformity, the importance of the sanction variables decreases as compared to the results of bivariate analyses (see Schumann, Berlitz, Guth, & Kaulitzki, 1987, pp. 127-130). This result can be registered not only for panel surveys but also for cross-sectional analyses using multivariate procedures. Usually the variables with the strongest explanatory power are those of moral commitment to norms and the acquaintance of delinquent persons (e.g., Silberman, 1976; Tittle, 1976).

Also with regard to a survey conducted by the author on 540 young men - 362 of whom were called to their compulsory military service in the Bundeswehr, 82 of whom were inmates of two detention centres; and 96 of whom were inmates of a prison for juvenile offenders - bivariate analysis revealed remote relationships between the perceived detection risk and delinquency for some criminal offenses (see Dölling, 1983). Using multivariate procedures, these relationships become even weaker. Some of the independent variables with the strongest explanatory power are the acquaintance of delinquent persons, the moral commitment to legal norms, and the probationer's readiness to run a risk.

In order to evaluate the survey studies the following should be pointed out: The explanatory power of the surveys must, at first, be relativized as a result of methodological considerations. During the interview, specific data of the respondents regarding the perceived detection risk and the expected severity of punishment are "produced". It is doubtful whether the subjects have exactly the same perceptions under real-life conditions under which committing a crime is considered as they indicate in the survey. Possibly in real life they do not even think of the fact that the criminal act might be punished and possibly their perceptions are not as clear as the information provided in the survey if they think of a punishment at all in real life. This especially applies to the interview methods that record punishment perceptions in a very detailed way on scales with numerous levels. This is how it might occur that one subject estimates the detection risk to be 30% and another subject may say 40%. This does not yet imply that the perceptions of those respondents differ substantially under realistic conditions. Probably both have the idea - which cannot be quantified more closely - that a certain risk of detection exists, and one subject expresses this idea with a value of 30% and the other with a value of 40%. If the estimation values do not differ strongly the lack of differences in the frequency of crimes does not necessarily mean that punishment perceptions are irrelevant for legal behavior. Possibly the perceptions of the respondents just do not vary relevantly in real life.

These considerations are particularly important because the groups interviewed in the survey studies were mostly homogeneous especially pupils and students. For these groups, it can be expected that the variances between the perceptions of sanction probability and severity of sanctions will be limited. Consequently, only weak relationships between punishment perceptions and delinquency are revealed in these surveys. Hence, the results of such surveys can not be generalized without reservations. Interviews of other groups in which punishment perception is dispersed more widely might yield quite different results.

But even if the sanction perceptions of the respondents are dispersed more widely, the explanatory power of the surveys is still limited. Drastic changes of the detection risk for which an effect of the punishment probability on the frequency of behavior is most probable are hardly covered by the surveys. It is, for example, reported that in

1956 car thefts in Sweden decreased considerably on weekends when a weekend driving ban was imposed during the time of the Suez canal crisis to save petrol (see Andenaes, 1974, p. 52). Furthermore, a massive increase in the number of police patrols is said to have caused a reduction in criminal offenses (see Cramton, 1969, p. 435; Gallagher, 1978, pp. 175-178). Such situations are not reflected adequately by the interview studies to date. It might be possible that the ranges of the thresholds at which changes in detection risk become relevant to legal behavior are so large that most of the perceptions provided in the surveys are well within these threshold ranges and that - as a consequence - the surveys cannot cover the significance of passing such thresholds.

In addition to this, surveys only cover the fact whether variances in the sanction perceptions affect behavior. It cannot be examined, however, whether the existence of a penal system as such has an influence on conformity. All persons interviewed or at least the majority of them assume that the behavior investigated in the surveys is punishable so that the independent variable practically does not vary with respect to the "if" of punishability. In order to investigate the importance of punishability of a behavior as such, circumstances must be compared in which a behavior is liable to prosecution or is not.

The significance of this aspect is demonstrated by historic examples in which criminal law was repealed de facto. During the arrest of the Danish police force by the German Wehrmacht in World War II and during a police strike in Montreal - that is to say under circumstances in which no prosecution by the police took place - a marked increase in specific crimes such as burglary and robbery was recorded (see Andenaes, 1974, pp. 16, 17, 51; Clark, 1969). Accordingly, in situations in which a behavior that had previously not been prosecuted publically was penalized, at least a temporary decrease in that behavior was reported. This was demonstrated, for example, when driving with a blood-alcohol concentration of 0.8 per mille and more became punishable by the Road Safety Act of 1967 in Great Britain and when not wearing seat belts became liable to prosecution in Switzerland (see Andenaes, 1974, pp. 95-102; Killias, 1985). This aspect of the existence of a serious public prosecution as such is neglected by surveys.

A cautious evaluation of the surveys is also necessary regarding the severity of sanctions. Most surveys yield the result that severity of punishment is of no or only minor importance for legal behavior compared with detection risk. First, it is doubtful how far the separation between perception of sanction probability and perception of sanction severity generally operationalised in surveys is realistic. Under realistic circumstances, many people possibly only have a perception of the punishability of a behavior, a perception in which the elements of certainty of punishment and severity of punishment are mixed in an intricate manner. Therefore, information on the perceived sanction probability may often have overtones of assumptions on the severity of sanctions.

Furthermore, variances in the perceptions of respondents might also be limited regarding the sanction severity, so that many surveys do not cover the relevant threshold values of the severity of sanctions. It might, for example, be irrelevant for the frequency of homicides whether the potential offender reckons with an imprisonment of seven or nine years. But if, in the future, a fine instead of imprisonment were imposed on homicides, an influence of such change in severity of the sanction on the rate of crimes is likely. The surveys to date therefore do not rule out that the severity of sanction could be relevant under certain circumstances. This might, for instance, apply if there are clear differences in sanction alternatives, if it is realistic to anticipate the implementation of the more severe sanction alternative and if potential offenders are concerned who rationally weigh advantages and disadvantages of committing a crime (see Beha II, 1977, regarding the impact of a law that came into force in Massachusetts in 1975 imposing a minimum imprisonment of one year on persons illicitly carrying firearms; when this law came into effect, it was accompanied by an intensive publicity campaign; the law was applied in court without trying to evade it).

Evaluation of the surveys must also take into account that most psychological laboratory experiments on the hypothesis of general prevention resulted in an influence of sanction probability and sanction severity on behavior frequency (e.g., Heisler, 1974; Horai & Tedeschi, 1969). The reason for this might be attributed to the fact that the tests used a given degree of sanction probability or severity of sanction for a specific situation that was so obvious to the subjects that it became relevant to behavior. The results of the laboratory experiments cannot be applied to real human life without problems, because in social reality the independent variables sanction probability and severity of sanction cannot be varied and thus cannot be intensified so easily as it was the case in laboratory experiments. Great efforts have to be made to organize penal law administration in such a way that a detection risk of a specific extent perceptibly exists or that punishments of a certain degree are very likely to be imposed on criminal offenses. If survey studies do not show an influence of sanction probability and severity of sanction, this does not have to imply that punishment variables are generally irrelevant for the frequency of a behavior. On the contrary, it may also imply that for the persons interviewed the conditions under which sanction probability or severity of sanctions become effective did not exist.

The explanatory power of surveys ist thus limited for methodological reasons. At least the surveys are an indication for a certain relevance of variances in the perceived punishment probability. Furthermore, evaluation of those studies has to take account of the possibility that they only refer to parts of the theory of general prevention. This might also contribute to relativization of the importance of the surveys. This will be discussed in the following.

Considerations Regarding the Theory of General Prevention

The empirical investigations to date hardly cover positive general prevention, that is to say, the impact of penal law on the legal consciousness of the population. Positive general prevention comprises a number of complicated correlations. The punishment of breaking the legal norms illustrates that the legal norms are still in effect and compliance with them is expected (see Jakobs, 1983, p. 7-8). Responding to crime with the punishment that the population considers to be just strengthens the public esteem of the legal system and thus the readiness of the people to comply with legal norms (see Roxin, 1979, pp. 304-306). Furthermore, punishment serves to illustrate the value of the infringed legal norm and the importance of the damaged object of legal protection and thereby to strengthen and to stabilize prevailing ethic standards (see Jescheck, 1988, pp. 4, 61). Finally, punishment appeals to the sense of responsibility of citizens. Everybody is reminded that he is responsible for his behavior and is called upon to conform to the legal system (see Otto, 1982, pp. 279-287).

The empirical examination of such hypotheses related to the theory of positive general prevention is extremely difficult. Some studies exist in which moral attitudes were investigated before and after an amendment to a law or in which ways of behavior were given to be punishable or not punishable, and correlations between such given classifications and the moral judgments of the ways of behavior by the persons interviewed were examined (Berkowitz & Walker, 1967; Walker & Argyle, 1964; for a summary see Schumann, 1989). Such studies, however, contain "snapshots" of punishment variables and moral attitudes. In contrast, the theory of general prevention states long-term effects of penal law on the moral consciousness of the population. Due to their selective approach, the cited studies do not allow any detailed judgment of the empirical substance of the theory of positive general prevention.

But also with regard to deterrence, the empirical studies to date might not be sufficient enough. They concentrate on the decision-making process of the offender in an individual situation and investigate how perceptions of the penal consequences of a violation of the law influence the decision for or against breaking the law. But it is also possible that the penal law is of significance not only to decisions in individual situations but also to long-term dispositions that determine future social behavior (see Dölling, 1990, pp. 9-14). Human actions do not constitute a chain of individual decisions which are made completely independently from one another but are also determined by more long-term attitudes and action strategies. Such strategies might be reversible but they influence actions for a certain period of time and thus the decisions in favor of legal or illegal behavior. In the course of human development, legal life-styles or life-styles with delinquent tendencies take shape (see Kaiser, 1990, for a discussion of the concept of life-style and its significance for criminology). People can set up their lives in a way that they try to reach their goals within the scope of the legal system and consequently learn legal action strategies to satisfy their needs (legal life-styles) or people can develop a life-style that includes committing criminal offenses (life-styles with delinquent tendencies).

Legal life-styles do not completely preclude criminal acts but reduce their probability. Those who master legal action strategies are less motivated to use criminal means. Those who are integrated in the conventional system of roles are more strongly shaped by the prevailing system of values and are to a larger extent subject to formal and informal control mechanisms.

Long-term attitudes and action patterns are shaped by socialization in the first place. Apart from this, penal law might also be of importance to the development of legal life-styles. Development of legal action patterns is more likely if conventional careers appear to be attractive and criminal careers unfavourable. A means to render criminal careers unattractive is penal law that provides that criminal careers are finally not worthwhile because they result in punishment related to loss of goods and social status. This mechanism does not require that every crime is detected and punished. A serious offender may remain undetected in some offenses but if he is detected for committing another offense later on and severely punished, then his criminal career is to be regarded as a failure.

The importance of these relations becomes obvious when societies are viewed in which criminal careers appear to be as attractive as or even more attractive than legal careers for parts of the population. South American societies can be mentioned as an example where a career as a drug dealer appears more worthwhile to many people than attempting to reach affluence and social advancement by legal means. In this case, both possibilities for successful legal careers as well as a sufficiently high pressure of sanctions against criminal careers are lacking.

Apart from the short-term impact of punishment on behavior in individual situations, a long-term impact of deterrence could be reached by penal law that favors the development of legal life-styles. This long-term impact, however, has not been covered by the empirical surveys to date. No or only weak correlations might exist between the perceptions of punishment of young people and their delinquency in juvenile age. But this does not preclude that in the course of growing-up - apart from the predominating socialization process - it is important for youth to know that criminality is not worthwhile in the long run because it leads to an isolated position in society while conventional careers promise to be sucessful. This question has not been settled in empirical studies so far.

Finally, another possible relationship between moral commitment to legal norms and the function of penal law to render criminal careers unattractive shall be pointed out: According to empirical investigations, a close relationship exists between the moral commitment to legal norms and conformity. Possibly the morally binding character of legal norms can only be maintained if people believe that a moral behavior is finally also worthwhile under cost-benefit aspects. If law-abiding citizens experience that breaking the law is worthwhile and if they lose when competing for desirable goods against those breaking the law they will be unable to afford conformity in the long run and will also use illegal methods. In order to guarantee the readiness to stick to conformity it might therefore be necessary to organize society in such a way - also by means of penal law - that conformity is worthwhile in the end. No empirical research has been made so far regarding these relationships.

To validate the outlined assumptions concerning the impact of penal law on long-term attitudes and action patterns, new empirical research approaches are necessary. An attempt should be made to investigate action strategies and life-styles and to correlate these variables with the "working" of criminal law and its perception by the population. If the outlined assumptions are correct, relations between efficiency of penal law and frequency of life strategies encouraging conformity will be obtained. Due to the complex structure of the research field, this empirical research is, of course, extremely difficult.

The considerations in this paper have shown that the results of empirical research on general prevention to date are limited. The significance of general prevention for practice and theory of penal law requires further investigations. Quick solutions to the problems are not likely, but perhaps it is possible to advance step by step.

References

Albrecht, H.-J. (1980). Die generalpräventive Effizienz von strafrechtlichen Sanktionen. In Forschungsgruppe Kriminologie (Ed.), *Empirische Kriminologie. Ein Jahrzehnt kriminologischer Forschung am Max-Planck-Institut Freiburg i.Br. - Bestandsaufnahme und Ausblick* (pp. 305-327). Freiburg i.Br.: Max-Planck-Institut für ausländisches und internationales Strafrecht.

Andenaes, J. (1974). *Punishment and deterrence.* Ann Arbor: The University of Michigan Press.

Anderson, A., Harris, A., & Miller, J. (1983). Models of deterrence theory. *Social Science Research, 12,* 236-262.

Avio, K.L., & Clark, C.S. (1978). The supply of property offences in Ontario: Evidence on the deterrent effect of punishment. *Canadian Journal of Economics, 11,* 1-19.

Beha II, J.A. (1977). "And nobody can get you out". The impact of a mandatory prison sentence for the illegal carrying of a firearm on the use of firearms and on the administration of criminal justice in Boston. *Boston University Law Review, 57,* 96-146, 289-333.

Berkowitz, L., & Walker, N. (1967). Laws and moral judgements. *Sociometry, 30,* 410-422.

Bishop, D.M. (1984). Deterrence: A panel analysis. *Justice Quarterly, 1,* 311-328.

Breland, M. (1975). *Lernen und Verlernen von Kriminalität. Ein lernpsychologisches Konzept der Prävention im sozialen Rechtsstaat.* Opladen: Westdeutscher Verlag.

Chauncey, R. (1975). Deterrence. Certainty, severity and skyjacking. *Criminology, 12,* 447-473.

Clark, G. (1969). What happens when the police strike? *The New York Times Magazine, November 16,* pp. 45, 176-185, 187, 194-195.

Cramton, R.C. (1969). Driver behavior and legal sanctions: A study of deterrence. *Michigan Law Review, 67,* 421-454.

Diekmann, A. (1980). *Die Befolgung von Gesetzen. Empirische Untersuchungen zu einer rechtssoziologischen Theorie.* Berlin: Duncker & Humblot.

Dölling, D. (1983). Strafeinschätzungen und Delinquenz bei Jugendlichen und Heranwachsenden - Ein Beitrag zur empirischen Analyse der generalpräventiven Wirkungen der Strafe. In H.-J. Kerner, H. Kury, & K. Sessar (Eds.), *Deutsche Forschungen zur Kriminalitätsentstehung und Kriminalitätskontrolle, Vol. I* (pp. 51-85). Köln: Heymanns.

Dölling, D. (1990). Generalprävention durch Strafrecht: Realität oder Illusion? *Zeitschrift für die gesamte Strafrechtswissenschaft, 102,* 1-20.

Gallagher, F. (1978). Appendix. An annotated bibliography of deterrence evaluations, 1970-1975. In A. Blumstein, J. Cohen, & D. Nagin (Eds.), *Deterrence and incapacitation: Estimating the effects of criminal sanctions on crime rates* (pp. 174-186). Washington, D.C.: National Academy of Sciences.

Greenberg, D.F., Kessler, R.C., & Logan, C.H. (1979). A panel model of crime rates and arrest rates. *American Sociological Review, 44,* 843-850.

Heisler, G. (1974). Ways to deter law violators: Effects of levels of threat and vicarious punishment on cheating. *Journal of Consulting and Clinical Psychology, 42,* 577-582.

Horai, J., & Tedeschi, J.T. (1969). Effects of credibility and magnitude of punishment on compliance to threats. *Journal of Personality and Social Psychology, 12,* 164-169.

Jakobs, G. (1983). *Strafrecht. Allgemeiner Teil. Die Grundlagen und die Zurechnungslehre.* Berlin: De Gruyter.

Jensen, G.F. (1969). "Crime doesn't pay": Correlates of a shared misunderstanding. *Social Problems, 16,* 189-201.

Jescheck, H.-H. (1988). *Lehrbuch des Strafrechts. Allgemeiner Teil,* 4th ed. Berlin: Duncker & Humblot.

Kaiser, G. (1988). *Kriminologie. Ein Lehrbuch,* 2nd ed. Heidelberg: C.F. Müller.

Kaiser, G. (1990). "Lebensstil". Entwicklung und kriminologische Bedeutung eines Konzepts. In H.J. Kerner, & G. Kaiser (Eds.), *Kriminalität, Persönlichkeit, Lebensgeschichte und Verhalten. Festschrift für Hans Göppinger zum 70. Geburtstag* (pp. 27-40). Berlin: Springer.

Killias, M. (1985). Zur Bedeutung von Rechtsgefühl und Sanktionen für die Konformität des Verhaltens gegenüber neuen Normen. In E.-J. Lampe (Ed.), *Das sogenannte Rechtsgefühl* (pp. 257-272). Opladen: Westdeutscher Verlag.

Maurach, R., & Zipf, H. (1987). *Strafrecht. Allgemeiner Teil. Teilband 1. Grundlehren des Strafrechts und Aufbau der Straftat. Ein Lehrbuch,* 7th ed. Heidelberg: C.F. Müller.

Minor, W., & Harry, J. (1982). Deterrent and experiential effects in perceptual deterrence research: A replication and extension. *Journal of Research in Crime and Delinquency, 19,* 190-203.

Nagin, D. (1978). General deterrence: A review of the empirical evidence. In A. Blumstein, J. Cohen, & D. Nagin (Eds.), *Deterrence and incapacitation: Estimating the effects of criminal sanctions on crime rates* (pp. 95-139). Washington, D.C.: National Academy of Sciences.

Otto, H.J. (1982). *Generalprävention und externe Verhaltenskontrolle. Wandel vom soziologischen zum ökonomischen Paradigma in der nordamerikanischen Kriminologie?* Freiburg i.Br.: Max-Planck-Institut für ausländisches und internationales Strafrecht.

Phillips, L., & Votey, H.L. Jr. (1972). An economic analysis of the deterrent effect of law enforcement on criminal activity. *The Journal of Criminal Law, Criminology and Police Science, 63,* 330-342.

Rettig, S., & Rawson, H.E. (1963). The risk hypothesis in predictive judgments of unethical behavior. *Journal of Abnormal and Social Psychology, 66,* 243-248.

Roxin, C. (1979). Zur jüngsten Diskussion über Schuld, Prävention und Verantwortlichkeit im Strafrecht. In A. Kaufmann, G. Bemmann, D. Krauss, & K. Volk (Eds.), *Festschrift für Paul Bockelmann zum 70. Geburtstag* (pp. 279-309). München: Beck.

Saltzmann, L., Paternoster, R., Waldo, G., & Chiricos, T.G. (1982). Deterrent and experiential effects: The problem of causal order in perceptual deterrence research. *Journal of Research in Crime and Delinquency, 19,* 172-189.

Schumann, K.F. (1989). *Positive Generalprävention. Ergebnisse und Chancen der Forschung.* Heidelberg: C.F. Müller.

Schumann, K.F., Berlitz, G., Guth, H.-W., & Kaulitzki, R. (Eds.) (1987). *Jugendkriminalität und die Grenzen der Generalprävention.* Neuwied: Luchterhand.

Schwartz, B. (1968). The effect in Philadelphia of Pennsylvania's increased penalties for rape and attempted rape. *The Journal of Criminal Law, Criminology and Police Science, 59,* 509-515.

Silberman, M. (1976). Toward a theory of criminal deterrence. *American Sociological Review, 41,* 442-461.

Sinha, J.B.P. (1968). A note on ethical risk hypothesis. *The Journal of Social Psychology, 76,* 117-122.

Stewart, C.H.M., & Hemsley, D.R. (1979). Risk perception and likelihood of action in criminal offenders. *The British Journal of Criminology, 19,* 105-119.

Tittle, C.R. (1969). Crime rates and legal sanctions. *Social Problems, 16,* 409-422.

Tittle, C.R. (1976). Sanction fear and the maintenance of social order. *Social Forces, 55,* 579-596.

Walker, N., & Argyle, M. (1964). Does the law affect moral judgements? *The British Journal of Criminology, 4,* 570-581.

Williams III, F.P. (1985). Deterrence and social control: Rethinking the relationship. *Journal of Criminal Justice, 13,* 141-151.

Part IV
Psychological Research on the Police

Psychologists and the Police

John C. Yuille

Introduction

This chapter examines both the benefits and the difficulties for psychologists who apply research findings within the context of police organizations. Psychologists play a variety of roles, from clinician to operational consultant, in that context and these are briefly discussed below. However, the emphasis here is on psychologists as researchers and, more importantly, as sources of practical knowledge for the police. Increasingly, psychologists are attempting to apply research results to police recruit selection, police training and police operations. These applications are the concern of this chapter.

The Applications of Psychology to Policing

Psychologists first began working directly with police in the 1960s by providing treatment services to police organizations (Reiser, 1986). Clinically trained psychologists were recruited to provide assistance to officers who had either general or specific job related problems, and this remains the major service that psychologists provide to police. Most of this clinical work has relied on the general clinical literautre for guidance since there have been few publications dealing specifically with clinical practice in the context of police departments. However, recently there have been a few reports which have dealt with clinical practice with police (e.g., Reese & Goldstein, 1986). This literature is characterized by practical discussions and case studies and it lacks a basic research focus. In short, the major activity of psychologists in police departments has little research basis specific to police needs. Although clinical work is not the focus of this article, the lack of a research foundation for this work reinforces my major concern: the lack of directly relevant research to guide psychologists who work with police.

During the 1970s, and accelerating in the 1980s, the job of the police officer changed. The traditional roles of law enforcer and protector of public safety have remained but to these have been added a new set of tasks. Police must now deal with community relations, including minority group issues; they must respond to domestic violence; they often deal with mentally ill individuals. In short, much of policing now involves the delivery of social services rather than strict law enforcement. One consequence of this change in the nature of policing is a change in the type of individual needed for the job. Communication skills and human awareness are now as important as physical fitness.

These changes in policing have led, perhaps too slowly, to modifications both in the procedures for selecting police recruits and in their training. Psychologists are now employed or consulted by police forces to assist in the development and presentation of these new selection and training techniques.

During the past 20 years police forces have increased their use of psychological tests in the selection of potential recruits (e.g., Inwald, 1986; Loo & Meredith, 1986). Often, as with the use of the MMPI, the test is simply borrowed from another area of psychology, in this case clinical assessment, and applied to police selection with little or no research on its predictive value for police forces. Although some research has guided the use of a few selection tolls (e.g., Inwald, 1986; Hargrave, 1986; Loo & Meredith, 1986), most of these tools are used without any directly relevant research with police. Although police selection is not a focus of this chapter, this activity of psychologists again supports the present concern: the application of psychological techniques to policing without the appropriate research basis.

In response to the changing nature of policing, many police forces have modified the content and style of their training (e.g., Yuille, 1986a). However, they rarely research the consequences of training alterations. New curricula are introduced, new pedagogical techniques are instituted yet there is no empirical basis to evaluate the results. This is an unfortunate state of affairs and reflects a basis shortcoming in the developing cooperation between psychologists and the police. The lack of research, in part, is a result of financial limitations. Police forces typically have budgetary constraints and they have no tradition of designating any funds for research purposes. More germane, however, is the fact that police management have little appreciation for the value of research. This is a problem psychologists should work to redress. If training changes routinely included a research component, training would improve and, in the long run, would be more cost effective as well.

One example of a project designed to evaluate police training demonstrates the value of such a research component. In the early 1980s, the London Metropolitan Police introduced a new facet in recruit training at their facility in Hendon (c.f., Poole, 1986). This component, called Human Awareness Training (HAT), was designed to improve communication skills and the awareness of recruits of the problems related to minority groups in the community. HAT includes several weeks of training at the Hendon facility. The police decided to evaluate the impact of the training and Ray Bull, a psychologist who was then at the North East London Polytechnic, and his colleagues have completed several evaluations in the past five years. They have employed a multi-method approach which has included paper and pencil tests (e.g., Bull, 1986) as well as on the job observations by researchers of those officers who had been trained (e.g., Bull & Horncastle, 1990).

The results of the HAT evaluations have indicated that this program has mixed effects. For example, although the attitudes of the recruits were positively affected by the training, those effects disappeared after several months of job experience (demonstrating the effects of what Bull (1986) has called the "canteen culture"). As a result of these and similar findings, the police have modified the program to more effective ends (Bull, 1990, personal communication). This example of cooperation between psychologists and policing clearly demonstrates the advantage of a research component in any training change. The inclusion of an evaluation encourages:

1. A clear statement of the goals of the changes in training.

2. The development of evaluation procedures by psychologists which are suited to the needs of police work (rather than simply of convenience to the researcher).

3. An examination of the actual (rather than hypothesized) effects of the training.

Unfortunately, the evaluation of HAT is the exception (see also, Dutton, 1986) rather than the rule. Most training changes are simply evaluated on their face validity or by informal feedback from the field. This is a real failure on the part of psychologists. The forte of the discipline is research but we have failed to communicate its value to police.

The Lack of Research

The three areas of applied police psychology reviewed above, clinical practice, recruit selection and recruit training, present a generally negative picture with respect to the absence of research in police psychology. The most basic strength of psychology as a discipline is critical thinking. Psychologists are trained to evaluate their assumptions and to test their interventions. They are now active in police organizations yet their major strength, critical thinking, exemplified in solid research, is strikingly absent. Psychologists have been unsuccessful, assuming they have tried, to convince police forces of the many advantages that research would produce.

Lack of research is only one problem with the police/psychology relationship. An additional, albeit related, problem is the facile application of research findings from other domains to police work. I am concerned that psychologists are too willing to apply the knowledge of their discipline to police work without advocating the need for research in the police context. Research results from cognitive and social psychology laboratories are often applied to policing (or, at least, their application is advocated) without any apparent concern for the generalizability of the results. I offer a detailed example of my basis for this concern with the examination of eyewitness memory research.

Eyewitness Research

I have chosen eyewitness research as a focus for two reasons. To begin with this is the major area of forensic research in psychology, major in the sense that more studies have been done in this area than any other forensic area. In fact, the amount of eyewitness research has been so great that the editor of the journal *Law and Human Behaviour* expressed exasperation at the disproportionate number of Journal submissions involving eyewitness studies (Saks, 1986). He encouraged researchers to focus on other topics, equally worthy of their attention. In addition, the eyewitness area precisely represents the problem that exists in the application of psychology to police work: a willingness to apply without having done the appropriate studies to test the generalizability of research findings from one context to another.

Eyewitness research has had two periods fo productivity in the past century. The first occurred around the turn of the century when French (e.g., Binet, 1900), German (e.g., Stern, 1910) and American (Münsterberg, 1908) researchers studied memory for a variety of events. The second period began in the late 1960s and has shown no decrease in activity to the present. Both periods have had the same general characteristics:

1. Research witnesses are usually uninvolved bystanders, most often undergraduate volunteers who are exposed to an event. The witnesses generally do not participate in

the event and, for obvious ethical reasons the event rarely has a negative impact on them (c.f., Yuille & Tollestrup, in press).

2. For the sake of consistency, and cost, the events are usually recorded (e.g., via a slide sequence or a video tape). However, during both periods of research there was, and is, a recognition that recorded events are rather artificial (e.g., Stern, 1910; Malpass & Devine, 1981). Concern with ecological validity led to the use of staged events in either controlled or field settings (s.f., Davies, 1990).

3. The memory of witnesses is usually tested immediately after the event. If any delay is included it is usually a maximum of a few days (in contrast, see Bull, Boon, Knox, & Flin, 1990).

4. The research eyewitness accounts have no consequences for either the witness or the "criminal" (Yuille & Wells, 1991). Actual witnesses of crimes stand in stark contrast to research witnesses.

The "real" witness has the following characteristics:

1. More than 70 percent of witnesses of crimes are victims of the crime (c.f., Yuille & Tollestrup, in press). Of the remainder, many are affected and even traumatized by the event. Uninvolved bystanders do exist, for example as witnesses to traffic offenses, but, in the realm of serious crime, they are relatively rare.

2. The events which real witnesses experience are complex, absorbing and very different from any recorded event and from most staged events.

3. "Real" witnesses often have their memory tested months and even years after the event.

4. In actual crimes, providing a description of an event and/or making a choice from a photo-spread or line-up has very real consequences for both the witness and the suspect.

It is apparent that there are major differences between the characteristics of witnesses studied by psychologists and those interviewed by the police. Further, there are differences between the contexts employed by psychologists and those which most witnesses to serious crimes encounter. However, these differences have not impeded psychologists in claiming that their research has application in police work and in criminal courts: such claims have been made in spite of the fact that, until recently, no research had been conducted to determine if witnesses behave in the same way in "real life" and in typical research contexts.

To date, there have been only a few studies of the memory of actual witnesses to serious crimes (Cutshall & Yuille, 1989; Fisher, Geiselmann & Amador, 1989; Yuille & Cutshall, 1986; Yuille & Cutshall, 1989; Yuille & Kim, 1987). The lack of this type of research is understandable. Studies of actual witnesses are very costly, time consuming and filled with practical difficulties (e.g., obtaining police co-operation, finding the witnesses, finding ground truth criteria, etc. see Yuille, 1986b). However, the results of these studies suggest that the generalization from controlled research to actual witnesses should be made with caution. Witnesses of serious crimes do not always show the memory weakness of their laboratory counterparts. In fact, Fisher et al. (1989) concluded that: "If this difference between laboratory and field studies continues to appear, one may question the validity of describing in court the accurarcy rates found in the laboratory as evidence of the general unreliability of eyewitness testimony in field cases." (p. 725)

Perhaps the most striking difference between controlled research and the field research findings relates to the strength and persistence of the memory of some witnesses to actual crimes. Several authors, on the basis of controlled research findings, have suggested that witnesses are typically fallible and that their memory deteriorates rapidly with the passage of time (e.g., Loftus, 1979; Yarmey, 1979). While this may characterize some witnesses of actual crimes, the limited field research indicates that it does not characterize all of them. In certain situations a witness may have a fairly detailed memory (detailed enough, at least, to include the core elements of the event), and he or she may retain that detail for months - or even years. Yuille and Cutshall (1989) proposed that such memories could be labelled remarkable memories: a memory for an event which is so striking or unusual that it will be retold (rehearsed) by the witness, assuring that the details will be retained.

The value of the remarkable memory concept must await further research. However, the concept was a result of the different performance found with actual witnesses. The concern about the generalizability of controlled research findings was not trivial. It turns out to be well founded.

Converging Paradigms

The fact that field research is producing results which are different from those of more controlled research should give psychologists reason for hesitation in generalizing results from one context to another. This is not an argument that field research is superior to controlled research but rather, it is the obvious argument for an empirical discipline: do not claim knowledge until the appropriate empirical test has been conducted. We have learned a great deal about how human memory operates in *controlled contexts* from eyewitness research. Much of this knowledge is of basic value and much of it may prove generalizable to other contexts, such as memory for actual crimes. But which findings are generalizable and which are not is an empirical question. It is simply inappropriate to take any other stand and continue to assert that psychology is an empirical discipline.

Making premature generalizations is not only inappropriate, it is dangerous to the discipline. When psychologists become too eager to apply their knowledge they risk the professional embarrassment of attacks by those more familiar with police work or the courts. For example, when Münsterberg (1908) claimed that the courts should be informed of the psychological knowledge of witnesses he was soundly and effectively attacked by the leading legal expert of the day (Wigmore, 1909). Wigmore's attack on the premature nature of Münsterberg's claims was instrumental in effecting a decline in eyewitness research. In the contemporary era, similar attacks have begun to appear. For example, Konečni and Ebbesen (1986), in a discussion of court teestimony by psychologists about eyewitness memory, concluded that the generalizability "problems seem sufficiently important that they should give would-be experts on these matters serious pause-on both ethical and scientific grounds-in deciding whether or not to testify." A more detailed examination of issues concerning expert psychological testimony in found in Yuille (1989).

Offering advice before we have an appropriate or sufficient data base also runs the risk of losing the respect of the potential consumers of our advice. An anecdote illustrates this point. Some time ago I attend a talk by a well known researcher in the eyewitness field. He reviewed an excellent series of studies concerned with the performance of witnesses in controlled research settings. Toward the end of his presentation the researcher offered police a number of proposals of how they should conduct their investigations with witnesses.

There happened to be several police officers present for this talk and they were astonished at these proposals. They observed that most of the researcher's proposals, although theoretically interesting, were impossible to achieve in the context of police work. That is, the police said that an officer answering a call for service would not have the luxury of using the researchers suggestions. In short, the proposals were simply impractical. The officers who attended the talk were offended that the psychologists had such little understanding of the practical demands of their job.

What is required to assure that the knowledge we offer to police and the courts has a firm foundation is a converging set of research studies. The controlled research of the laboratory needs to be combined with simulation studies carried out in field settings. These studies, in turn, need to be compared with archival research and with studies of actual victims and witnesses. All of this research must be interpreted with an understanding of the practical demands of police work.

Conclusions

Police departments have sought assistance from psychologists with increasing frequency in the past two decades. Although psychology has much to offer, a review of the types of applications psychologists have made raises a real concern. Whether one examines clinical work for police, the use of psychologists in police selection and training, or the application of psychological research to police operations (e.g., interviewing eyewitnesses) psychologists have gone well beyond their data base.

I believe that the results of psychological research have potential application and value for police. This application must be made cautiously and only after converging research methods have been employed. Psychologists must be sure that the phenomenon of concern has been examined in a variety of contexts, in particular, in the police context. A psychologist who attempts to apply knowledge derived from research must also have an understanding of the place in which the findings will be applied. Researchers and practitioners should display more caution and more sensitivity to the needs of police when offering assistance and advice.

References

Binet, A. (1900). *La suggestibilité*. Paris: Schleicher Frères.
Bull, R. (1986). An evaluation of police recruit training in human awareness. In J.C. Yuille (Ed.), *Police selection and training: The role of psychology* (pp. 97-122). Dordrecht, The Netherlands: Kluwer Academic.
Bull, R., Boon, J., Knox, A., & Flin, R. (1990). *The effect of five month delay on children's and adults' eyewitness memory*. Paper presented at the 22nd International Congress of Applied Psychology, Kyoto, Japan.
Bull, R., & Horncastle, P. (1990). *Evaluating police recruit training*. Paper presented at the 22nd International Congress of Applied Psychology, Kyoto, Japan.
Cutshall, J.L., & Yuille, J.C. (1989). Field studies of eyewitness memory of actual crimes. In D. C. Raskin (Ed.), *Psychological methods in criminal investigation and evidence* (pp. 97-124). New York: Springer.

Davies, G.M. (1990). *Influencing public policy on eyewitnessing: Problems and possibilities.* Paper presented at the Second European Conference on Law and Psychology, Nürnberg, Germany.

Dutton, D.G. (1986). The public and the police. Training implications of the demand for a new model police officer. In J.C. Yuille (Ed.), *Police selection and training: The role of psychology* (pp. 141-157). Dordrecht, The Netherlands: Kluwer Academic.

Fisher, R.P., Geiselmann, R.E., & Amador, M. (1989). Field test of the cognitive interview: Enhancing the recollection of actual victims and witnesses of crime. *Journal of Applied Psychology, 74,* 722-727.

Hargrave, G.E. (1986). Psychological standards research for California Law enforcement officers. In J.C. Yuille (Ed.), *Police selection and training: The role of psychology* (pp. 247-249). Dordrecht, The Netherlands: Kluwer Academic.

Inwald, R.E. (1986). Law enforcement officer screening: A description of one pre-employment psychological testing program. In J. Reese, & H.A. Goldstein (Eds.), *Psychological services for law enforcement* (pp. 51-80). Washington, DC: Government Printing Office.

Konečni, V.J., & Ebbesen, E.B. (1986). Courtroom testimony by psychologists on eyewitness identification issues. *Law and Human Behaviour, 10,* 117-126.

Loftus, E.F. (1979). *Eyewitness testimony.* Cambridge, MA: Harvard University Press.

Loo, R., & Meredith, C. (1986). Recruit selection in the Royal Canadian Mounted Police. In J. C. Yuille (Ed.), *Police selection and training: The role of psychology* (pp. 3-20). Dordrecht, The Netherlands: Kluwer Academic.

Malpass, R.S., & Devine, P.G. (1981). Guided memory in eyewitness identification. *Journal of Applied Psychology, 66,* 343-350.

Münsterberg, H. (1908). *On the witness stand: Essays on psychology and crime.* New York: Clark, Boardman, Doubleday.

Poole, L. (1986). The contribution of psychology to the development of police training in Britain. In J.C. Yuille (Ed.), *Police selection and training: The role of psychology* (pp. 77-96). Dordrecht, The Netherlands: Kluwer Academic.

Reese, J., & Goldstein, H.A. (Eds.). (1986). *Psychological services for law enforcement.* Washington, DC: Government Printing Office.

Reiser, M. (1986). Critical issues for the police psychologist in training police. In J. C. Yuille (Ed.), *Police selection and training: The role of psychology* (pp. 21-42). Dordrecht, The Netherlands: Kluwer Academic.

Saks, M. (1986). The law does not live by eyewitness testimony alone. *Law and Human Behaviour, 10,* 279-280.

Stern, L.W. (1910). Abstracts of lectures in the psychology of testimony and on the study of individuality. *American Journal of Psychology, 21,* 270-282.

Wigmore, J.H. (1909). Professor Münsterberg and the psychology of testimony: Being a report of the case of Cokestone v. Münsterberg. *Illinois Law Review, 3,* 399-434.

Yarmey, A.D. (1979). *The psychology of eyewitness testimony.* New York: The Free Press.

Yuille, J.C. (1986a). Meaningful research in the police context. In J.C. Yuille (Ed.), *Police selection and training: The role of psychology* (pp. 225-243). Dordrecht, The Netherlands: Kluwer Academic.

Yuille, J.C. (Ed.) (1986b). *Police selection and training: The role of psychology.* Dordrecht, The Netherlands: Kluwer Academic.

Yuille, J.C. (1989). Expert evidence by psychologists: Sometimes problematic and often premature. *Behavioural Sciences and the Law, 7,* 181-196.

Yuille, J.C., & Cutshall, J.L. (1986). A case study of eyewitness memory of a crime. *Journal of Applied Psychology, 71,* 291-301.

Yuille, J.C., & Cutshall, J.L. (1989). Analysis of the statements of victims, witnesses and suspects. In J.C. Yuille (Ed.), *Credibility assessment* (pp. 175-191). Dordrecht, The Netherlands: Kluwer Academic.

Yuille, J.C., & Tollestrup, P.A. (in press). A model of the diverse effects of emotion on eyewitness memory. In S. A. Christianson (Ed.), *Emotion and memory.*

Yuille, J.C., & Wells, G.L. (1991). Concerns about the application of research findings: The issue of ecological validity. In J.L. Doris (Ed.), *The suggestibility of children's recollections.* Washington, DC: American Psychological Association.

Predictors of Suspect and Interviewer Behaviour During Police Questioning

Stephen J. Moston and Geoffrey M. Stephenson

Introduction

How will a suspect respond initially when he or she is being questioned in connection with an offence? The answer is not determined solely by the actual guilt or innocence of the suspect. Not all guilty persons confess, and not all innocent people maintain their innocence. Moreover, some may genuinely not know whether they are guilty of a crime or not, and, in addition, in England, innocent and guilty people alike are made aware of their right to be silent.

Regardless of the individual's actual involvement in the offence of which he or she is accused, there appear to be three main sets of factors that will determine the suspect's initial response to an allegation: The background characteristics of the suspect (including their age, sex and criminal history) and case (the offence type and its severity); the contextual characteristics of a case (strength of evidence and legal advice) and an interviewer's questioning techniques. Interviewing techniques are in turn affected by the interviewer's beliefs and attitudes which are largely determined by the background and contextual characteristics of the case, as well as the characteristics of the suspect.

These factors are seen as having a direct bearing on a suspect's initial response to an allegation. That is, at the start of the interview the suspect has a predetermined strategy (e.g., deny everything). Consequently, if the interviewer should start the interview by directly accusing the suspect, that suspect would deny the allegation. Alternatively, if the accusation is not directly stated, the guilty suspect's responses to questions (e.g., their movements at the time of the offence) will incorporate an implicit denial, that is, they will lie. In fact, it is often assumed that guilty suspects will lie (or deny) at the outset of questioning and that it is task of the skilled investigator to manipulate the suspect's decision making in order to make them confess. Each of the factors that can affect the suspect's initial decision to admit or deny will be discussed in turn.

The characteristics of the suspect

The criminal history of the suspect. There is believed to be a relationship between the suspect's criminal record and their behaviour during interrogation. Those with more experience of interrogation and the legal system may respond differently to those without such experience (e.g., Mitchell, 1983). Additionally, the police interviewer may treat the suspect differently depending on their criminal history. For example, some well-known criminals may be treated with all the respect due a "professional".

Age of suspect. The age of the suspect may also predispose a suspect to make particular response. For example, older suspects may be more likely to deny an allegation because they are less intimidated by the police officer and the situation generally.

Sex of suspect. One area in which the "manuals" of interrogation are very weak is in their treatment of sex differences. Inbau and Reid (1967) and Royal and Schutt (1976) both offer what may be seen as slightly patronising advice concerning the interrogation of women. For example, Royal and Schutt suggest that women's emotional responses are different from men's and that they might be more ready to use "the white lie" as a defence. Although sex of suspect may not directly influence suspect behaviour, it may have a bearing on interviewing styles.

There are a number of other case characteristics that might also have a bearing on the behaviour of a suspect and the police interviewer including the suspect's race (Bishop & Frazier, 1988), personality (Inbau, Reid, & Buckley, 1986) and social class (Sparger & Giacopassi, 1986).

The characteristics of the offence

Offence type. Different interviewing techniques may be necessary depending on the offence type. The most significant example of this is rape cases. Interviewing techniques in any sexual offence cases may need to be different from the norm. Another way in which offence type may have a bearing on interviewing style and suspect behaviour is the extent to which evidence is available. For example, in an assault case, there may be little evidence to directly implicate a suspect. However, in a burglary there is more likely to be physical evidence such as stolen property. Different offence types may also be associated with differing levels of severity.

Offence severity. Dealing with serious cases may necessitate a quite different set of strategies to dealing with trivial cases. The pressure to obtain a confession in a trivial case is not quite so great. Serious cases offer a greater professional incentive for the interviewer to obtain a confession. However, serious cases are more likely to evoke a self-preservation instinct in the suspect since the consequences of confession are going to be extremely damaging (i.e., a long prison sentence).

Contextual case characteristics

Contextual case characteristics are a particular sub-set of case characteristics that may have a bearing on the behaviour of the suspect and the police interviewer. The main contextual factors are legal advice and evidence, though other factors such as the location of the police station, the number of interviews and time spent in custody might also be included in this category. Certain contextual factors may vary across time, for example, in one interview a legal representative might be absent, but present later.

Legal advice. A prime determinant of suspect behaviour is legal advice. A solicitor or their representative will directly advise their client on how to behave during interrogation. It is less clear to what extent that the presence of a legal representative has on the adoption of different interviewing strategies. It is possible that interviewers adopt more cautious styles when a solicitor is present, however, with tape recording now being used, this seems unlikely. The presence of a tape recorder is probably just as likely to encourage caution on the part of the interviewer as is the presence of a legal representative.

Strength of evidence. The strength of evidence against a suspect is likely to be a major determinant of both suspect behaviour and interviewing style. When there is weak evidence, there are a limited range interviewing strategies available, but with stronger evidence a greater range of possibilities emerge. The suspect's knowledge of the evidence against them is also likely to be a key predictor of how they will respond to an allegation. What is important here is the extent to which the suspect knows of the police evidence. That is, there is a relationship between how the suspect perceives the police evidence and how they will behave during questioning. For example, in a case where a suspect has been caught red-handed, the suspect knows that the police have strong evidence against him or her. Denying an allegation seemingly serves little purpose. However, if the suspect was arrested after an incident and is aware of no evidence that implicates them, such as the possession of stolen property, then their perceptions of the evidence are unclear. The police may well have strong evidence such as witnesses and fingerprints, but if the suspect is unaware of this, thinking he or she was not seen or had left no fingerprints, they may think the police case is weak. In such a scenario the suspect may begin an interview by denying any knowledge of an incident, but may later decide to confess as the police point out the evidence.

This relationship is central to the process of interrogation. The interviewer manipulates the suspect's decision making by using the available evidence as a persuasive technique. Irving (1980) suggests that evidence can be used to persuade suspects that the only available course of action is confession. Using the available evidence appropriately is the key to interrogation. The suspect's perceptions of the case and most importantly their perceptions of their chances of escaping custody can be affected by evidence.

When the police have only weak evidence, yet are seeking a confession, then they have to convince the suspect that they have a strong case. Lying about evidence, for example, by stating that the suspect's fingerprints have been found when they have not, is outlawed under the present legislation. Apart from presenting a bad image of police interrogation, it is a poor interviewing technique. For example, suppose an interviewer lies and tells a burglar that their fingerprints have been found at the scene of a crime. If that burglar had been wearing gloves then they would know this statement is a lie and they will probably view anything the interviewer says from that moment on with either contempt, or at least a high degree of cynicism.

The other option, instead of lying, is to imply that evidence may be found. For example, instead of saying "We have found your fingerprints", a more effective line would be "We are dusting for fingerprints, might we find yours?". If the burglar hadn't been wearing gloves then this statement might provoke a degree of anxiety on their part, stemming from a fear of being caught, in much the same way as the lie would have done. However, if the burglar had been wearing gloves then they would simply dismiss this statement and no 'harm' would have been done. One problem with using implied evidence is that the suspect may believe that the police are going to fabricate evidence.

To summarise, it is the suspect's perceptions of the police case that is important. It is not the degree of evidence itself. It is possible that if the police have a strong case, but through bad interviewing practices they convey the impression that it is weak, then the suspect will deny. Conversely, if the case is weak but the limited evidence is used effectively, it may persuade the suspect to confess.

The interviewer's beliefs, attitudes, and behaviour

The characteristics of the suspect and the case affect not only the behaviour of the suspect, but the beliefs and attitudes of the interviewer. This may, in turn, have a bearing on the detective's choice of interviewing strategy (as has already been shown in several of the earlier examples). Belief in a suspect's guilt or innocence is likely to be largely determined by the evidence available. For example, when a person is caught red-handed, the interrogator's belief in the suspect's guilt is going to be very high.

The interviewer is also likely to have a series of preconceived ideas concerning appropriate interviewing strategies. For example, a detective may have a favoured style of questioning that is used in a large number of cases, irrespective of any case or suspect characteristics.

Data Collection

Information concerning police interviews was collected from questionnaires distributed to nine Metropolitan Police stations. This questionnaire assessed a number of facts about each interview that took place. The variables (to be used as predictors of outcome of interview) identified in the questionnaires were as follows.

1. Strength of evidence against the suspect: The interviewer in each case rated the strength of evidence against the suspect. Three levels of evidence strength were coded: weak, moderate and strong. 2. Interviewer's perception of the offence's seriousness: In this study, offence seriousness was assessed by asking the interviewing officer to rate the seriousness of the offence. Three levels of severity were coded: trivial, moderately serious and very serious. 3. Offence type: Although there is a multitude of offences for which a suspect can be accused, these were divided into two basic categories, offences against property and offences against the person. 4. Age of suspect. 5. Sex of suspect 6. Criminal history: Suspects were categorised into those with and without previous convictions. 7. Use of Legal advice: Some suspects seek legal advice whilst others do not.

The final outcome of an interview was recorded as either an admission, a denial, or neither. Additional outcome measures such as the making of damaging statements and use of the right of silence were also recorded. For further details of the periods of data collection and types of suspects and cases featured in the study, see Moston, Stephenson, and Williamson (1990a; 1990b). Information on 1067 consecutive cases was collected.

One obvious limitation to the present findings is that the final outcome of an interview need not necessarily correspond to a suspect's initial response to the allegation. However, it is suggested here that in this sample the relationship between a suspect's initial and final response to an allegation are likely to be the same in the vast majority of cases. The reasons for this assertion are as follows. The Police and Criminal Evidence Act which governs the questioning of suspects places strict controls on the conduct of police interviewers. Many questioning practices, although accepted in other countries, such as lying to suspects through the distortion of facts, are explicitly prohibited and rigorous checks on the conduct of police officers are enforced. All interviews must be tape recorded and any signs of coercive questioning (a term not yet adequately defined) will almost certainly serve to invalidate any evidence obtained through questioning. The consequence of these conditions is that interviewers are reluctant to contradict a suspect's account of events and denials, even in the face of overwhelmingly contradictory information are thus accepted. There is little if any attempt to manipulate a suspect's decision to admit or deny.

Predictors of suspect behaviour

Overall, nearly 42% of suspects admitted committing an offence, a similar number denied and about 16% did not either admit or deny. Many of the suspects in this last category used their right to silence.

The next part of the analysis was to determine which case characteristics had a bearing on a suspect's decision to admit or deny. This analysis was carried out using hiloglinear analysis. The results of the analysis showed that only three main factors (evidence, offence severity and legal advice) were significantly associated with final outcome of an interview. Tables illustrating each of these factors will be shown in turn. Percentages are rounded to two decimal places. The other variables (age and sex of suspect, criminal history and offence category) were not significantly associated with the outcome of an interview.

Strength of evidence. Table 1 shows the effects of different strengths of evidence on suspect behaviour in interviews. Strength of evidence had a major association with the outcome of the interview (partial $\chi^2=307.642$; df=4; p<.0001). There is a marked effect of strength of evidence on full admissions. With strong evidence the admission rate reached two-thirds of all cases. However, with weak evidence denials reached an ever higher level (76.64%).

Table 1: Strength of Evidence and the Outcomes of Interviews.

Strength of evidence	No. of cases	Outcome of interview		
		% of admissions	% of denials	% of neither admit nor deny
Weak	274	9.85	76.64	13.50
Moderate	363	36.36	45.18	18.46
Strong	430	66.74	16.28	16.98

Severity of the offence. Table 2 shows how outcomes varied with an interviewer's rating of case severity (partial $\chi^2=9.704$; df=4; p<.0001). The most striking figure here are those in the neither admit or deny category. Such responses became more frequent with increasing offence severity.

Table 2: Interviewers Perceived Severity of the Offence and the Outcomes of Interviews.

Perceived severity	No. of cases	Outcome of interview		
		% of admissions	% of denials	% of neither admit nor deny
Trivial	164	37.20	50.00	12.80
Moderate	601	45.76	38.94	15.31
Very serious	302	36.42	42.38	21.19

Legal advice. There was a highly significant effect of legal advice on both the outcome of an interview (partial $\chi^2=64.388$; df=2; p<.0001). Table 3 shows that full admissions dropped by about 20% when a suspect has made contact with a legal representative.

Table 3: Legal Advice and the Outcomes of Interviews and the Use of Silence.

Legal advice	No. of cases	Outcome of interview		
		% of admissions	% of denials	% of neither admit nor deny
No legal advice	631	50.40	39.78	9.83
Has legal advice	436	29.36	44.27	26.38

Predictors of interviewers' beliefs and attitudes

The next step in the analysis was to identify which case and suspect factors affected interviewers' beliefs concerning the guilt or innocence of a suspect. Immediately prior to questioning, interviewers were asked to indicate whether or not they believed the person they were about to question was either innocent or guilty. Their response was then related to the seven case and suspect characteristics and statistically analyzed, again using hiloglinear analysis.

Not surprisingly, evidence was the biggest predictor of belief (partial $\chi^2=453.154$; df=2; p<.0001). Criminal history also showed an association with belief (partial $\chi^2=12.942$; df=1; p<.0005). No other variables were associated with belief (all p>.05).

When there was weak evidence, the interviewer was sure of the suspect's guilt in 31% of cases. With moderate evidence, interviewers were sure nearly 74% of the time and with strong evidence 99% of suspects were seen as guilty. When the suspect had no previous convictions, the interviewer was sure that nearly 69% of suspects were guilty whereas when the suspect had previous convictions, nearly 76% were believed to be guilty.

Predictors of interviewing strategies

The final part of this paper refers to the relationship between case and suspect characteristics and interviewing strategies. The following observations are based on the taped records of questioning and detailed analysis of these tapes is still in progress.

Despite our initial assumptions, there appear to be few obvious links between case characteristics and interviewing strategies. The only factors that appear to exert any obvious effect on interviewing strategies are strength of evidence and offence severity. In cases where there is strong evidence against the suspect there is a marked tendency towards accusatorial strategies of questioning (see Moston, 1990) where the suspect is confronted with the accusation against them at the very outset of questioning. In cases where there is almost certainly already enough evidence to obtain a conviction, without obtaining any additional information through questioning, interviewers appear to be concerned simply with obtaining an admission ("Yes, I did it"), without necessarily checking the validity of this admission. In some cases in which the suspect did confess at this stage, no further questions were put to the suspect leaving the possibility that the confession was either coerced (possibly through pre-interview intimidation) or unreliable. For example, a guilty suspect confronted with an accusation that is far less serious than the offence which they have really committed, might be all too eager to accept the opportunity to "confess" in order to forestall any additional investigation of the details of the offence.

Information gathering questioning strategies, characterised by the asking of 'open' questions intended to let the suspect describe their actions in their own words, are far more common in cases in which there is minimal evidence against the suspect. In such cases this strategy is essentially dictated by the circumstances, that is, the interviewer cannot confront the suspect with the 'proof' of their guilt because such evidence has not yet been obtained. This style of questioning is also commonly observed with serious offences, particularly sex related offences. In such cases the suspect's motive for committing an action might be a crucial aspect of an investigation.

Even though this aspect of the study is still continuing, the early indications are that there are few associations between case characteristics and interviewing strategies. The reason for this may lie with the fact that Metropolitan Police officers, and in fact most British police officers, typically receive no interview training whatsoever. Interviewing has traditionally been viewed as a skill that could only be learnt through experience. The introduction of training courses is a relatively new innovation which is still under-researched and under-resourced. Although it may be possible to predict the behaviour of a suspect depending on the characteristics of that person and the case, it is considerably harder to predict the behaviour of a police officer. The degree to which interviewing strategies and case characteristics interact to affect a person's decision making across an interview, or series of interviews, is something that this research will attempt to cover. The research reported here is thus a first step in trying to determine why a person should decide to confess to a crime. It is hoped that this work will illustrate the relative importance of interviewing strategies in relation to case and suspect characteristics in influencing this decision.

References

Bishop, D.M., & Frazier, C.E. (1988). The influence of race in juvenile justice processing. *Crime and Delinquency, 25*, 242-263.

Inbau, F.E., & Reid, J.E. (1967). *Criminal interrogations and confessions*, 2nd ed. Baltimore: Williams and Wilkins.

Inbau, F.E., Reid, J.E., & Buckley, J.P. (1986). *Criminal interrogation and confessions*, 3rd ed. Baltimore: Williams and Wilkins.

Irving, B. (1980). *Police interrogation: A case study*. Royal Commission on Criminal Procedure, Research study No. 2. London: HMSO.

Mitchell, B. (1983). Confessions and police interrogation of suspects. *Criminal Law Review*, 596-604.

Moston, S. (1990). *The ever-so gentle art of police interrogation*. Paper presented at British Psychological Society Annual Conference, University of Swansea.

Moston, S., Stephenson, G.M., & Williamson, T.M. (1990a). *Police interrogation styles and suspect behaviour*. Final report to the Police Requirements Support Unit (Home Office).

Moston, S., Stephenson, G.M., & Williamson, T.M. (1990b). *Suspects' use of the right of silence during police interrogation*. Final report to the Home Office.

Royal, R.F., & Schutt, S.R. (1976). *The gentle art of interviewing and interrogation*. Englewood Cliffs, NJ: Prentice-Hall.

Sparger, J.R., & Giacopassi, D.J. (1986). Police resentment of the upper class. *Criminal Justice Review, 11*, 25-33.

Perceived Credibility of the Communicator: Studies of Perceptual Bias in Police Officers Conducting Rape Interviews[1]

Frans W. Winkel and Leendert Koppelaar

Introduction

Victimological interest in the notion of secondary victimization has increased rapidly (Guidelines for Victim Support in Europe, 1987; Shapland, 1990; Viano, 1989). It is assumed that when crime victims communicate their experiences to others in their direct social environment or to the criminal justice system, they regularly encounter inappropriate responses. Through these responses, they are in a sense revictimized: They are wounded again. Preventing secondary victimization is considered a central objective of victim assistance (Guidelines for Victim Support in Europe, 1987):

> In all these practices prevention of secondary victimisation is central: the victim should not be victimised again as a result of treatment by agencies. Not only victim support networks should prevent this, but also police, welfare workers, probation officers and criminal justice authorities. Victim support has to inform these agencies on this subject. (p. 12)

Attempts to prevent or eliminate secondary victimization will be succesful only if we diagnose the problem correctly and have clear ideas about its roots and causes. Victimological analyses are incomplete, in the sense that a social-psychological perspective is notably absent. Ignorance, thoughtlessness, routine behavior, bad manners, a lack of consideration and empathy by those running the criminal justice system are generally seen as major causes of inadequate responding to crime victims. Davelaar van Tongeren (1980), expressing the dominant view, characterizes police behavior with regard to rape victims, for example, as follows:

> Insinuating remarks such as "did you lean him on?", unhealthy interest in intimate details, curiosity about the victim's private life, other policemen who come to "look over" the victim, endless questioning sessions to test her credibility, sudden, direct confrontations with the apprehended suspect to test victim reactions, in short: the very same arsenal of complaints as compiled in the American literature. The police are not your best friend; even worse; the vice squad is a horrible institute full of horrid little men. (p. 115)

In our view, more subtle causes of secondary victimization should be taken into consideration, too. Distrusting rape victims, or more generally, inadequate responding toward crime victims, might be the result of biases in the process of forming impressions

---

[1] All videomaterial discussed in this article was produced by the CIRCON- group for organization and training development (Amsterdam) under supervision of L. Koppelaar. The Netherlands Organisation for Scientific Research (NWO-Stichting Psychon), the Stichting Mens & Recht, the Ministry of Justice, and the Free University are gratefully acknowledged for funding the experiments.

of those victims, and in the process of making judgments about their statements. In this article, some empirical evidence is reported suggesting that at least three types of bias might be operative in police personnel conducting interviews with rape victims, namely a self-presentation bias, a referral bias, and a dishonest demeanor bias. These biases express the idea that irrelevant factors have a negative impact on the perceived credibility of the victim. Respectively a relationship is postulated between perceived credibility and (irrelevant) characteristics of the victim (style of self-presentation), situational characteristics present in the interview setting (prior credibility information), and characteristics of the suspect (style of denying charges). The notion of perceptually induced secondary victimization obviously calls for solutions in tackling the problem of secondary victimization that are different from those emanating from a "bad manners" approach.

Self-Presentation Bias

Getting over the negative effects of sexual victimization not only depends upon the victim, but upon others in the victim's environment (Cook, Smith, & Harrell, 1987; President's Task Force on Victims of Crime, 1986; Saunders & Size, 1986). There is broad psychological support for the hypothesis that the help of others is essential to overcoming these effects more thoroughly and rapidly (Brownell & Shumaker, 1984; Shumaker & Brownell, 1984; Steinmetz, 1984). Unfortunately, instead of getting help, many victims of sexual crimes are regarded with suspicion and mistrust; their integrity and credibility cast into doubt (Burt, 1980; Cann, Calhoun, Selby, & King, 1981; Gulotta & De Cataldo Neuberger, 1983; Schwendinger & Schwendinger, 1974). Victim-blaming can so seriously hamper the victim's coping process that it constitutes in effect a secondary victimization. Winkel and Koppelaar (1991) examined the question: "Under what conditions is a rape victim blamed for her rape?" The post-victimization demeanor of the victim appears to be an important variable, on which we will focus here.

Individual victims react differently in many respects (Fattah, 1984; Winkel, 1984, 1988, 1989), including the way in which victims inform others about their experiences (Brom, Kleber, & Defares, 1986; Horowitz, 1976; Ruback, Greenberg, & Westcott, 1984). Empirical studies have distinguished two basic styles of response to crime: One is a highly emotional self-presentation, in which the victim displays distress clearly visible to outsiders. The other style of self-presentation is more low-key, with feelings checked and controlled. In the first case, for instance, the experience is expressed in a trembling voice and is more often interrupted by fits of crying; while, in the second case, the victim makes a more numbed or resigned impression on the observer. The latter victims will express their experiences less emotionally, at least to all appearances. We will refer to these as the emotional and the numbed style of self-presentation (Brom, Kleber, & Defares, 1986). From the recent victimological literature it can be deduced that victims of criminal offenses also show such self-presentation styles (Frieze, Hymer, & Greenberg, 1987; Janoff-Bulman & Hanson Frieze, 1983; Kidd & Chayett, 1984). With regard to rape victims, Burgess and Holmstrom (1974) were the first to observe these two styles, which they respectively labeled as expressed and controlled.

In view of collective gender role stereotyping (Brownmiller, 1975; Krulewitz & Payne, 1978), combined with the social stereotype of a rape victim as a hysterical, crying, and shaking individual, the hypothesis was formulated that victims who express their experiences in an emotional way run less risk of secondary victimization, that is, undesired reactions from the environment, than rape victims who show a more numbed self-presentation. It should be stressed that this hypothesis comprises a perceptual distortion in observers. These biases can stretch the truth considerably. In fact, the style of self-presentation conveys no information at all about the realness or unrealness of the victimizing experience in itself (Wortman, 1983). One implication of this hypothesis is that a victim characterized by numbed self-presentation can count on less help from the environment in "working through" her experiences and is perceived as less credible than a victim who is characterized by an emotional self-presentation. This hypothesis was tested in the experiment outlined in Figure 1.

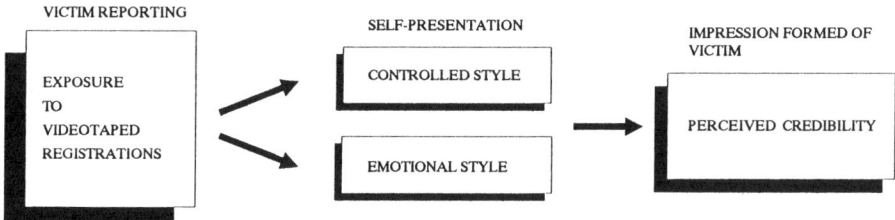

Figure 1: Experimental Design (Self-Presentation Effect).

Figure 1 shows that the most important independent variable was the self-presentation style of the victim. To operationalize the self-presentation of the victim, two videotapes were recorded, one of which showed an emotional self-presentation, the other a numbed self-presentation. In the former version, the victim experience was communicated in an extremely emotional manner, with some sobbing and in a trembling voice; in the latter version, all such outward signs of emotion were absent and the experience was communicated in an emotionally restrained manner. Both film versions were interrogated by a vice squad detective in which the victim announced she wanted to bring charges of rape. The role of the victim was played by a professional Dutch actress; her "opposite" player was a police officer who was actually employed by a juvenile vice squad. The subjects were shown edited versions in which only the victim could be seen and heard. Apart from the manipulated variable, both versions were identical and related to an event that actually took place.

The event was described by the victim as follows. She had given a party at her home. She had "invited" a vague acquaintance, a fellow apartment building tenant, who had helped her (after a chance encounter at the elevator) carry the groceries for the party. This tenant had once repaired her doorbell. After the party, when the rest of the guests had left, he stayed to help her with the dishes. After the dishes he went into the living room. There, according to the victim's reports, the rape took place. Some of the victim's statements were as follows:

> Yes, he stayed, to help with the dishes, he said. He dried, and all the while he had his hands all over me and things like that. I pushed him away and I said "We won't get anything

done like that." Well, finally the dishes were nearly done. He kept on hanging around and so I said, "I'll make some coffee," because I thought it might sober him up a little. He went and sat down in the living room. And I started pacing around, because I thought, "If I sit down next to him it will only get worse." So I went around emptying ash trays and wiping off tables. At a certain point, I walked past him and he grabbed me and drew me to him. What happened then? Then he raped me. We slid off the sofa. He pulled me back on the sofa. I lost my balance. And then the two of us slid down on the floor. I don't remember if he said anything or not. Of course a man is much heavier and much stronger when it comes to things like that. Finally he put his hand over my mouth because I was trying to scream.

Both film versions were shown to different subjects who were then asked to fill in a questionnaire about the victim.

To measure perceived credibility of the victim the following questions were posed: "How careful do you think the woman in the film was?" "In how far was the woman responsible for the situation?" "Do you believe the story of the woman?" "Do you think that this is a false allegation?" "In your opinion, did the woman speak the entire truth?" The subjects answered these questions on 9-point scales ranging from *definitely* (1) to *definitely not* (9); *definitely false* (1) to *definitely not false* (9); and so forth. All of these questions were used in a previous - rape vignettes - study (Den Ouden & Barentsen 1984), in which significant correlations emerged between scores on these items and scores on a revised and extended version of the Rape Myth Acceptance Scale (Burt, 1980; Schwartz, Williams, & Peppiton-Rockwell, 1981). Stronger acceptance of rape myths, for example, was positively associated with attributing more responsibility to the victim. Table 1 presents an overview of the major outcomes.

Table 1: Perceived Credibility by Style of Self-Presentation.

	Emotional self-presentation		Controlled self-presentation			
	M	SD	M	SD	F	p
Careful	4.21	2.6	2.46	2.0	11.30	.00
Not responsible	4.64	2.6	2.54	2.1	12.99	.00
Credible	7.65	1.6	6.25	1.7	14.06	.00
Report not phoney	6.50	2.7	5.0	2.7	2.89	.04
Telling the truth	6.69	1.9	5.96	2.7	2.05	.08

Note. Higher score represents stronger agreement with label

If we look at the means reported in this Table, we see a consistent picture: All means relating to the extent to which the style of self-presentation led to victimizing reactions agreed with the expectation expressed in the hypothesis. More specifically, it can be deduced from the table that the victim characterized by an emotional self-presentation was more strongly felt to be a woman who exhibited caution. She was more often described as a person who was not responsible for the situation. Less belief was attached to the story of the victim characterized by a numbed self-presentation than to that of the emotional victim: The perceived credibility of the numbed victim was significantly smaller. In addition, observers of the numbed victim more strongly tended to describe the charges as false. Lastly, a trend could be discerned toward describing an emotional victim more as a person who was speaking the truth.

Summarizing, the emotional victim made a considerably more credible impression on others than the numbed victim. The self-presentation style of the victim led to a perceptual bias in the observer in the sense that the numbed victim ran a higher risk of being treated with mistrust: A numbed self-presentation evoked stronger secondary victimizing reactions. Although more research is needed to unravel the precise psychological mechanisms underlying these styles, commentators do seem to agree that, in itself, the preferred style of self-presentation provides no information about the realness or unrealness of the victim experience (Brom et al., 1986; Burgess & Holmstrom, 1974; Wortman, 1983). However, from the present experimental results it may be concluded that others in the victim's environment may tend to attach more far-reaching conclusions to the style of self-presentation. Victims characterized by a numbed style of presentation are perceived as less credible.

Referral Bias: Transfer of Prior-Credibility Information

The referral effect suggests that prior expectancies, created during the transfer of tasks from one interviewer to another, bias the interview process toward these expectancies, and thus affect final judgments based on these interviews. Positive prior information will generally result in "favorable" postinterview impressions of the victim, while negative prior information will result in unfavorable postinterview perceptions of the victim. Conceptually, the referral bias is related to a number of other cognitive phenomena that are well documented in social psychological person perception studies, such as *anchoring* (adjusting initial judgments that serve as an anchor or reference point as more information is obtained), *belief perseverance* (sticking to one's initial beliefs, notwithstanding disconfirming evidence obtained later) and the *primacy effect,* suggesting that information that comes first in a sequence exerts a stronger influence than that which is acquired later (Nisbett & Ross, 1980; Schneider, Hastorf & Ellsworth, 1979; Winkel, 1986).

An applied perspective partially explains our interest in examining the referral bias. It particularly arises from the fact that actual rape reporting to the police organization, almost without exception, involves contacts with more than one professional. Vice squad detectives, specialists conducting the interviews with victims, and suspects are generally not the first ones with whom a victim comes into contact. Usually, these interviews are preceded by an "intake" made by a station officer, who then refers the victim to the specialist. During these referral procedures, the interviewer is provided with (oral or written) information containing some facts in brief about what has happened. Our field observations suggest that it is not uncommon for these referral sheets to also include personal impressions, comments, or observations from the station officer, for example, "please hurry up, because she is really upset." Sometimes, credibility information is provided, too. In these instances, a referral bias might be activated. Given a general tendency of observers to confirm their initial expectations, prior credibility information might influence the gathering (e.g., by types of questions asked) and processing (interpretation) of victim-provided information about the event, and result in strengthening or weakening the perceived credibility of the victim. In this regard, our referral bias is a special illustration of "confirmatory strategies" used by human observers in general (Leyens, 1989).

At a theoretical level, basically two mediating processes leading to the confirmation of an observer's expectancies about a target are postulated, namely: (1) the self-fulfilling prophecy or behavioral confirmation effect, and (2) the cognitive confirmation effect (Skov & Sherman, 1986). Darley and Gross (1983, p. 20) note that in the first process "perceiver's behaviors toward the individual for whom they hold an expectancy channel *the course of the interaction* (italics added) such that expectancy confirming behaviors are elicited from the other individual" (Snyder, Tanke, & Berscheid, 1977). Cognitive confirmation effects refer to "expectancy confirmation effects that occur in the absence of any interaction between the perceiver and the target person. In these cases perceivers simply *selectively interpret* (italics added), attribute, or recall aspects of the target person's actions in ways that are consistent with their expectations" (Darley & Gross, 1983, p. 20).

Notwithstanding the fact that studies performed by Snyder et al. (1977; Snyder & Swann, 1978) have been criticized by different authors on several grounds (Semin & Strack, 1980), there seems to be substantial empirical evidence sustaining the notion of behavioral elicitation/confirmation processes (Rosenthal, 1974; Rosenthal & Jacobson, 1968). Regarding the second process, Darley and Gross (1983) report findings that are consistent with a two-stage model of cognitive confirmation processes. As this model offers a promising perspective for scrutinizing referral biases, we will clarify this model first, before describing our own experimental procedure. In doing this, we will lean heavily on Darley and Gross (1983).

During the first phase, it is assumed that when perceivers have reason to suspect that the information that establishes an expectancy (e.g., a personal comment on a transferral sheet) is not diagnostically valid for determining certain of the target person's dispositions, they will refrain from using that information to come to diagnostic conclusions. The expectancies do not function as truths about the target person but rather as hypotheses about the likely dispositions of that person. If perceivers were asked to make a judgment about the target, they would probably report that they do not have sufficient information at this point. The second stage occurs when perceivers are given the opportunity to observe the actions of the labeled other (e.g., by personally interviewing the victim). They then can test their hypotheses against relevant evidence. This testing process provides the perceiver with a valid basis for making judgments about the target. If, however, perceivers use a confirmatory strategy during this testing process, they tend to find evidence supporting the hypothesis being tested. The error that perceivers make, according to this model, is in assuming that the behavioral evidence they have derived is valid and unbiased.

In the experiment to be reported, the referral bias was examined in more detail. In the first place, the hypothesis was tested that exposure to prior credibility information biases the final judgment about the victim, after having conducted a victim interview. We expected to observe a linear downward pattern in credibility assessments ranging from the positive/credible prior information, via the neutral or no information, to the negative/unreliable condition. Secondly, we were interested in exploring the relationship between prior credibility information and the categories of questions asked during the interview with the victim. Figure 2 presents an overview of the experimental procedure.

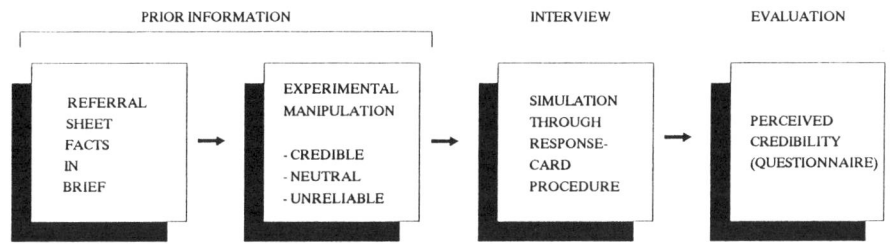

Figure 2: Procedure of the Referral-Bias Experiment.

The experimental procedure consisted of several phases. During "prior information", subjects were given some information about the report, including the experimental manipulation. The information was provided through a handwritten referral sheet, ostensibly made up by a female station officer who had already done the intake. The sheet read as follows:

> Richard, this morning a woman came to report a rape. Because you were not there, I welcomed her and had a first conversation. I do not completely trust her. I noted down some things for you: date of reporting: 26.11.88, 11:00 hours; name: Margreet; date of birth: 30.11.62; Dutch, not married; domicile: Utrecht. Margreet told me the following: She went to a her girlfriend Carla's party. C lives 30 km away. She went by bus. Wanted to take the final bus back home, but she was enjoying the party. She could not sleep at C's, but it was possible to sleep at Peter's place, a friend of C. Went home with P. Decided to sleep on the floor. Got sick and had to vomit. Went to the toilet and could not sleep any longer. Took her sleeping-bag and pillow to lie down next to P. She told that she was raped by him after that. Went back home in the morning by bus and came up here later. I am interested in how things proceed, Marjan.

The experimental manipulation was incorporated in the referral sheet. It merely consisted of the above sentence "I do not completely trust her" for subjects in the negative condition; "I do trust her" for those in the positive condition; while no such information was given in the neutral condition. Subjects were further told that all of the information they were given was based on a real victim report recorded at a Utrecht police station in 1988. Subjects were also provided with the text of art. 242 of the Dutch Penal Code, containing the legal definition of rape. They were then requested to interview the victim personally in order to find out whether the present situation constituted rape in a legal sense.

Table 2: Perceived Credibility of the Victim After Conducting the Interview.

	Unreliable		Neutral		Reliable		
	M	SD	M	SD	M	SD	F_{in}
Police personnel (n=30)							
Characterological attribution	5.27	1.35	5.11	1.05	5.00	2.06	< 1
Fake report	3.82	2.04	3.30	2.58	1.6	0.73	6.25 **
Incredibility	2.82	1.60	2.33	1.00	2.11	1.62	1.22
Victim's intention	3.18	2.27	2.00	1.70	1.56	1.01	4.26 *
Solidness of evidence (art 242 penal code)	4.09	1.87	6.70	2.63	7.11	2.62	8.45 **
Law students (n=90)							
Characterological attribution	5.25	1.72	4.60	1.90	4.32	1.26	3.50 *
Fake report	3.94	2.03	3.63	2.04	3.03	1.89	3.25 *
Uncredibility	4.34	2.10	3.33	1.88	2.68	1.81	11.65 **
Victim's intention	3.34	2.09	2.90	2.25	2.32	1.80	3.88 *
Solidness evidence in trial	3.75	1.85	4.37	2.24	4.97	2.51	4.78 **

Note. Higher score represents stronger agreement with label
* $p < .05$; ** $p < .01$

During the interview phase, no real victim was present. Instead, to simulate the interview, we utilized a specific procedure developed and tested in a number of previous studies (Bijl, 1986; De Winter & Mutsaers, 1990; Rekvelt, 1989). Subjects were instructed to ask as many questions as they wanted concerning any issue they considered relevant. Subjects could stop interviewing when they felt they had sufficient information to arrive at a final conclusion. Answers were provided by a female (extensively trained) experimenter through handing over a typed response card containing the answer to the question posed. The total set of response cards consisted of 905 possible answers. These answers corresponded to nine major categories of possible questions: (1) identity of the persons involved in the situation; (2) personal backgrounds of victim; (3) situation during the party; (4) situation during the party from the moment of getting acqainted with suspect until arrival at suspect's home; (5) situation at P's home until actual rape; (6) actual rape; (7) after the rape; (8) procedure; and (9) miscellaneous questions. After handing out a response card, the experimenter recorded the corresponding (sub)category.

Upon completing the interview, subjects were requested to fill out a questionnaire, which, amongst others, included items on perceived credibility of the victim, rape myth acceptance, and so forth. Perceived credibility was measured (using 9-point scales) through questions like: "Do you think this woman is a type of person to whom such a thing might happen again (characterological attribution)?" "Do you think this is a fake report?" "Does she appear to be a credible person?" "To what extent was it her intention to have things happen this way?" and "How solid/feasible is the legal evidence in pursuing this case to trial?"

Table 3: Mean Number of Questions Asked in the Victim Interview by Experimental Condition and "Type" of Interviewer.

	M	SD	F	p
Experimental condition				
Neutral	44.00	22.18	2.37	0.08
Unreliable	61.36	15.61		
Reliable	47.89	19.57		
Probability of fake reports in general				
Low	45.71	20.66	5.17	0.02
High	61.08	15.41		
Total	51.53	20.08		

In testing the hypothesis formulated, we utilized the data presented in Table 2. The means reported in Table 2 generally support our hypothesis. In both samples, a pattern emerges that is in line with the predicted linear trend. These data clearly suggest that prior credibility information does bias final judgments in the direction of the expectancy created. Impressions formed of the victim in the reliable condition tend to be more positive relative to the neutral condition, while the remaining impressions tend to be more negative. To find out whether this referral bias merely reflects differences in interpretation of the "evidence" gathered in the victim interview, or is rooted in different strategies of obtaining the evidence, a number of exploratory analyses were performed. Here we will confine ourselves to reporting some data pertaining to the police sample.

In the police sample, a total of 1,501 questions were asked, constituting a mean of 50 questions ($SD=20$) per interview. Table 3 suggests that the experimental condition had some impact on the number of questions posed. A prior expectancy that the victim was not completely trustworthy tended to stimulate questioning. A similar pattern emerges at the second entry of the table. Interviewers generally believing the percentage of fake victim reports to the police to be high asked significantly more questions than their counterparts. Unreliability thus appears to strengthen the need for more information. Analyses (Table 4) moreover revealed a significant relationship ($\chi^2=42.60$; $p=.00$) between type of question and type of prior information.

Table 4 shows the bulk of questions to be related to the situation directly before, during, or after the actual rape occurred (Categories 4, 5, 6, and 7). In these categories, some differences emerge between experimental conditions. In the unreliable condition, Categories 5 and 6 are somewhat underrepresented, while Category 7 is relatively overrepresented. It is noteworthy that a similar pattern emerges with regard to Rape Myth Acceptance scores. Subjects scoring high on this scale tended to pose relatively fewer questions within the Categories 5 and 6, while 7 is overrepresented again. Although further analyses (e.g., on the audiotaped interviews) are definitely needed, the present outcomes do suggest that the referral bias does not merely reflect differences in interpretation of victim-reported information but also involves different strategies in information gathering.

Table 4: Percentage of Questions per Category by Experimental Conditions.

Experimental condition	Question categories								
	1	2	3	4	5	6	7	8	9
Neutral	3.7	1.2	9.6	14.5	24.5	30.1	13.3	1.6	9.1
Unreliable	4.7	2.0	7.8	10.4	20.3	25.2	16.9	1.7	11.0
Reliable	2.1	1.4	5.1	10.5	23.8	29.7	13.3	1.9	12.1
Total	3.5	1.6	7.5	11.6	22.5	27.8	12.9	1.7	10.8

Note: All percentages based on total N in neutral condition

(Dis)honest Demeanor Bias: The Impact of Suspect Characteristics

Article 342 (sub2) of the Dutch Code on Criminal Procedure incorporates the "unus testis-nullus testis"-rule of evidence. The evidence that a suspect actually committed the alleged offense cannot be based solely on the statement of one witness (e.g., the victim), no matter how convincing that witness may be. One witness is no witness. In legal commentaries, it is noted that the legal significance of this article often comes up in rape cases, involving a persuasive statement of the victim and a suspect denying the charges. However, it is not considered a breach of this regulation to base a conviction on the statement of the victim that she was raped *and* on a statement of the suspect (denying the rape charge) that the girl was in his car at a particular moment (e.g., NJ 1955, 2:7; Supreme Court, penal dept, 19-10-1954). In particular, in these cases involving two conflicting statements without substantial auxiliary evidence, all sorts of "perceptual phenomena" might have a strong impact on police officers' decisions to continue juridical procedures. We assume that in these cases the perceived credibility of the victim is weighted against the perceived credibility of the suspect. A highly credible suspect might thus reduce the perceived credibility of the victim and vice versa. From this perspective it seems worthwhile to also examine characteristics of the suspect in studying secondary victimization. Here we will focus on the "demeanor bias".

Research by Riggio and Friedman (1983) and by Zuckerman, DeFrank, Hall, Larrance, and Rosenthal (1979) suggests that there is a demeanor bias. That is, some persons are judged more truthful or deceptive regardless of whether they are telling the truth or deceiving. Certain individuals with an honest overall appearance may be more succesful deceivers simply because they appear to be trustworthy. Riggio and Friedman (1986) provide empirical evidence suggesting that extraverted and expressive persons are judged to be more likeable speakers. On the basis of these studies, Riggio, Tucker, and Throckmorton (1987) predicted that extraverted and emotionally expressive individuals will be judged as more truthful regardless of whether they were deceiving or telling the truth. Riggio et al. (1987) conclude:

> Certain subjects appeared to be judged as more or less believable across conditions. Specifically, subjects scoring high on the SSI Social Control Scale and on the Extraversion scale of the SMS were judged as more believable regardless of whether they were sending

truthful, deceptive or neutral messages. Conversely, subjects scoring high on the Social Anxiety scale were judged as less believable across these three conditions .... These results indicated that possession of these basic social skills may be advantageous in certain social situations. Individuals possessing these particular social skills behaved in ways that made them appear honest to observers. Expressive, articulate, and socially controlled or tactful persons may be more successful in situations involving self-presentation or persuasiveness simply because they are generally perceived as more credible than individuals who lack these basic communication skills. (p. 575)

Table 5: Correlations Between Perceived Credibility and "Social Skills".

	Perceived credibility		
	Study 1 (n=176)	Study 2 (n=192)	Study 3 (n=172)
Social anxiety	-.15 (.01)	-.36 (.00)	-.23 (.00)
Introversion	-.19 (.00)	-.20 (.00)	-.22 (.00)

A number of our own studies, performed within a police context, point in the same direction (Vrij & Winkel, 1990). Vrij and Winkel (1990) conducted three studies in which police officers were exposed to videoclips showing a police officer interviewing a potential suspect of rape. After exposure, subjects were requested to evaluate amongst others the perceived credibility of the suspect by answering questions, like: "Would you invite him for a second interview?" "Do you think he is hiding the truth?" and "Does he make a suspect impression?" A number of items measuring introversion (Briggs, Check, & Buss, 1980) and social anxiety (Fenigstein, Scheier, & Buss, 1975) of the citizen interviewed were also incorporated in the questionnaire. Table 5 presents an overview of the correlations observed between these measures and the perceived credibility of the suspect.

Table 5 shows that in all three studies introversion and social anxiety correlated negatively with perceived credibility. Individuals scoring high on social anxiety and introversion thus might exhibit behavioral patterns that are generally seen as "dishonest." Extraverted or assertive individuals might automatically exhibit behaviors during a police interview that make them appear "honest." These studies, however, leave open the question whether such a (dis)honest demeanor bias does also have an impact on the perceived credibility of the victim. The experimental setup outlined in Figure 3 sheds some light on this issue.

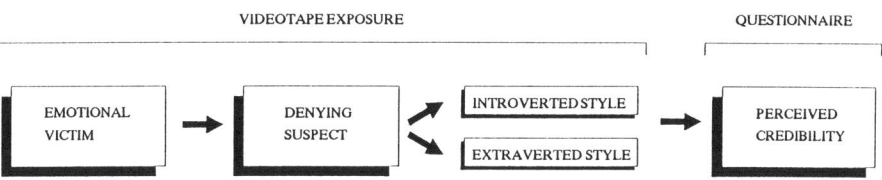

Figure 3: Introverted/Extraverted Style of Self-Presentation by Suspect.

In the "(dis)honest demeanor" experiment, all subjects, amongst others, a sample of male and female police officers, were first exposed to a videotape showing an emotional victim reporting a rape to the police. This videotape was the same as the one used in the experiment reported in Section 2 of this article. Upon completion of a questionnaire assessing the perceived credibility of this victim, subjects were further exposed to a videotape showing a denying suspect, telling his view of the incident to a police officer, by either exhibiting an extraverted or an introverted style of self-presentation. In the final questionnaire, mainly assessing the perceived credibility of the suspect, subjects were also asked to indicate to what extent they would now revise their beliefs about the credibility of the victim. Analyses revealed a significant interaction ($F=4.03, p<.05$), between subjects' sex and type of self-presentation. This interaction is graphically illustrated in Figure 4.

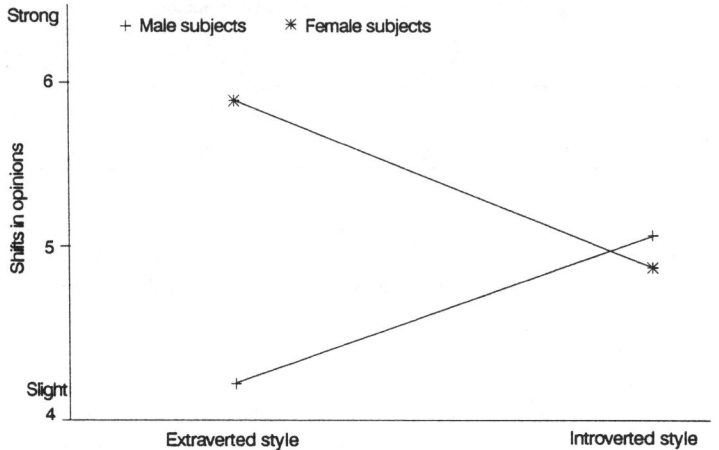

Figure 4: Shifts in Belief About the Victim After Exposure to Different Types of Suspects.

Figure 4 suggests that exposure to an introverted suspect denying the rape charges results in moderate revisions in male and female beliefs about the victim's credibility. Exposure to an extraverted suspect results in differential revisions. Female subjects more strongly revise their beliefs about the victim than males. In view of the fact that female subjects more strongly believe the extraverted suspect, the present interaction suggests that these subjects revised their beliefs about the victim negatively. Denials by an extraverted suspect thus appear to reduce the perceived credibility of the victim.

Conclusions

The empirical evidence reported here suggests that a numbed style of communicating about the victimization, prior information about the unreliability of the victim, and an extraverted style in denying rape charges by the suspect have an adverse impact on the perceived credibility of the victim. Perceptual biases might thus be operative in police officers conducting interviews with rape victims. A lack of consideration for crime victims of those working in the criminal justice system is not the only cause of secondary victimization; more subtle causes appear to be involved. Training programs, aimed at preventing secondary victimization, should not only stimulate officers' sensitivity for victims' needs, but should also address the issue of perceptual biases in information processing and in forming judgments about the credibility of the victim.

References

Bijl, P.A. (1986). *Waarom wilt U dat weten: Het slachtofferverhoor van een zedendelict gesimuleerd.* Unpublished master's thesis. Amsterdam: Department of Social Psychology, Free University Amsterdam.

Briggs, S., Check, J., & Buss, A. (1980). An analysis of the self-monitoring scale. *Journal of Personality and Social Psychology, 38,* 679-686.

Brom, D., Kleber, L., & Defares, P.B. (1986), *Traumatische ervaringen en psychotherapie.* Lisse: Swets & Zeitlinger.

Brownell, A., & Shumaker, S.A. (1984). Social support: An introduction to a complex phenomenon. *Journal of Social Issues, 40,* 1-10.

Brownmiller, S. (1975), *Against our will: Men, women and rape.* New York: Simon and Schuster.

Burgess, A.W., & Holmstrom L.L. (1974). Rape trauma syndrome. *American Journal of Psychiatry, 131,* 981-985.

Burgess, A.W., & Holmstrom, L.L. (1974), *Rape: Victims of crisis.* Bowie, MD: Brady, 1974

Burt, M.R. (1980). Cultural myths and support for rape. *Journal of Personality and Social Psychology, 38,* 217-230.

Cann, A., Calhoun, L.C., Selby J.W., & King, H.E. (Eds.) (1981). Rape. *The Journal of Social Issues, 37,* 1-162.

Comment (1968). Police discretion and the judgment that a crime has been committed: Rape in Philadelphia, *University of Pennsylvania Law Review, 117,* 277-322.

Cook, R.F., Smith, B.E., & Harrell, A.V. (1987), *Helping crime victims: Levels of trauma and effectiveness of services.* Washington DC: U.S. Department of Justice, National Institute of Justice.

Darley, J.M., & Gross, P.H. (1983). A hypothesis-confirming bias in labeling effects. *Journal of Personality and Social Psychology, 44,* 20-33.

Davelaar-Van Tongeren, V.H. (1980). *Verkrachting: Strafrechter, wat moet je er mee.* Arnhem: Gouda Quint.

Fattah, E.A. (1984). Victim's response to confrontational victimization: A neglected aspect of victim research, *Crime and Delinquency, 30,* 75-89.

Fenigstein, A., Scheier, M.F., & Buss, A.H. (1975). Public and private self-consciousness: Assessment and theory. *Journal of Consulting and Clinical Psychology, 43,* 522-527.

Frieze, I.H., Hymer, S., & Greenberg, M.S. (1987). Describing the crime victim: Psychological reactions to victimization. *Professional Psychology, 4,* 299-315.

Gulotta, G., & De Cataldo Neuberger, L. (1983). A systematic and attitudinal approach to victimology. *Victimology, 8,* 1-2, 5-16.

Guidelines for Victim Support in Europe (1987), *Report of the first European conference of victim support workers,* Utrecht: Landelijke Organisatie Slachtofferhulp (LOS).

Horowitz, M.J. (1976), *Stress-response syndroms.* New York: Aronson.

Janoff-Bulman R., & Hanson Frieze, J. (1983). A theoretical perspective for understanding reactions to victimization. *Journal of Social Issues, 39,* 1-17.

Kidd R.F., & Chayet, E.F. (1984). Why do victims fail to report: The psychology of criminal victimization. *Journal of Social Issues, 40,* 39-51.

Krulewitz, J.E., & Payne, E.J. (1978). Attributions about rape: Effects of rapist force, observer sex, and sex role attitudes. *Journal of Applied Social Psychology, 8,* 291-305.

Leyens, J.P. (1989). Another look at confirmatory strategies during a real interview. *European Journal of Social Psychology, 19,* 255-262.

Nisbett, R.E., & Ross, L. (1980), *Human inference: Strategies and shortcomings in social judgment*. Englewood Cliffs, NJ: Prentice Hall.

Ouden, M. den.,& Barentsen, C. (1984). *Beeldvorming rondom verkrachting*. Unpublished manuscript. Department of Social Psychology, Free University Amsterdam.

President's Task Force on Victims of Crime (1986). *Four years later*. U.S. Department of Justice, Office of Justice Programs. Washington, DC: Government Printing Office.

Rekvelt, K. (1989). *Politiele slachtoffer-ondervraging en oordeelsvorming: De invloed van informatie over de betrouwbaarheid van een verkrachtings-aangeefster op de informatie-behoefte, de vraagkeuze en de oordeelsvorming van zedenrechercheurs*. Unpublished manuscript. Department of Social Psychology, Free University Amsterdam.

Riggio, R.S., & Friedman, H.S. (1983). Individual differences and cues to deception. *Journal of Personality and Social Psychology, 45*, 899-915.

Riggio, R.E., & Friedman, H.S. (1986). Impression formation: the role of expressive behavior. *Journal of Personality and Social Psychology, 50*, 421-427.

Riggio, R.E., Tucker, J., & Throckmorton, B. (1987). Social skills and deception ability. *Personality and Social Psychology Bulletin, 13*, 568-577.

Rosenthal, R. (1974). *On the social psychology of self-fulfilling prophecy: Further evidence for pygmalion effects and their mediating mechanisms*. New York: Modular Publications, module 53.

Rosenthal, R., & Jacobson, L. (1968). *Pygmalion in the classroom*. New York: Holt, Rinehart & Winston.

Ruback, R.B., Greenberg, M.S., & Westcott, D.R. (1984). Social influence and crime victim decision making. *Journal of Social Issues, 40*, 51-76.

Saunders, D.G., & Size, P.B. (1986). Attitudes about woman abuse among police officers, victims and victim advocates. *Journal of Interpersonal Violence, 1*, 25-42.

Schneider, D.J., Hastorf, A.H., & Ellsworth, P.C. (1979). *Person perception*. Reading, MA: Addison-Wesley.

Schwartz, J., Williams, H., & Pepitone-Rockwell, F. (1981). Construction of a rape awareness scale. *Victimology, 6*, 110-119.

Schwendinger, J.R., & Schwendinger, H. (1974). Rape myths: In legal theoretical, and everyday practice. *Crime and Social Justice, 1*, 18-26.

Semin, G., & Strack, F. (1980). The plausibility of the implausible: A critique of Snyder & Swann (1978). *European Journal of Social Psychology, 10*, 379-388.

Shapland, J. (1990). *Guide for practitioners regarding the implementation of the Declaration of Basic Principles of Justice for Victims of Crime and Abuse of Power*. Helsinki: United Nations Publishing Service.

Shumaker, S.A., & Brownell, A. (1984). Toward a theory of social support: Closing conceptual gaps. *Journal of Social Issues, 40*, 11-36.

Skelton, C.A., & Buckhart, B.R. (1980). Sexual assault: Determinants of victim disclosure. *Criminal Justice and Behavior, 7*, 229-236.

Steinmetz, C.H.D. (1984). Coping with a serious crime: Self-help and outside help. *Victimology, 9*, 3-4, 324-343.

Skov, R.B., & Sherman, S.J. (1986). Information-gathering processes: Diagnosticity, hypothesis confirmatory strategies, and perceived hypothesis confirmation. *Journal of Experimental Social Psychology, 22*, 93-121.

Snyder, M., & Swann, W.B. (1978). Hypothesis-testing processes in social interaction. *Journal of Personality and Social Psychology, 36*, 1202-1212.

Snyder, M., Tanke, E.D., & Berscheid, E. (1977). Social Perception and interpersonal behavior: On the self-fulfilling nature of social stereotypes. *Journal of Personality and Social Psychology, 35*, 656-666.

Viano, E.C. (Ed.)(1989). *Crime and its victims: International research and public policy issues*. New York: Hemisphere.

Vrij, A., & Winkel, F.W. (1990). Sociale vaardigheden, perceptuele vertekeningen en 'verdachte' zijn, *Proces, 69*, 7/8, 181-190.

Williams, L.S. (1984). The classic rape: When do victims report. *Social Problems, 31*, 459-468.

Winkel, F.W. (1984). Changing misconceptions about rape through informational campaigns: A model. *Victimology, 9*, 262-272.

Winkel, F.W. (1986). Criminele toespelingen in de massamedia: Een rechtspsychologische analyse. In J. von Grumbkow, D. van Kreveld, & P. Stringer (Eds.), *Toegepaste sociale psychologie, deel 2* (pp. 89-101). Lisse: Swets & Zeitlinger.

Winkel, F.W. (1988). *Rape reporting to the police: Testing the social psychological impact of a persuasive campaign*. Paper presented at the 6th International Symposium on Victimology, Jerusalem, Israel.

Winkel, F.W. (1989). Responses to criminal victimisation: Evaluating the impact of a police assistance program and some social psychological characteristics. *Police Studies, 12*, 59-73.

Winkel, F.W., & Koppelaar, L. (1991). Rape victims' style of selfpresentation and secondary victimization by the environment: An experiment. *Journal of Interpersonal Violence, 6*, 29-41.

Winter, S. de, & Mutsaers, P. (1990). *Vooraf-informatie en oordeelsvorming: Wat is bij zedenverhoren de invloed van vooraf-informatie op de beoordeling van een vrouw die aangifte van verkrachting doet?* Department of Social Psychology, Free University Amsterdam.

Wortman, C.B. (1983). Coping with victimization: Conclusions and recommendations for furure research. *Journal of Social Issues, 33*, 195-221.

Zuckerman, M., DeFrank, R.S., Hall, J.A., Larrance, D.T., & Rosenthal, R. (1979). Facial and vocal cues of honesty and deception. *Journal of Experimental Social Psychology, 15*, 378-396.

Police Officers' Beliefs About Cues Associated With Deception in Rape Cases[1]

Luise Greuel

Introduction

Police interrogation of rape victims has been a focus of public discussion and criticism for the last decades. If psychological research is to set out to investigate this very complex problem, this can not be done without reflecting upon the institutional setting of police interrogation and its procedural goals in the context of the code of criminal procedure.

The central goal of police interrogation is the reconstruction of past events in order to produce conclusive evidence in criminal cases. In the situation of police interrogation, the detective has to lead the witness to reconstruct the criminal incident under consideration as completely and reliably as possible. Hence, the process and the result of police interrogation depends to a great extent upon the officer's communication skills and interactive competences. Besides this, the police interrogator has to perform complex tasks with regard to judicial decision-making and social impression formation, that is, (a) to subsume the incriminated event under a particular criminal law, and (b) to assess the credibility of the complainant's report. The latter aspect is the focus of the present research: the process of discriminating between truthful and deceptive testimonies at the initial investigative stage in processing rape charges.

Deceptions, that is, false pretences or claims of being victimized by a criminal offense that the deceiving witness knows to be false constitutes a criminal act according to German Law (§ 145d StGB). So far, judging a witness's complaint to be deceptive is of enormous judicial importance, because - in this case - the police now have to treat the alleged complainant as a defendant.

On the other hand, psychological research on "the impression side of credibility" (Köhnken 1989, p. 276) has shown that the overall accuracy rate in detecting deceptions falls at chance levels or levels slightly above chance (DePaulo, Stone, & Lassiter, 1985; Zuckerman, DePaulo, & Rosenthal, 1981). It is still unclear exactly which cues observers use as a basis for their credibility judgment.

The present study set out to investigate police officers' beliefs about cues associated with deception in rape cases. It is concerned with the decoder's perspective in discriminating between true and deceptive witness statements at the initial investigative stage of processing rape complaints. The two major questions addressed by the present research are:

    1. What patterns of cues do police officers perceive to be indicative of truthfulness and deception in the context of victim interrogation in rape cases?

---

[1] This research was supported by the Minister for Science and Research of the state of North Rhine-Westphalia (Az.: IV A 2 - 700 005 88).

2. Is there any relationship between the subjective confidence in deception detection and the sources of information on which credibility judgment is based?

Method

Subjects. Fiftyone police inspectors from eight police departments in the state of North Rhine-Westphalia were investigated. Within their sphere of duty, all of them are specifically engaged in the investigation of criminal sexual assault cases. Their gender distribution was 59% male and 41% female, their mean age was 38.6 years ($SD=8.6$; range 25-57). The mean length of service in the police force was 18.1 years ($SD=8.2$; range 6-37), and they have been dealing with sexual crimes for an average of 10.0 years ($SD=6.9$; range 1-25). Most detectives were married (74.5%) or single (19.6%) and only a relatively small number were divorced or widowed.

Standardized interview data. First, all subjects were interviewed concerning their beliefs about cues associated with deception in rape cases. Each interview was recorded and then transcribed by the investigator. A content analysis of the interview transcripts was conducted and these data were subjected to frequency analysis.

Protocol analysis. In a second step, authentic interrogation protocols of the interviewed detectives were subjected to content analysis. Subjects were explored regarding the last victim interrogation they had actually performed in a rape case. From 30 of the 51 rape cases, criminal files could be collected for further analysis.

Confidence rating. Subjects were asked to indicate their degree of subjective confidence in detecting deception on a 5-point rating scale ranging from *not at all* (0) to *always* (4). In their replies, 45.7% were mostly or always confident in detecting deception within the interrogation of alleged rape victims. These subjects were called "high-confident" detectives, whereas those subjects who indicated that they were at most sometimes confident in their judgment (54.3%) were called "low-confident".

Results

Cues associated with deception in rape cases

Table 1 presents the distribution of the subjects' answers to the explorative question, "On which cues do you base your judgment concerning the truthfulness of rape complaints?" It can be seen that characteristics of statement content, especially logical inconsistencies and a lack of plausibility are mentioned by the majority of the interviewed officers as significant cues in the process of lie detection within victim interrogation in rape cases. It should be noted that the detectives have referred to only 2 of the 19 reality criteria of the criteria-based statement analysis system as published by Steller and Köhnken (1989), that is, consistency of content (87.2%) and quantity of details (20.5%).

Table 1: Cues Interpreted as Indicative of Deception/Truthfulness (Percent Rates).

	Expressed in interview	Documented in protocol
Inconsistency of statements	87.2	17.5
Availability of other evidence	48.2	35.0
Atypical behavior of alleged rape victim	41.0	65.0
Complaint initiated by significant others/ motivation	38.5	40.0
Intuition, job experience	30.8	0.0

In second place, nearly 50% of the subjects indicated availability of other pieces of evidence to be basic cues in detecting deception. That means, nearly half of the officers tended to rely on external validation criteria when assessing witness credibility.

Forty-one percent of them declared that nervous or overcontrolled victim behavior evoked their suspicion. They proved to be oriented by the stereotype of the "real rape victim" being conceptualized as psychologically instabile, highly traumatized, and emotionally expressive.

Furthermore, nearly 40% believed that complaints initiated by significant others than the victim herself serve to evoke suspicion of being lied to, because this circumstance could be interpreted as indicative for a critical motivation to deceive. They expressed this belief without reflecting upon the empirical findings that consistently demonstrate that it is not unusual in the context of rape for parents, husbands, or intimates of the raped women to first inform the police - mostly by phone (Steinhilper, 1986).

Last, nearly one third of the interviewed police officers mentioned their subjective intuition, job experience or general knowledge of the world to be sufficient cues on which to base their credibility judgment.

Applied cues of credibility judgment as documented in interrogation protocols

As can be seen in Table 1, the ranking of lie detection cues revealed by interview data differs markedly from that revealed by protocol analysis. Looking at the criteria of credibility judgment as documented in protocol notes, the issue of victim behavior was the most frequent mentioned cue concerning deception detecting followed by the aspects of the victim's motivation to testify. In 65% of the analyzed protocols, officers based their credibility judgments upon significant aspects of victim behavior. Especially, they discussed affective instability and emotional expressiveness as indicators for the truthfulness of the victim's complaint. With regard to the complainant's motivation to testify, it can be shown that in 40% of the analyzed protocols, the issue who initiated the complaint was mentioned as an indicator of truthfulness. In those cases in which significant others first reported the victimization under consideration to the police, police officers expressed some suspicion concerning the truthfulness of the incriminated offense.

With a frequency of 35%, the practical relevance of other pieces of evidence for credibility assessment proved to be relatively stable. However, the actual relevance of statement criteria seemed to be dramatically diminished when comparing the number of mentions in the protocols (17.5%) with standardized interview data (87.2%).

Relationship between subjective confidence in deception detection and sources of information upon which credibility judgement is based

The next step analyzed whether there was any relationship between the attribution of subjective confidence in detection accuracy and the sources of information upon which credibility judgment is based. Table 2 shows the intergroup differences on assumptions about cues associated with deceptive rape complaints. It can be seen, that investigators with high subjective confidence in deception accuracy relied significantly more strongly on rather invalid deception cues such as atypical victim behavior ($\chi^2=4.84$; $DF=1$; $p \leq .05$), victim's motivation to complaint ($\chi^2=3.96$; $DF=1$; $p \leq .05$) and own intuition or job experience ($\chi^2=5.64$; $DF=1$; $p \leq .05$) than subjects with relatively low confidence.

Table 2: Relationship Between Perception of Deceptive Cues and Confidence in Lie Detection Accuracy.

	Expressed in interview		Documented in protocol	
	High confidence	Low confidence	High confidence	Low confidence
Inconsistency of statements	81.0	68.0	50.0	31.8
Availability of other evidence	28.6	52.0	11.1	54.5
Atypical behavior of alleged rape victim	42.9	20.0	27.8	9.1
Complaint initiated by significant others/motivation	47.7	20.0	72.2	59.1
Intuition, job experience	42.9	12.0	0.0	0.0

The results of protocol analysis (see Table 2) showed that police officers with high confidence tended to rely less on external evidence than low-confident detectives ($\chi^2=8.21$; $DF=1$; $p \leq .01$).

Conclusions

Police officers base their credibility judgment on valid as well as invalid cues to deception. Logical consistency and plausibility of the complaint is the most - and to a great extent only - statement-related cue mentioned in deception detecting. Standardized interview data indicate that police officers are somewhat aware of the relevance of criteria-based statement analysis. However, analyses of authentic interrogation protocols yield that police inspectors orient more toward victim behavior and other statement-unrelated cues than by the statement itself when assessing victim credibility in a particular case. To a great extent, police agents base their decision about the truthfulness of a specific rape complaint on behavioral cues that are stereotypically associated with deception but are not valid indicators of deception. For example, "nervous" behavior in the alleged rape victim could be identified as subjectivly relevant cue that allows an investigator to suspect that he or she is being lied to. On the other hand, in experimental research on lie detection Riggio and Friedman (1983) and Zuckerman et al. (1979) have proven, that nervous behavior is an invalid cue of deception detecting that does not discriminate between truthful and deceptive messages. Whereas "nervosity" has been identified as a general stereotype of lying (Köhnken, 1988), Kröhn (1984) has stated that it is a rape-specific myth to associate emotionally expressive, psychologically instable and highly affective behavior with the "typical rape victim". On the contrary, victimological studies have consistently shown that rape victims may behave just as well in a highly expressive as in an overcontrolled manner (Burgess & Holmstrom, 1974; Licht, 1989). Although empirical evidence has shown that the stereotype of the hyperexpressive, uncontrolled victim is an inadequate misconception of rape reality, police officers tend to orient toward this invalid conception when trying to detect false rape complaints.

Furthermore, there is a significant relationship between subjective confidence in accuracy of lie detection and subjective beliefs about cues associated with lie detection in rape cases. Officers who rely primarily on content unrelated and stereotypical cues to deception express higher confidence in their deception detecting than low-confident investigators. On the other hand, the credibility judgment of low-confidence detectives - as documented in the protocol notes - strongly rely more on comparisons with objective, external evidence.

These findings may be interpreted in the context of theories of social impression formation and information-processing as defined by Bodenhausen and Lichtenstein (1987). Police officers' implicit theories about rape and their stereotypical conceptions of cues to deception may be interpreted as cognitive heuristics (Sherman & Corty, 1984) that - on the one side - may establish subjective confidence and competence attribution on the decoder's side. On the other hand, these heuristics may determine judgment and decision-making by structuring perception and information-processing in accordance with the principle of "anchoring" (Tversky & Kahnemann, 1980) or the strategy of selecting heuristic-consistent cues (Greuel & Scholz, 1990).

Future research on the decoder's perception of credibility judgment should more strongly reflect these aspects of social decision-making in addition to the input variables produced by the witness. It may also be considered whether the overall insufficient effects of previous attempts to improve deception accuracy of so-called "professional detectors" through instructional training (Köhnken, 1987; Zuckerman, Koestner, & Colella, 1985) might be inferred by effects of those generally resistant stereotypes and cognitive heuristics.

References

Bodenhausen, G.V., & Lichtenstein, M. (1987). Social stereotypes and information-processing strategies: The impact of task complexity. *Journal of Personality and Social Psychology, 5*, 871-880.

Burgess, A.W., & Holmstrom, L.L. (1974). Rape trauma syndrome. *American Journal of Psychiatry, 131*, 981-987.

DePaulo, B.M., Stone, J.I., & Lassiter, G.D. (1985). Deceiving and detecting deceit. In B.R. Schlenker (Ed.), *The self and social life* (pp. 323-370). New York: McGraw-Hill.

Greuel, L., & Scholz, O.B. (1990). Deliktspezifische Kenntnisse und Einstellungen als psychologische Bedingungen des Urteilsverhaltens in Vergewaltigungsfällen. *Monatsschrift für Kriminologie und Strafrechtsreform, 73*, 177-183.

Köhnken, G. (1987). Training police officers to detect deceptive eyewitness statements: Does it work? *Social Behavior, 2*, 1-17.

Köhnken, G. (1988). *Subjektive Konzepte zur Glaubwürdigkeit und ihrer Verhaltenskorrelate: Ergebnisse einer Fragebogenstudie.* Unpublished paper presented at the 36th meeting of the German Psychological Association, Berlin, October 2-6.

Köhnken, G. (1989). Behavioral correlates of statement credibility: Theories, paradigms, and results. In H. Wegener. F. Lösel, & J. Haisch (Eds.), *Criminal behavior and the justice system* (pp. 271-289). New York: Springer.

Kröhn, W. (1984). Mythos und Realität sexueller Unterdrückung - Vergewaltigung im Spiegel der öffentlichen Meinungen. *Sexualmedizin, 3*, 129-136.

Licht, M. (1989). *Vergewaltigungsopfer. Psychosoziale Folgen und Verarbeitungsprozesse.* Pfaffenweiler: Centaurus.

Riggio, R.E., & Friedman, H.S. (1983). Individual differences and cues to deception. *Journal of Personality and Social Psychology, 45*, 899-915.

Sherman, S.J., & Corty, E. (1984). Cognitive heuristics. In R.S. Wyer, & T.K. Srull (Eds.), *Handbook of social cognition, Vol. 1* (pp. 189-286). Hillsdale, NJ: Erlbaum.

Steinhilper, U. (1986). *Definitions- und Entscheidungsprozesse bei sexuell motivierten Gewaltdelikten. Eine empirische Untersuchung der Strafverfolgung bei Vergewaltigung und sexueller Nötigung.* Unpublished doctoral dissertation, University of Constance, Germany.

Steller, M., & Köhnken, G. (1989). Statement analysis: Credibility assessment of children's testimonies in sexual abuse cases. In D.C. Raskin (Ed.), *Psychological methods in criminal investigation and evidence* (pp. 217-245). New York: Springer.

Tversky, A., & Kahnemann, D. (1980). Causal schemas in judgments under uncertainty. In M. Fishbein (Ed.), *Progress in social psychology, Vol. 1* (pp. 49-72). Hillsdale, NJ: Erlbaum.

Zuckerman, M., DeFrank, R.S., Hall, J.A., Larrance, D.T., & Rosenthal, R. (1979). Facial and vocal cues of deception and honesty. *Journal of Experimental and Social Psychology, 15*, 378-396.

Zuckerman, M., DePaulo, B.M., & Rosenthal, R. (1981). Verbal and nonverbal communication of deception. In L. Berkowitz (Ed.), *Advances in experimental social psychology, Vol. 14* (pp. 1-59). New York: Academic Press.

Zuckerman, M., Koestner, R., & Colella, M.J. (1985). Learning to detect deception from three communication channels. *Journal of Nonverbal Behavior, 7*, 188-194.

Police-Citizen Interaction and Nonverbal Communication: The Impact of Culturally Determined Smiling and Gestures[1]

Aldert Vrij and Frans W. Winkel

Introduction

Research data show that Dutch police discriminate against black (Surinamer) citizens (see for a review De Beer, 1988). Correspondence theory offers a possible explanation (Hyland, 1974; Winkel, 1981). According to this principle, lack of correspondence between the target (a Surinamer) and the observer (Dutch police officer) leads to a more negative assessment of Surinamer citizens. Literature usually considered two kinds of lack in correspondence: physical characteristics (skin color: Tajfel, 1978) and psychological traits (beliefs: Rokeach, 1960). However, a third type of lack in correspondence - in nonverbal behavioral patterns - is much neglected and thus needs some clarification.

Vrij and others (Vrij & Koppelaar, 1990a, 1990b; Vrij, Winkel, & Koppelaar, 1988) have examined nonverbal behavior of Surinamer and Dutch citizens during police questioning. These studies revealed many differences in nonverbal behavior. Surinamers make more speech disturbances, have a higher voice pitch, speak more slowly, answer more indirectly and less to the point, use less eye contact, smile more often and use more body language (movement of hands, arms, and torso and self-touching). Reviews by Zuckerman, DePaulo, and Rosenthal (1981) and DePaulo, Stone, and Lassiter (1985) indicate that white observers associate certain behaviors with deception: speech disturbances, a high-pitched voice, indirect answering, gaze aversion, frequent smiling, and excessive body language. Comparison of these results suggests that crosscultural police-citizen interaction is prone to misunderstandings between white police officers and Surinamer citizens concerning the meaning of the nonverbal behavior of the latter. Some nonverbal behaviors are both indicators of perceived deception and typical Surinamer nonverbal behavior. Hence, nonverbal patterns of behavior that are typical for Surinamer actors are interpreted by white observers as betraying attempts to hide the truth. Perhaps, therefore, negative treatment of Surinamers may be linked with nonverbal communication errors, that is, with faulty interpretation of characteristic black nonverbal behavior.

Consensus on the relative importance of the three above-mentioned factors is lacking. According to Tajfel (1978), negative evaluation is determined by skin color alone; Rokeach (1960) holds that beliefs are exclusively responsible. Others (Insko, Nacoste, & Moe, 1983; McKirnan, Smith, & Hamayan, 1983; Mezei, 1971; Moe, Nacoste, & Insko, 1981) take a middle position: Negative evaluation is determined by both factors, while beliefs contributing more than skin color. The factor nonverbal behavior was never introduced in this type of comparison.

---

[1] This project was in part supported financially by the foundation PSYCHON, which is subsidized by the Netherlands Organization for Scientific Research.

Closer analysis of the available studies (see Insko, Nacoste, & Moe, 1983 for a review) allows us to introduce the hypothesis that the relative influence of the three factors corresponds with the degree of social pressure on equal treatment of citizens of dissimilar ethnic background. Social pressure means that in the observers environment, negative treatment of ethnic minorities is not allowed, that is discrimination is socially and legally taboo. It seems plausible that an observer will be highly conscious of the skin color of the actor and less conscious of the nonverbal behavior displayed by the actor, while the consciousness of the factor beliefs will be intermediate between these two factors. Therefore, when social pressure is present, nonverbal behavior will be the most important factor in predicting negative assessment, skin color the least important, and beliefs will be intermediate. Disagreement in the literature indicates that if social pressure is absent the pattern is unpredictable.

We examined the relative influence of the three factors in two experiments. The major difference between the two is the nonverbal behavior displayed by the actors. The first experiment centered on smiling, the second on gestures. Subjects (white police officers) were exposed to a videotape of a citizen being interrogated. They were requested to evaluate the citizen through a questionnaire. The main dependent variable was the degree to which the citizen evokes suspicion. In addition, we assessed the impression the citizen gave of nervousness and unpleasantness. Together, the three variables constitute the core of the usual way in which police officers assess citizens (Angement, 1984).

The following eight hypotheses were tested: (1) White police officers assess a citizen with dissimilar (Surinamer) ethnic background more negatively (as more suspicious, unpleasant, and nervous) than they assess native Dutch citizens. (2) Citizens with dissimilar beliefs are assessed more negatively than citizens whose beliefs correspond with those of the police officers. (3) Citizens displaying black nonverbal behavior are assessed more negatively than citizens who display white nonverbal behavior. Certain interaction-hypotheses were formulated expressing mutual reinforcement of the above main effects: (4) Black nonverbal behavior is assessed more negatively than white nonverbal behavior, especially if the actor is a Surinamer. (5) Dissimilar beliefs lead to more negative assessment than simmilar beliefs, especially if the actor is a Surinamer. (6) Black nonverbal behavior is assessed more negatively than white nonverbal behavior, especially if the citizen has dissimilar beliefs. (7) Most negatively assessed is the Surinamer with both dissimilar beliefs and black nonverbal behavior. Finally, the relative weight of the three factors may be formulated as follows: (8) If the environment exerts social pressure (i.e., discrimination is held to be socially taboo), nonverbal behavior is the most important factor in predicting negative assessment, skin color the least important, and the factor beliefs is intermediate. This is the weak version of the hypothesis; the strong version is that the effect of the factor skin color is zero.

Experiment One: Smiling

Method

Subjects. A total of 176 police officers of lower ranks participated in the experiment, 91% of whom were male, 9% female. Average age in the sample was 34 years. The average period of employment with the force was 13 years.

Procedure. The study was conducted among local police forces. Subjects were shown a video clip, which began with shots of a street and a living room. A voice commented on the scenes, saying that a young woman was assaulted and raped, and that the police assumes that the offender lives in that street. Accordingly, police are calling door-to-door to have a brief interview with all the men. Part of an interrogation was shown, though presented without sound. A male citizen (actor) appeared in view, seated behind the table in his living room, evidently talking with a police officer, who remained invisible. The questions asked by the officer were given as subtitles. The answers took 20 seconds each time, the question, and hence the citizens listening period, lasted 10 seconds. In total, the fragment showed the citizen speaking for 80 seconds and listening for 40 seconds.

Independent variables. The independent variables were introduced in the video clips. The factor skin color was manipulated by showing both a Surinamer and a Dutch actor. We tried to select actors who seemed quite similar in other respects, especially in physical characteristics that are likely to be relevant to the way in which police officers assess people: relative to growth of a beard (Bond & Robinson, 1988), hair style (Willemse & Meiboom, 1979), dress (Kraut & Poe, 1980) and physique (Bull, 1983). The factor beliefs was introduced by manipulating the street in which the citizen lives, his home and his appearance. In the situation of dissimilar beliefs, the citizen lived on a run-down street, his room was untidy and uncared for, and he looked unkempt and alternative (unwashed and uncombed hair, earrings, a very large ring on his finger, a loud shirt with the logo Miami Vice on it). For the condition of similar beliefs the citizen lived on a neat street, his living room was clean and uncluttered, and he looked well groomed (clean-shaven, combed hair, no jewelry, and wearing a striped shirt). This manipulation was adopted from Walker and Campbell (1982). To construct the factor nonverbal behavior, we took our norm data from Vrij and Winkel (1990b), who registered that on average Surinamers smile 3.26 times per minute of speaking ($SD=2.2$) and Dutch persons 2.44 times ($SD=1.8$, $F(1,84)=3.91$, $p<.05$). Per minute of listening Surinamers smiled on average 1.64 times ($SD=1.3$) and Dutchmen 1.02 times ($SD=.9$, $F(1,84)=7.78$, $p<.01$). In the black smiling version of our experiment, the citizen smiled six times (five times during 80 seconds of speaking and once during 20 seconds of listening); and in the white smiling version, he smiled three times (during 80 seconds of speaking). Other than that, the citizen remained nonverbally unremarkable. He looked straight at the policeman, did not move his head or body, sat with arms crossed and kept his face neutral (showed no emotions: see Buck, 1984). The factor social pressure was varied by introducing information that it is against the law to suspect people simply because of the color of their skin. In the no social pressure version, this information was not given. The four independent variables were varied systematically in the video clips, such that we ended up with 16 video clips: 2 (skin color) x 2 (beliefs) x 2 (nonverbal behavior) x 2 (social pressure).

Dependent variables. To measure the degree of suspicion evoked by the citizen, five questions were asked such as Does this man give a suspicious impression? Does this man seem to hide the truth? and Would you want to interrogate him again later? Answers could be entered on a seven-point scale ranging from certainly not (1) to most certainly (7). To determine perceived unpleasantness we used seven semantic seven-point differentials

(Angenent, 1984) including cooperative - aggressive, sympathetic - unsympathetic, and self-possessed - uncontrolled. To determine perceived nervousness, we also used seven semantic seven-point differentials; examples are: the event did not disturb him - disturbed him greatly, calm - agitated, self-assured - insecure. To check manipulation of the factor skin color subjects were asked to indicate the ethnic background of the citizen (Dutch, Surinamer, dont know). To check the factor beliefs, subjects were asked how much they perceived themselves as different from the citizen on the following points: the street on which the citizen lives, the way the house is furnished and kept, dress, grooming, norms and values, beliefs. Answers could be given on a seven-point scale ranging from no different (1) to very different (7). To check manipulation of smiles, we asked how often the citizen smiled. These answers were also arranged on a seven-point scale from very seldom (1) to very often (7). The questionnaire concluded with background data (gender, age, level of education, position with the police, experience). For purposes of analysis, the sum of dependent variables was reduced to three indices. The six variables measuring the differences between policeman and citizen were reduced to one index. Reliability was sufficient: Cronbach's α were .89 for suspicious, .85 for unpleasant, .82 for nervous, and .79 for different beliefs.

Results

Manipulation checks. The ethnic background of the citizen was given correctly by 80% of the subjects; 2% were wrong; 18% were unable to recall. Further inspection revealed that 22% were unable to indicate the ethnic background of the black citizen and 10% failed with respect to the white citizen. A possible explanation for the relatively high percentage of dont know for blacks is that respondents cannot, by skin color alone, determine whether the citizen is a Surinamer or from the Antilles, for instance. To check for the influence of incorrect answers a covariance analysis was performed in which the subjects' answers were included as correct, dont know, and incorrect. But this yielded no different picture than the one presented in the text and the table. Univariate analyses of variance were used as manipulation checks for beliefs and nonverbal behavior. Results showed that the citizens with dissimilar beliefs were considered more unlike the subjects themselves than citizens whose beliefs were similar ($M=4.97$ versus $M=3.86$, $SD=1.10$, $F(1,174)=59.94, p<.01$).

Hypothesis-testing. Data analyses were conducted via an analysis of variance according to a 2 x 2 x 2 factor design. The factors were skin color (black or white), beliefs (similar or dissimilar), and nonverbal behavior (white or black). Dependent variables were the impressions of suspicion, nervousness, and unpleasantness. The mean scores and standard deviations relative to Hypotheses 1 through 3 are given in Table 1.

The pattern of the mean scores belonging to the factor ethnic background (Columns 1 and 2) ran counter to the hypothesis: In each case, the white citizen was evaluated a little more negatively, but the difference was never significant: (suspect: $F(1,160)=2.35$, $p=.12$; nervous: $F(1,160)=.99, p=.32$); unpleasant: $F(1,160)=.61, p=.43$). This means that the hypothesis should be rejected.

Table 1: Means and Standard Deviations on Hypotheses 1 through 3 (First Experiment).

| | Ethnic background | | | | Beliefs | | | | Smiling | | | |
| | White | | Black | | Similar | | Dissimiliar | | Seldom | | Often | |
	M[1]	SD	M	SD	M	SD	M	SD	M	SD	M	SD
Suspect	3.12	1.3	2.86	1.2	2.81	1.2	3.16	1.3	2.57	1.2	3.38	1.2
Nervous	3.69	1.0	3.56	1.0	3.86	0.9	3.37	1.0	3.39	1.0	3.85	1.0
Unpleasant	3.15	0.9	3.05	1.0	3.08	1.0	3.12	1.0	2.96	1.0	3.22	0.9

[1] A higher score means a more negative assessment (more suspect, etc.).

The pattern of the mean scores on the factor beliefs (Columns 3 and 4) was not consistent. In agreement with the hypothesis, the dissimilar citizen seemed more suspect than the citizen with similar beliefs, although the effect was weak ($F(1,160)=.1.87, p=.08$). In contrast to the hypothesis, however, the similar citizen was assessed as more nervous ($F(1,160)=15.41, p<.01$). The factor beliefs did not affect the degree to which a citizen gave an unpleasant impression ($F(1,160)=.00, p=.95$). Taking these results together we concluded that the second hypothesis received slight support.

The pattern of the means for nonverbal behavior (Columns 5 and 6) agreed with the hypothesis: Black nonverbal behavior (frequent smiling) impressed as more suspicious, more nervous and more unpleasant. For each aspect, the difference was significant (suspect: $F(1,160)=20.33, p<.01$; nervous: $F(1,160)=10.48, p<=.01$; unpleasant: $F(1,160)=3.18, p<.05$. This confirmed hypothesis 3.

Hypotheses 4 through 7 assumed that the main effects would reinforce each other. This proved to be the case in the effect of interaction between nonverbal behavior and beliefs (Hypothesis 5). Black nonverbal behavior was found to be more unpleasant than white nonverbal behavior, especially if the citizens beliefs were dissimilar to those of the respondent. But the effect was weak: M(dissimilar, black nonverbal)$=3.32, SD=.9$; M(dissimilar, white nonverbal)$=2.88, SD=.9$; M(similar, black nonverbal)$=3.12, SD=.9$; M(similar, white nonverbal)$=3.04, SD=1.0, F(1,160)=1.97, p=.08$. For the interaction between nonverbal behavior and skin color, the effect did not support the hypothesis: Black nonverbal behavior gave an impression of greater nervousness, especially if the citizen was white: M(white, black nonverbal)$=4.10, SD=.8$; M(black, black nonverbal)$=3.63, SD=1.0$; M(white, white nonverbal)$=3.29, SD=.9$; M(black, white nonverbal)$=3.49, SD=1.1, F(1,160)=4.62, p<.05$. The interactions skin color x beliefs and skin color x beliefs x nonverbal behavior showed no significant effects. Taking these results together, we concluded that Hypothesis 5 received limited support, while Hypotheses 4, 6 and 7 should be rejected.

To determine the relative weight of the factors that were part of evaluations, we performed stepwise regression analyses, one for the condition absence of social pressure and one for the condition social pressure present. Criterion was the main dependent variable degree of being suspect. Table 2 presents a summary of the regression analyses.

Table 2: Regression for the Three Factors Predicting Degree of Being Suspect (First Experiment).

	Social pressure absent			Social pressure present		
	β	t	p	β	t	p
Skin color	.04	.41	.68	.11	1.13	.26
Beliefs	.03	.33	.74	.17	1.73	.04
Nonverbal behavior	.25	2.22	.01	.34	3.59	.00
R^2	.06			.16		

The first regression analysis, to determine the degree of being suspect when social pressure is absent, indicated that just one factor - nonverbal behavior - was a predictor. Black nonverbal behavior was found to evoke more suspicion than white nonverbal behavior. This factor explained 6% of the variance. The second regression analysis provided insight into the empirical support for Hypothesis 8. The table shows that if there was social pressure, the degree of suspicion could be predicted on the basis of two factors, namely, nonverbal behavior and beliefs. Black nonverbal behavior was more suspicious than white nonverbal behavior. This factor bound 13% of the variance. And, dissimilar beliefs led to greater assessed suspicion than similar beliefs. The factor bound 3% of the variance. Results indicated that nonverbal behavior was the strongest predictor. The color of the citizens skin did not affect suspicion. This means that the strong version of Hypothesis 8 was confirmed. Comparison of the two regression analyses showed that presence of social pressure caused nonverbal behavior (compare the betas) and beliefs to become stronger predictors of suspicion.

Experiment Two: Gestures

Method

Subjects. A total of 192 police officers of lower ranks participated in this experiment, 88% were male, 12% were female. Average age in the sample was 30 years. Average experience with police work was 9 years.

Procedure. The procedure did not differ from the experiment on smiling.

Independent variables. The factors skin color, beliefs and social pressure were constructed as in the experiment on smiling. To construct the factor movement of hands and arms we took our normative data from Vrij and Winkel (1990b). Their study showed that Surinamers move their hands and arms, more frequently while speaking than Dutch people do (Surinamers: $M=7.33$, $SD=5.8$ gestures per minute of speech; Dutch: $M=4.59$, $SD=4.2$ gestures/minute; $F(1,84)=6.92$, $p<.01$). Hand and arm movement did not differ significantly during periods of listening (Surinamers: $M=1.20$, $SD=1.6$; Dutch: $M=1.47$, $SD=2.1$ movements/minute; $(F(1,84)=.47$, n.s.). In the black version of the experiment, the citizen moved hands and arms 10 times (all during 80 seconds of speaking); in the white version 6 such gestures were made (all during 80 seconds of speaking). As in the case of the smiling experiment, other nonverbal behavior was identical.

Dependent variables. Except for two items, we used the same questionnaire. The exceptions were measurements of the manipulation checks for skin color and nonverbal behavior. In view of the results of the smiling experiment we added three choices in response to the question What is the citizens ethnic background? These were: black, white, dont know. As a manipulation check on nonverbal behavior, we asked participants how often the citizen moved his hands and arms. The answer could be entered on a seven-point scale from very seldom (1) to very often (7). For purposes of analysis the sum total of dependent variables was reduced to three indices: suspicious, nervous, and unpleasant. In addition, the six questions relating to the perceived differences between the respondent and the citizen were reduced to one index: different beliefs Cronbach's α for the scales were .91 (suspicious), .80 (unpleasant), .83 (nervous) and .84 (different beliefs) respectively.

Results

Manipulation checks. The vast majority of the subjects noted the citizens ethnic background correctly (91%), 0% of the answers were wrong, while 9% said they did not recall. The ethnic background of the citizen had nothing to do with this: 9% failed to recall the background of either the white or the black citizen. The percentage of respondents who indicated the ethnic background of the black citizen was greater than it was in the smiling experiment, probably because one now had a choice between black and white rather than between Surinamer and Dutch. Manipulation checks for beliefs and nonverbal behavior were univariate analyses of variance. The results indicated that subjects attributed greater difference between themselves and citizens with dissimilar beliefs $M=4.90$ ($SD=1.0$) than between themselves and citizens with similar beliefs $M=3.97$ ($SD=1.0$; $F(1,190)=38.68$, $p<.01$). Respondents perceived more movement of hands and arms when exposed to the black gestures condition: $M=6.21$ ($SD=.9$) versus $M=5.01$ ($SD=1.7$; $F(1,190)=39.06$, $p<.01$).

Hypotheses-testing. Data analysis was performed with an analysis of variance with a 2 (skin color) x 2 (beliefs) x 2 (nonverbal behavior) factor design. Table 3 presents a review of the means and standard deviations relative to Hypotheses 1 through 3.

Table 3: Means and Standard Deviations on Hypotheses 1 through 3 (Second Experiment).

| | Ethnic background | | | | Beliefs | | | | Gestures | | | |
| | White | | Black | | Similar | | Dissimiliar | | Seldom | | Often | |
	M[1]	SD	M	SD	M	SD	M	SD	M	SD	M	SD
Suspect	3.72	1.2	3.39	1.4	3.46	1.2	3.63	1.4	3.09	1.2	4.05	1.2
Nervous	4.23	1.0	4.31	0.9	4.22	0.9	4.31	1.0	3.96	0.9	4.60	0.9
Unpleasant	3.70	0.8	3.82	0.9	3.65	0.7	3.85	0.9	3.71	0.7	3.81	0.9

[1] A higher score means a more negative assessment (more suspect, etc.).

The pattern of means relating to the factor skin color (Columns 1 and 2) is not consistent. In contrast to the hypothesis, the white citizen seemed more suspicious than the black citizen. Moreover, the difference was significant ($F(1,176)=4.47, p<.05$). In conformity with the hypothesis, however, black citizens impressed the subjects as more nervous and more unpleasant than their white counterparts. But the differences were not significant, (nervous: $F(1,176)=.14, p=.70$; unpleasant: $(F(1,176)=1.13, p=.29)$. Hence, Hypothesis 1 was rejected.

The pattern of means relative to beliefs (Columns 3 and 4) was consistent. The dissimilar citizen was considered more suspicious, nervous and unpleasant, as expected. But the effects were weak (suspicious: $F(1,176)=1.66, p=.09$; unpleasant: $F(1,176)=1.85, p=.08$) or even insignificant (nervous: $F(1,176)=.03, p=.85$). Accordingly, the results supported the hypothesis in a limited way only.

Nonverbal behavior showed a consistent pattern (Columns 5 and 6). Black nonverbal behavior (relatively frequent movement of arms and hands) was perceived as more suspicious, nervous and unpleasant. The effects were significant for suspicion ($F(1,176)=32.94 \, p<.01$) and for nervousness ($F(1,176)=26.21, p<.01$), and insignificant in the case of unpleasantness ($F(1,176)=.79, p=.37$). On the whole, though, Hypothesis 3 was confirmed.

Hypotheses 4 through 7 related to interaction effects. Hypothesis 5 was reflected affirmatively in significant interaction effects between nonverbal behavior and beliefs. Black nonverbal behavior seemed more nervous, especially if the citizens views were dissimilar (M[dissimilar, black nonverbal behavior]=4.73, $SD=.9$; M[similar, black nonverbal]=4.42, $SD=.9$; M[dissimilar, white nonverbal]=3.85, $SD=.9$; M[similar, white nonverbal]=4.07, $SD=.9$; $F(1,176)=4.25, p<.05$). Black nonverbal behavior impressed subjects as more suspicious, especially if the citizens beliefs were dissimilar (M[dissimilar, black nonverbal]=4.23, $SD=1.3$; M[similar, black nonverbal]=3.80, $SD=1.2$; M[dissimilar, white nonverbal]=2.98, $SD=1.2$; M[similar, white nonverbal]=3.20, $SD=1.1$; $F(1,176)=3.77, p<.05$).

The interaction between skin color and beliefs yielded a nonpredicted significant effect: If the beliefs of the citizen were dissimilar to those of the respondents, both white and black were viewed as equally suspicious; while when black and white citizens held similar beliefs, the black citizen was considered less suspicious than the white (M[dissimilar, black nonverbal]=3.62, $SD=1.4$; M[dissimilar, white nonverbal]=3.05, $SD=1.4$; M[similiar, black nonverbal]=2.84, $SD=1.2$; M[similar, white nonverbal]=3.74, $SD=1.0$; $F(1,176)=5.19 \, p<.05$). The interactions skin color x nonverbal behavior and skin color x beliefs x nonverbal behavior yielded no significant effects.

To determine the relative weight of these factors in assessments we executed stepwise regression analyses, one for the condition social pressure absent and one for social pressure present. Criterion was giving a suspicious impression. See Table 4.

When social pressure was absent, nonverbal behavior alone influenced the degree of being suspect; the citizen exhibiting black nonverbal behavior was considered more suspicious than the citizen exhibiting white nonverbal behavior. The factor explained 6% of the variance.

Table 4: Regression for the Three Factors Predicting Degree of Being Suspect (Second Experiment).

	Social pressure absent			Social pressure present		
	β	t	p	β	t	p
Skin color	.09	.92	.36	.20	2.16	.03
Beliefs	.01	.14	.88	.14	1.43	.08
Nonverbal behavior	.25	2.54	.01	.45	4.93	.00
R^2	.06			.27		

If social pressure was present, each of the three factors contributed significantly to the degree of being suspect. Strongest predictor was nonverbal behavior: black nonverbal behavior was considered more suspect than white. The factor explained 22% of the variance. The next strongest predictor was the citizens skin color, white evoked greater suspicion than black; variance explained was 3%. That is to say, when people are explicitly reminded that discrimination because of someones skin color is (legally) forbidden, the result is positive discrimination; the black citizen in our experiment was given a degree of preferential treatment because of the color of his skin whereas the white citizen was disadvantaged. Weakest predictor was beliefs. The dissimilar citizen impressed respondents as more suspicious. This factor explained 2% of the variance.

In sum, results are against the weak version of Hypothesis 8 (which says that a black skin contributes to negative evaluation), but they support the strong version of the hypothesis, which states that skin color may cause a positive effect to occur instead of a zero-effect only. Comparison of the two regression analyses shows, as in the former experiment, that application of social pressure makes nonverbal behavior and beliefs into stronger predictors of suspicion.

Conclusions

This article has examined the extent to which differences between Dutch and Surinamer citizens (differences in skin color, beliefs, and nonverbal behavior) would explain negative treatment of Surinamers by police officers. Since the outcomes of the two experiments overlap, they can be summarized together.

Hypotheses 1 through 3 relate to three main effects. Hypothesis 1, stating that a black citizen is evaluated more negatively than a white person, is rejected in both experiments. The second hypothesis is confirmed in both experiments: the citizen with dissimilar beliefs is judged negatively (more suspect in Experiment 1; more suspect and more unpleasant in Experiment 2). Both experiments provide support for Hypothesis 3: black nonverbal behavior is assessed as more negative than white nonverbal behavior (more suspect, more nervous, and more unpleasant in Experiment 1; more suspect and nervous in Experiment 2).

Hypotheses 4 through 7 predict interaction effects. The assumption in each case is that the main effects would reinforce each other. The results indicate only (limited) support for Hypothesis 5, which posits interaction between nonverbal behavior and beliefs. The citizen whose beliefs are dissimilar is evaluated negatively (unpleasant in Experiment 1; suspect and nervous in Experiment 2), especially if he displays black nonverbal behavior.

Hypothesis 8 deals with the relative weight of the three factors (skin color, beliefs and nonverbal behavior). The regression analyses concerns the condition of social pressure, applied via a statement to the effect that discrimination because of skin color is against the law. Results of both experiments support the strong version of the hypothesis: The degree of evoking suspicion is influenced especially by nonverbal behavior, less by the factor beliefs, and not at all (zero effect) by the factor skin color.

The regression analyses for the condition no social pressure presents a different picture. The degree of suspicion is determined by nonverbal behavior only, be it less evidently so than under the social pressure present condition. It can be said, then, that application of social pressure causes increased influence of beliefs and nonverbal behavior on assessments of seeming suspect.

We here encountered four unexpected effects: In the smiling experiment the citizen with similar beliefs is judged to be more nervous than the one whose beliefs are dissimilar to those of the respondent; in Experiment 2 (gestures), the factor beliefs does not affect the perceived degree of nervousness. This means that the relation between beliefs and nervousness remains unclear. In each of the other three unexpected effects, the factor skin color plays a role. We discuss these below.

Compared to earlier studies on discrimination we encounter two remarkable points: First, the fact that negative judgment of nonnatives in our study is caused especially by the black nonverbal behavior they display. Discrimination theory and research on prejudice has largely neglected this factor. In view of our results, however, it seems a good idea to make police officers aware of misunderstandings that can arise because of nonverbal behavior. For this reason we are now developing a training program on dealing with ethnic minorities, in which nonverbal behavior receives special attention. Remarkable, too, is the minimal influence of the factor skin color. None of our hypotheses relating to this (1, 4, 6 and 7) receive empirical support. On the contrary, we find that the black citizen is looked upon more favorably.

We have not ascertained the cause for this second point. Three explanations seem plausible:

1. Social desirability: Police officers are very much aware that discriminating because of skin color is neither desirable nor allowed; hence, to prevent a negative image for themselves and the police force generally, they will seek to avoid this kind of discrimination. But this explanation remains unsatisfactory, because in an earlier experiment (Vrij & Winkel, 1990c), in which white police officers were confronted with video clips showing Dutch and Surinamer citizens during interrogations, the Surinamers were assessed more negatively (more suspect) than the whites. We will refer to this study below.

2. By explicitly mentioning that skin color discrimination is illegal we in fact sought to eliminate the effect.

3. A third explanation has to do with the method used: Most studies that trace the influence of ethnic background on judgment provide respondents with *written texts* introducing black and white stimuli (negro and white person, Insko & Robinson, 1969; Rokeach, 1960; black person and white person, McKirnan, Smith, & Hamayan, 1983, Moe, Nacoste, & Insko, 1981). The problem then arising is that these terms stand for more than just ethnic background; for the observer they connote a variety of notions

(cognitive schemes) that lead to negative evaluation. In such cases, the negative judgment cannot simply be ascribed to the factor ethnic background (skin color) as such (McKirnan & Hamayan, 1984). In some experiments the black and white citizens are *filmed* (Hendrick, Bixenstine, & Hawkins, 1971; Mezei, 1971; Vrij & Winkel, 1990c). The problem here is that the factor ethnic background may be contaminated: Next to different color of skin there may have been other differences as well. For example, it may be that there were differences in nonverbal behavior, which actually caused the effect. This happened in our experiment (Vrij & Winkel, 1990c): As it turned out, the video clips showed that Surinamers exhibited different nonverbal behavior (typically Surinamer) to the Dutch. Although not mentioned in other research, contamination with nonverbal behavior may well have occurred. At least, our experience with videotape is that even professional actors find it hard to control their nonverbal behavior.

The argument of contaminating factors is underscored by the results of a study by Jussim, Coleman, and Lerch (1987). Their experiment was designed largely along the same lines as our own. They too, confronted respondents with blacks and whites, in which variation in skin color was the only difference. In this case, too, black citizens were assessed more positively than whites.

The question is: Why this more positive evaluation of blacks? One possible explanation is given by expectancy-violation theory (Jussim, Coleman, & Lerch, 1987), predicated on the principle that individuals have expectations regarding persons belonging to specific social categories. In general, white individuals attribute negative traits to black persons and positive traits to whites. The theory states that if persons deviate from these expectations, evaluation will be in the direction of the deviation, that is, black persons with positive traits will be assessed relatively positively (more positively than whites evincing the same traits), and white persons with negative traits will be adjudged relatively negatively (more negatively than blacks with the same negative traits). In both our study and the one by Jussim et al. the result is a more positive overall effect for black persons. Our study recods that two significant interaction effects relating to skin color support this theory. In the gestures experiment, this holds for the effect of skin color x beliefs. Black and white citizens espousing beliefs dissimilar to those held by the respondent are assessed similarly, while the black citizen with similar views is evaluated more positively (less suspect) than the white citizen. In the smiling experiment, nonverbal behavior x skin color also supports the theory: Black nonverbal behavior (frequent smiling) is looked upon as more negative (witnessing to greater nervousness) than white nonverbal behavior, especially if the citizen is white. It seems that much smiling, especially in whites, is seen as abnormal and hence invites more extreme assessment.

We would not exclude altogether that the influence of skin color should be taken into account when explaining unequal treatment of ethnic minorities. But it makes sense to divide the interaction processes that lead to such treatment into two phases: a selective and a communicative phase. The selective phase has to do with the person addressed, that is, who is asked to show his or her driving license during a routine investigation, whose luggage is searched at customs. The communicative phase refers to the police interview with a citizen, that is, subsequent to selection. It appears as if skin color does influence selection (see Bovenkerk, 1990) but, as our results indicate, does not affect the communicative phase.

References

Angenent, H. (1984). Met de politie op pad, oordeel en vooroordeel. *Tydschrift voor Crimilogie, 26*, 256-269.

Beer, P. de. (1988). Nederlandse studies naar de criminaliteit van etnische minderheden, *Migrantenstudies, 4*, 17-27.

Bond, C.F., & Robinson, M. (1988). The evaluation of deception. *Journal of Nonverbal Behavior, 12*, 295-308.

Bovenkerk, F. (1990). Misdaad en de multi-etnische samenleving. *Justitiële Verkenningen, 16*, 8-29.

Buck, R. (1984). *The communication of emotion.* New York: Guilford Press.

Bull, P. (1983). Summing up or assessing people. In Bull, P. (Ed.), *Body movement and interpersonal communication* (pp. 43-55). New York: Wiley & Sons.

DePaulo, B.M., Stone, J.L., & Lassiter, G.D. (1985). Deceiving and detecting deceit. In B.R. Schenkler (Ed.), *The self and social life.* New York: McGraw-Hill.

Hendrick, C., Bixenstine, V.E., & Hawkins, G. (1971). Race versus belief similarity as determinants of attraction: A search for a fair test. *Journal of Personality and Social Psychology, 17*, 250-258.

Hyland, M. (1974). The anticipated belief differences theory of prejudice: Analysis and evaluation. *European Journal of Social Psychology, 4*, 179-200.

Insko, C.A., & Robinson, J.E. (1967). Belief similarity versus race as determinants of reactions to negroes by southern white adolescents: A further test of Rokeachs theory. *Journal of Personality and Social Psychology, 7*, 216-221.

Insko, C.A., & Robinson, J.E. (1969). Belief similarity versus race as determinants of reactions to negroes by southern white adolescents: A further test of Roheach's theory. *Journal of Personality and Social Psychology, 7*, 216-221.

Insko, C.A., Nacoste, R.W., & Moe, J.L. (1983). Belief congruence and racial discrimination: Review of the evidence and critical evaluation. *European Journal of Social Psychology, 13*, 153-174.

Jussim, L., Coleman, L.M., & Lerch, L. (1987). The nature of stereotypes: A comparison and integration of three theories. *Journal of Personality and Social Psychology, 52*, 536-546.

Kraut, R.E., & Poe, D. (1980). On the line: The deception judgements of customs inspectors and laymen. *Journal of Personality and Social Psychology, 36*, 380-391.

McKirnan, D.J., Smith, C.E., & Hamayan, E.V. (1983). A sociolinguistic approach to the belief-similarity model of racial attitudes. *Journal of Experimental Social Psychology, 19*, 434-447.

McKirnan, D.J., & Hamayan, E.V. (1984). Speech norms and perceptions of ethno-linguistic group differences: Toward a conceptual and research framework. *European Journal of Social Psychology, 14*, 151-168.

Mezei, L. (1971). Perceived social pressure as an explanation of shifts in the relative influence of race and belief on prejudice across social interaction. *Journal of Personality and Social Psychology, 19*, 69-81.

Moe, J.L., Nacoste, R.W., & Insko, C.A. (1981). Belief versus race as determinants of discrimination: A study of southern adolescents in 1966 and 1979. *Journal of Personality and Social Psychology, 41*, 1031-1050.

Rokeach, M. (1960). *The open and closed mind.* New York: Basis Books.

Tajfel, H. (1978). *Differentiation between social groups: Studies in the social psychology of intergroup relations.* London: Academic Press.

Vrij, A., & Winkel, F.W. (1990a). Culturele verschillen in spreekstijl van Surinamers en Nederlanders: de relatie tussen zakelijkheid en misleiding bij een politieverhoor. *Recht der Werkelijkheid, 11*, 3-15.

Vrij, A., & Winkel, F.W. (1990b). The frequency and scope of differences in nonverbal behavioral patterns: An observation study of Dutch men and Surinamers. In N. Bleichrodt, & P.J.D. Drenth (Eds.), *Contemporary issues in crosscultural psychology.* Amsterdam: Swets & Zeitlinger.

Vrij, A., & Winkel, F.W. (1990c). *Sociale vaardigheden, etnische afkomst en verdacht zijn: Een experiment.* Amsterdam: Stichting Mens en Recht.

Vrij, A., Winkel, F.W., & Koppelaar, L. (1988). Culturele verschillen in non-verbaal gedrag: De persoonlijke ruimte van Nederlanders en Surinamers. *Migrantenstudies, 4*, 40-49.

Walker, W.V., & Campbell, J.B. (1982). Similarity of values and interpersonal attraction of whites towards blacks. *Psychological Reports, 50*, 1199-1205.

Willemse, H.M., & Meyboom, M.L. (1979). Personal characteristics of 'suspects' and stereotyping by the police, part 2: A laboratory experiment. *Abstracts on Police Science, 7*, 359-368.

Winkel, F.W. (1981). Beslissingen: Het rechtspsychologisch perspectief. *Delikt en Delinkwent, 11*, 506-521.

Zuckerman, M., DePaulo, B.M., & Rosenthal, R. (1981). Verbal and nonverbal communication of deception. *Advances in Experimental Social Psychology, 14*, 1-59.

The Effect of the Right to Silence on the Prosecution and Conviction of Criminal Suspects

Geoffrey M. Stephenson and Stephen J. Moston

Introduction

In England, it is a principle of common law that juries should not be invited by judges or prosecutors to draw adverse inferences from the fact that an accused person has refused to give evidence in his or her own defence. This applies as much to the response to questions put by the police as it does to testimony in a court of law. This right to silence, as it is called, occasions much controversy (Zuckermann, 1989). Those in favour of retaining the right argue that it helps protect wrongfully accused persons, whilst those in favour of abolishing the right claim that it inappropriately protects the guilty. The public debate over whether the Right to Silence should be abolished has raged since the Eleventh Report of the Criminal Law Revisions Committee proposed in 1972 that Courts should be allowed to draw "such inferences ... as appear proper" from a suspect's failure when charged by the police to mention facts which are subsequently relied upon to establish a defence, and that appropriate inferences should be drawn from an accused person's refusal to answer questions at trial (Greer, 1990). These recommendations have yet to be put into effect.

What are the effects of suspects using the right to silence at the point of interrogation by police officers? Police officers believe that the present state of the law is detrimental to prosecution, especially in serious cases (e.g., McKenzie & Irving, 1988), but the evidence for this is slim. There is no doubt that the present state of the law frustrates the police in their attempts to extract confessions from suspects, especially now that tape-recording of interrogations at police stations is being demanded. But, however irritating it may be for police officers to be faced with a silent suspect, does the right to silence seriously interfere with the process of prosecution? This study represents an attempt to provide some evidence that might contribute towards the fruitful discussion of this question.

In this paper we report an investigation of the use of silence in the context of police interrogation, and in particular we (1) examine how frequently and by whom the right to silence is exercised; (2) examine the interaction between police officers and suspects when silence is employed; (3) examine how the use of silence affects the decision by police to charge a suspect, and (4) assess what effect, if any, the use of silence has on the outcome of the decision to prosecute.

Method

Information concerning tape-recorded interviews by police detectives was collected from nine Metropolitan Police stations using a questionnaire completed by the interviewing officer. Seven key background variables were assessed.

1. *Strength of evidence against the suspect.* Three levels of evidence strength were coded: weak, moderate and strong.

2. *Interviewer's perception of the seriousness of the offence.* Three levels of severity were coded: trivial, moderately serious, and very serious.

3. *Offence type.* These were divided into two basic categories, offenses against property and offenses against the person. Property crimes included: robbery, burglary, theft, shoplifting, handling stolen goods, deception, criminal damage, arson and possession of firearms. Crimes against the person included: actual bodily harm, grievous bodily harm, murder, incest, indecent assault and rape.

4. *Age of suspect.* Four broad age groupings were employed: less than 17 years, 17-21 years and 32 years or over.

5. *Sex of suspect.*

6. *Criminal history.* Suspects were simply categorized into those with and those without previous convictions.

7. *Use of legal advice.* Two categories of legal support were coded: (a) no solicitor present with legal advice not given; and (b) solicitor present, or legal advice given.

At the end of the interview the outcome was recorded in four main categories as follows:

1. *Confession.* Three main outcomes were identified. The suspect could either confess, deny or do neither of these things, either because the right to silence was exercised, or because the interviewing officer did not make any kind of accusation against the suspect.

2. *Damaging admissions.* Damaging admissions may or may not accompany any type of confession outcome (admit, deny or neither).

3. *Exercise of right to silence.* A distinction was made between selective and complete right of silence. Selective right of silence means the suspect answered some questions, complete silence means exactly that: the suspect answered no questions. A suspect was said to have used their right of silence when they declined to answer a question either through evasion, silence, or by saying "No comment".

4. *Results of interview.* The action taken against the suspect was recorded. Suspects are typically either charged, cautioned, detained pending further enquiries, released for further enquiries, released with no further action or referred to the youth and community section.

It was initially intended that a questionnaire should be completed for every C.I.D. interview, at each of 9 Police Stations over a period of about 6 weeks. Checks of custody records found that about 90% of the intended cases were covered. The cases that were missed were typically those in which officers from stations not involved in the study interviewed suspects.

Results and Discussion

Data from a total of 1067 cases in which C.I.D. officers interviewed suspects, were obtained.

By whom is the right to silence exercised?

A number of commonsense hypotheses were unsupported by our data. For example, it might be supposed that strength of evidence would be associated with use of silence. When there is weak evidence there is little point in unnecessarily providing the police with an opportunity to obtain some, whereas when the evidence is strong the incentive, or temptation, to try to talk one's way out of it must be correspondingly greater. In practice there was no association between use of silence and strength of evidence. Similarly it has been assumed on commonsense grounds that younger persons and females would be less likely to employ silence than would older people and males. In practice neither age nor sex was associated with use of silence. Rather less surprisingly, offence category was not linked to exercise of the right to silence: those accused of property offenses were no more likely to remain silent than were those accused of committing offenses against the person. These four variables were eliminated in the first step of the hiloglinear analysis used in the examination of our data.

Altogether some 16% of the sample used either selective or complete silence (roughly 8% in each category). Use of silence was reliably associated with the remaining four factors whose effects we studied: (a) severity of offence, (b) giving of legal advice (c) a criminal history, and (c) the police station where the interview was conducted. Let us consider the effects of these variables in turn.

Severity of the case. The more serious the offence, the greater is the incentive to protect one's interests by keeping silent. This hypothesis was strongly supported. Severity of an offence was strongly associated with the use of silence. Figure 1 shows how use of the right to silence rose in line with increasing offence severity, from 8.5% for trivial offenses to nearly 23% for very serious offenses.

Criminal history. It is common-place that experienced ("professional") criminals are more likely to maintain silence in an attempt to avoid prosecution than are novices in crime. The suspect's criminal history did, indeed, have an effect on the use of silence; that is, there was greater use of silence in interviews by the suspects with previous criminal convictions. This is shown in Figure 2.

Legal advice. The police complain bitterly that legal advice consistently encourages use of silence by suspects, and the fear is expressed that improved access to legal advice will be detrimental to successful prosecution of offenders. Figure 3 shows that the right of silence was employed in nearly one-third of interviews in which legal advice was given as compared to less than 5% when it was not. This association was the strongest of all those observed, and fully confirms that the general drift of legal advice to suspects is that they do best to remain silent when questioned by police officers.

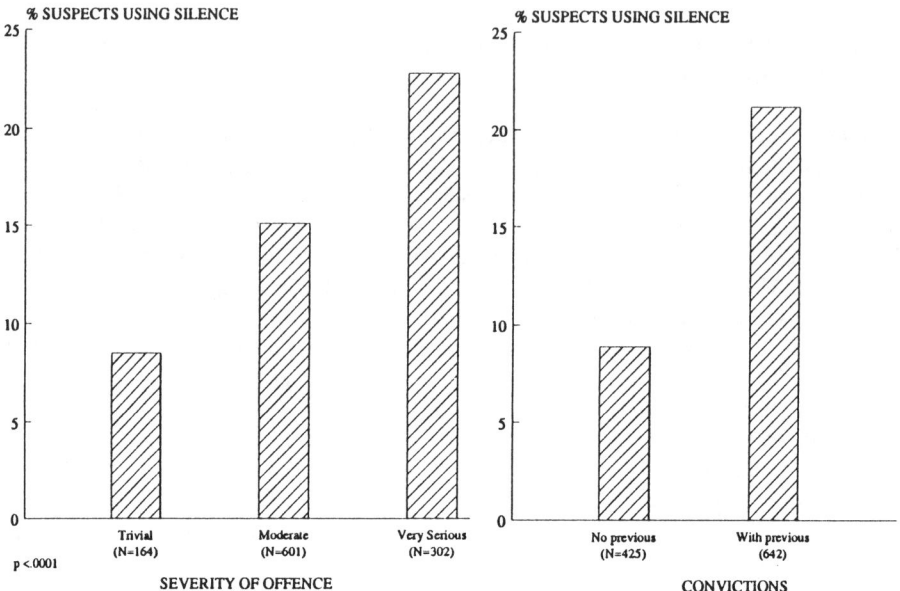

Figure 1: Relationship between Severity of Offences and the Right to Silence.

Figure 2: Relationship between Criminal History and Right to Silence.

Station. We had no particular reason to believe that there would be material differences in the use of silence by suspects interrogated at different police stations. However, use of the right to silence did show some variation by station as is shown in Figure 4. At Kingston, less than 9% of suspects used the right of silence in interviews. However, at Holborn the rate reached 25%. Police officers were inclined to attribute the variation to systematic differences in the nature of legal advice given in different areas, but it is possible that variations in police interrogation methods and the circumstances of interrogation may also play a part.

Interaction of police and suspects when silence is used. These results suggest that silence is used strategically by those who feel compelled, or are advised, to gain what advantage they can from so doing. Those who remain silent tend to be experienced offenders, accused of a serious offence and receiving legal advice. Some questions are, of course, more material to the offence than others, and it is to be expected that the use of silence will vary with type of question. It is difficult, and interpersonally offensive and perhaps inadvisable to remain silent in response to harmless, friendly questions.

During the main period of data collection large numbers of tapes were collected in order to validate the questionnaire details, as well as to allow analysis of the interaction. A total of 133 cases were examined in detail, and these were a random selection from the total of 174 right to silence cases described earlier.

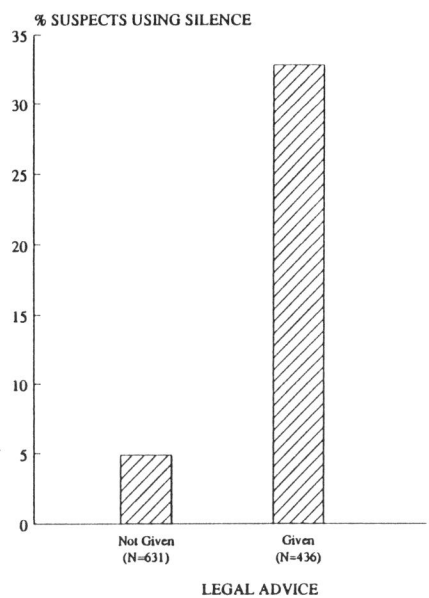
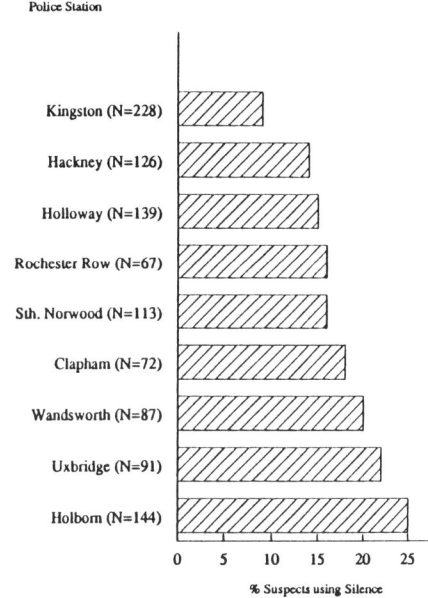

Figure 3: Relationship between Receiving Legal Advice and Use of Right to Silence.

Figure 4: Relationship between Police Station and Use of Right to Silence.

Four main categories of question types were identified:

1. *Procedural questions.* These include establishing the suspect's name, administering the caution, discussion of the taping procedure etc.

2. *Background questions.* Background questions are those which describe the suspect and his or her way of life without having any direct bearing on the offence under investigation.

3. *Offence related questions.* These include questions about the suspect's movements, the evidence in a case and the suspect's knowledge of the incident.

4. *Accusation questions.* These are questions in which the suspect is directly accused of a particular offence.

The responses of suspects to questions were classified into three categories: A full answer, a selective answer and not answered. Figure 5 below shows suspects' responses to each of the four question types, provided they were asked.

The association between use of silence and question type is apparent. A mere 6% of this sample of users of silence refuse to answer procedural questions, the proportion increasing through 19.5% for questions concerning suspect's background to 55.5% for offence related questions and 65.5% in response to the direct accusation. It should be noted that only procedural questions were asked of all suspects. Relatively few were asked questions about their background, and a significant number were not even directly asked about their involvement in the offence.

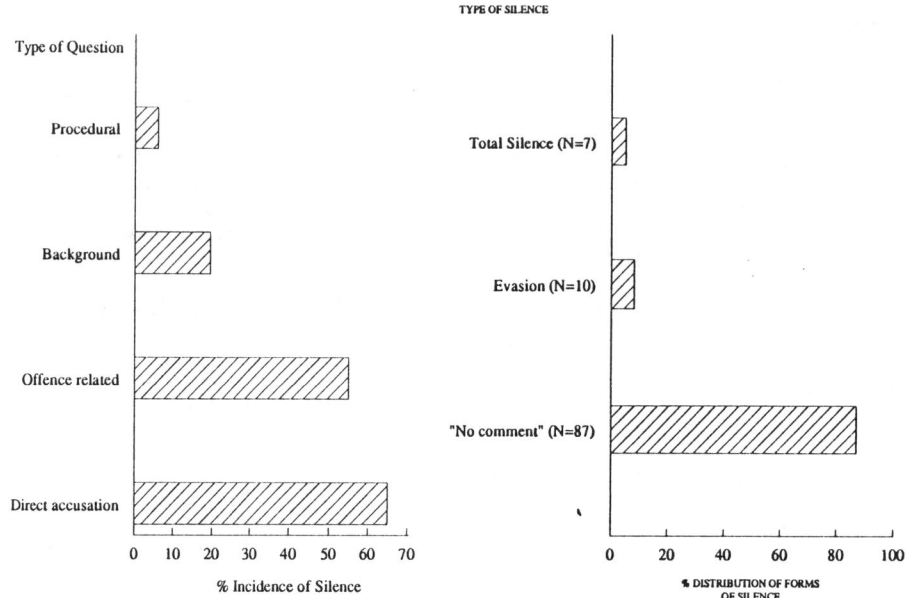

Figure 5: How Suspects Using Silence Respond to Different Types of Question.

Figure 6: Incidence of Different Types of Silence (Total=100%).

Figure 6 shows the ways in which suspects exercised their right of silence. There are three principal strategies: Total silence, that is, say nothing whatsoever; evasion, where the suspect typically claims to have forgotten ("I don't know", "Not sure"); and simply saying "No comment". This response category also includes statements such as "No answer" and "I don't want to answer that". The suspects' behaviours were categorized into a single predominating strategy for each person. In each case one of these forms of silence was more common. By far the most common form of silence (87% of cases) was the characteristically political response of "No comment". Total silence was relatively scarce.

How do police cope with a silent suspect?

There is no training given in what to do, and it is not surprising that the initial response of officers varied considerably. Five different coping strategies, or reactions to silence, used by police interviewers, were identified. They are listed in order of strategic complexity.

1. *Avoidance.* This occurs where an interviewer's immediate reaction is to conclude the interview, even if it has only just started, the suspect's use of silence being seen as preventing any form of questioning. In some interviews in which the avoidance reaction is observed, the suspect may not be asked a single offence related question.

2. *Persistence.* In this reaction the interviewer tries out a series of questions almost in a bid to jog the suspect's memory. The identical question may sometimes be repeated again and again, or questions in the sequence may be very similar in form and content;

sometimes quite different questions might be asked. The key aspect of the persistence reaction is that the interviewer does not use any of the available evidence in their questions. That is, nothing new is added to any of the questions that directly implicates the suspect and thus needs to be refuted if the suspect wishes to say that they are innocent.

3. *Downgrading.* If the suspect appears reluctant to talk about the offence, the interviewer may decide to shift the topic of conversations to a less stressful or controversial issue, such as the suspect's homelife or work. This switching of topics is referred to here as "downgrading", as the interviewer is seeking to establish some form of rapport through discussion of supposedly non-salient issues.

4. *Upgrading.* The "upgrading" reaction is characterized by the inclusion of evidence that implicates the suspect in a question, the assumption being that the suspect needs to reply to questions if they want to maintain that they are innocent.

5. *Rationalization.* There are common forms of rationalization. First, the interviewer might say something along the lines of, "It is your right not to answer questions, but I still have my duty to question you". The alternative or second step is to try and reason against the use of silence. For example, the suspect may be told that this is their opportunity to speak. The interviewer is not permitted to suggest that the use of silence will bring negative consequences for the suspect, nor can they suggest that cooperation will bring positive consequences. It may, however, be suggested that the suspect now has a chance to give their version of events, or that they might be able to help in recovering some stolen items. These five reactions to the use of silence serve as good means of characterizing how interviewers cope with the right of silence. The frequency of each type of initial reaction to silence is shown in Figure 7.

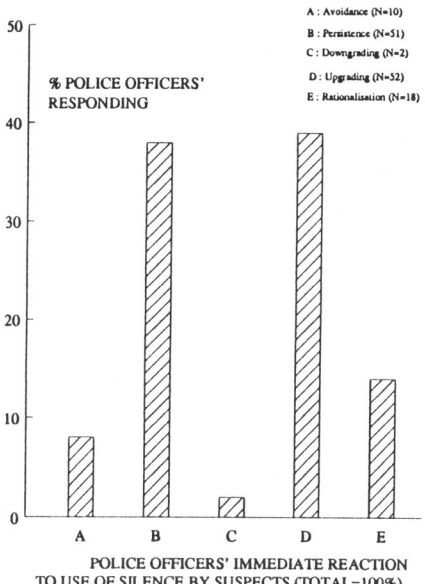

Figure 7: How Police Officers Respond to Use of Silence.

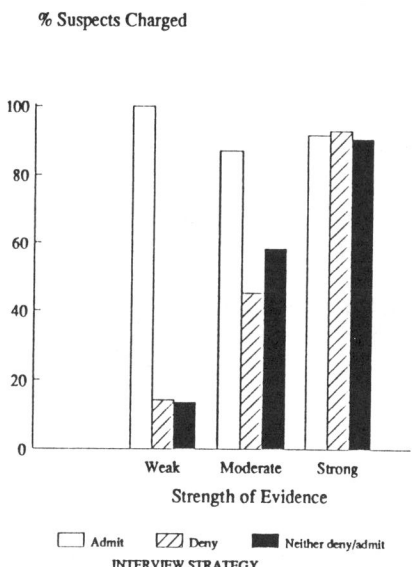

Figure 8: Relationship between Decision to Charge and Interview Strategy when Evidence is Weak, Moderate and Strong.

In about 38% of cases interviewers reacted to the use of silence by persisting with their earlier line of questioning. 39% upgraded their questioning by using the evidence against the suspect in an attempt to encourage a response. Only 13.5% of interviewers tried to reason against silence as their initial reaction. "Avoidance" and "downgrading" were relatively infrequent.

Police officers were not especially flexible in their response to silence, and in the majority of cases (58.6%) no new second reaction was observed. This suggests that interviewers have a certain degree of rigidity in their reactions to silence, that is, they try only one method of encouraging the suspect to answer questions. A total of 67 interviewers (50.4%) tried upgrading at some stage during questioning. A total of 35 (26.3%) tried rationalization at some stage.

It may be that part of the reason why interviewers do not employ more flexible strategies for dealing with silence is that they may believe that their behaviour will be labelled coercive. Consequently, interviewers will adopt what might be considered as cautious or safe interviewing strategies. The introduction of tape recording may be at the heart of this matter. Interviewers appear keenly aware that any mistakes they make in questioning could be advertised publicly in court.

Does use of the right to silence affect the decision to charge the suspect?

The use of silence does not directly influence the decision to charge a suspect. In the hiloglinear analysis used to predict the decision to charge a suspect, only four main factors predicted the result: strength of evidence, severity of offence, sex of suspect, and outcome of interview. Indirectly, however, use of silence may be said to have influenced the decision to charge via its association with the outcome of the interview. This can be seen in the statistically significant interaction between strength of evidence, outcome of interview, and decision to charge, portrayed in Figure 8. The figures to note are for those who "neither" admit nor deny their guilt, the category into which the majority of silence cases fall. When there is weak or strong evidence the "neither" category has results which are very similar to those of the "deny" group. This pattern is changed when the evidence is only "moderate". Silence would seem then to be taken by police officers to indicate guilt, and increases the chances of being charged.

Strength of evidence had by far the greatest effect on the decision to charge, followed by outcome of interview, with sex being the third most important factor. About 66% of men were charged compared with a figure of only 53% for women. This was a more important factor than the severity of offence, which had only a slight effect on the result, very serious offenses being more likely to result in a charge than less serious offenses.

What effect does use of silence have on prosecution and conviction?

Silence was used in 174 cases. Of these, 113 suspects (about 65%) were subsequently charged (or detained pending further enquiries). The majority of these 113 cases have now come to court, and it has thus been possible to examine the effects of silence on these cases. In order to assess the significance of the findings, a "control" group of comparable cases in which suspects who did not use silence, but were charged, was also examined. These control cases were matched with the silence cases on a number of important dimensions, ie, strength of evidence, severity of offence, type of offence, outcome of interview, damaging statements, and age group. Each of these factors is likely to be of major importance in determining how a case proceeds. Other factors, such as the suspect's criminal history, sex and use of legal advice during interrogation are perhaps less likely to have a bearing on the decision making of the Crown Prosecution Service or courts.

The only important difference between the control group and the silence group was the use of the right to silence. The control group did not use silence, the silence group did.

The Crown Prosecution Service prosecuted in 80% of cases and discontinued prosecution in 20%, but a matched comparison of silence and control groups suggests that there was no effect whatsoever of the suspect's use of right to silence during an interview on the decision making of the Crown Prosecution Service. However, a comparison of the Silence and Control cases that have come to court suggests firstly that Silence cases are more likely to plead guilty at the trial (67%) than is the case with the Control group, only 49% of whom pleaded guilty. A total of 80% of the Silence group was eventually found Guilty, and 77% of the Control group. These results certainly suggest that there is no clear advantage to the use of silence at the police station in terms of the ultimate verdict at court. The high proportion of Silence cases who ultimately plead Guilty might be taken to suggest that use of silence is a ploy - adopted for the most part by previously convicted offenders - which having failed to secure release from custody is abandoned in favour of a guilty plea when prosecution, probable conviction and (especially) sentencing are likely. In sum, the results as a whole suggest that the tactical advantages of using silence in response to police questioning are rather limited. They further indicate that whether guilty or not the tactic might backfire when the evidence the police have already gathered is no more than moderate in strength. Appearing to cooperate in such instances could well be the more effective strategy to adopt.

If the police find the right an irritant which frustrates them in the task of securing a confession, their policy of making a suspect's use of the right a reason to charge that suspect seems to pay off in court, where the confession withheld so steadfastly in the police station emerges as a decision to plead Guilty. It is also clear from our analysis of how police officers respond to a silent suspect that attempting to improve their interviewing skills would be helpful. Abolishing the right to silence might reduce the irritation felt by the police, but would probably do little to increase the number of successful prosecutions. It seems that accused persons who have remained silent already act as if adverse inferences will, indeed, be drawn should they continue to stay silent, or even plead Not Guilty. Our results suggest that the alarm and anxiety to which the continued existence of the Right gives rise are misplaced for the most part (see Criminal Law Review, 1989). The problem if there is one, has less to do with uncooperative suspects than it does with those features of the adversarial system which make conviction on good evidence a less than certain process. It is that which makes obtaining a confession such an important goal for English police officers, and the use of silence by suspects such a frustrating experience.

Part V
Research on Witness Testimony

Influencing Public Policy on Eyewitnessing: Problems and Possibilities

Graham Davies

Nowhere are the problems of the generalisability and reliability of research findings more acute than in the study of eyewitnessing. In the United Kingdom, changes in the rules governing the admissibility of children's evidence were prefaced by an official review of the existing psychological research on children as witnesses (Hedderman, 1987) and the specialist training given to police officers who produce composite pictures of suspects was developed by witness psychologists (Davies, Shepherd, Shepherd, Flin, & Ellis, 1986). In the United States, such researchers have played a controversial role as experts, normally appearing for the defense, in cases where eyewitness testimony plays a central role (Loftus, 1986).

Not surprisingly, the methodology and status of eyewitness research has been the subject of debate and controversy. Yuille (1986) has argued that much of the orthodox laboratory research on eyewitness issues is of little or no relevance to the real world and that only the study of real crimes is likely to yield generalisable findings. Conversely, Benaji and Crowder (1989) have argued that such retrospective studies are meaningless without any control over the conditions of observation. They call for a return to well-designed and tightly controlled laboratory research as the only basis for a sound understanding of memory in general and eyewitnessing in particular. Finally, McClosky and Egeth (1983) in their critique of the role of the psychologists as expert witnesses espoused both views: Laboratory bench studies were inconsistent and irrelevant and nothing of significance could be deduced from existing studies of real events.

This paper examines each of the four major methodologies which have emerged for the systematic study of eyewitness identification illustrating them, where necessary, with examples of recent research by the author and others. It is argued that no one research method can of itself provide a reliable data base for legislation or advocacy. Rather, problems need to be addressed from a number of perspectives, each of which makes a different compromise between ecological validity and methodological rigour. Only by pooling the results of these different varieties of study is a reliable psychology of the eyewitness likely to emerge.

Slide Shows: Latter-Day Picture Tests?

The great German pioneer, L.W. Stern (1910) reviewing a decade of studying eyewitnessing, distinguished between picture tests (recall from a static picture) and event tests (an unexpected event staged for an audience who are later asked to recall it). He made a plea for greater use of event tests as more closely approximating the "nearness to life" criterion.

In the field of identification, the latter-day equivalent of Stern's picture test is the slide show: the serial presentation of static photographs of faces which the witness must later recognise among other novel faces. As a technique for understanding the psychological processing of face stimuli such studies have proved effective and powerful in developing theories of face recognition in both normal and brain damaged populations (Young & Ellis, 1989). However, as an analogue for eyewitness identification such experiments have great limitations.

As one of the early critics pointed out:

> Pictures are static; criminal events are dynamic; pictures are information light; events are information dense; while pictures predispose focused attention, events of a criminal nature predispose diffuse attention. (Clifford, 1978, p.202)

Moreover, faces are exposed in multiple numbers divorced from a background context and the bodies which support them. Delays between study and test are unrealistically brief and recognition is based on prior familiarity alone (Davies, 1989).

Given these discrepancies between the laboratory and real life it is not too surprising that when slide presentation is compared to more realistic circumstances, systematic differences occur in outcome. False alarms (misidentifications) are much lower in slide studies than in staged events (Lindsay & Harvie, 1988) and recognition rates appear to be much lower in real life than in the laboratory slide show (Clifford & Bull, 1978; Devlin, 1976).

The reasons for such differences appear to be not that the cognitive processes involved in processing persons in events are substantially different to pictures, so much as cognitive factors are supplemented by other considerations. Specifically, motivational (Köhnken & Maass, 1985), affective (Malpass & Devine, 1980) and social (Macleod, 1989) factors operate in the real world of witnessing in such a way as to interact with and obscure the operation of more basic cognitive components. In order to provide a convincing and comprehensive account of eyewitness behaviour it is necessary to go beyond the two-dimensional world of the frozen face.

Incident Studies

But are Stern's "event tests" a sufficiently serviceable guide to reality? As Lindsay and Wells (1983) have noted the term covers a wide variety of situations from the most innocuous (in Brown, Deffenbacher, & Sturgill's 1977 study, a stooge entered the lecture theatre to assist the instructor) through to a violent and dramatic episode (in a study reported by Timm, 1981, the stooge posed as a gangland boss who was then "assassinated" in front of an unsuspecting audience). There are those who argue that only such confrontational studies have anything to contribute to the debate over eyewitness accuracy (Yuille, 1986). However, such an argument ignores the fact that many criminal encounters do not involve violent confrontation between witness and suspect: the doorstepping thief who misrepresents himself (they are predominantly male) as a public servant in order to gain access to an old person's house is an obvious example. However, all such event tests, whatever their intended level of arousal, do have their limitations as representations of reality.

Unlike the picture test, one can never be certain that all one's audience have the same view of the stooge or even look at him or her at the critical moment: there is evidence from social psychological research that persons observing an individual indulging in embarrassing or antisocial acts will often disassociate themselves as much as possible (Aronson, 1980). Moreover, the canons of ethical experimentation demand that participants be advised subsequent to the key incident that they have been observing a stunt in order that they can give their advised consent to taking part in an experiment, a procedure which inevitably casts doubt on the authenticity of their behaviour at any subsequent identification parade or photo search task (Malpass & Devine, 1980). When ethical canons have been stretched, results have been consistent in showing that debriefing subsequent to a parade yields changes in performance to that of prior debriefing (see Köhnken & Maass, 1985, for a review). A further problem for such studies is that, with the exception of those involving individual confrontations, subjects are bystanders rather than participants. Recent research points to the crucial influence of style of interaction with a target "suspect" as having an important influence on subsequent ability to recognise and recall both for real (Macleod & Shepherd, 1986) and simulated (Yuille & Davies, 1990) crimes. A final problem, common to both picture and incident studies is the use of samples of subjects which are unrepresentative of those involved in criminal investigations (Clifford & Lloyd-Bostock, 1983). Yuille and Cutshall (1986) calculate that of a representative sample of 38 studies published between 1974 and 1982, no less than 92% involved college students exclusively as subjects. Clearly, if one is to extrapolate to the performance of the population as a whole, then it is unwise to rely upon norms collected from such selected samples.

Field Studies

One way of ensuring a more representative cross section of the population is through "field studies": rather than bringing subjects into the laboratory, the experiment is taken to the subjects as they go about their daily lives. A number of eyewitness variables first studied systematically in the laboratory, have now been scrutinised in this way, with mixed results. As Table 1 shows, superior recognition of "own" over "other" face identification first demonstrated in the laboratory has now been shown in two field studies. Likewise improvements in recognition consequent upon reinstatement of cues, associated with the original witnessing context has made a successful transference. However, two other effects: pose at original observation and "unconscious transference" (mistaken identification of individual "Y" as person "X" based on sight of Y at or near the time when X was originally observed), have failed to make the transition. Allowance needs to be made for unpublished failures to replicate (Read, Tollestrup, Hammersley, McFadzen, & Christensen, 1990) but in general it seems the larger the effect size found in meta-analyses of laboratory results (Shapiro & Penrod, 1986), the more likely the successful transition from laboratory to field.

Of course, some eyewitness effects are not held to apply to the population at large but rather, to one specific component, the police. Policemen are widely held by the public and legal professionals to have special powers of observation and report (Yarmey & Tressilian-Jones, 1983). Early studies successfully refuted this simple generalisation (Clifford, 1976). However, as researchers in both Britain and North America have worked more closely with police officers in a training and development role, it has become evident that as eyewitnesses, policeman are not simply "civilians in uniform" (Yuille, 1986). Growing glasnost between police officers and psychologists is facilitating a range of field studies which utilise captive populations of police officers and recruits undergoing training (Yuille & Davies, 1990).

Table 1: Transfer of Laboratory Effects to Field Settings: Eyewitness Identification.

Variable		Laboratory findings	Field findings
Pose:	Full face vs. 3/4 vs profile	3/4 superiority (Krouse, 1981)	No clear superiority (Logie, Baddeley, & Woodhead, 1987)
Race:	Own vs. other	Own race superiority (Shepherd, Deregowski, & Ellis, 1974)	Weak own race effect (Brigham, Maass, Snyder, & Spaulding, 1982) Consistent own race effect (Platz & Hosch, 1988)
Context		Context reinstatement improves recognition (Davies & Milne, 1982)	Context improves recognition (Krafka & Penrod, 1985)
Unconscious transference		Transference achieved (Loftus, 1976)	No transference (Read et al., 1990)

Field studies are demanding in terms of time and logistics but there is no doubting their contribution to the external validity of the eyewitness literature. There is a case for arguing that wherever practical, variables which are the subject of expert testimony should be "road tested" in this way. One adds the caveat "whenever possible", because it is clear that there are limits on the range of variables which can be explored through the innocuous deceptions involved in field studies.

Factors associated with stress and arousal clearly create difficulties for such studies: one cannot contemplate research assistants systematically holding up local shopkeepers in the cause of exploring the impact of weapon focus! Recent studies of children's eyewitnessing abilities for the dentist who inspected their teeth (Peters, 1987) or the nurse who administered multiple inoculations (Goodman, Aman, & Hirschman, 1987) have demonstrated that stress is not automatically precluded as a variable in field studies. However, the very naturalism of their setting puts constraints on the matching of suspects, the range of variables which can be explored and the types of design which are feasible (Davies, Tarrant, & Flin, 1989). To explore the full range of variables field studies must be supplemented by other designs which actually sample the grainy realism of witnessing: archival research and case studies.

Archival Studies

In archival studies, actual data from police files are examined and categorised in terms of variables of interest to the researcher. Macleod (1987) examined 379 witness statements associated with some 135 cases of assault. Where actual injury occurred, women gave fewer details of their attacker compared to cases where no injury occurred, a result which serves to confirm an experimental finding (Clifford & Scott, 1978).

However, the major determinant of richness of recall was whether the witness was a victim or a bystander: bystanders in general gave less information both about appearance and events than did victims. Macleod's research is a good example of how archive studies of this kind can draw attention to major variables operating in the real world which have been largely overlooked by orthodox laboratory studies (see Hosch, Lieppe, Marchioni, & Cooper, 1984, for an exception).

I offer two other examples where archival research may serve to modify the conclusions of laboratory experiments, both derived from the work of a student of mine, Peter Bennett. Detective Sergeant Bennett is Scotland Yard's principle operator of the Photofit kit: the system which enables a witness to piece together a likeness of a suspect from an assortment of facial features. As a preliminary to that process, operators will normally secure from the witness a free verbal description of the suspect. Such free descriptions given under laboratory conditions from student volunteers describing faces from photographs have been used as a measure of the saliency of different facial features and as a guide for the production of protocols for witnesses reporting actual crimes (Shepherd, Davies, & Ellis, 1978).

Bennett identified some 117 cases for which he was called upon to act to produce Photofits of male suspects from witness descriptions in 1988. Of these, some 95 were for violent crimes, which included murder, rape, armed robbery, aggravated burglary and assault. The remaining 22 covered a range of serious but not violent crimes, principally deception and fraud. Bennett took as his model the laboratory study of Ellis, Shepherd, and Davies (1980) where 24 student volunteers had described one of two faces seen as photographs after delays of up to one week. Bennett caste his results in the same way as Ellis et al., expressing the frequency of each feature common to the two studies as a proportion of the total number of shared features.

A comparison of the crime and laboratory samples showed a reasonably good fit between the two ($r_{xy} = .66, p < .001$). It confirmed the overwhelming saliency of hair and of upper features relative to lower. The only serious departure on shared features was on shaving, where the very much larger sample of target faces, many with beards or moustaches yielded higher numbers of reports in real crimes. There were, however, a number of facial cues which were volunteered in significant numbers by witnesses, but which did not figure in the Ellis et al. list. Principle among these were attributions, either of character (evil eyes, mean mouth etc.) or attractiveness (ugly, good looking etc.). Disfigurements also figured significantly as did accessories such as spectacles or earrings: features which had been selected out in the interests of homogeneity in the original Ellis et al. study, but which are clearly present in significant numbers in the criminal population. The only facial features missing from the original protocol but present in significant numbers in Bennett's data were ears and teeth, an omission which again reflected the choice of the original laboratory stimuli. These two features apart, this particular piece of laboratory research holds up quite well to appraisal by actual witness data and provides a good example of the fruitful interplay between different research rationales.

A second laboratory finding fared less favourably. Ellis, Davies, and Shepherd (1978) worked with student volunteers and a single police Photofit operator in constructing likenesses from monochrome photographs of two caucasian males. These Photofits were then rated for likeness by a panel of judges. The components were rated both in their basic form and elaborated, that is with elaborations and modifications to the basic features drawn on in pencil by the operator. In the experiment, modifications did not improve rated likeness, which led Ellis et al. to discount artistic embellishment as an aid to identification.

Bennett's inspection of his own archive led him to suspect that this result reflected the lack of proper training of the original operator. As a test of his hypothesis he took six photographs of convicted persons from police sources and gave one to each of six operators to produce first as a basic Photofit and then in an enhanced and modified form. He then handed photographs of the original Photofit or its enhanced counterpart to groups of police trainees to select from a standard 12 man photospread, where the distracters bore the same degree of physical similarity to the target as in actual police photospreads. Under these conditions, five out of the six elaborated composites produced better recognition rates than their basic counterparts, supporting Bennett's assertion that training in artwork can lead to more recognisable photofits. The next step must be a fullscale archive study using actual witness composites in basic and elaborated forms to confirm and extend this revised picture.

Single Case Studies

The major problem with archive studies is the absence of data on the overall accuracy of the descriptions provided by witnesses. Even, as in a police archive, where description and perhaps some photographs of suspects are available, the data set are incomplete. There are no pictures or descriptions of those criminals who were never found or convicted. To answer this problem, Yuille and Cutshall (1986) have argued forcefully for the importance of "real crime" studies, case histories where a conviction has occurred and sufficient facts are available to check the statements of a substantial number of witnesses. On the basis of their analysis of a gun-shop shooting in Burnaby, Vancouver, they claimed that witness statements were substantially accurate with regard to action details and personal details, with the exception of height, weight and age estimates. Moreover, the subgroup of witnesses they were able to interview four to five months later gave information consistent with their original statements and were resistant to suggestion through leading questions. A subsequent study of 45 witnesses to serious crime also yielded accuracy rates of 82% for the subset of facts which were ascertainable - some 18% of the total (Yuille & Kim, 1987). Yuille and his colleagues concluded that such studies of actual crimes undermine the view derived from laboratory research that witnesses are invariably prone to error and thus "the only way for us to learn about the factors affecting eyewitness performance is to study real eyewitnesses" (Yuille, 1986, p.236).

Not surprisingly perhaps, Yuille's position has been subject to critical scrutiny. Many psychologists, while accepting the value and necessity for such studies, believe they have limitations. Macleod (1989) points to the problems of sampling: Only a minority (9 out of 21 witnesses) agreed to be interviewed in the Yuille and Cutshall study and there is a possibility that only the most confident and effective witnesses cooperated. The problem of viewpoint and attention already highlighted in relation to "event tests" apply equally to a consideration of how individual witness statements are to be aggregated to provide an overall measure of accuracy. Moreover as Davies (1989) has noted, every crime contains a unique set of features, the sum of which will determine whether witness accounts are overwhelmingly accurate or tarnished with error.

As a contribution to the debate over accuracy rates in case studies, I offer a case on which I was recently consulted. Like the Burnaby shooting it involved a shooting seen by a large number of potential witnesses. In November 1987, a robbery took place in a busy shopping centre in Birmingham, England, where the day's takings were snatched at the close of business. An energetic pursuit ensued during which shots where fired which resulted in two members of the public being injured. Over 30 witnesses came forward who had seen the man fleeing from the shop, gun in hand. A subsequent police enquiry led to the arrest of Hassan Khan, a 33 year old man of mixed European and Afghan parentage. Khan vigorously denied his guilt and claimed to have been in Wales at the time of the shooting.

A total of 14 witnesses were summoned to the identification parade of whom seven picked out Khan. This impressive figure needs to be set against the configuration of the line-up: Mr Khan was the only half-caste European/Asian on the parade along with five dark-skinned Asians, another dark skinned man of indeterminate race, a half-caste West Indian and a White man with the word "Skins" tattooed across his forehead. At the subsequent trial police relied upon these identifications coupled with a disputed "confession" allegedly taken down in the police car which conveyed the suspect to Birmingham from his brother's home in Wales. Mr Khan's defence relied upon alibi evidence (he claimed to have been in Wales throughout the robbery period) and the fact that six weeks previously he had lost two toes in a shotgun incident and was barely able to walk on crutches let alone scamper down the street shooting as he went as alleged by the Crown.

However, in accord with the eyewitness "over belief" hypothesis (Loftus, 1974), the jury convicted Khan. Khan subsequently appealed on the grounds of the admissibility of the confession and the disputed identifications. I was supplied with the witness transcripts which reveal a picture of much greater confusion and inconsistency than was present in the Burnaby shooting. Unlike the latter, we do not have a palpably guilty individual with whom to compare the information supplied, but the sheer contradictory nature of some of the descriptions makes the point adequately.

Witnesses could not even agree on the race of the offender. Of the 14 witnesses summoned to the parade, eight were convinced they had seen a Western European, two an Asian and two a Greek, while the remainder did not specify a racial origin. There was equal confusion on the suspect's hair, which as has been demonstrated is the most salient of cues in the laboratory or in the field. It was variously described as "black", "dark brown" or "jet black" in colour. Length at one extreme was "very short", "short" and at the other "collar length". Hair texture was either "wavy", "curly" or "straight". Statements such as this accord much more closely with the view of witnessing which emerges from laboratory research than that arising from the Burnaby study.

The Court of Appeal duly sustained Khan's appeal ironically, not on the basis of the eyewitness evidence but over the "confession" which forensic analysis demonstrated had been substantially amended at a later date.

Whose witnesses are more representative: Birmingham or Burnaby? One can cite various reasons why one incident should have produced more reliable and consistent data than the other. Perhaps the British gunman was of mixed race. Perhaps also the artificial lighting and time of day operating in the latter case may have contributed to error. Such arguments are intriguing but irrelevant: What is crucial is that the same problems of witness factors and event factors so painstakingly explored in the mundane setting of the laboratory appear to operate in the outside world. Case studies, however crucial and illuminating, do not open the doors to some alternative reality which will overturn all the findings of more traditional research.

Conclusion

In sum, there appears to be no one ideal method for studying eyewitness behaviour. Rather different methods have different strengths and weaknesses. We may summarise these by reference to Figure 1 which considers all the procedures surveyed as a function of the degree of control they offer and the potential for forensic realism. As has been demonstrated, each paradigm makes a different compromise between these two crucial factors. The position of any one experiment within each quartile will vary, depending upon the excellence of the design and the ingenuity of the experimenter.

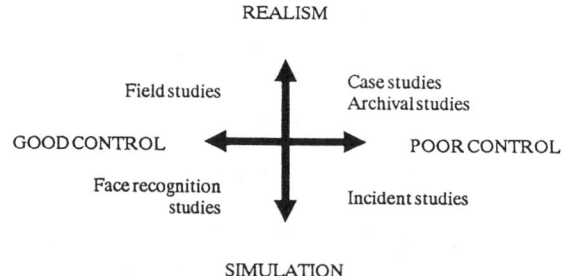

Figure 1: Eyewitness Identification Paradigms as a Function of Realism and Control.

Sometimes as in the studies of context and cross-racial identification, research may begin in the laboratory and then progress to field studies. In other instances, such as the differences in testimony between victims and bystanders, archival analysis or case studies may point to a neglected variable in field or laboratory studies. The direction of progression is not so important as ensuring that findings are replicated across a range of paradigms. Where repetition of an effect occurs - as in the cross-racial recognition and context reinstatement studies - we may feel confident in asserting a psychological truth in our training of police officers and statements to court officials. A failure of an effect to transfer to a "real world" setting will inevitably give rise to questions as to its robustness. Is it a weak effect, like the impact of face pose at presentation? Or is there a need for conceptual as well as empirical clarification, as in the case of "unconscious transference"? Clarification of such issues are essential if we are to satisfy our critics among lawyers (King 1986; Stone 1984) and our fellow psychologists (McCloskey & Egeth, 1983) of the validity of our science.

References

Aronson, E. (1980). *The social animal, 3rd ed.* San Fransisco: Freeman.
Benaji, M.R., & Crowder, R.G. (1989). The bankruptcy of everyday memory. *American Psychologist, 44*, 1185-1193.
Brigham, J.C., Maass, A., Snyder, L.D., & Spaulding, K. (1982). Accuracy of exewitness identification in a field setting. *Journal of Personality and Social Psychology, 42*, 673-680.
Brown, E., Deffenbacher, K., & Sturgill, W. (1977). Memory for faces and the circumstances of the encounter. *Journal of Applied Psychology, 62*, 311-318.
Clifford, B.R. (1976). The police as eyewitnesses. *New Society, 36*, 176-177.
Clifford, B.R. (1978). A critique of eyewitness research. In M. Gruneberg, P. Morris, & R. Sykes (Eds.), *Practical aspects of memory* (pp.199-209). London: Academic Press.
Clifford, B.R., & Bull, R. (1978). *The psychology of person identification*. London: Routledge & Kegan Paul.
Clifford, B.R., & Lloyd-Bostock, S.M.A. (1983). Witness evidence: Conclusion and prospect. In S.M.A. Lloyd-Bostock, & B.R. Clifford (Eds.), *Evaluating witness evidence* (pp. 285-290). Chichester: Wiley.
Clifford, B.R., & Scott, J. (1978). Individual and situational factors in eyewitness testimony. *Journal of Applied Psychology, 63*, 352-359.
Davies, G. (1989). The applicability of facial memory research. In A.W. Young, & H.D. Ellis (Eds.), *Handbook of research on face processing* (pp. 557-562). Amsterdam: North Holland.
Davies, G., & Milne, A. (1982). Recognition of faces in and out of context. *Current Psychological Research, 2*, 235-246.
Davies, G., Shepherd, J., Shepherd, J., Flin, R., & Ellis, H. (1986). Training skills in police Photofit operators. *Policing, 2*, 35-46.
Davies, G., Tarrant, A., & Flin, R. (1989). Close encounters of the witness kind: Children's memory for a simulated health inspection. *British Journal of Psychology, 80*, 415-429.
Devlin, Lord P. (1976). Report to the Secretary of State for the Home Department of the Departmental Committee on evidence of identification in criminal cases. London: Her Majesty's Stationery Office.
Ellis, H.D., Davies, G.M., & Shepherd, J.W. (1978). A critical examination of the Photofit system for recalling faces. *Ergonomics, 21*, 297-307.
Ellis, H.D., Shepherd, J.W., & Davies, G.M. (1980). The deterioration of verbal descriptions of faces over different delay intervals. *Journal of Police Science and Administration, 8*, 101-106.
Goodman, G., Aman, C., & Hirschman, J. (1987). Child sexual and physical abuse. In S. J. Ceci, M.P. Toglia, & D.F. Ross (Eds.), *Children's eyewitness memory* (pp. 1-23). New York: Springer.
Hedderman, C. (1987). *Children's evidence: The need for corroboration.* Home Office Research and Planning Unit Paper, No.41. London: The Home Office.
Hosch, H.M., Lieppe, M.R., Marchioni, P., & Cooper, S.D. (1984). Victimisation, self-monitoring, and eyewitness identification. *Journal of Applied Psychology, 69*, 280-288.
King, M. (1986). *Psychology in and out of court.* Oxford: Pergamon Press.
Köhnken, G. and Maass, A. (1985). Realism, reactance and instructional bias in eyewitness identification. In F.L. Denmark (Ed.), *Social/ecological psychology and the psychology of women* (pp. 141-163). Amsterdam: North Holland.
Krafka, C., & Penrod, S. (1985). Reinstatement of context in a field experiment on eyewitness identification. *Journal of Personality and Social Psychology, 49*, 58-69.
Krouse, F. L. (1981). Effect of pose, pose change, and delay on face recognition performance. *Journal of Applied Psychology, 66*, 651-654.
Lindsay, R.C.L., & Harvie, V.L. (1988). Hits, false alarms, correct and mistaken identifications: The effects of method of data collection on facial memory. In M. Gruneberg, P. Morris, & R. Sykes (Eds.), *Practical aspects of memory: current research and issues*, vol.1 (pp.47-52). Chichester: Wiley.

Lindsay, R.C.L., & Wells, G.L. (1983). What do we really know about cross-race eyewitness identification? In S.M.A. Lloyd-Bostock, & B.R. Clifford (Eds.), *Evaluating witness evidence* (pp.219-234). Chichester: Wiley.

Loftus, E.F. (1974). The incredible eywitness. *Psychology Today, 8*, 116-119.

Loftus, E.F. (1976). Unconscious transference in eyewitness identification. *Law and Psychology Review, 2*, 93-98.

Loftus, E. (1986). Ten years in the life of an expert witness. *Law and Human Behavior, 10*, 560-572.

Logie, R.W., Baddeley, A.D., & Woodhead, M. (1987). Face recognition, pose and ecological validity. *Applied Cognitive Psychology, 1*, 53-70.

McCloskey, M., & Egeth, H. (1983). Eyewitness identification: What can a psychologist tell the jury? *American Psychologist, 38*, 573-575.

Macleod, M.D. (1987). *Psychological dynamics of the police interview*. Unpublished Ph.D. thesis, University of Aberdeen.

Macleod, M.D. (1989). *Law and the psychology of testimony: The way ahead*. Unpublished manuscript. University of St. Andrews, Scotland.

Macleod, M.D., & Shepherd, J.W. (1986). Sex differences in eyewitness reports of criminal assaults. *Medicine, Science and the Law, 26*, 311-318.

Malpass, R., & Devine, P. (1980). Realism and eyewitness identification research. *Law and Human Behaviour, 4*, 347-358.

Peters, D.P. (1987). The impact of naturally occuring stress on children's memory. In S.J. Ceci, M.P. Toglia, & D.F. Ross (Eds.), *Children's eyewitness memory* (pp.122-141). New York: Springer.

Platz, S.J., & Hosch, H.M. (1988). Cross racial/ethnic eyewitness identification: A field study. *Journal of Applied Social Psychology, 11*, 972-984.

Read, J.D., Tollestrup, P., Hammersley, R., McFadzen, E., & Christensen, A. (1990). Are innocent bystanders ever mis-identified? *Applied Cognitive Psychology, 4*, 3-32.

Shapiro, P.N., & Penrod, S. (1986). Meta-analysis of facial identification studies. *Psychological Bulletin, 100*, 139-156.

Shepherd, J.W., Davies, G.M.,, & Ellis, H.D. (1978). How best shall a face be described? In M.M Gruneburg, P.E. Morris,, & R.N. Sykes (Eds.), *Practical aspects of memory* (pp. 278-285). London: Academic Press.

Shepherd, J.W., Deregowski, J., & Ellis, H.D. (1974). A cross-cultural study of recognition memory for faces. *International Journal of Psychology, 9*, 205-212.

Stern, L.W. (1910). Abstracts of lectures on the psychology of testimony and on the study of individuality. *American Journal of Psychology, 21*, 270-282.

Stone, M. (1984). *Proof of fact in criminal trials*. Edinburgh: W. Green.

Timm, H.W. (1981). The effects of forensic hypnosis techniques on eyewitness recall and recognition. *Journal of Police Science and Administration, 9*, 188-194.

Yarmey, A.D., & Tressilian-Jones, H.P. (1983). Is the psychology of eyewitness identification a matter of common-sense? In S.M.A. Lloyd-Bostock, & B.R. Clifford (Eds.), *Evaluating eyewitness testimony* (pp.13-40). Chichester: Wiley.

Young, A.W., & Ellis, H.D. (1989). *Handbook of research on face processing*. Amsterdam: North Holland.

Yuille, J.C. (1986). Meaningful research in the police context. In J.C. Yuille (Ed.), *Police training and selection* (pp. 225-243). Dordrecht: Martinus Nijhoff.

Yuille, J.C., & Cutshall, J.L. (1986). A case study of eyewitness memory for a crime. *Journal of Applied Psychology, 71*, 291-301.

Yuille, J.C., & Davies, G. (1990). *Eyewitness research with police trainees*. Paper presented at the 22nd International Congress of Applied Psychology, Kyoto, Japan.

Yuille, J.C., & Kim, C.K. (1987). A field study of the forensic use of hypnosis. *Canadian Journal of Behavioral Science, 193*, 418-435.

Comparison of One-Person and Many-Person Lineups: A Warning Against Unsafe Practices

Willem A. Wagenaar and Nancy Veefkind

Introduction

Lineup tests used for the identification of suspects by witnesses to a crime usually comprise the suspect and a number of innocent foils who fit the same general description. The rationale of the inclusion of foils is that witnesses who do not remember the perpetrator will either not make a choice or make a random choice. In the latter case there will be only a negligible probability that the suspect is chosen by chance, especially when there are more witnesses. Thus, the main purpose of a lineup confrontation is to construct a difficult test that cannot be passed by witnesses whose memory is less than perfect.

A closer analysis reveals that the paradigm serves two purposes simultaneously: (a) to ascertain that the suspect is the same person as the perpetrator observed by the witness at the scene of the crime, and (b) to verify that the witness' memory is reliable. The underlying assumption is that witnesses will consistently point at the suspect in the lineup if and only if both conditions are fulfilled. This assumption is quite often false, for instance, when the suspect bears a misleading resemblance to the perpetrator, or when the suspect is the only person who fits the prior description, or when the suspect was shown to the witness at an earlier occasion, or when the lineup contains only the suspect and no foils (see Wagenaar & Loftus, 1990, for an extensive discussion of conditions that endanger the assumptions of lineup tests).

On the other hand, the inclusion of foils is totally superfluous when it is certain that the witness' memory cannot be at fault, such as when I claim that in the middle of the night I saw my neighbor smash the windshield of my car and steal the radio set. There is no need to place my neighbor in a lineup with five unknown foils, as I will have no trouble remembering my neighbor; even when he is in fact innocent, it will be easy to identify him in a lineup. The many-person lineup test in such a situation is both unnecessary and insufficient. It can be useful to confront me with my neighbor in a one-person lineup, just to verify that the police took the right neighbor. But if there is doubt about the correctness of my observation in the middle of the night, neither a one-person nor a many-person lineup will prove my neighbor's guilt.

Hence, there are situations in which many-person lineups are indicated, and other situations in which one-person lineups are needed, and the two are not to be confused. It would be a serious mistake to convict my neighbor because I recognized him in a multi-person lineup. It would be equally harmful to rely on one-person lineups when the reliability of witnesses' memory is questioned. Yet, it was found in the Netherlands and in the United States that one-person lineups are frequently offered as evidence of both facts: that the suspect is guilty *and* that the witness is reliable (Wagenaar & Loftus, 1990). To defend such a practice, it is often argued that witnesses who do not have a clear recollection of the perpetrator, or who do not definitely recognize the suspect, will refrain from pointing at the suspect even in a one-person lineup. However, this argument is not backed by empirical evidence, simply because an experimental comparison of one-person and many-person lineups has never been made. Shapiro and Penrod (1986) discuss the effect of number of foils in a lineup only on the basis of comparisons across experiments. One-person lineups are not even part of their discussion. In the present study, we will try to fill this gap by two experiments, one in laboratory conditions, the other in a more realistic setting.

As pointed out by various authors (Lindsay & Wells, 1980; Malpass & Devine, 1984), a study of lineup procedures should always consider two different conditions: one in which the suspect is the same person as the perpetrator observed at the scene of the crime (target-present lineup), and one in which the suspect is not the perpetrator (target-absent lineup). In target-absent lineups, three types of errors can occur: not choosing at all, or choosing a foil, or choosing the innocent suspect. It is the latter type of error that should worry us the most, since it may lead to a wrong conviction. Therefore target-absent conditions should always be included in experimental studies of lineup procedures.

There is another reason for including both target-present and target-absent conditions. This is that they allow the computation of two useful scores characterizing lineup effectiveness. The first score is d-prime, a measure derived from the theory of signal detection (see Swets, 1964). d-prime reflects witnesses' ability to distinguish between guilty and innocent suspects. One of the basic tenets of the theory is that this ability can be measured independently of a witness' willingness to choose, which is expressed by the decision criterion *Beta*. This assumption is extremely important for research on lineup effectiveness, since the willingness to choose, for instance, in victims who have a strong desire to see the culprit punished or who trust that the police will not suspect the wrong person, is not easily simulated in a realistic manner. It is therefore essential that a measure of lineup effectiveness is obtained in empirical research that is independent of the subjects' decision criterion. For this reason d-prime scores will be used in the present research.

The second score based on target-present and target-absent conditions is the diagnosticity (or diagnostic impact) of a positive identification. This measure is derived from the Bayesian representation of a judge's decision problem. As explained by Wagenaar (1988), the Bayesian representation is based on the degree of belief in two mutually exclusive hypotheses, expressed by the probability that the suspect is guilty, $p(G)$, or not guilty, $p(NG)$. The judge's decision is determined by the ratio of these probabilities. Usually it is assumed that a judge will only convict if $p(G)/p(NG)$ is sufficiently large. The use of evidence (for instance the identification I) is implemented according to Bayes' rule:

$$p(G|I)/p(NG|I) = p(G)/p(NG) \times p(I|G)/p(I|NG) \qquad (1)$$

The vertical symbol | means "given". Thus $p(G|I)$ stands for the probability that the suspect is guilty, given the identification; $p(I|NG)$ stands for the probability of obtaining a positive identification, given that the suspect is not guilty. Left of the equality sign we see the *a posteriori belief*, expressed by the ratio of probabilities after reception of the evidence. To the right we see two parts. The *a priori belief*, expressed by the ratio of the probabilities before reception of the evidence, and the *diagnostic impact ratio*. The latter consists of two probabilities: the probability of a positive identification when the suspect is guilty, or not guilty. Or, in other words, the probability of identifying the suspect in a target-present or a target-absent lineup. It is clear that a diagnostic impact ratio of 1.0, which is obtained when the two probabilities are equal, will have the effect that the belief is not influenced by the identification. When the impact ratio is very large, a major change toward the belief of guilt is warranted.

Both scores of lineup effectiveness are useful for our purpose. The d-prime score, derived from the theory of signal detection, describes the ability of subjects (witnesses) to distinguish between innocent and guilty suspects. Computed for one-person and many-person lineups, this score provides an insight into how the two procedures affect the processes that are going on in the heads of our subjects. This is of major theoretical interest. The diagnostic impact score, derived from Bayesian statistics, describes the relevance of a positive identification to a judge's decision. This score is therefore more of interest to the practician faced with the difficult task of weighing eyewitness testimony.

The present study contains two experiments: one in laboratory conditions, one in a more realistic setting. The reason is that the manipulation of independent variables in identification experiments requires large numbers of subjects; many more than can be exposed to realistic crime simulations. Hence we are forced to resort to laboratory conditions, even though it means giving up a number of characteristic and desirable aspects of the situation. One of these aspects is that the subjects are aware of the experimental nature of the situation, even during the exposure to the crime. Another, that the subjects are not faced with a serious crime like rape or murder. A third, that the identification is known to have little or no consequence. For these and similar reasons it has been argued that laboratory studies on identifications are invalid (see McCloskey & Egeth, 1983). We feel that, although there is much truth in this argument, a partial solution can be obtained by securing laboratory studies to some anchoring points, obtained in more realistic conditions. We offer such an anchoring point by repeating only a small subset of the laboratory experiment in more realistic conditions.

Experiment 1

The purpose of this experiment is to compare one-person and many-person lineups. However, in order to gain some information about the desirable number of foils, lineup size is varied in four steps, from 1 to 10. Few countries prescribe the number of foils by law, but in practice a number around five foils is usual. Smaller and larger numbers are also found, usually without any justification. It would be reasonable to let the number of foils be determined by the effect it has on the witnesses' identification abilities and on diagnostic impact.

Another question studied in this experiment is whether similarity between target and foils affects the difficulty of the identification task. Two hypotheses present themselves here: One is that a high degree of similarity between the culprit and one of the foils in a target-absent lineup will mislead the subjects; this may cause an increasing number of false identifications in target-absent lineups. Another hypothesis, not excluding the first one, is that one highly similar foil in a target-present lineup, or two highly similar foils in a target-absent lineup, will have the effect of warning subjects about the difficulty of the task; this may lead to an increasing number of refusals. These hypotheses are studied by a systematic variation of the number of foils highly similar to the culprit.

Method

Material. Subjects were shown a series of 24 color slides, depicting the theft of Dfl. 25 from the till in our institute's cafeteria. Three slides showed the face of the thief; one of these showed only his face and nothing else. The target was a white male of 23, with light curly hair, average posture, no moustache or beard and no glasses. The 14 foils roughly fitted the same description.

Ninety-six photographic lineups were prepared, containing 1, 2, 6 or 10 pictures. The pictures were colored photographs of faces. Prior to the experiment, 10 subjects rated the faces of the foils according to similarity with the face of the perpetrator. The four faces rated highest were placed in the "high similarity group"; the four faces rated least similar were placed in the "low similarity group". The remaining six faces were placed in the "medium similarity group". The lineups numbered 1 to 24 contained only one picture: 12 showed a foil (four from each similarity group), the other 12 showed the thief. The lineups numbered 25 to 48 contained two pictures. The first 12 showed two foils (four with two faces from the high similarity group, four with one face from the high similarity group and one from the low similarity group, four with one face each from the medium and low similarity group); the remaining 12 sets showed one picture of the thief and one of a foil (four from each similarity group). The lineups numbered 49 to 72 contained six faces; the lineups numbered 73 to 96 contained 10 faces. Again half of the sets in these groups showed only foils, the other half foils and the thief. In each group of 12 there were four lineups with 2, 1, or 0 foils from the high similarity group.

The response sheet contained a question, and a number of responses from which the subject could choose one by placing a sticker in the appropriate circle. This response mode was chosen to prevent subjects from making pencil marks on the picture sheets, and to force them to give one and only one answer. The phrasing of the questions was as follows:

- (one picture) Is this person the thief who stole the 25 guilders? If not, put the sticker on "No". If yes, put the sticker on "Yes".
- (two or more pictures) Is one of these people the thief who stole the 25 guilders? If not, put the sticker on "No". If yes, put the sticker on the number corresponding to your choice.

Procedure. Subjects were run in groups of 25 to 50. First, they were told that they took part in a memory test. The first slide contained the title of the sequence: "The thief". The slide sequence was shown at a rate of 3s per slide. Then the subjects worked on other memory tasks for about 20 min. The material in these tasks was verbal and alphanumerical, so that no serious interference with the slide sequence could occur. Then they were asked six questions about the slide sequence that were unrelated to the identity of the thief. Finally, they received a sheet with the lineup pictures and a response sheet. Response time was unlimited, but usually subjects finished this task within one minute.

Subjects. The subjects were 548 visitors from outside the psychological institute, who visited the institute on an "open day" for citizens of Leyden. They were of all ages, with lower and upper limits of 6 and 75, and a normal spread inbetween. The subjects were randomly distributed over conditions.

Results

d-prime scores. Since none of the foils in the target-absent conditions was specially designated to represent the (innocent) suspect, the number of times that the suspect was falsely identified in target-absent conditions was obtained by dividing the frequency of choosing a foil by the number of faces shown. Thus, the hit rates with 1, 2, 6, and 10 faces (in target-present lineups) were 35%, 56%, 50%, and 42%. The corresponding false-alarm rates (in target-absent lineups) were 11%, 12%, 7%, and 5% respectively. The values of *d*-prime following from these rates were, for 1-, 2-, 6-, and 10-person lineups: .73, 1.29, 1.46, and 1.47. The increasing tendency is obvious, and the scores represent a significant difference.* Thus, increasing the number of foils facilitated the subjects' ability to distinguish between guilty and innocent suspects. The raw scores are presented in Table 1.

Table 1: Raw Scores of Experiment 1.

Response type	Number of pictures			
	1	2	6	10
Target-absent:	n=72	n=72	n=72	n=60
Choosing a foil	8	18	31	29
No choice	64	54	41	31
Target-present:	n=72	n=72	n=68	n=59
Choosing the target	25	40	34	25
Choosing a foil	n.a.	5	12	20
No choice	47	27	22	14

Diagnostic impact ratios. These scores are computed by taking the ratio of hit rate and false alarm rate. The results were, for 1-, 2-, 6-, and 10-person lineups: 3.1, 4.4, 7.0, and 8.8. Since the numbers that make up these ratios are exactly the same as those that contribute to the *d*-prime scores, there is no reason to compute again a level of significance. The increase of the number of foils in the lineup tests multiplied the impact ratio by a factor of almost three.

Similarity to the target. The number of high, medium, and low similarity foils chosen was 43, 39, and 41 (or 35%, 32%, and 33%). The opportunities for choosing high, medium, and low similarity foils across the conditions were, percentage-wise: 25%, 36%, and 39%. The difference between actual frequencies and opportunities was significant ($\chi^2 = 6.45$, $df=2$, $p<.05$). Thus, high similarity foils attracted more false identifications than expected.

Number of highly similar foils in the lineup. Since similarity had an effect, it made sense to analyze whether the number of similar foils in a lineup had an effect. The number of false recognitions in target-present lineups was, for 0, 1, and 2 highly similar foils: 8 (out of 89 subjects, or 9%), 15 (out of 68 subjects, or 22%), and 14 (out of 44 subjects, or 32%). The increase was significant ($\chi^2=11.15$, $df=2$, $p<.01$). The frequency of not choosing was, for 0, 1, and 2 highly similar foils: 30 (out of 89 subjects, or 34%), 16 (out of 68 subjects, or 24%), and 17 (out of 44 subjects, or 39%). The differences were not significant ($\chi^2=3.22$, $df=2$, $p=.20$). Thus there was no effect of restrain induced by an "embarrassment of choices". Introduction of highly similar foils while the target was present led to more false identifications, and no extra hesitance to choose.

For target-absent lineups, the number of false identifications was identical to the frequency of choosing. For 0, 1, and 2 highly similar foils the number of false identifications was 22 (out of 68 subjects, or 32%), 26 (out of 68 subjects, or 38%), and 30 (out of 68 subjects, or 44%). The increase was not significant ($\chi^2=2.00$, $df=2$, $p>.30$). Again there was clearly no beneficial effect of presenting difficult choices. A summary of these results is presented in Table 2.

Table 2: The Effect of Having 0, 1 or 2 Highly Similar Foils in the Lineup.

	Highly similar foils			χ^2
	0	1	2	(df=2)
% False alarms in target-present lineups	9%	22%	32%	11.15
% Choosing in target-present lineups	34%	24%	39%	3.22
% False alarms (=choosing) in target-absent lineups	32%	38%	44%	2.00

Discussion

The effect of lineup size on the ability to distinguish innocent and guilty suspects is systematic and significant. This result gains some extra weight when it is realized that the number of subjects in the eight groups (lineup size x target-present/absent) was not excessively large. Also, the laboratory conditions could have provided an extra warning, removing the suggestive nature of small lineups. This factor will be further examined in Experiment 2.

Similarities between target and foils have a straightforward effect: Highly similar foils attract false recognitions. There is no warning effect emanating from the presence of two or more highly similar pictures in the set. This excludes a possible extra advantage of larger lineups in practice, which are more likely to contain foils resembling the suspect (not in our experiment, because this factor was controlled).

When witnesses are to a greater or lesser degree guessing, larger lineups may in principle have two advantages: one is a declining guessing rate, the other is a decreased probability of hitting on the innocent suspect. From the choosing rates in target-absent lineups (see Table 1) it is obvious that the first advantage does not exist: There is more guessing with larger lineups. This increase is only partially compensated by the larger spread. The chances of hitting on the innocent suspect were, for size, 1, 2, 6, and 10: 11%, 12%, 7%, and 5%. Thus, the advantage of larger lineups is simply due to a diversion of responses to known foils. There are no other advantages.

The increased guessing rate with larger lineups may be related to the difference between absolute and relative comparison. In absolute comparison, each single picture is compared to the remembered image of the perpetrator, and an absolute judgment is made on whether the resemblance is high enough to warrant a positive response. In relative comparison, one identifies the picture that bears the highest similarity to the target without considering the absolute level of resemblance. Theoretically, one could reason that one-person lineups dictate the absolute comparison mode, while many-person lineups may invite the application of relative comparison. This may explain the higher guessing rates for the larger lineups. But there is no indication of a strict dichotomy, nor of an exclusive application of relative comparison in the larger lineups.

Experiment 2

The rationale of Experiment 2 is to provide an anchoring for Experiment 1, in conditions that are somewhat closer to reality. Therefore a relatively harmless but still violent event was staged in the classroom, much like the scenario presented by Malpass and Devine (1981). The differences with the laboratory situation in Experiment 1 are:

- During the exposure the witnesses do not know that they are engaged in an experiment, and that their memories will be tested.
- The retention period is a week.
- During the retention period the subjects do not know that they will be tested.
- In the lineup test it is suggested to the subjects that the experimenter does not know the correct answer.

Method

Materials. The test materials consisted of photographic lineups with either one or six pictures. Target-absence and target-presence were combined factorially with lineup size. There were six pictures of foils taken from a larger collection of black and white portraits. All foils fitted the general description of the criminal, such as white male, between 20 and 30 years old, no glasses, no moustache or beard. In the one-person condition, there was one target-present lineup, and six different target-absent lineups, each presenting one of the foils. In the six-person condition, there was one target-present lineup, showing the criminal and five foils, and one target-absent lineup, showing all six foils.

Procedure. The staged event took place in an introductory psychology class. A person unknown to the students (a student at the Theater School in Amsterdam) entered through a door in the front of the classroom, and asked whether he could say a few words about the Faculty Council elections (all students have a vote in these elections). The teacher (who was an accomplice, and with whom the scene had been rehearsed) protested modestly, and asked the intruder to wait 10 minutes, till class was over. The actor sat down, waited a few seconds, and started to play with the cable of a TV-camera that was standing to one side. The cable fell on to the floor, and the teacher reacted in a rather upset way. The actor then started to complain that he did not want to wait. The teacher replied that, in that case, it would be better for him to leave. The actor left, swearing and purposefully knocking over the TV-camera, that crashed to the floor. The whole scene lasted 85s. There was substantial reaction in the class; some students were truly shocked. Therefore the teacher announced an early break. After the break, one of the authors (not the teacher) told the students that they had witnessed a staged event. He explained that the staging was part of an experiment on remembering person descriptions, and asked all students to write down a description of the actor. Subjects thought that this was the end of the experiment. The descriptions were collected but not analyzed, as they only served to convince the subjects that the experiment was over. One week later, most of the students met again in small voluntary tutoring groups of about 25 students each. The second author visited these groups to test their memories again. Subjects were run individually. It was explained that others, who had not witnessed the crime, had picked some photos from a much larger set on the basis of the descriptions produced by the witnesses. Now they would be shown one (or six) of these selected pictures; their task was to indicate whether this was the correct picture (or whether one of the six was the correct picture, and if so, which one). It was stressed that the pictures selected by the others were not necessarily correct, and that the experimenter had not herself witnessed the crime and therefore did not know the correct answer. These instructions were meant to recreate as much as possible the situation of a photographic lineup at a police office, where pictures are preselected by the police, while the investigator does not know whether the wanted person is at all in the set.

Subjects. The subjects were first-year psychology students engaged in an introductory course.

Results

Of the 152 students present during the staged event, 144 produced a description of the actor. Out of these 144, only 99 attended the working groups one week later. All these students agreed to take part in the recognition test. The results are presented in Table 3.

d-prime scores. Again the number of times that a suspect was falsely identified was obtained by dividing the number of foil identifications in the target-absent conditions by the number of pictures in the set. The hit rates (in target-present lineups) were 50% and 75%, for 1- and 6-person lineups. The corresponding values of *d*-prime for 1- and 6-person lineups were 1.05 and 2.33. This difference was significant with $\chi^2=4.25$, $df=1$, and $p<.05$.[*] Thus, increase of lineup size led again to a greater ability to distinguish between innocent and guilty suspects.

Table 3: Results of Experiment 2.

Response type	Number of pictures	
	1	6
Target-absent:	(n=41)	(n=24)
Choosing a foil	6	7
No choice	35	17
Target-present:	(n=10)	(n=24)
Choosing the target	5	18
Choosing a foil	n.a.	2
No choice	5	4

Diagnostic impact ratios. The impact ratios for 1- and 6-person lineups were 3.4 and 15.4. Again, there was no need for a significance test, because the d-prime scores were already shown to differ significantly.

Discussion

Just like the laboratory study, this replication in more realistic conditions reveals a significant advantage for many-person lineups. Although the d-prime scores are slightly higher in Experiment 2, the difference between the two experiments was not significant ($\chi^2=2.78$, $df=1, p>.05$;).* The advantage for the larger lineup size is again not situated in a lower rate of choosing, but in a diversion of incorrect choices to a larger group of foils. In the target-absent group the rate of choosing is 15% for the one-person lineup, and 29% for the six-person lineup.

The attempt to establish an anchor point was quite successful: There is no strong indication that the adoption of more realistic conditions changes the essential results obtained in the laboratory.

General Discussion

On the basis of these results it can be concluded that one-person lineups are to be avoided as they increase the likelihood of false identifications. It must be feared that in actual practice the danger of one-person lineups is even greater, because the demand characteristics of a police investigation differ markedly from those of a psychological experiment. Subjects in a psychological experiment will realize that the experimenter is measuring accuracy, and that, for that purpose, target-absent lineups will be presented. Especially in the condition of one-person lineups this should lead to the adoption of a conservative criterion. In a police investigation there is no reason to assume that the police will knowingly present the wrong person. On the contrary, witnesses may trust the ability of the police to arrest the right person. On top of that, the police will quite often offer a strong suggestion that the suspect is indeed the wanted person. One way in which this may happen is through the wording of the invitation to come to the police station: "We arrested the man who robbed you, will you come and identify him?" Hence, although the ability to distinguish between innocent and guilty suspects may not decline in practical situations, it is still expected that a more lenient decision criterion will lead to a higher false alarm rate.

Another aspect that may render the practical situation more open to error is that innocent suspects are often tracked down through their resemblance to the perpetrator. Thus, the identity test is applied to people known to resemble the wanted person. The deceptive effect of a target-absent lineup in which one or more foils bear a high similarity to the perpetrator is especially large in one-person lineups.

Looking at the other end of the scale, there is no strong argument to prefer 10-person lineups over six-person lineups. The 10-person lineup is not included in Experiment 2, but the results of Experiment 1 can be accepted as sufficiently conclusive in this respect.

A matter of major concern is the low absolute level of performance in all conditions of both experiments. Even the best score in Experiment 2 involves almost 5% false identifications of an innocent suspect. One may appreciate this result by considering the corresponding diagnostic impact ratio of 15.4. Let us assume that the identification is the only evidence available. This means that, before the reception of the evidence, the prior belief of the judge, in formula (1) represented by $p(G)/p(NG)$, is determined by the benefit of the doubt generally awarded to suspects. It is not extreme to put this ratio at 1:20. Reception of a positive identification in a six-person lineup would change this degree of belief to $15.4 \times 1/20 = 1:1.3$. This means that the odds are still in favour of innocence, and far remote from "beyond any reasonable doubt." Hence, even a well-executed lineup test cannot contribute sufficient evidence for the establishment of identity. If an a posteriori belief in the guilt of a suspect is accepted as decisive when it reaches a value of 20:1, the ratio proposed by Wigmore (1931), a diagnostic impact of 400 is needed. An identification test carrying so much diagnostic power should allow a d-prime of more than 5.0. There is no reason to believe that witnesses will have that sort of discriminative ability, other than in exceptional conditions.

Of course there are many cases in which two independent witnesses identify the same suspect. But even then the diagnostic impact is only 15.4×15.4, or 237, which still falls short of the factor 400 that is needed. The legal custom of accepting two independent identifications as sufficient evidence should be challenged on this ground. This simple computation is in full accordance with the finding that errors in the identification of suspects by witnesses account for more than half of actual wrong convictions (Rattner, 1988).

The danger of one-person lineups is best illustrated by the fact that five independent identifications in one-person lineups are needed to create the minimally required diagnostic impact of 400. There will not be many cases in which five truly independent witnesses can be found. It should be kept in mind that one cause of interdependence is a high degree of similarity between an innocent suspect and the real culprit.

The logic of identity tests explained in the introduction does not in principle apply to one-person tests. The argument often heard in the courtroom, that uncertain witnesses will refrain from pointing at the suspect in a one-person lineup, carries some truth, in as far as the rate of choosing in target-absent lineups is lower for small lineup sizes. But the difference is not sufficiently large to compensate for the absence of decoys that attract some of the mistaken choices. Usage of one-person lineups should therefore be considered as an unsafe practice.

Endnote

* A convenient manner of testing the significance of differences between d-primes is by comparing the number of correct responses (hits + correct rejections) with the decision criterion in the neutral position, where Beta = 1. For example, in the condition of one-person lineups, this neutral point entails 64% hits and 64% correct rejections; altogether 92 correct responses and 52 errors. In the 10-person condition, the neutral criterion leads to 77% hits and correct rejections, or 92 correct responses vs. 27 errors. This difference yields a significant $\chi^2=5.91$, $df=1$, $p<.02$.

References

Lindsay, R.C.L., & Wells, G.L. (1980). What price justice? Exploring the relationship of lineup fairness to identification accuracy. *Law and Human Behavior, 4*, 303-314.

Malpass, R.S., & Devine, P.G. (1981). Eyewitness identification: Lineup instructions and the absence of the offender. *Journal of Applied Psychology, 66*, 482-489.

Malpass, R.S., & Devine, P.G. (1984). Research in suggestion in lineups and photo-spreads. In G.L. Wells, & E.F. Loftus (Eds.), *Eyewitness testimony: Psychological perspectives* (pp. 64-91). New York: Cambridge University Press.

McCloskey, M., & Egeth, H.E. (1983). Eyewitness identification: What can a psychologist tell a jury? *American Psychologist, 38*, 550-563.

Rattner, A. (1988). Convicted but innocent: Wrongful conviction and the criminal justice system. *Law and Human Behavior, 12*, 283-293.

Shapiro, P.N., & Penrod, S. (1986). Meta-analysis of facial identification studies. *Psychological Bulletin, 100*, 139-156.

Swets, J.A. (Ed.)(1964). *Signal detection and recognition by human observers.* New York: John Wiley, & Sons.

Wagenaar, W.A. (1988). The proper seat: A discussion of the position of expert witnesses. *Law and Human Behavior, 12*, 499-510.

Wagenaar, W.A., & Loftus, E.F. (1990). Ten cases of eyewitness identification: Logical and procedural problems. *Journal of Criminal Justice, 18*, 291-319.

Wigmore, J.H. (Ed.)(1931). *The principles of judicial proof.* Boston: Little Brown.

The Influence of Eyewitness Observation and Photographic Presentation on the Identification of Persons in Lineups

Michael Stadler, Hans Schindler, and Thomas Fabian

Introduction

In the course of preparations for the reopening of proceedings in a murder trial, the authors were asked to write an expertise, from the point of view of perceptual psychology, on whether, under given circumstances and after a lapse of nine months, an eyewitness has a high probability of actually being able to identify in a lineup procedure the driver sitting behind the wheel of a vehicle, after photographs of the accused had been presented in the interim period. The authors decided to examine this problem with an experiment in which the original situation was reproduced as accurately as possible. Since the problem is of general importance and the investigation shows the possibilities and difficulties of such a "realistic experiment", the result shall be presented here.

Observation, Photographic Presentation, and Lineup

Two days before the crime - a bank raid during which two persons were shot - the witness walked through a street in the German city of Kaiserslautern. On the opposite side of the street he saw an automobile parked in a conspicuous way. He passed the hood of the car at a distance of about 50*cm*. Inside, he could perceive nothing but - for a short moment - the face of the driver.

Three weeks later the witness read an article in a daily newspaper about the bank raid, with the picture of a person who was at that time being sought for questioning. The witness reported to the police and made his first statement about the observation described in the paragraph above. He was shown a folder with photographs. On one photograph he identified a face as belonging to the driver of the automobile in question.

Ten and a half months later, the witness took part in a police lineup. Five other persons stood beside the suspect in the lineup. The witness named Person 2 in the first trial and Person 4 in the second trial, the numbers with which the accused was actually marked.

Three and a half years later, at the main hearing, the witness was asked: "Just now you replied to the question whether you had been shown photographs and whether you recognized anything on them by stating: 'Yes, the man on the wanted person's photograph.' Did you recognize the photograph from the folder that had just been shown to you because you had already seen the wanted person's photograph or because you remembered the driver?" The witness replied to this question: "No, because I *also* remembered the driver."

Psychological Questions

From the psychological point of view, the following questions can be asked:

1. Is it possible, under the given observation conditions, to identify the driver of a car at a much later lineup?

2. What are the effects on someone's identification of a person who had originally been seen in a real situation, if a photographic presentation took place in the interim?

3. How great is the probability of an unconscious transfer (see Loftus, 1979)?

4. How sure is a person normally of his or her judgment who, under the given conditions, identifies someone? This shall be examined (a) after observation of a driver in an automobile (according to question 1) and (b) after observation of a driver in an automobile and a photographic presentation in the interim period (according to questions 2 and 3).

5. At what percentage is, under the given conditions, identification normally based on observation in the real situation and on a photographic presentation, respectively?

Experimental Examination of the Questions Raised

Design and implementation of the experiment

The experimental design was based on two premises:

1. By creating conditions as similar to the original conditions as possible, a direct transfer of the results of the experiment to the witness's situation in the court proceedings (realistic observation, presentation of photographs of the accused, lineup) should be possible.

2. Wherever, for practical reasons, the original conditions cannot be reproduced completely, the experiment should be designed in such a way that a suspect is more likely to be identified correctly in the later lineup on the basis of observation in the real situation. Since this is to be the zero hypothesis of the experiment, such a conservative test design is necessary so that in case of a possible later confirmation of the alternative hypothesis (correct identification is determined by photographic presentation), this result cannot be accounted for, entirely or in part, by the differently reproduced conditions of the experiment.

The experiment consisted of three phases:

1. Observation of a realistic situation corresponding to the original situation described above.

2. Photographic presentation two or three weeks after Phase 1; the photographs showed either the driver of the automobile (Phase 1) or another person who later also took part in the lineup (Phase 3).

3. Lineup, taking place a further two weeks later, that is, about five weeks after Phase 1. The lineup procedure was carried out according to the methodological principles demanded by Gniech and Stadler (1981, 1984).

To answer the questions raised above, a test design with several groups of test persons was chosen:

Group A: Subjects in this group took part in the observation of the realistic situation (Phase 1) and five weeks later in the lineup (Phase 3).

Group B: These subjects took part in the observation of the realistic situation (Phase 1), were later shown the picture of the driver of the automobile (Phase 2), and finally took part in the lineup (Phase 3).

Group C: Subjects in this group took part in the observation of the realistic situation (Phase 1). Two weeks later, they were shown a picture of a person who had *not* been sitting in the automobile while being told that this was in fact the driver (Phase 2), and then took part in the lineup (Phase 3).

Group D: This group did not take part in the observation of the realistic situation. They were only shown a photograph of the driver (Phase 2) with the comment that they would later be questioned about this person. Two weeks later, they took part in the lineup (Phase 3). Table 1 shows the conditions for the four groups.

Table 1: The Experimental Groups.

Group	(1) Real situation	(2) Photographic presentation	(3) Lineup right/wrong	N
A	yes	no	yes	8
B	yes	yes right	yes	5
C	yes	yes wrong	yes	8
D	no	yes right	yes	8

A detailed description of the observation situation, the photographic presentations, and the lineup is dispensed with here as these details have been published elsewhere (Schindler & Stadler, 1991). Originally, eight subjects were recruited for each of the four experimental groups. However, for various reasons (illness, etc.) only 29 out of the original 32 subjects were able to take part in all three phases of the experiment and supply analyzable data (see Table 1, last column). Test persons were paid for their participation.

Results

Table 2 shows the results of the lineup procedure. Among the eight subjects in Group A, who had seen the driver only in the realistic situation (Phase 1) and who had not been shown any photographs in the interim period, only one indicated a person other than the driver, and three stated that the driver was not among the persons present. In Group B, who differed from Group A only by being shown photographs of the driver in the interim, all five subjects identified the correct target person. However, two subjects emphasized particularly that they had identified the person on the photograph presented to them, who was not identical with the driver in the realistic situation. One subject indicated another person than the driver. The second subject, who had correctly identified the photograph, stated that the driver was not among the persons in the lineup.

Table 2: Results of the Lineup Procedure.

Group	N	Target person identified from real situation or photograph			Target person not identified	
		Real situation	Undecidable	Photograph	Wrong person	No identification
A	8	1	-	-	4	3
B	5	0	3	2	0	0
C	8	0	-	5	0	3
D	8	-	-	7	0	1

In Group C, who had in the meantime been shown the photograph of another person and been told that this was the driver, five of the eight subjects identified this other person from the photograph as the driver. Three subjects maintained that the driver was not among the persons in the lineup and therefore identified nobody. In the lineup experiment, none of the subjects in this group identified the driver who had been observed in the realistic situation.

In Group D, who had not observed the driver in the realistic situation (Phase 1), seven of the eight subjects identified the driver from the photograph. One subject did not recognize the target person because he - as the only one among 29 subjects - had misunderstood the written instructions.

In summary, Table 2 shows that of the 21 subjects from Groups A, B, and C who could have recognized the driver whom they had seen in the realistic situation, only a single one in Group A succeeded. When one of eight test persons identifies the correct target person from a lineup of six persons, this result corresponds approximately to a random chance. But our notes show that precisely this subject who was the only one to identify the driver had observed him in the realistic situation longer than any other subject, namely for 15 s. It is therefore quite possible to assume that this longer observation time is the cause of the correct identification.

A statistical check of these results is unnecessary because they are unequivocal. Every conceivable model about the expected frequency, in the separate groups or in all of them together, of identifying a person from the realistic situation would, compared with the frequency we found, result in a random probability of far below the $p < .001$ limit in a binomial test.

Table 3 shows that the results are also supported by including the degree to which the subjects were sure of their judgment and the question whether in their opinion the realistic situation or the photographic presentation was the decisive factor for the identification.

Table 3: Certainty and Attribution of Judgment.

Group	N	Certainty of judgment	Identification mainly from Real situation	Photograph
A	8	28%	-	-
B	5	88%	15%	85%
C	8	90%	16%	84%
D	8	73%	-	-

In Group A, the eight subjects assessed the certainty of their judgments with an average of 28%, varying between 10% and 50%. In Groups B, C, and D, the certainty of judgment averaged 88%, 90%, and 73%, varying between 20% and 100% in Group D. From this result we may conclude that certainty of judgment is high in those groups who had at least also been shown the photographs. In Group A, on the other hand, who could only refer to the realistic situation for their identification, the certainty of judgment is low.

Conclusion

With the results of the experiment available, the psychological questions formulated at the beginning of this article can be answered in detail as follows:

1. The question whether the driver of the automobile could be identified under the conditions prevailing in Kaiserslautern two days before the crime must be answered negatively. The only subject who identified the driver in our experiment under just these conditions had observed him much longer (15 s) than the witness at that time. All other subjects were not able to identify the driver solely on the basis of their observation in the realistic situation.

2. On the other hand, looking at a photograph is of considerable importance for a correct identification. Subjects who, similar to the witness at that time, had in the interim period been shown photographs of the person to be identified could in most cases identify him in the lineup.

3. The question whether an unconscious transfer is possible can definitely be answered affirmatively. More than half of the subjects in Group C identified a person whose photograph they had seen as the driver of the automobile, although he was in fact another person. On the other hand, not a single subject in this group identified the driver in the realistic situation, who was also among the persons in the lineup.

4. The question how sure people are of their judgments under the given conditions can also be answered relatively clearly: Whenever - as in groups B, C, and D - a photograph was shown, test persons are very sure of their judgment. When, however, as in Group A, they must come to a decision in the lineup solely on the basis of their recollection of the realistic situation, the certainty of judgment drops to one third. A high degree of certainty, such as that expressed by the witness at the time, therefore rather points to an identification on the basis of photographic presentations.

5. Identification by our subjects in Groups B and C was based on their recollection of the realistic situation with a proportion of 15% and on the recollection of the photograph with a proportion of 85%. When the witness said in the proceedings at that time that he had recognized the photograph from the folder of pictures because he *also* remembered the driver, this statement must be interpreted quantitatively against the background of the present results.

An important factor, which makes the identification of persons more difficult, is much more effective in forensic lineups than in all experiments that only simulate reality: Under stress, the ability of identification drops significantly (Dent & Stephenson, 1979; Gase & Köhnken, 1981). This means that an eyewitness who is confronted in the lineup with a number of possible suspects and, in addition, feels the social pressure of actually having to identify someone will more often give incorrect identifications than when he or she is asked to identify an accused only from photographic presentations. In an actual police lineup procedure, the probability of an incorrect identification should therefore be even greater than in our experiment because our subjects knew that the experiment was only simulated reality and were therefore only under slight stress.

According to the research results available, the possibility of identification from photographs is considerably greater than identification from real situations. Standing (1973) presented photographs of faces to his test persons for one second. At a later presentation, these photographs could be identified correctly from a series of other photographs in 90% of the cases. Persons acting in reality, however, were correctly identified in only 13% to 50% of the cases (see Clifford & Bull, 1978). The results of our experiment agree with this finding: Here too, persons could be identified much better from a photographic presentation than from observation in a realistic situation.

References

Clifford, B., & Bull, R. (1978). *The psychology of person identification*. London: Routledge & Kegan Paul.
Dent, H.R., & Stephenson, G.M. (1979). Identification evidence: Experimental investigation of factors affecting the reliability of juvenile and adult witnesses. In D.P. Farrington, K. Hawkins, & D.S. Lloyd-Bostock (Eds.), *Psychology, law, and the legal process* (pp. 195-205). London: MacMillan.
Gase, M., & Köhnken, G. (1981). Psychologische Probleme der Identifizierung von Tatverdächtigen durch Augenzeugen. *Kriminalistik, 18*, 514-521.
Gniech, G., & Stadler, M. (1981). Die Wahlgegenüberstellung - Methodische Probleme des kriminalistischen Wiedererkennungsexperiments. *Strafverteidiger, 1*, 565-570.
Gniech, G., & Stadler, M. (1984). Methodische Probleme beim kriminalistischen Gegenüberstellungsexperiment. *Zeitschrift für Sozialpsychologie, 15*, 194-198.
Loftus, E.F. (1979). *Eyewitness testimony*. Cambridge, MA: Harvard University Press.
Schindler, H., & Stadler, M. (1991). Tatsituation oder Fahndungsphotos - Ein experimentalpsychologisches Gutachten zum Dilemma des Zeugen in der Wiedererkennungssituation. *Strafverteidiger, 11*, 38-44.
Standing, L. (1973). Learning 10,000 pictures. *Quarterly Journal of Experimental Psychology, 25*, 207-222.

The Generation of Misinformation[1]

Hunter G. Hoffman, Elizabeth F. Loftus, Christine N. Greenmun, and Richard L. Dashiell

Although prosecutors would prefer to base their cases against alleged criminals on tangible evidence, sometimes the testimony of eyewitnesses is the only evidence that a crime has been committed. So it was with the case against California schoolteacher Raymond Buckey. Widespread accusations by McMartin preschool students that Raymond Buckey had sexually assaulted and terrorized them with satanic rituals led to the longest (33 months) and most expensive ($ 15 million dollars) criminal trial in U.S. history. Hundreds of these students went to a particular therapist to be interviewed and if necessary to get professional help. These taped interviews became the focus of the dispute over whether Buckey was guilty. Could the children's reports have been affected by the interviewing process and by new information communicated during that process?

The case against Buckey ended in acquittal on some charges and a hung jury on others. Eventually all charges were dismissed. Several jurors came to believe that some of the children may have been sexually fondled and abused, while other jurors remained unconvinced that the children's memories were accurate. The latter jurors were concerned that the children's memories had been contaminated, or perhaps even created by information encountered after the alleged events. Cases that hinge on the potential suggestibility of witnesses during interviews invite us to ask about the nature of suggestibility.

Factors that Influence Suggestibility

Under what conditions is a memory of an event vulnerable to contamination from suggestive postevent interviewing procedures and when are witnesses immune to suggestive influence? Experiments performed in the controlled environment of the memory laboratory have shed light on this issue.

The misinformation paradigm

Research using the "misinformation" paradigm involves a three stage procedure by which experimenters can study suggestibility in memory for events, such as bank robberies and auto accidents. The three stages are 1) the event, 2) the postevent narrative, and 3) a memory test. For example, subjects might watch a slide sequence in which a sports car goes through a stop sign at an intersection and gets into an accident (the event). Half

---

[1] The underlying research fundamental to the arguments made here was supported by a grant from the National Institute of Mental Health.

the subjects in these experiments then read a postevent narrative which accurately describes what occurred in the slides and the other half are deceived about a detail (i.e., they receive misinformation). For example, although the "event" slide shows a car go through a stop sign, subjects in the misled condition are told in the narrative that the car went through a yield sign. When later asked whether they originally saw a stop sign or a yield sign at the intersection, misled subjects perform much less accurately than control subjects. Specifically, misled subjects often claim to have seen a yield sign in the slides.

Using the misinformation paradigm, we can study how and when information encountered after an event contaminates a memory report and makes the report unreliable. A brief sample of recent publications shows the considerable research interest in the misinformation effect in laboratories around the world: in the United States Belli (1989), Bowman and Zaragoza (1989), Chandler (1989), Lindsay and Johnson (1987, 1989), Metcalfe (1990), Tversky and Tuchin (1989); in Australia Sheehan (1989); in Germany Köhnken and Brockmann (1987); and in the Netherlands Wagenaar and Boer (1987). Memory contamination resulting from exposure to postevent misinformation has caused subjects to remember seeing a clean-shaven man instead of a man with a mustache, curly hair instead of straight hair, a can of peanuts instead of a Coca Cola, and eggs instead of breakfast cereal. This systematic alteration in a person's recollection of an event is referred to as the "misinformation effect". Determining the circumstances in which exposure to postevent information is likely to distort memory reports is critical for theoretical models of forgetting, and for applied issues such as the validity of eyewitness testimony (Johnson & Hasher, 1987).

Theoretical implications of the misinformation effect

One of the most fundamental issues in the brain sciences can be addressed using the misinformation paradigm. The question is, how does the brain store information, permanently, or only temporarily? When misinformation is assimilated into our memory, what happens to the event memory? Or put another way, when we are tricked into remembering a yield sign in our recollection of a traffic accident, what becomes of the stop sign we would otherwise have remembered? Is the memory for the stop sign damaged, distorted, weakened or physically altered structurally in the architecture of the brain, or is it only anesthetized by the yield sign, and ready to reawaken when the right question is asked?

Over the past 15 years of research using the misinformation paradigm, several competing theories have emerged to explain what happened to the memory for the original critical item. One of the rockiest controversies is over whether misinformation actually affects memory, or whether the decrement in accuracy of misled subjects is a result of demand characteristics. That is, do subjects simply figure out the hypothesis and respond the way they think the experimenter wants them to.

Demand characteristics

The standard testing procedure in misinformation studies permitted subjects to respond to a test question with the misinformation itself. For example, if the subject originally saw a hammer in the slide sequence, and later received misinformation about a screwdriver, the traditional test is between hammer and screwdriver. With this "standard test" subjects readily chose screwdriver, but this could be happening because subjects think the experimenter wants that response, not because memory for hammer is impaired. To test their hypothesis that misinformation does not impair earlier memories, McCloskey and Zaragoza (1985; Zaragoza, McCloskey, & Jamis, 1987) introduced the "modified test". The modified test does not permit the subject to give the misinformation response, screwdriver. If the subject originally saw a hammer and later received misinformation about a screwdriver, the modified test might be between hammer and wrench (a completely novel item). Using the modified test, McCloskey and Zaragoza observed no effect of misinformation on performance and consequently concluded that the original memory trace was not affected by exposure to misinformation.

Source misattributions

Yet, as many researchers have pointed out (Belli, 1989; Johnson & Lindsay, 1987), there are several other hypotheses about memory interference that are not addressed by the modified test. For example, since the misleading item is not an option on the modified test, subjects are not given the opportunity to make source misattributions. They don't have the opportunity to get the slides and narrative mixed up and to say they saw the screwdriver in the slide show.

Familiarity

Other researchers have pointed out that subjects exposed to misinformation but tested with the modified test may respond correctly simply because they know what they have not seen. As mentioned earlier, the modified test offers the event item and a novel item as test alternatives. All that subjects need to know to get the answer correct is that they have not seen the unfamiliar novel item before (Tversky & Tuchin, 1989). Thus even if misinformation damages or weakens memory for the event item, this influence may go undetected as long as there is even a trace of familiarity left, and if the novel item seems very unfamiliar.

Misinformation effects with the modified test

Some laboratories have replicated McCloskey and Zaragoza's lack of a misinformation effect using the modified test (Loftus, Donders, Hoffman, & Schooler, 1989). However, Ceci, Ross, and Toglia (1987) found that children are especially susceptible to misinformation, and show decrements in performance even on the modified test. In another study using very different stimulus materials, Chandler (1989) also got a misinformation effect on the modified test. Why do some researchers get the effect while others don't? One important factor influencing whether a particular investigator gets the misinformation effect on the modified test may be the strength of the misinformation relative to the strength of the event information (Ceci et al., 1987; Loftus, Hoffman, & Wagenaar, 1992). Evidence suggests that the relative strength of someone's memory for an event, compared to the strength of their memory for the postevent information, is a crucial determinant of whether an observer will be misled. Let's look at an extreme case. Suppose a witness (call him

George) never encoded the critical item, say a stop sign, during the slide sequence, because he didn't happen to see the item in the slides. But further suppose that he clearly reads the misleading information in the narrative. It erroneously describes the sign as a yield sign. He will have no memory for the critical item from the event (i.e., the slides) but will undoubtedly remember the item presented in the narrative. For a variety of reasons, George may report that he saw a yield sign in the slides. This could happen if the postevent information creates a memory where none existed, and the witness embraces the misinformation as the real thing. This process is known as misinformation acceptance (Belli, 1989) and one consequence is an erroneous report. When asked to choose which sign, stop or yield, he saw in the slides, George may well confidently say he saw a yield sign, inferring that it existed and perhaps even believing he actually saw it in the slides.

Obviously we cannot claim that George's memory was impaired since there was no memory of the stop sign from the event in the first place. This particular information processing history has no implications for models of forgetting due to interference or memory impairment and should not result in a misinformation effect on the modified test. But misinformation acceptance is an interesting phenomenon in its own right. It relates to the important issue of how new, erroneous information is weaved into established memories (Loftus & Hoffman, 1989).

For another extreme situation, which is also not predicted to contribute to a misinformation effect on the modified test, consider a witness named Jeremy. Jeremy encodes the event information, but she does not see the critical misleading information in the postevent narrative. Her memory report is not likely to get contaminated. In fact, Jeremy's performance should be equivalent to that of a control subject who remembers an event in the absence of exposure to postevent information.

Somewhere between the experiences of George and Jeremy (misinformation acceptance and control performance on the event item), the memory strength for the event item can be varied by manipulating how long the slide remains on the screen, or by how much time is allowed to pass, and thus the extent to which the event item has a chance to fade before exposure to misinformation (Loftus, Miller, & Burns, 1978). Allowing the memory to fade decreases the possibility that the memory for the event item is so strong that the subject catches on that the experimenter is trying to deceive him in the narrative. The phenomenon of "catching on" has been called "discrepancy detection" (Tousignant, Hall, & Loftus, 1986). When subjects get suspicious, they are often hard to mislead, not only on that critical item, but on items that follow in the narrative. Subjects respond as if they had been warned that the narrative contains errors and that the narrative should be regarded with skepticism (Greene, Flynn, & Loftus, 1982; Zaragoza & Koshmider, 1989).

Multiple process histories

On the standard test, experimenters routinely got large misinformation effects. The magnitude of the effect likely reflects the contributions of a number of different information processing pathways that can alter memory reports: memory impairment, inaccessibility or memory interference, misinformation acceptance, source misattribution, and perhaps some demand characteristics. The modified test, on the other hand, appears to exclude all but one of these contributors, memory impairment. Thus it is likely that we will get a misinformation effect only under optimal circumstances, when the memory for the postevent item is strong. We hypothesize that the reason some previous researchers obtained a misinformation effect on the modified test while others did not is because of differences in the strength of the postevent information relative to the event information. This hypothesis suggested to us a need for a method that maximally strengthens the postevent information. In this way we might discover that misinformation effects are readily produced, and even impairments on the modified test might be observed.

One way to strengthen postevent information is to have subjects actually generate it. That is the innovation in the two new studies we describe here. In the first study, subjects were induced to generate the misinformation. They viewed a slide sequence depicting a burglary. They watched a thief rummaging through an office, looking into desk drawers for valuables, and finally hiding a stolen calculator under a hammer in his toll box. Later, subjects read a narrative describing the event. The narrative correctly described the event with the exception of a few minor details. The narrative misled subjects by saying the burglar put the calculator under an screwdriver in his tool box. We then "forced" subjects to generate screwdriver in a fairly subtle way. We had them complete sentences in which one word had several letters blank, which subjects were to fill in. The letters that they were given as cues constrained how they completed the misinformation. In this way for example, we "forced" subjects to generate the misinformation, screwdriver. Then subjects were tested with the modified test - hammer vs. wrench. We found an impairment in memory performance. Although suggestive, the data were open to multiple interpretations. A second study disentangled these interpretations.

Study 1: The Influence of "Self Generating" the Misinformation

In groups of from 2 to 10 subjects, 68 students from the University of Washington were shown slides using materials and procedure adapted from McCloskey and Zaragoza (1985).[2] Each subject saw one of three sets of slides depicting an office theft by a janitor. The slide sequence included four critical items: a coffee jar, a magazine, a soda can, and a tool. These four objects differed in the three slide versions. For example in one version subjects saw a Coke can and in another they saw a Seven-Up, while in a third version they saw a Sunkist Orange can. After viewing the slide sequence subjects were given a narrative describing the slide sequence. The narrative was composed such that for each slide sequence, two of the four critical details were described incorrectly and two correctly. Across subjects, each of the four critical items were equally often referred to correctly and incorrectly.

In the next phase we gave subjects a "test". The test was designed to increase the proportion of subjects who encode the postevent item and to strengthen that item. We did this by capitalizing on a well known phenomenon called the generation effect (Jacoby, 1978; Slamecka & Graf, 1978). The generation effect refers to the advantage in memory that has been observed for items that the subject has generated herself (e.g., from a word fragment), compared to items passively encoded. Like previous studies, we presented

---

[2] We are grateful to McCloskey and Zaragoza for generously lending us these slides and instructions.

misinformation in the narratives in a subtle fashion so that subjects wouldn't catch on that we were trying to trick them.

After the narrative, subjects were asked to take a word fragment completion test. To hide our true intentions, this task was described to subjects as a test of their ability to generate answers about the slide sequence from the context of sentences possessing varying amounts of retrieval cues. They were asked to read 14 sentences possessing varying amount of retrieval cues. They were asked to read 14 sentences and fill in the blanks to complete the missing words. The object of this test was not to evaluate memory for the slide sequence but was instead designed to "boost" the saliency of the misinformation items presented in the narrative. For example, some subjects were presented with a hammer in the slide sequence, and read a postevent narrative in which they were incorrectly informed they had seen a screwdriver. In this case, subjects were then lured into filling in the blanks of a word fragment in the sentence "The man put the calculator in a tool box under a *scre - dr ----*". For other subjects, this was a control item. These subjects also saw a hammer in the slide sequence, but read a postevent narrative describing it (accurately but vaguely) as a tool. These subjects were then lured into filling in the blanks in the sentence "The man put the calculator in a tool box under a *t--l*".

Finally, subjects took the modified test, requiring them to choose between hammer (the event item) and wrench (a novel item not previously encountered in the experiment). For each question, they were to indicate their choice between the two alternative answers by circling it with a pencil. A blank line followed each question and subjects were encouraged to mention any comments they had regarding the question and/or an explanation for their answer.

Results

How do subjects react when the answer they want is not offered as a test option? Subjects who are convinced that the answer is screwdriver might react with indignation. They might refuse to respond, becoming so convinced that they saw a screwdriver in the slide sequence that they can't even dust off the old hammer on the modified test anymore. This is in fact what we found.

As shown in Table 1, the percent correct was 43% for misled items and 63% for control items. This difference was statistically significant, $t(67)=3.15, p=.001$ (one-tailed). But the finding of a misinformation effect on the modified test occurs not because subjects are choosing the wrong response, but because many are refusing to answer. The percentage of incorrect responses did not increase with misinformation.

Table 1: Responses of Subjects.

	Misled	Control
Correct	43%	63%
Incorrect	24%	26%
Missing	33%	12%

What happened was that many subjects refused to follow instructions after misinformation. They failed to answer a test item after misinformation had been generated. Subjects were over twice as likely to refuse to answer a test item after misinformation had been generated. Many subjects indicted in their comments that their reason for refusing to answer was because they didn't think the item they remembered was offered as a possible choice. For example, several subjects who saw hammer in the slides, who generated screwdriver, and who were asked to choose between hammer and wrench refused to circle either choice and wrote "neither" or "screwdriver" in their comments.

Would we still get a misinformation effect on the modified test if subjects were forced to make a decision between the event item and a novel item? Or would misled subjects choose the event item just as often as control subjects, even though they don't like it? This question is addressed in study 2.

Study 2: Forced Decision on the Modified Test

In groups of from 2 to 8 subjects, 136 students from the University of Washington were shown one of three sets of slides (at $5s$ per slide) depicting an office theft by a janitor. The stimuli and procedure were similar to study 1 except that the narratives and test questions were computer controlled. After the paper and pencil word fragment completion task, subjects were asked to complete ten practice questions. They were instructed to place the index finger and middle finger of their right hand on the 1 and 2 buttons and the thumb of their left hand on the spacebar of the computer keyboard. Recognition testing for each question involved two phases: a reading phase and a test phase. In the reading phase, subjects read a sentence with a word missing (e.g., The man put the calculator in a tool box under a --------."). After reading one question they pressed the space bar. Doing so initiated presentation of the test phase and activated the timer. In the test phase subjects were presented with two alternatives (e.g., hammer, wrench) and had to decide as quickly as possible which alternative correctly corresponded to what they had seen in the slide sequence. Subjects indicated their responses by pressing the 1 or 2 key. After every question, subjects entered their confidence about the accuracy of that response on a 5-point rating scale, one meaning "not at all confident" and five meaning "extremely confident". The next question followed the confidence response by $1.5s$. Subjects were instructed to take as much time as they wanted to decide their confidence but that the amount of time they took to read the questions and select a test alternative would be measured so they should respond to the test questions as fast as possible without sacrificing accuracy. Following the test, subjects were debriefed and given class credit.

Results

The mean percent correct was 59% for misled items and 70% for control items. A paired samples t-test revealed that the difference was significant, $t(135)=2.57, p<.01$, one-tailed. Overall, subjects responded to misled items more slowly than to control items ($3757ms$ versus $3313ms$). To test statistically for the differences between the means, the following analysis was done. For each subject, two scores were calculated. the first score was the mean reaction time for the 2 misled items, and the second score was the mean reaction time for the 2 control items. A paired samples t-test revealed that the difference was significant, $t(135)=2.36$, $p=.01$, one-tailed. Thus, there was an overall tendency for subjects to respond more slowly in the face of misinformation. Overall, mean confidence was the same for misled as for control subjects (3.03 vs. 3.11). A sign test revealed that subjects were not significantly more confident in their responses to misled items than in their responses to control items, $z<1$.

Generation boosted the efficacy of the post-event misinformation. Not only did misled subjects take longer to respond on the modified test, but a significant percentage of memory reports suggest unsuccessful retrieval attempts. Response accuracy was poorer in the misled condition than in the control condition. When the test was administered on a computer forcing subjects to choose between the event items and a novel item before continuing, some subjects were still often unable to dredge up their memories for the event item.

Discussion

We found a misinformation effect on the modified test by utilizing the "generation effect" to strengthen memory for the misinformation item. One important issue remains unresolved. Perhaps generating the control item in the word fragment completion task elevated control performance on the recognition test, contributing to the misinformation effect. Brainerd and Reyna (1988) have argued that exposure to the neutral word "tool" in the narrative can act as a powerful retrieval attempt which results essentially in a study trial for the control item. This "retention enhancement effect", as they call it, would be even more likely when the neutral item had to be self-generated. For example, if the narrative was neutral with respect to the tool seen in the slide sequence, subjects filled in the missing letters in the following sentence: The man put the calculator under a *t--l* in his tool box. When filling in the blank, subjects may retrieve the hammer shown in the slides, enhancing subsequent control memory performance and increasing the difference between control performance and misled performance. To test this possibility, further research is needed.

One technique for future research would be to systematically delete two generation questions from each subject; one misled item generation and one control item generation. This would leave one boosted misled item and one boosted control item. Boosted versus unboosted performance within subjects could be assessed to determine the contribution of retention enhancement of the control items, and the detrimental impact of generating the misleading item, to the misinformation effect found on the modified test. An attempt was made in our laboratory to perform this experiment, but the results were uninterpretable. For reasons that remain unclear we failed to replicate the misinformation effect obtained in the two studies reported here. This failure suggests some caution is needed in interpreting the package of results reported here.

How would the generation of misinformation influence the size of the misinformation effect on the standard test, that is, on a test that gives a choice between hammer and screwdriver, where subjects are allowed the misinformation option? Based on the current results, we would expect a larger than usual increase in the proportion of subjects choosing the misinformation item on the test. Are subjects who have generated misinformation more likely to believe they actually saw the misinformation item in the slide sequence? The issue of true belief is one of the key issues presently being debated in the misinformation paradigm (Lindsay, 1990). One could investigate the influence of generation on belief that the information came from the event (slides) by first getting subjects to generate misinformation and then giving a source attribution task. To briefly consider the source attribution task, consider the following example. Subjects are shown a slide sequence and receive a misleading narrative. Instead of taking a recognition test, subjects categorize the source of origin of various items presented in the study as (roughly) 1) from the slides, 2) from the narrative, 3) from both the slides and the narrative, or 4) neither from the slides nor the narrative (Johnson & Lindsay, 1987; Lindsay, 1990; Lindsay & Johnson, 1989; Zaragoza & Koshmider, 1989). In addition, one can further ask subjects to bet on the accuracy of their responses. If generating the misinformation truly leads subjects to be more adamant that they actually saw the misinformation in the slide sequence, this should be evident from these source monitoring tests. Subjects who generate misinformation should be more likely to misattribute the source of their memory for the misinformation to the slides, and should be more willing to bet on the veracity of these memories than control subjects.

References

Belli, R.F. (1989). Influences of misleading postevent information: Misinformation interference and acceptance. *Journal of Experimental Psychology: General, 118,* 72-85.

Bowman, L.L., & Zaragoza, M.S. (1989). Similarity of encoding context does not influence resistance to memory impairment following misinformation. *American Journal of Psychology, 102,* 249-264.

Brainerd, C.J., & Reyna, V.F. (1988). Memory loci of suggestibility development: Comment on Ceci, Ross, & Toglia (1987). *Journal of Experimental Psychology: General, 117,* 197-200.

Ceci, S.J., Ross, D.F., & Toglia, M.P. (1987). Suggestibility of children's memory: Psycholegal implications. *Journal of Experimental Psychology: General, 116,* 38-49.

Chandler, C.C. (1989). Specific retroactive interference in modified recognition tests: Evidence for an unknown cause of interference. *Journal of Experimental Psychology: Learning, Memory, and Cognition, 15,* 256-265.

Greene, E., Flynn, M., & Loftus, E.F. (1982). Inducing resistance to misleading information. *Journal of Verbal Learning and Verbal Behavior, 21,* 207-219.

Jacoby, L.L. (1978). On interpreting the effects of repetition: Solving a problem versus remembering a solution. *Journal of Verbal Learning and Verbal Behavior, 17,* 649-667.

Johnson, M.K., & Hasher, L. (1987). Human learning and memory. *Annual Review of Psychology, 38,* 631-668.

Johnson, M.K., & Lindsay, D.S. (1987). *Despite McCloskey and Zaragoza suggestibility effects may reflect memory impairment.* Unpublished Manuscript.

Köhnken, G., & Brockmann, C. (1987). Unspecific postevent information, attribution of responsibility, and eyewitness performance. *Applied Cognitive Psychology, 1,* 197-207.

Lindsay, D.S. (1990). Misleading suggestions can impair eyewitnesses' ability to remember event details. *Journal of Experimental Psychology: Learning, Memory and Cognition, 16,* 1077-1083.

Lindsay, D.S., & Johnson, M.K. (1987). Reality monitoring and suggestibility: Children's ability to discriminate among memories from different sources. In S.J. Ceci, M.P. Toglia, & D.F. Ross (Eds.), *Children's eyewitness memory* (pp. 92-121). New York: Springer.

Lindsay, D.S., & Johnson, M.K. (1989). The eyewitness suggestibility effect and memory for source. *Memory and Cognition, 17,* 349-358.

Loftus, E.F., Donders, K., Hoffman, H.G., & Schooler, J.W. (1989). Creating new memories that are quickly accessed and confidently held. *Memory and Cognition, 17,* 607-616.

Loftus, E.F., & Hoffman, H.G. (1989). Misinformation and memory. *Journal of Experimental Psychology: General, 118,* 100-104.

Loftus, E.F., Hoffman, H.G., & Wagenaar, W.A. (1992). The misinformation effect: Transformation in memory induced by postevent information. In M.L. Howe, C.J. Brainerd, & V.F. Reyna (Eds.), *Development of long-term retention.* New York: Springer (in press).

Loftus, E.F., Miller, D.G., & Burns, H.J. (1978). Semantic integration of verbal information into a visual memory. *Journal of Experimental Psychology: Human Learning and Memory, 4,* 19-31.

McCloskey, M., & Zaragoza, M. (1985). Misleading postevent information and memory for events: Arguments and evidence against memory impairment hypotheses. *Journal of Experimental Psychology: General, 114,* 1-16.

Metcalfe, J. (1990). Composite holographic associative recall model (CHARM) and blended memories in eyewitness testimony. *Journal of Experimental Psychology: General, 119,* 145-160.

Sheehan, P.W. (1989). Response to suggestions of memory distortions in hypnosis: Sampling cognitive and social factors. In V.A. Gheorghiu, P. Netter, H.J. Eysenck, & R. Rosenthal (Eds.), *Suggestion and suggestibility: Theory and research* (pp. 295-303). Berlin: Springer.

Slamecka, N.J., & Graf, P. (1978). The generation effect: Delineation of a phenomenon. *Journal of Experimental Psychology: Human Learning and Memory, 4,* 592-604.

Tousignant, J.P., Hall, D., & Loftus, E.F. (1986). Discrepancy detection and vulnerability to misleading post-event information. *Memory and Cognition, 14,* 329-338.

Tversky, B., & Tuchin, M. (1989). A reconciliation of the evidence on eyewitness testimony: Comments on McCloskey and Zaragoza. *Journal of Experimental Psychology: General, 118,* 86-91.

Wagenaar, W.A., & Boer, H.P.A. (1987). Misleading postevent information: Testing parameterized models of integration in memory. *Acta Psychologica, 66,* 291-306.

Zaragoza, M.S., & Koshmider, J.W. (1989). Misled subjects may know more than their performance implies. *Journal of Experimental Psychology: Learning, Memory and Cognition, 15,* 246-255.

Zaragoza, M.S., McCloskey, M., & Jamis, M. (1987). Misleading postevent information and recall of the original event: Further evidence against the memory impairment hypothesis. *Journal of Experimental Psychology: Learning, Memory, and Cognition, 13,* 36-44.

Effects of Detailed Imagery on Simulated Witness Recall

Debra A. Bekerian, John L. Dennett, Kathleen Hill, and Rosalind Hitchcock

The beneficial effects of imaging at learning have been documented regularly in the literature on adult human memory (see Marschark & Surian, 1989; Richardson, 1980). One would anticipate that imagery would be similarly beneficial if used at the time of recall. Imaging at the time of recollection is potentially powerful as a memory enhancement technique. The process of imaging should help to reinstate features present at the time the event was originally experienced, which should increase the likelihood of accessing event-related information (c.f., Encoding Specificity Principle, Tulving & Thomson, 1973).

As a memory enhancement technique, imagery is an easy technique to employ in applied settings, such as interviews with witnesses. The process of imaging can be performed by a real eyewitness almost as easily as it can be by a person in a memory experiment, and so is not difficult to use in real settings. However, there is a paucity of work done on the effects of imagery at the time of remembering. Thus, although plausible, the arguments have little empirical support.

There is research that provides some indirect experimental evidence for the effects imagery may have on memory of more realistic events. This comes from the data reported by Geiselman, Fisher and their associates (e.g., Geiselman et al., 1984). It is important to stress that the focus of this work has not been on imaging, per se, but rather on a combination of memory enhancing techniques, known collectively as "the cognitive interview technique." The following represents an attempt only to summarize the major components, as the actual methodologies used in the various papers are quite different. The generality of the findings across different methodological variables used in different studies will also be noted.

The general designs is as follows. Individuals view (and/or hear) an event. Some time later, they are asked to recall the event. Individuals are divided at recall into groups, representing different instructional conditions. At least one group of individuals are given standard memory instructions, which require the individual to recall as much as s/he can remember of the event. Another group is given elaborated instructions that highlight the use of at least four different memory mnemonics. These will be identified in key phrases: (a) reinstate the context; (b) report everything; (c) recall events in different order, and (d) change perspectives.

The consistent findings is that the cognitive interview technique results in the individual remembering more correct information without increasing, absolutely or proportionally, the number of errors. Further work has established that two of the four components used in isolation, context reinstatement and report everything, also have beneficial effects (see Geiselman, Fisher, MacKinnon, & Holland, 1986). However, the effects are not as great as those found with the complete cognitive interview technique.

It is important to note the reported generality of these findings. The cognitive interview technique[1] is reported to increase correct number of items without increasing errors across a wide range of variables, as reviewed across different papers. Examples of these are shown below:
- Type of event (live vs. video)
- Length of event (15s vs. 4 min)
- Type of learning (incidental vs. intentional)
- Time of recall (immediate vs. delayed)
- Number of recall attempts (single vs. multiple)
- Mode of recall (written vs. spoken)
- Nature of interview (interactive vs. noninteractive)
- Status of the rememberer (participant vs. observer)
- Age of rememberer (college students vs. older adults)
- Gender of rememberer (male vs. female)
- Type of methodology (field vs. experimental).

However, the cognitive interview technique can only be cited as indirect support for the present purposes as imagery is only one of many components. In the absence of any other data, this study attempts a simple comparison of different imagery instructions at recall. The findings should provide further evidence for the effects of imagery, with particular reference to the recall of highly enriched materials, such as videos or staged events. Additionally, such data may help to clarify how an imaginal component contributes to the overall effects of the cognitive interview technique. This general attitude is shared by Fisher, Geiselman, and Amador (1989): "We invite other researchers to tease apart the various components to determine their relative efficacy and to help refine the technique even further" (p. 6).

It was decided to manipulate imagery by encouraging some individuals to form highly vivid and clear images of details, before they reported the details (referred to as *Imagers*). So, for example, if an individual had recalled a man carrying a stick, the instructions encouraged this individual to form an image of the man, including his physical and other distinguishing features; an image of the stick; an image of the man carrying the stick, for examples. Only when these images had been clearly constructed was the individual to report the details. Other individuals received standard recall instructions, where imagery was not mentioned (referred to as the *Non-Imagers*).

The particular type of imaging that was encouraged is regarded as "molecular", in that detailed or molecular features were being emphasized (see Bekerian & Conway, 1988). This can be contrasted with the type of imaging where more general or molar features of the event are being constructed, like specific placement of people, general environmental factors like the weather, overall physical appearances of individuals, general actions, and so on (e.g., Smith, 1979). Both molecular and molar imaging seem to be relied upon in the context-reinstatement component of the cognitive interview technique.

---

[1] The complete cognitive interview technique relies on a variety of other components, for example, interactive interviewing where the interviewer is trained to phrase questions in image-compatible ways (e.g., Fisher, 1989).

It will be interesting to determine whether or not the specific of the information being imaged becomes a crucial factor in determining memory enhancement.

One final point should be made. There is no suggestion that *Non-Imagers* will fail to have the phenomenal experience of imaging. In fact, there is every reason to suspect that all individuals will spontaneously experience images when remembering, although there are likely to be individual differences. Consequently, the interpretation of any results cannot be ones that contrast imaging with not imaging. Rather, any effects that are found must be viewed in light of the distinction between positively encouraging individuals to form highly detailed images and not encouraging individuals to do so.

Method

Video event

The stimulus was a 3 minute video depicting a suspected burglary that resulted in a shopkeeper being found dead. The video was an reconstruction of real crime and highly enriched in detail. The video contained general location noises (e.g., sounds of traffic) as well as dialogue. There were two main characters, the victim and the alleged murderer/burglar who was posing as a local gas workman. Eight other characters were indentifiable in the video. The video was divided into eight scenes, with scenes determined by the presence of a new character, a new location and/or a shift in action.

Procedures

People were seated in front of a 14 inch TV monitor and asked to pay close attention to a video, as they would be asked questions about it later. Neither the nature of the video nor of the memory test was specified in advance. The experimenter was out of sight of the person while s/he was watching the video. After watching the video, individuals were given one of two instructions.

Non-Imagers. People were asked to describe as much as they could of the video they had just viewed. They were told not to worry about making their account into a coherent story. Instead they were asked to recall whatever they could remember in whatever order they wished. People were encouraged to guess about details even if they were not sure.

Imagers. Identical instructions were given, with the following addition. People were asked to try and form a very clear and detailed image of whatever they remembered *before* they actually recalled it. They were told that they should try to make sure that they had a very clear picture of what it was they were going to recall before mentioning it. They were told that once they had formed the image, they should then recall the detail. An example was then given using items not present in the video.

All individuals were recorded on audio tape. During the recall period, the experimenter was not in view and did not interact in any way. This was done so as to ensure that the experimenter would not interrupt an individual's concentration on the remembering task (e.g., Fisher, Geiselman, & Raymond, 1987, p. 180). Individuals informed the experimenter when their recall was finished. After debriefing, people were asked to give informal comment about any strategies that they may felt they had been using during recall.

Subjects

Forty-eight people were recruited via an advertisement and were paid for their participation in the experiment. The mean age was 25.6 years. An approximately equal number of males and females appeared on both conditions. Assignment to condition was random. All testing was done individually.

Results

Protocol analyses

All tapes were transcribed and protocols were subjected to discourse analyses procedures detailed in Bekerian and Dennett (1990b). Basic units of analyses corresponded to complete thoughts. Opinionated responses were not scored, as in accordance with Geiselman, Fisher, MacKinnon, and Holland, (1985). Errors were defined as information that occurred in the video but were incorrectly reported (e.g., wrong hair colour).

The analysis were conducted on three measures: overall = the total number of features recalled regardless of their correctness (correct features + errors); correct = the total number of correct features; errors = the total number of errors. The mean values for these measures are represented in Figure 1.

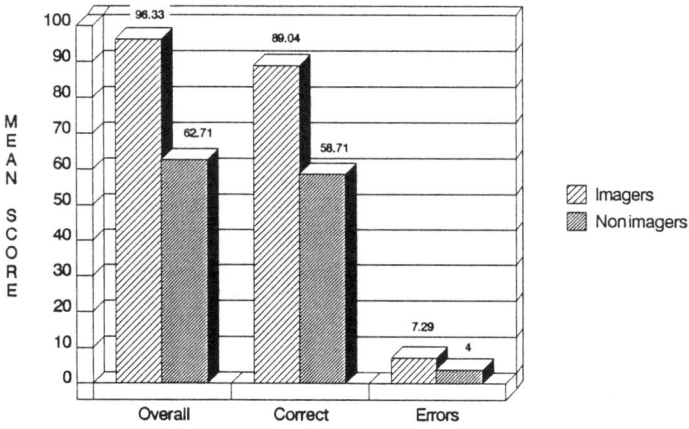

Figure 1: Mean Number of Features Recalled.

The pattern of results across the three measures of overall, correct and errors were similar. The *Imagers* recalled significantly more features overall and recalled more correct feature than did the *Non-Imagers* ($F(1,46)=21.31$ and 21.06, respectively, both $p > .05$). However, the *Imagers* also recalled more errors in their accounts than did the *Non-Imagers*

($F(1.46) = 6.22, p > .05$). Thus, *Imagers* gave more information, both correct and errors; and, the enhancement was equivalent across the different measures.

Analyses on the proportion error scores showed that an account produced by an Imager had about seven percent errors; an account produced by a Non-Imager contained about six percent errors ($F < 1$). Thus, detailed image instructions did not elicit proportionally more accurate accounts.

Discussion

The experiment was designed to examine the effects that detailed image instructions have on memory for a highly enriched event. Our findings suggest that although instructions which encouraged people to image increased total recall, the effects were equivalent across correct and incorrect information. In other words, imagery increased the absolute number of correct and incorrect information recalled by a subject. This increase in absolute number of errors is not typically reported in studies examining the cognitive interview technique (e.g., Geiselman et al., 1984).

One explanation for these data comes from a comparison of the memory strategies that might be used to initiate recall. We will assume, as do many theories of cognition and memory, that people adopt strategies that directly influence what they remember of an event, and how (e.g., Morton, Hammersley, & Bekerian, 1985; Norman & Bobrow, 1978; Schank, 1982; Schank & Abelson, 1977). The strategy will be sensitive to all the pragmatic conventions known to influence memory (e.g., Bekerian & Dennett, 1990b; Dritschel, 1990; Edwards & Middleton, 1986a, 1986b).

We will suggest that *Non-Imagers* adopted a "story-telling" strategy, in spite of the fact that they were explicitly asked not to conform to that style of reporting (or strategy of construction). However, the event being recalled here (i.e., the video) had narrative cohesiveness: e.g., it's characters spanned across different scenes with dialogue providing intentions and motives of the characters. Consequently, *Non-Imagers* could assume, reasonably, that the goal (of remembering) was to report the gist or overall theme of the story (see Kintsch, 1974). Perceptual details would still be recollected and would not be "suppressed" in recall. However, for the *Non-Imagers*, the primary task of remembering was to convey general thematic information about the story.

In contrast, *Imagers* were confronted with a slightly different situation. Thematic information was still regarded as important. However, in addition there was an implied emphasis on recalling finer details, e.g., perceptual features. Thus, because of the instructions, *Imagers* were led to believe that detailed descriptions of information were not only important in the account, but also expected, in some senses, by the experimenter. This difference in initial strategies and goals of remembering can easily account for the *Imagers* giving more information overall and more correct information. These results confirm those reported in experiments and studies using variants of the cognitive interview technique (e.g., Fisher et al., 1989).

In contrast, the increase in errors reported here are not typically found in studies using the cognitive interview technique. However, the findings are reminiscent of results reported by Bartlett (1932). Bartlett stated that individuals claiming to have frequent and highly vivid images of the to-be-remembered material were most likely to report erroneous information. Bartlett was cautious in over-interpreting such findings; however, he remarked, tentatively, that visualization (sic imagery) as a method of recall "... favours the introduction of material from an extraneous source ...." (1932, p. 61). Given that memories are constructed, imaging promotes filling-in-details that are otherwise inaccessible at the time of recall. Thus, Bartlett would predict that errors would increase when detailed imagery was encouraged, which was the finding.

Another point should be addressed. It might be argued that the differences between *Imagers* and *Non-Imagers* were due to amount of time, or effort, given to recall. That is, *Non-Imagers* may have "tried less hard". The most direct response to this criticism would require conditions where *Non-Imagers* were encouraged to expend great effort (e.g., take their time) in their recall. While the present experiment cannot address this comment, there is some evidence that suggests that increased motivation does not enhance memory performance (see MacKinnon, O'Reilly, & Geiselman, 1990). However, the possibility of motivational differences is currently being examined (see Bekerian & Dennett, 1990a).

A contrast between the present findings and those reported in the cognitive interview technique lead to some interesting questions that have theoretical importance as well as practical consequences. Comparisons must be qualified, of course, as it is acknowledged that the cognitive interview technique is comprised of many component processes.

First, there is the nature of the imagery instructions. The cognitive interview technique seems to rely on molar images as well as molecular details. It would seem to encourage imaging "a restaurant at noon in the summer" as well as imaging "a man in a red and white waistcoat". In contrast, the instructions used here stressed molecular images. Molar features were not emphasized. The present findings suggest that molecular images provide at least some information that enables the person to recall more (i.e., the difference between *Imagers* and *Non-Imagers*). However, molecular features of autobiographical events have been suggested to be less well-integrated into general event structures than molar features of an event (see Conway & Bekerian, 1987). Thus, molecular images will be less efficient at organizing memory than molar images. This may explain why the results on errors are different than those typically reported for the context-reinstatement component of the cognitive interview. A direct comparison of both types of imaging is currently being conducted to explore this further (see Bekerian & Dennett, 1990a).

A second issue is the nature of the event to be remembered. The characteristics of the event have already been demonstrated to influence the effects of the cognitive interview technique. The event used here could be regarded as lacking density in action, i.e., not too many things were going on at one time. Interestingly, Geiselman et al. (1985) reported that memory enhancement with the cognitive interview technique was greater with scenarios where many actions were occurring simultaneously.

Unfortunately, this finding was not pursued by those authors, although no other study reports such differences. However, given our findings and those of Geiselman et al. (1985), it is important to see whether the nature of the event will influence the consequences of using imagery.

Finally, let us comment on the potential application of these findings to techniques used in the interviewing of real witnesses. The conclusion, albeit tentative, depends on the assumptions one is prepared to make about information and its importance. One obvious interpretation is that molecular imaging is a good technique, in that more correct information was remembered, although not proportionally more errors. Thus, if the interviewer can get more correct information, s/he will be prepared to live with an increase in errors. This would seem to be a sensible conclusion, provided certain conditions are met. First, one must assume that the type of correct information recalled is important or case-relevant; second, one must assume that all errors being produced are not important, or case-irrelevant. If either one of these assumptions is incorrect, the interviewer might do well to reconsider the practical value of the technique.

References

Bartlett, F.C. (1932). *Remembering.* Cambridge: Cambridge University Press.

Bekerian, D.A., & Conway, M. (1988). Everyday contexts. In G. Davies, & D. Thomson (Eds.), *Memory in context: Context in memory* (pp. 205-318). Chichester: John Wiley & Sons.

Bekerian, D.A., & Dennett, J.L. (1990a). *Imaging molar and molecular details.* Manuscript in preparation.

Bekerian, D.A., & Dennett, J.L. (1990b). Spoken and written recall of visual narratives. *Applied Cognitive Psychology, 4,* 174-187.

Conway, M.A., & Bekerian, D.A. (1987). Organization in autobiographical memory. *Memory and Cognition, 15,* 119-132.

Dritschel, B. (1990). *The role of autobiographical memory in describing commom activities.* Manuscript submitted for publication.

Edwards, D., & Middleton, N. (1986a). Joint remembering: Construction an account of shared experience through conversational discourse. *Discourse Processes, 9,* 423-459.

Edwards, D., & Middleton, N. (1986b). Text for memory: Joint recall with a scribe. *Human Learning, 5,* 125-138.

Fisher, R.P. (1989). *Enhancing eyewitness memory with the cognitive interview.* Miami Seminar Notes.

Fisher, R.P., Geiselman, R.E., & Amador, M. (1989). Field test of the cognitive interview: Enhancing the recollection of actual victims and witnesses of crime. *Journal of Applied Psychology, 74,* 722-727.

Fisher, R.P., Geiselman, R.E., & Raymond, D. (1987). Critical analysis of police interview techniques. *Journal of Police Science and Administration, 15,* 177-185.

Geiselman, R.E., Fisher, R.P., Firstenberg, I., Hutton, L.A., Sullivan, S.J., Avetissian, I.V., & Prosk, A.L. (1984). Enhancement of eyewitness memory: An empirical evaluation of the cognitive interview. *Journal of Police Science and Administration, 12,* 74-80.

Geiselman, R.E., Fisher, R.P., MacKinnon, D.P., & Holland, H.L. (1985). Eyewitness memory enhancement in the police interview: Cognitive retrieval mnemonics versus hypnosis. *Journal of Applied Psychology, 70,* 401-412.

Geiselman, R.E., Fisher, R.P., MacKinnon, D.P., & Holland, H.L. (1986). Enhancement of eyewitness memory with the cognitive interview. *American Journal of Psychology, 99,* 385-401.

Kintsch, W. (1974). *The representation of meaning in memory.* Hillsdale, N.J.: Erlbaum.

MacKinnon, D.P., O'Reilly, K.E., & Geiselman, R.E. (1990). Improving eyewitness recall for licence plates. *Applied Cognitive Psychology, 4,* 129-140.

Marschark, M., & Surian, L. (1989). Why does imagery improve memory? *European Journal of Cognitive Psychology, 1,* 251-263.

Morton, J., Hammersley, R.H., & Bekerian, D.A. (1985). Headed records: A model of memory and its failures. *Cognition, 20,* 1-23.

Norman, D., & Bobrow, D. (1978). Descriptions: An intermediate stage in memory retrieval. *Cognitive Psychology, 11,* 107-123.

Richardson, J.T.E. (1980). *Mental imagery and human memory.* London: Macmillan Press Ltd.

Schank, R. (1982). *Dynamic Memory.* New York: John Wiley.

Schank, R., & Abelson, R. (Eds.) (1977). *Scripts, plans, goals and understanding: An inquiry into human knowledge structures.* Hillsdale, NJ: Lawrence Erlbaum.

Smith, S. (1979). Remembering in and out of context. *Journal of Experimental Psychology, 5,* 460-471.

Tulving, E., & Thompson, D. (1973). Encoding specificity in episodic memory. *Psychology Review, 80,* 352-373.

Racial and Gender Issues in Facial Recognition[1]

Norine L. Jalbert and Jeanette Getting

Introduction

Research spanning the past two decades has resulted in the general conclusion that witnesses to crimes are not as reliable as we might intuitively believe, yet they play a major role in the conviction rate of juries (Blau, 1984; Buckhout, 1974; Loftus, 1979; Penrod, Loftus, & Winkler, 1982; Wells, 1987). Of particular interest to researchers has been the question of eyewitness identification - specifically, how accurate and reliable is eyewitness testimony and what factors influence the accuracy and reliability of an eyewitness. The research in this area has produced diverse studies with diverse results. For example, Clifford and Scott (1978) found higher recall accuracy in witnesses who viewed the crime rather than having the crime described to them. Ellis and Deregowski (1981) found transformations in the appearances of faces to affect identification accuracy. Hosch and Platz (1984) found high self-monitoring individuals to be more accurate in identifying a person they had previously seen. Lipton (1977) found that subjects are more accurate but less complete when they are asked for "unstructured" testimony, while the opposite is true for subjects who are asked for "structured" testimony. Shapiro and Penrod's (1986) meta-analysis of facial identification studies found the following factors to also have an impact on facial identification performance: context reinstatement, depth of processing, elaboration, the target present/absent variable, exposure time, subject age, retention interval, pose, and cross-racial identification.

The present study on eyewitness reliability focuses on the main or interactive effects of race and gender of the subject and the stimulus person on subsequent identification tasks. A substantial body of research has been reported that focuses on racial and cross-racial identification (e.g., Cross, Cross, & Daly, 1971; Luce, 1974; Malpass & Kravitz, 1969) with the general conclusion that cross-racial identifications are more difficult, less accurate, and therefore less reliable than within-race identifications (Bothwell, Brigham, & Malpass, 1989; Penrod et al., 1982; Shapiro & Penrod, 1986; Wells, 1978, 1987). A recently published meta-analysis by Bothwell et al. (1989) on cross-racial identification produced data indicating that own-race bias was quite consistent for both black and white subjects.

While there appears to be increasing agreement among researchers regarding the greater difficulty of cross-race versus own-race identifications, much less attention has been paid to gender as an influencing variable in eyewitness identification/facial recognition research. Recent studies including gender as a variable have produced inconsistent results. For example, Cunningham and Bringmann (1986) found no significant sex differences with regard to subjects' recall accuracy or resistance to suggestibility. Lindsay (1986) also found no significant sex differences due to sex of subject or sex of target on either

---

[1] The research reported here was supported by a CSU-AAUP research grant.

identification accuracy or confidence. On the other hand, studies by Shapiro and Penrod (1986), Lipton (1977), and Howells (1938) all found accuracy rate of subjects to be higher for females than for males. Clifford and Scott (1978), however, found a sex of subject x situation interaction such that female subjects were less accurate than male subjects after viewing a violent incident but equally accurate as male subjects after viewing a nonviolent incident. Cross et al. (1971) found a significant sex of subject x sex of stimulus person interaction such that male subjects recognized male and female stimulus persons equally well while female subjects recognized female stimulus persons better than male stimulus persons. Shapiro and Penrod (1986) reported more correct identifications for same gender targets than cross-gender targets but no differences for false identifications.

To date, there appears to be no research focussing on the possible interactive influences of race and gender. In a period of history when increasing numbers of sexual assault crimes are being brought to trial and where cross-gender and/or cross-racial identification issues are often critical to the disposition of a case, the absence of clear evidence regarding the possible influences of gender and/or race on eyewitness testimony is a serious omission. The present study therefore attempts to address three questions: (1) Does race or gender of stimulus persons influence their identifiability; (2) does race or gender of subjects influence their identification accuracy; and (3) are there any interaction effects between race or gender of the stimulus person and the subject?

The question of eyewitness reliability as a function of race or gender is viewed within the broader arena of the psychology of eyewitness testimony. As stated in the beginning of this paper, research spanning the past two decades has generally concluded that witnesses to crimes are not as reliable as we might intuitively believe, yet they continue to play a major role in the conviction rates of juries, and, *regardless of accuracy,* the more confident an eyewitness, the more likely the jury is to believe that eyewitness (Cutler, Penrod, & Stuve, 1988; Deffenbacher, 1980; Fox & Walters, 1986; Lindsay, 1986). In a society as diverse as the United States, where defendants and witnesses are likely to differ in racial and/or gender characteristics, it is both practically and theoretically important to investigate the extent to which such individual characteristics affect the judicial process. If we also consider that expert witnesses are more and more often being called upon to instruct the court and jury about the fallibilities and/or limitations of eyewitness testimony, thereby potentially affecting the outcome of trial deliberations, then it becomes even more pressing that the base of knowledge from which these experts draw their conclusions be broadened.

Method

Subjects

114 subjects participated in the study, 13 black males, 31 white males, 7 black females, and 63 white females. All Ss were students at Western Connecticut State University whose classes were invited to participate in the study. Student participation was voluntary, and any student who did not wish to participate was free to leave at any time.

Stimulus photographs

Stimulus faces were taken from the high school yearbook of a large metropolitan public high school. Black and white slides were made of 80 senior class pictures which were selected in a more or less random fashion. True random selection was not possible because of the use of several selection criteria - specifically, anyone with unusual facial expression, posture, hairstyle, jewelry, or clothing or anyone who wore glasses was not included in the study. Additionally, an attempt was made to exclude white students with light blonde hair coloring in order to maintain some consistency in hair coloring of stimulus persons. Of the 80 photos that were selected, there were 20 in each of the following four groups: black males, white males, black females, white females.

Procedure

Students were approached during their regularly scheduled class meeting by the same female experimenter and invited to participate in a group study of their ability to recognize faces. Seven different introductory level social sciences or humanities classes were used with group size ranging from 8 to 31. Students who agreed to participate were given a brief written description of the study and asked to sign an informed consent form. They then completed a short biographical questionnaire in which they indicated, among other things, their gender and their ethnic identification. Although all students who wished to participate were allowed to do so, only the data of black and white Ss were analyzed. Upon completion of the biographical questionnaire, Ss were given the following instructions:

> In measuring your ability to accurately recognize faces, two series of slides of males and females will be projected on the screen with a 1 - 2 minute interval between the two series. The first series of slides will consist of 20 photographs, and each will be shown for a time span of 2 seconds. Your only task will be to view the faces of the individuals with your full attention. The second series of slides will consist of 80 photographs - the original 20 slides from the first series randomly distributed among 60 new photographs. Each will be shown for a time span of 4 seconds. Your task will be to view the faces of the individuals and to determine whether or not each particular photograph is one which you had previously viewed in the first series.

Following these instructions, Ss viewed the first series of 20 slides. The 20 stimulus slides were randomly selected from the pool of 80 slides with the criteria that there be no more than three slides in a row of any race or gender and there be no more than two slides in a row of any race x gender combination. For each of the seven sessions, a different set of stimulus slides was selected. After the stimulus slides were shown, the E gave Ss the following instructions:

> Please turn to page 4 of your booklet. You should each have a Response Sheet before you. Upon viewing each photograph, you must decide whether or not the face is one which you previously viewed in the first series of slides. If you recognize the face, fill in Circle A on the response sheet to denote a YES response. If you do not recognize the face, fill in Circle B to denote a NO response. You must respond for each of the 80 slides to be projected. The order in which the photographs will be presented corresponds to the numbers on the response sheet. Therefore, a response to photograph Nr. 1 is marked

as Nr.1 on the response sheet, and so on. Maintaining both attention and speed will be very important during the projection of the second series of slides. Your full attention to each photograph will help to assure the accuracy of your responses. Since each slide will only be projected for 4 seconds, speed is essential so that you do not fall behind and lose track of what number photograph is being presented. Each slide of the second series will only be projected once.

Results and Discussion

Ss' responses were scored for number of correct and incorrect identifications, then transformed into proportion scores for analysis. Correct and incorrect identifications were analyzed separately in a 2 x 2 x 2 x 2 ANOVA with two repeated measures (S sex x S race x SP sex x SP race). Table 1 presents the means and standard deviations for proportions of correct and incorrect identifications of stimulus photos.

Table 1: Means and Standard Deviations for Proportions of Correct and Incorrect Identifications of Stimulus Persons.

		Stimulus persons							
		Male				Female			
		Black		White		Black		White	
		Correct i.d.	Incorrect i.d.	Correct i.d.	Incorrect i.d.	Correct i.d.	Incorrect i.d.	Correct i.d.	Incorrect i.d.
Male	Black	.785[a]	.185	.569	.241	.815	.123	.692	.267
	n=13	.191[b]	.099	.281	.205	.128	.105	.225	.202
	White	.729	.271	.774	.142	.645	.198	.703	.217
	n=31	.234	.196	.205	.136	.229	.187	.199	.192
Female	Black	.657	.162	.600	.181	.829	.114	.657	.191
	n=7	.190	.176	.231	.210	.138	.183	.299	.245
	White	.625	.203	.746	.100	.733	.168	.756	.141
	n=63	.181	.141	.260	.113	.172	.150	.226	.143

a = means
b = standard deviations

Analysis was performed on an IBM PS/2 computer using the Crunch interactive statistical package, CRISP. Because WCSU has a predominantly white student body, there were very few black Ss compared to white Ss. The statistical program's default correction for the unequal N's adjusted the between Ss sums of squares in hierarchical fashion (i.e., each between Ss is adjusted for previous effects and ignores subsequent effects).

Correct identifications

The ANOVA results revealed no between Ss effects due to S sex or S race and no within Ss main effects due to SP sex or SP race.

Table 2: Analysis of Variance of Proportion of Correct Responses of Black and White, Male and Female Ss Exposed to Black and White, Male and Female Stimulus Photos.

Source	df	MS	F
Between Ss	113		
Sex of S (A)	1	.0002	.003
Race of S (B)	1	.007	.089
A x B	1	.015	.199
Ss wGps	110	.076	
Within Ss	342		
Sex of SP (C)	1	.084	2.354
A x C	1	.250	6.969**
B x C	1	.201	5.619**
A x B x C	1	.036	1.017
C x Ss wGps	110	.036	
Race of SP (D)	1	.084	2.271
A x D	1	.120	3.219
B x D	1	.659	17.768***
A x B x D	1	.005	.124
D x Ss wGps	110	.037	
C x D	1	.064	1.820
A x C x D	1	.126	3.574
B x C x D	1	.006	.181
A x B x C x D	1	.009	.241
C x D x Ss wGps	110	.035	

* $p < .05$
** $p < .01$
*** $p < .001$

However, there were some noteworthy within Ss interaction effects. There was a significant interaction effect between S sex and SP sex ($F(1,110)=6.969; p<.009$) such that male Ss correctly identified more males SP's than female SP's. Female Ss, on the other hand, correctly identified more female SP's than male SP's. A close examination of the means in Table 1 would further suggest that it is the white male Ss who are contributing to the higher accuracy scores for male SP's than female SP's since black male Ss show slightly higher accuracy for female SP's than male SP's. These findings contradict Lindsay (1986) who found no sex differences and Lipton (1977) and Howells (1938) who concluded that female Ss were more accurate that male Ss. The findings corroborate the conclusion drawn by Shapiro and Penrod (1986) that accuracy is greater for same-gender targets than cross-gender targets and partially corroborate Cross et al.'s (1971) findings that female Ss recognize female SP's better than male SP's. However, the present data failed to replicate Cross et al.'s finding that male Ss recognized male and female SP's equally well.

A significant S race x SP sex interaction was found ($F(1,110)=5.619; p<.01$) indicating that black Ss demonstrated higher accuracy for female SP's than male SP's. While white

Ss showed a similar pattern of response, the difference in their mean accuracy scores was much weaker.

Lastly, a very strong S Race x SP race interaction was found ($F(1,110)=17.768; p<.001$) which corroborates earlier research findings indicating that blacks are more accurate in their identification of black SP's and whites are more accurate in their identification of white SP's. The robustness of the interaction effect lends strong support to the mounting evidence that cross-racial identifications are more difficult than same-race identifications.

False identifications

The ANOVA of Ss' false identification scores yielded a between Ss main effect for sex of S ($F(1,110)=5.193; p<.02$). Specifically, the data suggest that male Ss ($M=.206$; $SD=.178$) make more false identifications than female Ss ($M=.154; SD=.148$).

Table 3: Analysis of Variance of Proportion of Incorrect Responses of Black and White, Male and Female Ss Exposed to Black and White, Male and Female Stimulus Photos.

Source	df	MS	F
Between Ss	113		
Sex of S (A)	1	.295	5.193*
Race of S (B)	1	.0002	.004
A x B	1	.002	.039
Ss wGps	110	.057	
Within Ss	342		
Sex of SP (C)	1	.0002	.011
A x C	1	.0008	.060
B x C	1	.006	.468
A x B x C	1	.000	.003
C x Ss wGps	110	.014	
Race of SP (D)	1	.155	9.606**
A x D	1	.055	3.426
B x D	1	.294	18.245***
A x B x D	1	.007	.401
D x Ss wGps	110	.016	
C x D	1	.262	22.631***
A x C x D	1	.021	1.83
B x C x D	1	.008	.647
A x B x C x D	1	.002	.143
C x D x Ss wGps	110	.012	

* $p < .05$
** $p < .01$
*** $p < .001$

A within Ss main effect for SP race was also found ($F(1,110)=9.606; p<.002$) indicating that black SP's ($M=.192; SD=.160$) are more frequently misidentified than white SP's ($M=.156; SD=.162$).

A strong interaction between S race and SP race was found ($F(1,110)=18.245; p<.001$) which, as in the case of correct identifications, corroborates earlier research suggesting that cross-racial identifications are more difficult than same-race identifications. The present data indicated that black Ss falsely identify white/black SP's more than white SP's and white Ss falsely identify black SP's more than white SP's. Of greater interest is the significant interaction found between SP sex and SP race ($F(1,110) = 22.361$; $p < .001$) which indicated that black male SP's are the most frequently misidentified group while white male SP's are the least frequently misidentified group. Along these same lines, it is interesting to note that although the S sex x SP race interaction was not significant ($F(1,110) = 3.426$; $p < .06$), the data do suggest a tendency for male Ss to misidentify black and white SP's equally whereas female Ss, even though they show a much weaker tendency to make false identifications overall, do make more false identifications for black SP's than for white SP's.

The results of the present study lend robust support to the notion that cross-racial identifications are more difficult and, therefore, perhaps less reliable than same race identifications. Ss were not only more accurate in recognizing members of their same race, they also demonstrated a tendency to more often misidentify members of another race. While the present study did not attempt to test the validity of various explanations for own-race bias, it should be noted that failures to find strong support for any explanation of own-race bias (e.g., Brigham & Malpass, 1985) may be due in part to the failure of earlier studies to examine race biases in conjunction with sex differences. It is in the area of sex differences that this study makes its biggest contribution. While in no way conclusive, the data suggest that there is a wealth of information yet to be explored dealing with the interactive influences of S sex, S race, SP sex, and SP race. Further research is needed in this area to establish the reliability of findings that indicate that males can more correctly identify other males and females can more correctly identify other females; that males have a greater tendency to make false identifications than females; that blacks, especially black males, are more often misidentified than whites; and that females misidentify blacks more frequently than they misidentify whites. In the real world of judicial proceedings, such patterns in eyewitness behavior are not insignificant.

References

Blau, T.H. (1984). *The psychologist as expert witness*. New York: John Wiley & Sons.

Bothwell, R.K., Brigham, J.C., & Malpass, R.S. (1989). Cross-racial identification. *Personality and Social Psychology Bulletin, 15*, 19-25.

Brigham, J.C., & Malpass, R.S. (1985). *Journal of Social Issues, 41*, 139-155.

Buckhout, R. (1974). Eyewitness testimony. *Scientific American, 231*, 23-31.

Clifford, B.R., & Scott, J. (1978). Individual and situational factors in eyewitness testimony. *Journal of Applied Psychology, 63*, 352-259.

Cross, J.F., Cross, J.,, & Daly, J. (1971). Sex, race, age and beauty as factors in recognition of faces. *Perception and Psychophysics, 10*, 393-396.

Cunningham, J.L., & Bringmann, W.G. (1986). A re-examination of William Stern's classic eyewitness research. *Perceptual and Motor Skills, 63*, 565-566.

Cutler, B.L., Penrod, S.D., & Stuve, T.E. (1988). Juror decision making in eyewitness identification cases. *Law and Human Behavior, 12*, 41-55.

Deffenbacher, K.A. (1980). Eyewitness accuracy and confidence: Can we infer anything about their relationship? *Law and Human Behavior, 4*, 243-260.

Ellis, H.D., & Deregowski, J.B. (1981). Within-race and between-race recognition of transformed and untransformed faces. *American Journal of Psychology, 94*, 27-35.

Fox, S.G., & Walters, H.A. (1986). The impact of general versus specific expert testimony and eyewitness confidence upon mock juror judgment. *Law and Human Behavior, 10,* 215-229.

Hosch, H.M., & Platz, S.J. (1984). Self-monitoring and eyewitness accuracy. *Personality and Social Psychology Bulletin, 10,* 289-292.

Howells, T.H. (1938). A study of ability to recognize faces. *Journal of Abnormal and Social Psychology, 33,* 124-127.

Lindsay, R.C.L. (1986). Confidence and accuracy of eyewitness identification from lineups. *Law and Human Behavior, 10,* 229-239.

Lipton, J.P. (1977). On the psychology of eyewitness testimony. *Journal of Applied Psychology, 66,* 79-89.

Loftus, E.F. (1979). *Eyewitness testimony.* Cambridge, MA: Harvard University Press.

Luce, T.S. (1974). Blacks, whites and yellows: they all look alike to me. *Psychology Today,* November, 105-108.

Malpass, R.S., & Kravitz, J. (1969). Recognition for faces of own and other race. *Journal of Personality and Social Psychology, 13,* 330-334.

Penrod, S., Loftus, E., & Winkler, J. (1982). The reliability of eyewitness testimony: a psychological perspective. In N.L. Kerr, & R.M. Bray (Eds.), *The psychology of the courtroom* (pp. 119-168). New York: Academic Press.

Shapiro, P.N., & Penrod, S. (1986). Meta-analysis of facial identification studies. *Psychological Bulletin, 100,* 139-156.

Wells, G.L. (1978). Applied eyewitness-testimony research: System variable and estimator variables. Reprinted in L.S. Wrightsman, C.E. Willis, & S.M. Kassin (Eds.) (1987), *On the witness stand* (pp. 139-156). Newbury Park: Sage.

Wells, G.L. (1987). The eyewitness. In S.M. Kassin, & L.S. Wrightsman (Eds.), *The psychology of evidence and trial procedure* (pp. 43-66). Beverly Hills: Sage Publications.

Eyewitness Memory and Time of Day

Margarita Diges, Maria E. Rubio, and Maria C. Rodriguez

Introduction

Increasing interest in individual differences in eyewitness performance has shown that people differ in terms of total accuracy, confidence in their own recall, and even in suggestibility (e.g., Ward & Loftus, 1985). Some of these differences are thought to reflect varied degrees of basal arousal, as in the case of introverts and extroverts, because differences in arousal underlay some variations in cognitive processing.

The relationships between arousal levels and memory performance are not clear (Eysenck, 1982) but one must take into account two additional facts:

1. Individual differences might vary due to change in time of day. For example, introverts reach their arousal peak sooner than extroverts.

2. There are differences in memory performance throughout the day: the morning being better for immediate or short-term memory, verbatim and ordered memory, and shallow processing of verbal material. On the contrary, the evening favours delayed memory, prose memory (not verbatim) and semantic or deep processing.

The purpose of the present experiment was to explore another individual difference variable that is related both to changes in time of day and to eyewitness memory performance. The "morningness-eveningness" dimension refers to people with preferred life schedules. Morning-type subjects reach their arousal peak 3 hours before evening-type subjects (Kerkhof, 1985). Also morning-type subjects (so called larks) perform better in the morning than in the evening, and evening-type subjects (so called owls) perform better in the evening than in the morning in free recall (Lancry, cited in Lecont, 1988).

This leads to the prediction that subjects in their "best moment" (morning- and evening-type in the morning and in the evening, respectively) will show higher (optimal) arousal levels and better eyewitness memory than subjects in their "worst moment" (morning- and evening-type subjects in the evening and in the morning, respectively).

Method

Subjects

Twenty morning- and 20 evening-type subjects (larks and owls, respectively) were selected on the basis of their scores (> 59 or < 41) on Horne and Ostberg's questionnaire (1976). These were 31 females and 9 males, all of whom were undergraduate psychology student volunteers.

Materials

Two scales (Fatigue and Vigor) from the *Profile of Mood States* (POMS; McNair, Lorr, & Droppelman, 1971) were used as subjective arousal estimators. A silent traffic accident film (27 s duration) was employed as stimulus material. Recall performance was assessed by means of a questionnaire on different aspects of the filmed event (cued recall). Free recall narratives were analyzed in terms of accuracy (numbers of micropropositions recalled, distortions) and quality (exaggerations, personal judgments, cognitive operations, dubitative expressions, length of the narrative, etc.).

Design

The design involved two between-subjects factors, type of person (morning- or evening-type), and time of day (10:00 and 20:00). Consequently, 10 morning-type and 10 evening-type subjects were assigned randomly to 10:00, and the remaining subjects performed the eyewitness memory task at 20:00.

Procedure

Oral temperature and Vigor and Fatigue scales were self-measured at 1-hour intervals from the time the subjects got up until 20:00. In all cases, individual typical scores (obtained from the scores of the subject along the day) for test time were used in statistical analyses. Subjects were first shown the film. Immediately, arousal variables were measured, so that they served as a filling task. Then, eyewitnesses were asked to write their recall in their own words. Finally, they filled in the cued recall questionnaire.

Results

Free recall narratives were scored by two independent judges who used the same criteria to assess accuracy and quality of recall. They tried to reach agreement when they did not share the same view, and if agreement could not be reached, the information was eliminated.

Results from the questionnaire (cued recall) were scored by counting the number of items answered correctly. In both cases (free recall and cued recall), the filmed event could be considered as made up of: *introduction, complication and resolution* of the story. Then, scores for each part as well as for the total recall were calculated.

Analyses of variance were performed on the arousal, free recall and cued recall variables, and significant effects were found for type of subject, time of day, and, finally, their interaction.

The following variables showed significant effects (see Table 1).

Morningness-eveningness had a significant effect on cued recall on film duration estimation, $F(1,36)=7.64$, $p<.01$, morning-type subjects being higher in their estimations.

Time of day had a significant effect on the following variables of cued recall: introduction, $F(1,36)=3.64, p=.065$; complication, $F(1,36)=12.56, p<.01$; and total, $F(1,36)=9.14$, $p<.01$. In all these cases, subjects in the morning remembered more details than subjects in the evening. This independent variable also had significant effects on variables of free recall: introduction, $F(1,36)=4.02, p=.052$; complication, $F(1,36)=10.79, p<.01$; and total, $F(1,36)=7.92, p<.01$. Again, subjects in the morning remembered more details than subjects in the evening.

Table 1: Differences in the Dependent Variables Between Owls and Larks in the Morning and Evening Condition.

	Larks		Owls	
	Morning	Evening	Morning	Evening
Estimated time of film duration (in seconds)	123.5	150.0	49.7	67.5
Accuracy in cued recall:				
Introduction	15.5	13.2	15.7	13.0
Complication	5.5	3.7	6.9	4.2
Resolution	3.9	3.0	3.7	3.5
Total	25.5	20.7	26.8	21.0
Free recall scores				
Introduction	7.1	6.4	8.0	5.7
Complication	4.9	3.4	5.0	4.2
Resolution	1.9	1.1	1.3	1.9
Total	13.9	10.9	14.8	11.6
Irrelevant information	1.2	1.7	2.3	0.8
Arousal variables (in individual mean scores):				
Temperature C°	0.86	0.12	-0.44	0.34
Fatigue	-0.48	0.86	-0.27	-0.35
Vigor	0.84	-0.28	-0.24	0.65

The interaction morningness-eveningness x time of day had a significant effect on the following variables of free recall: resolution, $F(1,36)=4.12, p<.05$; and irrelevant information, $F(1,36)=5.348, p<.05$. In the first case, subjects in their "best moment" recalled more resolution details. Regarding irrelevant information, subjects in their "worst moment" remembered more irrelevant details. The interaction also had significant effects on variables of arousal: temperature, $F(1,36)=4.36$, $p<.05$; fatigue, $F(1,36)=5.02$, $p<.05$; and vigor, $F(1,36)=11.78, p<.05$. For all arousal variables, subjects in their "best moment" showed higher arousal than subjects in their "worst moment".

Discussion

The results obtained indicate that the main factor affecting eyewitnesses (free and cued recall) is the time of day, irrespective of type of eyewitness. In free recall, eyewitnesses in the morning show higher scores in *total and complication* recall (and marginally in the introduction) than in the evening. The same pattern is found in cued recall. Interaction (morningness-eveningness x time of day) affects arousal variables, as expected, and the recall of event *resolution and of irrelevant* information, both in free recall. So, arousal data fit the expected pattern; morning subjects being more aroused in the morning (their best moment) than in the evening (their worst moment), and evening subjects showing the opposite pattern. It seems that subjects in their best moment are able to discriminate important details from irrelevant information when reporting their recall. On the contrary, subjects in their worst moment have less resources to make such a discrimination, as also suggested by data from narrative length.

The effect of time of day on the remaining recall variables does not fit the expected pattern. There was a systematic superiority of the 10:00 (testing time) as compared with the evening test at 20:00.

If we only look at morning-type subjects, interaction effects appear as expected, namely, better recall and better report of relevant details in their best moment than in their worst.

What needs an explanation is the recall of evening-type eyewitnesses in the morning. They write more words than the other groups (although differences are not significant); they report more accurate details but fail to discriminate the important ones (from the irrelevant information); and, finally, a close analysis of recall questionnaires reveals that they mistake the relative speeds of cars involved in the accident in the film, attributing the superior speed to the nearly stopped car. These speed distortions are significantly higher in this group as compared to the remaining groups in which they were hardly ever observed.

We suggest that the strange behaviour of evening-type eyewitnesses in the morning might be explained in terms of their low basal arousal at that moment. Low arousal level is related to scarce cognitive resources, which would result in an impaired processing of the information available at the scene.

Scarce cognitive resources may permit one to "catch" a lot of accurate details of the event but they do not guarantee that the details will be properly integrated in a factual way.

However, morning-type eyewitnesses in the evening also have a low arousal level. The reason for the difference between the two groups is the way in which they face the task with few resources. Evening-type people show a tendency towards the extroversion dimension of personality (Kerkhof, 1985), which, in turn, is related to assertiveness and self-confidence. These characteristics could result in a lower decision criterion when extroverts report their recall. Consequently, they write longer reports, perform hastily and make mistakes when trying to integrate the information. After all, they recall a lot of details!

As a consequence of our results, we would like to stress the importance of qualitative analysis when evaluating eyewitness memory; they can reflect some subjects' mistakes that remain hidden when a simple questionnaire methodology is used. Also, our results, specially in the case of evening-type subjects, suggest that individual differences must continue to be explored in eyewitness memory research.

References

Eysenck, M. (1982). *Attention and arousal. Cognition and performance.* Berlin: Springer.

Horne, J.A., & Ostberg, O. (1976). A self-assessment questionnaire to determine morningness-eveningness in human circadian rhythms. *International Journal of Chronobiology, 4,* 97-110.

Kerkhof, G. (1985). Interindividual differences in the human circadian system. A review. *Biological Psychology, 20,* 83-112.

Lecont, P. (1988). Les rhythmicités de l'efficience cognitive. *L'Année Psychologique, 88,* 215-236.

McNair, D.M., Lorr, M., & Droppelman, M. (1971). *Manual for the profile of mood states (POMS).* San Diego: Educational and Industrial Testing Service.

Ward, R.A., & Loftus, E. (1985). Eyewitness performance in different psychological types. *Journal of General Psychology, 112,* 191-200.

"Phenomenal Causality" in Eyewitness Report

Katharina Dahmen-Zimmer and Martina Kraus

Introduction

When judging the veracity of an eyewitness report, we have to investigate whether the critical event could actually be observed correctly and remembered by the witness. A lot of investigations deal with witness memory processes and the occurrence of possible errors in them (e.g., Loftus & Ketcham, 1983), whereas research on perception processes in witnesses is scarce. When investigating these processes, we have to consider both the physiological limits of human visual perception and the perceptual laws controlling event perception. Especially Gibson's (1979) "ecological approach to visual perception" deals with event perception. As he points out, perception is not based on "having sensations" but is based on the active "pick-up of information". That is, perception is purposeful, the organism searches for information in order to know about and to control his/her environment. Of course, it is most important for an organism to know if and how ongoing events are connected and especially if a change in his/her environment is caused by a particular event.

In everyday life, we are usually highly capable of correctly perceiving physical causations. But we can be mistaken in situations that are unfamiliar and/or provide only impoverished information, as demonstrated by the experiments on "phenomenal causality" (Michotte, 1963). In his experiments, subjects typically viewed a display with simple geometrical objects like a square or a circle. The speed and constellation of the moving objects was varied systematically. In his Experiment 1, for instance, a black square moved toward a red square at a constant speed and stopped when touching it; at this moment, the red square started moving at the same speed or at a lower speed. The observers reported that they saw the black square giving an impulse to the red square and thereby causing its subsequent movement. This causal impression depends on the temporal, spatial, and formal properties of the display. Bassili's (1976) experiments with computer-generated displays have confirmed the finding that an interaction between two moving geometrical objects is perceived if there is a temporal contingency between their changes in direction. Whether an intention is attributed to the objects (e.g., one chases or follows the other) depends on the spatial contingencies. Yela (1952) has demonstrated that a moving object seems to cause the movement of another object even without actually touching it. While Michotte (1963) concluded that this "phenomenal causality" is always perceived directly, other authors stress the role of the observer's perceptual and cultural experience of the world (e.g., Bruce & Green, 1985).

There are other specific situations in which organisms can be fooled about the reality of causal relations: A time-dependent delivery of positive reinforcement can result in superstitious behavior in animals (Skinner, 1948) and humans (Catania & Cutts, 1963). A contiguous presentation of a stimulus and a positive reinforcement can generate autoshaped behavior in animals (Brown & Jenkins, 1968) and humans (Dahmen, 1988). In the social domain, cultural expectations, prejudices, and personal expectations about the behavior of other people may affect perception of causation (Allport & Postman, 1958; Hastorf & Cantril, 1954).

The following experiment studied whether observers of an ambiguous social event could be induced to perceive physical causal relations that were not actually present. That is, whether and in which way eyewitness reports of an ambivalent social situation could be distorted by erroneous causal perceptions or conclusions. Moreover, we examined if and how the following variables influenced the outcome: (a) The mental state of the observed person (angry vs. neutral), which might influence the individual expectations; (b) the kind and amount of information given (visual vs. visual plus acoustic); (c) the delay between observation and interrogation (immediately vs. some days later); and (d) whether the consequences of the event were presented or not. In order to perform this investigation, subjects were shown a videotape of an event sequence ending with an accident. Afterwards, the subjects had to answer questions on what they had seen.

Method

Subjects were 102 volunteers, 98 college students and 4 employees, 70 females and 32 males, mean age 22;6, range 19 to 40 years.

The videotape

The videotape showed a woman in a telephone booth: She talks, laughs, and drops more money into the apparatus. A second woman is waiting in front of the booth. Another woman arrives, and the two women begin to talk. Finally, the woman in the telephone booth puts the receiver down and, taking her purse with one hand and her bag with the other hand, tries to push open the door with her back. The waiting woman hurries to her and opens the door from the outside. Both women are close together now, moving in opposite directions. It is not visible, however, if they really touch each other. While trying to leave the booth, the woman falls down on her back, dropping both her purse and bag. The film lasts about 73 s.

The mental state of the first waiting woman was featured in two different ways: In one version of the film, she is very angry about the long time she has to wait ("angry version"), and in the "neutral version" she does not care about the length of the phone call. An additional videotaped scene (7 s) depicted the consequences of the fall: The woman sits on the pavement with a painful face and rubs her knee.

The questionnaire

The subjects were first asked to report the content of the videotape; afterwards to describe the persons and their actions, and to estimate the duration of the videotape. The next items were crucial for this investigation: They referred to the fall of the person who left the booth: Was there a connection between the fall and the behavior of another person? (Item "connection"). Was another person particularly to blame for causing the fall? (Item "cause"). Finally the subjects were asked to imagine being a witness in the case of an insurance claim by the injured person (Item "witness"). Here the crucial question concerned the physical contact between the two persons involved. The subjects also had to draw in the position of all persons on a ground plan.

Experimental design

Four different factors were manipulated to investigate their influence on the perception of causation in the social domain: (a) The mental state of the waiting person (neutral vs. angry toward the woman in the telephone booth); (b) the presentation of only visual versus visual plus acoustic information (film with or without sound); (c) the time elapsed between observation and interrogation (immediately vs. some days later); and (d) whether the consequences of the fall (hurting her knee) were presented or not. The sample of subjects was divided into 10 groups, each containing 10 or 11 members. Subjects in Groups 1-5 saw the "neutral version" of the film; those in Groups 6-10 the "angry version". Subjects in Groups 1, 2, 3, 6, 7, and 8 saw the film with sound; those in Groups 4, 5, 9, and 10 without sound. Subjects in Groups 1, 2, 4, 6, 7, and 9 were interrogated immediately; those in Groups 3, 5, 8, and 10 were interrogated some days later. The consequences of the fall were presented to subjects in Groups 2 and 7, while they were left out for other groups (see Table 1 for an overview of the experimental design).

Table 1: Experimental Design.

Group	Number of Ss	Mental state	Sound	Interrogation	Consequences
1	10	neutral	with	immediate	no
2	10	neutral	with	immediate	yes
3	10	neutral	with	delayed	no
4	10	neutral	without	immediate	no
5	11	neutral	without	delayed	no
6	10	angry	with	immediate	no
7	10	angry	with	immediate	yes
8	11	angry	with	delayed	no
9	10	angry	without	immediate	no
10	10	angry	without	delayed	no

Procedure

The whole experiment lasted about 30 minutes. It was introduced to the subjects as an experiment on perception. Groups of two to four subjects saw the videotape together.

Following the presentation, one-half of the subjects answered the questionnaire immediately, the other half were interrogated a few days later (mean 4.3 days, range 2 to 7 days).

Results

Details and errors in subjects reports

Concerning the mode of reporting, it was found that free reports were less complete ($t(102)=-3.9, p<.001$) but also less erroneous ($t(102)=-11.06, p<.001$), than answers to specific questions. In their free reports on the contents of the videotape, subjects who were interrogated at once (Groups 1, 2, 4, 6, 7, 9) did not differ from the subjects who were interrogated later (Groups 3, 5, 8, 10) in the mean number of given details. However, subjects in groups with delayed interrogation made significantly more errors ($t(102)=2.36$, $p<.02$). Furthermore, they were less able to give specific descriptions of the persons in the videotape than subjects interrogated without delay ($t(102)=-4.45, p<.001$).

Subjects in Groups 1-5, who saw the waiting person acting in a neutral state, and subjects in Groups 6-10, who saw the waiting person acting in an angry mood, did not differ in the number of details remembered or in the number of errors.

In all groups, the duration of the videotape was very much overestimated. While it actually lasted about 73 s (for all groups except Groups 2 and 7) or 80 s (Groups 2 and 7), the mean estimation of the duration across all subjects was 244 s, with a standard deviation of 100.3 s.

Reported causes of the fall

In the free reports, no subject mentioned a cause for the fall. When asked whether there was a *relation* between the fall and the behavior of another person, 34 subjects (33.3% of all subjects) were affirmative, of whom 15 (14.7%) asserted and 19 (18.6%) assumed this connection, whereas 35 subjects (34.3%) answered in the negative. Thirteen subjects (12.8%) said that another person wanted to help, the rest (20 subjects) did not express themselves. When asked whether another person had *caused* the fall, 34 subjects (33.3%) were affirmative, of whom 13 subjects (12.8%) asserted, and 21 subjects (20.5%) assumed this connection, whereas 57 subjects (55.9%) answered in the negative. The rest (11) did not express themselves.

Under the instruction to imagine being a *witness* for an insurance claim, 32 subjects (31.4%) affirmed the physical contact, of whom 19 (18.6%) asserted and 13 (12.8%) assumed the physical contact; 6 (5.9%) reported a contact as an attempt to help; whereas 44 (43.1%) denied any contact between persons (see Table 2).

Subjects were highly consistent in answering the items on the cause of fall, tending to be more consistent when interrogated later than when interrogated at once.

For each item, it was tested whether the groups differed in the reported causes of the fall, that is, could these differences be attributed to the mental state of the waiting women: neutral (Groups 1-5) versus angry (Groups 6-10); to the kind of information: visual (Groups 4, 5, 9, 10) versus visual plus acoustic (Groups 1-3, 6-8); to the time elapsed between observation and interrogation: immediately (Groups 1, 2, 4, 6, 7, 9) versus delayed (Groups

3, 5, 8, 10); and to the presentation of the consequences of the videotape: depicted (Groups 2, 7) versus not depicted (Groups 1, 3-6, 8-10).

Table 2: Reported Causes of the Fall.

Item "connection": Was there a connection between the fall and the behavior of another person? Item "cause": Was particulary another person to blame for causing the fall? Item "witness": Did you see any physical contact between the two persons involved?

Item	Kind of answer (percentage of Ss)				
	affirmative		negative	attempt to help	no opinion
	asserted	assumed			
connection	14.7	33.3 / 18.6	34.3	12.8	19.6
cause	12.8	33.3 / 20.5	55.9	-	10.8
witness	18.6	31.4 / 12.8	43.1	5.9	19.6

With regard to the relation between the fall and the behavior of another person, no differences between groups were found. However, in items on the causes of the fall and physical contact between the persons in the videotape, more subjects with only visual information tended to be affirmative compared to subjects with visual and acoustic information.

Discussion

The general results on the details and the kinds of error in the subjects' reports fit well into the relevant literature on eyewitness memory. That is, (a) free reports are usually less complete but less erroneous than questionnaires; (b) witnesses usually remember more details when interrogated immediately than after a delay; (c) a postponed interrogation yields more errors; and (d) the duration of an observed sequence of events is usually overestimated.

The following results refer to the main topic of this study, namely, the characteristics of eyewitness perception. The results concerning the attributed causes of the fall show that about one third of all subjects "see" a connection to the behavior of a person nearby. Moreover, these subjects affirm that the bystander caused the fall. When imagining to give evidence as a witness, they affirm that the falling woman had been touched by the bystander. That is, although it is actually not possible to see a physical contact between the persons, such a contact is reported by about one third of the subjects. They even report a causal relation between the fall and the behavior of another person.

Therefore, many subjects seem to be influenced by their "observation" of a causal relation, which physically did not exist. It can be concluded that this effect takes place while subjects are perceiving the scene, for the result is independent from additional information that would fit into a plausible causal schema, namely, that the waiting person is angry. Apparently, subjects do not reconstruct the scene according to a naive frustration-aggression hypothesis, expecting an aggressive act from the side of an angry person. This is also supported by the differences between the groups with only visual versus with visual plus acoustic information. Subjects hearing the angry complaints of the waiting woman tend to report that she is to blame for the fall even less often than those subjects who only view the scene. Furthermore, the results are independent from memory effects (e.g., elaboration), because it does not matter whether subjects are interrogated at once or some days later.

In summary, this indicates that subjects who report a causal relation directly perceive this "phenomenal causality" in the same way as in Michotte's experiments. There is no cognitive judgment involved, because neither additional information fitting into a "physical assault script", nor a longer time delay allowing for elaboration, influence the probability of a causal relation being reported. Neither conscious nor memory processes need to be involved.

Therefore, even eyewitnesses striving to give a correct report may fall into this trap. As a consequence of these results, "implicit schemata" as well as "phenomenal causality" should be taken into account when judging the veracity of eyewitness reports. It is important that these distortions are not observed in free reports. Thus, free reports are more correct not only concerning details but also concerning the conception of the event as an unity. Further research should investigate the special conditions that promote the perception of "phenomenal causality", and the question why only a certain portion of the observers perceive this "phenomenal causality".

References

Allport, G.W., & Postman, L.J. (1958). The basic psychology of rumor. In E.E. Maccoby, Th.M. Newcomb, & E.L. Hartley (Eds.), *Readings in social psychology* (pp. 54-65). New York: Holt, Rinehart, & Winston.

Bassili, J.N. (1976). Temporal and spatial contingencies in the perception of social events. *Journal of Personality and Social Psychology, 33*, 680-685.

Brown, P.L., & Jenkins, H.M. (1968). Auto-shaping of the pigeon's key-peck. *Journal of the Experimental Analysis of Behavior, 11*, 1-8.

Bruce, V., & Green, P.R. (1985). *Visual perception: Physiology, psychology and ecology.* London: Lawrence Erlbaum.

Catania, A.C., & Cutts, D. (1963). Experimental control of superstitious responding in humans. *Journal of the Experimental Analysis of Behavior, 6*, 203-208.

Dahmen, K. (1988). Von der Wahrnehmung zum Handeln. Verhaltenskontrolle durch "Affordances". *Gestalt Theory, 10*, 35-45.

Gibson, J.J. (1979). *The ecological approach to visual perception.* Boston: Houghton Mifflin.

Hastorf, A.H., & Cantril, H. (1954). They saw a game: A case study. *Journal of Abnormal and Social Psychology, 49*, 129-134.

Loftus, E.F., & Ketcham, K. (1983). The malleability of eyewitness accounts. In S.M.A. Lloyd-Bostock, & B.R. Clifford (Eds.), *Evaluating witness evidence* (pp. 159-172). Chichester: Wiley.

Michotte, A. (1963). *The perception of causality*. London: Methuen. (Original work published in 1946).

Skinner, B.F. (1948). "Superstition" in the pigeon. *Journal of Experimental Psychology, 38*, 168 - 172.

Yela, M. (1952). Phenomenal causation at a distance. *The Quarterly Journal of Experimental Psychology, 4*, 139-154.

Deception Detection and Reality Monitoring: A New Answer to an Old Question?

María L. Alonso-Quecuty

Research into lie detection can be grouped under three general headings: (a) The study of physiological changes that coexist with lying; (b) behavioral research into body changes, movements, facial expressions, tone of voice, pauses, and so forth; and (c) the analysis of verbal content that examines the semantic and stylistic changes associated with lying (length of the statement, content, etc.; see Yuille, 1988).

The study of the physiological changes produced by lying has, as a common denominator, the use of the polygraph. However, detection errors (false-positive error) have brought into question the convenience of its usage (see Wrightsman, 1987, for a summary).

On the other hand, behavioral research into behavioral changes and language prosody occasionally presents contradictory results. This is the case with two variables of great interest: the number of pauses and the length of the statement. While some authors (Harrison, Halek, Raney, & Fritz, 1978) maintain that the length of false statements is greater than that of true ones, others (Kraut, 1976) have obtained the opposite result. In our opinion, a factor that might affect these variables is the amount of time between the perception of the criminal act and the taking of the statement. The study of this modulating effect of time on false statements is one of the objectives of this work.

Within the third research area (semantic and stylistic analysis of the statements), the works of Undeutsch (1982, 1984, 1988), which focus on the production of a system for the evaluation of the credibility of witnesses and their testimonies (Statement Reality Analysis), stand out. Moreover, in recent years, a new method of analysis has appeared, based on the differentiation between perceived and imagined reality (Johnson & Raye, 1981). According to these authors, it is possible to distinguish between perceived memories (generated externally) and imagined memories (generated internally). Those which are the result of perception include more contextual information (spatial and temporal) and more sensory details. On the other hand, imagined memories are the result of mental and imaginative processes and, therefore, they will include subjective idiosyncratic information.

Schooler, Garhard, and Loftus (1986) have performed an interesting study in which qualitative differences were found between suggested memories (post-event) and real memories: Individuals used more words in the description of suggested memories, they used more expressions of doubt and they mentioned more cognitive processes; besides, they mentioned fewer sensory attributes of the suggested object (Stop). As can be seen, it is possible to establish a parallelism between suggested and imagined memories, and between nonsuggested memories and reality.

Intuitively, it also seems correct to establish a new parallelism between imagined memories and lies, as well as between perceived memories and truth. But, is it possible to identify imagined memories and lies? The other objective of this research study is to answer this question.

Thus, our study focused on two goals:

1. To analyse the modulating effect that the time elapsed between the perception of the criminal act and the taking of the statement could have over two variables traditionally studied in lie detection (i.e., number of pauses, length of the statement).

2. To verify whether the dichotomy, memories of internal versus external origin established by Johnson and Raye (1981) is valid for the differentiation between true and false testimonies. Likewise, we have tried to study to what extent efficiency would be affected by the delay in the taking of the statement.

Method

Subjects

Twenty-two undergraduate students of psychology at the University of La Laguna (11 females and 11 males) participated voluntarily in the experiment.

Material and apparatus

Materials were a videotaped sequence of approximately three minutes duration in which a criminal act was presented from beginning to end, and which could be fully understand in the absence of the context of the film. The sequence was taken from the American series, Hill Street Blues. The sequence begins with a demonstration against abortion in front of an abortion clinic. One of the demonstrators attempts to attack a doctor from the clinic. By mistake, a young pregnant woman is hit. The sequence ends when the aggressor apologises to the victim while he is being arrested. Two further cassettes were used to record true and false statements. There was also a protocol for the transcriptions of the tapes and a protocol of the evaluation of the dependent variables by the judges.

Design

A 2x2 factorial design with the following variables was manipulated:

Independent variables. 1) The value of truth of the subjects' statement; this variable had two levels: true and false. 2) The time of preparation of the statements; this variable had two levels: immediate and delayed.

Dependent variables. 1) Length of the statements (number of words). 2) Number of detected pauses in the statements. 3) Analysis of the contents of the true and false versions: detection of the presence versus absence of the categories proposed by Johnson and Raye (1981).

Controlled variables. 1) Sex of the subjects: 50% females and 50% males. 2) Order of request for the true and false statements: in 50% of the cases the true version was requested first followed by the false version. In the other 50%, the order was reversed.

Procedure

The sample was divided into two groups making sure that the proportion of both sexes was the same.

Subjects in Group 1, having seen the film, made a statement of what they had really seen. Having finished the first statement, they had to retell the facts, but, on this occasion, changing them in such a way that the aggressor was acquitted.

They were not allowed time to elaborate upon this false version, which they had to produce immediately. Half of the subjects were asked to give both their statements in this order (true-false), and the other half in the opposite order (false-true).

Subjects in Group 2 received the same treatment, but, in this case, they were allowed about 10 minutes to prepare their false statement.

Our hypotheses were as follows: (1) The detection of deception, by means of the traditional variables of the number of pauses and the length of the statement, would be facilitated by the delay in the taking of the statement. Only where the delayed statements were concerned would the false versions show a greater length and a greater number of pauses than the true versions. (2) The detection of deception by means of the distinction between imagined reality versus perceived reality would be impaired by the delay in the taking of the statement. Only in the immediate statements would the true versions have more sensory and contextual information and less subjective idiosyncratic information than the false versions.

Results

First, the length of each statement (number of words) and the number of nonprosodic pauses it contained were measured. Later, two expert judges carried out a content analysis of the statements of each individual with the aim of detecting the presence/absence of elements from the categories proposed by Johnson and Raye (sensory, contextual and idiosyncratic information). In the analyses, the only observations taken into account were those on which the judges reached an agreement.

Then, we calculated the mean value in the five dependent variables for each one of the four experimental groups (immediate true statement, immediate false, delayed true and delayed false; see Table 1).

The tendency is opposite according to which of the following are used: either the variables number of words and number of pauses, or the categories proposed by Johnson and Raye. Thus, in the immediate statements, the number of pauses and the length of the statement seemed to be good lie detectors. On the other hand, in the delayed statements, the detection of deception was facilitated by the hypotheses of Johnson and Raye: There was more sensory and contextual information in the true versions and more subjective idiosyncratic information in the false versions.

The results for the five dependent variables were analysed separately. For both length of statement and number of pauses, the interaction Type of statement x True was significant, $F(1,36) = 9.82, p < .01$ and $F(1,36) = 7.02, p < .05$, respectively. In both cases, the false version had more words/pauses then the true one but only in the delayed statement. In of deception was facilitated by the hypotheses of Johnson and Raye: There was more sensory and contextual information in the true versions and more subjective idiosyncratic information in the false versions.

The results for the five dependent variables were analysed separately. For both length of statement and number of pauses, the interaction Type of statement x True was significant, $F(1,36)=9.82, p<.01$ and $F(1,36)=7.02, p<.05$, respectively. In both cases, the false version had more words/pauses then the true one but only in the delayed statement. In the immediate statement, the greatest number of words/pauses corresponded to the true version.

Table 1: Mean Value for Each Type of Statement in Each One of the Dependent Variables (*=Follows the Expected Tendency).

Type of statement	Value of truth	Number of words	Number of pauses	Sensorial	Contextual	Idiosyn-cratic
Immediate	true	64.88	6.11	1.22*	4.00*	0.22
	false	55.11	4.88	0.33	2.22	2.44*
Delayed	true	112.77	5.00	0.55	5.88	1.22
	false	139.55*	7.00*	1.33	7.00	1.44*

For sensory information, a new interaction Type of statement x True was significant, $F(1,36)=17.36, p<.01$, and the same happened with the contextual information, $F(1,36)=14.12, p<.01$. In both cases, the true version had more sensory/contextual information than the false one but only in the inmediate statement. When the statement was delayed, the greatest sensory/contextual information corresponded to the false version.

Finally, when the idiosyncratic information was used as dependent variable, this interaction was nonsignificant, $F(1,36)=0.08$. In this case, only the main effect of Type of statement was significant, $F(1,36)=22.30, p<.01$. The delayed statement had more idiosyncratic information than the immediate one.

Lastly, a main effect of true was not found.

Discussion

Our results agree with those obtained by Harrison et al. (1978), as the extent of the false statements is greater than that of the true ones. Likewise, Yerkes and Berry's (1909) classical hypothesis that "pauses are associated with lying" is confirmed. The number of pauses is also greater in the false statements than in the true ones. However, and here the new development of this study is found, this only happens in the delayed statements and not in those taken immediately after the video sequence was watched. This difference may be due to the fact that, with the passing of time, the individual creates a very rich mental setting, which is reflected in a greater length of statement. However, lying implies that there is a parallel process amounting to a double discourse, the true and the false, with the subsequent cognitive cost. It follows that there are a greater number of pauses

The significant interactions found between both types of statement (immediate and delayed) confirm the trends observed in our data. The length of the statements may be a good detector of deception when the individual has disposed of the necessary time to elaborate them. Where the immediate statements are concerned, it might be better to make use of the categories proposed by Johnson and Raye.

Nevertheless we must not forget that a main effect of true was not found.

Our work is an exploratory study and should be considered as such. However, it is clear that the period of delay in the taking of the statement should not only be taken into account when considering the processes of memory. It also plays an important role in the study of lying.

References

Harrison A., Halek, M., Raney, D.F., & Fritz, J.G.(1978). Cues to deception in an interview situation. *Social Psychology, 4,* 156-161.

Johnson, M.K., & Raye, C.L. (1981). Reality monitoring. *Psychological Review, 88,* 67-85.

Kraut, R.E. (1976). *Verbal and nonverbal cues in the perception on lying.* Paper presented at the annual meeting of the American Psychological Association.

Schooler, J.W., Garhard, D., & Loftus, E.F. (1986). Qualities of the unreal. *Journal of Experimental Psychology: Learning, Memory and Cognition, 12,* 171-181.

Undeutsch, U. (1982). Statement reality analysis. In A. Trankell (Ed.), *Reconstructing the past* (pp. 27-56). Deventer, NL: Kluwer.

Undeutsch, U. (1984). Courtroom evaluation of eyewitness testimony. *International Review of Applied Psychology, 33,* 51-67.

Undeutsch, U. (1988). The development of statement reality analysis. In J.C. Yuille (Ed.), *Credibility assessment* (pp. 101-120). London: Kluwer Academic Publishers.

Wrightsman, L.S. (1987). *Psychology and legal system.* Pacific Grove, CA: Brooks Cole Publishing Co.

Yerkes, P.M., & Berry, C.S. (1909). The association reaction time method of mental diagnosis. *American Journal of Psychology, 20,* 22-37.

Yuille, J.C. (1988). *Credibility assessment.* London: Kluwer Academic Publishers.

Part VI
Children as Witnesses and Victims in the Justice System

The Truth in Content Analyses of a Child's Testimony

Debra A. Bekerian and John L. Dennett

This paper will discuss a general class of psychological assessment procedures that are used to determine the validity/reliability of evidence given by child witness. This class of procedures has been most vigorously discussed in the context of child abuse cases. However, the general arguments advanced could be applied to any cases where a child is giving evidential fact.

Assessment procedures require a number of stages and rely on information from a variety of sources, e.g., child's testimony, forensic evidence, socio-economic status, family history, etc. On the basis of all available information, an informed decision is given as to the likelihood that the allegations are true. Depending upon the legal system in question, assessment may take the form of expert opinion.

The scope of this paper extends only one source of information used in assessment procedures: the analysis of the information contained in the child's account. For the present purposes, we will describe the procedure through which a child's testimony is analysed as content analyses. Of necessity, we will only provide a schematic version of content analyses, bearing in mind that many versions have been proposed.

The basic working hypothesis of all versions of content assessment is that truthful accounts will differ in fundamental, consistent and observable ways from those accounts in which confabulated information is included (see Trankell, 1972; Undeutsch, 1982; see also Köhnken, 1989a,b; Raskin & Steller, 1989; Raskin & Yuille, 1989; Yuille 1988). Specific criteria are used to assess features of truth. Each version of content analyses has its own idiosyncrasies. However, there would appear to be criteria that are regularly used in most versions. These are included in the following (see next page). It should be remembered, however, that there are variants associated with each particular approach to content analysis.[1]

It is important to point out that these criteria are meant to be discriminators of truthful accounts. That is, it is assumed that a truthful account will be more likely to contain features corresponding to these criteria. So, for example, an account that is truthful will be more likely to be reproduced in an unstructured manner (e.g., criterion 2) and/or have comments that indicate the child's uncertainty in his/her account (e.g., criteria 14-16).

---

[1] For example, Undeutsch (1982) includes Trankell's "Bilateral Emotion Criteria" which is not immediately obvious in other versions of content analyses.

General characteristic.	1.	Logical structure
	2.	Unstructured production
	3.	Quantity of details
Specific contents.	4.	Contextual embedding
	5.	Descriptions of interactions
	6.	Reproduction of conversation
	7.	Unexpected complications
Peculiarities of content.	8.	Unusual details
	9.	Superfluous details
	10.	Accurately reported details not understood
	11.	Related external associations
	12.	Accounts of subjective mental states
	13.	Attribution of perpetrator's mental state
Motivation-related content.	14.	Spontaneous corrections
	15.	Admitting lack of memory
	16.	Raising doubts about one's own testimony
	17.	Self-deprecation
	18.	Pardoning the perpetrator
Offence-specific elements.	19.	Details characteristic of the offence

Before going further, a few points will be clarified. They concern a) definitions of truth; b) issues of measurement; c) limitations of the techniques and d) validation of the techniques. First let us consider the definition of truth. It would appear that there are a number of ways in which proponents define truth in the context of content analysis. There is the definition that relies on a distinction between real memories vs. imagined ones (e.g., Raskin & Steller, 1989; Raskin & Yuille, 1989). Another definition relies on the difference between intentions to tell the truth and intentions to deceive (e.g., Köhnken, 1989a; Undeutsch, 1982.). A third definition relies on the difference between accounts that contain accurate information vs. those that contains errors (Köhnken, 1989a; Undeutsch, 1982).

Of course, these definitions are not mutually exclusive. However, it would seem that most agree on a definition of truth or validity where congruence with a real event is stressed, e.g., accuracy. Errors, either resulting from intentional or unintentional factors, are associated with false/fictitious statements. This seems to suggest that false accounts produced by spontaneous, unintentional misremembering will be similar to those produced when the child intents to deceive. This suggestion needs further and close examination.

Next let us turn to issues of measurement or scaling. How does content analysis assess a child's account? The more recent attempts at content analyses have provided some information to this end. Criteria may be judged on a present/absent basis; or the statement can be rated in terms of the strength extent to which criteria are met (e.g., Köhnken, 1989b; Raskin & Steller, 1989; Raskin & Yuille, 1989; Yuille, 1988). At this time, there are no specific rules about the number of criteria that need to be met in order for a statement to be considered as valid. Nor would there appear, as yet, to be any criteria that are uniformly weighted as more important than others, although there is some suggestion that accounts must be logical and unstructured before a conclusion of validity is reached (Yuille, 1988, 1990). Also, most proponents are careful to point out that measurement reflects only a probabilistic assessment that the alleged event had been experienced, e.g., caution against using "quasi-objective measures or cut-off scores" (Raskin & Steller, 1989, p. 299). However, it must be remembered that the probabilistic assessment of content analyses, when used as expert evidence in the court-room, is taken as being an objective one in the sense that it is scientific and free from subjective bias.

Let us now discuss the limitations of the criteria. Most proponents would agree that content analyses can be applied only to statements that are extensive (i.e. complex events); and, that such things as age, education level, socio-demographic background and verbal competency will determine the appropriateness of certain criteria. Raskin and Yuille (1989) warn:

> Relatively simple events...described by a child who has well-developed cognitive abilities and access to sexual information or experience produce less definitive results than do complex descriptions by a young child who has limited experience with such matters. (p. 197)

Additionally, content analyses cannot be used if the child is not willing to disclose abuse. Further, and importantly for the present purposes, negative assessment does not equal deception. The absence of features corresponding to the criteria does not mean that the child's testimony is false (e.g., Yuille, 1988). This will be important later when specific content criteria are discussed.

Finally, let us consider the issue of validity. Is content analysis a reliable technique to index the truth? Most proponents argue that validation must come from different sources, including experimental and case/field studies (e.g., Yuille, 1988, p. 259), as well as data analyses such as multivariate statistics. For example, Undeutsch's particular version of content analyses "...has been submitted to unremitting scrutiny by trials courts since a quarter of a century" (1982, p. 49). We eagerly await any documentation of the evidence from the relevant legal cases in question.

Experimental evidence from the psychological literature seems to show systematic differences between truthful and confabulated accounts (e.g., Johnson, 1988; Schooler, Clark, & Loftus, 1987; Schooler, Gerhard, & Loftus, 1986). The actual details of the Schooler et al. findings are interesting. Schooler et al. compared recall from individuals who had actually seen various details in the original event with recall from people who had been exposed to the details only through verbal, post-event information. The findings were that people who only received post-event information were less detailed in their accounts. Such findings would seem to support the notion that details will be present in accounts based on real perceptual experience (criterion 3). However, Schooler et al. make a comparison between individuals who perceptually *experienced* the details and those who *experienced the details in a verbal form*. Those individuals receiving post-event information can, in no way, be argued to have imagined the details.

Thus, it is unclear as to the relevance of the Schooler et al. findings to issues of distinctions between real and confabulated memories. The data are more useful in helping to clarify differences between real and suggested memories, e.g., a child being primed to accuse an adult falsely.

The data reported by Johnson (e.g., 1988) on reality monitoring would seem more pertinent to the distinction between real and imagined events. Individuals are asked to imagine events. Later they are asked to recall these imagined events. When compared with the recall of actually experienced events, the recall of imagined events contains less detail, supporting the contention that real and imagined events are distinguishable by virtue of the number of features included in the accounts (e.g., criterion 3). However, it should be pointed out that Johnson (1988) remarks that the mode of recall may be an important factor: the differences between real and imagined memories are different depending upon whether the individual writing his/her account, or speaking it. Therefore, although the Johnson (1988) findings do support the notion of distinctive characteristics of memory for real and imagined events, the reliability of such differences would seem to be sensitive to pragmatic and communicative conventions.

Recent unpublished reports by Yuille (1990), of both field and experimental studies, suggest that the presence of criteria in accounts is in complete accordance with the child giving a truthful account. That is in all cases either where the child was thought to be telling the truth (e.g., through independent evidence such as confessions or physical evidence) or where the child was known to be telling the truth (e.g., experimental studies), the evaluation through content analysis was 100% reliable. Unfortunately, the details of these cases/empirical findings (e.g., details of the sexual abuse; nature of instructions) are not available for examination.

Let us summarise. Proponents of content analyses suggest that truthful accounts can be differentiated from untruthful accounts through the presence or absence of specific features. Untruthful accounts are those that are misremembered, either intentionally or unintentionally. Truthful accounts are typically associated with the presence of certain features, although their absence cannot be taken as an indication of deception. Proponents claim that the criteria are valid and reliable, although the support for such a claim would appear to be largely anecdotal, or in preperation. Most proponents suggest that the technique will be sensitive to certain variables, e.g., age/mental competency of child, type of incident.

In the absence of any documentation, comments on content analyses must be restricted to theoretical concerns. To this end, we will attempt to discuss content analyses at two levels. One will concern the meta-theoretical assumptions made by the general class of techniques. The second will attempt to discuss a few of the specific criteria, focusing on compelling theoretical reasons for anticipating their absence in otherwise truthful accounts. It seems equally important to understand and explain when the criteria may not be expected to occur in a truthful account, although the Yuille (1990) data seem to suggest that this will never be the case. Nonetheless, if one attempts to define these limiting conditions, one may be in a stronger position to argue for the relative appropriateness of specific criteria.

Three meta-theoretical assumptions seem to be held by all examples of content analyses. The first concerns the assumption about reality and the objective description of it. Most proponents make the implicit assumption that one can translate "real" entities into language which, in turn, has objective status, i.e., is right or wrong. So, for example, it is assumed, that details of a real event (e.g., a man) can be represented in language (e.g., by the child recalling "a man"), objectively identified as such (e.g., by the interviewer) and then counted as though one were counting the actual perceptual entities themselves. Proponents of content assessment must hold this assumption, given, for example the emphasis placed on the presence or absence of details in an account (see criterion 3). One first has to decide what constitutes a detail in the real world, before one can identify it in an account. This decision of reality is meant to be objective.

However, it is worthwhile to consider why such a decision might not be objective. Each investigator must decide what s/he considers to be a detail and how this detail gets manifested in an account. Seemingly objective decisions about real details are as subjective as any other measure (e.g., Murphy & Medin, 1985). In fact, Edwards and Middleton (1986a, 1986b) argue that consensual agreement between raters about details reflects more about the processes of social interaction than it does about the representation of real events into language. According to this argument, content analysis cannot represent itself as an objective index of reality.

The second assumption concerns the nature of memory representations. Most of the work on memory uses, as its general framework, a spatio-temporal metaphor: things get "put" into memory (see Hinton & Anderson, 1981, for a discussion of the spatio-temporal metaphor). Remembering, in turn, requires the reading out or accessing of this information from its spatio-temporal store. Following this logic, quantitative measurements, such as the number of details in an account, will reflect the number of details in memory. If one can motivate the child to tell the truth, "...the accurate recounting of essential details requires only very low cognitive abilities on the part of the victim. " (Undeutsch, 1990, pp. 33/34). The belief that memory is a relatively stable store, from which information need only be accessed, would appear to underlie most versions of content analyses.

However, it has been recently argued by a number of researchers working in such diverse areas as artificial intelligence (e.g., Gammack, 1988; Hinton & Anderson, 1981), human memory (e.g., Barsalou, 1988; Bekerian & Dennett, 1990; Dritschel, 1990; Edwards & Middleton, 1986b), concept learning (e.g., Murphy & Medin, 1985) and social cognition (e.g., Potter & Weatherhall, 1987) that knowledge is constructed for the particular goals of the situation. This general alternative approach stresses that each recollection will be vulnerable to many factors occurring at the time the recollection is requested. Following this argument, quantitative measures (e.g., counting the number of details in an account) do not give one an indication of what is in memory. Instead, they provide only one index of the factors that were directing the person's account at that particular interview (see, for example, Bekerian & Dennett, 1990).

Finally, there is the assumption about the relationship between knowledge and language. Most proponents generally assume that language reflects knowledge, in some systematic way. That is, the assumption is that the characteristics of the account are, in some way, isomorphic to characteristics of the memory representation. Proponents of content analysis must make this assumption, given that they argue, for example, that logical consistencies in an account (the language) represent logical consistencies in memory; or, that statements connoting uncertainty (e.g., "I think") reflect the information's meta-memorial status.

The immediate challenge to this assumption is that the child giving an account (i.e., its language) is subject to constraints beyond those imposed by individual cognitive operations. For example, when someone uses the phrase "I think", this does not necessarily mean that s/he is always referring to some meta-memorial belief. This general argument is further supported by research that has shown how many memory phenomena are sensitive to such things as pragmatic conventions, modes of reporting and other features of the socio-linguistic environment (e.g., Bekerian & Dennett, 1990; Edwards & Middleton, 1986a, 1986b; Tannen, 1982). Thus, one can challenge the assumption that the presence of criteria in an account (as depicted by the language) reflects characteristics of memory or knowledge.

These comments attempt to draw attention to meta-theoretical assumptions made by proponents of content analysis about the nature of reality, memory and the relationship between language and memory. Each of these assumptions have been challenged. The opposing arguments have been convincingly made across not only different methodologies, but also different fields of science. There must be rigorous debate about the appropriateness of the meta-theoretical assumptions underlying the approach.

Now let us turn to a few of the specific criteria. Again the intention is here to discover whether there are any theoretically motivated reasons for suggesting the absence of some criteria in otherwise truthful accounts. This should help further define the conditions under which criteria from content analyses might be most appropriately applied.[2]

The first criterion considered is that of unstructured productions. It is assumed that unstructured accounts are more likely to be based on real experiences. As suggested by Yuille (1990), "...Real memories have a spontaneous character to them... each time...it's a little different...it might come out in a slightly different order...". In contrast, accounts based on confabulated events are likely to be structured and lacking in detail, if one believes that only schematic information will be available (see, for example, Bekerian & Conway, 1988; Johnson-Laird, 1983; Schank 1982; Schank & Abelson, 1977).

Raskin and Yuille (1989) suggest that this general criterion will not apply when the event in question is simple or short. We would like to suggest another factor that may conditionalise the use of the criterion further. This factor is frequency of experience with an event. Experimental findings as well as case studies of memory for repeated or frequently occurring events suggest that people produce very schematic or structured accounts, in some circumstances.

In the adult literature, Neisser (1981) makes note that frequent events may be recounted in a merged fashion, sampling across otherwise different events. Neisser referred to this as "repisodic memory" and suggested how these processes were operating in John Dean's testimony about conversations held with the then President of the United States, Richard Nixon. Dritschel (1990) also reports that common every day activities which are ritualised and occur frequently will be described in a highly schematic, structured manner, depending upon the pragmatics at the time. Thus, adults sometimes produce very structured accounts, either when they believe they are telling the truth (e.g., John Dean) or when they are known to be telling the truth (Dritschel, 1990; see also Brewer, 1988; Linton, 1986; Pillemer, Rhinehart, & White, 1986).

Studies of children's memory for autobiographical events suggest similar processes. Data from Hudson (1986) suggest that frequency of experience can result in more complete,

---

[2] The criteria of unusual and superfluous details (criteria 8 and 9) also prove somewhat problematic, in that both would seem to require decisions as to what the event is, in the first instance, before one can make decisions about unusualness or superfluousness. Given that the child's testimony may be the only evidence pertaining to the event, it is difficult to see how one could establish, a priori, the nature of the event, so as to then make subsequent decisions about the status of details, e.g., unusualness.

but less accurate recall: Pre-school children were reported to merge individual episodes, becoming confused about special details. Nelson (1988) summarises data that suggest that frequent experiences with an event lead to more general or schematic accounts seemingly irrespective of the nature of the questioning (e.g., whether the child is asked about a specific event or a general event). Nelson (1988) suggests that these findings show how children construct repisodic memories when events are more frequent, and how frequency can lead to schematic accounts. Therefore, there are reasons for expecting that frequently experienced events (even complex ones) will be recounted by children in a rather structured manner under certain circumstances.

The criterion of unstructured production can thus be argued to be non-evaluative under circumstances of short/simple events (Raskin & Yuille, 1989) and frequently experienced events. What seems necessary is to pursue this line of investigation further, both experimentally as well as through case studies. For example, it would be expected that the mood of the person will be another powerful factor in producing schematic accounts. Williams and Broadbent (1986; see also Williams & Dritschel, 1989) report that extreme feelings of hopelessness/depression seem to be associated with impoverished, rigid accounts of autobiographical memories. This suggests that negative mood at the time of recollection will increase the likelihood of repeated events being recounted in a structured fashion.

The criterion of quantity of details has also been suggested as being inconclusive for accounts of simple/short events (e.g., Raskin & Yuille, 1989). Another limiting factor that should be considered with respect to this criterion will be the pragmatics of the conversation, and remembering. One can anticipate that otherwise enriched events will be recounted with little detail, depending upon the pragmatics of the interview. This is due to the effects of communicative rules or maxims, which govern why, how, how much and when people include information in their account. Such maxims enable the process of communication to proceed more smoothly and be cooperative (c.f., Grice, 1975). Application of Gricean maxims to memory for visual and verbal narratives has shown that speakers will sometimes omit quite essential details, if they think the interviewer is already aware of the details (i.e., the Maxim of Quantity - don't give more than is necessary) and/or if the question directs them accordingly (i.e., the Maxim of Relevance - don't give what isn't asked for)(e.g., Bowers, 1986; Tannen, 1982).

Adherence to any conversational maxims certainly develops with age, so the concerns may be greater with older chidren. Nonetheless, the developmental literature suggests that children are capable of manipulating and responding to conversational interactions from a very early age (see Menig-Peterson, 1975; Sachs & Devin, 1976; Shatz, 1983). Therefore, the quantity of detail present in any child's account is as likely to be determined by the particular pragmatics operating at the time as by the real (or imagined) nature of the event being remembered. Content analyses procedures do acknowledge some effects of pragmatics, e.g., admonishing the use of leading questions. However, the inherently social nature of communication needs to be considered initially, as the criterion of quantity may be more an evaluator of the pragmatics of the interview, rather than of the truth of the memory being described.

Lastly, we will consider two criteria associated with the "motivation-related component" - the child's willingness to raise doubts about the accuracy or the completeness of his/her account. Raskin and Yuille (1989) suggest that

> ...admitting lack of memory or 'raising doubts about one's own testimony'...are unlikely in accounts that are fabricated... because they tend to be perceived by the speakers as...pointing out possible objections to [the testimony's] accuracy. (p. 199)

The authors' acknowledge that the age of the child will have something bearing on the extent to which s/he makes such comments. As suggested by Flavell (1971), part of the development of a child's memory system is an increased ability to assess his/her own memory performance. So, younger children may be less likely to make such comments than older children.

More interesting is Raskin and Yuille's (1989) suggestion that chidren who are lying will not wish to suggest doubt in their memory, since the listener may then infer dishonesty. It is unclear why the exact same arguments cannot and should not be applied to a child who is telling the truth. Evidential interviews, and disclosure of abuse, are associated with great costs. Given that a child has decided to tell the truth, s/he will be concerned that the listener believes that the account is true. Should the child think that comments indicating uncertainty are likely to jeopardise the listener's reactions, such comments may be avoided. Thus, motivation-related criteria may be as equally sparse in both truthful and fabricated accounts.

Let us summarise our arguments. We have suggested that content analysis, as a class of procedures, makes assumptions about the nature of reality, memory and the relationship between language and memory. We have provided reasons for challenging these meta-theoretical assumptions. We have also suggested that a few, important criteria used in content analyses will not be good evaluators of the truth, in all circumstances. We have provided theoretical arguments and psychological evidence to support these claims. It is certainly true that some versions of content analyses do conditionalise the use of specific criteria. However, other factors not previously considered would also seem to restrict the generalisation of criteria even further. We submit that content criteria will prove effective as discriminators of truth, only to the extent that they are regarded in light of detailed documentation of real evidential interviews and of empirical findings that are relevant to the issues. This general opinion would seem to be shared by all proponents. However, at this time, such documentation is not available. Consequently, we suggest that while assessment procedures have proven useful, the specific content criteria, themselves, cannot be uncritically accepted.

It must always be remembered that an evidential interview is a vehicle for communication. Communication is a social behaviour that is governed by an enormous number of factors. Without explicit and a priori identification of factors known to contribute to this social behaviour, any attempts at assessment may serve to camouflage the truth, rather than clarify it.

References

Barsalou, L. (1988). The content and organization of autobiographical memories. In U. Neisser, & E. Winograd (Eds.), *Remembering reconsidered* (pp. 244-276). Cambridge, UK: Cambridge University Press.

Bekerian, D.A., & Conway, M. (1988). Everyday contexts. In G. Davies, & D. Thomson (Eds.). *Memory in context; Context in memory* (pp. 305-318). Chichester: John Wiley & Sons.

Bekerian, D.A., & Dennett, J.L. (1990). Spoken and written recall in visual narratives. *Applied Cognitive Psychology, 4*, 175-187.
Bowers, J. (1986). Schema theory. Doctoral dissertation. University of Cambridge, England.
Brewer, W. (1988). Memory for randomly sampled autobiographical events. In U. Neisser, & E. Winograd (Eds.), *Remembering reconsidered* (pp. 21-90). Cambridge: Cambridge University Press.
Dritschel, B. (1990). *The role of autobiographical memory in describing common activities*. Manuscript submitted for publication.
Edwards, D., & Middleton, N. (1986a). Joint remembering: Constructing an account of shared experience through conversational discourse. *Discourse Processes, 9*, 423-459.
Edwards, D., & Middleton, N. (1986b). Text for memory: Joint recall with a scribe. *Human Learning, 5*, 125-138.
Flavell, J. (1971). What is memory the development of? *Human Development, 14*, 272-278.
Gammack, G.J. (1988). *Eliciting expert conceptual structure using psychological techniques*. Doctoral dissertation. University of Cambridge, England.
Grice, H. (1975). Logic and conversation. In P. Cole, & J. Morgan (Eds.), *Syntax and Semantics, vol. 3, Speech Acts* (pp. 1-20). New York: Academic Press.
Hinton, G., & Anderson, J. (Eds.) (1981). *Parallel models of associative memory*. Hillsdale, NJ: Lawrence Erlbaum.
Hudson, J. (1986). Memories are made of this. In K. Nelson (Ed.), *Event knowledge: Structure and function in development* (pp. 97-118). Hillsdale, NJ: Lawrence Erlbaum.
Johnson, M. (1988). Reality monitoring: An experimental phenomenological approach. *Journal of Experimental Psychology: General, 117*, 390-394.
Johnson-Laird, P.-N. (1983). *Mental models towards a cognitive science of language, inference, and consciousness*. Cambridge: Cambridge University Press.
Köhnken, G. (1989a). Behavioural correlates of statement credibility: Theories, paradigms, and results. In H. Wegener, F. Lösel, & J. Haisch (Eds.), *Criminal behaviour and the justice system; Psychological perspectives* (pp. 271-289). New York: Springer.
Köhnken, G. (1989b). *Psychological approaches to the assessment of the credibility of child witness statements*. Paper presented at the International Conference on Children's Evidence in Legal Proceedings. Cambridge, England.
Linton, D. (1986). Ways of searching and the contents of memory. In D. Rubin (Ed.), *Autobiographical memory* (pp. 50-70). Cambridge: Cambridge University Press.
Menig-Peterson, C. (1975). The modification of communicative behaviour in preschool-aged children as a function of the listener's perspective. *Child Development, 46*, 1015-1018.
Murphy, G., & Medin, D. (1985). The role of theories in conceptual coherence. *Psychology Review, 92*, 289-316.
Neisser, U. (1981). John Dean's memory: A case study. *Cognition, 9*, 1-22.
Nelson, K. (1988). The ontogeny of memory for real events. In U. Neisser, & E. Winograd (Eds.), *Remembering reconsidered* (pp. 277-282). New York: Cambridge University Press.
Pillemer, D., Rhinehart, E., & White, S. (1986). Memories of life transitions: The first year in college. *Human Learning, 5*, 109-123.
Potter, J., & Wheatherhall, M. (1987). *Discourse and social psychology: Beyond attitudes and behaviour*. Sage: London.
Raskin, D.C., & Steller, M. (1989). Assessing credibility of allegations of child sexual abuse: Polygraph examinations and statement analysis. In H. Wegener, F. Lösel, & J. Haisch (Eds.), *Criminal behaviour and the justice system: Psychological perspectives* (pp. 290-302). New York: Springer.
Raskin, D., & Yuille, J. (1989). Problems in evaluating interviews of children in sexual abuse cases. In S. Ceci, D. Ross, & M. Toglia (Eds.), *Perspectives on children's testimony* (pp. 184-207). New York: Springer.
Sachs, J., & Devin, J. (1976). Young children's use of appropriate speech styles in social interaction and role-playing. *Journal of Child Language, 3*, 81-98.
Schank, R. (1982). *Dynamic memory*. Cambridge: Cambridge University Press.

Schank, R., & Abelson, R. (1977). *Scripts, plans, goals and understanding; An inquiry into human knowledge structures*. Hillsdale, NJ: Erlbaum.

Schooler, J., Clark, C., & Loftus E. (1987). Knowing when memory is real. In M. Gruneberg, P. Morris, & R. Sykes (Eds.), *Practical aspects of memory: Current research and issues*, vol. 1 (pp. 83-88). Chichester: John Wiley & Sons.

Schooler, J., Gerhard, D., & Loftus, E. (1986). Qualities of the unreal. *Journal of Experimental Psychology: Learning, Memory and Cognition, 12*, 171-181.

Shatz, M. (1983). Communication. In P. Mussen (Ed.), *Handbook of Child Psychology, 3: Cognitive Development* (pp. 201-230). New York: John Wiley & Sons.

Tannen, D. (Ed.)(1982). *Spoken and written language: Exploring orality and literacy*. Norwood, NJ: Ablek.

Trankell, A. (1972). *Reliability of evidence*. Stockholm: Rotobeckmann AB.

Undeutsch, U. (1982). Statement reality analysis. In A. Trankell. (Ed.), *Reconstructing the past* (pp. 27-56). Stockholm: Norstedt & Soners.

Undeutsch, U. (1990). Conference at Leeds University, 12 January. *The testimony of a child*.

Williams, J.M., & Dritschel, B. (1989). *Categoric and extended autobiographical memories*. Manuscript submitted for publication.

Williams, J.M., & Broadbent, K. (1986). Autobiographical memory in attempted suicide patients. *Journal of Abnormal Psychology, 95*, 144-149.

Yuille, J. (1988). The systematic assessment of children's testimony. *Canadian Psychiatry, 29*, 247-262.

Yuille, J. (1990). Conference at Leeds University, 12 January. *The testimony of a child*.

The Credibility of Children as Witnesses and the Social Denial of the Incestuous Abuse of Children

Herman E.M. Baartman

Introduction

The answer to the question to what extent a child can be taken seriously as a witness in lawsuits is partly based on our daily experiences with children. Furthermore, we try to base the answer as much as possible on the results of developmental psychological research. However, complementary and mutually corrective experience and research by no means completely determine the answer. This becomes particularly clear in lawsuits where children are not just witnesses but both witness and victim at the same time. I am referring here to sexual abuse and, more specifically, incestuous sexual abuse. My thesis is that the extent to which one is prepared to take a child seriously as a witness in such matters is largely determined by the extent to which one considers the occurrence of incestuous abuse of young children in particular, boys as well as girls, to be a serious problem. The less seriously the problem is considered, the more negatively the competence of child witnesses will be assessed; the more the problem is considered, the more positively this competence will be assessed. In the former case, there is a risk of underestimating this competence; in the latter case, there is a risk of overestimating it. Whether or not the existence and seriousness of sexual abuse of children is taken seriously is to a large extent determined by the existence or absence of conceptual frameworks within which violence against children can be discussed and of social frameworks within which it can be dealt with. I will demonstrate this from three angles. The first is concerned with the significance that physicians have attached to venereal diseases among children in the past. The second involves the meaning attached by physicians to clearly visible injuries on young children, such as fractures of the bone and subcutaneous hemorrhages. Indeed, a venereal disease can be an indirect signal that a child has been sexually abused. And a broken arm or a bruise can indirectly indicate the physical mistreatment of the child. The third approach is concerned with direct signals: the direct story told by the child itself, that he or she has been sexually abused.

Venereal Diseases

Most publications on venereal diseases among children date from after 1860 (Taylor, 1985). A large number of these publications describe children with venereal diseases of, for instance, the genitalia, the mouth, or the anus, whose father, or (one or more) other relatives, suffered from a sexually transmitted disease as well. With reference to the literature of the late 19th and early 20th centuries, Taylor has analyzed 381 such cases. They did not concern congenital syphilis through intrauterine contagion but cases of acquired venereal disease. In only 40 out of these 381 cases (10%), did the doctor recognize the possibility that the child's venereal disease had been caused by sexual contact. It is remarkable that 26 of these cases were highlighted by the New York Society for the Prevention of Cruelty to Children, an organization that formed a social framework within which the possibility of sexual abuse of children could be recognized. In most cases, the child's venereal disease was ascribed to indirect contact, for example, via toilets, towels, drinking utensils, and shared bedclothes. Even if such a child shared a bed with a syphilitic older brother, the possibility of infection through direct sexual contact was usually not suggested. One of the best-known child psychiatric manuals of the early 20th century (Ziehen, 1917) speaks in 19 different instances of syphilis as a cause of mental disturbance among children. Nearly all these cases concern congenital syphilis. Acquired syphilis is mentioned only twice (pp. 23 and 186), and, in both cases, the book only refers to the wet nurse and the dry nurse as important potential sources of infection. When Scholz (1922) writes about acquired syphilis, he too points only to the possibility of a syphilitic wet nurse (pp. 23 and 222). This reminds one of the well-known stories about nursemaids and governesses seducing students placed in their care.

In 1909 the Swedish physician Welander described the transfer of gonorrhea and syphilis by parents to their children. It is only very rarely in our society that gonorrhea is passed on to young girls through sexual contact, he wrote. In an exceptional case, which involved a little boy, the nursemaid turned out to be the source of evil. In cases where both parents suffer from a sexually transmitted disease, it is, according to Welander, nearly always the mother who is the source of the child's infection because mothers have more physical contact with their children than fathers. For many decades, physicians confronted with a child suffering from a venereal disease hardly considered the possibility that the child was being sexually abused by an adult, although that abuse was taking place, as it were, in front of their very eyes. "Although they attributed identical symptoms among adults to sexual contact, they ascribed children's symptoms to some form of innocent contact" (Taylor, 1985, p. 439). Welander wrote, for instance, that syphilitic disorders occur mainly on the mucus of the mouth and the genitalia and are passed on from there to other people. It is, however, scarcely considered a possibility that this could also happen to children. On the one hand, the overestimation of innocent contact as a source of infection made it possible to treat venereal disease among children as a purely medical matter. Parents could go to a doctor with their sick children without risk of suspicion. If, nonetheless, the possibility of incestuous abuse had to be faced, as was the case in the Societies for the Prevention of Cruelty to Children, which existed in nearly all U.S. states at the end of the 19th century, then, on the other hand, the overestimation of innocent contact made it possible for a physician to relate incest to situations of filthiness and slovenliness in "overcrowded" households; in other words, to life on the fringes of society (Gordon, 1988; Taylor, 1985). In both cases, physicians were able to ignore the possibility of incestuous abuse within the bourgeoisie - of which they themselves were a part - with its Victorian common decency and its disdain toward the lower classes.

There are two possible explanations for this consistent and widespread denial. In the first place, there was no proper conceptual framework within which incestuous abuse could be recognized. The legal provisions with regard to rape in New York around 1880 may serve as an example. They speak only of female victims; the possibility of sexual abuse of boys is not mentioned at all in this conceptual framework (Taylor, 1985). Another example can be found in an article from 1880 written by the French physician Fournier (1880/1986). In his article, Fournier amplifies how incorrect it is to link venereal diseases or other disorders or injuries of the genitalia in children too easily to sexual abuse. Very often, these disorders develop spontaneously, he writes. In addition, he gives various examples that are meant to demonstrate that the injuries were deliberately caused by the child him- or herself or the mother in order to support false accusations of sexual abuse. At the time, Fournier was considered an outstanding authority on the subject of sexually transmitted diseases. This is why in 1889 the physician Bulkley, referring to Fournier, was able to write:

> In the light of our present knowledge of the disease and the frequency with which it is communicated innocently (. . .) we are no longer justified in regarding it as an accompaniment of vice or the scourge of those who have committed sexual errors. (Bulkley, cited in Taylor, 1985, p. 444)

Gordon (1988) points out that a physician working for the Massachusetts Society for the Prevention of Cruelty to Children concentrated solely on examination of the hymen in cases of suspected sexual abuse of girls. "The physical evidence was objective, "scientific"; the victim's statements were not", Gordon writes (p. 216).

As an instruction for physicians dating from 1913 he said:

> It is always a good working rule to be guided only by the physical conditions that present themselves to your eye and finger, and to forget what the sense of hearing has suggested. (p. 356)

This form of medical examination meant that, with regard to sexual abuse, attention was paid only to direct penetration and not to other forms.

In the second place, there was the difficult position in which the physician was placed should he diagnose or suspect incestuous abuse in a society in which child protection services, confidential doctors, child protection legislation, and child abuse laws were not yet heard of. Social frameworks within which the problem could be dealt with were almost nonexistent. In this respect, it is clear that there is a mutual relationship between the existence or absence of a conceptual framework on the one hand, and a social framework on the other. They mutually reinforce one another.

Radiology and Cruelty to Children

It was not just the diagnosis - to speak in medical terms - of incestuous abuse that was missed by physicians for many years, when in our eyes and within our conceptual frameworks the facts were so unmistakably clear. It was also the diagnosis of physical cruelty to children that was for a long time consistently overlooked.

The radiologist Caffey was, in 1946, the first to write about "the frequent association of chronic subdural hematoma and fractures of the long bones". In the early 1950s, publications on the same phenomenon appeared in Canada, France, and the United States. There were five publications in all, none of which related these data to the possibility of physical violence on the parents' side. In Great Britain, Astley wrote about the subject in 1953, and he too did not suggest this possibility. "This despite the coincidental presence of retinal separation, easy bruising, black eyes, compressed vertebrae and the more usual types of fractures" (Woolley & Evans, 1955, p. 539). The traumas that could be made visible through X-ray diagnosis were attributed to "metaphyseal fragility of the bones". Usually, these cases concerned very young children showing unmistakable traces of physical violence, that is to say, unmistakable within our conceptual frameworks, but the physicians did not recognize them. For a long time, such injuries were mistaken, for example, for rachitis, scurvy, or "osteogenesis imperfecta" (Radbill, 1987). Silverman, a radiologist, was in 1953 among the first to suggest an explanation of such injuries that was not purely medical, and he reproached physicians with laxity and naivity in this respect. He was one of the authors that cooperated in Henry Kempe's classic article (1962) that coined the phrase "battered child syndrome".

Again, one may wonder why this diagnosis was missed for so many years. Of course, various factors played a part in the matter. I will mention only one of them here: the existence of a conceptual framework within which the use of violence by parents toward their children was regarded as a generally accepted means of education. It was associated with the high degree of autonomy and privacy assigned to the family by society. Children were seen as the exclusive property of their parents, and society respected the way parents handled this property. Kempe's article brought about substantial cracks in this conceptual framework. In consequence, within no more than five years, every state in the U.S. had legislation concerning cruelty to children, a social framework within which child abuse was not only discussable, but also possible to deal with. Moreover, it was a framework that protected the position of medical doctors by obliging them to report suspected child abuse to certain authorities.

Ignored Testimonies

We have until now been concerned with the denial of indirect signals of child abuse; signals on the body of a child. However, children have also made direct signals, more specifically, they have told adults that they were being sexually abused. Historical research reveals that the coexistence of four conceptual frameworks formed an obstacle to taking these children's stories seriously. The first conceptual framework concerned the cognitive incompetence of children. For a long time, research into a child's competence as a witness was basically aimed at proving that, because of inadequate cognitive development, a child was an incompetent witness, and therefore highly dangerous. For instance, in 1907 Baginsky (at the time an unquestioned authority in the field) wrote:

> True experts in the field of child psychology declare children's testimonies in lawsuits to be absolutely null and void, without any value or meaning. They are all the more meaningless and invalid, as the more often the child repeats its testimony, the more firmly it will stick to the same statements" (p. 20). "That is why we should get rid of children's testimonies in court. (p. 21)

In 1911, the Belgian Varendonck asked himself when, as a civilized nation, we would stop listening to children in lawsuits (Goodman, 1984).

Research emphasized very one-sidedly the suggestibility of children, their failures of memory, and their incomplete ability to distinguish fantasy from reality. This form of research aimed to show children's incompetences rather than their competences (see, e.g., Van Raalte, 1911). Bleuler (1937) pointed out that one should be very careful with children as witnesses, and that judges are inclined to give credence to children's testimonies far too easily. In his view, this has led to many unjust sentences concerning indecent offenses. Remarkable in this respect is the stereotyped way in which differences between boys and girls were referred to. "Upright, practically minded boys may well deserve our credence. This is much less true of girls, especially teenage-girls, whose heads are turned by blossoming romance" (p. 162). Brown's principle was that children are more suggestible than adults, and that women are more suggestible than men (Goodman, 1984).

In addition to that concerning their cognitive unreliability, a second conceptual framework involved the moral unreliability of children. The previously mentioned article by Fournier (1880/1986) was titled: "Simulation of sexual attacks on young children" (Simulation d'attentats venériens sur des jeunes enfants). The article opens as follows:

> We will be dealing with sad things and sad people. But public interest demands that we speak of them. This is a duty from which the physician, by profession the witness to such ignominies, must not recoil. What I have in mind is the simulation of sexual abuse of young children, a simulation inspired by the profit its originator hopes to gain from his criminal plans. (p. 106)

Bourdin wrote in 1882: "It is up to educators and particularly medical doctors to destroy the myth of the infallible sincerity of the child." (Bourdin, cited in Masson, 1984, p. 48). Within this conceptual framework, children's stories about sexual abuse were usually interpreted as conscious lies, to which they were incited by immoral parents. This is why a Dutch monograph on the child as witness, dating from 1911, had as its subtitle: "Bad children and bad parents". The child psychiatrist Strohmayer (1910) wrote about "adolescent girls with depraved sexual phantasies, who, by giving invented evidence, put innocent people in the dock for sexual offenses" (p. 42). Almost prototypical for the literature from about 1880 onward, are case descriptions of girls accusing an adult man - often referred to by the author as a respectable person - of sexual abuse. The girls are then exposed as little impostors.

A third conceptual framework functioning as an obstacle was that of the disturbed child. Within this framework, the simple fact that a child told this kind of story was easily regarded as a sign that he or she was mentally disturbed. When looking in old child psychiatric manuals for information about sexual abuse or incest, it is best to look in the index under "H" for hysteria or "P" for pseudologia fantastica. Within this framework, one did not consider the possibility that the sexual abuse of a child was the very cause of his or her behavioral disturbances. Usually, the disturbance itself was enough to determine the story as a hysterical figment of the child's imagination.

Finally, a fourth conceptual framework involved that of the erotically seductive child. In 1931, Frieda Fromm-Reichmann wrote an article about a 30-year-old woman who was receiving therapy from her. As a child, this woman had, from the third to the fifth year of her life, been repeatedly sexually abused by her father. The abuse stopped from one day to the next when another child was born into the family. Fromm-Reichmann then writes that, in the case of this child, from the third to the fifth year of her life, the oedipal desires which every girl has for a sexual relationship with the father had been satisfied. But suddenly these desires were no longer fulfilled. Fromm-Reichman relates the now adult woman's sense of inferiority not to the fact that she had been abused by her father, but to the fact that, in her own eyes, she was suddenly no longer thought worthy of the satisfaction of her oedipal desires. For many decades, the picture sketched by psychoanalysis of the child as seducer acted as an impediment to taking reports of incestuous abuse seriously. As Bender and Blau wrote in 1937:

> The history of the [incestuous] relationship in our cases usually suggested at least some cooperation of the child in the activity, and in some cases the child assumed an active role in initiating the relationship. (p. 516)

In 1982, a 24-year-old man was given a three-year suspended sentence for the sexual abuse of a five-year-old girl. The judgment was: We have to do with an exceptionally promiscuous young lady, and this man just did not manage to resist her advances (Hechler, 1988). To be clear, psychoanalysis did not discover this conceptual framework, it just gave it a semblance of having a scientific character.

Conclusions

Where the conceptual and social frameworks for recognizing indirect physical signs of sexual abuse did not exist, we find that interpretation of the direct signals - the children's own stories - was equally blocked by persistent and biased conceptual frameworks emphasizing the unreliability of child witnesses. For many centuries, discussion of the incestuous abuse of children was under a very strong taboo. On the one hand, it was the taboo itself that caused biased conceptual frameworks to become persistent. On the other hand, these frameworks themselves provided a rationalization for maintaining the taboo.

It may even be the case that the general resistance in society toward considering the sexual abuse of children, and particularly incestuous abuse, as a serious problem has formed an impediment to providing an unbiased answer to the question of children's competence as witnesses. Even today, we can still see how these four conceptual frameworks are applied to avoid facing the broad social problem of incestuous abuse. Whereas, previously, a victim's story of incestuous abuse was easily judged to be nothing but a symptom of hysteria, today, publications appear that try to reduce the current social attention to the sexual abuse of children to a form of mass hysteria. Anyone presenting the results of developmental psychological research into children's competence as witnesses will have to take this resistance into account. Especially in lawsuits, full use is still made of these four conceptual frameworks. It is true that stories told by children as witness/victim are sometimes difficult to interpret. However, anyone who is not, in principle, prepared to take them seriously can continue to use unsubstantiated biases about the unreliability of child witnesses.

References

Astley, R. (1953). Multiple metaphyseal fractures in small children (metaphyseal fragility of bone). *British Journal of Radiology, 26*, 577-583.

Baginsky, A. (1907). Die Impressionalität der Kinder unter dem Einfluss des Milieus. *Beiträge zur Kinderforschung und Heilerziehung (Heft XXVII)*.

Bender, L., & Blau, A. (1937). Reactions of children to sex relations with adults. *American Journal of Orthopsychiatry, 7*, 500-518.

Bleuler, E. (1937). *Lehrbuch der Psychiatrie*. Berlin: Springer.

Caffey, J. (1946). Multiple fractures in the long bones of infants suffering from chronic subdural hematoma. *American Journal of Roentgenology, 56*, 163-173.

Fournier, A. (1986). Simulation of sexual attacks on young children. In J.M. Masson (Ed.), *A dark science: Women, sexuality and psychiatry in the 19th century*. New York: Farrar, Straus, & Giroux. (Original work published 1880)

Fromm-Reichman, F. (1931). Zur Entstehungsgeschichte "sozialer Minderwertigkeitsgefühle". *Zeitschrift für Psychoanalytische Pädagogik, 5*, 19-29.

Goodman, G.S. (1984). Children's testimony in historical perspective. *Journal of Social Issues, 40*, 9-31.

Gordon, L. (1988). *Heroes of their own lives: The politics and history of family violence*. New York: Viking.

Hechler, D. (1988). *The battle and the backlash: The child sexual abuse war*. Lexington: Lexington Books.

Kempe, H.C., Silverman, F.N., Steele, B.F., Droegemuller, W., & Silver, H.K. (1962). The battered-child syndrome. *Journal of the American Medical Association, 181*, 17-24.

Masson, J.M. (1984). *The assault on truth: Freud's suppression of the seduction theory*. New York: Farrar, Straus & Giroux.

Raalte, F. van (1911). *Getuigenissen van kinderen: Slechte kinderen en slechte ouders*. Rotterdam: Nijgh en Van Ditmar.

Radbill, S.X. (1987). Children in a world of violence: A history of child abuse. In R.E. Helfer, & R.S. Kempe (Eds.), *The battered child*. Chicago: The University of Chicago Press.

Scholz, L. (1922). *Anomale Kinder*. Berlin: Karger.

Silverman, F.N. (1953). The roentgen manifestations of unrecognized skeletal trauma in infants. *American Journal of Roentgenology, 69*, 414-426.

Strohmayer, W. (1910). *Vorlesungen über die Psychopathologie des Kindesalters für Mediziner und Pädagogen*. Tübingen: Laupp'sche Buchhandlung.

Taylor, K.J. (1985). Venereal diseases in 19th century children. *The Journal of Psychohistory, 12*, 432-463.

Welander, E. (1909). Über den Einfluss der venerischen Krankheiten auf die Ehe sowie über ihre Übertragung auf kleine Kinder. *Beiträge zur Kinderforschung und Heilerziehung* (Heft LV).

Woolley, P.V., & Evans, W.A. (1955). Significance of skeletal lesions in infants resembling those of traumatic origin. *Journal of the American Medical Association, 158*, 539-543.

Ziehen, Th. (1917). *Die Geisteskrankheiten des Kindesalters*. Berlin: Reuther & Reichard.

Injustice to Children and Families in Child Abuse Cases

Dennis Howitt

The concern of this paper is disputed child protection decisions. The sense in which the term "error" applies has to be one of the issues addressed. While these "errors" may well be the "false positives" beloved in positivistic views of psychological research (e.g. Brown & Saqi, 1988), the problem is deeper than that conceptualization implies. The processes by which "disputed" decisions come to be made need close examination. "Error" needs understanding in terms of its social meaning in the context of statutory child protection activities. A second major task of the paper is to discuss some elementary theory about the nature of "errors". It is important not to regard such "errors" and "proper" decisions as having different aetiologies without evidence of this. To do so would be to accept that "tinkering" with procedures or practices would eliminate such "hiccups" in the system. This is far from self-evident.

Much of the paper will be taken up with a single case study selected from over twenty carried out for the research. The reasons for choosing a case study presentation are numerous. Particularly important are the desire to examine "processes" which are difficult to present in terms of aggregate data, the interactive involvement of many different elements in the process, the importance of the wider picture of the effects on the family, and that such an approach gives substance to the issues.

"Errors" in Child Protection

Child abuse and child sexual abuse are modern conceptions. The use of the terms has only emerged in the last 25 years or so, child sexual abuse being even more recent. What is not so clear is the extent to which they are terms which refer to homologues of "events" which have a much longer standing. Of course, violence and sexual violence against children have a extremely long history (Daly & Wilson, 1988), but there remains the question of the special nature of the social constructs of child abuse and child sexual abuse. They are not the same, for example, as corporal punishment and incest. Child abuse and child sexual abuse are social constructs which impose meanings and understandings which are not implied by the older terms. Child abuse is a radically different social construct from "baby battering" from which it partially emerged. One history of the social construction of child abuse is found in Parton (1985), but here it is possible only to note what the constructs overlay:

1. They impose a relatively unproblematic moral imprint. Child abuse contains within it no question of a moral dilemma. The appropriate societal reaction comes ready built into the term "abuse". This is particularly important as it allows simple defining

characteristics (such as a small bruise) to be used as an indicator of an abuse, or even characteristics of a potential abuser as a substitute. Baby battering could not be so all-encompassing nor does it have the dilemma free characteristic.

2. Child sexual abuse changes the metatheoretical framework significantly from the idea of incest. Not only does it also avoid a moral quandary, it effectively moves away from the biologized issue of incest (where the typical 20th century concern was with genetic degeneration) to one which is intimately related to sexual politics (Hechler, 1988). That is, paedophiliac activities are seen as part of a continuum which includes many other issues (such as pornography) which are of great concern in the feminist literature (Ellis, 1989).

These changes are not trivial matters but ones of great substance. To claim that child abuse and child sexual abuse are social constructs does not mean (as some authors imply) that they refer to social realities which had to be gradually uncovered or revealed (sometimes it is argued that in the past they have been effectively hidden by families). Instead it means that ways of seeing the world, defining situations, explaining, researching and predicting are generated through social processes. What is constructed is not some basic reality which has been detected, say, through scientific investigation or professional involvement. Child abuse cannot be fully understood without reference to the historical, social, and institutional context in which the ideas were developed. As such, it is not something which resides in the actions of an individual or a family. It does not have such an independent existence.

It is probably easier to understand this by reference to other social issues such as drug abuse. The history of drug abuse turned what was a fairly everyday activity in 19th century Britain, into essentially a "monster" created by the state and the medical profession (Berridge & Edwards, 1981; Howitt, 1990b). Drug use became drug abuse and imbude with criminality and a medicalized social problem. As a consequence, it is impossible to differentiate the pharmacological effects of a drug from its legal, medical, and social overlay. In other words it is not possible to understand the use of drugs distinct from their socially constructed nature (e.g. Auld, 1981). Other examples of social issues treated in this way include Szasz (1986) on suicide.

Consequently, it is not possible to properly speak of "errors" since this is to try to isolate a "fact" from the social processes involved in the construction of child abuse. This might appear to be particularly pedantic since it is not unknown for public hearings to report mistakes, to attribute blame, and to criticize individuals. But these are not decisive to the argument, partly because they are rare events, but also because they have no social reality independent of the social issues which they emerge to deal with.

"Error" Processes

Formal theories of "errors" in professional judgement are conspicuously missing. There are a number of reasons for this. Probably the most important is the "top-down" approach of social scientific research which is overwhelmingly financed and facilitated by the state and component institutions for their own purposes. In these circumstances "errors" tend to be seen as the product of individual inexperience, sloth, and communicative failures. The nature of the institutions and the nature of the social construct of child abuse not being a matter for particular question. The solutions in this formulation are improved managerial structures (typically at the lower levels of management) or improved "inter-agency" cooperation, links, communications, or understanding. It is worth noting Howitt's (1990a) account of a case of alleged child sexual abuse in which a clinical psychologist prepared a report for a legal hearing, based on an interpretation of a child's story written for school. In this report sexual abuse was heavily hinted at despite the psychologist never seeing the child. However, the story was simply a slightly modified version of a book and television programme! Perhaps this suggests that professional training in itself is no guarantee that the standards of the profession will be applied.

Alternatives to these rarely come from the social sciences literature. Examples of non-social scientific approaches are Bell's (1988) witch-hunt theory, which sees child abuse "errors" as being on a par with the mass "trials" of women accused of witchcraft, and Pride's (1987) right-wing ideological account of "errors" which construes them as essentially (but perhaps paradoxically given the notion of child protection) the by-product of an anti-child/anti-family ideology. One perhaps could also include Campbell's (1988) feminist of "errors" as being "non-errors" in these terms too. That is to say that she sees the reaction against some child protection activities as being the real "error". Probably too little is known to confidently reject any of these accounts. Indeed, in many ways, given the sparcity of psychological approaches to professional "errors", they cannot simply be dismissed. Social sciences have tended to regard errors as essentially random events in a diagnostic system - that is as "statistical error" due to the unreliability of predictors. Indeed to describe them as false positives draws heavily on the medical origins of this conceptualization. One psychological approach (Evans, 1989) is to see "errors" as being basically the outcome of normal human cognitive functioning, one of his ideas, metacognition, being particularly useful. This basically refers to the tendency of humans to be "overconfident" in their judgements - the belief that one is right. Given that many of the disputed cases demonstrate great difficulties in reversing, undoing, or abandoning the involvement of child protection agencies in such cases, explanations of this apparent resistance to change ultimately are needed.

In this paper three broad explanatory principles are discussed which can be adduced to explain "errors". These do not emerge out of the single case study to be presented but help to organize the bulk of the cases interviewed in the research project. It needs to be stressed that these explanatory principles are not intended as an exhaustive list by any means. They are chosen because of their apparent near universality in the various case studies. No claim is made that the processes to be described constitute sophisticated theory. However, it would seem that the child abuse literature is lacking any theoretical integration and that even rudimentary attempts at theoretical understanding ought to be a priority for researchers. The three principals can be termed "templating", "justificatory theorizing", and "ratcheting". They all are processes rather than predictor variables as such. To what do these refer?

Templating

This is closely related to stereotyping. The fundamental and major difference is that stereotyping involves the attribution of features to individuals on the basis of their broad classification. So, for example, stereotyping might be the assumption of criminality in a member of the classification Afro-Carribeans. Templating is different in that it involves checking the individual against a "social template" to see whether or not the individual fits that template. So for example, although the literature is replete with the advice that child abuse can occur in all sectors of society, it is part of the template of the child abuser if that individual is a step-parent. A stereotyping process would assume that step-parents are child abusers, a templating process involves an instigating event (such as a bruise or scratch detected on a child by a health visitor) which then involves the "suspect" being compared with the template. It is noteworthy, that in the full study virtually all, if not all, cases demonstrated some relevant instigating factor, no matter how trivial. With possibly one exception, all of the families involved were single-parent, step-parent, unemployed, unmarried, or young, or combinations of all of these things. Most of these are the typical demographic predictors of abusing families (Brown, Davies, & Stratton, 1988).

Justificatory theorizing

There is considerable evidence that child protection decisions are theory led. While one could argue that templating is based on empirical evidence (personal or research), many "errors" are dependent on theoretical explanations which justify decisions. The classic example of this in my research is what might be termed the "contrition" theory. This assumes that in order for a family or a family member to be "treatable" (i.e., "they can be worked with" in the professional parlance), evidence has to be shown that the full implications of what has happened are understood and acceptance of responsibility confirmed. Without this evidence then the individual or family is deemed "not workable with" and the risk of the family and child being separated, increased. What is poignant about this is that if the family denies the abuse when none has occurred, this is indistinguishable from denying the abuse when it has occurred. Some families prefer to risk losing their children even though they know that if they lie and claim responsibility, they are more likely to keep their family intact.

Ratcheting

This is very clearly a description of a process. It really refers to the tendency of the child protection processes to move in a single direction - unwinding, undoing, or going back on a decision tends not to happen even in circumstances where this might seem appropriate. An example of this process at work is reflected in the difference between taking-into-care decisions and coming-out-of-care decisions. It might be common-sensical to assume that the factors which lead to children being returned to their homes are simply the reverse of those which led to the child being taken into care in the first place. For example, a child may enter care to give the parents a respite but when the parents feel able to cope this is not sufficient signal for the child to return home. Sometimes new criteria may be introduced to determine release from care which have nothing or little to do with the taking into care criteria. Ratcheting has a "never going back" quality which possibly may help protect the professionals from the risk of taking a decision which may attract criticism.

Although not an exhaustive list, the above processes seem to help organize many of the cases studied in the research, one should not assume them to be totally independent of each other in particular instances. This is fairly evident in the case study.

The Case Study

Mrs King, who provided the case study material, was 29 years at the time of interview, her 32 year old husband was a blue-collar worker, and her son, Tim, 5 1/2 years. Since the time of the alleged abuse the couple have had a baby son who was 5 1/2 months at the time of interview. The story started two years previously, just after the family had moved into a new home. Perhaps two key facts should be mentioned. The boy, Tim, was from a previous relationship of Mrs King, so Mr King was his step-father. Already in the story is the key information for "templating" to take place - the family initially was a single-parent one and then a step-parent relationship becomes involved. The couple were married about five-weeks before the precipitating incident took place. (Names have been altered in the following account. Direct quotations are in double inverted commas and italics.)

Tim (3 1/2 years) was in bed as it was about 10.30 at night. According to his mother, he got up to go to the toilet. Climbing over a safety gate at the top of the stairs, his foot caught and he fell down the stairs. The parents were alerted by his call and picked him up. They found a friction or carpet-burn graze on one side of his knee. However, the next morning he complained of having a "headache" (he called it "a tummy ache in his head"). Given the possibility of concussion, he was examined further but only "two tiny little bruises on his rib cage" were found in addition. Mrs King telephoned her doctor who suggested that she should visit his surgery. Coincidentally the health visitor arrived (Mrs King was pregnant) and "took them to the doctor".

"So we got there and he examined Tim, and he said to Tim: How have you done this? And Tim said: I fell down the stairs last night because I climbed over the safety gate and I was naughty, you know... and then the doctor said to him: Has your mummy hit you? And Tim said no. And he said has your daddy hit you? And Tim said no... [The doctor] said I"m very sorry to say this but I think either you or your husband has abused your son."

He told her to take the child to the hospital to see a paediatrician who after examining the child said "This is just a waste of time since the injuries and the story were perfectly consistent and that there is no evidence in my opinion that this child has been abused at all". She was told to go home. But:

"... there was a knock at the door and a nurse said: Could she have a word with the paediatrician ... So he went out, he was gone for 5 minutes, and he came back in. And he said I'm very sorry Mrs King, but your doctor has rang the Social Services and informed them that he thinks that the child is at risk, and a social worker was there at the hospital...in the space of two hours, this was, Social Services have been to a magistrate and they've taken a Place of Safety order, just on the say-so of my doctor."

Notice that the ratcheting process has begun. Essentially the general practitioner and the paediatrician are in fundamental disagreement as to the cause of the child's injury. A process of child protection has begun and cannot be stopped let alone undone on the opinion of the paediatrician. Not only does the no-abuse opinion from a more senior medic carry little weight now compared to the other opinion claiming abuse offered by the general practitioner despite the fact that he had referred the case to the paediatrician (presumably as being more expert), but the child's account seems to be also dismissed. According to the interviewee the social workers' view was "we don't think these injuries are explained".

In the meantime, the police arrive and interview the woman. Her parents have been called and are now present. Finally, after a lengthy period of time has passed, her husband arrives at the hospital and he is arrested immediately and taken to the police station. While the events in the hands of the police are complex and disturbing, more important in the context of the present discussion is an example of justificatory theorizing. This seems to be used as an interviewing ploy but also presumably as an explanation of why the husband might have abused the child. Notice that it is more than simply an empirically established relationship between step-parenthood and abuse but a theory of why it should happen. It might have also provided the justification for keeping the man in a police station for 24 hours and apparently subjecting him to force and strong psychological and other pressures:

"They also tried a tactic which sounds pretty disgusting but I have to say it, of going in and this policeman sat by him and tried to be pally with him and gave him a cigarette, and he said: I can't say as I blame you mate, he said: Because after all he's not yours is he. And my husband said: Well, no he's not mine but, you know, I think of him as my son. And he said: Imagine that, he said, somebody's been with your wife before you, how does that make you feel? He said: I bet you hate that child."

In this instant, the templating process has allowed the emergence of a justificatory theory which is then used as a persuasive technique. This is not uncommon and there is no sense in which justificatory theorization can be seen as an abstraction - it is often part of the exchange between the child protection agencies and the family.

While the father was not prosecuted, their story has a long way to go before it comes to an end. Within a few days the mother miscarries. This she attributes to the accusations and specifically she claims no prior nor later history of miscarriages. Within four weeks of the intervention (this is under the previous legislation) a court application for an interim care order was made but the lack of evidence resulted in just a two week adjournment. After this time no evidence of substance was provided by the solicitors for Social Services and on the other side was the evidence of the paediatrician. Virtually the same justificatory theorization was the substance of the Social Services case:

"All they said was: We've visited Mr and Mrs King in their home and we feel because the father is not the natural father, we believe that he, the son, is at risk from the step-father, because he isn't the natural father, and the family have, they're a new family, they've only just been married, they've only just moved into this house, and we feel that the son is at risk and should remain on the at risk register which he'd been put on from the word go, that's automatic, and that they should have this care order."

Essentially "risk-indicators" are being used to justify what "diagnostic signs" cannot support. This is not a trivial matter, clearly, and it should not be forgotten that in some instances attempts at intervention have been made on the basis of "risk-indicators" alone - for example, where the parent had been abused as a child this is taken of a sign that their child is at risk of abuse. At root, this is the cycle of deprivation thesis pushed to limits which would not apply to other offences for which there are similar predictors.

But the King family had reached a stage which is not available to many other families - that is, the court decided not to grant a care order and, in the interviewee's view, "gave the Social Services quite a severe ticking off". This may be construed as evidence of innocence. Many families do not have this possibility as opportunities to put the case before a court of law do not exist. Typically, because cases of abuse have to be reported to the police, the outcome of the police investigation is seen as part of the process of achieving a sense of justice, as confirming innocence just as it was in this case. The decision of the police not to prosecute is seen as validation of innocence, not as a matter of insufficient evidence. The family was also fortunate in that both partners were together when the precipitating incident occured. A residue of suspicion otherwise may be left which can be extremely painful.

But justice is not the sole prerogative of courts of law and feelings of injustice can be engendered by other actions after what might be seen as a successful court appearance. Tim was kept on the at-risk register by Social Services. This is not a neutral matter as, for example, Mrs King was prevented from involvement with a play group of which she had been a committee member for several years because of Tim's name being on the at-risk register.

All of this is part of the ratcheting process whatever the original justification for being concerned about the child. In this case, the only known professional concern about the child was based on six injuries during the period of being on the at-risk register. However, these clearly must have been reconstrued by the Social Services in a rather novel way since they had happened at the local Social Services day nursery and had been recorded as such in the records of that day nursery. In other words, it could be argued that the child was being kept on the register because of injuries which could be attributed to the negligence of the Social Services department itself! Eventually, the child's name was removed from the at-risk register. This seemed instigated by the threat of litigation by the family but even after this more followed:

"... in March of this year, my ex-husband - my husband's ex-wife, was contacted by the Social Services where she lives ... she had this note saying would she please telephone this particular social worker... So she went along and the social worker told her that her ex-husband had been accused of child abuse, and that in his opinion he didn't think that the children should be allowed to come down here and see their father unless it was in the presence of their grandmother, like my husband's mother."

All through the period of being on the at-risk register, these children from the previous marriage had visited for overnight stays!

Coda

The fundamental problem of the case study is the initial actions of the general practitioner who sent Mrs King to the hospital and reported his views to the Social Services department. Why did he act so precipitantly? Why the rush? Gergen (1985) has written of socially constructed ideas:

> ... the objective criteria for identifying such "behaviors", "events", or "entitities" are shown to be either high circumscribed by culture, history, or social context or altogether nonexistent. (p. 266)

The difference between abuse and non-abuse did not lie in the actions of the King family since once Mrs King had contacted her doctor's surgery she had entrained far more than reassurance over her concern about concussion. Nor could the family shed the child protection processes no matter what other judgements or decisions were taken in courts of law or elsewhere. Pressed in the interview about the involvement of the doctor, the following emerged. Mrs King recounts her visit to this doctor after her miscarriage:

> So I went in and he opened this letter [from the hospital] and he read it - oh, you've lost a baby - oh well, in view of what's happened it's probably best anyway. And I - but the thing is, now, I'm repeating this in confidence - the thing is, about 3 years ago, if - yes - 3 or 4 years ago - my doctor, my particular doctor, was actually taken to court for sexually abusing his own daughter. Right. And he was found guilty, in fact he pleaded guilty. He was fined pounds 1,000, and the case was like - he was found guilty but he still had to go before the - I don't know if it's the GMC or the BMA or whatever. .... He blamed it, he said he'd been depressed and he'd been taking tranquilizers and he didn't know what he was doing, but he still carried on being a doctor.

While this would appear to reveal the motive of an individual actor, the involvement of this one doctor is not responsible for all that follows. Without the social construct of abuse and the institutional arrangements, that doctor's telephone call to Social Services could have no effect of the sort it did.

Can anything be learnt from this case? Can we cut the bad parts out of the system? One might be tempted to the view that awareness of the risk and nature of "errors" reduces that risk. But with so many individuals and so many agencies involved in this instance, so many opportunities to back-track on the process, and so few signs of this happening, the suspicion remains that "errors" and "successes" are not due to distinct processes and are inseparably intertwined. Indeed, it might be suspected that templating, justificatory theorizing, and ratcheting are also central to non-disputed cases also. Their utility in the wider context might provide a degree of self-validation which explains their continuation and acceptance by practitioners. For this reason, amongst others, it is possible that answers to questions like "what can we do to prevent errors?" will need to be more radical than most practitioners would be prepared to countenance currently. To reconstruct the idea of child abuse so that the qualities of imperativeness, child centredness, moral panic, and crude interventionism are replaced by less risky precepts may benefit from the understanding of "errors". However, this is not to suggest that from the study of "errors" will come means of modifying the child protection system. Such a quest may be built on the failure to understand the child protection process and the social construction of child abuse.

References

Auld, J. (1981). *Marijuana use and social control.* London: Academic Press.
Bell, S. (1988). *When Salem came to the Boro.* London: Pan.
Berridge, V., & Edwards, G. (1981). *Opium and the people: Opiate use in nineteenth century England.* London: Allen Lane.
Brown, K., Davies, C., & Stratton, P. (Eds.) (1988). *Early prediction and prevention of child abuse.* Chichester: John Wiley.
Brown, K., & Saqi, S. (1988). Approaches to screening for child abuse and neglect. In K. Brown, C. Davies, & P. Stratton (Eds.), *Early prediction and prevention of child abuse* (pp. 57-85). Chichester: John Wiley.
Campbell, B. (1988). *Unofficial secrets: Childhood sexual abuse - The Cleveland case.* London: Virago.
Daly, M., & Wilson, M. (1988). *Homicide.* Hawthorne, NY: de Gruyter.
Ellis, L. (1989). *Theories of rape: Inquiries into the causes of sexual aggression.* New York: Hemisphere.
Evans, J.St.B. (1989). Some causes of bias in expert opinion. *The Psychologist, 2,* 112-114.
Gergen, K. (1985). The social constructionist movement in modern psychology. *American Psychologist, 40,* 266-275.
Hechler, D. (1988). *The battle and the backlash: The child sexual abuse war.* Lexington, MA: Lexington.
Howitt, D. (1990a). Expert opinion: Risky sexual abuse diagnosis. *The Psychologist, 3,* 15-17.
Howitt, D. (1990b). Britain's "substance abuse policy": Realities and regulation in the United Kingdom. *The International Journal of Addiction, 25,* 1087-1111.
Parton, N. (1985). *The politics of child abuse.* London: MacMillan.
Pride, M. (1987). *The child abuse industry.* Winchester, IL: Crossway.
Szasz, T. (1986). The case against suicide prevention. *American Psychologist, 41,* 806-812.

Child Witnesses in Sexual Abuse Cases: Psychological Implications of Legal Procedures

Max Steller

During the past years, child sexual abuse has become a topic of increased public and professional concern. Some countries (e.g., the US) have experienced an enormous increase in reported cases. In many countries, the growing numbers of relevant publications, media reports, conferences, as well as the formation of child supporting agencies can be considered as signs of an awakening awareness that child sexual abuse is a topic that merits the highest possible efforts of interdisciplinary prevention and treatment. From the perspective of overlapping problems in the areas of law and psychology, potentially negative psychological influences on children who serve as witnesses in child sexual abuse cases seem to be of special importance. Considering the juridical practice in most countries, the provocative question whether courts abuse children (Davies & Drinkwater, 1988) cannot yet be answered satisfactorily by an unqualified "no".

Otherwise well-established judicial procedures and rules of evidence might be inappropriate for the needs caused by the specific constellation of sexual offenses against children in which a child's statement very frequently constitutes the only available evidence. In the following chapters, experts from Canada, Great Britain, Israel, Norway, and Germany will discuss the psychological implications for children as witnesses in the investigative and legal procedures in their countries. The term "psychological implications" was chosen to include discussions of secondary victimization effects of legal procedures (and methods to prevent them, respectively) as well as regulations concerning the introduction of expert testimony in child sexual abuse cases.

The organizer of this symposion has been engaged in court-appointed assessments of the credibility of child witnesses in sexual abuse cases since 1970. In Germany - as described in the paper by Renate Volbert - working as a court appointed expert witness includes the opportunity to read casefile information, to interview the child, and to question third persons. All findings are summarized to a credibility assessment of the child's statement. On a regular basis, the psychologist is asked to deliver a written report as well as to give oral testimony in court about his or her findings and evaluations. Doing this kind of work, a psychologist inevitably encounters experiences with juridical procedures in dealing with child witnesses that are not only positive. The psychologist's naive reflections about the adequacy of certain procedural rules and juridical practice are reinforced when he or she learns that routines in one country would not be allowed in other countries and vice versa.

Assume a case in which a psychologist interviewed a child witness and thereby received a convincing statement about sexual abuse. The interview was conducted with the use of an appropriate interview technique in the psychologist's office and it was videorecorded. The case went to trial, and the child was called as a witness. Procedural delays led to a long waiting time in the lobby of the court house. The court went into recess, and the handcuffed defendant was led back to his prison cell accompanied by two well-armed officers, thereby passing the waiting child. The trial was continued later the same day. Called into the witness stand, the child was not able or willing to testify. The whole situational context was such that even adults would have had difficulties in overcoming internal thresholds like anxiety, shyness, or any other reason for being inhibited about talking in front of a large audience that was subjectively experienced by the witness as unresponsive, not to say hostile. After a sophisticated legal discussion, the psychologist's tape was not allowed to be introduced as evidence. The case ended with an acquittal.

This simple but realistic example is meant to illustrate two types of problem in dealing with child witnesses: A first type of problem could be summarized as lack of thoughtfulness among legal professionals. These mainly organizational problems should be easy to overcome - but nevertheless they frequently do occur not only in German practice (see the description in Rhona Flin's chapter). The second types of problem are institutionalized problems, problems of procedural laws for which there are no easy solutions. Procedural laws are valuable safeguards against false convictions and they should not be changed hastily and without good reasons. On the other hand, as indicated above, comparing the laws in different countries helps us to remember that procedural laws are man-made and therefore capable of improvement.

The following reports about different legal procedures in various countries are meant as contributions to the ongoing international debate (e.g., Spencer, Nicholson, Flin, & Bull, 1990) about defining those legal rules that promise an optimal achievement of two goals that appear to be antagonistic: strengthening the (traditionally weak) position of child witnesses, and, at the same time, not jeopardizing safeguards against false convictions as formulated in procedural laws. To identify potential positive and negative aspects of different approaches, a comparison that includes legal systems of the adversarial as well as the inquisitorial type seems especially worthwhile.

It seems as if there is no one and only adequate solution for legal procedures, but that all jurisdictions could benefit by reflecting their weak points and by adopting good aspects of other countries' procedures. Therefore, the following makes no attempt to describe a "model procedure" that would constitute an artificial composition. Instead, a few selected issues will be addressed. Some of the problems appear especially urgent and require serious reflection regarding their compatibility with the above mentioned goals. Most outstanding are the unique difficulties in the Netherlands that are imposed on psychologists who intend to offer contributions to forensic interventions in child sexual abuse cases (unfortunately, the judicial situation in the Netherlands is not covered by the following chapters). In the Netherlands, there exists the rule that an expert witness must not receive any information about the case prior to conducting an interview with the alleged victim of sexual abuse. It can only be speculated whether this strange practice can be traced back to particular contributions in the American literature (e.g., Underwager, Wakefield, Legrand, Bartz, & Erickson, 1986; White, Strom, Santilli, & Halpin, 1986). It would be discouraging if these publications were to contribute to judicial practice in the Netherlands, because such recommendations for "blind" interviewing are contrary to the reasoning of the majority of experts who state that it is crucial for professionals conducting interviews to obtain complete information about all case facts (Jones & McQuiston, 1989; MacFarlane & Krebs, 1986; Steller & Boychuk, 1992).

The recommendation for blind interviews is based on a concern about interviewer biases created by knowledge of background information. However, maintaining open-mindedness and flexibility, that is, staying aware during the interview that the child may have been (not was) sexually abused (Jones & McQuiston, 1989) cannot be achieved by ignoring available information about the alleged incident and its surrounding circumstances. Lack of that information places an interviewer in the almost impossible position of trying to obtain a statement on something about which he or she is unable to formulate a strategy for the questioning procedure or for assessing incoming information. The problem with the blind interview approach is that, through ignorance, the interviewer might miss important information or fail completely to elicit any forensically relevant information from the child.

In German-speaking countries, there is a long tradition for forensic use of statement analysis as an evaluation procedure to assess the credibility of child statements about sexual abuse (Undeutsch, 1982, 1984, 1989). The content of child statements is thoroughly analyzed as to the presence of so-called reality criteria, that is, features that appear in truthful reports about experienced events but are missing in fabricated accounts. In connection with systematizing statement analysis under the name of Criteria-Based Statement Analysis (Steller, 1989; Steller & Köhnken, 1989), interview strategies have been designed to maintain objectivity on the part of the interviewer while maximizing the amount of useful information obtained from the child during the interview (Steller & Boychuk, 1992). The interview is structured as a hypothesis-testing problem-solving process (see also Wegener, 1989). From the available information, the interviewer generates a complete set of alternative hypotheses that might explain the origin of the child statement's content in contrast to the basic hypothesis that the statement is about an experienced event. During the course of the interview, all alternative hypotheses are followed up, thereby assuring that the interview does not just aim at reassuring a present agenda.

Turning a professional investigative interview into a layman's fishing expedition, that is, an unprepared, open-ended, trial-and-error process, would not only mean to minimize the forensic usefulness of the interview but also possibly to maximize the length and number of interview sessions necessary to achieve any useful information from the child interviewee. This contrasts sharply with the aim of reducing the danger of secondary traumatizations from forensic procedures.

The need for systematized, theoretically and empirically founded interview strategies corrresponds with the plea for documentation of the initial interviews by means of audio or video recordings. The most elaborated proposal on the use of videotaped evidence is described by Rhona Flin in her chapter on the child witness in British courts. Renate Volbert complains about the lack of documentation of the initial interview and the corresponding need for repeated interviews of the child witness by the expert witness in the German system. The picture of a police officer simultaneously typing a record on an old-fashioned typewriter while interviewing a child witness seems archaic but is present reality in Germany. Police reports in Germany frequently demonstrate everything ranging from the police officers' attitudes toward sexual matters, fears to talk about them with children, up to language problems of the police interrogators, but they contain only little from the child's actual wording. Of course, Criteria-Based Statement Analysis, which basically makes use of a sentence-by-sentence or a word-by-word analysis of the child's statement, cannot be applied to a summary police report about the statement. A verbatim transcript of the statement itself is needed. Repeated undocumented interviews by parents, police, and prosecution attorneys not only weaken or totally destroy the discriminating power of Criteria-Based Statement Analysis but also lay the ground for suspicion that the child's statement might be contaminated by unknown influences during the undocumented interviews. Repeated undocumented interviews therefore not only constitute an avoidable burden for the child witness but also enhance the probability of false negative legal decisions, that is, dismissals or acquittals in cases where child sexual abuse actually did occur.

Tamar Morag's paper on the progressive revision of the Israeli law of evidence from 1955, which introduced the youth interrogator who is allowed to substitute a child witness in court, describes how this child protection measure might be responsible for relatively low conviction rates. According to a recent amendment, all youth interrogations must now be recorded in order to enable judges and juries to assess the credibility of the child's statement by themselves. As Tamar Morag points out, mandatory audiotapes or videotapes should be combined with training in proper interview techniques. There would be only limited advantage in documenting interviews that do not allow for forensic conclusions other than that the interview was poorly conducted. On the other hand, even documentations of poor interviews might add to defining characteristics of interview techniques that are useful for forensic purposes. They could also help to overcome the myth that children in general are unreliable witnesses by proving that confusions in child statements are frequently introduced by poor interview techniques.

Toril Havik in her paper also critically mentions the lack of training and skills in interview techniques on the side of the various professionals involved in child interviewing in sexual abuse cases in Norway. The observation of a mutual distrust among professionals from different backgrounds (e.g., law, psychology, child welfare) is certainly not a Norwegian peculiarity. Interdisciplinary projects accompanied by research - as mentioned in several of the papers - are well-suited to overcome such barriers.

It is an interesting detail in Mary O'Neill's chapter that judges in Canada are no longer allowed to warn juries about the unreliability of children's evidence in general but only with respect to particular circumstances in a particular case, thereby treating children no differently from adult witnesses. Focusing on interview characteristics helps to avoid resurrecting the fruitless debate from the beginning of the century on whether children in general can be reliable witnesses. After Stern's (1902, p.327) misleading overgeneralization of experimental findings that neglected both task and context variables, false statements (by children) were thought to be the rule and accurate statements to be exceptions. There is a need, therefore, for the rehabilitation of the child witness (Steller, 1991). Adequate treatment of child-victim witnesses also includes that a policy should be developed to instruct child witnesses about the need and meaning of procedural requirements and legal standards such as assumption of innocence, burden of proof, and reasonable doubt.

Overall, the experts' chapters make it clear that legal rules and procedures for interviewing and assessing child witnesses in sexual abuse cases offer a wide field for a beneficial cooperation between law and psychology in research and practice, not only within national jurisdictions but also in an international perspective.

References

Davies, G., & Drinkwater, J. (Eds.)(1988). *The child witness - Do the courts abuse children? Issues in criminological and legal psychology*, No. 13. Leicester: The British Psychological Society.

Jones, D., & McQuiston, M. (1989). *Interviewing the sexually abused child*. Oxford: Alden Press.

MacFarlane, K., & Krebs, S. (1986). Techniques for interviewing and evidence gathering. In K. MacFarlane, & J. Waterman (Eds.), *Sexual abuse of young children* (pp. 67-100). New York: Guilford Press.

Spencer, J.R., Nicholson, G., Flin, R., & Bull, R. (Eds.)(1990). *Children's evidence in legal proceedings. An international perspective*. Cambridge: University Law Faculty.

Steller, M. (1989). Recent developments in statement analysis. In J. Yuille (Ed.), *Credibility assessment. A unified theoretical and research perspective* (pp. 135-154). Dordrecht: Kluwer Academic Publishers.

Steller, M. (1991). Rehabilitation of the child witness. In J. Doris (Ed.), *The suggestibility of children's recollections* (pp. 106-109). Washington, D.C.: American Psychological Association.

Steller, M., & Boychuk, T. (1992). Children as witnesses in sexual abuse cases: Investigative interview and assessment techniques. In H. Dent, & R. Flin (Eds.), *Children as witnesses* (pp. 47-71). Chichester: John Wiley & Sons.

Steller, M., & Köhnken, G. (1989). Criteria-based statement analysis. In D. Raskin (Ed.), *Psychological methods in criminal investigation and evidence* (pp. 217-245). New York: Springer.

Stern, W. (1902). Zur Psychologie der Aussage. *Zeitschrift für die gesamte Strafrechtswissenschaft, 22*, 315-370.

Underwager, R., Wakefield, H., Legrand, R., Bartz, C., & Erickson, J. (1986). *The role of the psychologist in the assessment of cases of alleged sexual abuse of children*. Paper presented at the 94th Annual Convention of the American Psychological Association, Washington, D.C.

Undeutsch, U. (1982). Statement reality analysis. In A. Trankell (Ed.), *Reconstructing the past* (pp. 27-56). Stockholm: Norstedt & Soners.

Undeutsch, U. (1984). Courtroom evaluation of eyewitness testimony. *International Review of Applied Psychology, 33*, 51-67.

Undeutsch, U. (1989). The development of statement reality analysis. In J. Yuille (Ed.), *Credibility assessment. A unified theoretical and research perspective* (pp. 101-119). Dordrecht: Kluwer Academic Publishers.

Wegener, H. (1989). The present state of statement analysis. In J. Yuille (Ed.), *Credibility assessment. A unified theoretical and research perspective* (pp. 121-133). Dordrecht: Kluwer Academic Publishers.

White, S., Strom, G.A., Santilli, G.S., & Halpin, B.M. (1986). Interviewing young sexual abuse victims with anatomically correct dolls. *Child Abuse and Neglect, 10*, 519-529.

Child Witnesses in British Courts

Rhona H. Flin

> The courtroom ordeal of child victims. (The Independent 9.7.90)
> Plea for children's evidence on video as case collapses. (The Times 22.6.90)
> Move to ease witness ordeal for children. (The Scotsman 28.7.90)

Headlines such as these have appeared with depressing regularity in British newspapers since the media became interested not only in sexual abuse but also in the problems which child victims experience in our criminal courts. Although children have given evidence in Scottish and English trials for centuries, it was not until the early 1980s that the problems faced by child witnesses became the focus of attention. This concern appears to have been the result of (a) increasing numbers of child sexual abuse allegations (mirroring similar trends in other countries), (b) a series of spectacularly unsuccessful prosecutions of child sexual abuse which attracted extensive press coverage, and (c) the development of victim support organisations, which began to complain about the insensitive treatment of adult victims, particularly rape victims, at the hands of our criminal justice system. The increase in child abuse allegations is generally attributed to an increase in reporting as opposed to a rise in the incidence rate of these crimes. Whatever the true cause of this effect, as the numbers of reported cases rose, many professionals became increasingly worried about children's ability to cope with the demands of criminal proceedings.

Legal Systems of Scotland and England

The Scottish and English legal systems are entirely separate and have many distinctive features (for example their rules of evidence and their child care laws), yet both criminal justice systems are accusatorial (adversarial) in nature (for a detailed description see, Spencer & Flin, 1990). This means that a child who has witnessed a crime or who has been victimised must appear in court to give evidence at a formal trial which will involve a legal examination and cross-examination by opposing lawyers in the presence of the defendant. There are no formal age limits for the admission of children's evidence and competence is assessed by the presiding judge: In Scotland, children as young as three years of age have given evidence in criminal proceedings. In England, until very recently, it was unusual for the evidence of children under the age of 8 years to be admitted as competent, the latest judgements have indicated that 5 and 6 year olds may be deemed competent. Expert evidence from psychologists and psychiatrists on witness credibility or the traumatic effects of sexual abuse is generally deemed inadmissible in criminal proceedings.

Many adult witnesses find their day in court to be a difficult experience and for some children the demands of the trial are so overwhelming that they create an impediment to justice. On occasion, children have been so upset that their evidence is incomplete or incoherent and in other cases child victims have been unable to give any evidence at all. This situation is obviously unsatisfactory both in terms of the quality of evidence being presented to the court and in regard to the child's psychological wellbeing.

There appears to be little doubt that many children suffer from anxiety both before and during the trial and that some children will experience negative effects in the longer term (Goodman et al., 1992; Spencer & Flin, 1990). However, it is difficult to estimate the size of this problem: In neither Scotland nor England are there any official statistics which record the numbers of children called to the criminal courts to give evidence as witnesses. While child sexual abuse victims appear to constitute the majority of English child witnesses, in Scotland significant numbers of children are called to give evidence for crimes they have witnessed as bystanders, such as assaults or road accidents. In the city of Glasgow (pop. 800,000), for example, a total of 1,440 children under the age of 16 years were cited as witnesses in a 12 month period (Flin, Bull, Boon, & Knox, 1992). Under Scot's Law all evidence requires to be corroborated and this may account for the numbers of non-victims called to give evidence. In England there is no general corroboration rule and it seems that fewer child bystander witnesses give evidence. (The specific requirement in England that children's unsworn evidence must be corroborated was abolished in the Criminal Justice Act of 1988, however the judge still has a duty to warn the jury of the dangers of convicting on the uncorroborated evidence of a sexual complainant - and many child abuse victims will find themselves in this category).

Before contemplating legal reform, it is first necessary to determine the principal causes of stress for child witnesses required to give evidence in British criminal courts. Some of these problems will be specific to the demands of the adversarial trial (e.g. confronting the accused or cross-examination) while others may also be found in jurisdictions with a more inquisitorial approach (pretrial delays, giving oral evidence).

There are three main sources of information on the causes of stress for witnesses in the accusatorial systems of United Kingdom and of North America: (a) anecdotal accounts from witnesses reported in articles or the press, (b) reports and case studies from social workers, prosecutors, psychologists and psychiatrists (e.g. Burgess & Holmstrom, 1978), (c) systematic interview studies of professionals working with child witnesses (Flin, Davies, & Tarrant, 1988; Whitcomb, Shapiro, & Stellwagon, 1985), and (d) interviews with child witnesses themselves (Flin et al., 1988; Goodman et al., 1992).

In any attempt to evaluate the psychological impact of the child's involvement in legal proceedings, it is important to distinguish effects attributable to the legal process from post traumatic stress related to the crime itself. This problem of confounding variables can be tackled by studying matched cases of child sexual abuse and comparing those children who go to trial with those who are not required to testify (Goodman et al., 1992). Another technique is to study the total population of child witnesses, that is bystanders who have not been directly victimised as well as victims (Flin et al; 1992). Drawing from these various sources of information a reasonably clear picture of the consistent stress factors begins to emerge (see Figure 1).

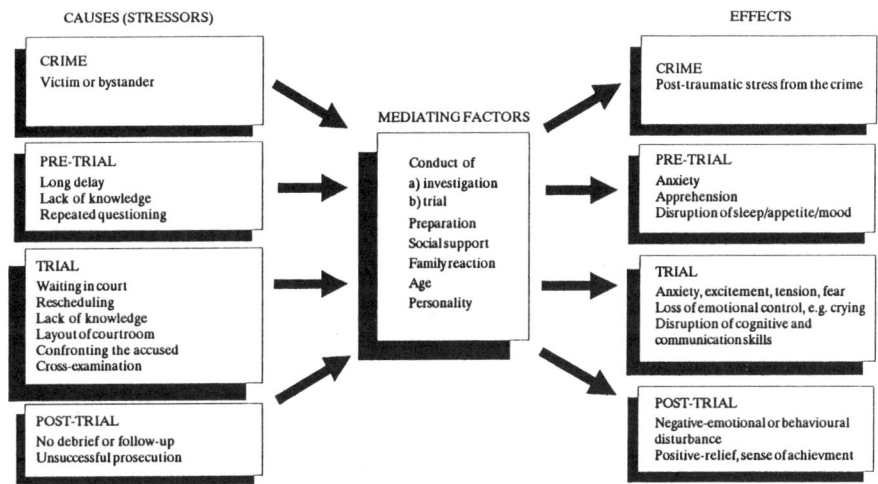

Figure 1: Model of Stress Factors for Child Witnesses (from Spencer & Flin, 1990).

Stress Factors

The major sources of stress (or stressors) can be subdivided on a temporal basis into (1) pre-trial, (2) the trial, and (3) post-trial stages. These will be outlined briefly, for a more detailed account see Spencer and Flin (1990).

Pre-trial

Children who witness criminal offences may have to wait many months before they are called to give their evidence in court. There are no official figures of the delays experienced by child witnesses in England (likely to be in the order of 4 - 6 months or longer), although it is widely believed that the present delays are unacceptable and that child abuse cases should be prioritised for a speedy disposition (Plotnikoff, 1990). In Scotland, the average delay between witnessing a crime and the trial is in the order of 5 to 6 months (Flin, Boon, Knox, & Bull, in press). Such delays can pose two problems for child witnesses, namely the anxiety of waiting to be examined in court and also the risk of memory fade over this period. A recent study has suggested that younger children may forget more information than older children and adults over a 5 month delay (Flin et al., in press).

A related difficulty for child witnesses is their lack of relevant legal knowledge. This has been identified in a number of countries including Scotland (Flin, Stevenson, & Davies, 1989), the United States (Saywitz, 1989; Warren-Leubecker, Tate, Hinton, & Ozbek, 1989) and Australia (Cashmore & Bussey, 1990). Children's ignorance of legal proceedings can result in fear of the unknown as well as misapprehensions about the format or purpose of the trial. If the child misunderstands the roles of the lawyers involved in an adversarial trial this may also influence the child's behaviour in the witness box. The third issue which has received a great deal of professional attention is the necessity for the child to be repeatedly interviewed by a number of agencies, e.g. police, social workers, paediatricians, lawyers. The stress this can cause to the child victims has been well documented and has led to a number of innovative approaches, such as videotaped interviews or joint-agency investigations.

The Trial

Criminal courts in Britain were not designed to be user-friendly environments for obvious reasons. They are often located in buildings which are old and too small for their present volume of business. Waiting facilities are often quite unsuitable for children particularly where there is a risk of the child encountering the accused before the trial. Parents unfamiliar with the criminal courts do not expect to have to wait for hours before their child is called, and unforeseen delays and schedule changes can contribute to a witness's anxiety.

Once the child has been called into the courtroom, she may be asked to stand alone in the witness box, in full view of the defendant. The courtroom is often large and imposing, and the lawyers and judge may be wearing wigs and gowns. Although the court can be cleared of the public at the discretion of the judge when a child gives evidence, this is not always done. Even if the public are excluded, the lawyers, court officials and the jury (12 in England, 15 in Scotland) may amount to a large audience of 20 to 30 strangers.

The specific features of a formal trial that appear to trouble children are: (a) standing alone in the witness box, (b) proximity of the defendant, (c) the elevation of the judge, (d) the audience, (e) the lawyers' formal dress, and (f) the necessity of projecting one's voice across a very large room. Most if not all these difficulties can be avoided without the necessity of major legal reform. Procedural changes and practical devices which have been implemented or are currently under consideration are discussed below.

The procedure in an adversarial trial is that the prosecuting lawyer will lead the witness's evidence (the examination in chief), which is intended to be favourable to the prosecution's case. (Child witnesses are almost always called by the prosecution.) Then the defence lawyer will conduct the cross-examination in which he or she will try to elicit evidence which damages the prosecution's case or at least destroys the credibility of the witness. The prosecuting lawyer may then re-examine the witness to clarify or consolidate the prosecution case. In the case of multiple accused, the child may be cross-examined several times by different lawyers. There is little doubt that many witnesses, both adults and children find this to be a traumatic process, especially the cross-examination which is designed to discredit the prosecution evidence, for example by accusing the witness of lying. A related problem for small children and (possibly some adults) is that they find the formal language used by lawyers in court difficult to understand (Brennan & Brennan, 1988; Flin et al. 1992).

Post-trial

After the child has given evidence it may still be necessary to provide information and support for the family. If the prosecution has been unsuccessful the child may feel personally responsible that the case has failed, even although other factors may have been instrumental in the final verdict.

Psychological Effects

As Figure 1 illustrates there are many factors which may cause stress, but whether or not a particular child experiences anxiety in the short or long term will depend on a number of other factors, shown as mediating factors. Judges have a reasonable degree of discretion in determining the conduct of a trial and may be prepared to dispense with unnecessary formalities in the courtroom in order to make the child feel more at ease. An individual's ability to cope with a potentially stressful situation will also depend on their personality, previous experiences and the degree of social support provided by others.

While it is well known that many witnesses experience anxiety before or during a trial, the longer term effects of being examined in court are more difficult to assess. There have been very few well controlled studies of children who have given evidence at formal trials. Gail Goodman has just completed a study of 46 child sexual abuse victims who were required to testify during the legal process and she found that at seven months after the initial testimony, (in the USA children may have to testify at several stages of the process), the children who testified showed greater behavioural disturbance than the children who did not testify, especially if the 'testifiers' took the stand several times, were deprived of maternal support and lacked corroboration of their claims. However once the prospect of giving evidence was finally behind them the adverse effects of testifying were diminished (Goodman et al., 1992). It therefore appears that the after-effects for most victims will be in the short rather than the long term. Nevertheless it should be remembered that most of these children will have waited many months before the trial took place and may have experienced anxiety during this period.

Table 1: British Options for Reducing Children's Stress.

Stress factors	Possible solutions
Pretrial anxiety	Pretrial preparation Leaflets for children
Repeated interviews	Videotaped evidence Joint interviews Professional training
Delays	Videotaped evidence Expedite cases
Courtroom	Videotaped evidence Videolinked evidence Reduce Formality
Confronting Accused	Videotaped evidence Videolinked evidence Screens
Adversarial examination	Videotaped evidence Child examiner Legal training

Proposals for Reducing Stress

At the present time, there is widespread international interest in the problems of gathering and testing children's evidence, especially in abuse cases. Lawyers and psychologists are surveying with great interest legal reforms proposed or enacted in other jurisdictions. Last year an international conference of lawyers, psychologists and other professionals was held in Cambridge in order to examine how very different legal systems attempt to solve the same problems. (A complete collection of the conference papers can be found in Spencer, Nicholson, Flin, & Bull, 1990).

Returning to the principal sources of stress identified in Figure 1, some of these can be eliminated or minimised by simple procedural changes, while others require changes to existing legislation, for example to permit the use of relatively modern technology.

A brief summary of possible strategies for improving the adversarial system for child witnesses is given above in Table 1. This is a British version of the summary presented several years ago for the United States by Whitcomb et al. (1985), and is similar in content to her updated proposals (Whitcomb, 1990).

The Present Position in the UK

Scotland

In Scotland, the Lord Advocate asked the Scottish Law Commission in 1986 to look at the particular problems relating to children's evidence. They produced a Discussion Paper for consultation in 1988, and when all responses had been considered, they published a final report "The Evidence of Children and Other Potentially Vulnerable Witnesses" (Scottish Law Commission, 1990). This was a carefully argued set of proposals which included practical measures such as the removal of wigs and gowns, the use of screens in court and allowing the child to give evidence sitting in the well of the court with the lawyers. There were also more radical recommendations for the use of videolink systems and prerecorded videotaped depositions at the discretion of the judge. This deposition would be recorded close to the time of the trial in the judge's chambers and the child would still be examined by prosecuting and defence counsel, however the accused is excluded and has to observe the proceedings through a one way mirror or videolink, although he would have a direct sound link with his counsel. While they advised that videotapes of early interviews made by non-lawyers should be admissible, this was only if the child also gave evidence. It was not suggested that these should be used in place of the child's live evidence at trial. To date the only change that has resulted from these proposals is that the Lord Justice General has issued (July, 1990) a practice direction to judges which gives guidelines for reducing courtroom formality for child witnesses. These include removing wigs and gowns, seating the child outwith the witness box, allowing a supporting adult to sit beside the child and clearing the courtroom. While these guidelines are helpful they simply endorse what the more enlightened judges have been doing in recent years. They do not solve the basic problems of delays, attending court or adversarial examinations. It is hoped that the more advanced recommendations will be enacted in the not too distant future.

England

South of the border a similar review of procedures for taking children's evidence has been undertaken by the English Home Office. A number of changes have already occurred through the Criminal Justice Bill of 1988 (amendments to the corroboration rules and the introduction of live videolink system on an experimental basis in Crown Courts); in addition, several important judgements have created new case law on the question of young children's competency (4, 5 and 6 year olds deemed competent).

The videolink system whereby children give their evidence in a room adjoining the courtroom by means of close circuit television is currently being evaluated by a team of psychologists led by Professor Graham Davies of Leicester University.

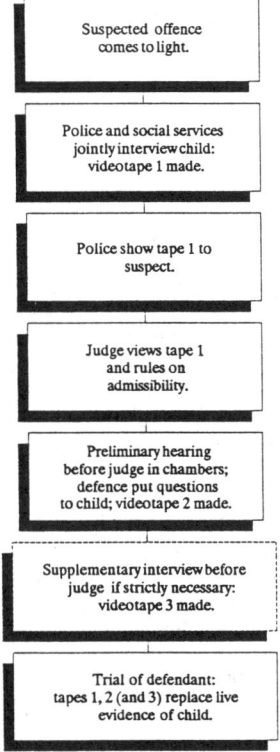

Figure 2: The Pigot Committee Scheme (from Spencer & Flin, 1990).

In response to mounting public pressure, the Home Office set up a special committee chaired by Judge Pigot to consider the possible use of videotaped evidence. This committee produced a very radical report (Home Office, 1989) which recommended that the first interviews conducted with a child victim are recorded on videotape. If this tape is deemed admissible by the judge then the child's evidence would be taken at a preliminary hearing where the initial tape would be shown. At this stage a tape would also be made of the child's examination and cross-examination and at the trial these two tapes could be used in place of the child having to give live evidence (see Figure 2).

This proposal has a number of advantages, for instance the early tape preserves the original and freshest account and the child is not required to wait months before having to attend court to be examined in the witness box or through the videolink. As in Scotland, these proposals are still under consideration and may or may not see the light of day.

Conclusion

It is an unfortunate probability that children will continue to find themselves in the roles of victims and witnesses to crime in the coming decades. There is a pressing need for more psychological research in to the problems children encounter when they are required to give evidence at a criminal trial and on the possible impact of new procedures. Lawyers should be prepared to listen to the fruits of such research because in the 1990s attempts to reform the law should be founded on solid empirical evidence as well as on accumulated legal wisdom.

References

Brennan, M., & Brennan, R. (1988). *Strange language*. Wagga Wagga: Riverina Literacy Centre.

Burgess, A., & Holmstrom, L. (1978). The child and family during the court process. In A. Burgess, A. Groth, L. Holmstrom, & S. Sgroi (Eds.), *Sexual assault of children and adults*. Lexington: Lexington Books.

Cashmore, J., & Bussey, K. (1990). Children's conceptions of the witness role. In J. Spencer, G. Nicholson, R. Flin, & R. Bull (Eds.), *Children's evidence in legal proceedings* (pp. 177-188). Available from Cambridge University Law Faculty.

Flin, R. Boon, J., Knox, A., & Bull, R. (in press). The effects of a five month delay on children's and adults's eyewitness memory. *British Journal of Psychology*.

Flin, R., Bull, R., Boon, J., & Knox, A. (1992). Children in the witness-box. In H. Dent, & R. Flin (Eds.), *Children as witnesses* (pp. 167-179). Chichester: Wiley.

Flin, R., Davies, G., & Tarrant, A. (1988). *The child witness*. Report to the Scottish Home and Health Department.

Flin, R., Stevenson, Y., & Davies, G. (1989). Children's knowledge of legal proceedings. *British Journal of Psychology, 80*, 285-297.

Goodman, G., Taub, E., Jones, D., England, P., Port, P., Rudy, L., & Prado, L. (1992). *Emotional effects of criminal court testimony on child sexual assault victims*. Society for Research in Child Development Monographs (in press).

Home Office (1989). *The use of videotechnology at trials of alleged child abusers*. London: Home Office.

Plotnikoff, J. (1990). Delay in child abuse prosecutions. *Criminal Law Review*, 645-647.

Saywitz, K. (1989). Children's conceptions of the legal system. In S. Ceci, D. Ross, & M. Toglia (Eds.), *Perspectives on children's testimony* (pp. 131-157). New York: Springer.

Scottish Law Commission (1990). The evidence of children and other potentially vulnerable witnesses (SLC No. 125). Edinburgh: HMSO.

Spencer, J., & Flin, R. (1990). *The evidence of children*. London: Blackstone.

Spencer, J., Nicholson, G., Flin, R., & Bull, R. (Eds.) (1990). *Children's evidence in legal proceedings*. Available from Cambridge University Law Faculty.

Warren-Leubecker, A., Tate, C., Hinton, L., & Ozbek, N. (1989). What do children know about the legal system and when do they know it? In S. Ceci, D. Ross, & M. Toglia (Eds.), *Perspectives on children's testimony* (pp. 158-183). New York: Springer.

Whitcomb, D., Shapiro, C., & Stellwagon, E. (1985). *When the victim is a child.* Washington: National Institute of Justice.

Whitcomb, D. (1990). When the victim is a child: Past hope, current reality and future prospect of legal reform in the United States. In J. Spencer, G. Nicholson, R. Flin, & R. Bull (Eds.), *Children's evidence in legal proceedings* (pp. 133-146). Available from Cambridge University Law Faculty.

Child Witnesses in Sexual Abuse Cases: The Juridical Situation in Germany

Renate Volbert

In Germany[1], as in other countries, increased attention directed toward child sexual abuse over the past years has, from time to time, raised the question as to whether the existing legal systems and procedures, as well as general legal practice itself, are appropriate for dealing with the child witnesses involved (e.g., Diesing, 1980). However, in contrast to other countries (see, e.g., Davies & Drinkwater, 1988; Goodman, 1984; Heddermann, 1987; Melton, 1984; Naylor, 1989; Parker, 1982; Spencer & Flin, 1990), there is no current noteworthy debate in Germany on strategies for improving or strengthening the position of child witnesses, nor have significant considerations been made on changes in legislation. This situation may be due to two factors: First, Germany already follows legal procedures that offer relatively great protection to child witnesses when compared to many other countries. Second, during the last decade, there has been no increase in Germany in the number of charges or convictions involving child sexual abuse. On the contrary: Until recently, statistics have reflected a decrease in reported cases.

The following provides information on these two complexes, as well as on preliminary results of an ongoing study dealing with prosecution in cases of child sexual abuse.

Legal Situation in Germany

Criminal law

According to German criminal law, children under the age of 14 are under no circumstances considered capable of consenting to sexual activity of any kind (Penal Code, § 176). Sexual acts with persons under 18 are subject to punishment under certain conditions, primarily if the juvenile is a biological, adopted, or foster child of the perpetrator, or if the juvenile is in a state of dependence owing to an educational or instructional relationship (Penal Code, § 174).

Pretrial procedure. If an allegation of child sexual abuse is reported to the police, subsequent interrogations of the child are made only by the responsible police officers themselves. Child welfare officers will be informed, but, in general, there is no coordination such as joint interviews with the child. It is also very uncommon to appoint an expert witness at this stage of the investigation. Police officers who interview children normally have not received training for such tasks. In larger German cities, however, special police

---

[1] All statistics refer to the territory of the former FRG, excluding the former GDR.

departments exist that deal only with child sexual abuse cases. According to official guidelines, police officers are expected to draw up records as literally as possible. In practice, this means that very often the police officer who interviews the child is at the same time typing the record. Audio- or videotapes of interviews are very uncommon.

In all cases in which the defendant is a relative of the child, the child has the right to withhold testimony. This must be explained to the child before the interview. If the child is able to understand the sense of the right to withhold testimony, his or her decision to testify or not is relevant. If the child is not able to understand, the parents must make the decision. But even if they allow their child to testify, the child is still allowed to refuse testimony. If one of the parents is accused and the child is not able to understand the right to withhold testimony, it is possible to appoint a receiver to make the decision whether or not the child should testify.

If a court proceeding takes place, the period between police interview and court trial is often longer than one year. In cases of alleged incest, an interrogation of the child by a judge is sometimes made during this period. The reason for this is as follows: If a child witness decides to withhold testimony during the trial, former statements can be used as evidence only if the interrogation had been made by a judge. Interrogations by the police are not admissible.

Trial procedure. Special rules are in force for dealing with child witnesses in court proceedings in Germany. First, all cases in which children are involved as victim witnesses - most of them, sexual abuse cases - can be tried by a juvenile criminal court (Constitution of Law-courts, § 26). Most trial proceedings are conducted in this manner.

In comparison with judicial systems in other countries, the position of child witnesses in Germany is more favorable because the German criminal justice system is not adversarial in nature. According to German law governing criminal procedure, all proceedings are dealt with in an inquisitorial manner. This system provides the basis for special rules. Pertaining to child witnesses up to the age of 16, the following rules are in force in Germany:

1. Only the presiding judge is allowed to direct questions to a child. Other participants concerned in the case have no right to interrogate the child, but they may insist that the judge directs certain further questions. Other participants may request the right to interrogate a child, but this is rarely granted (Code of Criminal Procedure, § 241a). This means that there is no cross-examination of children in Germany.

2. The trial can be held in camera, with exclusion of the general public, while a child witness is testifying (Constitution of Law-courts, § 172).

3. It is also possible to send the accused out of court while a child witness is testifying, if otherwise considerable detriment to the child's well-being is feared, or if it is expected that the child will not tell the truth in the presence of the accused (Code of Criminal Procedure, § 247).

Currently in Germany, children are normally required to give evidence in all cases in which the accused does not admit guilt. A minimum age for testifying is not fixed, and children as young as three years of age have been called as witnesses. The use of video technology in courtrooms is very uncommon.

In support of a child, she or he may be represented by a lawyer, who will then act as a third party during the trial; that is, the lawyer can direct questions to witnesses, propose the calling of further witnesses, and the like.

Expert witnesses. Quite often an expert witness (mostly a psychologist) is appointed by the court or the prosecution attorney to testify to the credibility of a child's statement. With respect to the inquisitorial system, the role of the expert is a neutral one. Appointing an expert implies on the part of the expert the right to have access to all facts of the case - that is, to the whole case file - and the right to interview the child outside the courtroom. Except for cases in which parents are accused, one or both parents will also be interviewed. The expert witness participates at the trial from the very beginning in order to become aware of all evidence presented in court. During the trial, the expert witness has the right to direct questions to all witnesses. After taking all evidence, the expert is asked to judge the credibility of the witness's statement. (In most cases, the expert will have already delivered a preliminary written expertise after examining the child - a procedure that usually takes place before the beginning of the trial.)

However, participation in the examination is voluntary, and no witness can be compelled to cooperate. If the witness refuses to submit to examination, the expert witness can also be asked to deliver the expertise as part of participation in the court trial. The courts are not, however, bound to act in accordance with the opinion of the expert. Instead, they are obliged to assess the expertise and reach an independent final judgment on the credibility of the witness's statement (see Köhnken & Steller, 1988).

The psychological assessment of the credibility of statements consists of a complex diagnostic approach, including an analysis of the individual characteristics and motives of the child witness and an analysis of the content of the statement itself, which is the crucial part of the credibility assessment. This content analysis is conducted according to a prescribed set of criteria (Steller, 1989; Steller & Köhnken, 1989).

There are no official figures on how often expert witnesses are appointed. In a decision of the German Supreme Court in 1954, it was ruled that expert witnesses must be called to assess the truthfulness of children's or juveniles' testimonies in cases in which such testimony represents the sole, or main, evidence, and if it is not corroborated by other evidence (Supreme Court, Criminal Branch, 1955, 7, 82-86). Since this decision, however, a great number of Supreme Court decisions have weakened this procedural rule and have principally limited its use to extraordinary and complicated cases. Nevertheless, such expert testimony is currently very often requested in court.

Frequencies of Charges and Convictions in Cases of Child Sexual Abuse

Police statistics supplying information on the frequency of charges show that, until recently, there has been a decrease in the number of charges filed on child sexual abuse (Figure 1). Since 1988, however, we have observed a moderate increase in reported charges. Currently, the police solve an average of 60% of these cases. Ninety-eight percent of all suspects are male. On average, there are 1.5 complainants filed for each suspect. According to police data, in two-thirds of all cases, the child and the alleged perpetrator did not know each other before the alleged acts.

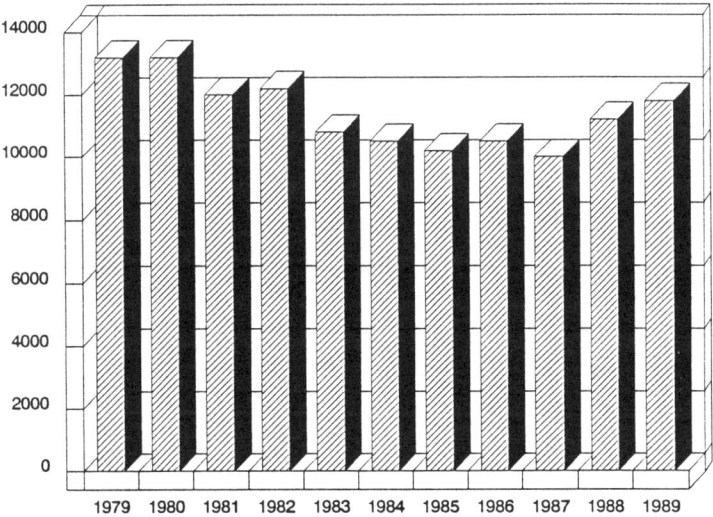

Figure 1: Police Statistics 1979 - 1990.

In less than 5% of cases, child and alleged perpetrator are relatives. These statistics are in clear contradiction to studies outside the context of judicial action, which emphasize the typical close relationship between child and perpetrator (e.g., Finkelhor, 1979) and indicate an underreporting of child sexual abuse within the family in official crime statistics. Seventy-five percent of the complainants are female, and less than 10% are younger than six. Figure 2 presents information on the number of court proceedings and convictions.

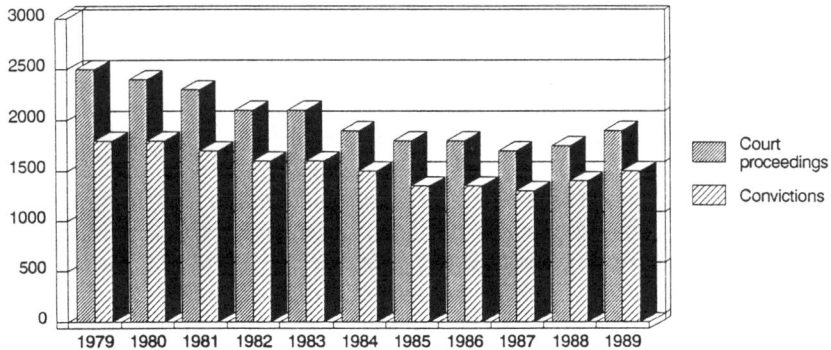

Figure 2: Court Proceedings and Convictions in Cases of CSA.

There was also a decrease of court proceedings and convictions in cases of child sexual abuse until 1987, followed by a slight increase in 1988. In 20 to 30% of all cases in which the main proceedings were opened, the accused was acquitted or the charges were dropped.

Because of different modes and periods of registration, the two groups of statistics cannot be compared directly. Nevertheless, a general comparison does allow limited conclusions. Upon study of both statistics, the discrepancy is striking between the number of cases reported to the police and the number actually tried in court (Table 1).

Table 1: Charges, Court Proceedings and Convictions in Cases of Child Sexual Abuse.

	Police statistics		Court statistics			
	Charges	Suspects	Court proceedings	Percentage of all suspects	Convictions	Percentage of all proceedings
	N	N	N		N	
1979	13200	6300	2500	40%	1800	72%
1980	13200	6300	2400	38%	1800	75%
1981	12100	5800	2300	40%	1700	74%
1982	12300	5800	2100	36%	1600	76%
1983	10900	*	2100	*	1600	76%
1984	10600	4800	1900	40%	1500	79%
1985	10400	4600	1800	39%	1400	78%
1986	10600	4600	1800	39%	1400	78%
1987	10100	4300	1700	39%	1300	76%
1988	11400	4700	1800	38%	1400	78%
1989	11800	5000	1900	38%	1500	79%

* Due to problems connected with a new mode of registration number of suspects was not published in 1983.

In about 60% of cases in Germany for which police have located a suspect, charges are dropped between police investigations and court proceedings. This means that a bill of indictment is not filed in 60% of cases. If one further takes into account the number of acquittals in cases actually handled by courts, the result is that almost 70% of all suspects located by the police are eventually released without conviction. Since extensive studies do not exist here in Germany, clear insights have not been gained in to why charges are dropped so often.

Studies in other countries have revealed similar data on the initial prosecution process, although the conviction rate appears to be slightly lower in Germany (Bradshaw & Marks, 1990; Cashmore & Horsky, 1988; Conte & Berliner, 1981; MacMurray, 1988). Such differences may, however, be chiefly attributable to different systems of criminal justice.

A Pilot Study

As described above, there is a lack of information concerning the frequency with which children testify in courts, the types of event they testify about, and the frequency with which - and the reasons why - cases are dropped, dismissed, or lead to acquittals or convictions. To provide further information, a comprehensive analysis is now being prepared by the author on the way cases of child sexual abuse are dealt with in the German criminal justice system, from the first filing of a charge to the final decision. Research is now being directed toward (a) identifying variables that influence the prosecution process and the final decision, and (b) analyzing expert credibility assessments.

The following presents the results of a pilot study conducted in West Berlin. This study utilized case files gathered by the Institute of Forensic Psychiatry of the Free University of Berlin. These were all cases in West Berlin in which members of the Institute were appointed as experts on the credibility of child witnesses. Included were all such cases between 1980 and 1989 in which the victimized witness was under the age of 16. Altogether, there were 98 cases involving a total of 107 alleged offenders and 140 children. In the same period in West Berlin, about 900 trials were conducted on child sexual abuse (involving an unknown number of children). Since expert testimony on the credibility of child witnesses is also provided by other institutions in the city, it is not possible to determine the extent to which experts are actually appointed.

Characteristics of the alleged offenders

Ninety-five percent of the defendants were male. Their average age was 38.0 years at the time of the first alleged offence and 38.9 years at the time when the current charge was filed. Defendants ranged in age from 14 to 73 years. Information on prior criminal records was limited and was unavailable in 25% of the files. In 46% of those cases in which information was available, the accused had a previous conviction record for one or more sexual offenses, mostly to the prejudice of a child. More than one person was accused in less than 5% of cases studied.

Characteristics of the complainants

The majority of complainants were female (59%). This share, however, was clearly less than the proportion of female victims reported by the police (75%). The average age at the onset of the alleged offense was 9.9 years, the youngest being 2 years old. The average age was 10.8 when the charge was filed.

Characteristics of the alleged offenses

Table 2 shows a breakdown of alleged sexual acts. There was no case in which only exhibitionism was alleged. Physical violence was involved in about 15% of all cases, and 65% involved allegations of multiple incidents over periods of time ranging from a few weeks up to seven years.

Relationship between alleged offender and complainant

The majority of alleged offenders were known to their victims. Only 10% were total strangers. In 21% there was a nodding acquaintance. The percentages in these two groups are even less if one considers only complainants younger than 14. About 30% of alleged offenders were members of the victim's family or household, 15% close friends of the family, 10% neighbors, and 10% acquaintances. Biological fathers comprised 66% of defendants in cases involving family members. These figures are not in line with offender-complainant relationships as reported in police statistics. These evidence only a very small proportion of related or acquainted suspects.

Table 2: Characteristics of Alleged Offences.

Sexual acts	Total number N=213	Percentage related to number of incidents N=213	Percentage related to number of children N=140
Fondling for a sexual purpose	92	43%	65%
Masturbating the adult	35	16%	25%
Sexual intercourse	32	15%	23%
Oral-genital contact	19	9%	14%
Indecent exposure	18	8%	13%
Anal intercourse	10	5%	7%
Exposure of pornographic films or pictures	7	3%	5%

The expert evidence

Eighty-seven percent of all children and juveniles were actually examined by experts outside courtrooms. The remaining children, or their parents, refused to submit to the examination. More than 30% of all expert opinions were delivered only orally. Since, in most of these trials, case files provided no information on the experts' conclusions, Table 3, which shows experts' conclusions, was therefore prepared from the remaining cases.

Table 3: Experts' Assessments on Witnesses' Capability to Provide Accurate Testimony and on the Credibility of their Statements.

Assessments on	Positive	Positive with reservations	Challenged	Negative
Capability to provide accurate testimony, N=80	67 (84%)	12 (15%)	-	1 (1%)
Credibility, N=66	45 (68%)	16 (24%)	3 (5%)	2 (3%)

Normally, part of the expert opinion concerns the child's ability to provide accurate testimony. In 84% of these cases, the children were assessed to be able to do so without reservation, and a further 15% with certain reservations. Only one out of 80 children was assessed as not being able to provide accurate testimony.

Sixty-eight percent of all statements were evaluated as unreservedly credible, and a further 24% were judged as basically truthful. In 5%, the truthfulness of statements was challenged; and in two cases (3%), the statement was assessed as not credible. With regard to the nature of the sample, it must be taken into consideration that it is not random. Rather, it presumably includes cases in which assessment of credibility was held to be so problematic that an expert witness had been appointed. One would expect the proportion of noncredible statements to be even smaller in a random sample.

Judicial decisions

In 5% (4) of those cases in which the case files provided information about the final decision (85), the case was dismissed after the expert opinion had been delivered. Eleven percent (9) of the cases were terminated without a formal court conviction, by paying a fine. In the remaining 84% (72), main proceedings were opened. Of this number, 26% (19) were acquitted. Of the remaining 53 defendants who were convicted, 11% (6) were required to pay a fine, 43% (23) received a custodial sentence suspended on probationary terms, and 45% (24) received custodial sentences (see Figure 3).

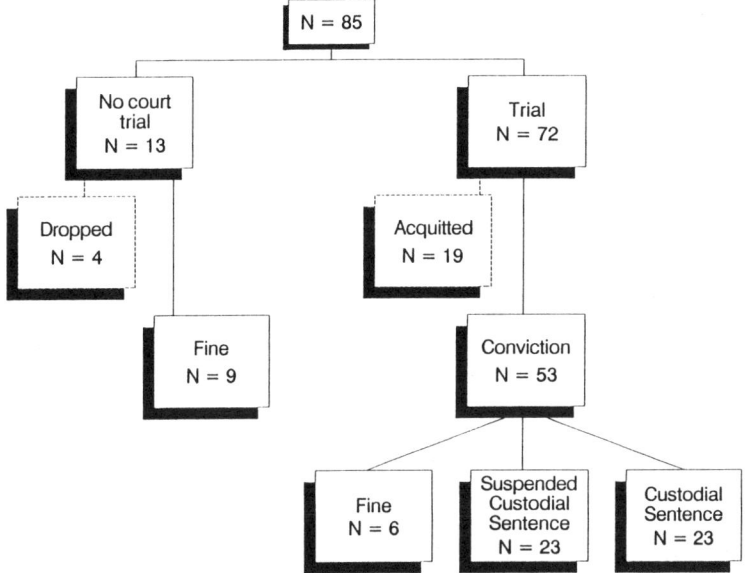

Figure 3: Judicial Decisions.

The average length of the suspended custodial sentence was 12.9 months, with a range from 4 to 24 months. The average length of the imprisonment sentence was 28.8 months, with a range from 6 to 96 months. (The maximum penalty for child sexual abuse is 10 years according to the German Penal Code.)

Whether or not a trial results in conviction is associated with the following factors: Defendants who had a record of previous sexual offenses were more likely to be convicted than those who did not have such a record ($\chi^2=13.72$, $df=1$, $p<.000$). Cases with multiple alleged incidents were also more likely to result in a conviction than single offences

($t(99) = 2.72$, $p < .01$). Cases in which physical violence occurred were more likely to end in conviction ($\chi^2 = 5.14$; $df = 1$, $p < .05$). Conviction cases were also more likely than nonconviction cases to involve either very young children (younger than 6) or older complainants (older than 10), whereas conviction was less likely when children were between 6 and 10 ($t(112) = 2.16$, $p < .05$). And, finally, conviction cases were more likely to involve defendants who were a member of the complainant's family or household than others ($\chi^2 = 10.05$, $df = 4$ $p < .05$).

The influence of experts' assessments on the credibility of children's statements and on their capability to provide accurate testimony could not be analyzed because there were so few negative assessments.

The length of the prison sentence increased significantly with the frequency of accused incidents ($F(3,124) = 8.26$, $p < .000$). Incidents with physical violence against the complainants also resulted in higher sentences ($F(3,124) = 3.24$, $p < .05$). Defendants with records of previous sexual offenses were not only more likely to be convicted but also received longer sentences ($F(2,95) = 12.80$, $p < .000$).

Concluding Remarks

Specific shortcomings are frequent in child sexual abuse cases during the pretrial period. Children are mostly interviewed by police officers who are not specially trained for these tasks, and these interviews are insufficiently documented. Long delays come about between police interviews and court trials, leading to the risk of fading memory and anxiety about waiting to be called into court (see Flin in this volume). If an expert witness is appointed during the pretrial or trial procedure, this always results in repeated interviews. This is due to the lack of proper documentation of police interrogations, as well as to the fact that police officers generally do not use interview techniques that elicit lengthy narratives. Such methods, however, are necessary for an assessment by means of statement analysis (Raskin & Steller, 1989). Professional training and improved documentation of interrogations and/or an appointment of expert witnesses at the time of police investigations could help to avoid repeated interviews and to reduce the above-mentioned problems connected with delays between police investigations and trials.

Compared with many other countries, trial procedure in Germany features regulations that offer some protection and support for child witnesses. At the same time, however, these procedures do not seem to be well-suited to the needs and capabilities of very young children, especially not to those of preschoolers. Moreover, it may be assumed that shortcomings in the pretrial period (e.g., poor interview techniques, insufficient documentation, long delays) pose problems especially for this group of very young children (e.g., Flin, Boon, Knox, & Bull, 1992). The results of the reported pilot study indicate, on the other hand, that cases of alleged child sexual abuse involving children of preschool age lead more often to convictions than cases involving children at primary school age, once these cases reach the courts (see, in contrast, Finkelhor, 1983).

Very few studies exist that deal with child witnesses' reactions to pretrial and trial procedures (Baurmann, 1983; Diesing, 1980; Wegener, 1989). There is still a lack of information that includes basic knowledge on how often and at what age child witnesses are called into courts, which kinds of event they testify about, and about how often and why expert witnesses are appointed. Hardly any information exists on variables that allow the prediction of judicial decisions (Filthaut, 1962). This fact also means that little is known about the actual influence of expert witnesses' credibility assessments (Prahm, 1972). And, finally, little knowledge exists on difficulties that arise from special pretrial or trial procedures for the child witness and for the criminal justice system.

References

Baurmann, M. (1983). *Sexualität, Gewalt und psychische Folgen.* (BKA-Forschungsreihe Band 15) Wiesbaden: Bundeskriminalamt.

Bradshaw, T.L., & Marks, A.E. (1990). Beyond a reasonable doubt: Factors that influence the legal disposition of child sexual abuse cases. *Crime and Delinquency, 36,* 276-285.

Cashmore, J., & Horsky, M. (1988). The prosecution of child sexual assault. *Australian and New Zealand Journal of Criminology, 21,* 241-252.

Conte, J.R., & Berliner, L. (1981). Prosecution of the offender in cases of sexual assault against children. *Victimology: An International Journal, 6,* 102-109.

Davies, G.M., & Drinkwater, J. (1988). *The child witness: Do the courts abuse children?* Leicester: Division of Criminological and Legal Psychology of the British Psychological Society, Occasional Paper No. 13.

Diesing, U. (1980). *Psychische Folgen von Sexualdelikten bei Kindern.* München: Minerva.

Filthaut, W. (1962). *Der Freispruch bei Unzucht mit Kindern (§176 Abs.1 Ziff 3 StGB). Eine Untersuchung über die Gründe des Freispruchs.* Unpublished doctoral dissertation, Universität Münster.

Finkelhor, D. (1979). *Sexually victimized children.* New York: The Free Press.

Finkelhor, D. (1983). Removing the child - Prosecuting the offender in cases of sexual assault against children: Evidence from the National Reporting System for Child Abuse and Neglect. *Child Abuse and Neglect, 7,* 195-205.

Flin, R., Boon, J., Knox, A., & Bull, R. (1992). The effects of a five month delay on children's and adult's eyewitness memory. *British Journal of Psychology* (in press).

Goodman, G.S. (1984). Children's testimony in historical perspective. *Journal of Social Issues, 40,* 9-31.

Hedderman, C. (1987). *Children's evidence: The need for corroboration.* London: Home Office, Research and Planning Unit, Paper 41.

Köhnken, G., & Steller, M. (1988). The evaluation of the credibility of child witness statements in the German procedural system. In G.M. Davies, & J. Drinkwater (Eds.), *The child witness: Do the courts abuse children?* (pp. 37-45). Leicester: Division of Criminological and Legal Psychology of the British Psychological Society, Occasional Paper No. 13.

MacMurray, B.K. (1988). The nonprosecution of sexual abuse and informal justice. *Journal of Interpersonal Violence, 3,* 197-202.

Melton, G.B. (1984). Child witness and the First Amendment: A psychological dilemma. *Journal of Social Issues, 40,* 109-123.

Naylor, B. (1989). Dealing with child sexual assault. *British Journal of Criminology, 29,* 395-407.

Parker, J.Y. (1982). The rights of child witnesses: Is the court a protector or a perpetrator ? *New England Law Review, 17,* 643-717.

Prahm, H. (1972). *Die ärztlich-psychologische Beurteilung der Glaubwürdigkeit Minderjähriger und ihre Berücksichtigung im Gerichtsverfahren.* (Kriminologische Studien Band 10). Göttingen: Otto Schwartz & Co.

Raskin, D.C., & Steller, M. (1989). Assessing credibility of allegations of child sexual abuse: Polygraph examinations and statement analysis. In H. Wegener, F. Lösel, & J. Haisch (Eds.), *Criminal behavior and the justice system. Psychological perspectives* (pp. 290-302). New York: Springer.

Spencer, J.R., & Flin, R. (1990). *The evidence of children. The law and the psychology.* London: Blackstone.

Steller, M. (1989). Recent developments in statement analysis. In J. Yuille (Ed.), *Credibility assessment - A unified theoretical and research perspective*. (NATO ASI Series, Series D: Behavioural and Social Sciences, Vol. 47, pp. 135-154). Dordrecht: Kluwer Academic Publishers.

Steller, M., & Köhnken, G. (1989). Criteria-based statement analysis. In D.C. Raskin (Ed.), *Psychological methods for investigation and evidence* (pp. 217-245). New York: Springer.

Wegener, H. (1989). The present state of statement analysis. In J.C. Yuille (Ed.), *Credibility assessment - A unified theoretical and research perspective*. (NATO ASI Series, Series D: Behavioural and Social Sciences, Vol. 47, pp. 121-133). Dordrecht: Kluwer Academic Publishers.

Children's Evidence in Child Abuse Proceedings under the Israeli Legal System: The Law of Evidence Revision

Tamar Morag

In 1955, following public criticism of cases in which children were harshly interrogated in court regarding sex offenses, the Knesset (the Israeli Parliament), enacted the Law of Evidence Revision (Protection of Children). The purpose of this law, as expressed in its name, is to protect children from possible harm during police courtroom interrogation.

Although 35 years have passed since this law was enacted, it is still considered one of the most innovative and unique pieces of legislation in this field. It has drawn much attention and discussion in Israel as well as abroad.

In this short presentation, I will discuss the main provisions of this law and how they were accepted, interpreted and implemented in Israel.

The Law

The law applies to children who are under 14 years of age and who are required to testify in court regarding a sex offense or an offense that was committed against them by one of their parents. It relates mainly to cases in which the child was a victim of the crime but also applies to cases in which the child is a suspect or an eyewitness of a sex offense.

The law established the function of the "youth interrogator", a new function that did not exist before the law was enacted. The youth interrogator is empowered to decide whether, and under what conditions, the child may testify in court. The interrogator is the only one who may interrogate the child and take his or her testimony.

After interrogating the child, the youth interrogator must decide whether or not to allow the child to testify in court. If the interrogator believes that testifying in court may psychologically damage the child, testimony will be forbidden. In this case, the testimony of the child taken by the youth interrogator becomes admissible in court. The interrogator presents the child's testimony to the court and testifies as to the circumstances in which the testimony was taken and as to his or her own impression of the child's credibility.

The defense and the prosecution, as well as the judge, may request that the interrogator reexamine the child and ask other specific questions. Yet, the youth interrogator has the right to refuse to ask questions that may be harmful to the child.

In those cases in which the youth interrogator does allow the child to testify in court, the court may stop the child's testimony if the youth interrogator believes that continuing the testimony would harm the child.

The main innovation of this law clearly lies in the creation of an exception to the rule excluding hearsay evidence and to the right of the accused to cross-examine the witness. In order to compensate for any potential harm to the rights of the accused, the law provides that no person may be convicted on the basis of a child's testimony submitted through a youth interrogator, unless it is corroborated by other evidence.

The Law's Implementation

According to figures provided by the Ministry of Welfare, Illana Karniel (1989), until 1988, approximately 1,000-1,200 children were interrogated every year by youth interrogators. Recently, as a result of an increase in public awareness of the issue of child abuse and the enactment of a reporting law, there has been a significant rise in the number of cases reported and referred to interrogation. In 1989 alone, 1,600 children were interrogated. It is particularly interesting to note the increase in the number of incest cases reported. While, in 1988, only 37 incest cases were reported, in 1989, 132 cases were reported.

About 80% of the children who were interrogated were themselves the victims of the crime, 14% were eyewitnesses, and 6% were suspects. In about 85% of the cases, the youth interrogator did not allow the child to testify in court.

The Youth Interrogator

It is clear that the central figure and the key to the success or failure of this law is the youth interrogator; who are the youth interrogators? How are they appointed? What are their qualifications, and what are their roles?

When the Minister of Justice presented the law to the Knesset in 1955, he remarked that "The ideal would be for a youth interrogator to combine in his personality the psychologist and the lawyer". But, he added "Unfortunately this is an unattainable ideal"(17 Divrei Haknesset, Knesset Protocols, 262).

In order to avoid the establishment of unattainable requirements, the legislator decided not to include in the law conditions for qualifications; rather, the law empowers the Minister of Justice to appoint interrogators upon the recommendation of a statutory committee.

At first the Minister appointed mainly policemen, but they seemed to lack the treatment skills that are required for the interrogation of children. The Minister then began to appoint people who had educational or treatment skills, such as social workers or teachers. In 1982, the responsibility for youth interrogation was transferred from the Police Department to the youth probation division in the Department of Welfare. Almost all youth interrogators are now probation officers and social workers by profession.

The Role of the Youth Interrogator

The major role of the interrogator is to take the child's testimony. This is done with the aid of therapeutic techniques such as the use of anatomic dolls, drawings, and play-acting. The investigation is conducted in a relaxed atmosphere that enables the child to open up. The youth interrogators are allowed to ask the child leading questions, yet they are required to write down everything that is said or that happens during the interrogation.

One of the most important questions that the Israeli courts have to deal with in interpreting the law, is whether the role of the interrogator is completed in taking down the child's testimony and presenting it to the court, or whether it is also part of his or her role to assess the child's credibility. This question was debated extensively in the Isaeli courts and has reached the Supreme Court several times.

During the first years after the law came into force, the courts tended not to admit as evidence the opinion of the youth interrogator as to the child's credibility (see *Yehudai v. The Attorney General*, 1957; *Gondler v. The Attorney General*, 1959). The courts stressed that determining the credibility of a witness was the unique and exclusive role of the court and could not be transferred to any other agent. However, this view has been revised (see *Danino v. The State of Israel*, 1986). Today the opinion of the interrogator as to the child's credibility is not only admissible but also required. According to the Supreme Court, only the court is authorized to assess the credibility of a child as a witness, yet, there is no stronger or more important evidence in determining the child's credibility than the impression of the youth interrogator.

The opinion of the youth interrogator is therefore a dominant factor in determining the child's credibility. Yet, the court is not bound by this opinion and may reach a different conclusion.

Apart from interrogating the child, the interrogator now has an additional role: to assess the child's credibility. This is a role that requires much experience and expertise. The youth interrogator who testifies in court is questioned and has to undergo cross-examination regarding not only the child's testimony but also his or her opinion of the child's credibility.

The Controversy Surrounding the Law

Ever since its enactment, the Law of Evidence Revision has been highly debated and controversial. What are the arguments raised for and against this law?

The arguments of those who support the law may be divided into two major categories:

(a) Arguments that concern the protection of children, and (b) arguments that concern the enforcement of law and justice.

The major purpose of this law is to protect children from harm during police or courtroom interrogation. Testifying in court, particularly regarding sex offenses and offenses committed by those to whom this child is emotionally attached, may be harmful to the child and add to the trauma that he or she has already suffered. The main advantage and importance of this law, stressed by its supporters, lies in its success in minimizing the emotional damage caused to the child as a result of testifying.

The other type of argument raised by those who support the law is that is has improved the possibilities of prosecution in child abuse cases. Before the law was enacted, many parents were hesitant to report cases of child abuse to the police. They wanted to protect their child from further harm that might be caused by the interrogation. Even in those cases that were reported, the Attorney General's office often decided not to prosecute in order to save the child the trauma of interrogation. It is evident that the enactment of the law has brought an increase in the number of cases reported and prosecuted.

Another argument presented in this context is that the interrogation of the child by a competent professional, in a relaxed atmosphere, increases the probability of arriving at the truth and receiving a full and accurate statement from the child.

The arguments of those who oppose the law may also be divided into two major categories: (a) the law harms the rights of the accused, and (b) the law harms law enforcement due to the difficulty of convicting on the basis of a testimony that is presented through a youth interrogator.

As I have mentioned earlier, the law creates exceptions to criminal law and evidence law principles: the rules that exclude hearsay evidence and the right to cross-examination. It is therefore argued that the law infringes on the rights of the accused and may lead to the conviction of innocent people.

Criticism of the law from an almost opposite direction is expressed by those who argue that it hinders the enforcement of justice, as, in practice, many judges find it difficult to reach a conviction based on a child's testimony that was submitted through a youth interrogator.

The difficulty in convicting stems from a variety of factors. The first and most important factor is the corroboration requirement - a requirement that does not usually exist when the child testifies in person. Until now, if a child had testified in court and was sworn to the truth, the testimony was equivalent to that of an adult. A bill on the weight of child evidence is being discussed currently by the Knesset's Legislative Committee. According to the proposed bill, the court will not be allowed to convict a person on the basis of a testimony of a child who is under the age of 12 (the age of criminal responsibility) unless the court finds "something to strengthen" the child's testimony. This is a lesser evidentiary requirement than the corroboration requirement.

The corroboration requirement is often a difficult one to meet in the case of child abuse offenses[1] - as these offenses are frequently committed within the privacy of the home, with no witnesses, and few, if any, visible scars.

A second obstacle to conviction is the fact that some judges are still not at ease with the law. Many of them find it difficult to base a conviction on testimony presented through a youth interrogator. A good illustration of these hesitations can be found in the following quotation from an appeal court's equitable decision (see hon. judge H. Ben-Ito, Tel-Aviv district court, on criminal appeal no. 906/83; from Hanon, 1988).

Status of the Law Today

Do these debates succeed in creating a threat to the law? The answer seems to be no. Despite all controversies, the status of the law is firm, and drastic changes in it are not expected.

This was specifically demonstrated in the 1987 recommendations of the committee that examined the subject of sex offenses against minors (The Melamed Committee Report,

---

[1] The court's interpretation of the corroboration requirement was severe. This view was well expressed by hon. Supreme Court Judge Landei in the case of Yehudai, where the court stressed that the corroboration required is more than a technical one (see also C.A. 192/56 *Yehudai v. The State of Israel*, 1957).

1987). In discussing the law, the committee stated that its enactment was an important achievement for the Israeli legislator and that the law must remain untouched.

There also seems to be quite widespread agreement that the legislators' fear that innocent people would be convicted has been proven false. On the contrary, the main problem of the law seems to lie in the difficulty or reaching convicting sentences.

Recent Admendments to the Law

The firm position of the law was demonstrated once again in the following amendments enacted in 1989:

Until 1989, the law applied only to sex offenses. For years, those who supported the law had argued that its restriction only to sex offenses was illogical. It was argued that there is no justification for the distinction between physical, mental, and sexual abuse, and that the law should apply to all child abuse cases.

It was also argued that the law should make special provisions for those children who are required to testify in court, either because the interrogator has allowed their testimony, or because the law does not apply to them as they are over 14, or because the offense is not a sexual one.

The amendments enacted in 1989 give at least a partial answer to these criticisms. As a result of the first amendment, the law applies not only to sex offenses but also to any offense committed against a child by one of his or her parents.[2]

The second amendment[3] deals with those children who do testify. The law empowers the judge to remove the offender from the court when a child is giving testimony on incest. If the judge chooses to do so, the attorney of the accused may remain in court and cross-examine the child. This amendment was enacted following a few incest cases in which the child had much difficulty or was unable to testify in the presence of the offender.

A third amendment[4] to the law has come into force only recently. According to this new amendment, all youth interrogations must be recorded. The amendment was enacted in order to improve the credibility of the child's testimony and to enable the judge to obtain a better impression of the child.

Proposals for Improvements in the Law and Its Implementation

Despite all the controversies, it is now apparent that the law is here to stay. The debates center therefore on ways of improving the law and its implementation. What are the steps that should be taken in order to improve the law and to better implement it?

An area that still attracts much criticism with regard to the operation of this law is the qualifications and training of youth interrogators. The interrogators, who are social workers, put much emphasis on the child's well-being. Yet, at times, they lack sufficient

---

[2] 1989 Amendment to the Law of Evidence Revision (Protection of Children), see Appendix.

[3] Section 2A to the Law of Evidence Revision (Protection of Children) enacted in 1989.

[4] Section 3A to the 1956 regulations of the Law of Evidence Revision, which was enacted in 1989.

techniques, and this may lead to the omission of crucial questions. The interrogators' lack of adequate legal knowledge may also damage the interrogation and even lead to the disqualification of the entire testimony. The need to assess the child's credibility also requires much expertise. The interrogators, who are cross-examined in court regarding their opinion on this issue, sometimes find it difficult to defend their opinion.

It is therefore essential that the level of training and supervision of youth interrogators be improved, and that they be required to participate in an intensive course as a prerequisite to their appointment.

Another suggestion that is often raised, and that seems to be the next step after the audiotape-recording requirement, is to videotape all or some of the interrogations through a one-way mirror. This would undoubtedly improve the credibility of the testimony but would also require sufficient funding.

Another area that requires revision involves children who are required to testify in court, either because the interrogator has allowed their testimony, or because the law does not apply to them. These children are required to face harsh cross-examination and enjoy almost no special protection.

Attention must be given to these children as well, and special arrangements should be made for their testimony. Such arrangements could include testifying through a closed video circuit, or requiring that the questions the child is asked will be approved by the judge before the hearing.

Conclusion

With the enactment of the 1955 Law of Evidence Revision a process has begun, a process that involves much debate and discussion.

In this process the Israeli legal system is learning to accept and appreciate this unique and innovative law.

Although 35 years have passed since its enactment we are still in the midst of this process. Serious implementation and discussion of the law have developed mostly over the last 10 years. In recent years, we have intensively discussed and debated this law, rethinking its implementation, and reevaluating its advantages and drawbacks.

Despite all controversies and possible hesitations, I believe that this is a good law. It is sensitive to the needs of children and effective in balancing the various interests involved.

References

Danino v. The State of Israel, 40 P.D. 1249, 259-260 (1986).
Gondler v. The Attorney General, 13 P.D. 1495 (1959).
Harnon, E. (1988). Examination of children in sex offenses; The Israeli law and practice. *Criminal Law Review*, 263-271.
Karniel, I. (1989). Annual Report on the Work of the Youth Interrogator.
Nizan, S. *Childrens' Testimony in Sex Offenses - A Reevaluation*. 189 Mishpatim, 297.
Yehudai v. The Attorney General, 11 P.D. 365, 367 (1957).

Appendix: *Law of Evidence Revision Protection of Children*

1. Definitions

    In this law - "child" means a person under 14 years of age; "offense against morality" means any of the offenses enumerated in the Schedule.

2. Hearing of child as a witness

    (a) Save with the permission of a youth interrogator, a child shall not be heard as a witness as to an offense against morality committed upon his/her person or in his/her presence, or of which he/she is suspected, and a statement by a child as to such as offense shall not be admitted as evidence.

    (b) Where a youth interrogator has permitted a child to be heard as a witness, no person shall be present at the taking of the evidence except the prosecutor, the accused, the youth interrogator, and any person whom the Court has permitted to be present.

    (c) The Court may order the taking of evidence or receipt of a statement under subsection (a) to be discontinued if, after hearing the youth interrogator, it is of the opinion that the continuance thereof may cause mental harm to the child.

3. Appointment of youth interrogators

    (a) The Minister of Justice shall appoint youth interrogators for the purpose of this law.

    (b) A youth interrogator may be appointed only after consultation with the Committee.

    (c) The Committee shall consist of five members, namely:

    1. A judge of a Magistrate Court currently serving as a judge for the purposes of a Juvenile Offenders Ordinance. 1937 appointed by the Minister of Justice;

    2. A mental hygiene expert appointed by the Minister of Health;

    3. An educator appointed by the Minister of Education and Culture;

    4. A child and youth care expert appointed by the Minister of Social Welfare;

    5. A superior officer of police appointed by the Minister of Police.

    (d) The judge shall act as chairman of the Committee.

    (e) The Committee shall prescribe the rules for its deliberations and work in so far as they have not been prescribed by regulations.

4. Examination by youth interrogator only

    Except for an examination as a witness permitted by a youth interrogator under section 2, a child shall not be examined as to an offense against morality save by a youth interrogator; but this provision shall not apply:

    (1) to questions put at the time or immediately after the commission of the offense or as soon as a reasonable suspicion arises that such an offense has been committed;

    (2) to questions put by the father, the mother, the guardian, the person having supervision or control of the child, or a physician.

5. Presence at examination

    No persons shall be present at the examination of a child by a youth interrogator, save with the latter's permission.

6. Publication

    (a) A person shall not publish anything calculated to reveal the identity of a child who has been examined as to an offense against morality or has been examined as to an offense before a court, save with the permission of the court.

    (b) A person who contravenes this section is liable to imprisonment for a term of six months or to a fine of 250 pounds or to both such penalties.

7. Presence of child at investigation operations

    Where, in the course of a police investigation into an offense against morality, it appears necessary to carry out an act requiring the presence or participation of the child, such act shall not be carried out save in accordance with the directions of a youth interrogator.

8. Report to police

(a) Where an examination as to an offense against morality has been held by a youth interrogator at the request of the police, the youth interrogator shall disclose to the police the particulars of the examination and lay his/her conclusions before them.

(b) The provisions of section 6 shall apply mutatis mutandis to a report of a youth interrogator under this section.

9. Admissible evidence

Evidence as to an offense against morality taken and recorded by a youth interrogator and recorded by a youth interrogator and any minutes or report of an examination as to such an offense prepared by a youth interrogator during or after the examination, are admissible as evidence in Court.

10. Additional examination

Where the taking of evidence or receipt of a statement has been discontinued under section 2(c) or where evidence as referred to in section 9 has been submitted to the Court, the accused of the prosecuted may require, and the judge may order, that the youth interrogator reexamine the child and ask him/her a particular question, but the youth interrogator may refuse to ask all or any questions so required if he/she is of the opinion that asking them is likely to cause physical harm to the child.

11. Supporting

A person shall not be convicted on evidence under section 9 unless it is corroborated by other evidence.

12. Implementation and regulations

The Minister of Justice is charged with the implementation of this law and may make regulations as to any matter relating to such implementation.

13. Commencement

This law shall come into force on the 4th Tishrei 5716 (20th September, 1955).

SCHEDULE
(Section 1)

Offenses against sections 208, 209, 210, 211, 345(A), 346, 347, 348, 349, 337, 368(B), 368(C), to the Criminal Code.

Yitzchak Ben-Zvi	Moshe Sharett	Pinchas Rosen
President of the State	Prime Minister	Minister of Justice

Official Ideals and Current Practice in Work With Child Witnesses in Sexual Abuse Cases in Norway

Toril Havik

Introduction

In Norway, as in other Western countries, there has been a growing acknowledgment that children are victims of sexual abuse. In 1985 a nationwide survey (Saetre, Holter, & Jebsen, 1986) found that every sixth person had been subjected to sexual abuse as a child. Of these, 20% had been victimized by a parent, stepparent, or other close relative. However, due to methodological difficulties, the authors consider that their results might represent a conservative estimate of the actual occurrence of child sexual abuse.

Figures of the Central Bureau of Statistics do not tell how many sexual abuse cases involving children are reported to the police each year. Nor do they tell how many of the reported cases are investigated. While official statistics state that 472 cases were investigated in 1989 (Criminal statistics of the Central Bureau of Statistics of Norway, 1990), a separate survey sent directly to all police districts found the number to be closer to 1,000 (Kobbhaug, 1990).

As there are approximately 900,000 children in Norway who are 15 years old or younger, this latter figure gives an annual police investigation rate somewhere between 0.5 and 1.0 per 1,000 children.

Many of the cases categorized in the official figures as sexual abuse against children do not, however, actually involve children. These figures also include young women reporting abuse committed to them during their childhood. As a consequence, we do not have exact information about the number of children actually involved in police investigation and court proceedings, nor do we know the exact ages of the children involved.

We do know, however, that police investigation of child sexual abuse cases is very time-consuming. On average, it seems to take between 18 months and 3 years from a case being reported until it comes to trial or is dismissed (Skaar, 1989).

Furthermore, we also know that many of the investigated cases never reach the courts. Figures indicate that in Oslo, the capital of Norway, only 1 out of 10 reported cases do so (Holt, 1990).

Official Ideals for Working With Child Sexual Abuse Cases

In 1988, a committee appointed by the Minister of Justice made recommendations for the police investigation of child sexual abuse cases (NOU, 1988). These recommendations underline the importance of coordination between the police and the social and health-care system, with the goals of (a) ensuring the investigation, and (b) reducing the burdens on the child.

The police and the childcare system are both given responsibility for coordination. When a case is reported to the police, they are supposed to notify the childcare office, and vice versa. Furthermore, to secure a clear agreement about the involved parties' responsibilities and about explicit contingency plans for protecting and helping the child and other family members, a meeting is supposed to be arranged (see Figure 1).

The recommendations state that the childcare system should not investigate the case nor interrogate the child or any of the family members. The *investigation* of the accusation is strictly defined as a police matter.

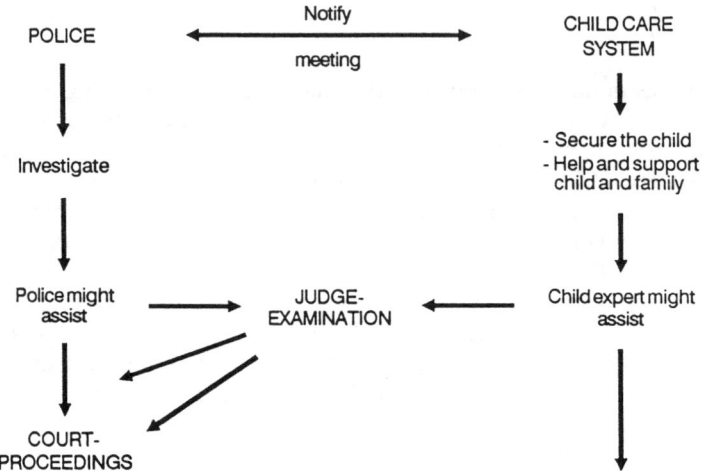

Figure 1: Recommended Model of the Investigation.

Furthermore, the recommendations underline that the child should not be subjected to several interrogators, and that the number of interrogations should be kept as low as possible. To reach this goal, it is recommended that the police do not themselves interrogate the child in any detailed way, but arrange for what is called a judge examination to take place soon after a case is reported to the police.

A judge examination is a meeting between the judge and the child. The aim of this meeting is to secure (a) as detailed a description as possible of what act(s) have taken place, and (b) the factual circumstances surrounding the abusive act(s).

The judge examination is supposed to be video- or audiotaped. The taped material may be used in the further police investigation and, together with a written protocol of the meeting, it may be used in the courtroom as the child's court testimony.

Children below 15 years of age cannot give testimony in court. A young child can therefore not be cross-examined by the counsel for the defendant. Thus the quality of the judge examination is especially important.

A child of 15 years or older will usually give testimony in court. The child will usually then have a legal custodian appointed to her or him. The legal custodian is present during the court hearings to protect the child from being overtaxed by the court proceedings. The accused might be sent out of the courtroom when the child gives testimony.

To promote the quality of the judge examination, it is recommended that the judge has assistance in conducting this. In fact it is recommended that the judge examination should be conducted by a specially educated police officer or by a psychologist or psychiatrist experienced in child sexual abuse cases. The judge might, if she or he thinks it preferable, be rather passive in conducting the interview, even to the extent of sitting behind a one-way mirror. However, it is the judge who has the sole responsibility of deciding who will conduct the judge examination.

The recommendations contain no explicit guidelines for how the interview should be conducted, only that the child should not be asked any leading questions. If leading questions are deemed necessary, the judge must give her or his explicit permission. Drawings, pictures, and anatomically correct dolls can be used for clarification.

Current Practice in Working With Child Sexual Abuse Cases

So far I have described what might be called the official Norwegian ideals for reducing the burden on the child of police investigation on the child, while, at the same time protecting the judicial aspects of the investigation.

The problem in Norway is not these recommendations. The problem is that these recommendations are not used in practical work with cases of child sexual abuse.

There are several reasons for this. Partly, this is due to practical and economic considerations (for one thing: travel distances in Norway are considerable and quite time-consuming), but it also reflects a lack of knowledge both about child sexual abuse *and* about the recommendations. However, it is my experience that difficulties in trusting other professions than one's own is an equally important reason why good ideals are not realized in everyday work.

If we look at the reality of the situation in Norway, it is my impression that the modal, or typical, routines are as shown in Figure 2.

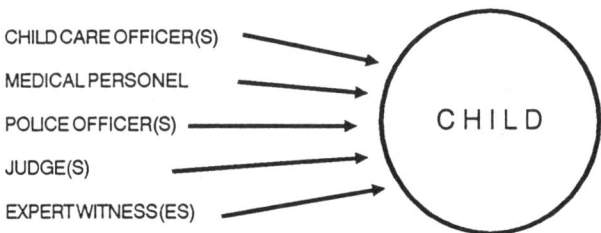

Figure 2: Current Practice of the Investigation.

1. The childcare system contacts the police only after they themselves have investigated the case so thoroughly that they are quite certain that the child has been sexually abused and who the offender is.

That is, childcare personnel tend *not* to contact the police when they have a suspicion but to wait until they feel they have a justified conviction. The police claims that this makes their investigation hopeless, as, by this time, legal evidence is destroyed or distorted.

2. On the other hand, when the police receive a complaint about child sexual abuse, they very seldom contact the childcare system. Consequently, an early coordination meeting

is seldom arranged, and no plans for helping the child and other family members are made.

3. Furthermore, as a rule rather than an exception, the police interrogate the child as part of their police investigation, and do not arrange for an early judge examination. In part, this is due to the long travelling distances and to the heavy workload of judges. But it is also due to lack of trust. Many police officers maintain that judges, usually being older men, have little competence in interviewing children. And although professionals (i.e., psychologists) are recognized as having special competences in interviewing children, they are also viewed as asking leading questions and as being preoccupied with feelings and circumstantial evidence rather than with concrete information and specific acts.

In summary, and to focus on the problems we often meet: The different parties involved, (i.e., childcare professionals, psychologists, police, and judges) all seem to feel that only their interviews will not harm but help the child, and that only their way of interrogating will bring clarification and secure evidence and proof.

Psychologists' Work as an Expert Witness

According to the legal system in Norway, the professional is defined as an expert witness only if she or he is appointed and paid by the court. The main reason for this is to ensure the neutrality of the expert witness. For the same reason, two expert witnesses are usually appointed. We have no statistics showing how often the court appoints psychologists as expert witnesses, but it seems the court do so more and more often.

As a rule, the expert witness should not know the child beforehand and should, furthermore, have had no therapeutic relations with the child or the child's family. However, if the child or the family has been in psychotherapy, the therapist is usually asked to give testimony. Sometimes the therapist is also appointed by the court as an expert witness. According to my experience, the use of the child's therapist as an expert witness invariably hinders the case, since defence lawyers use this to question the neutrality of the psychologist.

There are no explicit guidelines as to what the psychologist ought to give an expert opinion about or the working methods she or he ought to adopt. Sometimes the psychologist is asked to give her opinion of the child's more general mental and emotional status, sometimes she is asked to give her opinion on the compatibility of the child's symptoms with those usually found in sexual abuse victims, and sometimes she is asked to give her opinion on the credibility of the child as regards the specific sexual abuse acts. The expert witness has access to all casefiles. She can interview the child as many times as she deems necessary. The expert witness submits a written report to the court. She has to be present and follow the court proceedings, and will be asked follow-up questions by both the judge and the defence lawyer.

According to my general impression, psychologists as expert witnesses in Norway tend to function primarily as general experts in clinical child psychology. There has been little discussion within the psychological profession about the "whats" and the "hows" of doing good expert witness work.

If we look at Sweden, our neighboring country, the scene is quite different: There we find a lively and heated discussion about how psychologists ought to work, and what they ought to give weight to, as expert witnesses. Sweden has a long tradition in "witness psychology" based on the work of Trankell (1963/1971) and Holgerson (1989, 1990). In this debate we find that psychologists specializing in the principles of witness psychology are often in sharp disagreement with psychologists specializing in clinical child psychology. On the one hand, clinical child psychologists tend to maintain that the strict rules of "formal structure analysis" used by witness psychologists are not appropriate for work with children. On the other hand, experts in witness psychology tend to maintain that clinical child psychologists overidentify with the child, give too much weight to general clinical judgment, and are not analytical enough in their evaluation of the child's statements of what has happened.

The Norwegian courts do not have any statistics on how often psychologists are used as expert witnesses, and we do not know to what degree their opinion as expert witnesses is followed by the court. Psychologists seem to feel that this happens too seldom, lawyers seem to feel that this happens all too often.

However, data from Sweden indicate that the expert witness' opinion may have a strong impact on the ruling of the court. Lindegren (1990), in a summary of 120 child sexual abuse cases evaluated at the "Research Laboratory for Witness Psychology", from 1979 to 1989, reported the figures shown in Table 1.

Table 1: Impact of Expert Witness' Opinion on the Ruling of the Court (after Lindegren, 1990).

	The laboratory found suspicions		
	Grounded	Ungrounded	Either/or
Ruling of the court			
Found guilty	54	-	3
Acquitted	7	7	1
Dismissed	1	31	6
Case not reached court	4	2	2
Lost data	2	-	-
	68	40	12

The figures indicate that, in the majority of cases, the rulings of the court followed the expert witness' opinion.

Concluding Remarks

At present, Norwegian ideologies as regards reporting child sexual abuse cases to the police seem to be changing. It is my impression that there is a growing concern that the prolonged police investigation and the high rates of dismissal and acquittal create very significant traumas for the child and the child's family. As a consequence, childcare officers and health personnel are becoming more reluctant to report cases to the police, whereas, only a few years ago, there was general agreement that all suspected sexual abuse cases should be reported routinely. In the present situation, there seems to be a feeling, shared by social workers, psychologists, and the police, that cases should be reported only if there is a reasonable chance that the offender will be found guilty.

It is also my impression that psychologists, childcare officers, and lawyers more often than before recommend that the case be brought before the childcare system rather than the court. This is so because the childcare system can act on the principle of "the child's best interest" rather than on the principle of proving the guilt of the accused. That is, the uncertainty and doubt will benefit the child and not the adult. Likewise, many cases are recommended raised as custody cases, where the same principle of deciding in "the child's best interest" is followed.

In conclusion, there is an obvious need for more knowledge and for a more open sharing of knowledge. There is a need to develop more trust between the many institutions involved. These needs have long been recognized. However, it seems to be a rather long path from the identification of needs to the change of actual routines.

Hopefully, a national project aiming at the education and coordination of health or social personnel and institutions working with child sexual abuse cases will contribute to shortening the path. This government-funded project is coordinated by a central project leader and a team of experts appointed by the Minister of Health and Social Affairs. In the different regions of Norway, the project is being led and coordinated by regional project leaders. It started in 1990 and it will run for a 2-year period.

References

Holgerson, A. (1989). *Ett barn far illa*. Stockholm: Psykologiforlaget.
Holgerson, A. (1990). *Fakta i målet*. Stockholm: Pedagogiska Institutionen.
Holt, A. (1990). *Derfor dømmes ikke fedrene*. Verdens Gang (3. February).
Kobbhaug, W (1990). *Spørreundersøkelse ved landets politikammer*. Oslo: Oslo Politikammer.
Lindegren, I.R (1990). Vi ser til utsagans - inte persones - troverdighet. *PsykologTidningen, 14*, 5-7.
Norges Offentlige Utredninger (1988). Etterforskning av incestsaker. NOU 1988:29.
Skaar, T. (1989). *Kva er eit kvinneliv verdt ? Ei bok om seksuelt misbruk av barn*. Oslo: Samlaget.
Saetre, M., Holter, H., & Jebsen, E. (1986). *Tvang til seksualitet. En undersøkelse av seksuelle overgrep mot barn*. Oslo: Universitetsforlaget.
Trankell, A. (1963/1971). *Vittnespsykologins arbetsmetoden*. Stockholm: Libere.

Juridical Situation of Child Witnesses in Canada

Marie J. O'Neill

Introduction

Under Canada's legal system, the federal government has authority for the criminal law and the provincial and territorial governments have responsibility for the administration of justice. The Criminal Code and the Canada Evidence Act are two federal laws covering criminal justice matters (Wells, 1990). Changes were made to the law creating new sexual abuse offences and expanding the opportunities for courts to receive children's testimony in cases of child sexual abuse in January, 1988. The meaning of many terms used in the new law (named Bill C-15, Statutes, 1987) will no doubt become the subject of interpretation and scrutiny by judges across Canada. It is expected that some time will elapse before the full impact of the new legislation is known.

In Canada, sexual offences against children and youth only began to be fully recognized in the late 1970's. It was not until December, 1980 that Parliament established a committee to make a concentrated enquiry into the matter. The Badgley Report (1984) confirmed child sexual abuse as a problem of major proportions for Canada's children. The Committee found that, at some time during their lives, about one in two females and one in three males had been victims of unwanted sexual acts, almost all committed against them when they were children or youths. Almost all abusers were male, more than 75% being known to the victims. A majority of the victims or their families did not seek help from public services (Wells, 1990). It was in consideration of the Badgley Report that the major reforms were proposed, making it easier to prosecute child sexual abusers and increasing the opportunities for children to testify in court. Previously, i.e., before 1988, Canada's laws on the rules of evidence and the rules of procedure usually did not provide younger children with the chance to testify.

There are now 16 sexual offences in the Criminal Code that could apply to child sexual abuse. Children under 12 years are never considered able to consent to sexual activity. Children of 12 or more, but under 18, are protected from sexual exploitation.

The court system is basically the same across Canada. Generally, the courts deal with both "civil" and "criminal" matters. The court that hears a case is usually determined by the nature of the matter. The Criminal Code of Canada divides offences into two categories: (1) summary conviction offences (generally less serious offences) and (2) indictable offences, which are more serious and which may be tried by a judge sitting alone, or by a judge sitting with a jury.

Categories of child sexual abuse offences are described as summary, hybrid and indictable. The maximum sentence for the new sexual abuse crimes (invitation to sexual touching, touching for a sexual purpose and sexual exploitation) is ten years in prison. The maximum sentence for aggravated sexual assaults is life imprisonment. When an incident of child sexual abuse is reported to the police they will conduct an investigation. Reporting is mandatory in Canada. The specific procedures are determined locally. In general, the investigation is done in cooperation with child welfare officers conducting a simultaneous child protection investigation. The police decide whether charges should be laid and the police make the first contact with the accused. My impression from the literature is that social workers are more involved in the majority of cases than are psychologists. Psychologists may be called as expert witnesses, either side having the freedom to call these persons.

The child victim is regarded, under the new laws, as a key witness who gives evidence of the offence to the court. In general, the victim does not attend the first court appearance, but usually gives evidence at the preliminary inquiry and the trial. The law allows child victims and child witnesses to request that their names or information that would identify them not be published or broadcast by the media. When a non-publication order is requested by a victim or a witness under 18 in a child sexual abuse case, the court is *required* to make the order. In a situation where the accused is a young person, the publication ban is automatic.

Children's Testimony

Corroboration

The corroboration rule as it previously stood meant that it was frequently impossible to convict someone unless the Crown provided evidence that met highly technical constraints of being independent evidence. This was different from evidence which merely supported the testimony of the victim. Section 274 of the new Bill C-15 allows that it is not essential to have additional evidence to corroborate the testimony of a child victim or witness in order to convict someone of sexual offence. The evidence of the victim or witness may be sufficient to secure a conviction. Guilt must be proved beyond a reasonable doubt. This section of the law acknowledges that child sexual abuse usually takes place in private and that there is usually little physical evidence (Wells, 1990). The new rule suggests that no judge should automatically assume that all children are inherently suspect as witness. The judge may still comment to the jury on the reliability of any particular witness in any criminal case. A statement produced by the Institute for the Prevention of Child Abuse (1990) charges professionals with the duty of monitoring and documenting any instances where judges may, either through direct comments or through their tone of voice, continue to warn juries about the unreliability of children's evidence.

Recent complaint

The "recent complaint rule" has been revoked for all sexual assault offences (1983) and with respect to child sexual abuse offences (1988). This rule allowed the court to make an adverse inference against the credibility of a victim in the erroneous belief that actual victims of sexual assaults would complain at the first opportunity. "Changing the law on recent complaint acknowledges a new understanding about the reluctance of sexual abuse victims to come forward" (Wells, 1990). Some writers still consider that the proper interpretation of the new provision will continue to prove controversial among judges and lawyers.

No evidence concerning sexual activity

Bill C-15 provides that the statutory rule generally precluding questions about a child victim's prior sexual activity with others will apply to the new child sexual offences. Some exceptions may be allowed, e.g., to prove that the actual offender is someone else. Only under fairly limited circumstances is it possible to ask a child victim about prior sexual activity. Advance written notice of the intention to ask the court to allow such questions must be given to the Crown Prosecuter. Counselling may be needed by a child under these circumstances.

Reputation evidence

Bill C-15 states that "evidence of sexual reputation, whether general or specific is not admissible for the purposes of challenging or supporting the credibility of the complainant" (Statutes, 1987, p. 640). As sexual promiscuity may be an indicator of sexual abuse, it may be necessary under some circumstances for experts to give testimony to this effect that a particular child has been sexually abused.

Testimony outside the courtroom

The law allows that, where "the complainant is, at the time of the trial or the preliminary enquiry, under the age of 18 years, the presiding judge or justice, as the case may be, may order that the complainant testify outside the courtroom or behind a screen or other device that would allow the complainant not to see the accused, if the judge or justice is of the opinion that the exclusion is necessary to obtain a full and candid account of the acts complained of from the complainant" (Statutes, 1987, p.640). This allowance is made only for the child victim and only if the accused is able to hear and watch the testimony and communicate with his or her lawyer at all times. Arrangements must be made in such a way that the judge and jury also are able to view the testimony. Closed circuit television is recommended for this purpose, but not all courts are yet fitted out.

Videotaped evidence

A videotape may be made and used which contains the testimony of a child victim, if the tape is made "within a reasonable time after the alleged offence," (Statutes, 1987, p.641) if the complainant was under the age of 18 years at the time the offence is alleged to have been committed, in which the complainant describes the acts complained of. The child must take the witness stand and agree that the statements on the tape are substantially correct, i.e., the child "adopts" the contents of the videotape. This consideration applies only to offences of a sexual nature. Many issues are involved here, especially: training in investigative interviewing; consideration of the emotional impact of the method on the child; the security of the tape and the quality of the tape; the difficulties of incremental disclosure and the necessity of presenting only one tape within a time limit; the location of the interview and the circumstances prevailing for the interview.

Child Witnesses

Children under 14 years of age or persons whose mental capacity is challenged will be asked by the court whether they understand the meaning of an oath or a solemn affirmation. The judge will decide whether the witness is "able to communicate the evidence" (Statutes, 1987, p.642) and may ask the child to promise to tell the truth if the child does not understand the meaning of "oath" or "affirmation". The evidence of a child testifying after promising to tell the truth may be considered as acceptable as other evidence. There is no legal requirement for corroboration.

Bill C-15 also allows that,

> A party who challenges the capacity of a proposed witness of 14 years of age or more has the burden of satisfying the court that there is an issue as to the capacity of the proposed witness to testify under an oath or a solemn affirmation. (Statutes, 1987, p.642)

This legislation allows quite young children to testify (children as young as three years have testified recently). From the psychologist's point of view, knowledge of the younger child's developmental level and of the child's emotional state or potential are important factors which could assist the police or the Crown Prosecutor in their decision to count a particular child to act as a credible witness. It would be reasonable to demand the child witness should be treated like any other witness, as an individual.

Nicholas Bala, of the Faculty of Law at Queen's University, Kingston, has pointed out that "there never has been a documented case where a person in Canada has been falsely convicted of sexually abusing a child" (Bala, 1990).

Conclusions

Recommendations about further improvements in the laws relating to children as victims and witnesses have been made by Rix Rogers, a Special Advisor to the Minister of National Health and Welfare, after examining more than 1600 submissions on the subject. Specifically, he recommends that "the Federal Department of Justice should monitor challenges to Bill C-15 under Canadian Charter of Rights and Freedoms and actively defend the legislation against constitutional attack" (Rogers, 1990, No. 28).

Further, Rogers recommends that "Parliament reform the laws governing child sexual abuse prosecutions." He also makes recommendations which would shorten the time between complaint and hearings by giving priority in court scheduling to child sexual abuse cases and that provincial and territorial governments amend their legislation "to facilitate the giving of evidence by children...and at least ensure that child witnesses receive all the benefits of Bill C-15" (Rogers, 1990).

The report by Rogers will form part of the planned review of the legislation which is to be completed as soon as possible after January, 1992. In order to ensure the success of the new legal procedures, professionals in the field are being actively encouraged to learn more about the mechanisms of the law, while those in the legal professions are even more actively encouraged (by the psychologists) to understand the needs of children. In essence, the 1988 amendments to the Criminal Code and the Canadian Evidence Act concerning child sexual abuse signal an intent in Canada to provide greater protection to children, especially against re-abuse and the "trauma of testifying" (Lebel, 1989).

References

Badgley, R. (1984). *Sexual Offences Against Children. Report of the Committee on Sexual Offences Against Children and Youth*. Ottawa: Government of Canada.

Bala, N., & Stewart, C. (1990). *Understanding Criminal Prosecutions for Child Sexual Abuse*. Bill C-15 and the Criminal Code. Toronto: The Institute for the Prevention of Child Abuse.

Lebel, J.G. (1989). *Reducing the Trauma of Testifying. Bill C-15 and The Child Victim. Keynote address given at the Bill C-15 Forum*. Toronto: The Institute for the Prevention of Child Abuse.

Rogers, R.G. (1990). *Reaching for Solutions*. Summary Report of the Special Advisor to the Minister of National Health and Welfare on Child Sexual Abuse in Canada. Ministry of Supply and Services Canada.

Statutes of Canada (1987). Chapters 1-48, Vol.35-36 Elizabeth II, Vol. 1. An Act to Amend the Criminal Code and the Canada Evidence Act, pp. 633-643.

Wells, M. (1990). *Canada's Law on Child Sexual Abuse*. Ottawa: Department of Justice, Canada.

Some Areas of Interface Between Psychology and the Guardian Ad Litem Programs in Juvenile and Domestic Relations Settings

Sandra B. McPherson

Introduction

In the Child Abuse Prevention and Treatment Act (PL 93-247) enacted 1974, provision was made for appointment of a guardian ad litem (GAL) in every juvenile court case involving child abuse or neglect. Subsequently, the states developed GAL programs to serve both the juvenile and domestic relations (DR) spheres. GALs serve to advocate for the best interests of the child. In order to do so they may utilize the services of mental health professionals (MHPs). Additionally, MHPs have been used in the training of GALs to increase psychological insight and knowledge.

In Cuyahoga County, the GAL program began as an unstructured semi-volunteer effort of lawyers and judges. The Federation for Community Planning in conjunction with the County Bar Association recognized and developed a structured program to formalize assignment and training (Freedheim & Kurtz, 1980). The need to augment legal education with mental health/social service knowledge was recognized and met. Initially, this program provided training for GALs in both juvenile and DR. Approximately nine years ago the DR administrative judge decided the need for specialized DR GALs would be best met in a separate program.

Procedure

Semi-structured interviews were conducted with as panel of experts including past and present directors of the juvenile GAL program, current director of the DR GAL program, six DR GALs (x yrs. experience = 14), seven forensic MHPs (x yrs. experience = 9), two juvenile judges, one juvenile referee, four DR judges, three DR referees, directors of the juvenile court clinic and the DR Family Conciliation Service, a community planner who was instrumental in development of the GAL program, and two administrators of the juvenile court. Results from the 28 interviews were analyzed for agreement and divergence and reported in narrative form.

Results

MHP perspectives

DR court. The most frequent role played by MHPs is visitation and custody evaluator but the mediator role is increasingly in evidence. MHPs also engage in training new GALs. Other roles include treating therapist sometimes by court order post decree, sex abuse evaluator, and visitation monitor. While the sample favored court apointed or jointly agreed upon evaluators, MHPs have functioned as evaluators hired by a side.

Recognizing that MHPs often lack training for the courtroom, the sample was asked what was most helpful to them in dealing with the legal arena. The one psychiatrist in the sample indicated two exceptional formal training experiences. Otherwise, the sample importantly ranked input from GALs who guide the MHP on how to respond to the legal system and assist in interpreting in what the system requires, ongoing continuing education, and consultation with colleagues.

The sample was asked to reflect upon the GAL-MHP interface with regard to characteristics that enhanced or impeded success. The most commonly noted traits of a successful GAL were high activity, ability to get information, and MHP-GAL collaboration with complementary activities and minimal duplication of effort. Other positive traits included the GAL's ability to communicate with parties' counsel and legal expertise in the courtroom. Several MHPs noted the child's interest were brought out through the planning of the courtcase and questioning of the witness by the GAL. Creative strategizing was characteristic of successful complex cases. For an MHP relatively unaccustomed to the courtroom situation, a good GAL provided tutoring and some protection so the MHP could fulfill the role desired by the court. Therapists can uncover needs of the children which may run counter to an existing court order on visitation. Involvement of GALs facilitated obtaining changes in the order to reflect current realities of the child or children. As MHPs become more experienced, they tended to take more pro-active positions rather than simply responding to the GAL and the court system. Their capacity to develop with the GAL both formal and informal strategies increased.

On the negative side, problem situations included the inactive GAL or the GAL who too quickly takes a position favoring one side or the other, becoming closed to emerging contrary data. Some less than effective guardians will seek settlement at all costs, being more interested in working out an agreement without litigating even where the result may conflict with child interests. However, a GAL and a MHP do not always have to agree and, in fact, may dynamically work together to develop information for contrary theories.

Juvenile court. At the time the GAL program started, available mental health input from the court clinic was limited and it was not uncommon to call upon outside consultants. As a function of community and legal pressures, the court's clinic was measurably upgraded and placed under a full time director who restructured aspects of its function so that it is more problem focused and efficient. Information available from other community agencies is systematically collected. At this point, external MHPs only occasionally serve this court. Such MHPs may provide second opinions as to mental status or parenting capacity. In bindover cases, particularly in high profile crimes, and in civil cases, additional MHPs are obtained. Finally, external MHPs may interface with GALs and the courts as part of their work as child or family therapists either before, during, or after the court has acted.

In reflecting on GAL role and function, the following concerns emerged. GALs may move too quickly or impulsively to remove children from their homes. Such decisions may lead to further litigation and questions of violation of parental rights. The area of parental rights is a particularly thorny one which is not easily addressed on the basis of precedent and requires careful case by case reasoning. In a similar way, a GAL can get into an alliance with one of the parties too quickly and lose sight of the best interests of the child. Conversely, a good GAL emphasizes objectivity, is very involved in generating information, teams well ... the MHP, but is a good lawyer who can deal with the rather complex legal issues that continue to emerge in the area of parent and child rights.

A GAL is often capable of evaluating mental health aspects against prevailing legal requirements and developing creative solutions. An area of GAL functioning which needs further development and implementation and which requires a combination of psychological and legal skills, involves explaining to youngsters their legal position and the judicial process.

MHPs who render psychological opinions in regard to issues of custody and placement without adequate data on family and situation without awareness of how the legal system works and what its likely responses will be were singled out for criticism. Obtaining that kind of information, especially for a forensically inexperienced MHP, may be a corrective function of the GAL.

GAL perspectives

GALs perceived many roles for MHPs in the court system including therapist, mediator, visitation supervisor, custody/visitation evaluator, catalyst/intervener (an informal role which develops out of evaluation and which pushes the system toward a reasonable and effective resolution), election assessment which is an issue of competency as well as evaluation of externals in some cases, and sex or physical abuse assessment. GALs noted MHPs may appear in court as therapists called upon to provide information from that perspective. On occasion MHPs are hired by each side with a "battle of experts" ensuing, which frequently contributes to problems in the situation.

GALs in more than one case indicated the MHP was a tool for shaping up the system. They look to the MHP for answers, for theories, for ways to construe the case, for predictions of behavior and for specific recommendations as to intervention or outcome. GALs are unhappy when MHPs equivocate, but there was some recognition the data may not allow for an unqualified conclusion. GALs feel MHPs can fail to understand the potential impact of what they say and do in the system. On occasion MHPs, rather than erring on the side of being less definitive, will make pronouncements based on inadequate information which then lead the system to act in high impact ways such as removal of a child from a parent.

In looking at best and worst case scenarios, a number of interesting traits emerged. Often the GAL has a pretty good idea after interviewing children and looking at the total situation as to how the child's best interests may be served. However, the GAL may need the expert testimony which contributes to evidence on the basis of which the court will then act. In many cases in DR court, GAL-MHP teamwork can make the difference between long litigation versus settlement or resolution with minimal costs, both monetary and emotional, to the family and children involved. Sometimes the kind of teaming up which takes place involves the dynamics of the courtroom itself. One attorney known for adversarial toughness was essentially controlled by the prehearing planning which took place between the GAL and the MHP. On the negative side, the kinds of qualities, traits, and activities that emerged included the venial or self-serving, the naive of borderline competent, or the biased MHP. The area of sex abuse allegations has become particularly difficult for DR cases. It has been documented there is a strong potential for false allegations. One GAL cited the MHP who testified that in almost all, if not all cases, children who make statements alleging sexual abuse are fully credible including in contested custody cases. The same specialist also stated on cross that she had had only one instance in all the investigations she had performed where sex abuse had not occurred. Her testimony was discounted by the court and served only to complicate an already out of control legal *and* psychological situation.

While juvenile court is well served by its clinic, GALs noted specialists need to be more frequently accessed in specific cases. GALs highlighted the importance of external MHPs being familiar with juvenile and criminal justice systems in cases involving competence to testify, bindover, and dangerousness.

Judicial perspectives

DR court. Judges varied in their approach to GAL appointments. Factors favoring appointments were judicial perception of need based on child(ren)'s situation or a request by both parties. Perceived need occurred when the parties' positions re the children were not clear, when there were allegations of sexual or physical abuse, and with children having special needs, older children resisting visitation, or in allegations of parental alienation. Appointment of an MHP was likely when requested by the GAL, although a request for an MHP can arise where an attorney wishes to avoid the legwork involved in working through a case. DR judges avoid unnecessary GAL/MHP involvement which is expensive and can elongate the process.

Judges generally supported the attorney GAL model perceiving the need for a legal advocate who can professionally and competently represent child interests in the court, but did not rule out special situations - especially post decree - where an MHP might best serve a GAL function. Judges preferred MHPs who would provide a definitive conclusion, even though, as one judge dryly noted, he may not endorse the opinion.

In considering problem areas, one example was the nonresolvable case where parties are determined to litigate. Part of judicial decision-making is knowing when to relinquish efforts to use expensive professionals where no results can be reasonably expected. In such cases it was seen as often better to let the parties periodically reappear in the court and obtain the rulings they seek rather than burdening that process with additional hearings and interventions conducted by well-meaning but essentially powerless professionals.

Not surprisingly, referees' opinions did not diverge from those of judges. Referees look to GALs for help when the parties' attorneys cannot communicate. They can use GALs as judicial extenders, obtaining information and empowered to make interim decisions in specific areas. Referees want MHPs who are objective and case focused rather than implementing personal agendas such as rights of fathers or reduction of sexism. An area cited for MHP contribution was that of inappropriate stepparent involvement. There was a definite preference for the court appointed or jointly agreed upon expert over persons hired by each side. One referee indicated willingness to talk directly to the court's expert but would delegate to the GAL the task of answering questions or facilitating appropriate requests of an expert from one side.

Referees supported the lawyer GAL model but noted GALs need psychological skills and insight. In looking at GAL-MHP interface, MHPs could lack insight into the GAL role. GALs were seen as most effective when they gathered data for the MHP while obtaining feedback on mental health factors. When a GAL and an MHP arrived at opposite conclusions, the situation required special management with professionals working together to reduce differences or coming to a mutual understanding of the reasoning process while allowing the court to sift through the positions. Effective MHPs knew some law and how to testify. MHPs can perform intervention functions including dealing with visitation questions, especially in cases of parental alienation and sometimes in facilitating case settlements.

Juvenile court. In this setting, there is less judicial discretion on GAL appointment. All cases of abuse, neglect permanent custody, and permanent or temporary surrender are assigned a GAL. GALs are frequently required in delinquency adjudications where statutory guides exist defining appointment conditions (Cuyahoga County Bar Association, 1989). The involvement of an MHP is typically by request of the GAL, but the court clinic may initiate more differentiated mental health involvement. Some examples of mental health input which can be helpful to the juvenile court included assessment of parenting potential, particularly where there was question as to whether a child should be returned to a parent, questions of mental health status of parents or child as those might impact upon developing a rehabilitation plan, and development of differentiated mental health treatment plans.

In regard to some of the problems that MHPs may create in the courtroom situation, one judge was particularly critical of the consultant who specifies treatment needs which may have psychologically valid antecedents and be appropriately reasoned in the situation but which have no potential for realization. From the standpoint of the court, it is frustrating to be given an answer which cannot be implemented. Another problem is inappropriate assumption of expertise, either in the course of testimony or as treating personnel.

In regard to the use of MHPs as GALs, respondents noted the advantage a lawyer has in situations requiring the exercise of legal skills and expertise, especially given the GAL program's backup resource bank for mental health and other professional input. It was generally felt coordinated GAL-MHP teamwork contributed strongly to the work of the court while maintaining legal protections. One judge registered specific disappointment for inactive GALs, pointing out he had had to continue a case to the detriment of the child because of the lack of GAL preparation. It was his feeling that GAL functioned "acording to the Woody Allen formula: 90 percent of success is simply showing up." The judge did not endorse the standard.

Administrative structures and perspectives

DR court. Family Conciliation Services (FCS) has been in existence 11 years. Staffing consists of a director, four social workers, a half time psychologist, and a part time psychiatrist. The unit receives cases both pre and post decree and the emphasis is on preventive mental health. Towards that end, staff works to promote agreement between parties, to reduce litigation and even on occasion to achieve reconciliation. However, there is an overriding evaluative function such that where the mediation or intervention process is not successful in resolving issues, a report becomes available to the court.

Staff occasionally testifies. It is not uncommon for FCS to collaborate not only with GALs but also with external MHPs.

A formally structured DR-GAL program with coordination has improved training and performance of GALs. The lawyer/GAL model was viewed as essential for the legal complexities of this court and mental health input as best obtained on a case by case basis. One service of the GAL program has been to develop resource lists of various specialists, especially in cases needing sex abuse assessment or supervision of visitation. New legislation relating to grandparent rights has increased the need for GAL/MHP collaboration. Quality of GAL service is enhanced by follow up evaluations performed within the DR program by the coordinator. There is ongoing input of initial training and updating of skills by MHPs who volunteer service in this area as well as serving on the advisory committee. Unlike juvenile GALs, it is not unusual to collect full fees for GAL work; a fund for indigent clients pays a token $ 200 per case.

Juvenile court. Mental health input to the Juvenile program included direct service, training, and service on the advisory board. The court clinic emphasizes timely response, important because of recent statutory demand for processing of cases. (Hearings must be held within 24 hours with decisions in 90 days depending upon circumstances.) It was noted there may be underutilization by GALs of available MHP input, especially outside of the court clinic, where insurance support systems would permit greater use of the private sector. In looking at the GAL program itself, there were some pros and cons seen to the way it was set up. The token pay ($ 200 per case) allows some symbolic reinforcement only since GALs may be responsible for the legal needs of a child up until his/her age 18. Administrators supported the attorney GAL model, but saw attorneys needing more insight into subtleties of guardian over straight advocacy roles.

Problem areas included the question of ultimate issue testimony, an area of ambiguity in juvenile proceedings. Some judges preferred not to have professionals make ultimate issue statements; others expected an opinion would be rendered and were irritated if the MHP attempted to "duck." Bindover cases, where the question is whether or not the child will benefit from continued treatment in the juvenile system, were particularly difficult. Professional recommendations require knowledge of available resources, both of court and community and careful communication of conclusions. Fine tuned communication between GAL and MHP on testimony and knowledge of judicial expectations was seen as fundamental, particularly in publicized and/or politicized cases.

Conclusions

Juvenile court was originally established to provide a haven for adjudication of minors apart from the adult criminal system (Smith & Meyer, 1987). With *in re Gault* (1967) and subsequent legislation, due process was enhanced as a balance to benevolent authority in order to secure the rights of children (Reznek, 1970). In DR courts, another dilemma presented-children became prawns in civil adversarial proceedings. The development of GAL programs has enhanced the status of children and their potential to be heard in these two court systems. Involvement of MHPs has allowed GALs to more effectively represent children's interest which can have subtle referents.

In this study, although questions varied slightly depending upon the role of the respondent, all members of the sample were asked to reflect upon the layer vs. lay person GAL models and all were asked to consider best and worst case scenarios involving GAL and MHP work. Analysis of responses indicated support for the following:

1. Legal rights and mental health needs of children are significantly enhanced by the existence of well structured GAL programs in the DR and juvenile courts and by use of ancillary MHPs as needed in specific cases.

2. The lawyer GAL model best serves the needs of these urban court system in most situations.

3. GALs need mental health perspectives and MHPs need forensic sophistication to best function in these areas.

4. MHPs serve best as independent experts; working with the GAL enhances that potential.

5. When MHPs founder in the court system it is more likely to reflect inadequate scientific practice than legal naivete.

6. The major failing of GALs is insufficient activity on cases.

7. There are substantial differences in needs between juvenile and DR courts insofar as both GAL and MHP functioning are concerned.

Differences pertained on individual points about MHP and GAL appointments. Judicial expectations insofar as MHP testimony is concerned can vary and MHPs need to know something of the specific character of the courts in which they serve; close collaboration with GALs enhances MHP ability to respond in this regard. Although a rule of thumb in forensic mental health work has been to avoid responding to ultimate issue questions, in point of fact in both juvenile and DR settings there may be an expectation for such responding; understanding whether that expectation exists is one of the necessary informal skills of an MHP.

References

Cuyahoga County Bar Association. (1989). *Revised Training Manual for Cuyahoga County Juvenile Court*. Juvenile Court Guardians Ad Litem.

Freedheim, G., & Kurtz, W. (1980). Family law (the guardian ad litem for children project); *Trial, 4*, 56-57, 163.

In re Gault, 387 US 1, 36 (1967).

Reznek, D. (1970). The rights of juveniles. In N. Dorsen (Ed.), *The rights of Americans*. New York: Random House.

Smith, S., & Meyer, R. (1987). *Law, behavior, and mental health: Policy and practice*. New York: New York University Press.

Part VII
Juridical Procedures and Decision-Making

Methodological Issues in Research on Legal Decision-Making, With Special Reference to Experimental Simulations

Vladimir J. Konečni and Ebbe B. Ebbesen

Introduction: Undue Optimism About Legal Psychology?

Rather optimistic appraisals of the status of the "interface" between the law and psychology are frequent. Optimism is implicitly present in the highly regarded volume dealing with the use of social science data in the law (Monahan & Walker, 1985), careful and level-headed as this volume is. One certainly finds it in the "concordance of experts" surveys of psychologists who have acted as expert witnesses in court. At least on the surface, such surveys are impressive in terms of the sheer number of polled experts and the frequency of their court testimony (for example, 63 experts with a total of 478 court appearances, in a recent survey by Kassin, Ellsworth, & Smith, 1989), and, more importantly, in the experts' high agreement about the scientific reliability of the issues on which they testify (Kassin et al., 1989; Yarmey & Jones, 1983). And one finds favorable assessments of the status of the field in numerous published reports (e.g., Tanford & Tanford, 1987), as well as in the present volume, for example, in the papers by Farrington, Kaiser, and Loftus, among others.

Some of the reasons for the optimism are: (1) The exuberance that often characterizes the early stages of development of interdisciplinary fields, an exuberance that blinds researchers to the fact that the interface sometimes consists of the inferior components of the two fields; (2) The social desirability of overemphasizing the positive features of the interdisciplinary effort at conferences and in journals that are specifically set up to promote the interface; (3) A neglect of the sociology and economics of science (cf., Konečni & Ebbesen, 1986, p. 120): The incentive system in which legal psychologists function - in terms of both research grants and expert-witnesses fees - encourages an optimistic view of the interdisciplinary enterprise (a rarely discussed, taboo topic; cf., Yuille's paper in this volume); (4) The hope that the theoretical conceptualizations developed in psychology - notably cognitive and social psychology - will be of considerable substantive and heuristic value in the domain of the law (cf., Konečni & Ebbesen, 1984); and (5) The belief that by using experimental simulations to answer questions pertaining to the law, one will automatically reap the rewards that the experimental method has unquestionably brought to the physical and natural sciences.

Points 1 - 3 are, on our opinion, self-evident and need not be elaborated here. A frank airing of these problems should remedy them as the interdisciplinary effort matures. Point 4 is more intricate and deserves a separate article. But it is Point 5 - the use and validity of experimental simulations in legal psychology - that is the primary concern of the present paper.

It is important, however, to acknowledge that one's stance on Points 4 and 5 is necessarily shaped by one's view of what legal psychology ought to do at the present stage of its development. Thus, our skepticism about the value of importing psychological theory and experimental simulations to the domain of the law can be traced to our biases about what the fundamentals of a sound psychology of law should be.

The plan of the paper is to describe briefly the essential core of legal psychology first. We will then discuss some new data on "death-qualified" juries to show that conclusions based on simulations can be not only irrelevant, but actually socially harmful and ethically questionable (if upholding the law of the land is the objective), when accompanied by an overzealous (or ideologically biased) presentation of results or expert testimony. The possibility that the incentive system and ideological bias actually affect the *design* of simulation studies will also be mentioned - with reference to new data regarding the confidence-accuracy relationship in eyewitness identification. Finally, our view of the role that experimental simulations should play in the overall research effort in legal psychology will be described.

The Core of Legal Psychology: A Proposal

The approach we favor at the present stage of development of legal psychology has previously been described in detail (Ebbesen & Konečni, 1982b; Konečni & Ebbesen, 1982b), so that only the main features will suffice here. The approach consists of a socio-systemic, descriptive/predictive, decision-making analysis of the law and the development of causal models and a meta-theory of the legal system's operation.

We define the legal system as a temporally ordered and interconnected network of "nodes" occupied by classes of decision-makers (legal participants) who have discretionary powers (i.e., a range of decision options with, at best, vague guidelines describing how these options are to be selected). The links among nodes are seen as causal pathways, many of which involve social influence.

From our perspective, a descriptive and predictively useful account of the operation of the legal system requires a number of steps (cf., Ebbesen & Konečni, 1982b, pp. 7 - 21). (1) Information is obtained about the aspects of the legal system's operation that are, and are not, constrained by the rule of law. (2) Classes of decision-makers are defined in terms of the type of decisions they make. For example, offenders decide whether or not to commit a crime. Police officers, district attorneys, defense attorneys, and judges make the arrest, prosecutorial, plea-bargaining, bail and sentencing decisions, respectively. (3) The range and details of decision options available to each class of legal participants are specified. (4) Information available to the respective classes of decision-makers at each point in time is identified. (5) The subjective values and weights of the various types of information is empirically obtained. (6) The percent of variance (in the processing of cases by the system as a whole), accounted by a particular node, is calculated. (7) Multi-tiered causal models - decision rules used by participants at various nodes - are formulated.

> If all of these components have been correctly defined and estimated, the result is a predictively accurate *theory* of the particular ... (legal) ... system being studied. If any of these steps are missing, or if the empirically derived solutions at a given step are in error (e.g., an important influence channel has been overlooked, or a particular type of information has been greatly underweighted at a given node), the theory will generally

> provide unsatisfactory predictions of the behavior of participants in the system. (Ebbesen & Konečni, 1982b, p. 11)

Because our approach so strongly emphasizes the importance of understanding the operation of the real-world legal system (jurisdiction by jurisdiction, if necessary), it is not surprising that we have been rather preoccupied with issues of external validity (e.g., Konečni & Ebbesen, 1979, 1982; Ebbesen & Konečni, 1980). Similarly, our concern with the day-to-day administration of criminal justice has led us to question repeatedly the wisdom of the hugely disproportionate amount of research effort and theoretical attention devoted in legal psychology to issues such as (simulated) jury decision-making and eyewitness identification - disproportionate, that is, to their relative unimportance (in terms of the percent of variance they account for) in the real-world processing of criminal cases.

Above all, however, our real-world concerns have led us to probe the pervasive and uncritical use of unvalidated experimental simulations in legal psychology.

Experimental Simulations in Legal Psychology

In principle, one's intention to understand how a real-world system (*any* system) operates or to test the performance of a theoretically-based application (be it a machine or a new law) by no means precludes the use of simulations. They are convenient and relatively cheap and safe, in comparison to the real thing. In aeronautics, for example, simulations ranging from wind-tunnel tests of aircraft wings to flights operated by test pilots fall along a continuum of similarity to the eventual intercontinental flight with 350 passengers. The graded sequence of simulations allows the adjustment of a multitude of variables and this is necessary even in engineering ventures that are based on intimately understood principle of physics. The goal of the continuum of simulations is a gradual approximation to the fully loaded passenger flight; the final test-pilot simulation is still cheaper - in terms of the number of lives lost if the plane crashes - than the first passenger flight. What one has here are *validated* simulations.

Taking shortcuts in this sequence of simulations makes it cheaper, but carries a considerable risk. Specifically, a series of simulations can be considered fully validated *only if* all the main effects and *all the higher-order interactions* of all the relevant variables are tested. Even in highly sophisticated space engineering efforts, the failure to test the higher-order interactions in simulations can have dire or very costly consequences.

For example, in describing the reasons why the camera on the $ 1.5 billion Hubble Space Telescope would not be fully usable due to the faulty mirrors, Mr. J. Olivier, deputy project manager, was quoted as saying:

> Separately, each mirror tested perfectly before launching ... and the flaw became apparent only when they were used together in space ... The mirrors were not tested in combination on the ground ... Doing so would have required mounting them on an elaborate structure that would have cost additional hundreds of millions of dollars. (Leary, 1990)

There are important methodological lessons here for the social sciences, in general, and legal psychology, in particular. It is dangerous and bordering on the irresponsible to draw conclusions and make recommendations to the legal system on the basis of simulations which examine effects independently of their real-world contexts (i.e., on the basis of unvalidated simulations or those that are not designed to examine the higher-order interactions). And *all* legal decisions take place in highly complex contexts and are very costly (in both human and economic terms). Moreover, as we put it in an earlier paper,

> ... human social behavior - legal and illegal - is governed by a host of genetic, economic, personality, organismic, social, and cultural factors (and) [it] is precisely this complexity of antecedents of the more interesting and socially important aspects of human social behavior that makes the ... accurate prediction of such actions so difficult. (Konečni & Ebbesen, 1984, p. 5)

The *only* way to validate a simulation properly is to carry out a real-world study as well (and this in each jurisdiction to which one wishes to generalize). Over the years, we have studied many different criminal and civil legal decisions (cf., Konečni & Ebbesen, 1984). In some of the projects (e.g., the setting of bail, the processing of mentally-disordered sex offenders, the sentencing of convicted adult felons), several different methodologies were used (as many as six in the case of sentencing, of which four were different simulations and two were real-world studies). In *none* of the projects did the results of the experimental simulations (and of the non-experimental approaches, such as interviews, questionnaires, and rating scales) match those obtained by methods (coding of hearings, archival analysis) that were applied to real-world data.

Results of simulations may be valuable to some social scientists regardless of how well they match real-world data. For example, for someone studying judicial attitudes, the judges' notions of what influences their sentencing decisions are of considerable interest. But if one wants to understand how the real-world criminal-justice system operates, an experimental simulation of sentencing (whether with judges or students as subjects) has merit only to the extent that it successfully duplicates real-world findings and thus provides information about the judges' real-world sentencing behavior - but does so cheaply, conveniently, and flexibly (more on this later).

From the latter point of view, a poor simulation is useless at best. At worst, when poor or unvalidated simulations are used as a basis for influencing the legal system, they are not simply useless, they are conceivably dangerous - as we well show in the next two sections.

Research on the Death Penalty and Juror Verdicts

One example of the potentially serious consequences of asserting external validity for unvalidated simulations is the "death-qualification" of jurors in capital-crime cases. In such cases, in the State of California, the same jurors decide, first, whether the defendant is guilty or not guilty (the verdict) and, second, if the person is convicted of first-degree murder, what the sentence should be (life imprisonment without parole or death). The goal of the death-qualification portion of *voir dire* (the jury-selection process) is to identify those individuals (veniremen) whose attitudes toward the death penalty prevent them from reaching either a verdict or a sentence based solely on the evidence presented in open court. The exclusion of veniremen who oppose the legally available capital-punishment option regardless of the merits of the case has lead many to argue that the resulting juries are unfairly skewed toward conviction in the verdict phase of the trial (see Bersoff, 1987, for a review).

So great is the tendency to accept weak and inconsistent results when they support one's favorite policy position that the California Supreme Court cited a single, unpublished study by Haney (it was published four years later, in 1984) as the key factor in their decision to require individual sequestration of prospective jurors for the death-qualifying portion of *voir dire*. (The ostensible purpose of sequestration is to prevent the eventual jurors from being more conviction-prone in the verdict phase by virtue of knowing that other jurors also do not oppose capital punishment.) The opinion, written by then Chief Justice, Rose Bird,[1] included:

> In order to minimize the potentially prejudicial effects identified by the Haney study, this court declares, pursuant to its supervisory authority over California criminal procedure, that in future capital cases that portion of the *voir dire* of each prospective juror which deals with issues which involve death-qualifying the jury should be done individually and in sequestration. (*Hovey v. California*, 1980)

The *Hovey* decision changed the way capital-crime juries are selected in California adding, at minimum, time and expense to the process.[2] (Slow justice is poor justice, in principle, and also because the passage of time lowers the probability that the truth about the case will be discovered in court, for example, because key witnesses for both sides may become unavailable for a variety of reasons.) While this kind of direct impact has been rare, it demonstrates a potential problem when findings from research, the external validity of which remains to be established, are used as an aid to legal reasoning and judicial action in real cases.

A review of the work done in the area and our own research (see below) convince us that the U.S. Supreme Court was right when, in a more recent decision (*Lockhart v. McCree*) it concluded - contrary to the *Hovey* decision - that the evidence on this issue is not yet sufficient to support the claim that the death-qualification *voir dire* increases the conviction-proneness of juries. In a sharp attack on the American Psychological Association's willingness to submit unsubstantiated *amicus* briefs, Elliott's (in press) analysis of the studies cited in the Association's *Lockhart* brief concluded that their results do not, in fact, support the brief's conclusion that the death-qualified juries are more conviction-prone. He also reported that the overall correlation between the death-penalty attitudes

---

[1] Chief Justice Rose Bird and two other California Supreme Court Justices, Joseph Grodin and Cruz Reynoso, failed to be re-elected (under confirmation law) by the people of California in 1986. It is generally agreed that this occurred because of the Court's frequent reversal of death-penalty verdicts in a State where 80 % of the electorate favors capital punishment. Fifty-two of 55 death-penalty decisions heard by the court during the tenure of these Justices were reversed (Lacayo, 1986).

[2] For example, while we were doing research on this topic, jury selection was in progress at a murder trial in the San Diego Superior Court (*California v. Lucas*). Sequestered *voir dire* under the guidelines mandated by the Hovey (1980) decision was in its fourth month and expected to continue for at least two additional months. From an original pool of 500 veniremen, half had been excused for hardship and 109 had passed the death-qualification *voir dire*. General *voir dire* would not begin until the Hovey phase of the selection process was completed.

and verdict decisions averaged between .05 and .12 and barely accounted for 2% of the variance in verdict decisions.

Even if much higher correlations were the norm, however, another feature of the research in the area raises serious concerns about its external validity. In particular, none of the research (including Haney's 1984 study, and the Cowan, Thompson, & Ellsworth's 1984 study) has empirically examined the following rather obvious question: What is the effect of the death-penalty attitudes on verdicts in the context of variations in (a) the nature of the case and (b) in the strength of the evidence against the defendant?

With this in mind, we (Hock, Konečni, & Ebbesen, 1990) recently conducted three simulation experiments in which the above two factors were varied. We used simulation methodology on purpose, so that our results could be more readily compared to those obtained in other simulations, the external validity of which we were questioning. We thought, for example, that the size of the correlation between the death-penalty attitude and the verdict choice might vary with the specific features of the case (e.g., gruesomeness), which would raise doubts about the correctness of generalizing the claim that the death-penalty attitudes influence verdict decisions even across studies *within* the simulation paradigm. However, in all three studies, the strength of the evidence dominated verdict decisions to such an extent that in not one study did the pre-trial death-penalty attitudes account for a significant portion of the variance in individual verdict decisions. This occurred despite the fact that these same attitudes accounted for a large portion of the variance in sentencing decisions. In short, our results were consistent with the notion that even if the death-penalty attitudes are related to verdict decisions, the relationship is so weak that it would be obliterated by many case-factor configurations that are encountered in the real world.

One is tempted to conclude that some psychologists and justices have behaved as they claim jurors do: Their private attitudes against capital punishment have caused them to ignore the strength of the evidence and to assert external validity for a conclusion the truth of which as a scientific fact had been far from being established.

Research on the Confidence-Accuracy Relationship in Eyewitnesses

To us, it seems striking that someone would want to talk about the relationship between the death-penalty attitudes and conviction-proneness on the basis of studies that do not vary something as obvious as the strength of the evidence is in the real-world capital cases. Is this merely ineptness (on the part of investigators, and journal reviewers and editors) or do personal biases (policy, ideological, etc.) interfere with the very design of experiments from the drawing-board stage on?

In regard to this issue, it is of interest to examine the research on the confidence-accuracy relationship in eyewitnesses. In *Neil v. Biggers* (1972), the U.S. Supreme Court commonsensically concluded that one of several factors that could be used to decide whether an eyewitness's identification was reliable was the confidence that the witness expressed in the identification. However, the previously mentioned recent survey of researchers and experts who testify in court about the reliability of eyewitnesses (Kassin et al., 1989) clearly suggests that most of them believe that the relationship between confidence and accuracy is weak or nonexistent. For example, over 80 % felt that the evidence for the claim, "An eyewitness's confidence is not a good predictor of his or her identification accuracy," was reliable enough to testify about in court (presumably for the defense, as 93% of them had previously done, according to the survey). But what is the research basis for this consensus?

There is, in fact, a rather large and heterogeneous collection of simulation studies that report correlations between the eyewitness confidence and accuracy of identifications (see the reviews by Bothwell, Deffenbacher, & Brigham, 1987; Deffenbacher, 1980; Fleet, Brigham, & Bothwell, 1987; Wells & Lindsay, 1985). And although one review (Bothwell et al., 1987) found the correlations to average around .20, the variability in the size of the correlations across studies is quite large: At one end one finds statistically significant negative correlations and at other correlations well above .50.

More importantly, as in the death-qualification area, the researchers on whose work the expert consensus is based have failed to design the experiments and to analyze the results in a manner that takes into account the everyday functioning of the legal system. In particular, the researchers have ignored the simple fact that the prosecution overwhelmingly relies only on witnesses who express high confidence that they can identify the culprit(s) correctly. Witnesses who admit that their identifications are "just guesses" are virtually never used in court because of the ease with which their testimony can be destroyed by defense attorneys in cross-examination; yet, data obtained from such "witnesses" are routinely included in simulation studies.

Therefore, the correct test of the Supreme Court's reliance on the witnesses' confidence as one of the criteria for estimating their identification accuracy is to ask whether the variation in accuracy that is produced by such commonly studied variables as the duration of exposure and the retention interval can be explained by knowing how confident the witness is. And in a recent study of just this issue (Ebbesen, Konečni, & Boucher, 1990) we indeed found that the confidence that people expressed in their identifications accounted for all of the (highly significant) variation produced by the length of the retention interval and by the duration of exposure to the "culprit".

Thus, because of some elementary flaws in their reasoning about the role that the eyewitnesses' confidence plays in the legal system, and because of not being (or not wanting to be) aware of the differences between their studies and the real world, the researchers' published claims and the "experts'" litanies in court have potentially tilted the scale of justice toward unjustified acquittals by lowering the jurors' quite justified reliance on the witnesses' confidence.

The Proper Role for Simulations in Legal Psychology

Based on the use to which simulations are typically put, one can surmise that many researchers believe that a good simulation is one that has "face validity", that is, the procedures somehow "look like" the contexts to which one wishes to generalize. For example, investigators frequently claim - explicitly or implicitly - that their studies have high external validity because videotapes of a simulated trial, rather than written summaries of the evidence, are used as stimulus materials, or because the subjects are somehow deceived to believe that their decisions will have "real" consequences. The face validity of such studies may be high, but their external validity remains *entirely* untested.

A puzzling extension of confusing face with external validity is the argument that one can test the degree of the latter in a given simulation with low face validity by comparing it to other simulations, with apparently greater face validity, along a single dimension (such as the representativeness of the subject sample) and showing that there are no differences in the pattern of results (O'Rourke, Penrod, Cutler, & Stuve, 1989).[3] The obvious logical flaw, again, is that face validity simply does not guarantee external validity. Merely because a result from one simulation (the external validity of which is not known) matches the result of another simulation, differing from the former along one dimension, does not establish that both results reflect a process operating in real-world legal settings.

Were legal settings readily available for observation, accurate measurement, and controlled field experimentation, the only reason to conduct simulations would be their lower social and economic cost. But because research is not built into the legal system, some argue that simulations provide the only way to discover whether causal relations exist among certain variables and that the simulation should therefore be the primary data-collection method in legal psychology. However, knowing that a causal relationship exists in one setting does not guarantee that it accounts for any variance in the legal settings to which psychologists and lawyers wish to generalize. Other variables (that were held constant at arbitrarily chosen levels in the simulation) may completely control the behavior of the participants in the legal setting, leaving virtually no variance left to be explained by the "discovered" causal process.[4] Alternatively, the causal process may have a limited range of values over which it operates, such that when the levels of other variables change, the causal process is no longer operative.

Despite these criticism, we are not arguing that there is no role for simulations in legal psychology, but rather that they should be more thoughtfully and carefully used. In our opinion, in psycho-legal research, the first step should always be that the existence of a relationship (for example, the probation officer's recommendation and the judge's sentence are identical 87 % of the time) be established on real-world data by means of archival or observational research methods. A family of simulations can then be carried out, using

---

[3] O'Rourke et al. (1989) used virtually identical stimuli, tasks, instructions and contexts as were used in five prior experiments on eyewitness identification accuracy. These procedures asked subjects to view a videotape of a simulated robbery in which the robber was present for 75 s and then seven days later make identifications from a serially presented videotaped lineup. The authors simply replicated prior procedures with a sample of subjects broader than college students. That the identification results did not vary with the age of the subjects was used to suggest that the effects of various factors (weapon presence, disguise, and context reinstatement) were externally valid. This claim was made despite the fact that no tests had been carried out to see whether the lack of an interaction with the age factor might not depend on the duration that the robber was present, the length of the retention interval, the nature of the instructions the subjects received, and so on.

[4] Other variables may dominate for a number of different reasons. They may simply control more of the variance, that is, the causal connections may be stronger. The range of values of the factors manipulated in the simulation may be very small compared to the range of values of other factors that occur in the real world, or the range of values of the variables studied in the simulation may simply never occur in the real world.

the range of values of variables that had been discovered in real-world legal data.[5] The simulations would be finely honed (in terms of the type of subjects, instructions given to them, method of presentation of stimuli, supposed consequences of the subject's decisions, and so on) until the pattern of results obtained with real legal data can be reliably duplicated. Once this has been accomplished, further simulations can be carried out to tease apart hopelessly confounded processes. To insure that these additional simulations continue to capture the basic relationship, they can be tested on both the original and new real-world legal data, collected specifically for this purpose.

The co-occurrence pattern of the variables is equally important. For example, when studying bail-setting (Ebbesen & Konečni, 1975, 1982a), we found that the amount of bail recommended by the district attorney was highly correlated with the amount recommended by the defense attorney. A simulation that varied the district attorney's recommendation from $ 1,000 to $ 10,000 and the defense attorney's recommendation from $ 0 to $ 5,000 would produce several combinations of levels (e.g., the district attorney recommends $ 1,000 and the defense recommends $ 5,000) that never occur in the real world, despite the facts that the simulation met every criterion for a well-designed factorial experiment and that the range of variables matched those that most frequently occur in the real bail hearings.

In our view, in legal psychology - a field where enormous human and economic costs are potentially at stake - simulations can be relied on as a source of information for the legal system only if they are fully validated. The best way to insure this is to incorporate them into a coherent, carefully conceived real-world/simulation/real-world alternating sequence. Real-world data and (ideally) archival methodology (see Konečni & Ebbesen, 1979) should be used as standards against which to test, repeatedly, the results obtained in such a sequence of simulations.

Conclusion

The general approach to legal psychology that we have been recommending for over ten years, and the archival methodology itself, are labor-intensive and often painfully slow. Thousands of cases have to be meticulously coded by a well-trained army of coders, and patience and cooperation by the various agencies of the legal system have to be cultivated. The unorthodox locations and style of this type of research, as well as the methodological and statistical sophistication, also require a different approach to graduate education in legal psychology. The models of legal decisions that have been developed in this work are characterized by a degree of predictive power and simplicity that are rather counterintuitive, in reference to both legal and lay truisms. However, the *contents* of the models, that is, the variables that are uncovered, are sometimes reacted to by researchers (those who have excellent hindsight) with an "I could have told you so" shrug. Yet, for example, our three-tiered causal model of sentencing (e.g., Ebbesen & Konečni, 1981;

---

[5] It makes little sense, for example, to study the effects of duration of exposure on eyewitness memory in simulations that vary exposure duration from .25s to 2.0s, if the shortest duration of exposure that occurs in real crimes is 15s and the longest is several days. The duration-accuracy function may be flat after 10s of exposure.

Konečni & Ebbesen, 1982a, 1984) containing a total of five variables, was not, and possibly could not have been, revealed by any other than archival methodology. The postscient researchers simply mistake their familiarity with individual variables for knowledge of the details and the intricate causal features of the overall model. Moreover, the model is just as interesting for the variables that it *excludes*, many of which are at the heart of popular theories in criminology, sociology, and psychology, especially those of the social-activist variety.

In our opinion, it is the laboriousness and slowness of the approach advocated here, the change in research orientation and training that are required, the academic incentive system as currently constituted, and the inertia of blind faith that what (sometimes) works in physics must work in legal psychology, which jointly maintain the continuing popularity of experimental and other simulations. And - we apologize for having to say this - because of the speed with which they can be carried out, simulations are a convenient way to disseminate one's ideological views on legal policies and procedures.

However, if one's goal is to understand how the legal system operates *in vivo*, simulations - except under carefully delineated conditions - are useless, and, if applied uncritically in the legal system, potentially detrimental to fairness, justice, and the rule of law.

If societies were sincerely interested in fairness and justice, their legal systems would incorporate methodologically sophisticated procedures for keeping data on their own performance. The on-line data collection and the development of continually adjusted causal decision models would insure that the legal participants and agencies (individually and collectively) behave in accordance with the rule of law. Such innovations would also make much of what we discussed in this article and what is currently being done in legal psychology superfluous. The logistics, trained manpower, and computing power for these procedures already exist in Western societies. What is lacking in these societies is the collective will to make their powerful, self-satisfied, and inert legal systems more self-analytical. Psychologists of law and other scientists should prod their societies and legal systems in this direction, but they can do so authoritatively and honestly only on the basis of a solid body of data about legal decisions, not the esoteric, irrelevant, or partisan findings obtained in inept simulations.

It is possible that the emerging democratic structures in Eastern, Central, and Southern Europe will give their legal systems the flexibility, open-mindedness, and enthusiasm that are needed to adopt the innovative, self-analytical stance we are recommending. Our remarks - at the Second European Conference on Law and Psychology in Nürnberg and in this article - are therefore to a large extent directed at our colleagues from these fledgling democracies. These colleagues are finally free to join the international community of psychologists of law, but they should ignore the fact that the latter are currently busy doing simulations.

References

Bersoff, D.N. (1987). Social science data and the Supreme Court: *Lockhart* as a case in point. *American Psychologist, 42*, 52-58.

Bothwell, R.K., Deffenbacher, K.A., & Brigham, J.C. (1987). Correlation of eyewitness accuracy and confidence: Opimality hypothesis revisited. *Journal of Applied Psychology, 72*, 691-695.

Cowan, C.L., Thompson, W.C., & Ellsworth, P.C. (1984). The effects of death qualification on juror's predisposition to convict and on the quality of deliberation. *Law and Human Behavior, 8,* 53-79.

Deffenbacher, K.A. (1980). Eyewitness and confidence: Can we infer anything about their relationship? *Law and Human Behavior, 4,* 243-260.

Ebbesen, E.B., & Konečni, V.J. (1975). Decision making and information integration in the courts: The setting of ball. *Journal of Personality and Social Psychology, 32,* 805-821.

Ebbesen, E.B., & Konečni, V.J. (1980). On the external validity of decision-making research: What do we know about decisions in the real world? In T.S. Wallsten (Ed.), *Cognitive processes in choice and decision behavior.* Hillsdale, N.J.: Lawrence Erlbaum.

Ebbesen, E.B., & Konečni, V.J. (1981). The process of sentencing adult felons: A causal analysis of judicial decisions. In B.D. Sales (Ed.), *Perspectives in law and psychology: The jury, judicial, and trial process, Vol. 2.* New York: Plenum.

Ebbesen, E.B., & Konečni, V.J. (1982a). An analysis of the bail system. In V.J. Konečni, & E.B. Ebbesen (Eds.), *The criminal justice system: A social-psychological analysis* San Francisco: W.H. Freeman.

Ebbesen, E.B., & Konečni, V.J. (1982b). Social psychology and the law: A decision-making approach to the criminal justice system. In V.J. Konečni, & E.B. Ebbesen (Eds.), *The criminal justice system: A social-psychological analysis.* San Francisco: W.H. Freeman.

Ebbesen, E.B., Konečni, V.J., & Boucher, R. (unpubl.)(1990). *Expert testimony about eyewitness memory: A premature entry of psychology into the legal system?* University of California, San Diego.

Elliot, R. (in press) (1992). Social science data and the APA: The Lockhart brief as a case in point. *Law and Human Behavior.*

Fleet, M.L., Brigham, J.C., & Bothwell, R.K. (1987). The confidence-accuracy relationship: The effects of confidence assessment and choosing. *Journal of Applied Social Psychology, 17,* 171-187.

Haney, C. (1984). On selection of capital juries: The biasing effects of the death qualifying process. *Law and Human Behavior, 8,* 121-132.

Hock, R., Konečni, V.J., & Ebbesen, E.B. (unpubl.) (1990). *Factors affecting simulated jurors' decision in capital cases.* University of California, San Diego.

Kassin, S.M., Ellsworth, P.C., & Smith, V.L. (1989). The "general acceptance" of psychological research on eyewitness testimony: A survey of experts. *American Psychologist, 44,* 1089-1098.

Konečni, V.J., & Ebbesen, E.B. (1979). External validity of research in legal psychology. *Law and Human Behavior, 3,* 39-70.

Konečni, V.J., & Ebbesen, E.B. (1982a). An analysis of the sentencing system. In V.J. Konečni, & E.B. Ebbesen (Eds.), *The criminal justice system: A social-psychological analysis.* San Francisco: W.H. Freeman.

Konečni, V.J., & Ebbesen, E.B. (1982b). Social psychology and the law: The choice of research problems, settings, and methodology. In V.J. Konečni, & E.B. Ebbesen (Eds.), *The criminal justice system: A social-psychological analysis.* San Francisco: W.H. Freeman.

Konečni, V.J., & Ebbesen, E.B. (1984). The mythology of legal decision making. *International Journal of Law and Psychiatry, 7,* 5-16.

Konečni, V.J., & Ebbesen, E.B. (1986). Courtroom testimony by psychologists on eyewit-ness identification issues: Critical notes and reflections. *Law and Human Behavior, 10,* 117-126.

Leary, W.F. (1990). Mirror flaw means telescope camera will not be usable. *International Herald Tribune,* June 29, 1990.

Monahan, J., & Walker, L. (1985). *Social science in law: Cases and materials.* Mineola, NY: The Foundation Press.

Neil v. Biggers, 409 U.S. 188 (1972).

O'Rourke, T.E., Penrod, S.D., Cutler, B.L., & Stuve, T.E. (1989). The external validity of eyewitness identification research: Generalizing across subject populations. *Law and Human Behavior, 13,* 385-395.

Tanford, J.A., & Tanford, S. (1987). Better trials through science: A defense of psychologist-lawyer collaboration. *The North Carolina Law Review, 66,* 740-780.

Wells, G.L., & Lindsay, R.C.L. (1985). Methodological notes on the accuracy-confidence relation in eyewitness identification. *Journal of Applied Psychology, 70,* 413-419.

Yarmey, A.D., & Jones, H. (1983). Is the study of eyewitness identification a matter of common sense? In S. Lloyd-Bostock, & B. Clifford (Eds.), *Evaluating eyewitness evidence.* New York: Wiley.

Justification and Goals of Punishment and the Attribution of Responsibility in Judges

Margit E. Oswald

Introduction

In the context of sentencing, possible justifications of punishment are discussed with much emotional arousal, particularly among theorists of penal law, judges, and criminologists. The point of the discussion is the defence of basically different philosophical positions and the question which position is linked to a more authoritarian attitude and a more punitive sentencing behavior. Among psychologists, this discussion is held in a purely rational manner, in cold blood, so to speak, but, actually, psychologists do not have to cope with the problem of justifying institutionalized punishment. Variables studied in this context, often and in various combinations, are goals and philosophy of punishment, attitude toward punishment, authoritarianism, attribution of responsibility, and sentencing behavior. However, the state of the art seems to be such that, upon closer inspection, theoretical relations are unclear, and empirical studies demonstrate only that "somehow" everything correlates with everything (see Carroll, Perkowitz, Lurigio, & Weaver, 1987). This paper takes a closer look at the relation between justification and goals of punishment and the attribution of responsibility. A theoretical approach will be presented and empirically tested in interviews with criminal court judges.

Theoretical Considerations

Criminal court judges, who considerably affect the lives of offenders by their sentencing decisions, are more concerned than others about the justification and goals of punishment. Traditionally, we may distinguish between two main directions of justifying penal sanctions: On one side, we might take the position that punishment has got to be useful for the offender and for society; that is, it should be imposed only if it can prevent criminal acts, directly or indirectly (= utilitarian position). On the other side, we might take the position that a penalty should be imposed to compensate a damage for which the offender is held responsible (= retributional position). Of course, judges will not take one or the other position exclusively, and have different considerations in different cases. And yet, we assume that, on average and seen over many cases, there are individual differences in the preference for one or the other justification of punishment. That is, we assume that persons do have a tendency to take either a more pragmatic position, oriented toward utility, or a more moral attitude, emerging from considerations of a just retribution.

Among theorists of penal law and criminologists, discussion on these two justifications of punishment is highly controversial (see Kim, 1987). This is essentially the case because (a) the positions are not considered in their own right but rather connected with authoritarianism and a punitive attitude, and (b) specific goals of punishment are attributed exclusively to either one or the other position of justification. It is assumed that a preference for one of the aims at the same time unveils to which tribe of penalty justification a person belongs. Both assumptions are to be analyzed critically in the following.

Theorists of penal law and criminologists with different positions in the controversy blame each other for fostering a problematic reality in penal law. Utilitarians blame retributionists for being a stumbling stone on the way toward a human penal law. The offender is nailed to his or her guilt, and it is said to be a characteristic of authoritarian penal law that the corresponsibility of society is turned over only to the offender (see Hassemer, 1983). Retributionists, on the other hand, accuse utilitarianists that, from their view, it would be justifiable to punish innocents or to inflict exorbitant penalties whenever this could achieve the aim of crime prevention (see Ten, 1987). In my view, this debate neglects that the preference for one of the possible justifications of punishment does not say anything about how severely a judge will sentence. As Hart (1984) emphasizes, it is an error to confound problems of justification of punishment with problems of severity. Hassemer (1983), for example, assumes that the affirmation of a moral justification of punishment necessarily implies that responsibility for the crime is attributed only to the offender. The basis for this line of argument seems to be the close connection of the retributional position with a theory of retaliation (see Kim, 1987).

However, this connection appears questionable, since the principle of just retribution does not exclude a priori that a corresponsibility of society is seen. From a psychological point of view, the search for a just balance settles neither where nor to what extent moral responsibility is assessed. Nor is it to be mixed up with a person's hypothesis of a just world (see Lerner, 1980), because a judge who justifies punishment primarily under the retributional aspect does not have to believe, in general, that everybody gets what he or she deserves. Similar considerations, with respect to the independence of punitiveness and justification of punishment, exist in connection with the utilitarian position. We can imagine that a pragmatically oriented person may be convinced of the effectivity of severe punishment, but the contrary may be the case as well. Respectively, we would expect a more severe or a more lenient sentencing behavior.

Let us come back to the second point, which refers to systematic connections between justification and goals of punishment. In the current view, atonement and retaliation are considered as goals of a retributive theory of punishment. Other goals like rehabilitation, deterrence of the actual offender, general deterrence, and consolidation of standards, are named as goals of a utilitarian theory of punishment. This list of goals has grown historically, in a certain sense, and thus may differ at different times in history and between different cultures of law. As pointed out above, the references quote only atonement and retaliation as retributive goals of punishment but not restitution. Moreover, American references mention the additional goal of "incapacitation" which is mainly locking the offender away from the rest of the population. But, more important than these considerations is the fact that the unique connection of goals to principles of justification of punishment is questionable in itself. As an example, let us consider the goal of consolidation of standards. For some people, consolidation of standards may be just a side effect of general deterrence, since, in their opinion, consolidation of standards is causally connected to a low overall crime rate. Other people assume that consolidation of standards does not depend on severity of punishment but on a thorough prosecution of criminal offenders. And, finally, consolidation of standards may be understood as the fact that punishment satisfies penal claims, and, thus, people's belief in justice. Thus, although consolidation of standards is traditionally categorized as an utilitarian goal of punishment, its equation with a more or less complete satisfaction of penal claims would be a clear expression of restitution. The same holds for the goal of rehabilitation. Whereas rehabilitation means for many people the acquisition of new standards and values, for others, it may be directly associated with the idea of restitution. According to their opinion, insight and the possibility of a new beginning are enabled by a restitutional act. These examples should demonstrate that different goals of punishment may have different meanings, and that it is by no means clear from the beginning whether they result from an utilitarian or from a retributive orientation.

Following the analyses up to now, we might get the impression that the different justifications of punishment are irrelevant from a psychologist's point of view. This impression would be wrong. On the other hand, the position is held that they can be used only in connection with other psychological dimensions to predict attribution of responsibility, punitiveness, or preferred goal of punishment. Let us consider, again, the different goals of punishment with respect to the differences between them.

We notice not only that punishment can be justified in different ways (utilitarian/ retributional) but also that it can be evaluated from very different points of view. Thus, the different goals of punishment reflect the respective readiness to judge the offense and the consequences of punishment more from the offender's, or more from the (potential) victim's point of view. The point of view to judge the criminal act changes with the goal of punishment: With the goals of retaliation and general deterrence, the point of view of the offender seems to be far out of sight, whereas the focus is on the (potential) victim's point of view. We could also say that the preference for these goals of punishment implies the general readiness to give up the offender's concern, for reasons of crime prevention, or to satisfy general claims for punishment. With the goal of rehabilitation, on the other hand, the (potential) victim's interests are far from sight, and those of the actual offender are in the focus. The goal of consolidation of standards could be located between these two poles of offender/victim points of view, as far as this goal is not understood as pure retaliation or general deterrence.

Following our consideration above, we come to a new categorization of goals of punishment (see Table 1). Contrary to current opinion, many goals cannot be associated uniquely with one or the other justification of punishment. Instead, we have to ask in each single case in what sense the goals are used, for example, rehabilitation or consolidation of standards. Furthermore, it becomes clear that the justification of punishment preferred enables predictions of goals only in connection with another dimension, and cannot be associated automatically with features like authoritarianism or punitiveness. This additional dimension refers to the readiness of the judge to see offenses more or less from the offender's point of view and will be labeled offender-victim perspective.

The analysis so far, and in particular the elaboration of the dimension "offender-victim perspective," permits some interesting considerations about why persons may hold an offender responsible for his or her actions to different degrees. The concept of attribution of responsibility is used in very different meanings, which has led to rather frequent misunderstandings (see Fincham & Jaspars, 1980). In particular, we have to differentiate between causal responsibility, role responsibility, moral responsibility, and legal responsibility. In the following, we will talk only about moral responsibility, as defined by Heider (1958), and which could be used synonymously with personal guilt.

Table 1: Classification of Goals of Punishment.

	Preferred justification of punishment	
	Retributional position	**Utilitarian position**
Perspective of offender	Rehabilitation by restitution	Rehabilitation by learning "positive" standards
Perspective of offender and (potential) victims	Offender related compensation of penal claim	Stressing the validity of standards
Perspective of (potential) victims	Damage related retaliation	General deterrence

Research on attribution has shown that persons in comparable situations differ in their inclination to attribute responsibility to offenders by judging either forseeability, intentionality, or justification of an action in different ways (see Carroll & Payne, 1977; Furnham, 1988; Shaver, 1985). Also, we know that the different perspectives of actor and observer lead to distictly different results of attribution. Jones and Nisbett (1972) have proposed the hypothesis that actors have a strong tendency to attribute their respective behavior to the requirements of the external circumstances, whereas observers of the very same behavior are more inclined to attribute it to internal traits of the actor. A fundamental explanation of this effect is seen in the focus of the perception of possible causes that changes with the perspective of either the actor or the observer (see Fiske & Taylor, 1984; Monson & Snyder, 1977).

Applying this line of reasoning to our problem, we arrive at the conclusion that adopting the perspective of the offender will be connected to an increased attentiveness to external influences upon the action, whereas adopting the perspective of (potential) victims will increase the attentiveness to internal traits of the offender. According to Heider (1958), a cause leads less to the attribution of moral responsibility the further it is distant from the actor. Thus, we can predict: A judge who tries to sentence from the perspective of the offender will attribute less responsibility than a judge who sentences more from the perspective of the (potential) victim, since he or she focuses more on external causes in his or her explanation of the action. From a juridical point of view, we could say that the search for personal guilt of the defendant is increasingly focused on his or her respective conditions of life. A judgment from the perspective of the (potential) victim, however, suggests an "objective" scale in which the opinion of the so-called average citizen serves as the criterion for the assessment of responsibility. With offenses committed mainly by lower social class offenders, according to the official records, like, for example, theft, this will result in an unquestioned assumption of responsibility of the offender, such that the charge is mainly dependent on the severity of the offense.

Based on the deliberations above, one possible objection is that the relation proposed between offender-victim perspective and attribution of moral responsibility holds only for persons who follow retributive goals of punishment. For persons with more pragmatic goals of punishment, the attribution of responsibility should not be very important, in general. Contrary to that, it is assumed that attribution of responsibility is a very elementary process that operates in each person, and, as such, also in persons with a preponderantly pragmatic justification of punishment (see Heider, 1958). For example, if a judge is convinced that penal law should aim at rehabilitation, he or she will be only little inclined to hold the offender responsible. Independent of that, however, he or she could be of the opinion that, for example, rehabilitation should be achieved by restitution or by different kinds of training. In this sense, it is highly possible that the respective preference for a justification of punishment constitutes a secondary judgmental process that is rather independent of the offender-victim perspective taken and of the responsibility attributed to the offender.

Let us finally get to the question of punitiveness. Last, not least because of consequences from attribution theory, we have to assume that punitiveness increases the more, the more the readiness to judge the action from the offender's perspective decreases. However, it cannot be excluded that severe punishment may sometimes be proposed in spite of an adoption of the offender's perspective, with the aim of individual deterrence. This could be the case particularly in judges who prefer a pragmatic justification of punishment and who are convinced of the effectiveness of severe punishment. How far this possibility exists in reality, and is not based on an only pretended adoption of the offender's perspective, would be a question for further research.

Empirical Study

The present empirical study tested whether the preferred justification of punishment is independent of the offender-victim perspective taken, and whether the latter dimension is related systematically to the inclination to attribute more or less responsibility to the offender.

During individual interviews with 36 criminal court judges, who all came from magistrate's courts, we presented standardized questionnaires as well as open and prestructured questions. Most judges came from two courts at big cities in West Germany. At these courts, we reached a participation rate of 80%. Only 10% of the judges refused explicitly, and the remainder of them were sick or on vacation at the time of the interview, so that we can hardly assume any bias of the results due to systematic self-selection of the sample.

Operationalization of variables

The preferred justification of punishment and the offender-victim perspective of the judges were assessed by means of a semistructured interview. This time-consuming procedure was considered neccessary to avoid replies oriented toward social desirability or a desired self-image. Individual tendencies in the attribution of responsibility were collected by means of a standardized questionnaire (see Oswald & Bilsky, 1991). But even here, the weighting of the dimensions relevant for the attribution of responsibility (see Heider, 1958; Weiner, 1980) was assessed only indirectly. Criminal actions to be discussed here were offenses that are usually the business of magistrate's courts.

Justification of punishment. As mentioned above, judges do not stick exclusively to one or the other justification of punishment but, at most, prefer either a pragmatic or a moral line of reasoning. We assumed that confrontation with a dilemma of justification would be most useful for unveiling their respective preferences. The following dilemma was presented to the judges: Assume an actual case, in which a major offense has been committed, for example, an aggravated assault, but in which it can be assumed almost certainly that a penalty would have no preventive effect at all. Would you be inclined, in this actual case, to withdraw a punishment because of its uselessness?

In addition to an immediate reply to this question, we asked for reasons for this reply. Counter-questions of the interwiever ascertained whether the given justification could be categorized into one of the four following categories (see Table 2).

Table 2: Prototypical Reactions to the Dilemma Concerning the Justification of Punishment.

	No resignation of punishment	Resignation of punishment
Retributional position	No, because the criminal offence is too high and restitutional demands have to be considered. (N = 16)	Yes, if punishment does not change the individual, the personal guilt must be low. (N = 4)
Utilitarian position	No, because I do not believe in the premise. Punishment has always an effect, at least for society. (N = 13)	Yes, if punishment has no effect, I cannot see any reason for punishment anymore. (N = 3)

As far as judges made clear, in both the confrontation with the dilemma as well as in some additional questions about justifications of punishment that the idea of retribution played an important role in their assessment of penalty, we classified them to a retributional position. A typical utterance for a retributive justification of punishment is: "Well, you know, I really do not think about the consequences of punishment, I only want to restore a state of justice." In cases in which we could deny both criteria, we assumed a predominantly utilitarian position of justification.

Offender-victim perspective. In this dilemma, the offender's concern was opposed to that of the (potential) victim. The judges were asked to assume that the frequency of a certain crime (e.g., burglary) has increased considerably, and that this threat to public peace could be countered by a considerable increase in the penalty for this crime. The consecutive question was whether the judge would be inclined to raise the degree of sentence severely (1). Further important indications of the adoption of an offender-victim perspective were (2) whether the judge was generally inclined to raise sentences severely with increasing crime rate, (3) if the justification of punishment assigned an important role to the consolidation of standards, and (4) if he or she emphasized the need to exert some positive influence on the defendant in the framework of the penal law system.

Attribution of responsibility. For the assessment of the judge's tendency to attribute more or less responsibility, a questionnaire has been developed (see Oswald & Bilsky, 1991) that should cover the main dimensions of layman's explanations of criminal behavior. In a pretest with 212 judges and students of law, 68 possible causes of criminal behavior were rated on 5-point Likert scales with respect to their importance in causing criminality. The data were processed by means of a factor analysis. According to conventional criteria (scree-test, eigenvalue, explained variance, stability of solution, parsimony, and item content), we chose a four-factor solution for describing the item pool that explains 32% of variance. Inspection of items with substantial loadings suggested the following factors labels: Destructive Motivation, Societal Factors, Lack of Planning and Future, Marginal Position in Social Life. Marker items that load at least .40 on one of the factors were used to construct the scales of the questionnaire with corresponding labels (see Table 3).

Table 3: Scales of Responsibility Attribution.

Scale	Variable (abbreviated)	Item-analysis r_{it}*	r_{tt}**
I.	**Destructive motivation**		.82
	Desire for excitement and adventure	.58	
	Revenge	.43	
	Exaggerated desire to show off	.75	
	Missing reference to reality	.39	
	Weakness of character	.42	
	Pathological aggressiveness	.44	
	Criminal energy	.43	
	Act under influence of emotion	.44	
	Longing to self-affirmation	.62	
	Feeling of hatred	.58	
II.	**Societal factors**		.78
	Coincidence of disastrous conditions	.49	
	Selectivity of police control	.50	
	Lack of educational opportunities	.45	
	Achievement-orientated society	.50	
	Impoverishment of population	.47	
	Not enough room for self-realization	.64	
	Consumer society	.55	
	Criminalization by penal legislation	.48	
	Stigmatizing reactions	.48	
III.	**Lack of planning and future**		.80
	Intellectual deficits	.71	
	Early leaving parent's house	.28	
	To live at random	.54	
	Broken partnership	.35	
	Sense of mental vacuum	.61	
	Disordered life-style	.61	
	Miserable prospects of life	.67	
IV.	**Marginal position in social life**		.80
	Anti-social background	.40	
	Failure in professional career	.54	
	Poor social integration	.58	
	Belonging to a subculture	.43	
	Insufficient tradition of values	.41	
	To be in a state of neglect	.71	
	Broken home	.62	

* r_{it} = Corrected item-total correlation
** r_{tt} = Cronbach's α (internal consistency reliability)

In accordance with Heider (1958) and Weiner (1980), the scales represent very clearly either external causes (Scales 2 and 4) or internal causes (Scales 1 and 3) of crime. A comparatively clear distinction of variable/stable and controllable/uncontrollable could not be detected. However, the external causes seem to be differentiated into those that work more proximally (Scale 4), or more distally (see Kidder & Cohn, 1979). On the other hand, internal causes seem to differ according to whether they describe a more active (threatening) or a more passive offender. Starting from attribution theory, we have to assume that the attribution of responsibility increases with the emphasis on internal causes and decreases with the emphasis on external causes. The latter causes should exculpate the offender more if these causes are localized further away from him or her.

Table 4: Percentage of Judges in the Categories of the Dimension Offender-Victim-Perspective.

	Perspective of offender	Perspective of offender and (potential) victims	Perspective of (potential) victims
General positive attitude toward severe punishment in favour of (potential) victims	0%	0%	100%
Positive attitude to punish burglary more severely if crime rate increases	0%	severely: 36% slightly: 23%	severely: 100%
Emphasizing the consolidation of standards	50%	54%	85%
Emphasizing the goal of rehabilitation	90%	30%	29%
	N = 10	N = 13	N = 13

Results of the Study

Let us first talk about the indications for the assessment of the offender-victim perspective. In the items listed again in Table 4, we assumed that they indicate the position of the respective judge on the dimension offender-victim perspective. While an indirectly assessed preference for the goal of rehabilitation (i.e., the judge emphasizes the need to exert some positive influence on the defendant) indicates the adoption of an offender's perspective, the readiness to react to a high crime rate by increasing the severity of sentencing speaks more for an adoption of the victim's perspective. An MDS (Multidimensional Scaling) approach has shown that the items can be scaled on one dimension according to our assumption. The location on the dimension of offender-victim perspective was differentiated into three categories. Critical for this categorization was the judge's reaction to the given dilemma and the generality of his or her inclination to raise the degree of sentence with increasing crime rates.

The central hypothesis that the offender-victim perspective adopted preponderantly by the judges is independent of his or her preference for a more pragmatic or more moral justification of punishment could be confirmed (see Table 5). The χ^2 test did not lead to a significant result.

Table 5: Relationship Between Justification of Punishment and Offender-Victim-Perspective.*

	Retributional position	Utilitarian position
Perspective of offender	7	3
Perspective of offender and (potentional) victims	6	7
Perspective of (potentional) victims	5	8

* $\chi^2=2,37$; $df=2$; $p>.30$

Finally, let us come to the second hypothesis, that is, that the adoption of a perspective is related to the attribution of moral resonsibility. In Figure 1 (see next page), we have arranged the data in a so-called box plot (see McGill, Tukey, & Larsen, 1978). The configuration of the display show the respective medians, 1st and 3rd quartiles of the group, and their upper and lower extremes. Except for Scale 4, all data point in the direction predicted. But the differences between group means reach statistical significance only for Scale 2, Societal Factors. Here we will have to wait and see how trends develop with increasing sample size. Finally, a remark about Scale 4 (Marginal Position in Social Life): The 36 judges interviewed at different magistrate's courts are sentencing almost only misdemeanors, and these are almost exclusively offenses involving property. Their clientele comes mainly from socially marginal groups. For this reason, it may be understandable that all groups of judges with this professional experience emphasize Scale 4 most and we are dealing with a ceiling effect.

Summary

In previous references, it has been speculated again and again that certain propositions about judges' punitiveness, authoritarianism, or inclination to attribute responsibility could be inferred from their justification of punishment. However, if we differentiate justifications of punishment into preferences for retributive (moral) or utilitarian (pragmatic) justifications, we can show empirically that neither preference allows any inference. Only the introduction of a second central dimension, called offender-victim perspective, makes it possible to categorize individual goals of punishment, and to make predictions about punitiveness and inclinations to attribute guilt. This dimension indicates the readiness of the judge to see the criminal act either more from the offender's perspective or more from the (potential) victim's perspective. Furthermore, assumptions from social psychology about differences in attribution between actor and observer enable the prediction that judges will attribute more responsibility to the offender, the more they are ready to adopt the perspective of the (potential) victim. This hypothesis has been confirmed empirically. However, whether corresponding predictions about the punitiveness of the judges hold is open to further research.

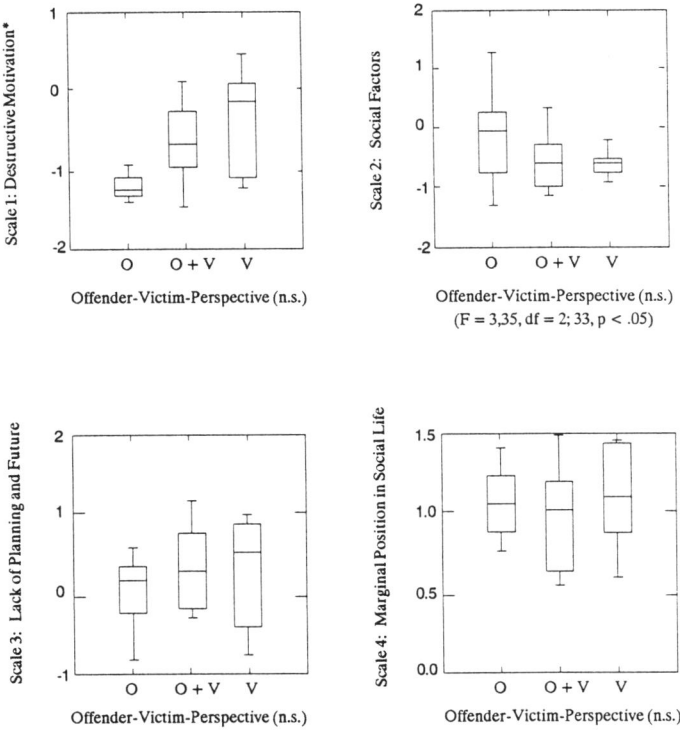

* Judges' scores on the scales were z'-transfomed to represent the relative importance of each scale.

Figure 1: Influence of Judge's Perspective on the Attribution of Responsibility.

References

Carroll, J.S., & Payne, J.W. (1977). Judgments about crime and the criminal: A model and a method of investigating parole decision. In P.D. Sales (Ed.), *Perspectives in law and psychology: Criminal justice system, Vol. 1* (pp. 191-239). New York: Plenum.

Carroll, J.S., Perkowitz, W.T., Lurigio, A.J., & Weaver, F.M. (1987). Sentencing goals, causal attributions, ideology, and personality. *Journal of Personality and Social Psychology, 52,* 107-118.

Fincham, F.D., & Jaspars, J.M. (1980). Attribution of responsibility: From man-the-scientist to man-as-lawyer. In L. Berkowitz (Ed.), *Advances in experimental social psychology* (pp. 82-138). New York: Academic Press.

Fiske, S.T., & Taylor, S.E. (1984). *Social cognition.* New York: Random House.

Furnham, A.F. (1988). *Lay theories.* Oxford: Pergamon.

Hart, H.L.A. (1984). *Punishment and responsibility.* Oxford: Clarendon Press.

Hassemer, W. (1983). Alternativen zum Schuldprinzip. In H.M. Baumgartner, & A. Eser (Eds.), *Schuld und Verantwortung* (pp. 26-39). Tübingen: J.C.B. Mohr.
Heider, F. (1958). *The psychology of interpersonal relation*. New York: Wiley.
Jones, E.E., & Nisbett, R.E. (1972). The actor and observer: Divergent perceptions of the causes of behavior. In E.E. Jones, D.E. Kanouse, H.H. Kelley, R.E. Nisbett, S. Valins, & B. Weiner (Eds.), *Attribution: Perceiving the cause of behavior* (pp. 79-94). Morristown, NJ: General Learning Press.
Kidder, L.H., & Cohn, E.S. (1979). Public views of crime and crime prevention. In I. Frieze, D. Bar-Tal, & J.S. Carroll (Eds.), *New approaches to social problems* (pp. 237-264). San Francisco: Jossey-Bass.
Kim, Y.-W. (1987). *Zur Fragwürdigkeit und Notwendigkeit des strafrechtlichen Schuldprinzips*. Ebelsbach: Gremer.
Lerner, M. (1980). *The belief in a just world: A fundamental delusion*. New York: Plenum.
McGill, R., Turkey, J.W., & Larsen, W.A. (1978). Variations of box plots. *The American Statistican, 32*, 12-16.
Monson, T.C., & Snyder, M. (1977). Actors, observers, and the attribution process. *Journal of Experimental Social Psychology, 13*, 89-111.
Oswald, M.E., & Bilsky, W. (1991). Subjektive Theorien über Kriminalitätsursachen und richterliche Schuldzuschreibung. *Monatsschrift für Kriminologie und Strafrechtsnorm, 74*, 129-145.
Shaver, K.G. (1985). *The attribution of blame*. New York: Springer.
Ten, C.L. (1987). *Crime, guilt, and punishment*. Oxford: Clarendon Press.
Weiner, B. (1980). *Human motivation*. New York: Holt, Rinehart & Winston.

Verdicts of Psychosocially Biased Juries

Ramón Arce, Jorge Sobral, and Francisca Fariña

Introduction

Great confusion has reigned as regards the influence of psychosocial variables on the decisions of juries. Conservatism, for example, has been reported to affect jury decisions by some researchers (Bray & Noble, 1978; Mitchell & Byrne, 1973; Sobral, Arce, & Mirón, 1988) but not by others (Hastie, Penrod, & Pennington, 1983; Penrod, 1980), and much the same goes for other personality variables and for sex (Sobral & Arce, 1990). In reviewing the relationship between psychosocial variables and jury function as a whole, it has generally been concluded that these variables have no adverse effect (Gerbasi, Zuckerman, & Reis, 1977; Hastie, Penrod, & Pennington, 1983; Kaplan, 1982), or that any slight effect they might have is removed in the course of joint deliberation by the jury (Kaplan & Miller, 1978). Most of the studies on which these conclusions were based used techniques such as multiple regression analysis or discriminant analysis to investigate the relationship between psychosocial variables and the verdicts or sentencing recommendations of individual jurors (Feild, 1978; Hastie et al., 1983; Hepburn, 1980; Penrod, 1980; Saks, 1977), finding that, although the influence of certain variables was significant, their weight was negligible (except in Feild's study). Other studies, in which the behavior of mock juries had been investigated (see the revision of Sobral, Arce, & Fariña, 1989), had often reached mutually contradictory conclusions.

In our initial work in this field, we used statistical techniques of the kind mentioned above to identify certain multivariable psychosocial profiles that appeared to be related to the verdict and sentencing behavior of individual jurors (Arce, 1989; Sobral, Arce, Fariña, & Vilán, 1988). We then selected juries whose members all exhibited the same profile, and studied their behavior in trying several re-enacted court cases; we found that juries with opposite personality profiles arrived at opposite verdicts in some cases but not in others (Arce, Sobral, & Fariña, 1990; Sobral, Arce, & Fariña, 1989) and interpreted this as showing that personality variables required particular circumstances for their effects to be manifested. Upon re-reading the literature, we noted that previous mock jury studies had almost exclusively looked for the effects of single personality variables rather than complete profiles (Davis, 1989), and that there was virtually no methodological consistency among the different studies as regards the type of case tried or the firmness of the evidence presented. We concluded that their mutual contradictions might well have been due largely to methodological differences and the consideration of isolated variables.

We furthermore hypothesized that the small but significant influence of personality variables detected in correlation studies might well influence the information handling ability of the juror in such a way that bias in the consideration of evidence presented in court and arguments wielded during joint deliberation might be amplified by positive feedback. The contrary view was held by Kaplan and Miller (1978), who opined that the bias of individual jurors would disappear during joint deliberation.

We report here a more thorough analysis of the experiment performed with mock juries that were homogeneous as regards the psychosocial profile of their members.

Procedure

Psychosocial profiles were defined on the basis of the results of a study of the verdicts and sentence recommendations of 311 individual subjects. Sentencing recommendations were regressed on the personality variables considered, and verdicts used for discriminant analysis in the personality space. The profiles defined were as follows (see Table 1).

Table 1: Psychosocial Profiles.

		Variable	Score
A)	**Attribution profiles**		
A1)	Internal attribution	Internal locus of control	High
		External locus of control (chance)	Low
		External locus of control (powerful others)	Low
A2)	External attribution	Internal locus of control	Low
		External locus of control (chance)	High
		External locus of control (powerful others)	High
B)	**Ideological profiles**		
B1)	Conservative	Political stance	Right-wing
		Conservativism	High
		Dogmatism	Low
		Attitude toward delinquency	Hard
B2)	Progressive	Political stance	Left-wing
		Conservativism	Low
		Dogmatism	Low
		Attitude toward delinquency	Soft

Nine-member juries were formed, in each of which all members had the same psychosocial profile. They were shown videotaped re-enactments of the court proceedings (with judge, public prosecutor, defence lawyers, witnesses, expert witnesses and accused) of two cases taken from real life, one a case of rape and murder and the other a case of criminal negligence involving a surgeon. Immediately after viewing each case, before deliberation, the jurors gave their individual verdicts, and they then deliberated together in a room equipped with a video camera (with sound recorder) that was controlled by a member of the research team who viewed the deliberation process from an adjacent room through a one-way mirror. The jury was asked to reach an unanimous verdict. The recorded deliberation processes were analysed using a modified version of the Relational Communicational Control Coding System (Rogers & Farace, 1975). In our version, each juror utterance was represented by a five-digit code. Digit 1 identified the juror speaking, Digit 2 the form of the utterance, Digit 3 its communication control function, Digit 4 its factual content and Digit 5 its legal content (see Hastie et al., 1983).

Results

Verdicts

The juries constructed on the basis of ideological profiles (the progressive and conservative juries) reached the same postdeliberation verdict in the criminal negligence case (guilty) but different verdicts in the rape and murder case.* The juries constructed on the basis of their locus of control characteristics (the internal attribution and external attribution juries) reached the same verdict in the rape and murder case but different verdicts in the criminal negligence case.

Deliberation style

The juries constructed on the basis of ideological content variables differed in joint deliberation style from those constructed on the basis of personality style variables. Thus differences in psychosocial profile led not only to differences in verdict, but, on the way, to differences in interaction style. Furthermore, in the case in which the two juries representing opposite profiles for the same group of variables reached the same verdict, their deliberation style was also the same; but in the case in which they reached different verdicts, one of the juries maintained the same deliberation style as for the other case, and the other adopted a different deliberation style. The verdict of the jury with stable deliberation style agreed with those of the other two juries and with that of an experienced magistrate, so that deviation in deliberation style was accompanied by a deviant and apparently erroneous verdict (see Arce et al., 1990; Sobral, Arce, & Fariña, 1990).

Content

Similar results were obtained for the content of the jury deliberation processes: Juries with opposite psychosocial profiles reached the same verdict when their deliberation content was the same, and different verdicts when they differed in deliberation content (see Arce et al., 1990; Sobral et al., 1990).

Discussion

The literature on the jury is among the most prolific in the field of social psychology, since the reliability of this institution is continually being questioned and has been considerably improved in the light of objective research findings (Pennington & Hastie, 1990). Nevertheless, numerous gaps remain in our understanding of the jury process; research in this area is not easy, because situational factors play a very important role in the behavior of jurors.

In this work we have found indications that juries may exhibit latent bias, that is, bias that is manifested in certain types of case and in the face of a certain minimum degree of inconclusiveness in the evidence, but not otherwise. In keeping with its psychosocial profile, the external attribution jury fails to accept what for all the others (and for the collaborating magistrate) is sufficient evidence of the accused surgeon's guilt, preferring instead to believe that his patient's death had been due to causes beyond his control; but the same jury would very probably not have erred in the face of unequivocally condemning evidence, and does not err in the rape and murder case, in which it reaches the same verdict as the majority of the other juries (in this case, it is the conservative jury whose verdict differs from those of the others). This latency in personality-induced jury bias, or interaction between personality and circumstantial variables such as the type of case and the balance of evidence, seems likely to have been largely responsible for many of the contradictions in the literature in this field.

Finally, we point out that the threshold of doubt that must be exceeded before personality-induced jury bias is realized is easily reached. It is, after all, only doubtful cases that come to trial by jury.

Endnote

* For practical reasons, it was not possible to sequester the juries until an unanimous verdict was reached. Here and in what follows, "different" therefore refers to a significant difference as regards the ratio of guilty to not guilty votes within the jury at the end of the deliberation period, as estimated by the χ^2 test; "same" refers to the absence of a significant difference.

References

Arce, R. (1989). *Perfiles psicosociales, veredictos y deliberación en jurados legos*. Unpublished doctoral dissertation. University of Santiago de Compostela, Spain.

Arce, R., Sobral, J., & Fariña, F. (1990). Análisis gráfico/descriptivo de la toma de decisiones judiciales. *Actas del II Congreso del Colegio Oficial de Psicólogos, 9*, 111-117.

Bray, R.M., & Noble, A. (1978). Authoritarianism and decisions of mock juries: Evidence of jury bias and group polarization. *Journal of Personality and Social Psychology, 36*, 1424-1430.

Davis, J.H. (1989). Psychology and law: The last 15 years. *Journal of Applied Social Psychology, 19*, 199-230.

Feild, H.S. (1978). Juror background characteristics and attitudes toward rape: Correlates of jurors' decisions in rape trials. *Law and Human Behavior, 2*, 73-93.

Gerbasi, K.C., Zuckerman, M., & Reis, H.T. (1977). Justice needs a new blindfold: A review of mock jury research. *Psychological Bulletin, 84*, 323-345.

Hastie, R., Penrod, S., & Pennington, N. (1983). *Inside the jury*. Cambridge, MA: Harvard University Press.

Hepburn, J.R. (1980). The objective reality of evidence and the utility of systematic jury selection. *Law and Human Behavior, 4*, 89-102.

Kaplan, M.F. (1982). Cognitive processes in the individual juror. In N.L. Kerr & R.M. Bray (Eds.). *The psychology of the courtroom*. New York: Academic Press.

Kaplan, M.F., & Miller, L.E. (1978). Reducing the effects of juror bias. *Journal of Personality and Social Psychology, 36*, 1443-1455.

Mitchell, H.E., & Byrne, D. (1973). *Minimizing the influence of irrelevant factors in the courtroom: The defendant's character, judge's instructions and authoritarianism*. Paper presented at the meeting of the Midwestern Psychological Association, Chicago, USA.

Pennington, N., & Hastie, R. (1990). Practical implications of psychological research on juror and jury decision making. *Personality and Social Psychology Bulletin, 16*, 90-105.

Penrod, S. (1980). *Evaluating social scientific methods of jury selection*. Paper presented at the meeting of the Midwestern Psychological Association, St. Louis, USA.

Rogers, L.E., & Farace, R.V. (1975). Analysis of relational communication in dyads. New measurement procedures. *Human Communication Research, 1*, 222-239.

Saks, M.J. (1977). *Jury verdicts*. Lexington, MA: Heath.

Sobral, J., & Arce, R. (1990). *La psicología social en la sala de justicia. El jurado y el testimonio*. Barcelona: Paidós.

Sobral, J., Arce, R., & Fariña, F. (1989). Aspectos psicosociales de las decisiones judiciales. Revisión y lectura diferenciada. *Boletín de Psicología, 25*, 49-74.

Sobral, J., Arce, R., & Fariña, F. (1990). Grupos ideológicamente sesgados: Toma de decisiones judiciales. Análisis de la interacción. *Actas del II Congreso del Colegio Oficial de Psicólogos, 9*, 117-123.

Sobral, J., Arce, R., Fariña, F., & Vilán, M. V. (1988). Influencia de la Ideología sobre el proceso de discusión y toma de decisiones de los jurados legos. Premio de Investigación en Psicología Jurídica "Emilio Mira y López". University of Santiago de Compostela, Spain.

Sobral, J., Arce, R., & Mirón, L. (1988). *Formaciones ideológicas y predicción de veredictos en jurados*. Paper presented at II Congreso Nacional de Psicología Social, Alicante, Spain.

Psychometric Evaluation of Two Scales Assessing Fitness to Stand Trial

R. Michael Bagby and Robert Nicholson

Introduction

Beginning in the 1960s, profound changes in the rights of the mentally ill were instituted, fuelled by legal activism and heralded by such landmark decisions as *Lake v. Cameron* (1966), and *Wyatt v. Stickney* (1975). An abiding concern both of caselaw and legislative reform was the provision of due process safeguards for psychiatric patients, a radical departure from the insular paternalism of past years. Among patients held involuntarily for indefinite periods were mentally disordered offenders who had been adjudicated as incompetent to stand trial. In far reaching decisions, the U.S. Supreme Court established standards for determining what constituted competency to stand trial (*Dusky v. United States*, 1960) and limited the duration of hospitalization for unfit defendants (*Jackson v. Indiana*, 1972).

The *Dusky* standard, concomitant with the rise of forensic psychology as an accepted subspeciality, demanded that clinicians address legally relevant constructs (Roesch & Golding, 1980), beyond the familiar parameters of typical psychiatric/psychological evaluations (Roesch, 1979). The development of standardized measures to assess fitness to stand trial emerged naturally in response to the needs of the courts. Initially, checklists were recommended to ensure coverage of the legally relevant issues (Bukatman, Foy, & DeGrazie, 1971; Robey, 1965). Additional standardization efforts in this direction came from the Community Mental Health-Law Program at Harvard which produced two noteworthy measures: the Competency Screening Test (CST; Laboratory of Community Psychiatry, 1974; Lipsitt, Lelos, & McGarry, 1971) and the Competency Assessment Instrument (CAI; Laboratory of Community Psychiatry, 1974). The CST is a 22-item sentence completion task intended as a screening measure to divert competent individuals from the assessment process. The CAI is a structured interview with scales for quantifying 13 functions associated with competency to stand trial. A Canadian version of the CAI, termed the Fitness to Stand Trial Interview Test (FIT) has also been developed (Roesch, Webster, & Eaves, 1984). A more recent development is the Georgia Court Competency Test (GCCT; Wildman et al., 1978). The expanded Georgia Court Competency Test, Mississippi State Hospital Revision (GCCT-MSH; Nicholson, Robertson, Johnson, & Jensen, 1988) includes 21 questions designed to assess ability to communicate with counsel, and understanding of the charges, range of penalties, and courtroom process. The purpose of the present study was to examine the psychometric properties of the GCCT-MSH and the FIT with a large sample of defendants referred to an outpatient assessment centre.

Method

The sample consisted of defendants remanded to the Brief Assessment Unit (BAU) of the Metropolitan Toronto Forensic Service (METFORS), Clarke Institute of Psychiatry. The Brief Assessment Unit was established in 1978 with the specific mandate of providing consultation service to the courts. It receives referrals primarily from the Metropolitan Toronto Courts and the defendants are evaluated by a team of workers, including a psychiatrist as team head, nurses, correctional officers, psychiatric assistants and psychologists. Defendants are evaluated in the morning and returned to their respective detention center in the afternoon. The evaluations were conducted over a 10 month period (June, 1989-March, 1990).

A psychiatrist conducted a standard diagnostic interview, which typically included several questions regarding fitness to stand trial. Following this interview the GCCT-MSH was administered by either one of four forensically trained clinical psychologists (3 Ph.Ds, 1 ABD) or a clinical psychology intern who had completed one full year rotation through METFORS. Judgements about a defendant's competency was made following the administration of the GCCT-MSH and was based on a team decision, although the final disposition rested entirely with the psychiatrist, as they were solely responsible for the report that was returned with the defendant to court.

A total of 353 defendants were seen, of these 42 (11.9%) refused to answer any questions or were so psychotic as to be unable to participate in the interview in a coherent fashion. Of the remaining 311, 267 (85.8%) were male and 44 (14.2%) were female. Two hundred thirty-four (75.2%) were White, 61 (19.6%) were Black, 13 (4.2%) were Asian, and 6 (1.9%) were Canadian (Native) Indian. The average age at the time of the evaluation was 32.1 years ($SD=9.9$) and the mean education level was 10.0 years ($SD=1.4$). One hundred sixty-eight (54.4%) received a diagnosis indicating psychosis, and 7 (2.3%) received a diagnosis of mental retardation. One hundred ninety-one (61.4%) were returned to court as competent and 121 (38.9%) were returned to court as incompetent.

Results and Discussion

Table 1 summarizes some of the psychometric characteristics of the FIT and GCCT. Both scales have excellent internal consistency. The mean inter-item correlation was also calculated as an additional measure of item homogeneity. The optimal level of item homogeneity occurs when the mean inter-item correlation is in the .20 to .40 range. The magnitude of the mean inter-item correlation for the FIT, at .56, is clearly above this range and indicates that the items on the scale are overly-redundant and may not represent the domain of the construct adequately. On the other hand, the mean inter-item correlation for the GCCT-MSH, at .34, indicates that the items on this scale strike a suitable balance between bandwidth and fidelity.

Table 1: Scale Properties of FIT and GCCT-MSH.

Properties	Competency test	
	FIT	GCCT-MSH
Mean	106.00	55.50
Standard deviation	39.40	26.80
Alpha	0.96	0.88
Mean inter-item r	0.53	0.34
Criterion r	0.49	0.52

The intercorrelations among the items for the GCCT-MSH and FIT are appropriately reflected in the factor structures of the respective scales. (See Tables 2 and 3).

Table 2: Factor Structure of the GCCT-MSH.

	Item	General legal knowledge	Courtroom layout	Specific legal knowledge
1.	Judge seat		.45	
2.	Jury seat	.36	.67	
3.	Defendant seat		.52	
4.	Defense seat		.60	
5.	Prosecution seat		.48	
6.	Witness seat		.49	
7.	Viewers		.52	
8.	Judge role	.56		
9.	Jury role	.64		
10.	Defense role	.62		
11.	Prosecution role	.62		
12.	Witness role	.68		
13.	Viewer's role	.70		
14.	Defendant role	.54		.39
15.	Attorney name			.57
16.	How contact			.65
17.	Help lawyer	.36		.38
18.	Charge	.38		.64
19.	Meaning	.49		.58
20.	Consequences	.51		
21.	Circumstances	.46		.37

Note: Only factor loadings > 0.35 are displayed.

The GCCT-MSH, with a moderate level of intercorrelation among the items, produced a clear three factor solution. Factor 1, which accounted for 31.2% of the variance, is comprised of items primarily associated with what can be described as General Legal Knowledge (e.g., What does the judge do during the trial? What will your lawyer do?

What do witnesses do?, etc.). Factor 2 accounted for 5.0% of the variance and consists of items relating to the courtroom layout. For these items the defendant is shown a drawing of the courtroom and asked to point out the various parts and positions of the key figures in the courtroom. For example, defendants are asked to point out where the judge sits, where they will sit, and where their lawyer will sit. The final factor, Factor 3, which accounted for 4.0% of the variance, consists of items relating to Specific Legal Knowledge (e.g., What are you charged with? What are the consequences if you are found guilty of these charges? How can you help your lawyer defend you? etc).

Table 3: Factor Structure of the FIT.

	Item	Comprehension of court process	Defendant mental capacity
1.	Arrest process	.62	
2.	Charge	.72	
3.	Arrest procedure	.69	.35
4.	Legal process	.61	.50
5.	Defense	.71	
6.	Prosecution	.69	.38
7.	Judge	.74	.35
8.	Jury	.51	.54
9.	Defendant	.57	.48
10.	Witness		.83
11.	Police		.78
12.	Psychiatrist	.53	.57
13.	Capacity to disclose	.58	.39
14.	Relating to lawyer	.53	.44
15.	Appreciation of penalties	.69	
16.	Outcome	.63	
17.	Legal defenses	.66	.50
18.	Legal strategy	.66	.40
19.	Challenge prosecution	.64	
20.	Testify relevantly	.73	.44
21.	Self-defeating motivation	.77	.54
22.	Unmanageable behavior	.41	

Note: Only factor loadings > 0.35 are displayed.

In contrast, the FIT, with a high level of intercorrelations among the items, produced a two factor solution, with very few unique item loadings and many items loading significantly on both factors. Factor 1, which accounted for 54.1% of the variance can be best labelled as a Comprehension of Court Process factor. It consists of items such as "Can you tell me how you came to be here in jail?"; "If the prosecuting attorney asks you questions, what is he/she trying to accomplish?" The second factor which accounted for 4.4% of the variance seems specifically related to the defendant's mental capacity, although this particular factor is anything but clear. Such items as the capacity to testify relevantly, and the ability to instruct counsel seem to capture this factor best.

Tables 4 and 5 display the correlations of the FIT and GCCT-MSH and the respective factors of these scales with a number of defendant characteristics. In general, diagnosis appears to be the most closely associated variable with the scores on the FIT and GCCT-MSH.

Past research has indicated the predictive power of legally irrelevant characteristics such as demographic and clinical variables. Perhaps a more standardized approach to competency evaluations is needed to reduce the potential for bias and argue for the use of instruments specifically designed to assess defendant's psycholegal abilities. To examine if standardized instruments such as the FIT and GCCT-MSH do, in fact, eliminate bias in competency decisions, the FIT and GCCT along with the non-legal variables presented in Tables 4 and 5 were analyzed using direct discriminant analysis. The court report indicating the defendant's competency served as the criterion. Table 6 displays the canonical Rs for each of the variables with the derived discriminant function.

Table 4: Correlations between Defendant Characteristics and FIT and GCCT-MSH.

Characteristic	Competency test	
	GCCT-MSH	FIT
Age	-.00**	-.24**
Sex	-.17**	-.08
Race	-.07	-.07
Education	.15**	.14*
Diagnosis	.35**	.32**
Type of offense	-.09	-.06

* $p < .05$; ** $p < .01$

Table 5: Correlations between Defendant Characteristics and the GCCT-MSH and FIT Factor Scores.

	GCCT-MSH			FIT	
	F1	F2	F3	F1	F2
Age	-.08	-.29**	-.08	-.24**	.06
Sex	-.15	-.18*	-.01	-.17	-.08
Race	-.07	.09	.02	-.07	-.10
Education	.26**	.12	.03	.22**	-.09
Diagnosis	-.25**	-.13	-.23**	-.42**	-.12
Offense type	.02	-.09	-.07	-.01	-.03

* $p < .05$; ** $p < .01$

Note: GCCT-MSH - F1 = General legal knowledge, F2 = Courtroom layout, F3 = Specific legal knowledge; FIT - F1 = Comprehension of court process, F2 = Defendant mental capacity.

As is clearly evident, the correlations for the standardized legal measures are of much greater magnitude than the demographic variables. In comparing the overall classification rates, demographic variables had a 61.4% accuracy rate, in contrast to the standardized legal measures which had a 74.2% accuracy rate.

Table 6: Canonical Correlation between Criterion and Demographic and Psychological Measures.

Variables	Canonical
GCCT	.963
FIT	.869
Education	-.224
Diagnosis	.176
Offense	-.165
Race	-.073
Sex	-.067
GCCT-MSH-Factors	
General legal knowledge	.648
Courtroom layout	.221
Specific legal knowledge	.432
FIT-Factors	
Comprehension of court process	.625
Defendant Mental Capacity	.494

The bottom half of Table 6 summarizes the canonical Rs for each of the factor scores from the GCCT-MSH and FIT. What these results indicate is that of the psycholegal variables, General Court Knowledge and Comprehension of Court Process are the best predictors of fitness.

Conclusions

In conclusion, the results of this study suggest that the use of standardized psycholegal measures in the assessment of fitness to stand trial, when administered, reduce the influence of non-legal demographic variables in the determination of fitness. In our opinion the GCCT-MSH is the measure of choice for such evaluations. It appears to be less redundant, casts a broader nominological net over the construct of fitness and is relatively independent of potentially influencing non-legal variables.

References

Bukatman, B.A., Foy, J.L., & DeGrazie, E. (1971). What is competency to stand trial. *American Journal of Psychiatry, 127,* 1225-1229.
Dusky v. United States, 362 U.S. 402 (1960).

Jackson v. Indiana, 406 U.S. 715 (1972).
Laboratory of Community Psychiatry (1974). *Competency to stand trial and mental illness*. New York: Jason Aronson.
Lake v. Cameron, 364 F.2d 657 (D.C. Cir. 1966)
Lipsitt, P.D., Lelos, D., & McGarry, A.L. (1971). Competency for trial: A screening instrument. *American Journal of Psychiatry, 128*, 137-141.
Nicholson, R.A., Robertson, H.C., Johnson, W.G., & Jensen, G. (1988). A comparison of instruments for assessing competency to stand trial. *Law and Human Behavior, 12*, 313-321.
Robey, A. (1965). Criteria for competency to stand trial: A checklist for psychiatrists. *American Journal of Psychiatry, 122*, 616-623.
Roesch, R. (1979). Determining competency to stand trial: An examination of evaluation procedures used in an institutional setting. *Journal of Consulting and Clinical Psychology, 47*, 542-550.
Roesch, R., & Golding, S. (1980). *Competency to stand trial*. Urbana-Champaign: University of Illinois Press.
Roesch, R., Webster, C.D., & Eaves, D. (1984). *Fitness to stand trial*. Toronto: University of Toronto Press.
Wildman, R.W., Batchelor, E.S., Thompson, L., Nelson, F.R., Moore, J.T., Patterson, M.E., & deLaosa, M. (1978). *The Georgia Court Competency Test: An attempt to develop a rapid, quantitative, measure of fitness for trial*. Unpublished manuscript, Forensic Services Division, Central State Hospital, Milledgeville, GA.
Wyatt v. Stickney, 325 F. Supp. 781 (M.D. Ala. 1971).

Beyond the Ultimate Issue

David Carson

Unlike ordinary witnesses, expert witnesses are entitled to express opinions on subjects where they have a special expertise (Hodgkinson, 1990). But this creates a number of tensions. For example, it is for judges and juries to make the decisions. If expert witnesses are involved their influence may be so great that, in effect, they make the decision. So rules of evidence have developed to regulate, sometimes to exclude, experts' evidence. These tensions and issues are common to all legal systems but the more exclusionary rules are associated with adversary trial procedures (Spencer & Flin, 1990). In England and Wales moves towards a more investigatory trial procedure are being considered by a Royal Commission, established after a number of convictions in prominent cases were discovered to be unsafe. It might recommend changes in the role of expert witnesses. However there is a scepticism of experts in investigatory procedures and with court appointed neutral experts (Howard, 1991; Spencer, 1991).

This paper questions the reasons given for limiting the role of expert witnesses. It argues that the present rules constitute an historically and culturally specific balance or "bargain." On one side is lawyers' and judges' desire to retain control over the "shape," cost and length of court proceedings. On the other side is lawyers' and courts' need for expert witnesses to legitimate the court process, with associations of being scientific, and for help in individual cases. The paper argues that expert witnesses should have a wider role, including being allowed to give evidence on the ultimate issue that the court has to decide, balanced by the introduction of a more appropriate system for testing the quality of expert evidence and increased accountability for expert witnesses.

Doubtless some expert witnesses have been incompetent in court. But were they incompetent as experts or as witnesses? They may have been confused, or their evidence misrepresented, by a lawyer's questioning techniques (Carson, 1990b). It may be the system for assessing expert witnesses' evidence that is at fault. For example a lawyer may pose, innocently or otherwise, an inappropriately dichotomous question so that the expert witness responds with a hedging reply. But research indicates that those who use hedging answers lose status and credibility (O'Barr, 1982).

The division of evidence into facts or opinions, the rationale for expert evidence, involves an inappropriate dichotomy. Every statement of fact, for example the colour of a banana, involves the expression of an opinion as to which words are adequate and sufficient to describe it. But the fact versus opinion dichotomy is of considerable tactical significance. It is easier to cross-examine a witness who emphasises the opinion rather than the factual nature of their evidence (Evans, 1983; Napley, 1970). There are practical advantages, for lawyers, in maintaining the current rules.

Inconsistency and the Ultimate Issue Rule

The "ultimate issue" is the core question(s) that the judge or jury must decide, for example the credibility of witnesses. Expert witnesses should not give evidence on, should not express opinions about, these ultimate issues (Hodgkinson, 1990). Whilst the principle has been that expert witnesses must not supplant the judge and jury, this has been considerably relaxed for civil proceedings in England and Wales, (Civil Evidence Act 1972, section 3). And practice is inconsistent. Psychiatrists, for example, regularly give evidence about the presence of mental disorder, which determines the ultimate issue of whether such defences as insanity and diminished responsibility are allowed (Hodgkinson, 1990; Mackay & Colman, 1991).

The ultimate issue rules might be justified if they worked well in practice. But one of their effects is to remove the protection of the law from some (presumed) victims. The ultimate issue will often concern the credibility of a witness, for example the alleged victims of rape or child abuse. As there will often only be one witness to such crimes, the victim, her or his credibility will be on trial. As this is the ultimate issue that the court must decide, expert witnesses should not give expert opinion evidence, at least in criminal proceedings in Britain, on the victims' credibility. Although expert witnesses can give evidence on credibility in other countries, for example based upon statement reliability analysis, (e.g. Undeutsch, 1989) this is not permissible in Britain. If victims are not believed - and in criminal cases the degree of proof required is high - then crimes go unpunished. Perpetrators can learn to commit crimes which, by leaving minimal evidence, will require the courts to rely upon the victim's credibility. Victims, fearing inquiries into their credibility in court, may not report the crime. Prosecutors, knowing the problems of demonstrating credibility, may decline to bring prosecutions. The more at social risk the victim or witness is, for example if the victim of a rape has a learning disability, the more defenceless the law will make that person as their credibility will be treated more sceptically.

Given their pervasiveness and their apparent status as matters of principle, these rules might be expected to apply to all cases. But the majority of cases are settled, or are otherwise dealt with, before they reach court. The rules restricting expert evidence do not apply in pre-trial proceedings. Prosecutors - amongst many other "gate-keepers" to the court system - may decide not to take a case further, for a variety of reasons. Social workers, who originally contemplated obtaining a court order giving them some powers over a child, might decide on a different course of action. On receiving an expert witness' report a claim for compensation may be dropped. In making their decisions the gate-keepers may consult a range of expert witnesses, whose "evidence" - at this stage - may breach the rules with impunity. The admissibility and relevance of such evidence is not questionned in pre-trial discussions except, doubtless, when a final decision has to be made about whether there is sufficient admissible evidence to provide a sufficient chance of success. Expert evidence, on issues such as credibility, is inadmissible in the courts even though there would be lawyers there to test it critically, judges and juries to assess it independently, and the possibility of other experts to contradict it. Nevertheless such evidence can be relied upon in pre-trial or extra-trial proceedings where there are no such protections!

The exclusionary rules regulate court proceedings. They are a product of lawyers' frameworks about what are core legal tasks. The courts deal with the cases brought before them; they are not, directly, concerned with decisions made before they enter the explicitly court arena. Lawyers have focused upon a part of the total process whereby disputes arise, are articulated, formulated into a legal issue, where evidence that is perceived as relevant is collected, is presented and argued over. The exclusionary rules may have more to do with a desire, conscious or otherwise, to maintain control over the court part of the proceedings. As Saks (1990), in a Presidential Address to the American Psychology-Law Society said: "The pretrial phase may tell us much about the structure of the legal process and may reveal its underlying norms in ways that a look at the trial does not."

Problems, such as these, cannot be remedied by largely symbolic changes in the law, such as providing a wider discretion to use expert evidence. For example in civil proceedings, in Britain, expert evidence may be given "... on any relevant matter ..." (section 3, Civil Evidence Act 1972). But there is still the question of what will be considered "relevant." If expert evidence is considered to be of low probative value it will be regarded as irrelevant (Hodgkinson, 1990). How are judges to learn of the value of experts' evidence if they do not hear it?

The exclusionary rules affect the quantity as well as the quality of cases that reach courts. If the rules were changed, for example the ultimate rule abolished and experts allowed to give opinions on the credibility of witnesses, defendants and victims, then it would affect gate-keeping decisions. Stereotypes and preconceptions about individuals, such as the competence of children and the suggestibility of people with learning difficulties, could be challenged. More defendants, if they knew that their victims' evidence and credibility might be positively assessed, might plead guilty and thereby minimise the distress caused to so many victims and witnesses by court proceedings. This is not to argue that defendants should lose any of their rights to present a vigorous defence, but it is to argue that courts should be helped by assessments of individual witnesses' credibility given by people who, outside of court, are regularly trusted and relied upon to make some very important decisions.

The Rationale for Scepticism of Experts

The principle justification for the ultimate issue rule is that litigants are entitled to have their disputes decided by a judge and/or jury, rather than by experts (Tapper, 1985). But can there be an "entitlement" when there is no choice? Litigants cannot choose trial by expert, unless they can get the other party to agree to a private arbitration. The majority of civil litigants, in Britain, are not "entitled" to have their disputes decided by a judge or jury as most are settled before the case ever gets to trial. (The British legal system could not cope with all disputes being tried.) Before a settlement is reached at least one expert, a lawyer, will use his or her expertise to decide, and advise, whether it is worth proceeding to trial. The rules are made for courts; if people wish to settle their disputes in other ways then there is no objection to experts deciding the ultimate issues.

Responsibility for decisions, many expert witnesses would agree, should not pass from the deciders of fact, the judge and/or jury, to experts. But that need not happen. The judge and jury can consider the experts' factual and opinion evidence, on the ultimate issue, but decide for themselves. They do that with other forms of expert evidence. Responsibility need not pass. Experts' opinions are, and would remain, open to criticism and contradiction even on evidence about ultimate issues. Experts, in an adversarial trial system, are kept "on their toes" as their opinions may be challenged by another expert (Howard, 1991). The ultimate issue rule protects judges and juries from hearing certain information; it is not designed to maintain their responsibility for making decisions.

But some argue (Tapper, 1985) that juries may be "unduly influenced" by expert witnesses' evidence on the ultimate issue.

> If a cardinal of the Roman Catholic church is testifying before a jury mainly composed of Catholics, and states that, in his opinion, the defendant was driving negligently, it can hardly be supposed that the verdict would be other than for the plaintiff. (Landon, 1944)

Certainly such a witness' eminence, with associations of moral rectitude, may aid a judge and jury when they have to determine credibility. Being a police officer - amongst many other occupations - can lead to similar associations being made. But high clerical office has nothing, directly, to do with ability to judge driving qualities; the cardinal would not be an expert witness. However, as an ordinary witness, the cardinal could give an opinion in the form of a quick summary arising from a number of inferences from facts (Tapper, 1985). So if a non-expert may express an opinion, in this way, surely the argument for allowing an expert to express an opinion on an ultimate issue must be greater.

Another justification for the ultimate issue rule is that expert evidence is often unnecessary.

> An expert's opinion is admissible to furnish the court with scientific information which is likely to be outside the experience and knowledge of a judge or jury. If on the proven facts a judge or jury can form their own conclusion without help, then the opinion of an expert is unnecessary. (*R. v. Turner*, 1975)

Judges and jurors are presumed to have sufficient knowledge of normal behaviour and only to need assistance with abnormal behaviour (Hodgkinson, 1990; Tapper, 1985). Allowing expert evidence, when a witness has been assessed as having an intelligence quotient of 69, but rejecting it where assessed as 72, (*Masih*, 1986) is bound to create problems, even if questions about the accuracy of the test measures are ignored. Rejecting expert evidence where the diagnosis is "abnormal personality" (*Weightman*, 1991), but allowing it where the diagnosis is "psychopathy," (*Byrne*, 1960) is difficult to understand, especially when the terms may overlap or be used inter-changeably. Such dichotomizing, dividing concepts into exclusive categories, normal or abnormal, mentally ill or not mentally ill, is a typical feature of lawyer's thinking or analytical processes (Aubert, 1963; Campbell, 1974). But such simple distinctions cannot be drawn between what judges and jurors can and cannot manage upon their own (Mackay & Colman, 1991).

Further problems arise when lawyers do not know what science and experts are able to offer, and do not set up procedures to ensure that they are informed. This enforced ignorance should prove embarrassing. For example a psychologist was not allowed to express an opinion upon the likelihood that a witness was telling a lie because, *inter alia*, he was not medically qualified (*R. v. Mackenny*, 1981). Doctors do not, *per se*, have special skills in diagnosing lies. Judges may overvalue one profession in relation to another, for example psychiatry rather than psychology or nursing. (The most appropriate expertise in many cases concerning human behaviour - for example in risk or dangerousness decisions - should be inter-disciplinary and inter-professional.) By distinguishing the normal from the abnormal, before permitting possibly counter intuitive information, the courts are protecting themselves from having their versions of "commonsense" or "ordinary knowledge" contradicted. But "commonsense" is often wrong. It is especially important that counter-intuitional information is made available to judges and juries (Fitzmaurice & Pease, 1986; Sheldon & MacLeod, 1991). Perhaps the most dramatic example of this concerns children's evidence. Formerly there was a taken-for-granted assumption that children readily lied and fantasised about being assaulted. Children's evidence was to be suspected, at the very least. Now, after much heartbreak, there have been major changes and children's evidence is much more readily accepted (Spencer & Flin, 1990).

Regulating Expertise

It is submitted that the exclusionary rules are the result of dynamic "tensions" between lawyers and expert witnesses over the regulation of trials, and between "legality" and "science." Lawyers wish to regulate experts in order to maintain practical and ideological control. These "tensions" are universal, as inherent in the process of litigation, but their variation between countries is explicable in terms of different stages of development and the trial process adopted. Allison (1971) has isolated three core models of decision making processes. The choice of model has significant effects upon the content of individual analyses. The most popular he termed the "Rational Actor Model." Here it is assumed that organisational decisions can be analyzed in the same way as individuals' decisions. Organisations are assumed to think and decide in the same way as individuals, which includes having one voice and consensual decisions. His second model, the "Organization Process Model," denies that the individuals in an organisation form a unity. Different views are mediated - largely to maintain the organization - and collective views are enunciated. In due course these decisions become predictable. The short-term needs of the organisation tend to dominate over long-term planning. His third model, the "Government Politics Model," suggests that organisations' decisions are best understood as the result of bargains made, and "games played," by the various individuals involved.

Hall (1980) has added further insights. He argues that the rational actor model is based upon assumptions that are basic to economics; the correct decision is the most efficient one that optimises the actor's objectives. The legal system also assumes that there are correct answers, for that is its product, which can be discovered by following a procedure. The organizational process model predicates insights from sociology and social psychology; the goal, frequently unstated or assumed, is to endorse, protect and sustain the organization. In this sense lawyers' organisational decisions may be seen as designed to preserve the dignity and integrity of the system. The third model, Hall argues, draws upon psychology and its interface with political science. Individuals within organisations play games, often for short-term benefits, and bargain with each other whilst following different agendas. He sees analogies with risk assessments, trading-off different outcomes and likelihoods. Here, it is suggested, it would be wiser to analyze a series or sequence of decisions rather than to abstract particular decisions from their dialectical context.

Adherents to the rational actor model are likely to accept the rationales provided for the ultimate issue and related rules. Adherents to the organizational process model are likely to emphasise the ways in which the rule supports the legal system, lawyers and legal analyses. Those attracted by the political bargaining model may emphasise an historical perspective and argue that what happens in practice - for example the admission of evidence that ought to have been excluded (Hodgkinson, 1990, Mackay & Colman, 1991) - is more important, and relevant, than the rules in books. They will regard the current ultimate issue rule as just a staging post and open to amendment, not just in practice, if an appropriate "bargain" can be struck. Whilst acknowledging that judges and other lawyers genuinely believe in the reasons given for excluding and restricting expert evidence, not just on the ultimate issue, it is submitted that organisational processes and "political" bargaining better explain the position.

There will always be (and should be) concern about the cost and duration of litigation. Despite all the romantic images and media portrayals, there has to be a limit to the time and money invested in a court's decision. This is, generally, related to the perceived seriousness of the case. We allow social perceptions of the seriousness of the case to determine what the legal system's organisational response ought to be. Consider Hall's (1980) analogy with risk assessments. The homicide charge, the insider dealing allegation and the claim for compensation for tetraplegia, all "require" and receive more time and resources because of the "seriousness" of the allegations or outcomes. The courts are perceived as taking a greater risk of getting these decisions wrong. These "serious" cases are decided in courts higher in the hierarchy even though the difficulties in interpreting the law, and the problems in determining proof, may make them much easier cases to deal with than many cases perceived as, and deal with as, less serious.

There has, in practice, to be a trade-off between "justice" and the time and expenditure to achieve it. Certainly there are cases where exceptional expenditure of time and money occurs. Those cases help to sustain the illusion that "justice" is priceless. But note how different bargains - or standards - have been set in different countries and at different times. For example, Great Britain and the United States of America have common cultures, legal systems and beliefs in "justice." And yet the bargain, or standard, appears quite different with a much greater willingness to invest time and money to get the right answer, through litigation, in the United States. The distaste for expert testimony appears much more pronounced, and rationalised, in the United States (Faigman, 1989). There appears to be an implicit fear that, if expert witnesses were allowed to give more opinion evidence it would increase the time and other expenditure of courts. It may be feared that, from being an optional extra, experts would become indispensable members of forensic teams.

It may also be feared that expert witnesses would undermine judges' self-esteem. Experts would challenge judges' confidence in their tried and tested techniques of determining ultimate issues. The frequently unscientific and unreliable techniques used by judges and juries would become pronounced. Simply acknowledging that a witness is an "expert" acknowledges that the judge and jury are not experts. It would involve a major challenge to the authority of judges for experts to give evidence on the ultimate issue, for example about what normal behaviour involves. Where would it end? If expertise, citing science, is allowed on the ultimate issue then we may find ourselves questioning the jury system! More people may want to know why small groups of adults are entrusted, as a jury, with major decisions and yet, in Great Britain at least, research to check whether they actually carry out their responsibilities in a responsible manner is restricted (Lloyd-Bostock, 1988).

The different uses of "probability," between empiricists and lawyers, would be dramatised if expert evidence was admitted more thoroughly. Scientists seek to state propositions, or make predictions, in terms of the probability of a future occurrence. Occasionally a very precise statement of high probability can be made. The ability to do this depends more upon the discipline concerned than the witness. Probability is also a core concept for lawyers, used in stating the level of proof that must be achieved. It is most commonly used when looking backwards (Aubert 1963). How probable is it that that defendant had that state of mind at that time? How probable is it that that witness saw what he or she claims to have seen, or that the witness is telling the truth as he or she perceives it? But it is also used when considering whether it is probable that a child will be abused again, or whether a patient will cause harm in the future.

Lawyers are most reluctant to utilise scientists' probability statements (Dant, 1988; Eggleston, 1978; Floud & Young, 1981). They argue that, even if it is probable that, for example, 95 per cent. of the population would forget certain information after a particular period, we cannot be sure that the particular witness, in the unique case being considered, would have forgotten it. We cannot be sure whether the defendant or witness falls within the 95 or the five per cent group. Information about what others have done, sometimes under control conditions, is not considered to be relevant evidence about the particular people the court is concerned with (Stone, 1984). Even writers who favour a greater role for expert evidence seek to develop distinctions to justify the exclusion of some probabilistic evidence. Sheldon and MacLeod (1991), for example, (see also Dant, 1988) distinguish "positive" and "normative" data. For them positive data "attaches" to the defendant and normative data does not. How are we to decide what does, and does not, attach? Why must we have another dichotomous category? There may be a point in doubting the relevance of an opinion based, solely, upon a defendant sharing certain characteristics with a research population, but that does not justify excluding that kind of information whilst accepting other "positive" information, say of an eye-witness, which may be of less value.

Statistical techniques and Bayesian theories of probability are regularly used in many other professions' decision-making processes, such as doctors' diagnoses, (Dowie & Elstein, 1988) and we rely upon their judgments. It has been argued that the techniques are also applicable in legal contexts but, as a leading textbook on the law of evidence states, "[much] of this debate is, to say the least, remote from the practical concerns of lawyers" (Tapper, 1985, p. 150).

If the ultimate issue requires a decision as to whether the defendant is more likely to fall within a 95 per cent. group (which might be called "the vast majority of people" or "highly probable," if figures are not available), or the five per cent. group (which might be called "the small minority of people" or "highly unlikely") then the most sensible decision - the decision most likely to be correct - must be to conclude that it is most likely that the defendant is a member of the most likely group! That five per cent. chance might, in a criminal trial, be sufficient to constitute a "reasonable doubt" so that a finding of guilt would not be appropriate. That exact statistics rarely exist is an insufficient objection to their use. Bands of probability or confidence levels (Dowie, 1990) may be used. That all the characteristics, of someone before a court, will rarely be exactly matched in the particular combination of variables that were the subject of a research study, also misses the point. Such research should not be cited to prove, conclusively, that something did or did not happen, unless - such as with some uses of blood samples - it is capable of such uses. Rather it should be cited as more evidence of likelihood, and be paid special attention when it is counter intuitive. Courts can never be certain that they acquit, convict and find for the right people but they can, and should, use the assistance that is available. They might find it easier to accept decision theories and probability assessments if they saw their task not so much as making the correct decision but as making the least number of wrong decisions (Carson, 1990a).

Some lawyers reject scientists' probability statements because they are based upon research where certain variables have been controlled. Whilst this may be a good research method it is of no value to the courts who cannot control the variables of their customers (Stone, 1984). This argument is also inappropriate. Judges also reason with variables. When deciding whether a precedent case is binding upon them they consider whether certain features, variables, are distinguishable. Are the significant facts sufficiently dissimilar that the precedent ought to be distinguished? A legal system involves a trade-off between adopting "rules of thumb" - or general principles - and accepting and accommodating to the individualistic features of cases. Increasingly expert evidence will be able to isolate the most significant variables (Meehl, 1989); indeed it will be able to state the cumulative significance of each variable. As it does so it will threaten lawyers' roles, and livelihoods, in emphasising the idiosyncratic features of their clients' cases in order to suggest that different decisions should be made. As it does so it will tackle a major source of erroneous decisions, paying insufficient attention to prior probabilities and too much attention to idiosyncratic features of particular cases (Fitzmaurice & Pease, 1986; Rachlin, 1989). The more predictable that legal decisions are the less is the need to employ lawyers to seek alternative outcomes.

Playing Games with Experts

The courts decide whom, and which disciplines, are to be acknowledged as experts. In doing so they dispense power and prestige. Clearly there are degrees of expertise with, for example, psychiatrists being more regularly utilised as experts, in cases concerned with mental disorder, than psychologists or nurses irrespective of their numbers, the nature of the expertise sought or the extent or quality of their observations of patients. History and tradition will largely explain this as certain professions, such as medicine, have a longer history than others and have become regarded as peer professions to law. Lawyers require a better education as to which experts can appropriately offer expert evidence, to which degree of reliability, on different issues. That the debate, about the role of expert witnesses, is more developed in the United States (see Saks, 1990) may be related to their legal education being postgraduate, in marked contrast to British legal education.

But even within disciplines such as medicine, different specialities will generate different expectations of expertise. Psychiatrists' expertise tends to rated lower, by lawyers, than that of, for example, a surgeon. A major reason for this is the extent to which expert witnesses are able to present their evidence as factual rather than opinionated (Carson, 1990b). It is easier to cross-examine expert witnesses who express opinions (Evans, 1983;

Napley, 1970). Surgeons' evidence tends to be more factual, concrete, emphatic and certain. Facts, such as broken bones, can be more easily demonstrated. Psychiatrists' evidence, which requires them to express more opinions, is less certain. Lawyers have an interest in emphasising the opinion nature, rather than factual or scientific nature, of experts' evidence.

Saks (1990) began his research with an expectation that the law would have worked out what it wanted and expected of expert witnesses. "But the more I have inquired, the more I have discovered that the law itself is confused about what it expects of expert witnesses, or has continually changing expectations" (p. 292).

King's research (1991), into perceptions of giving expert evidence, emphasises the "game" nature of giving expert evidence. This "game" analogy replicates findings of Smith, Wynne (1989) and colleagues who undertook a number of case-studies in the recognition and organisation of expertise. Whilst they do not claim that their insights also apply to "... decision making involving human or social science expertise,.." (p. 10) it is submitted that they do. They start from the general observation that no observation can be entirely free or independent of the observer's interpretations. Studying drug addicts necessarily involves deciding what is to count as a "drug;" does it include prescribed anti-depressants or nicotine? But they do not develop this familiar observation in a nihilistic fashion, as if to deny the relevance or value of any observation or research, but to stress that judgments have to be made about what is to count as adequate knowledge. (Here again we return to the image of organisational decisions being a balancing-act between competing claims.) Their case-studies indicate how the legal system shapes and controls what is to count as adequate knowledge for the courts. But the courts never make it explicit that they are authorising and recognising certain kinds of incomplete and partial knowledge for the special status of "expert" knowledge.

> Decision making always involves the management of uncertainty, scientific uncertainty included. This will continue, regardless of what developments in scientific or technical understanding are forthcoming. (Smith & Wynne, 1989, p. 8)

Three of the points, that Smith and his colleagues make, are particularly important to this discussion. First, the legal system enforces a "... firm structuring and classification of problems ..." (p.3). Lawyers' basic - and false - dichotomy between facts and opinions demonstrates this.

> Legal institutions therefore seek to frame the problem at issue in factual terms, to rely on experts to discover what the facts are, and then to apply rules to the facts to determine what course of action to follow. (Smith & Wynne, 1989, pp. 3-4)

This helps the courts to be efficient. It also adds to the prestige of experts as they are called in to answer specific questions, to solve rather than to point out the further complications of the issues in question. The question effectively asked, in a professional negligence case, is "Would a reasonably competent co-professional have done the same?" This avoids questions about what the particular person should have done - the test being objective - or the organisation of the various systems, for example, training, monitoring and information feedback loops.

Secondly, this emphasis upon a narrow issue involves uncertainties and doubts being silenced. All, for example, the epistemological doubts surrounding the very possibility of objectivity are silenced. It is not for the expert witness to tell the court what he or she considers the issues to be but just to answer the lawyers' questions. The expert might prefer a different perspective on the issue - more resources could help with many different problems - but the expert needs to acknowledge the narrow, depoliticized, perspective he or she is given. "A 'good' expert therefore is someone who can subordinate his or her technical view of the relevant question to that defined by the court." (p. 4)

Of course particular experts benefit from this approach, in that it emphasises their ability to offer answers rather than just develop further problems, methodological or substantive.

Thirdly, Wynne develops the notion of the "closure" of uncertainty:

> ... all decision making, even the most 'expert', requires a social agreement about when a conclusion, even if it be only a fact, has authoritative status. All knowledge requires 'closure'. Evidence alone is never enough to achieve this, independent of social acceptance that it *constitutes* acceptable evidence. (p. 13)

The courts cannot, or do not wish to, cope with experts parading their uncertainties. Psychiatrists have, much more effectively, "closed" the legal debate about the relevance, reliability and predictability of their science than, say, psychologists. This, it is suggested, is largely because they are frequently called as experts on "their" cases, where their evidence will determine what will happen to the patient, and where their evidence may be a necessary pre-requisite for further steps being taken. In this sense the expert witness is providing the court with a "receipt," or "ticket," which justifies a particular disposal of the case. Psychologists do not have so much control over the placement of clients or resources as psychiatrists.

These points are clearly related to the ways in which lawyers' thinking is different from scientists' (Aubert, 1963). These include the tendencies to dichotomise, to reify, to categorise, to relate to past rather than future events, to individualise. But this derives from the pragmatic imperative of dealing with individual cases in courtrooms (Campbell, 1974). But courtrooms are only the tip of a legal iceberg in terms of legal influences upon human behaviour. There are many opportunities for collaboration, involving the recognition of the relativity of the quality, relevance, reliability and predictability of experts' evidence, outside courtrooms (Carson, 1988).

Questioning Judges

The current rules on experts' evidence are the product of an uneasy "political" balance. Courts, *inter alia*, gain from association with expertise and science, but lawyers are anxious about allowing experts to have a bigger role in court. Because the focus is upon the public part of legal proceedings - court hearings - it does not matter that experts effectively determine the ultimate issue in the many cases that never get to court. In those cases the courts' self-esteem, their time and other balances are not threatened. What would be threatening, to the courts, would be a sustained assault on the source and quality of judicial expertise and the "science" of their decision-making. For example an expert's evidence can be criticised, in cross examination, by concentrating upon the limits of all scientific evidence, upon the ways in which that evidence is not fully objective, has limits, is only probabilistic, is based upon controlled research or necessarily limited experience. The cross-examiner simply has to re-open the controversies that he or she, and the court, ordinarily accept are "closed" in relation to the discipline in question (Smith & Wynne, 1989). A range of techniques are available that can improperly misrepresent expert evidence (Carson, 1990b). But when a court has to justify its own decision, its own expertise, it will rely upon the same kind of incomplete, non-objective methodology that it has just heard challenged.

> Even after deconstruction within the local legal setting, when it comes to presenting the decision more widely (in judgments or inquiry reports), explanation and justification often use just that style of natural, revealed knowledge which has previously been pulled apart in the relative privacy of legal proceedings. (Wynne, 1989, p. 37)

That such cross-examination of expert witnesses is relatively rare, and that many expert witnesses are disinterested in challenging a system which gives them considerable status, does not affect the analysis. Expert witnesses' "science" is generally acceptable and valuable to the legal system, but kept in check by occasional, often famous, challenges on lawyers' terms. We ought to consider the quality of courtroom processes.

Judges, when justifying their inductions, can rely upon a number of processes or appeals to conceptual constructs. "Common sense" is popular, often appealed to but, unfortunately, not always common. Take, for example, a legally uncontroversial appeal against a finding that a nurse had not been racially discriminated against in a promotion decision. An industrial tribunal, which heard the witnesses, expressed the opinion that an interview panel, involving five senior employees, would be less prone to racial prejudice. The Employment Appeal Tribunal (*Elahi* v. *Bristol and Weston Health Authority*, 1990) found no error in this because there was "... something to be said for safety in numbers ..." and "... a responsible attitude is perhaps more reasonably to be expected from senior than from relatively junior employees." It is not just that research evidence might show that older people are more likely, or as likely, to discriminate racially, or that groups of people are more likely, or just as likely, to develop extreme views as individuals. The point is also that a court could equally well have said the opposite and, because the implicit appeal is to common sense - which we are reluctant to challenge without appearing foolish - few would have questioned it. "We all know that older people tend to become set in their ways and therefore, even where there is no malice, they are liable to be less open to new ideas, new relationships, ways of workings, cultures and people." "Whilst a group of people may curb the excesses of one person it can also provide an audience which leads him or her to further excesses." Pick your "common sense" observation.

Meehl (1989) has advised against the uncritical judicial use of "fireside inductions." He finds no easy answers; indeed he suggests that statistical significance tests have been oversold. Very significantly he recognises the judge's pragmatic imperative of having to give a decision. He draws an analogy with clinicians who also have to give an answer in terms of providing a treatment. How far, he asks, are clinicians entitled to rely upon their clinical experience when that is contradicted by research? There is an important difference, however. Most clinicians are able to alter or "remedy" their treatment decisions in the light of experience. They work dialectically, moving from one situation to another in a broad pre-planned direction. Judges, in marked contrast, usually make once-and-for-all decisions (Carson, 1990c). Clinicians can, usually, take account of uncertainty by delaying, by undertaking further investigations or by taking smaller steps such as less radical treatments, smaller dosages. Judges cannot, usually, avoid dramatic decisions. In a civil case they must decide for plaintiff or defendant. In a criminal case they can use their uncertainty to decide that the prosecution has not satisfied its duty to prove to a high enough standard. However that is still a "dramatic" decision in that it is clear cut, it is an end of the matter.

Judges can also seek to justify their decisions with a claim upon "logic." However their decisions do not demonstrate regular reliance upon the principles of deductive or inductive logic, or statistical analysis. It would, at least, be surprising if lawyers were able to analyze the world of social events and human behaviour in terms of logical relations when so many others feel empirical or interpretative research is necessary, or desirable. Indeed, as Hart (1963) noted, courtroom argument is closer to rhetoric than reason.

Judges may rely upon their knowledge. The problem is knowing what they do and do not know. This is exemplified by the sexual abuse of children. When a large number of children were removed from their parents, in one town, within a relatively short period, because the statutory authorities believed that they had been sexually abused, the government appointed a High Court judge, Mrs Justice Butler-Sloss, as she then was, to head an inquiry. To this day we do not know which children were and were not abused. The inquiry's report, (Butler-Sloss, 1988) has acquired a form of "official knowledge." It is well known by judges and they expect child protection agencies to be familiar with it and to follow it (Spencer & Flin, 1990). But there are many other books and studies on child sexual abuse and good professional practice. The publicity attached to this report, and the fact that it was chaired by a senior judge, has led to it acquiring an "official," higher, status than other studies. So, just as common sense is not always common, so may judges' knowledge bases be different, and partial. In many arguments we take our knowledge base as given, we have no need to cite or explain it, so errors cannot be detected. Similar arguments can be made about judges' inferences or arguments based upon their experience or their interpretation of history.

Renegotiating the Contract for Expert Evidence

If the focus of attention was moved from the problems with experts' evidence to the problems with judges' decisions, then it might be possible to "renegotiate" the bargain on when, and on what, experts may give evidence. A number of dramatic cases of unsafe convictions, in England and Wales, have led to considerable public loss of confidence in the legal system. They were dramatic offences where considerable time, effort and money was put into the prosecution. It may be fair to anticipate a higher error rate where fewer resources were invested in the prosecution. A review of judicial fact-finding and assessing processes (Stone & McLean, 1990), including a reassessment of the role of experts and scientific insights, might lead to greater public confidence.

Faigman (1989) argues that:

> Suppositional science should not be presented to jurors through expert testimony, .., because such experts can provide little or no assistance to fact-finders who have their own (and possibly equally valid) suppositions concerning the factual questions they must resolve. (p. 1013)

Are those suppositions - that fact-finders suppositions are equally valid - equally valid? At least if expert evidence is heard it can be tested, and judges and jurors made aware that there is, at least, a contrary view. Faigman (1989) presumes that it is the duty of experts to justify their contribution rather than the duty of the courts to ensure that the make the best use of the aids to decision making available.

> The legal relevance of social science findings should depend upon their scientific strength, that is, on the ability of social scientists to answer validly the questions posed to them. (pp. 1009-1010)

But this approach has many problems. Faigman is prepared to acknowledge the contribution of "proper" science "... valid research findings can provide valuable assistance to legal decision makers ..." (p. 1013). He appreciates some of the epistemological issues involved in determining what is entitled to the label "scientific" and the courts' roles in selecting and shaping official "expertise." Certainly there are problems with the authority, quality and relevance of research. But we are not dealing with dichotomous categories of one perfect and one imperfect system, the courts and science respectively. We are dealing with two imperfect systems and we are duty bound to seek the best possible procedures, to learn, and to concede that future research and ideas may invalidate today's. The question is whether we have done our best today with a constant eye to ways to further improve. Even experts' "suppositional" or "commonsense" science, indeed even that which can, currently, only merit the term "experience," should be made available to courts. Where it coincides with judges' or juries' assumptions then that confirmation is surely valuable and meaningful. Where it does not coincide then an issue is raised which, at the very least, can sensitise the judge and jury and encourage fuller analysis and more rigorous thought.

Mackay and Colman (1991) argue that experts' evidence should be more widely available. Their test would be whether "... the expert evidence could make a significant contribution to the jury's understanding ..." but they agree that experts should not give evidence on "... matters that are well understood by ordinary people ..." (p. 809). This would replace one set of problems with others; how to decide whether a contribution would be "significant" and whether juries, in general or in particular, have sufficient understanding of a particular issue. We need to look further.

Monahan and Walker (1988) propose that "social authority" - in contrast to Faigman's "scientific validity" - should be the paradigm for courts' recognition of scientific research. They suggest that some research findings have gained such authority (which could be gained through the quality of research, its replication or critical assessment), to justify that the "... courts treat social science research much as they would legal precedent under the common law" (p. 466). Just as legal precedents can be reversed or distinguished, so it would be possible to reverse or distinguish the application of research findings. "Methodology can be treated like law, and the application of methodology can be treated like fact" (p. 469).

But this approach would have unfortunate side-effects. It would add a scientific gloss to the legal system, rather than challenge lawyers to review the quality of their system and the soundness of their premises. This approach would lead to certain research findings and methodologies finding judicial favour and others disfavour. It would lead to "closure," using Smith and Wynne's (1989) term, on certain forms of research and findings. It would enforce, particularly given lawyers' tendencies to dichotomise, distinctions between approved and disapproved research. That may seem appropriate but the subject matter of the research, surely, must be taken into account. Some issues are not amenable to traditional empirical research with close control over key variables. And yet people working in those areas may have something valuable to contribute to the courts. Consider a clinician who has developed a body of experience through his or her work. Colleagues might confirm that they have similar experience or at least empathise with it. He or she then uses that experience in making decisions. Those decisions usually have a beneficial outcome. Are courts to be denied the benefit of that experience just because it cannot fit into preconceptions about - or judicial precedents about - correct research?

Whilst the limits of, and the doubts about, any research methodology should be raised, the courts should particularly benefit from experts' evidence in areas where traditional empirical research is difficult, or unethical, to undertake. To which research, for example, should the courts give legal and social authority in relation to the assessment of dangerousness? Should it be the research that emphasises clinical variables (Monahan, 1988) or that which emphasises purely actuarial data, which claims a better prediction record (Dawes, Faust, & Meehl, 1989). Whilst we can never be sure that a court has made the correct decision, for the courts are inextricably involved in managing and minimising uncertainty, there are a number of steps that can be taken to minimise the likelihood of error.

(1) Expert evidence should be tendered whenever it may reduce the likelihood of a decision error. The limits of the research and any controversy in relation to it should be frankly conceded, as should the courts concede their difficulties with other forms of knowledge and reasoning, such as inductions from "common sense."

(2) In a practical sense, and for pragmatic motives, a measure of "closure" should be effected upon disputes which are not, epistemologically, open to final resolution. It is easy, as Smith and Wynne demonstrate (1989) to attack scientific method in court or in learned journals. But, at certain times and stages, a decision must be made whether to utilise an insight or research finding. (We hope that clinicians will.) "Experts" should acknowledge a pragmatic duty to make use of current knowledge to aid people rather than be theoretically pure or nihilistic. The conclusions, for example, of the research on eye-witness testimony may not be agreed and the research may be criticised for being conducted upon university students. But those findings should, at the very least, be better than nothing in sensitising a judge and jury to issues they might not otherwise have considered.

(3) The minimum standard for giving expert evidence should be understood, not just as a matter of law, as not being negligent. This standard is valuable because it emphasises (a) the duty to consider what other professionals would say, (b) duties to be well informed, and (c) that standards are not absolute but should improve over time. Being wrong is not necessarily negligent; we can learn from errors.

(4) Professional and other bodies should encourage the development of protocols on current states of knowledge, including methodology, on areas of expertise commonly sought by courts. These protocols should not be mere statements but include procedures for dissemination and encourage productive dissension, to encourage debate and research and to ensure that there is information feedback into review of protocols and systems.

(5) The protocols should encourage the use of probability statements. Where explicit statements cannot be made, either because of the nature of the issue or the state of the research, then either a range of likelihoods could be provided or the statement could be based upon a "consensus" of experts. This should also be done where the question is the likely relevance of some research. How probable is it that the findings of eye-witness testimony research, carried out on university students, would equally apply to other research subjects? This is not to exclude other questions about, or assessments of, the quality of the individual expert's evidence, or the basis for that evidence, but to stress the common language of probability. Lawyers' reluctance to handle statistical inferences will, however, need to be tackled.

(6) The implications of decision theory and research, for judges' and juries' decisions, should be drawn out and taken account of in expert evidence (Fitzmaurice & Pease, 1986). In particular emphasis should be placed on avoiding the under valuation of base rates, or actuarial information, and over valuation of subjectively isolated idiosyncratic variables.

> Many faulty signs remain popular because disregard of base rates and associated principles of probability preclude an accurate determination of their worth. (Faust & Ziskin, 1988 p.33)

Lawyers, with their emphasis upon distinguishing and emphasising the individualistic features of each case and their distaste for statistical inferences, must be particularly prone to this error. Decision research also emphasises the important of feedback information systems (Rachlin, 1990). Courts get very little information about the outcome of their decisions and that which they do get, such as in the criminal courts, tends to be about failures such as repeated offenders. This must affect perceptions and understandings of common behaviour.

(7) Lawyers' and courts' needs for efficiency and economy in the administration of justice should be recognised by experts appreciating the legal issues to be determined, in a particular case, and organising their evidence accordingly. However experts should not meekly accept lawyers' premises, methods and questions. They should explain how alternative approaches may be more useful. For example they should indicate the kinds of cross-examination question which would be appropriate to vigorously test the value and relevance of different kinds of evidence. They should "sell" their particular kind of "critical thinking" to lawyers. This might best be achieved via protocols developed by professional groups.

(8) Experts should ensure that lawyers understand both the proper ambit of their expertise and its limits. They should publish information about how their expertise can be, appropriately, tested. Professional bodies might organise continuing education courses, for lawyers, on how they assess the strength and quality of a colleague's opinion. Whilst this might lead to some very difficult questions being asked in court, and some experts being shown to be incompetent, the questions would be appropriate to the discipline.

(9) Experts should recognise that there is a continuum between that which we commonly regard as a fact and as an opinion. Without accepting the false dichotomy between them, they should emphasise the "factual" qualities of their evidence. Besides it being more difficult to misrepresent "factual" evidence, in cross-examination, it is of greater value to courts. It is easier to "see" its relevance. Instead of, for example, expressing an opinion that a child's evidence is credible because it satisfies certain of the criteria in statement reliability theory (Undeutsch, 1989), the expert should help a court understand how and why he or she believes in, and uses, that theory. (It might be wisest to drop the whole notion of "theory.") For example a court's commonsense knowledge, or inference, may be that people who change their evidence are liars. However an expert, instead of just contradicting this with another opinion, could explain to the judge how anyone who suddenly has to translate a dramatic experience - say being raped - into words, is likely to have difficulties in deciding which are going to be (a) the most appropriate words, (b) the most appropriate order and (c) what is and is not relevant to the listener. Thus a "better" "common sense" inference is that people who have recently been through such an experience are likely "to change" their evidence, to describe events in a disjointed order and include superfluous and irrelevant detail. This sort of "factual" and "commonsense" approach to explanation is likely to be much more powerful than an emphasis upon expertise and prestige.

(10) Systems should be developed to make expert witnesses accountable for what they say to courts. This could include an accreditation system or code of ethics. Professional bodies could develop a system for auditing a random sample of reports to courts. It should be possible for an expert witness to be professional disciplined for the quality of evidence given to a court. However lawyers should be required to reduce the extent to which they treat expert witnesses as partisan. "The law says be a witness, but the process by which experts become witnesses sends them the opposite message" (Saks, 1990). For example expert witnesses should be entitled, and encouraged, to send any reports that they prepare, but which are not used by the lawyer who requested them, possibly because insufficiently in the interests of the lawyers' client, to the trial judge. The judge might then have a discretion to admit them at the trial, to avoid injustice.

If these steps were taken by expert witnesses then it might be possible to renegotiate the role of experts and, in particular, recognise their role in relation to the ultimate issue. All involved have a common interest - and duty - to use their skills and knowledge to minimise the risk of erroneous decisions by courts.

References

Allison, G.T. (1971). *Essence of decision: Explaining the Cuban missile crisis.* Boston: Little, Brown and Company.
Aubert, V. (1963). The structure of legal thinking. In J. Andenaes (Ed.), *Legal essays: A tribute to Feide Castberg on the occasion of his 70th birthday* (pp. 41-63). Boston: Universitetsforlaget.
Butler-Sloss (1988). *Child abuse in Cleveland 1987.* London: H.M.S.O.
Byrne, 2 Q.B. 396 (1960).
Campbell, C. (1974). Legal thought and juristic values. *British Journal of Law and Society, 1,* 13-31.

Carson, D. (1988). Psychologists should be wary of involvement with lawyers. In P.J. van Koppen, D.J. Hessing, & G. van Den Heuvel (Eds.), *Lawyers on psychology and psychologists on law* (pp. 27-34). Amsterdam: Swets & Zeitlinger.
Carson, D. (1990a). Reports to court; A role in preventing decision error. *Journal of Social Welfare Law*, 151-163.
Carson, D. (1990b). *Professionals and the courts, a handbook for expert witnesses*. Birmingham: Venture Press.
Carson, D. (1990c). From risk policies to risk strategies. In D. Carson (Ed.), *Risk-taking in mental disorder; Analyses, policies and practical strategies* (pp. 59-69). Chichester: SLE Publications.
Dant, M. (1988). Gambling on the truth: the use of purely statistical evidence as a basis for civil liability. *Columbia Journal of Law and Social Problems*, 22, 31-70.
Dawes, R.M., Faust, D., & Meehl, P.E. (1989). Clinical versus actuarial judgment. *Science*, 243, 1668-1674.
Dowie, J., & Elstein, A. (Eds.) (1988). *Professional judgment: A reader in clinical decision making*. Cambridge: Cambridge University Press.
Dowie, J. (1990). Clinical decision making: risk is a dangerous word and hubris is a sin. In D. Carson (Ed.), *Risk-taking in mental disorder; Analyses, policies and practical strategies* (pp. 28-39). Chichester: SLE Publications.
Elahi v. Bristol and Weston Health Authority, Lexis, May 9 (1990).
Eggleston, R. (1978). *Evidence, proof and probability*. London: Weidenfield & Nicholson.
Evans, K. (1983). *Advocacy at the bar*. London: Financial Training Press.
Faigman, D.L. (1989). To have and have not: assessing the value of social science to the law as science and policy. *Emory Law Journal*, 38, 1005.
Faust, D., & Ziskin, J. (1988). The expert witness in psychology and psychiatry. *Science*, 241, 31-35.
Fitzmaurice, C., & Pease, K. (1986). *The Psychology of judicial sentencing*. Manchester: Manchester University Press.
Floud, J., & Young, W. (1981). *Dangerousness and criminal justice*. London: Heinemann.
Hall, P. (1980). *Great planning disasters*. London: Weidenfield & Nicholson.
Hart, H.L.A. (1963). Introduction. In C. Perelman, *The idea of justice and the problem of argument* (pp. VII-XI). London: Routledge.
Hodgkinson, T. (1990). *Expert evidence: Law and practice*. London: Sweet & Haxwell.
Howard, M.N. (1991). The neutral expert: A plausible threat to justice. *Criminal Law Review*, 98-105.
King, M. (1991). Children and the legal process: Views from a mental health clinic. *Journal of Social Welfare Law*, 13, 269-284.
Landon, P. A. (1944). Review of *Opinion Evidence in Illinois* (King W L, and Pillinger D, 1942, Chicago: Callaghan) *Law Quarterly Review*, 60, 202.
Lloyd-Bostock, S. (1988). *Law in practice*. London: Routledge.
Mackay, R.D., & Colman, A.M. (1991). Excluding expert evidence: A tale of ordinary folk and common experience. *Criminal Law Review*, 800-810.
Masih, Crim. L. R. 396 (1986).
Meehl, P. E. (1989). Law and the fireside inductions (with postscript): some reflections of a clinical psychologist. *Behavioral Sciences and the Law*, 7, 521-550.
Monahan, J. (1988). Risk assessment of violence among the mentally disordered: generating useful knowledge. *International Journal of Law and Psychiatry*, 11, 249-257.
Monahan, J., & Walker, L. (1988). Social science research in law: a new paradigm. *American Psychologist*, 43, 465-472.
Napley, Sir David (1970). *The technique of persuasion*. London: Sweet & Maxwell.
O'Barr, W.M. (1982). *Linguistic evidence: Power and strategy in the courtroom*. New York: Academic Press.
Rachlin, H. (1989). *Judgment, decision and choice: A cognitive/behavioral synthesis*. New York: Freeman.
R. v. Mackenny, 76 Cr. App. Rep. 271 (1981).
R. v. Turner, Q. B., 834, 841 (1975).
Saks, M.J. (1990). Expert witnesses, nonexpert witnesses, and nonwitness experts. *Law and Human Behavior*, 14, 291-313.

Sheldon, D.H., & MacLeod, M.D. (1991). From normative to positive data: Expert psychological evidence re-examined. *Criminal Law Review*, 811-820.
Smith, R., & Wynne, B. (1989). *Expert evidence, interpreting science in the law*. London: Routledge.
Spencer, J.R. (1991). The neutral expert: An implausible bogey. *Criminal Law Review*, 106-110.
Spencer, J.R. and Flin, R. (1990). *The evidence of children, the law and the psychology.* London: Blackstone.
Stone, M. (1984). *Proof of fact in criminal trials*. Edinburgh: W. Green & Son.
Stone, M., & McLean, I. (1990). *Fact-finding for magistrates*. London: Fourmat.
Tapper, C. (1985). *Cross on evidence*. London: Butterworths.
Undeutsch, U. (1989). The development of statement reality analysis. In J. Yuille (ed.), *Credibility Assessment* (pp. 101-119). Dordrecht: Kluwer.
Weightman, Crim. L. R. 204 (1991).
Wynne, B. (1989). Establishing the rules of laws: constructing expert authority. In R. Smith, & B. Wynne, *Expert evidence, interpreting science in the law* (pp. 23-55). London: Routledge.

Part VIII
Forensic Psychology in Civil Law

The Child in the European Legal System

Adelheid Kühne

The following report will give a short survey on the legal position of the child in different European countries. It is a comparison of the continental European countries of the Federal Republic of Germany, Austria, and Switzerland on the one side with England (Scotland, Wales) and Spain on the other side.

A Brief Historical Survey

In recent centuries, child development correlates with social changes. The increase in industrialization, the persistence in an agricultural way of life in some regions like the south of Spain, or confessional relationships have influenced the way of life. Industrialization and forced economic development have created better work opportunities for all family members. The level of female education increased, and life in the city encouraged other needs and activities than country life. The paternally oriented "extended family", in which parents, children, and unmarried relatives lived together, was replaced by the small family. Worksharing in the sense of the housewife budget management and the husband work slowly changed toward a new role distribution. Gainfully employed women increasingly reduced their dependence on the family. The principle of equality has become important for the changes in family life in the last decades.

German family law - in the Bürgerliches Gesetzbuch (BGB) of 1900 - permitted divorce based on the principle of fault. German law followed Roman law with the main sentence of the "patria potestas". According to this, the main authority is incumbent to the husband and father and only personal custody remained for the mother.

An amendment to family law came into effect on April 1, 1953. Since then, "joint parental authority" is mentioned, but, at first, the principle of equality from July 18, 1957, called for a regulation of the law of parent and child. The position of the child was discussed for the first time in the 1950s; at the same time, the principle of equality gave parental authority also to the mother of an illegitimate child.

The Austrian legal position is closely associated with German law. As in Germany, it is possible to divorce. Family law is codified in the Allgemeines Bürgerliches Gesetzbuch (ABGB) of 1811. Since then, the principle of cancelling the difference between legitimate and illegitimate children has been raised. A serious discussion of this problem first started in 1951 with the "Richtlinien 1951". But indeed, at that time, it became clear that reformations of the law are only possible in small steps. A satisfactory settlement of the illegitimate child law came into effect in 1970. It is important to note that the proportion of illegitimate children in Austria has remained higher than in other European countries. Only 35% of illegitimate children grow up in a family community (Bartels, 1986). The aim of the law should be to compensate for the socialization deficits in a complete community.

First directives to determine the statutory law of the illegitimate child date back to 1951. The approximation of the legal position of illegitimate and legitimate children came in effect in 1970 when the problems of the incomplete families and divorce orphans became evident.

Even though there are analogous developments in the legal systems of Germany and Austria, a principle of equality has existed in Austria only since 1975. The legal equality of man and woman had immediate consequences for the law of parent and child. That means that on June 30, 1977, the "authority of the father" was eliminated in the text of the law. Today, the rights of the illegitimate child are nearly the same as those of the legitimate.

First efforts to codify the civil law in Switzerland - Zivilgesetzbuch (ZGB) - started in 1798, but only the constitution of the Federal Republic of Switzerland in 1848 started efforts toward legal unification. The amendment of civil law came into effect on January 1, 1912. In the constitution of Switzerland the family has a marginal role. It says nothing about the status of parents, children, and the relationships between them; it is only interested in the problems of religious education (Brauchli, 1982). Coester remarks (1983, p.52) that there is broad social agreement on the organization of matrimony and family. In 1930, the women's societies demanded a revision of the illegitimate child law to improve its status. This revision failed because of resistence from welfare organizations.

Unlike the laws in continental European countries, English law for England, Scotland, and Wales is not codified. Following the English law tradition, it is mostly a so-called common law. Since the middle ages, the development of the common law followed the adjunctions of the Royal Court of Justice that dominated over regional customs.

In former times, there was the opinion that adjunctions of the law court confirmed socially existent but unwritten rights. Nowadays, the activities of the legislator in Great Britain are more considerable. Parliament has started to reform family law but this is not yet finished.

Even today, the so-called judgment laws, which give large discretion to judges, are fundamentals of English law. Cases are quoted in the law report under the names of the parties and the references. The reasons for the decision contain the different judges' opinions; dissenting opinions also have to be published. On several occasions, these dissenting opinions have been precursors of future legal opinions. The "doctrine of stare decises" says that a judgment will bind other judgments beyond the decided case. Every law court is obliged to the decisions of the next higher court. Statutory law - enacted by the parliament - has priority over case law. The most important differences between English and continental European laws can be seen in the interpretation of the law. The strained interpretation of a statue remains only in the verbal interpretation.

For many centuries, there was no interest in the development of children in family and society. Families used their children for their own profit or the profit of their social class in order to consolidate their economic position. The resulting problem was exploitation of children with authorian means.

There was no protection for children against their parents, because cruelties were so private that the law could not reach them (Eekelaar, 1983). Only the Poor Law Amendment Act of 1868 demanded sanctions against parents who neglect their children. But there were no instructions on how to detect guilty acts or take children away from their environments. A Poor Law Guardian was in charge of neglected children; custody was awarded to him or her, and he or she could decide about all interests of the child except the religious education.

The first Children's Charter of 1889 tried to extend the protection of law to all children, but it failed. For many centuries, illegitimate children have been a social problem in England. The mother in the upper class took care of her child, but in the lower class, the child was a problem for welfare and aid institutions. For prevention, the father had to pay maintenance; in extreme cases, it was possible to demand a constraint marriage with the mother. But the general opinion was that such modes of acting damaged the image of marriage. After the Poor Law Amendment Act of 1938, it was forbidden for the mother to demand maintenance. Eekelaar (1983) remarks that there was no adequate support for illegitimate children in either the 19th or 20th centuries, and he sees consequences for the development of delinquency.

At the end of the 19th century, private religious welfare organizations took care of children. Since then, they speak about "adoption". But there was no draft of a law to arrange adoptions like today; at any time it was possible for parents to demand their children. The child could remain in the foster family only if his or her property is endangered in the family of origin. Since the Adoption of Children Act in 1926, it was possible to award custody to the foster family with the agreement of the parents. A law court can substitute for the remission of parents after the abandonment of the child. Eekelaar (1983) has mentioned that, even today, adoptions still remain the best instrument for protecting children in England.

Developments in Spain were rather different compared to the other European countries. It was the priest of the Roman Catholic Church who sealed the marriage, the so-called canon marriage. Civil marriage was only possible if both partners denied Catholic beliefs. But both forms of marriage were undissolvable. Divorce was initially possible between 1932 and 1938 but a so-called Divorce Act did not come into effect until 1976. There exists no family law in our sense.

The Legal Position of the Child Today

The best interest of the child

The last few decades have seen the growth of the opinion that the legal positions of the child should be assimilated to the reality of the family and the society. Children should no longer be the objects of "parental authority". After World War II, discussions started on the status of the illegitimate child and the situation of divorce orphans in the Federal Republic of Germany and in Austria.

The main statement of the dogmatism of family law was the idea of the "best interest of the child". However, even today, the idea is no precise legal definition. Common sense is therefore the definition of Goldstein, Freud, and Solnit (1973, p.49) for "the best interest of the child" is to find the "less damaging alternative for the child".

The empirical study of Plessen and Bommert (1986) shows how the different professions vary in their opinion of the "best interest of the child". Results show a large agreement between social workers in welfare institutions (91%), psychologists (98%), and public opinion (95%). For these three groups, the "will of the child" is the main factor in the best interest of the child. In contrast, for judges at the family law court (39%) and solicitors (37%), the will of the child is not so important. The second main factor is the continuity of the child's environment, relatives, and playfellows. On this point, opinions among the different professions differ from 4% of judges who believe that the child must stay in its well-known surroundings and 88% of solicitors.

The legal position of the child in the Federal Republic of Germany

Since the marriage reform law (1977), the principle of broken marriage is the only reason for divorce. Since January 1, 1980, there is an act to regulate "parental custody" instead of "parental authority". Welfare institutions and the Federal Constitutional Court pushed the reform law. The law court had to allocate personal custody from the viewpoint of the best interest of the child. The parent who is not entitled to custody has the right of access to the child, if there are no serious reasons for withholding such a decision. A report from a social worker in a welfare institution is compulsory. In contested cases, the law court can order a psychological expert opinion. Children over the age of 13 have to be heard; but the judge can also hear younger children.

Awarding custody to a third person or institution is possible, if both parents are not able to educate the child. Since the decision of the Federal Constitutional Court on November 5, 1982, joint custody is possible if both parents agree (Luthin, 1987).

In the Federal Republic of Germany there is no right of access for an illegitimate father, but the guardianship court can deliberate upon it after a petition (Zenz, 1978).

The legal position of the child in Austria

Preliminary issues of the civil law in Austria are the rights and duties of parents and children (§ 137, §§ 140 - 154 ABGB). It is the duty of parents to educate the child, to promote the child's personality, interests, and cognitive abilities, and also to learn at school and train for employment. The rights of the father and mother are equal.

After the withdrawal of parental custody, it is possible for grandparents to be awarded custody. This view is very different from German law in the FRG. During divorce proceedings, parents can propose the allocation of personal custody under the primary view of the best interest of the child. A 10-year-old child must be heard. The parent who is not entitled to custody can claim access.

The rights of the illegitimate child in Austria and the FRG differ significantly. Care, education, and the choice of name are the rights of the mother. If the fatherhood of the illegitimate father is stated as a fact, he takes over all duties from the mother, if she dies, is put under care or cannot be found since several months. With regard to access, illegitimate fathers have equal rights. In the FRG, the father can only legitimate or adopt his child by marrying the child's mother.

The legal position of the child in Switzerland

The foundation of civil law in Switzerland is the unit of the child's relationships, and it differentiates between complete and incomplete families instead of legitimacy and illegitimacy. The tenor of the law is the best interest of the child, which is the highest standard for any decision.

If the father recognizes his illegitimate child, he is the child's relative. Rights and duties of reciprocal support, consideration, and esteem follow on from this relationship. Custody proceedings in Swiss civil law correspond closely to German law. However, the illegitimate father in Switzerland has the right of access, although this can be restrained in the interest of the mother.

The legal position of the child in England

The foundation of English law is the Matrimonial Custody Act of 1973 and the Children Act of 1975 and the adjunctions in cases (see above). The divorce sentence is initially a so-called decree nisi and then, in the second step - if the law court is convinced that the solution concerning the child's future is satisfactory - the final dissolution of the marriage is reached only then when custody, rights of access, and the maintenance of the child have been resolved. In contested cases, the best interest of the child and the equality of father and mother are the main points. The so-called not-fault parent gains some privileges, but he or she is not directly rewarded for good behavior by receiving custody. In principle, a "bad" wife may be a good mother and the behavior of the father during the time of the marriage says nothing about his interests in his child.

Adjunctions follow the decision of the cases and the law given by Parliament. The following arguments, taken from cases, give hints on judges' decisions: Young children up to the age of 6 years need the mother or an equal substitute, known since the day of birth. The mother has more time to spend with the child, because she is usually not employed. Current adjunctions try to avoid the child becoming a "key child". For girls, it is better to live with the mother; boys after the age of 8 need the care of the father because he has more understanding of sports and juvenile hobbies. The English educational tradition continues to favor football and cricket playing for boys. Brothers and sisters should not be separated, and a change in living conditions is to be avoided.

The will of the child is important when it seems necessary for the judge. But there is no legal claim for the child to be heard. Some judges prefer to hear the child, but others argue against such a hearing because it is unreasonable to ask a child to testify against his or her own parents. Important for the judge is the personal impression of father and mother during the trial. Even if the current opinion is that it is best for a child to live in a family, it is possible to award custody to a third person, for example, a welfare institution or grandparents. Economic factors do not play an important role, but the judge has to ask about housing conditions. For example, if a parent is working and living in a bar, custody cannot be awarded to him or her.

Religious aspects are important when extreme sectarian communities, such as Jehovas' witnesses, are involved, to avoid risks for the child because the ideology rejects medical treatment. Joint custody is possible since 1978.

In all cases, it is very important to consider the particular problems of the singular situation (Turner & Davis-Ferid, 1983).

The legal position of the child in Spain

The Código civile (CC), Art. 92 sect. 2, regulates the judge's decision regarding custody and education. The highest principle is the best interest of the child, and personal custody is to be awarded to the parent who can provide the best conditions for positive development. Important are economic conditions and the parents' relationships to others. Brothers and sisters should not be separated. The fault of one parent should not be taken into account. After the age of 12, the judge has to hear the child to know its will. Art 159 CC proposed personal custody to the mother of children under the age of seven. It is also possible to award personal custody to a third party and also to withdraw custody from the parents. Before adopting a child, parents in Spain have to prove their unexceptional life-style. Following the last edition of the civil law, legitimate and illegitimate children have equal rights (Langner, 1984).

Conclusion

On April 5, 1990, the German Bundestag passed a bill containing two amendments to international custody right (Mansel, 1990). The European convention regulates the recognition and execution of sentences concerning personal custody. With the Convention of Den Haag, the laws having legal force become effective in cases of kidnapping. Both conventions help to improve the situation of the child in those countries accepting the agreements.

The report gave a small survey over the legal situation of the child in some European countries. In the last few years, there has been an approximation of the position of the legitimate and illegitimate child, personal custody, and access to the child in European countries. It is to be hoped that the European Community will provide new perspectives for children in the future and also a better communication between psychology and law.

References

Bartels, T. (1986). *Die vollständigen und unvollständigen Familien im Kindschaftsrecht - Eine vergleichende Betrachtung der familienrechtlichen Regelungen in der Bundesrepublik Deutschland, der DDR, Österreich und der Schweiz*. Frankfurt: Peter Lang.
Brauchli, A. (1982). *Das Kindeswohl als Maxime des Rechts*. Zürich:
Coester, M. (1983). *Das Kindeswohl als Rechtsbegriff*. Frankfurt: Alfred Metzner.
Eekelaar, J. (1983). *Familienrecht und Sozialpolitik*. Berlin: Duncker & Humblot.
Goldstein, A., Freud, A., & Solnit, A. (1973). *Beyond the best interest of the child*. New York: Free Press.
Langner, D. (1984). *Eheschließung und Ehescheidung nach spanischem Recht*. Frankfurt: Peter Lang.
Luthin, H. (1987). *Gemeinsames Sorgerecht nach der Scheidung*. Bielefeld: Ernst & Werner Gieseking.
Mansel, H.P. (1990). Neues internationales Sorgerecht. *Neue Juristische Wochenschrift, 35*, 2176 - 2178.
Plessen, U., & Bommert, H. (1986). Empirische Untersuchungen zum Begriff des "Kindeswohls". In A. Schorr (Ed.), *Bericht über den 13. Kongreß für Angewandte Psychologie, Bonn, September 1985, Vol. 2*, (pp. 323 - 335). Bonn: Deutscher Psychologenverlag.
Turner, J.N., & Davis-Ferid, H. (1983): *Englisches Familienrecht*. Frankfurt: Verlag für Standesamtswesen.
Zenz, G. (1978). Das "Kindeswohl" in der richterlichen Entscheidung. *Psychosozial, 2*, 69 - 95.

Diagnostic Judgment on Parental Custody as a Decision-Making Process

Marie-Luise Kluck

Performing psychological expertises on questions of parental custody after divorce involves a complex diagnostic process. The diagnostic process as a whole includes the following stages: (a) the judge's question or questions as a starting point; (b) the "translation" of these questions into psychological hypotheses; (c) planning the diagnostic procedure; (d) carrying out the planned diagnostic procedure; (e) a descriptive report of the diagnostic results and other informations important for the present diagnostic problem; and (f) combining and weighing these results; that is, answering the judicial questions by deciding on each of the psychological hypotheses. Stages (c) and (d) are not reported in an expertise.

Single Stages of the Diagnostic Process

Decisions on planning the diagnostic process

First, when we receive a mandate from the family court to compile a report on psychological aspects of parental custody after divorce, we have to decide whether the judicial questions are presented in a proper form for psychological treatment. Some of the decisions that the expert has to make at this stage are: (a) Are the judicial questions unequivocal or ambiguous? (b) Am I the adequate expert to answer these questions? (c) Is there sufficient knowledge in psychology to answer these questions? (d) Is it morally acceptable for me to deal with these questions (i.e., ethical considerations)? The diagnostic process only proceeds to the next stage when - perhaps after a reformulation - all the above questions can be answered affirmatively. This second stage is the translation or transformation of judicial questions into psychological hypotheses (to avoid misunderstandings, we shall call these hypotheses "psychological questions"). These hypotheses have to focus on the "demand profile" that describes the so-called "best interest of the child." Criteria for this (given by the legal system, and not as psychological constructs or variables) are (a) the personal attachments of the child (or children); (b) the continuity of personal care and the continuity of the child's environment; (c) fostering the child's personality development; and (d) the child's own wishes regarding where he or she prefers to live (see Goldstein, Freud, & Solnit, 1974; Klussmann, 1981).

Each of these criteria contains a bundle of psychological variables that we have to inspect. This confronts the psychological expert with a great risk of systematically ignoring important variables that determine the behavior in question; due, for example, to the psychologist's own prejudices, values, aims, or general expectations. Our main issue here is to look for the least harmful conditions for the further physical and psychological development of the child. To avoid systematic errors in planning the diagnostic investigation, the following "search structure" of the conditions and psychological variables that influence and determine behavior in general is very helpful.

Conditions influencing and determining human behavior

These include both "nonpsychological" conditions and psychological conditions and variables.
Nonpsychological conditions are:
Living environment (E). This can include dwelling conditions, financial resources, communication facilities, and so forth.
Organism (O). This can concern the presence of, for example, chronic diseases, handicaps, or addictions.
Psychological conditions and variables are:
Cognition (C). For example, intelligence, social competence, and problem-solving skills.
Emotions (Em). These are feelings like anxiety, guilt, jealousy, or love.
Motivation (M). This involves not only single motives but also norms, values, goals, wishes, and expectations.
Social conditions and variables (S). For example, significant others, social contacts, attitudes.

Behavior (B) can then be conceived as a function (f) of all these conditions and psychological variables and their mutual interactions: $B = f(E, O, C, Em, M, S)$. When dealing with parental custody after divorce, we can check all these conditions and variables of behavior for their contribution to the child's welfare by matching them with the demand profile of the best interest of the child (see above). This leads to diagnostic hypotheses (or psychological questions). Attachment, for example, deals primarily with the child's close emotional relationships. Our hypotheses about "emotional" and "social" aspects of the general judicial question of custody have to refer to the (theoretical and empirically valid) knowledge that psychology can supply on "attachment." We only take into account psychological findings that have proved to be reliable and valid for the questions we have to answer. We examine only those variables that are relevant to the individual diagnostic problem. When performing this task, we are not attached to a single psychological theory or "school." Our general orientation is directed toward theoretically founded empirical psychology; behavior includes overt behavior as well as covert behavior such as cognitions, feelings, attitudes, and so forth.

Hypotheses on problems of parental custody have to refer to (a) the child or children in the family; (b) each of the parents; and (c) the child's significant others, who may be other relatives, close friends, nurses, teachers, foster parents, or others with whom the child maintains a close socioemotional relationship.

When we have translated each judicial question into psychological hypotheses, we have to plan the diagnostic procedure for the particular single case. We have to choose adequate instruments for obtaining the required data, and we have to fix the concrete procedure to be used in the diagnostic investigation.

We choose those diagnostic instruments that are (a) objective, (b) reliable, and (c) valid for the variables we want to assess.

For expertises on parental custody, it is generally found that systematic, semistandardized interviews and systematic observation of the "relevant" behavior (e.g., the "strange situation" designed by Ainsworth, 1978, for the measurement of attachment quality) deliver the greatest amount of the information needed to answer the diagnostic questions. As yet, there are only very few standardized tests that can contribute to dealing with the problems of recommending a certain solution of parental custody from a psychological point of view. Some questionnaires can be helpful here. Examples of "useful" diagnostic instruments that have been developed for German-speaking populations are the PF 11-14 (Westhoff, Geusen-Asenbaum, Leutner, & Schmidt, 1982): This questionnaire helps 11- to 14-year-olds to verbalize their problems. The Kiphard grid for siblings and very young children (1987), the HAVEL (Wagner, 1981), and the MVL (Ehlers, Ehlers, & Makus, 1978) ask parents about the usual behavior of their children. Q-sort-like "tests", for example, the FRT (Bene & Anthony, 1957; German adaptation from Flämig & Wörner, 1977), help children to verbalize their incoming and outgoing feelings about all members of the family. Projective techniques involve many and severe dangers regarding the validity of the results obtained (Hörmann, 1964a, 1964b). Therefore, we cannot recommend their use in systematic diagnosis. When planning diagnostic procedures, we select those procedures that can enhance and add to the information we have obtained already from other sources. Here, we balance the costs of a special diagnostic procedure, for example, a test, and its utility. Of course, this involves the consideration of not only material but also nonmaterial costs and benefits for all participants in the diagnostic process (Cronbach & Gleser, 1965).

The diagnostic investigation and its results

During the actual implementation of diagnostic procedures, it may become apparent that supplementary hypotheses are needed, former hypotheses need to be amended, or the remaining diagnostic strategy needs to be changed. The diagnostic process we describe here includes the options of recurring to an earlier stage in the process and of "sequential testing" (Cronbach & Gleser, 1965). The core of a psychological expertise is the final "diagnosis," that is, the psychological expert's answer to the judicial questions. This answer develops from combining and weighing all the individual pieces of information we have obtained on the persons who are investigated in the individual case. On this level of the diagnostic process, mistakes may arise due to a number of influences. The most inportant are: (a) logical errors; (b) improper weighing of single pieces of information (e.g., alcoholic mothers should never obtain parental custody of their children; each child needs his or her own room); and (c) all the influences we know from social psychology research on the processes of person perception and social perception in general (Hastorf, Schneider, & Polefka, 1970; Preiser, 1979; Schneider, 1973).

Distortions of diagnostic judgment due to these types of error can be avoided or at least minimized by: (a) thoroughly planning the whole diagnostic process and every single stage in this process; (b) making explicit decisions at each stage of the diagnostic process and describing these decisions so that a third person can test them; and (c) training students and experts to plan and perform diagnostic investigations, to decide on diagnostic hypotheses, and to monitor themselves during the whole diagnostic process.

With this method of "decision-oriented diagnostics" we have been able to confirm the effectiveness of training both students and colleagues over a period of 15 years. This effectiveness has been confirmed in many fields of psychological diagnosis that range beyond decisions on parental custody. The strategy integrates theoretical and empirical results of psychological research from various areas of basic and applied psychology. This includes research on decision-making (Janis & Mann, 1977; Kreitler & Kreitler, 1982), "judgment under uncertainty" (Kahneman, Slovic, & Tversky, 1982), person perception (Hastorf et al., 1970), and diagnostic judgment in a narrow sense (Lüer & Kluck, 1983). The conception has proved to be useful in other areas of legal psychology, in educational and clinical psychology, as well as in personnel selection. We have written a monograph in which first attempts to found a general "theory of psychological diagnostics" are described on the basis of Guttman's (1981) guidelines for theory construction as well as the feedback we have obtained on the effectiveness of decision-oriented diagnostics in many areas of applied psychology (Westhoff & Kluck, 1991).

References

Ainsworth, M.D.S., Blehar, M.C., Waters, E., & Wall, S. (1978). *Patterns of attachment: A psychological study of the strange situation.* Hillsdale, NJ: Erlbaum.

Bene, E., & Anthony, J. (1957). *Family Relations Test, Children's Version,* 1978 Revision. Windsor: The NFER-Nelson Publishing Co. Ltd.

Cronbach, L.J., & Gleser, G.C. (1965). *Psychological tests and personnel decisions,* 2nd ed. Urbana: University of Illinois Press.

Ehlers, B., Ehlers, Th., & Makus, H. (1978). *Die Marburger Verhaltensliste (MVL).* Göttingen: Hogrefe.

Flämig, J., & Wörner, U. (1977). Standardisierung einer deutschen Fassung des Family Relations Test (FRT) an Kindern von 6 bis 11 Jahren. *Praxis der Kinderpsychologie und Kinderpsychotherapie, 26,* 5-46.

Goldstein, J., Freud, A., & Solnit, A.J. (1974). *Jenseits des Kindeswohls.* Frankfurt: Suhrkamp.

Guttman, L. (1981). What is not what in theory construction. Paper presented to the 8th annual meeting of the Israel Sociological Association. In I. Borg (Ed.), *Multidimensional data representations: When and why* (pp. 47-64). Ann Arbor, Michigan: Mathesis Press.

Hastorf, A.H., Schneider, D.J., & Polefka, J. (1970). *Person perception.* Reading, MA: Addison-Wesley.

Hörmann, H. (1964a). Aussagemöglichkeiten psychologischer Diagnostik. *Zeitschrift für Experimentelle und Angewandte Psychologie, 11,* 353-390.

Hörmann, H. (1964b). Theoretische Grundlagen der projektiven Tests. In R. Heiss (Ed.), *Handbuch der Psychologie, Vol. 6, Psychologische Diagnostik* (pp. 71-112). Göttingen: Hogrefe.

Janis, I.L., & Mann, L. (1977). *Decision-making - A psychological analysis of conflict, choice, and commitment.* New York: The Free Press.

Kahneman, D., Slovic, P., & Tversky, A. (Eds.)(1982). *Judgment under uncertainty: Heuristics and biases.* Cambridge: Cambridge University Press.

Kiphard, E.J. (1987). *Wie weit ist ein Kind entwickelt?* Dortmund: modernes lernen.

Klussmann, R. W. (1981). *Das Kind im Rechtsstreit der Erwachsenen.* München: Ernst Reinhardt.

Kreitler, H., & Kreitler, S. (1982). The theory of cognitive orientation: Widening the scope of behavior prediction. In B. Maher, & W.B. Maher (Eds.), *Progress in experimental personality research,* Vol. 11 (pp. 101-169). New York: Academic Press.

Lüer, G., & Kluck, M.-L. (1983). Diagnostische Urteilsbildung. In J. Bredenkamp, & H. Feger (Eds.), *Enzyklopädie der Psychologie, Vol. 3, Messen und testen, Serie Forschungsmethoden* (pp. 727-798). Göttingen: Hogrefe.

Preiser, S. (1979). *Personwahrnehmung und Beurteilung.* Darmstadt: Wissenschaftliche Buchgesellschaft.

Schneider, D.J. (1973). Implicit personality theory: A review. *Psychological Bulletin, 79,* 294-309.

Wagner, H. (1981). *Hamburger Verhaltensbeurteilungsliste (HAVEL).* Göttingen: Hogrefe.

Westhoff, K., Geusen-Asenbaum, C., Leutner, D., & Schmidt, M. (1982). *Problemfragebogen für 11- bis 14jährige.* Braunschweig: Westermann.

Westhoff, K., & Kluck, M.-L. (1991). *Psychologische Gutachten schreiben und beurteilen.* Heidelberg: Springer.

Fire-Setting: Age Trends and Psychometrical Diagnosis of Competency Criteria for Liability[1]

Wilfried Hommers

The following studies are related to the competencies of minors relevant in German civil law. However, they are specialized in several other respects. First, as a specialized field of competencies, tort law competencies of minors have been chosen, which are only part of the larger field of developmental assumptions related to the age limit of seven years in German civil law. These are regulated by § 828 BGB (German civil code of 1900) and its legal implications. Undeutsch (1967) has summarized the Supreme Court rulings on the competency criteria for liability of minors since the beginning of this century. The two principle interfaces between psychology and law in this field are de lege lata and de lege ferenda (Wegener, 1981). The former looks at cognitive development related to issues of forensic competency evaluations of minors in tort (delictual) law suits (§ 828 II BGB), whereas the latter looks at the delictual (§ 828 I BGB) and contractual (§ 104 I BGB) law assumptions of the seven-year age limit in German civil law. Hommers (1983, 1989) has reviewed the available empirical evidence, which was only indirectly concerned with this problem, and has discussed methods for further examinations. Relevant empirical aspects of both interfaces are consequently pursued in the present approach directly, but still restricted to tort law competencies.

The Supreme Court criteria for tort law (delictual) capability of minors in German civil law rest on the preassumption that the individual child has one or both of two competencies when having reached the age of seven years: knowledge of right and wrong when doing harm and some understanding of the duty to make recompense for harm. As a consequence, an individual minor may be exempted from damages only if an expertise proves that he or she did not have the necessary capabilites at the time of the tort. On the other hand, if the expertise found that the individual child had the capability to know right and wrong, the second preassumption, understanding the duty to make recompense, will not be questionable. Instead, it is assumed that the capability to know right and wrong proves the understanding of the duty to make recompense. Thus, jurisprudence implicitly assumes that the duty to make recompense is understood earlier in cognitive development than the knowledge of right and wrong in a specific case. Aside from the developmental sequence, it is also possible to test the diagnosticity assumption of whenever knowledge of right and wrong is present, understanding the duty to make recompense is also present. However, the use of the specification "some understanding" in the Supreme Court rulings

---

[1] Acknowledgements: The empirical studies reported were funded by a grant from the German Research Society, Bonn (DFG Ho 920/2-2) to the author. Mr. Dipl.-Psych. K. Feld assisted with the data analyses. Mrs. Pirkner typed the manuscript and the tables.

on the recompense competency shows that no high standard is held that has to be proven for attributing the necessary cognitive ability to a child.

Both competencies have intellectual and emotional-evaluative components as the Supreme Court ruled. The former may be operationalized with respect to the appreciation of the wrong against the harmed person. Thus, scores on certain IQ subtests may be used as substitutes if more direct assessment of appreciation is not feasible. For the latter, the classical notion of discernment may be the basis for its operationalization. Since no specific assessment approaches were used for the latter, the present contribution is concerned with testing the developmental assumptions for discernment in cases of purposeful and negligent torts. According to the classical discernment concept (Waibel, 1970), the right-wrong capacity may be assessed by judgment differences between negligent and inadvertent fire-setting or by judgment differences of purposeful versus inadvertent fire-setting, other variables kept constant. These differences can be measured with ratings of single stimuli presented successively or with choices between two stimuli presented simultaneously. Moreover, the low standard of the Supreme Court on the understanding of the recompense duty allowed the extension of the classical discernment notion. Therefore, the recompense capacity may also be assessed by judgment differences and in particular with judgment differences between apology conditions and no apology conditions, other conditions kept constant.

In cases of negligent torts, two capacities of the average child of the same age as the harmdoer are relevant in addition to those two discussed above. Following from § 276 BGB (culpa of the harmdoer) and § 254 BGB (contributory negligence), knowing the dangerousness of the harmful act and performing up to these cognitive capabilites is necessary for attributing liability to a minor as well as to every person. However, here an average standard is used in which an individual child's competencies are irrelevant. Thus, psychological research on average age trends of relevant cognitive and volitive competencies are of interest. However, the Supreme Court used two concepts (Waibel, 1970) for the risk-oriented cognitions involved, one being the general duty to avoid negligent acts (relevant for § 828 BGB), the other being the concrete part related to the actually existing danger (relevant for § 276 BGB). Thus, individual competency criteria, in particular of the knowledge of right and wrong, apply also to cases of minors' negligent torts.

Finally, the special tort of arson is chosen (Canter, 1980; Prins, 1986). Children's fire-setting may be of interest for practical reasons, either because it is a behavioral problem of children and juveniles (Achenbach & Edelbrock, 1981) requiring prevention and modification (Ell, 1983; Holland, 1969), or because the size of the losses involved frequently results in civil law suits against minors, in which the capacity of the minor might be tested (Dauner, 1980; Ell, 1983). Also, there are empirical results from such expertise cases (Dauner, 1980) that indicate that the relevant cognitive abilities of the minors may develop differently across different torts. Thus, arson appeared as an ecologically valid choice.

For forensic expertise judgments, procedures for the assessment of individual differences in judgments of children are apparently of interest. But, the main problem for making forensic diagnoses is methodological: to obtain estimates of reliability and to show that the assessment of delictual capacities cannot be replaced by other measures like general intelligence. Therefore, two original empirical studies employed culpa and post-act information suitable for testing the preassumption of some understanding of the recompense duty and for individual diagnoses of the discernment of negligent and purposeful fire-setting in comparison with inadvertent fire-setting. In these studies, choice responses and rating responses were used for data collection, and direct and indirect psychometric assessment of the measurement errors (Huber, 1973) were employed for competency diagnoses. Moreover, scores on some subtests of intelligence were determined for testing their independence from the results on discernment diagnoses.

Experiment 1

The main points of the first study were to compare the mean age trends of the culpa effect and of the post-act-behavior effect, to provide results on the reliabilities of these effects in individual assessments, to test the two implicit hypotheses about the relation between knowledge of right and wrong and understanding the duty to repair, and to examine the correlations between these individual effects and intelligence measures.

Method

Twelve illustrated stories on incidents of fire-setting by a child were used as stimuli. They were presented to four groups of male and female preschool students ($N=33$, 5- to 6-year-olds), elementary school students ($N=38$, 7- to 10-year-olds), secondary school students ($N=37$, 11- to 15-year-olds) and adults ($N=40$). The stories factorially combined two damage levels (totally burnt doghouse, partly burnt barn), two culpa levels (inadvertently, when helping to search for a wallet lost by a farmer and striking a match to cast light in a dark corner; purposefully, becoming angry with the farmer who told the child to tidy up the barn as a punishment for stealing cherries), and three levels of post-act behavior (no apology by turning one's back on the farmer, apology by shaking hands with the farmer, helping to repair the burnt building). The two culpa levels were illustrated by two pictures each, the levels of the other factors by one picture each. Each picture was accompanied by a short text that was verbalized during the instruction by the examiner and later on by the subject. During the training phase of the rating task, subjects were presented all stimuli levels of each one of the stimuli factors simultaneously (damage first, followed by post-act behavior, and then culpa), and they rated them on a good-bad rating scale consisting of 13 black (right side of the scale) and 13 white bars. These bars were 0.5 cm thick and increased in size up to 6.0 cm from the middle to the ends. Afterwards, four complete story stimuli were arranged in correct order and were rated by the subjects.

The session started with the subtest MT (Block Design) of the HAWIK-R (Tewes, 1983). Afterwards, subjects entered the training phase. After two additional complete trial stimuli, which were used for retest reliability measures of the ratings, the subtest WT (Vocabulary) of the HAWIK-R followed. Then the twelve stimuli were presented. These were given in two sequences, each to half of the subjects. Finally, the subtest AV (Comprehension) of the HAWIK-R was administered.

Results

There were three main results: the age trends of the means, the assessments of individual effect differences, and correlations between individual effect differences and IQ subtest scores. Figure 1 presents the comparison of means for preschool and elementary school children as a function of three stimulus informations: Damage with levels "burnt dog-house" or "partly burnt coach-house" (horizontal axis), post-act behavior of the minor with the levels "no apology", "apology", and "helping with the repair" (curve parameters), and the culpa of the minor with the levels "inadvertend when helping with a burse search" and "purposeful as a revenge" (left and right part of each graph). Mainly, a strong effect of apology, a small effect of culpa, and a twofold disordinal age trend of apology and help with damage in the purposeful-level are visible. The means of the two older age groups resembled the 7- to 10-year-olds fairly well.

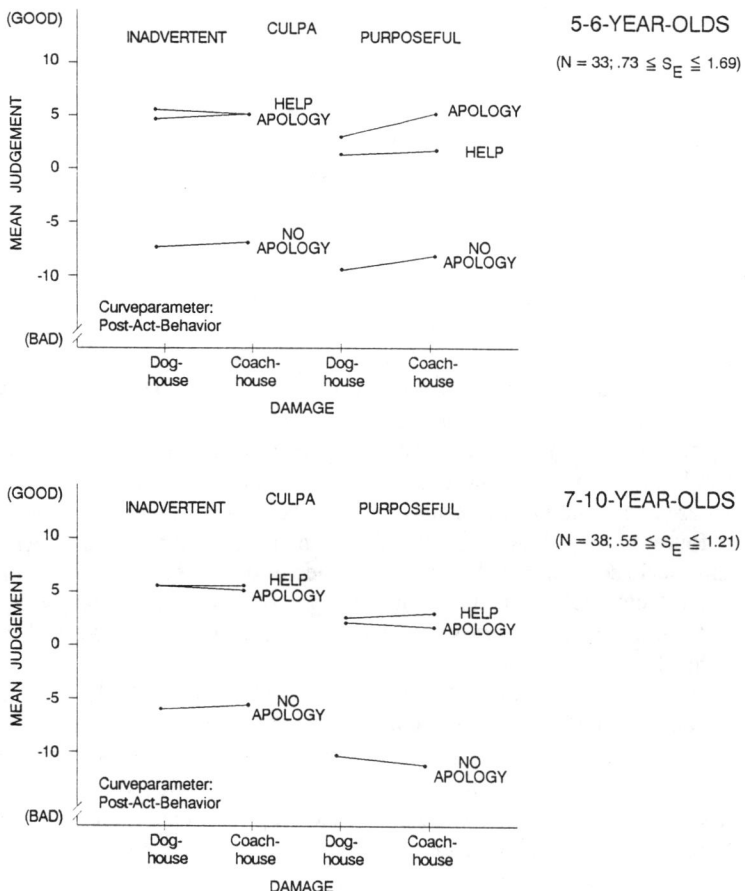

Figure 1: Means of Good-Bad-Judgements of two Age Groups on a Fire-Setting of a Minor as a Function of three Stimulus Informations.

The clearly visible main effect of culpa and of the difference between no apology and apology will be discussed with other results later (Table 1). Primarily, Figure 1 shows the results of the group means related to the 7-year age limit. As one can see, there are two "disordinal" effects in the preschoolers' means. To apologize for a purposeful fire-setting appeared better to the preschoolers than to help repair the damage. Similarly, to apologize for the larger damage appeared in their judgment better than to apologize for the smaller damage. This latter result was supported statistically by a significant triple age x damage x culpa interaction, $F(1,144)=4.178, p=.007$, and in part by a significant age x damage interaction, $F(3,144)=6.021, p<.001$. These two disordinal age trends around the age of seven years may indicate that preschoolers judge from a different recompense morality than elementary schoolers. The former may take into consideration the subjective efforts that the recompense implicates for the harmdoer, whereas the latter may center on the effect to the victim of the harm. Since similar disordinal age trends were found with various forms of another scenario (Hommers, 1986a, 1986b) and when comparing homogeneous age groups of 6- and 8-year-olds, this reliable result on the development of the understanding of the duty to make recompense seems to support the seven-year civil law age limit. However, this support exists aside from the presence of understanding the duty to make recompense up to the standard of "some understanding", as shown by results discussed below.

The mean data structure of secondary school children and adults was very similar to the elementary school children in Figure 1, except that the difference between repair help and apology was larger (see also the third column of Table 1) and their damage effects (which took the expected direction) were significant ($p<.05$ or $<.001$) in both older groups. Also, there was no main effect of age in contrast to Irving and Siegal (1983) who found a decrease of punishment as a function of age (4 groups from 7 to 17) with an arson scenario. Thus, no moral evaluation, but only punishment differences may exist in arson cases across age groups. However, age did influence the effect sizes of the stimulus components, as shown in Table 1 on the basis of individual effect sizes.

Table 1: Retest-Reliabilities (r_{tt}), Cronbach's α, Group Means (M) and their Standard Deviation (SD) of the Averaged Local Effect Sizes of the Individual Subjects for Four Groups.

	N	r_{tt}	Culpa (6 "Items")			Apology (4 "Items")			Repair-help (4 "Items")		
			α	M	SD	α	M	SD	α	M	SD
Preschool	33	.64	.50	-2.5	4.3	.78	12.6	7.65	-.35	-1.1	3.44
Elementary	38	.95	.78	-3.4	4.03	.94	12.4	7.67	-.01	0.7	2.39
Secondary	37	.95	.88	-6.3	4.71	.88	9.4	5.26	.27	1.9	2.19
Adults	40	.92	.81	-5.4	3.28	.91	8.2	5.81	.40	1.6	1.99
Total	148	.89	.77			.88			.11		

Because there were no further disordinal interactions, rating differences for apology and no apology or for helping with the repair and apology as well as the differences for inadvertent and purposeful fire-setting were determined for the assessment of the delictual capacities which was eventually based on the reliability of the differences estimated with Cronbach's α. As the comparison of the α-coefficients for individual effect sizes and the retest-reliabilities for judgments (first column of Table 1) show, ratings and effect sizes had reliabilities comparable to psychometric personality tests. Table 1 also presents the mean age trends in the three individual effect sizes and the relevant data for the standard error of measurement derived from the reliability as estimated from the α-coefficient and the standard deviations for the averaged individual differences of each group.

The culpa effect increased with age, $F(3,144)=6.452, p<.001$, although it was already significant in preschool students ($p<.01$), as seen in the lefthand side of Table 1, where standard deviations of the four age groups and α-coefficients for individual culpa effects are given. Whereas the former decreased, the latter increased with age, roughly speaking.

There was already a large effect of apology in preschool students, as expected from previous results with other scenarios of property damage (Leon, 1982), theft, personal injuries, and smearing stamps of a peer's collection (Hommers, 1988a, 1988b).

However, the stability of the effect of apology across age reported for other scenarios was not found in the arson scenario. Instead, the effect of apology on judgments decreased from preschool students to adults, $F(3,144)=3.965, p=.009$, as can be seen in the center of Table 1. This result was replicated in several independent studies not reported here, which varied some of the methodological features of this study by employing the arson scenario. In part, this scenario specificity in the mean age trend of the apology effect may be interpretable from the relations between victim and harmdoer or from the severity of the harm. In the arson scenario, the victim was an adult, whereas in the previously used scenarios, the victim was a peer of the harmdoer. Thus, adult subjects may identify with the victim and regard apology to be insufficient for arson.

There was also clear evidence that there is a development of the capability to understand the duty of recompense. On the one hand, there were the disordinal effects discussed above. On the other hand, there was an age-correlated increase in the distinctions made between helping to repair the damage on the one side and apology on the other, $F(3,144)=9.854, p<.001$, as seen in the righthand side of Table 1. According to the Supreme Court standard, this development is irrelevant for both purposes (de lege lata and de lege ferenda) of the civil law competency of understanding the duty to repair harm. But, it is in line with the low standard for understanding the duty to make recompense. Interestingly, the reliability data for these individual effects showed that there is no psychometrical basis for interpreting individual effect sizes of the difference between helping with repair and apology, although the reliability and standard deviations of individual effect sizes show the same age trend as in the two other ones.

Despite the arson-scenario-specific decreasing age trend of apology, the results clearly support the prior finding that preschool children already have some understanding of the duty of recompense, since they showed such a strong consideration of apology information (Hommers, 1988a, 1988b) or of harmdoer-compensation information (Hommers, 1986a, 1986b). As the reliability estimates and standard deviations for individual apology effects showed, however, this conclusion can be drawn individually on a psychometric basis. Thus, the results did speak directly and positively to the legal assumptions of cognitive development. In contrast, individual culpa effects were frequently nonsignificant in preschool students, as indicated by the mean, standard deviation, and reliability in the lefthand side of Table 1. Thus, the Supreme Court's developmental hypothesis concerning the developmental relation of the two cognitions appears valid.

Individual diagnoses of the two competencies require the determination of the error level of a wrong diagnosis. The following argument leads to the choice of a high error probability: First, the burden of proof is on the harmdoing minor. Thus, already weak signs of the presence of competency should speak against him or her. Second, one can use the probability of the adults for the randomly produced individual effect size of one, that is, literally speaking, "making an average distinction", as index for the error probability. Since the adult probabilities were $p=.24$ for culpa effects and $p=.28$ for apology effects (the error values for this cut-off score in the other groups were, in order of age, $p=.37$, $p=.30$, $p=.27$ for culpa and $p=.39$, $p=.30$, $p=.29$ for apology), it turned out that application of the adult error level of $p=.24$ would set the cut-off score for the diagnosis of knowledge of right and wrong to 2.14, 1.32, or 1.14; and for the duty to make recompense to 2.51, 1.32, or 1.28, in terms of averaged individual judgment differences of scale points for the three age groups respectively.

Another advantage of the reliability estimates for individual effect sizes is that they may be applicable to the ratings of the instruction phase. Those may present the original state of the individual better, whereas the ratings of the three- factorial stimuli may be overtrained. However, in the instruction, the method of contrasting the levels in the presentation was used, which may not be ecologically valid for the one-act-related competency diagnosis in a law suit. Applying the above cut-off score criteria showed that 11 preschool and 3 elementary school students were not showing knowledge of right and wrong in the instruction phase (3 preschool and 1 elementary school student for duty to make recompense). In the main phase of the investigation, there were 17 out of 33, 15 out of 38, 4 out of 37, and 4 out of 40 subjects (in order of age) below those age-specific cut-off scores for individual culpa effects; and only 4, 0, 1, and 3 for individual apology effects. Thus, the contrasting procedure used in the instruction phase may have made just the diagnoses of knowledge of right and wrong more likely, thereby supporting the implicit theory of the Supreme Court that at least one capacity is developed well enough at the age of seven.

The psychometrically based diagnoses of knowledge of right and wrong and of understanding the duty to make recompense were cross-classified to test the legal assumption that existing knowledge of right and wrong proves the understanding of the duty to make recompense. For comparison, this was done with two one-sided error levels ($p<.05$ and $p<.20$) for the wrong diagnoses. As the frequencies in Table 2 show, there were very few cases, five (with $p<.05$) or two (with $p<.20$) in total (all except one of them were in the adult group), in which understanding the duty to make recompense was present as a diagnosis and the knowledge of right and wrong diagnosis was not present. In contrast, 41 ($p<.05$) or 58 of the children and 30 ($p<.05$) or 33 of the adults had both diagnoses. Statistically the comparison of these frequencies (test of the hypothesis) with the two remaining cross-tabulations of the three minor groups with an absence of knowledge of right and wrong (conditional base rates) was significant ($\chi^2=7.96$ for the 5%-level and 5.04 for the 20%-level, $df=1$, $p<.05$). Thus, the validity of the implicit developmental theory that understanding of the duty to make recompense is developed ahead of the knowledge of right and wrong is supplemented by the validity of the hypothesis on the strong conditional association of the individual diagnoses.

Table 2: Cross Tabulated Psychometrical ($p<.05$ and $p<.20$ for the Numbers in Parantheses) Diagnoses of Right-Wrong-Knowledge and of Understanding the Repair-Duty on the Basis of Quantitative Judgments of Three-Factorial Descriptions of a Minor's Fire-Setting for Children and Adults.

		Children		Adults	
		Right-wrong-knowledge present			
		Yes	No	Yes	No
Understanding the recompense-duty present	Yes	41 (58)	53 (46)	30 (33)	5 (4)
	No	1 (0)	13 (4)	4 (0)	1 (1)

Finally, there were only two (out of 27) significant ($p<.05$) correlations between the three HAWIK-R scores and the three individual effect measures in the three groups. Only one of them was in the preschool student group and might have indicated that, at this age, some association between vocabulary and the knowledge of right and wrong as measured by the individual culpa effect may exist ($r=.45$). The other significant correlation was in the secondary school student group between block design and the culpa effects, and had no relevance for the legal questions since it was negative ($r=-.37$). The results on the multiple regression analyses involving sex and age additionally showed that the individual effect assessments could not be replaced by the intelligence measures, although there were statistically significant overall associations as indicated by the multiple regression coefficients for the three criteria variables ($p<.001$, $p<.05$, and $p<.001$). Thus, applying confirmative statistical standards, the correlations of judgments and intelligence showed that intelligence does not allow a prediction of reliable and valid individual differences in the moral rating task. Thus, the evaluative capacities of liability competency may not be replaced with intelligence testing.

Experiment 2

The main point of the second study was to involve the diagnosis of understanding the duty to avoid negligent acts as a topic of the procedure. This means that an interpretation of this moral knowledge is made that generalizes the discernment approach of Experiment 1 to the assessment of the evaluative component of knowledge of right and wrong of negligence. Thus, ratings on a negligent fire-setting were added.

Method

The picture for the negligent fire-setting showed a child making a fire near the barn, when the accompanying text added the information that the child had recently been told not to do this. This stimulus was presented as a third level of the culpa stimuli factor in addition to the levels of inadvertent and purposeful fire-setting. However, instead of the apology effect, two new aspects were included: Another kind of stimulus information was combined with the culpa levels, and the influence of methodological variations of the individual assessment per contrasting procedure was investigated. First, the stimuli were factorial combinations of the three culpa levels mentioned before with the two levels of the post-act event factor, which had a third-party compensation level (the picture showed a farmer in an insurance office receiving money) and the apology level of Experiment 1. Second, two judgment procedures were used instead of the single rating procedure in Experiment 1.

On the one side, subjects had to give two ratings during the assessment task. Thus, a direct assessment of the standard error of measurement could be used by a repeated measurement approach aside from the indirect consistency approach to reliability estimates of Cronbach's α (indirect assessment of the standard error of measurement) used in Experiment 1. On the other side, subjects gave their ratings after six paired comparisons of culpa levels with constant post-act event conditions. All three paired comparisons with the three apology stimulus combinations and all three paired comparisons with the three third-party-compensation stimulus combinations were given. Thus, two ratings were available for each of the six stimulus combinations and each pair of culpa levels was used twice. During the training phase, subjects were presented all of the stimuli levels of each one of the stimuli factors simultaneously (the two damage levels of Experiment 1 first, followed by the two post-act events, and then the three culpa levels) and rated them on the good-bad rating scale as in Experiment 1. Additionally, there were three pretrials of paired comparison, in which subjects first arranged the two correct story sequences and then indicated which of the two story events was better. Half of the subjects proceeded with the high damage level, the other half with the low damage level. This produced no effects on the results. After the main phase, a simplified procedure was run in a third phase to check its effect on the results. A damage level was shown and afterwards the three culpa levels were added verbally and subjects had to rate the combination of visible and auditory stimuli each. Subjects were twenty-five 5- to 6-year-olds, twenty-three 7-year-olds, and thirty-nine 8- to 9-year-olds, as well as 49 parents of the children. For adults, the procedure was shortened to a questionnaire format in which only ratings had to be made.

Three IQ subtests of the AID (Kubinger & Wurst, 1985) were given to each child similar to Experiment 1. Two of them were analog to the AV- and MT-subtests of the HAWIK-R used in Experiment 1, the third was the BO equivalent (Picture Arrangement). Since correlations and multiple regression analyses yielded no contradictory results to those of Experiment 1 (instead even nonsignificant multiple regression coefficients), these results are not discussed further in the result section of Experiment 2. However, the replicated absence of the correlations supported the conclusion that intellectual and emotional-evaluative components of the delictual capacity criteria have to be assessed with different methods.

Results

The mean age trends showed no main effect of age for the doghouse condition, but adults rated more harshly in the coachhouse condition, $F(1,70)=7.90$, $p=.006$. Both results once more contradicted Irving and Siegal (1983), who found a decrease in punishment with age. Also, the culpa effect was stronger in adults with the damage condition coachhouse, $F(2,140)=3.37$, $p=.037$. Within the groups of children, age had no effect on mean judgments of culpa levels. Furthermore, there was an age-correlated increase of the difference between ratings on the apology combinations and the third-party-compensation combinations. The conditions with third-party compensation by an insurance company were rated significantly worse than the conditions with apology only by the adults, and independently of the damage condition, $F(1,102)=21.86, p<.001$. This effect paralleled the increase in the distinction between apology and helping with repair found in the prior study. The means (standard deviations) of the children were -8.8 (2.9), -5.8 (4.4), and 1.2 (5.2) for purposeful, negligent, and inadvertent conditions (negative signs for the bad side of the scale), data for adults were -9.5 (2.4), -7.8 (2.9), and 1.4 (4.7). Thus, the negligent stimulus generally seemed to be definitely bad to all groups. There were clear, reliable individual differences in the evaluations when both types of measurement error were employed (see below). Also, clear age trends in the measurement error indicated that preschoolers' data were not reliable enough to make individual assessments of capacities. Thus, after taking into consideration the psychometric information, an age trend associated with the ratings of the culpa levels turned out to exist.

The analyses on the methodological aspects showed that the examined methodological aspects were irrelevant for the results. Group reliability estimates of the ratings and of the three rating differences among the culpa levels showed that children's ratings (0.76, 0.79, and 0.80 for decreasing culpa) and their rating differences (0.42, 0.76, and 0.72 for purpose-negligence, purpose-inadvertence, and negligence-inadvertence) were somewhat less reliable than adults' (0.86, 0.88, and 0.89 as well as 0.81, 0.85, and 0.88 for ratings and rating differences respectively), but high enough for the purpose-inadvertent and negligent-inadvertent differences (0.76 and 0.72) to have diagnostic impact. The standard deviations of the differences were 2.7, 5.8, and 5.5 for children and 2.2, 4.5, and 4.9 for adults. Among children, α estimates of reliability increased with age, but considerably more in the purpose-negligent differences (about 0.4) than in the two other differences (about 0.1). Similarly, across all age groups, direct assessments of the standard error of measurement decreased with age (6.9, 4.6, 2.9, and 2.3 in average, and 13.4, 10.6, 9.3, and 4.6 in the maximum individual standard error in the sequence of age). Finally, paired comparisons of children became more consistent in the choice tripels and in retests within their age range. Thus, the applicability of the procedure for the assessment of delictual competencies of minors of at least 7 years of age appeared to be psychometrically sound. In particular, the psychometrically based diagnoses of the direct and indirect assessment methods for the standard error of measurement produced less than 18% of discrepancies in the 85 children (versus 6% in adults). Also, diagnoses on the basis of ratings were the more secure diagnostic decisions, because the paired comparison procedure less frequently yielded (10%) contradictory results in cases of rating-based diagnoses (versus 36% the other way round). Comparison of the instruction phase, the main phase, and the final phase showed that in the final phase the same frequency of diagnoses for the distinction between purposeful and inadvertent (58 of 84 children) was obtained, whereas the two other diagnoses occurred slightly less often (5 to 6 depending on the standard error used). But, still, 42 children distinguished with $p<.05$ between the negligent and the inadvertent fire-setting in their judgments of the final phase. Thus, it appears that learning would not account for much of the competency diagnoses. Table 3 presents the main advantage gained from the reliability assessment in terms of revealing an age trend in the differences among the culpa levels that was not visible in the mean data and also not visible in the arbitrarily chosen numeric difference of one scale unit (lefthand side of Table 3) used as a measure of the knowledge of right and wrong as assessed by the rating response.

Table 3: Frequencies of Distinction Capacity Diagnoses of 4 Age Groups for 3 Assessment Procedures: Numeric Comparison of Individual Judgments, Psychometric Decision on the Basis of the Individual Measurement Error (Direct), Psychometric Decision on the Basis of Group Reliability (Indirect).

	Numeric					Psychometric									
						Direct ($p < .10$)					Indirect ($p < .05$)				
	Children				Adults	Children				Adults	Children				Adults
	5-6	7	8-9	Σ		5-6	7	8-9	Σ		5-6	7	8-9	Σ	
Purpose worse negligence	7	11	25	(43)	24	3	3	10	(16)	11	3	3	9	(15)	14
Elsewise	18	12	15	(45)	25	22	20	30	(72)	38	22	20	31	(72)	35
Purpose worse inadvertance	20	17	37	(74)	48	9	15	34	(58)	44	12	15	31	(58)	45
Elsewise	5	6	3	(14)	1	16	8	6	(30)	5	13	8	9	(30)	4
Negligence worse inadvertance	20	18	37	(75)	47	6	12	32	(50)	38	8	14	25	(47)	40
Elsewise	5	5	3	(13)	2	19	11	8	(38)	11	17	9	15	(41)	9

Table 3 shows that the number of individuals who can clearly ($p < .10$ as well as $p < .05$) be diagnosed to distinguish between purpose and inadvertent and between negligent and inadvertent fire-setting on psychometric grounds increased with age independently of the method of estimating the standard error of measurement. In particular, most preschoolers cannot be diagnosed as having the necessary capacities of judgment only if one of the two psychometric procedures is employed. Moreover Table 3 shows that, in contrast to the preschool students, the majority of 7-year-olds can still be diagnosed to have distinguished between inadvertent fire-setting and purposeful or negligent fire-setting, when psychometric procedures are applied to the judgments. This age trend drastically underlines another empirical part of the validity of the 7-year-age limit in the tort law of Germany, that is, the increase in the feasability of the assessments on the individual level.

These psychometrically based results add to those of Schleifer, Shultz, and Lefebre-Pinard (1983) who found, only reporting means of 5- and 7-year-olds, an onset of the distinction between inadvertent and voluntary as well as foreseeable damages but not between voluntary and foreseeable. Since the distinction between purposeful and negligent fire-setting was rare in children, in the reported psychometrically based diagnoses the conclusion was also substantiated that there may be no clear concept of negligence up to 10 years of age. Hook (1989), using a refined broken-cup task from Piaget (1932), claimed so merely on the basis of group means. However, employing the present methods allowed a more precise statement on an individual level. Finally, these results are in sharp contrast to

Tisak and Turiel (1984), who found no developmental trends (6 to 10 years) in several interview variables about a prudence incidence describing a child cutting the knee due to running too fast and falling down. The difference may be a consequence of several methodological dissimilarities in the approaches. But, it may indicate also that moral knowledge about negligence with respect to one's own damage develops earlier than moral knowledge about negligence with third-party damages. It is interesting that this was assumed by an Upper German Court (OLG Celle 1968, see Hommers, 1983, p. 26) with respect to a contributory negligence case in which the victim was a child. However, this cross-study conclusion would need direct research.

Discussion

To summarize the results on the two aspects for research of legal psychology in the tort law competencies:

De lege ferenda in support of the 7-year-age limit was found in the results: (a) two "disordinal" age trends in the means of preschool and elementary school students; (b) the presence of the apology effect in preschool students; and (c) in accordance with the low standard qualification "some understanding", signs of an ongoing development of that duty which is not taken to be relevant by the Supreme Court, i.e., the decrease of the rating differences between apology and no apology with age as well as the increasing distinction between the levels of apology and of helping with repair and between the levels of third-party compensation and of apology; and (d) the increase in the reliability of individual effect sizes from preschool to elementary school age.

De lege lata was relevant in the results (a) that the standard error estimates were sufficient for individual diagnoses from the age of seven years on; (b) that the psychometrically based distinction between the two or three culpa levels increased within elementary school age but was only rarely present in preschool students; (c) that the implicit Supreme Court theory on the indicativeness of knowledge of right and wrong for understanding the duty to make recompense was valid; and (d) that the diagnosis of competencies on the basis of indirect or direct reliability estimates was independent of intelligence measures and of learning within the task.

As a general consequence for forensic psychology, criticisms like those of Bresser (1988) against a trend in forensic or legal psychology that uses psychometrical, statistical, and mathematical-experimental methods seems unqualified. Apparently, such legal psychology can provide tools and results that are clearly useful for any scientifically defined de lege ferenda or de lege lata interface of psychology and law (see Steller, 1989, for another reply to Bresser's biographical position). Thus, even today, one should follow Marbe's (1913) example of introducing experimental and statistical procedures to the civil law expertise work of psychologists.

In contrast, the previous simplification strategy of basing expertise judgments on IQ measures alone (Bresser, 1972; Ell, 1983) is highly questionable. Conceptually, it misses the standards set by the Supreme Court. These are twofold: intellectual (use of adequate IQ subtests) and emotional-evaluative (use of the moral judgment task employed here). Empirically, it is in contrast to the zero correlations between the measures of the two standards. However, it is true that forensic expertise needs more complex (multi-method) integrational diagnostic reasoning than that involved in any one single diagnostic tool, as has been outlined by Wegener and Steller (1986) and Steller (1988). In support of their well-taken broad approach to forensic expertise judgments, it appears recommendable to extend the psychometrical research approach as employed here for a first time in a meaningful manner to other forensic fields in the interface between law and psychology.

References

Achenbach, T.M., & Edelbrock, C.S. (1981). Behavioral problems and competencies reported by parents of normal and disturbed children aged four through sixteen. *Monographs of the Society for Research in Child Development, 46*, (1, Serial No. 188).

Bresser, P.H. (1972). Die Beurteilung der Jugendlichen und Heranwachsenden im Straf- und Zivilrecht. In H. Göppinger, & H. Witter (Eds.), *Handbuch der Forensischen Psychiatrie*, Vol. 2. (pp. 1284-1313). Berlin: Springer.

Bresser, P.H. (1988). Über die Grenzen psychiatrischer Dokumentation: Was wird nicht abgebildet? *Forensia, 9*, 163-173.

Canter, D. (Ed.) (1980). *Fires and human behavior*. Chichester: Wiley.

Dauner, I. (1980). *Brandstiftung durch Kinder. Kriminologische, kinderpsychiatrische und rechtliche Aspekte* Bern: Huber.

Ell, E. (1983). *Wenn Kinder zündeln. Vorschläge zur Feuererziehung*. Tübingen: Katzmann.

Holland, C.J. (1969). Elimination of fire-setting in a seven-year-old boy. *Behaviour Research and Therapy, 7*, 135-137.

Hommers, W. (1983). *Die Entwicklungspsychologie der Delikts- und Geschäftsfähigkeit*. Göttingen: Hogrefe.

Hommers, W. (1986a). Non-Additivität als Beleg für die moralische Natur der Integration von Schaden und Ersatzleistungen. *Archiv für Psychologie, 138*, 71-90.

Hommers, W. (1986b). Zusammenwirken von Schaden und Ersatzleistung im moralischen Urteil. *Zeitschrift für Entwicklungspsychologie und Pädagogische Psychologie, 18*, 12-21.

Hommers, W. (1988a). Entschuldigung und Entschädigung für einen Diebstahl. *Zeitschrift für Entwicklungspsychologie und Pädagogische Psychologie, 20*, 121-133.

Hommers, W. (1988b). Die Wirkungen von Entschuldigung und Entschädigung auf Strafurteile über zwei Schadensarten. *Zeitschrift für Sozialpsychologie, 19*, 139-151.

Hommers, W. (1989). Die Entwicklung der Einsicht in das Delikt. In S. Bäuerle (Ed.), *Kriminalität bei Schülern: Ursachen und Umfeld von Schülerkriminalität*, Vol. 1 (pp. 97-116). Stuttgart: Angewandte Psychologie.

Hook, J.G. (1989). Heider's foreseeability level of attribution: Does it come after intentionality? *Child Development, 60*, 1212-1217.

Huber, H.P. (1973). *Psychometrische Einzelfalldiagnostik*. Weinheim: Beltz.

Irving, K., & Siegal, M. (1983). Mitigating circumstances in children's perceptions of criminal justice: The case of an inability to control events. *British Journal of Developmental Psychology, 1*, 179-188.

Kubinger, K.D., & Wurst, E. (1985). *AID. Adaptives Intelligenzdiagnostikum*. Weinheim: Beltz.

Leon, M. (1982). Rules in children's moral judgments: Integration intent, damage, and rational information. *Developmental Psychology, 18*, 835-842.

Marbe, K. (1913). Psychologische Gutachten zum Prozeß wegen des Mülheimer Eisenbahnunglücks. *Fortschritte der Psychologie und ihrer Anwendungen, 1*, 339-374.

Piaget, J. (1932). *Le jugement moral chez l'enfant*. Paris: Alcan.

Prins, H. (1986). *Dangerous behavior, the law, and mental disorder*. London: Tavistock.

Schleifer, M., Shultz, T.R., & Lefebre-Pinard, M. (1983). Children's judgments of causality, responsibility, and punishment in cases of harm due to omission. *British Journal of Developmental Psychology, 1*, 87-97.

Steller, M. (1988). Standards der forensisch-psychologischen Begutachtung. *Monatsschrift für Kriminologie und Strafrechtsreform, 71*, 16-27.

Steller, M. (1989). Gemälde oder Bauwerke? Anmerkungen zur Objektivierung der forensischen Begutachtung. *Monatsschrift für Kriminologie und Strafrechtsreform, 72*, 155-159.

Tewes, U. (1983). *Hamburg-Wechsler-Intelligenztest für Kinder, Revision 1983*. Bern: Huber.

Tisak, M.S., & Turiel, E. (1984). Children's conceptions of moral and prudential rules. *Child Development, 55*, 1030-1039.

Undeutsch, U. (1967). Delikthaftung junger Menschen. In U. Undeutsch (Ed.), *Forensische Psychologie* (pp. 567-597). Göttingen: Hogrefe.

Waibel, E. (1970). *Verschuldensfähigkeit*. Berlin: Duncker & Humblot.

Wegener, H. (1981). *Einführung in die Forensische Psychologie*. Darmstadt: Wissenschaftliche Buchgesellschaft.

Wegener, H., & Steller, M. (1986). Psychologische Diagnostik vor Gericht. Methodische und ethische Probleme forensisch-psychologischer Diagnostik. *Zeitschrift für Differentielle und Diagnostische Psychologie, 7*, 103-126.

The Legislation of Organ Donation

Dick J. Hessing, Henk Elffers, and Frank T. de Charro

Introduction

With great regularity, newspaper stories appear about the extreme shortage of donor organs for transplantation, recently accompanied by the mention of unsavory practices. At the end of 1988, one could read about the sale of organs from Third World countries for large amounts of money, especially in West Germany. In the summer of 1989, advertisements appeared in Dutch newspapers in which large sums of money were offered in exchange for organs. These developments can hardly be surprising for those who are familiar with the backgrounds to the shortage in organs. The number of people in the Netherlands waiting for a kidney transplant is more than twice as high as the number of transplants performed each year, resulting in waiting times of several years before a transplantation can take place.

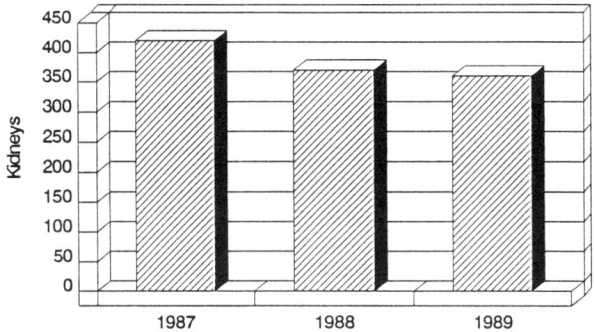

Figure 1: Kidneys Retrieved in the Netherlands 1987 - 1989.

As can be seen in Figure 1, the number of kidneys that became available after post mortem organ donation in the Netherlands decreased from 417 in 1987 to 361 in 1989. This explains the decreasing number of patients who could receive a post mortem donor kidney from 413 in 1987 to 366 in 1988.

The shortage in donor organs can possibly be related to the lack of a law regulating the donation of organs. Some months ago, an Organ Donation Bill was announced that will be based on an opting in system. The consent of a person to donate his/her organs for transplantation after death will be the criterion: If such a will - positive or negative - is missing, the relatives will be asked for their consent. One of the aims of this bill is to increase the supply of organs.

Opting in or Opting out?

Ever since the discussion on a legal regulation of organ donation started, the adherents of two systems have opposed each other: those who favor an opting in system and those who are in favor of an opting out system.

In the strict opting in system, the organs of the deceased may only be taken out when the deceased him/herself has given permission through a donor card or through a commitment in a central register. In a strict opting out system, the explantation of organs is permitted unless the deceased him/herself has made objections. So, neither system has reserved a place for the relatives! However, in daily practice, we can observe that, almost always, a variation of either system is used in which surviving relatives are consulted, and the differences between both systems are small indeed in these situations. In fact, only the question that is put to the relatives will differ. Therefore, the discussion between the adherents of both systems seems to be a theoretical-dogmatic discussion, and not a practical one. Moreover, this discussion has become obsolete through the practice in other (European) countries: Contrary to expectations the supply of organs in countries with an opting out system is not always larger than the supply in countries with an opting in system. Both systems - in the way they are implemented and used - do not by themselves guarantee an optimal harvesting of donor organs. This calls into question the choice made in the Organ Donation Bill: Which factors should be taken into account in a new law, when one of the aims of that law, is to increase the supply of donor organs?

The Attitude Toward Organ Donation

Quite apart from the question regarding which system the government will choose in the end, the attitude of the population toward organ donation remains the essential point. A law that will not be in keeping with that attitude is doomed to fail.

Since the beginning of the 1970s, research has been undertaken into the attitudes and behavior of the Dutch people with regard to organ donation. In 1977, only 3% carried a donor card; in 1988, this had increased to 8% (Hessing, 1983); and, at present, 20% report that they have signed a donor card. Research shows that about 50% do indeed carry such a card regularly, which results in 10% effective donor card carriers.

In recent years, there seems to have been hardly any change in this pattern. Only the commotion about the (alleged) sale of organs - at the end of 1989 - resulted in a slight downward trend, but this trend has already been corrected. Both at the end of 1989 and in May 1990, samples of the Dutch population (220 and 1,007 respectively) were asked the following question: "How do you feel about donating your organs after your death?" (Hessing, de Charro, & Akkermans, 1991). The results are presented in Table 1.

The following picture of the donor card carrier emerges from these studies: young, well-educated, belonging to a higher professional level, not a churchgoer, and often a blood donor. With regard to the personality of the donor card carrier, it was observed that they are - more than others - directed toward the interests of the community, less egocentric/egoistic, and they feel less alienated from society.

Table 1: Willingness to Donate Organs 1989 - 1990 (%).

		1989	1990
A	I am willing to donate and I have signed a donor card	20	20
B	I am willing to donate but I do not have a donor card	26	32
C	I doubt whether I want to or not / I have never thought about it	44	41
D	I refuse to donate	9	7

This profile exactly resembles the profile described by Hessing (1983) and again emphasizes the conclusion that there is a maximum to the number of people who are (or will be) willing to sign and carry a donor card, and that that maximum has probably been reached by now. This observation, coupled to the fact that at least 50% of the total population must carry such a card before shortages in this field can be brought to an end, leads to the conclusion that - at least under the current bill - the problem of shortages will never be solved.

The Attitude Toward Organ Donation: A Closer Look

The data in Table 1 give an impression of the willingness to donate. In order to make an analysis of the effects of variants of systems of organ donation, several additional assumptions must be made. These assumptions represent a further elaboration of the pattern presented in Table 1. It especially involves splitting up Groups B, C, and D that are differentiated in Table 1. This is relevant since part of the Organ Donation Bill is a system of national registration of donors. The goal is to present an estimate of the effective donor percentage, which will be defined as the percentage of donor reportings in which - based on the legal system and the behavior of the surviving relatives - organ donation can take place (apart from medical criteria!).

To be able to create Table 2, we make the simple assumption for Groups A and B that all of Group A will register as donors and none of Group B will register as donors in the national registration. To avoid fictitious precision, Group A will be set at 20 % and Group B at 30%. By registering as a donor, there will be a group with an "explicit positive" attitude, which will be Group 1 in Table 2; and a group with an "implicit positive" attitude, which will be Group 2 in Table 2. In general, direct surviving relatives will be informed about the positive attitude. However, explicit legal evidence is lacking here.

Group C requires a further analysis, because the doubt expressed here can have different sources. This group contains - see Table 1 - about 40% of the total number of respondents. One of the sources for doubt can be that the person prefers to leave the decision to his/her surviving relatives. The decision in this case is therefore implicitly delegated. Also the pros and cons of organ donation can be in balance for the person. In this case, doubt can be defined as a neutral position. In all other cases, doubt can be related to a resistance to organ donation that one is unwilling to express, and the doubt is in fact a cloak for a negative attitude. The three implicit sources for doubt - delegation, neutrality, and covert resistance - are, for the sake of argument, set at 15, 15, and 10% (together again 40%) of the total number of respondents in Table 1. These groups can be found in Table 2 as the groups *implicitly delegating* (Group 3), *implicitly neutral* (Group 4) and *implicitly negative* (Group 5).

Table 2: Attitude of Six Groups Toward Organ Donation.

Group	Attitude	Proportion (%)
1	Explicitly positive	20
2	Implicitly positive	30
3	Implicitly delegating	15
4	Implicitly neutral	15
5	Implicitly negative	15
6	Explicitly negative	5
	Total	100

Those people that are not willing to donate will probably lack the motivation to have themselves registered. This underestimation of refusals in a national registration must for the sake of the analyses lead to a splitting up of Group D (respondents who are not willing to donate) into a part that will have his/her opinion registered, and a part that will not do so. In general, relatives will be informed of the opinion of the deceased when no registration has taken place. This underregistration will be implemented in the analyses by dividing Group D into two equally large groups (both 5%) of persons who will and persons who will not register. The part that will register will be added to the group of doubting persons in Table 2 whose attitude actually was implicitly negative. The result is that Group 5 in Table 2 has an implicit negative attitude that has two sources: 10% doubters and 5% refusers who are unwilling to register.

The results presented in Table 2 offer the possibility of evaluating different legal organ donation systems with regard to their effectivity in supplying organs for transplantation.

From Table 2 it can be surmised that only 25% of the population will reach an explicit position. This can be related to the psychological barriers that keep people from taking an active position with regard to organ donation after death (Hessing, 1983). Any law on organ donation is therefore mainly a law for cases in which the will of the deceased is not fixed. Only 5% of the population are explicit opponents to organ donation after death. The support for organ donation is much greater than the resistance against donation, but it is made manifest with great difficulty. If the legislator wants to increase the number of organs for transplantation, the task of activating the passive support of the population through a legal decisional framework must inevitably be faced. This can be done by introducing a strict opting out system or by giving the surviving relatives a delegated power of decision in which they can either give consent or make objections against donation. There is no a priori reason on ethical grounds to prefer one system to the other.

Legal Systems for Donation of Organs

To describe the effects of several systems for organ donation, a classification of 12 organ donation systems (A to H) is presented. When calculating the consequences, two alternatives were supposed for the outcome of the possible judgment of surviving relatives. The first alternative is based on an opting in or opting out rate of the surviving relatives of 50%, the second alternative on a rate of 65%.

The systems differ not only in a strict legal division of decisional power but also with regard to the expectation about the extent to which relatives - if they are qualified - take into account in their own judgment the judgment of the deceased. We are dealing here therefore with combinations of legal characteristics and behavioral patterns, as - as a matter of fact - is always the case in the formation of a judgment on legal systems.

The systems of organ donation are classified as follows:

A   *a strict opting in system*, in which post mortem organ donation is only possible in the cases belonging to Group 1 in which the deceased has made an explicit positive will.

B   *a limited additional opting in system*, in which the wills of Group 1 and Group 6 are being observed and relatives decide in cases belonging to Group 2.

With 50% positive decisions of relatives, the effective rate of donation will be 35% (20+0.5 x 30) of all cases.

C   *a broad additional opting in system*, in which the wills of Group 1 and Group 6 are observed and relatives decide in cases belonging to Groups 2, 3, and 4.

With 50% positive decisions of relatives, the effective rate of donation will be 50% (20+0.5 x (30+15+15)) of all cases.

D   *a limited replacement opting in system*, in which the wills of Group 1 and Group 6 are observed and relatives decide in cases belonging to Groups 2, 3, 4, and 5.

With 50% positive decisions of relatives, the effective rate of donation will be 57.5% (20+0.5 x (30+15+15+15)) of all cases.

E   *a broad replacement opting in system*, in which the wills of Group 1 and Group 26 are not recognized and relatives decide in the cases belonging to Groups 1 to 6.

With 50% positive decisions of relatives, the effective donation rate will be 50%.

F   *a limited additional opting out system*, in which the wills of Group 1 and Group 6 are observed and relatives decide in cases belonging to Group 5.

With 50% positive decisions of relatives, no opting out will take place in 87.5% (100-5-0.5 x 15) of all cases.

G   *a broad additional opting out system*, in which the wills of Group 1 and Group 6 are observed and relatives decide in cases belonging to Groups 3, 4, and 5.

With 50% positive decisions of relatives, no opting out will take place in 72.5% (100-5-0.5 x (15+15+15)) of all cases.

H   *a limited replacement opting out system*, in which the wills of Group 1 and Group 6 are observed and relatives decide in cases belonging to Groups 2, 3, 4, and 5.

With 50% positive decisions of relatives, no opting out will take place in 57.5% (100-5-0.5 x (30+15+15+15)) of all cases.

I   *a broad replacement opting out system*, in which the wills of Group 1 and Group 6 are not recognized and relatives decide in the cases belonging to Groups 1, 2, 3, 4, and 5.

With 50% positive decisions of relatives, no opting out will take place in 50% of all cases.

    J   *a strict opting out system*, in which post mortem organ donation is only impossible in cases belonging to Group 6 in which the deceased has made an explicit negative will.

    K   *a complete decision system within an opting in system*, in which the wills of Group 1 and Group 6 are observed and permission for post mortem donation is denied by law in all cases belonging to Groups 2, 3, 4, and 5. This system is in essence identical to system A.

    L   *a complete decision system within an opting out system*, in which the wills of Group 1 and Group 6 are observed and by law there is permission for post mortem donation in all cases belonging to Groups 2, 3, 4, and 5.

The effective donor percentage can now be calculated for the above-mentioned systems for both levels of permission of surviving relatives and is presented in Table 3.

Table 3: Classification of a Number of Legal Systems for Organ Donation.

System	Definition	Effective donation rate (%)	
		Permission rate of relatives of deceased (%)	
		(50)	(65)
A	Strict opting in system	20.0	20.0
B	Limited additional opting in system	35.0	39.5
C	Broad additional opting in system	50.0	59.0
D	Limited replacement opting in system	57.5	68.8
E	Broad replacement opting in system	50.0	65.0
F	Limited additional opting out system	87.5	89.8
G	Broad additional opting out system	72.5	79.3
H	Limited replacement opting out system	57.5	68.8
I	Broad replacement opting out system	50.0	65.0
J	Strict opting out system	95.0	95.0
K	Complete decision system + opting in system	20.0	20.0
L	Complete decision system + opting out system	95.0	95.0

It can be observed that the effective donor percentage always remains between 50 and 95%, except for systems A, B, and L. Systems F to K result in a relatively high donation percentage when - next to the negative will - explicitly positive wills are also observed. Percentages of organ donation are higher in systems in which the relatives play a part (B to I) when they have a more positive attitude toward organ donation. In these systems, the legal system is a slightly better reflection of the dynamics in society with regard to the attitude toward organ donation. The Dutch Organ Donation Bill shows the characteristics of System D. When one is optimistic about the attitude of the relatives in cases in which the deceased had an implicit positive attitude toward donation, the Organ Donation Bill will show more similarities with System G, because the relatives cannot use their power of decision to obstruct an implicit positive attitude of the deceased.

The legislator could also opt for an opting out system in which relatives are presented with the possibility of objecting to donation when there is no known positive or negative will - donor card or registration. In that situation, it is more clearly indicated that it is desired to observe a not explicit but yet positive attitude of the deceased.

More Organs?

An important question is whether the Dutch Organ Donation Bill will result in an increase in the number of organs for transplantation. In answering this question, several factors should be taken into account. First, sending donor cards will only be effective for those people who currently report that they are willing to donate but do not have a donor card (yet). After all, given the enormous number of donor cards that have already been distributed and given all the advertisements on radio and television in recent years, it is unlikely that that people who are now doubting or refusing to donate, will be persuaded by simply sending a donor card. However, success with implicit positive persons, who do not carry a card but are willing to donate, will also be small. Many of these deliberately do not carry a card. The (small) gain that can be obtained with persons that doubt and persons who are willing to donate but not carrying a card could be destroyed by the emergence of a "reactance" under present donor card carriers: the phenomenon that people show when behavior becomes (more) mandatory: they will resist (more). This reaction could be the result of the loss of the altruistic element in the behavior, and consequently a part of them will not be willing to send in a signed donor card.

There also remains the question whether the present donor card carriers (and those who now report that they are willing to donate but nonetheless do not carry a card) will appreciate such a registration. It is highly possible that they regard such a registration as too compulsory, too absolute, with negative consequences.

One of the aims of the Organ Donation Bill is to increase the number of transplantable organs. By choosing some form of consent system, this aim will not be effective. The conclusion must be that there is a grave danger that once this bill will come into force a decrease in the supply of organs will result if no supplementary measures will be taken.

Required Consultation

The number of potential (kidney) donors is much greater than the number of donor reportings. The attitude of people working in hospitals is therefore crucial for harvesting organs. This notion was the reason for Caplan (1984) to advocate a "Required Request" system in the United States. This required request system implies that, after a patient (who could be a suitable donor) has been declared brain dead, the body-preserving measures may not be stopped before it is checked whether the deceased did have a donor card or not. When such a card is not found, the family must be asked if they consent to organ explantation for transplantation.

Legislators of different states in the USA have implemented this required request system (or a variant of it) into their legal system. The first was implemented in Oregon in 1985. A required request law also came into force on a federal level. This law makes payments out of such funds as Medicare and Medicaid to a certain hospital dependent on whether that hospital has a required request protocol or not.

Next to the required request system, a "Routine Inquiry" system was suggested. In the first system, relatives *must be asked* to consent or object; in the second system, they *must be offered* the possibility to donate the organs. A third variant is the "Routine Referral" system, in which external specialists on the field of organ donation (e.g., a transplant coordinator) must be brought in in a case of death in a hospital.

Since in the Netherlands many people are in favor of a legal power of decision for surviving relatives, some form of required consultation or required request system deserves serious attention. The required consultation/request system as such is not linked exclusively with either an opting in system or opting out system, when, in the less strict variants of these systems, consultation with the relatives takes place.

The Dutch population has a positive attitude toward the introduction of a required consultation/request system. This can be concluded from the results of another question asked in the May 1990 study (Hessing et al., 1991). The question was:

> There is a great shortage in donor organs for transplantation in the Netherlands. Amongst other things this is because many people who are willing to donate still have not signed a donor card. Therefore, it is considered to introduce a new law. This law will state that, when the attitude of the deceased is unknown, doctors in hospitals are obliged to ask the surviving relatives whether they consent to donation. The relatives may then consent or they may object. What is your attitude toward such a law?

Among those who under the present system are willing to donate after death we find significantly more supporters of a required consultation/request system than under the doubters and refusers. The opponents of a required consultation/request system stem mainly from the group that already has more problems with donating organs after death. It can be suggested that their attitude toward such a system is partly the result of their attitude toward donation itself.

Table 4: Relation Between Willingness to Donate and Attitude Toward a Required Consultation/Required Request System.

	A good system	No opinion	Not a good system	Total
Willing to donate (with/without donor card)	352 (67%)	24 (5%)	152 (29%)	528 (52%)
Doubting or refusing to donate	215 (45%)	104 (22%)	160 (33%)	479 (48%)
Total	567 (56%)	128 (13%)	312 (31%)	1007 (100%)

Introduction of a required consultation/request system can take place as an addition to an opting in or opting out system. Only in the case in which there is no place for surviving relatives, there is no use for a required consultation/request system. Prior to the obligation to approach relatives, there can be an obligation to consult the donor registration or to search for a donor card.

Conclusions

It seems highly improbable that the supply of organs will increase significantly by registering positive and negative wills only. It even must be feared that the registering of something that is so strongly associated with one's own death will remain an insurmountable barrier for many people. In these cases, required consultation or request seems to offer a solution. We prefer a variant in which there is an obligation to inform the relatives of the possibility to donate organs of the deceased. In exceptional cases, it should be possible to deviate from this obligation, for instance, when it is already known that surviving relatives have religious objections or will develop great emotional problems. Given the predominant positive attitude of the Dutch population toward the introduction of some form of required consultation with surviving relatives, this seems an adequate solution of the Dutch shortage.

It can be expected that the system that will eventually be introduced in the Netherlands will in any case observe the written negative decision of the deceased. As a result of that, the system will be a regulation for those cases in which there is no written opinion of the deceased. No matter what, in these cases one would like to let the result of the benefit of the doubt be in favor of donation. After all, otherwise the number of donations would drop to the very low level in which the deceased gave explicit permission. We firmly believe that the legislator should also explicitly state that organ donation will be given the benefit of the doubt. This can be done by taking the opting out system as the point of departure for consultation with surviving relatives.

References

Caplan, A. L. (1984). Ethical and policy issues in the procurement of cadaver organs for transplantation. *New England Journal of Medicine, 311*, 981-983.
Hessing, D. J. (1983). *De onsterfelijkheid benaderd: Een onderzoek naar de bereidheid tot postmortale orgaandonatie* [An approach to immortality: A study into the willingness to donate organs after death]. Lisse: Swets & Zeitlinger.
Hessing, D.J., de Charro, F.Th., & Akkermans, P.W.C. (1991). Psycholegal aspects of organ procurement systems. In W. Land, & J.B. Dossetor (Eds.), *Ethics, justice, and commerce in organ replacement therapy* (pp. 289-292). Berlin: Springer.

Jung's Psychology Adopted in Law

Martin Usteri and Georges Baur

Introduction

As a result of its dominant position in nature and the history of evolution, humanity is unique: It is the sole creature capable not only of understanding and influencing its environment but also of dominating it (Jakob, 1987, p. 9).

After the satisfaction of basic drives, what most interests humanity is living together with others. This is why the question of rights and justice is one of the oldest problems of the human race.

That the results of thinking in terms of law, the making of law, and the application of law are not merely products of conscious reason applied to objective facts might be illustrated by the following quotation from Montesquieu. Not only did he, the French national philosopher, have a tremendous influence upon his own and subsequent generations, but also his major work, "De l'Esprit des Lois" (1748) proved him to be a protagonist of constitutional state research. "Les lois rencontrent toujours les passions et les préjugés du legislateur. Quelquefois elles passent au travers, et s'y teignent; quelquefois elles y restent et s'y incorporent" (Montesquieu, 1973, p. 298).

This perception can be applied in particular to public and to constitutional law. Even the Greek philosophers of Antiquity concerned themselves with the phenomenon of "the State." Plato asserted that "in the form of the outer community the forces determining the inner human" could be recognized (Imboden, 1974, p. 142). From this fundamental idea, Johann Jakob Bachofen coined the phrase, "The State derives from the innermost nature of the human" (Imboden, 1974, p. 142).

The following example may help to illustrate: The building of the French State went as far as the "Grande Peur" before being surrounded by Habsburg, and later Spain and Germany. This is confirmed by statements made by Napoleon I (1808), Chateaubriand (1822), and the Foreign Minister of Napoleon III (1870). The latter led, in connection with the disputed Spanish succession of the throne of 1867, to the French-German War. In his comprehensive work on Richelieu, Carl J. Burckhardt (1967) shows in minute detail how this great statesman skillfully utilized the fear of the French to construct the powerful centralist state appropriate to this fear. Burckhardt recognized in this fear of being surrounded by enemy powers one of those collective states of fear that certainly can initially be caused by objective events, but that also are transmitted and reactivated long after the concrete event is past history. Thus, for example, one sees in the background of recent events the renewed fear in France of a united Germany.

The goal of the method to be described here today is to provide some thoughts for research into unconscious spiritual impulses influencing law.

History

That law derives not only from the common sense of human beings but is also influenced by their irrational acts, as suggested above, is not a new idea: Plato had already established this in classical Antiquity and Augustine applied it to Christianity (see Imboden, 1974, p. 140). Later references are found in the writings of Bodin, Montesquieu, Rousseau, and Tocqueville. Also continuing this tradition were many others, including the historical Savigny school of law, as well as some Swiss, such as Bluntschli, Hilty, Troxler and Huber, to name but a few (Schindler, 1975, pp. 17-30). The "actual" psychologists of law should also be mentioned, that is, those who, in contrast to the authors named above, placed psychology at the center of their investigations. Here, above all, Ernst Rudolf Bierling, Wilhelm Wundt, and Leon von Petrazycki should be mentioned (Jakob, 1987, pp. 12-14).

Particularly in Switzerland after the middle of the 1930s, well-known jurists developed psychological theories of law oriented to a large extent toward the psychology of C. G. Jung. Of note are Fehr, Schindler, Imboden, and Marti (see Imboden, 1974, p. 143; Pahud de Mortanges, 1987, pp. 187-190).

The Psychology of C. G. Jung

The psychology of C. G. Jung, along with the theories of Freud, has proven to be a most useful resource for interpretation and insight.

Central to Jung's psychological ideas is the interpretation of dreams. Their use in the treatment of individual conflicts is a matter of course in psychological circles and founded on the premise that dreams consist of the generally known and spontaneous impulses of the unconscious (Abt, 1978, p. 27).

Freud postulated that the dream speaks of the affairs of the soul in veiled forms, which then need to be uncovered. Jung responded that the dream indeed "speaks" to us unclearly and that something meant as a warning, for example, is often perceived as such only after an accident. This, however, is not, as Freud thought, due to a "censor preventing the messages of the dream from passing through directly," but rather corresponds to the phenomenon we can observe when we switch on an electric light next to a burning candle: Clarity and sharpness fade and dreams appear to us "only as vague analogies." By its very definition, however, a dream would never be able to provide a clear thought, for then it would not be a dream but a thought crossing over the threshold of consciousness (von Franz, 1972, pp. 116-117).

As an aid to the understanding of Jung's method of dream interpretation, a brief presentation of his ideas about the contents of the human psyche, the personal and the collective unconscious and the archetypes, will now be given:

The personal unconscious is the superficial layer. It consists of the wishes, thoughts, and impulses that slumber in everyone, contents that are rejected by consciousness, for we are able to consciously grasp only very few contents at any one time; these can, however, be raised to consciousness again at any time. Others have been repressed because they are unpleasant for various reasons or simply forgotten or subliminally perceived, as with further thoughts and feelings of every kind. We think, for example, of those who complain about military service today and then tomorrow describe it as the happiest time in their lives: They have repressed the unpleasantnesses!

The personal unconscious rests upon a deeper layer, the so-called collective unconscious, which is not individual but rather, as the name implies, of a more general nature. That is to say, it contains, in contrast to the personal psyche, contents and behavior patterns found everywhere and equally in everyone. The following can serve to define the term "collective unconscious":

The collective unconscious is a part of the psyche that can be negatively distinguished from a personal unconscious by the fact that it does not, like the latter, owe its existence to personal experience and consequently is not a personal acquisition. While the personal unconscious is made up essentially of contents that have at one time been conscious but that have disappeared from consciousness through having been forgotten or repressed, the contents of the collective unconscious have never been in consciousness, and therefore have never been individually acquired, but owe their existence exclusively to heredity (Jung, 1959, p. 42).

The contents of the collective unconscious are the archetypes. These are general patterns and images that have existed since far back in time and are also present in myths, sagas, and fairy tales, and have symbolic character. Theodore Abt (1978) defines them as follows:

> If we understand instincts as typical behavior patterns, then the archetypes, as the inner aspects thereof, are typical patterns of imagination. They constitute inborn structural dispositions, which become topical in the inner field of vision of the individual as feelings, ideas, representations of the imagination, opinions, etc., which are universally human and thus the same or similar in everyone. The fact that mythological, religious and moral representations or rules are found in similar or identical form in peoples known to be not in any form of cultural connection shows this clearly, as does the fact that we can regularly observe the surfacing of dream symbols, representations, etc., of which the dreamer does not have a clue that they are examples of collective images or ideas that have already been known somewhere and sometime before. (p. 22)

Jung employed the so-called amplification method for bringing forth the meaning and significance of such images in dream interpretation.

The Amplification Method

Jolande Jacobi (1984), a pupil of Jung, described the amplification method as follows:

> Amplification, in contrast to the Freudian method of reductio in primam figuram, is not an unbroken chain of causally connected associations leading backward, but a process by which the dream content is broadened and enriched with the help of analogous images. The associations - and here again it differs from the "free association" method - are not provided only by the patient or dreamer but also by the analyst. Indeed, the analogies contributed by the analyst often determine the direction of the patient's associations. With all their rich variety, these images and analogies will be reasonably close to the dream content that is to be interpreted, whereas there is no way of controlling free association and preventing it from straying too far from the dream content . . . . Amplification must be applied to all the elements of the dream if we are to form a total picture from which the "meaning" can be deciphered. In Jung's amplification method the various dream motifs

are enriched by analogous, related images, symbols, legends myths, etc., which throw light on their diverse aspects and possible meanings, until their significance stands out in full clarity. Each element of meaning thus obtained is linked with the next, until the whole chain of dream motifs is revealed and the whole dream as a unit can be subjected to a final verification (pp. 87-89).

Why should we not also make an attempt of this sort in the field of law? On the basis of this definition, Usteri (1987, p. 419) has coined the term "amplificatory method of law."

The Amplificatory Method in Law

The Amplificatory Method in Law is based, as mentioned previously, on extending our view of law to the irrational elements of human existence. The unconscious, consciousness, language, feelings, sensations and spirit are all active in the life of the individual and the community (Marti, 1958, pp. 8-9). If, in the text of Jolande Jacobi on the amplification method, we replace the term "dream content" with "legal norm" or "legal problem," the possibility of an application to the science and practice of law becomes apparent (Usteri, 1987, p. 419).

In the example of the witch hunt, we recognize a rationally unexplainable reaction in the unconscious of a collective group that fears certain persons behaving in ways that perhaps do not conform to societal norms. If we were to analyze the relevant (fear-) dreams, we would probably get inconclusive, vague results. With the assistance of the archetype, that is, the common mystical fear (of magicians, witches, etc.), and by making a comparison with fairy tales (Hansel and Gretel and Snow White, to name some very simple examples) of a corresponding sort, the subliminal fears and apprehensions of the populace of the Middle Ages and their resulting reactions become much more understandable.

Archetypes play an important role in law. Criminal law is a legal area in which a knowledge of archetypal representations contributes greatly to answering the question of why certain acts have always been considered criminal or have been considered by a society as deserving punishment.

One example of such an "archetypal offense" is incest (Pahud de Mortanges, 1987, p. 197), which is prohibited in nearly every culture. Rationally this may be explained as the attempt to prevent degeneration of the species, but psychologically behind this we find the so-called Oedipus-complex, the drive of the soul for security. This would appear to be confirmed by the fact that the "classical" Oedipal constellation (mother-son) has always been considered criminal, whereas incest between father and daughter or between siblings has only "frequently" been so (Pahud de Mortanges, 1987).

Other "archetypal crimes" are, for example, abortion, euthanasia, and murder in general. "Banning," or forcing a member out of the social group to which he or she belongs, corresponding to "psychic death," must be considered "archetypal punishment." This institution has been preserved down to the present and can be seen today in the form of the loss of civil rights (recently in part rescinded) or the banning of a foreigner from a country (Article 55, § 1 of the Swiss Penal Code). Other forms of punishment such as imprisonment or the death penalty can also be traced back to archetypal images (Pahud de Mortanges, 1987, pp. 198-204).

In the laws of marriage, the principle of monogamy can also be explained archetypally: It is the form appropriate for life. Polygamy is an exception found only in situations of overpopulation or war-caused or other decimation of one of the sexes (Fechner, 1987, p. 130).

Finally, one also finds in contract law, for example, the principle of reciprocity. In the case of an obvious disproportion of performance, Article 21, § 1 of the Swiss Law of Obligations allows for withdrawal from a contract. This corresponds to a basic principle also found in many other systems of law with archetypal content (Pahud de Mortanges, 1987, p. 193).

At the outset, we expressed particular interest in the reasons for the specific form of a constitution or type of State. At this point, Hans Marti's (1958) study of the background of the Swiss Federal Constitution, a study representative of several others, shall be looked at more closely.[1] Marti concentrates on what he considers to be three most important archetypes: the "great mother," the "great father", and "transformation."

The archetypal image of the "great father" (Marti, 1958, pp. 30-70) mediates by means of its "liberal economic character" the patriarchal-conservative ideas of freedom and risk, for example, in the area of the economy or strict conformity to the constitution in the area of constitutional law. In stark contrast stands the form of the "great mother" (pp. 96-142) the protective motherly element. Foremost here are existential help in the present and safeguards for the future, as well as greater emphasis on the collective rather than protection of the individual. According to Marti both are static aspects of law. A third component is the archetypal image of "transformation" (1958, pp. 71-95). This archetype embodies the dynamic aspect of law, for example, revisions of law or the constitution. Today in this connection, we often encounter the problem of bureaucracy or an increase of interventions by the State. According to Marti's interpretation, these problems can be explained psychologically by the opposition of the "great father" and the "great mother" archetypes. Greatly simplified, one could say: The increasingly all-providing State corresponds to the ever greater presence of the "great mother" archetype, which presumably can be attributed to growing uncertainty and a fear of responsibility in the collective unconscious.

> The increase of matriarchal components in the legal constitutional order shows ... this double aspect: on the one side, there is evidence of a deficient flight to the great mother; on the other, however, there are indications of a conscious appreciation of the motherly world and thus also for a tendency toward a truly human order that does not attempt an - impossible - synthesis between matriarchal and patriarchal components, but rather recognizes both in a balanced relationship of tension, an order allowing both the masculine and the feminine sides of the human being to unfold.

This was written by Hans Marti in 1958 while under the influence of the strongly patriarchal system dominant in Switzerland at that time. In the subsequent 30 years, the scale has

---

[1] Although not specifically mentioned, it may be assumed that this has made use of the method described here.

visibly tilted strongly to the side of the "great mother" while the "masculine" side has retreated to the background.

We can agree with Marti's vision of a truly human order on the condition that this always consists of a truly desirable goal (Wunschbild), and that it continues to be one. The knowledge of its complexity is the real secret of a functioning State (Imboden, 1974, p. 220). This would also be a step toward an anthropoetic State (Usteri, 1987, p. 418).

References

Abt, T. (1978). *Entwicklungsplanung ohne Seele?* Bern: Hallwag.
Bossard, R. (1985). *Recht und Psychologie*, Referat gehalten anlässlich des Seminars "Recht und Psychologie" der Uni Zürich, Einsiedeln.
Burckhardt, C. J. (1967). Aenaeas-Silvius Lecture on: Richelieu, 3 volumes (1935, 1961, 1966, München: Callwey). In *Basler Nachrichten, 487,* 6.
Fechner, E. (1987). Rechtsphilosophie. In R. Jakob & M. Rehbinder (Eds.), *Beiträge zur Rechtspsychologie*, (pp. 125-133). Berlin: Duncker & Humblot.
Franz, M.- L. von (1972). *C. G. Jung.* Frauenfeld: Huber.
Imboden, M. (1974). *Politische Systeme.* Basel: Helbling & Lichtenhahn.
Jacobi, J. (1984). *Die Psychologie von C.G. Jung.* Frankfurt/M.: Fischer.
Jakob, R. (1987). Rechtspsychologie. In R. Jakob & M. Rehbinder (Eds.), *Beiträge zur Rechtspsychologie*, (pp. 9-23). Berlin: Duncker & Humblot.
Jung, C. G. (1959). *Collected works, Vol. 9/1.* Princeton: Princeton University Press.
Marti, H. (1958). *Urbild und Verfassung.* Basel: Helbling & Lichtenhahn.
Montesquieu, C. L. de S. (1973). *De l'esprit des lois,* tome II. Edition R. Dérathe. Paris: Garnier.
Pahud de Mortanges, R. (1987). *Die Archetypik der Gotteslästerung als Beispiel für das Wirken archetypischer Vorstellungen im Rechtsdenken.* Fribourg: Universitätsverlag.
Schindler, D. (1975). Schweizerische Eigenheiten in der Staatslehre. *Neujahrsblatt, 138,* 17-30.
Usteri, M. (1987). Beiträge der Tiefenpsychologie zur rechtlichen Ordnung von Eigentum und Raumgestaltung. In *Festschrift für Alois Troller zum 80. Geburtstag* (pp. 417-424). Berlin: Duncker & Humblot.

Part IX
History and Development of Legal Psychology in Different Countries

Highlights of the History of Forensic Psychology in Germany

Udo Undeutsch

The cradle of experimental psychology stood in Germany: It was the Psychological Laboratory, founded in 1875 by Wilhelm Wundt at the University of Leipzig. The pioneer generation of experimental psychologists soon recognized that the well-established findings of experimental research could have enormous social relevance. One of the first areas to which experimentally obtained findings were applied was the judicial process. For decades, the concern of pychologists focused on criminal proceedings to the effect that Forensic Psychology became almost identical with the application of psychological techniques and knowledge to the investigation and adjudication of criminal cases. This application to the pursuit of criminal justice goals still is and, probably, will remain the core of Forensic Psychology.

The processes of criminal justice require, for the kind of social sorting in which they result, an allocation of responsibility to one or another of the actors who are involved in an offense. The system then imposes on the socially and psychologically complex set of relationships between two actors the role of defendant or criminal for one and the role of plaintiff or victim for the other.

Because of this polarization, Forensic Psychology, as applied to the investigative phase of criminal proceedings, shows a quasi natural bifurcation: One part of it is dealing with the identification of the actual perpetrator of the offense under investigation, the other part deals with the accuracy of eyewitness testimony (including person identification). Both branches of Forensic Psychology originated at the turn of the century from the work of German-speaking psychologists.

Wilhelm Wundt, stimulated by Galton (1897), introduced into experimental psychology a simple experiment that has been called the "association experiment." Completely independently of one another, Max Wertheimer (Wertheimer & Klein, 1904) and C. G. Jung (1905) within very different research contexts and at different places recognized simultaneously that this technique might have the potential to be used for the identification of the actual perpetrator of a crime under investigation.

At the turn of the century, the Austrian Hans Gross taught Criminal Law and Criminology at the German Karls University in Prague. Among his students was Max Wertheimer, at that time studying law. Hans Gross was the originator of the discipline of criminal psychology. This triggered in Wertheimer an interest in psychology which he studied at Würzburg with Külpe.

In 1904 Wertheimer and Klein published an article on "Psychologische Tatbestandsdiagnostik." This term is a monster or - as Cesare Ferrari (1908), editor of the Rivista di psicologia, put it - "is one of those words without meaning, at least for us, that only the Germans can coin."

In the literature, English translations of this mysterious term are "the psychological diagnosis of facts" or "the psychological diagnosis of evidence." My translation would be "the identification of the perpetrator by psychological means." Wertheimer and Klein discussed the possibility of finding, through the accused's associations, the emotionally charged remembrance of a crime committed in the past. In order to have as large a spectrum of behavioral responses at hand as possible - hereby increasing the reliability of the assessment of guilt - the authors suggested that concomitant involuntary bodily responses to the stimulus words be also simultaneously monitored by psychophysiological means. They proposed the use of the pneumograph and sphygmograph and Sommer's tremometer.

At the same time in Zurich at the psychiatric hospital Burghölzli, Eugen Bleuler was experimenting with a list of stimulus words on all types of psychosis, and in 1901 inspired his then assistant medical director C. G. Jung to collect material on associations in normal subjects and at the same time to study the primary conditions involved. Jung conducted an impressive series of experimental studies on the word association test (now jointly republished in Volume II of his "Collected works", 1973). He too, not knowing about Wertheimer's ideas, had the idea that this technique might be useful for the identification of the perpetrator and that the use of additional psychophysiological measures like respiration and skin conductance response would increase the reliability of the technique. One day in 1905, Jung had the opportunity of applying the word association test to a criminal suspect, with a striking success. Jung himself was so enthusiastic about this that on the night of the test he wrote a report that was published the same year. Jung later applied the technique in two more criminal cases: in a theft case with 3 suspects (1910) and in a murder case (1937).

The psychology of eyewitness testimony has its roots in cognitive psychology. The originators were, in France, Alfred Binet with his studies on interrogative suggestibility (1900) and, in Germany, William Stern. Stern, at the beginning of the century, conducted a considerable amount of research on adult and child subjects. He was interested in individual differences in the ability to report accurately and completely what had been witnessed. He initiated a series under the title "Contributions to the Psychology of Testimony" (1903-1906).

Of major concern to the pioneer generation of forensic psychologists were the statements of underage witnesses who claimed to have been sexually abused. In the vast majority of cases, the statement of the alleged victim would be the only basis for a conviction. Stern's first courtroom appearance took place in 1903. Under the impression of the results from the laboratory that perfectly correct remembrance is not the rule but the exception (Stern, 1902, p. 327), psychological expertise was for decades clearly biased against the truthfulness of statements from actual victims. This negativistic, overly skeptical attitude of forensic psychologists was, however, in conflict with the daily experience of the trial courts in which children often gave reliable and valid testimony about the sexual abuse to which they had been subjected.

Things changed after World War II within the framework of the restoration of the German criminal justice system after its deterioration during the Nazi period.

The Juvenile Justice Delinquency Act (JGG), enacted in 1953, established in section 121 the jurisdiction of Juvenile Courts not only for the adjudication of offenses committed by juveniles and adolescents but also for offenses committed against children and juveniles. Interestingly enough, the more knowledgeable and experienced these courts were or became, the more they felt the need for psychological experts to be called in. I myself was one of those experts frequently called into child sexual abuse cases. We very quickly learned from our experience in the courtroom that in not a few cases in which the psychologist had many reasons to doubt the reliability of the statement of the victim/witness, a subsequent confession indicated that the doubts were not justified. We had to learn that the credibility of children and juveniles testifying to a sex offense committed against them had been grossly underestimated by psychologists in the past. It became obvious that a different methodological approach was needed that would enable the expert psychologist not only to cast doubts on the reliability of a victim's testimony where those doubts are justified but also to render the diagnosis of truthfulness when the testimony actually is a true and authentic reflection of a self-experienced real event.

For this objective, two steps had to be taken: (1) The focus of attention had to shift from the ability to report a complex event or course of events accurately and completely to the willingness or intention of the victim/witness "to tell the truth, the whole truth, and nothing but the truth." (2) In assessing the truthfulness of testimonial statements the focus had to shift away from the credibility of the witness toward the veracity of the statement, in other words, from the character of the witness toward the characteristics of the statement. I introduced this new approach in my presentation at the 19th Convention of the German Psychological Association held in Cologne September 28th to October 2nd, 1953. A set of relatively easily identifiable, semiobjective, dependable criteria was developed, all of them derived from forensic experience, meant to be discriminators of truthful accounts. The criteria can be said to be "descriptive" in that the definitions of the criteria are generally limited to descriptions of the features of the testimonial statement that require a minimal amount of inference on the part of the examiner (Undeutsch, 1967, 1989). This approach very quickly gained widespread acceptance among forensic psychologists, first of all in both parts of Germany and then in Sweden and after that, in the aftermath of the first international conference on Witness Psychology, held in Stockholm in September 1981 (Trankell, 1982), in the English-speaking countries. Initially, however, the assessment of the truthfulness of a victim's testimony by psychological experts was vehemently opposed. It was considered not applicable to judicial practice, being "an invasion into the province of the jury," "trespassing on the jury's domain," being "improperly preemptive of the act of judgment (of the trier of fact) on the issue of credibility" and so forth. (I have a very long list of those niceties). The most frequently cited authority in the history of Anglo-American law, Master John Henry Wigmore (1978), dismisses these phrases, calling them "a mere bit of empty rhetoric"(7, § 1920 at 18). (He changed his mind since his satirical article of 1909).

It was only a matter of time until the Supreme Court of the Federal Republic of Germany had to take its stand with respect to the supposed nuisance of psychological experts "meddling into evidentiary matters." In 1954 a District Court submitted the following question to the Supreme Court: *What different resources exist for the expert witness who conducts an out-of-court examination and for the trier of fact during the trial within the courtroom by the determination of the credibility of the testimony of a child witness (especially in trials for sexual abuse)?*

Since the five Justices of the Court felt they did not have sufficient knowledge of the procedure followed by psychological experts to assess the truth value of a testimonial statement, they resorted to something extremely unusual: They decided to hold a hearing on the topic and summoned a small group of experts: a senior police officer, the presiding judge of a Juvenile Court, a psychiatrist, and myself as psychologist. In order to demonstrate the superiority of the psychological methods for assessing the truth and ascertaining the truth value of a testimonial statement in child sexual abuse cases, I selected from my files a case of forcible rape committed on a 14-year-old girl by three young men, acting in concert.

The girl witness testified in the trial before a Court of First Instance that she had been raped by the three defendants. During the police interrogation, the defendants denied any sexual activities with the girl, but during the trial they admitted they had had sex with her but claimed that it was completely consensual. In order to determine the truthfulness of the testimony of the girl, the court summoned the headmaster of the school and the vicar of the church and appointed a medical expert to examine the girl and to render an opinion as to her credibility. They all unanimously testified to the effect that the victim was a perfectly honest, trustworthy, and believable witness. The three defendants were convicted of forcible rape and sentenced to one year imprisonment, suspended on probation. The three defendants appealed their conviction. In preparation of the retrial, the District Court called me into the case. During the probing interview that I conducted with the girl, she admitted to some exaggeration in her previous testimony and changed some details in her account.

Since the Court of First Instance had done everything legally possible, but in spite of that was not able to get to the complete truth, this case was a good one to demonstrate the superiority of psychologically sophisticated interviewing techniques in obtaining an accurate, complete, and truthful report from the victim/witness. In the hearing, held by the Supreme Court on December 14, 1954, I included in my testimony a replay of the tape of my interview with the alleged victim. The five Justices of the Court were deeply impressed by the demonstration. They were convinced that in assessing the truthfulness of the testimony of a child or juvenile witness, an expert psychologist conducting an out-of-court examination has "other and better resources" than the court within the framework of formal courtroom proceedings. The Supreme Court held that an expert psychiatrist or psychologist must be called upon to testify on the subject of the truthfulness of the witness' account, particularly in child sexual abuse cases, if the conviction hinges primarily or exclusively on the testimony of an underage witness or if the witness testimony is not substantially corroborated by other evidence (BGHSt, 1955, 7, pp. 82-86)[1].

This decision must be viewed as a milestone in the development of the rules of evidence in Germany. From that time on, failing to call in an expert in sexual abuse cases can be a reversible error.

Since this landmark decision of 1954, psychologists in Germany have been called into sex cases rather regularly, appointed by the District Attorney in the investigative phase and by the court in the adjudicative phase. This procedure is the prerequisite for a completely objective, neutral, impartial acting of an expert witness. Having court-appointed experts avoids the practice of "shopping for experts" and "the battle of the experts" during the trial. This is one of the good things about the inquisitorial system.

---

[1] BGHSt = Entscheidungen des Bundesgerichtshofes in Strafsachen = official criminal case reports of the Supreme Court of the Federal Republic of Germany.

When it is certain, based on the evidence produced in the case at hand, that the accused is the actual perpetrator of the offense charged, the question of criminal responsibility has to be answered. Every adult person is considered by law to be responsible for any criminal conduct. Only the conditions of infancy and exceptional states of mind relieve the perpetrator of criminal responsibility. The rules for the defense of lack of mental responsibility are basically the same in most civilized countries. To achieve the necessary foundation to resolve the vital issue of lack of criminal responsibility, a two-step approach usually is provided:

A first step is to examine whether at the time of the commission of the offense charged the defendant was afflicted with an exceptional or abnormal mental condition. A second step attempts to determine whether "as a result" of such abnormal psychological condition, defendant lacked (a) the capacity to appreciate the criminality, that is, the wrongfulness of his/her conduct, and/or (b) the capacity to conform his/her conduct to the requirements of law.

The German penal code provides two degrees of lack of mental responsibility: Total lack of mental responsibility and diminished mental responsibility. The rules for a finding of total lack of criminal responsibility are provided in section 20 of the Penal Code: A person is not responsible for criminal conduct if at the time of such conduct because of a pathological mental dysfunction, a mental retardation or dementia, a pathological personality disorder, or a severe consciousness disorder, he/she is unable to appreciate the unlawfulness of his/her conduct or to conform his/her conduct to this insight.

The rules for diminished criminal responsibility are provided for in section 21 of the Penal Code: If, as a result of one of the mental conditions mentioned in section 20, the capacity either to appreciate the unlawfulness of his/her conduct or to conform his/her conduct to this insight is substantially impaired, punishment can be reduced in accordance with the provisions for an attempt to commit a crime.

This two-step approach to the assessment of lack of criminal responsibility, however, created problems in those cases which psychiatric experts found no indication of a mental disease or defect in a clinical sense but at the same time had to admit that the defendant when committing the crime of which he/she is accused probably lacked substantial capacity either to appreciate the criminality of his/her conduct or to conform his/her conduct to the requirements of law. A psychiatrist would conceptualize "mental disorder" in the sense of the DSM-III-R as "a clinically significant behavioral or psychological syndrome or pattern that occurs in a person" (p. XXII). He/she would not consider, for example, "the heat of passion" or an "emotional wildfire" as a clinically significant syndrome or pattern and, therefore, would deny that the defendant, when acting in such a state of mind, did suffer from a mental disease or defect, even though his/her capacity to appreciate the criminality of his/her conduct or the capacity to conform his/her conduct to the requirements of the law may have been substantially impaired as a result of high emotional arousal. For this reason, the accused's criminal responsibility would be affirmed.

The dilemma with the two-step approach is: When the actor lacked substantial capacity to appreciate the criminality of his/her conduct or to conform his/her conduct to external demands, then he/she did not possess the mens rea - the necessary guilty mind - when committing the crime charged. The concept of mens rea is based on the assumption that a person has a capacity to control his/her behavior and to choose between alternative courses of conduct. Thus, the sanctions of the criminal law are meted out in accordance with the actor's capacity to conform his/her conduct to society's standards through the capacity for choice control that he/she possessed with respect to his/her act.

To resolve this conflict - no findings indicative of mental disease or defect, yet lack of one of the two substantial capacities - two options are available: to dispense with the first step (which is the most consequent and radical proposal) or to broaden the scope of the concept of mental disease or defect beyond the scope of its use in clinical psychiatry. Since the terms used in section 20 for the abnormal mental conditions being a prerequisite for the assumption of lacking or diminished mental responsibility are not technical terms as used in contemporary psychiatry or psychology, they are open to a wide range of interpretations by case law. This is in particular true for the mental condition called "consciousness distortion", which is a kind of residual diagnostic class.

States of very high emotional arousal, as we know just as well from the experience of life as from experimental research, can cause a substantial impairment of either the capacity to appreciate the criminality of the conduct or the capacity to conform the conduct to the requirements of law. Emotional wildfires, therefore, certainly can be considered to form a specific manifestation of the residual and merely symptomatic class of "consciousness disorder."

Whenever there is a lack of one of the two substantial capacities that constitute fundamental prerequisites for criminal responsibility, I thought we could resort to this residual diagnostic class.

A homicide case tried in the year 1956 before the District Court of Dortmund gave occasion for this. I cannot possibly present the case fully. His wife was unfaithful to him, caused him a lot of worry and humiliations to the effect that eventually the accused in a state of rage killed her by stabbing her three or four times with a small kitchen knife. Details of the case are reported in de Boor (1966, 131-132, 166-192).

For assessing the criminal responsibility of the defendant, he was referred to the Public Health Office for psychiatric evaluation. The psychiatrist rendered the opinion that the defendant did not have a mental disease or defect at the time of the offense and, consequently, was fully responsible for the crime charged. This is where "the battle of the experts" started.

The defense appointed a famous experimental psychologist, Wolfgang Metzger, at that time professor of psychology at the University of Munster, who came to the conclusion that the defendant acted in the heat of passion and momentarily lacked substantial capacity to control his behavior. He stated that the defendant acted in a state of diminished criminal responsibility. The district attorney appointed two outstanding authorities in the field of Forensic Psychiatry: Kurt Schneider and Hans Gruhle. Kurt Schneider reached the conclusion that the accused at the time of the crime was likely to have suffered from a temporary "consciousness disorder" with the possibility of concomitant lack of substantial capacity to conform his conduct to the requirements of law.

Hans Gruhle, at that time already a giant in the field of Forensic Psychiatry, reached the conclusion that no signs of the existence of any mental disease or defect at the time of the crime could be found and, consequently, the accused had to be considered fully responsible for what he had done.

The court, on its own motion, appointed me as expert witness of its own selection. Based on my evaluation of the case facts and examination of the accused, I concluded that there was no indication of a mental disease or defect in the defendant, but that the instant crime behavior represented an isolated incident in his life, triggered by massive stress and an unusual juxtaposition of environmental and internal occurrences. He had acted in a state of an emotional wildfire of rage and uncontrolled passion and, consequently, did lack substantial capacity to conform his conduct to the requirements of law.

The court concurred with my conclusions and found the defendant "not guilty - only by reason of lack of mental responsibility." Needless to say, the state attorney appealed this decision.

The Supreme Court of the Federal Republic of Germany reviewed the case, endorsed the principles upon which my conclusions regarding lack of criminal responsibility were based, affirmed the decision of the District Court, and handed down a policy decision to the effect that the term "consciousness disorder" was not confined to psychopathological mental conditions, but includes any abnormal condition of the mind that has a potential to substantially affect mental or emotional processes and substantially impairs behavior controls (BGHSt, 1958, 11, 20.26). This decision opened the way for psychological evaluation and testimony on the vital issue of criminal responsibility. In assessing lack of criminal responsibility following that decision, two questions had to be answered: At the time of the alleged criminal conduct, (a) did the accused have a mental disease or defect in a psychopathological sense (which is clearly a psychiatric domain)? (b) Did the accused have a temporary exceptional mental condition substantially affecting mental or emotional processes and substantially impairing the capacity to conform his/her conduct to the requirements of law, as can occur under unusual life conditions even in otherwise normal human people (which is a psychological domain)?

From that point in time on, in an increasing number of cases - mostly homicide cases - an initially small number of specialized psychologists have been ordered by the courts to examine the accused and to draw assessment conclusions regarding cognitive and volitional competencies and impairments. In order to provide a scientifically defendable basis for assessing mental capacity versus total incapacity or substantially diminished capacity, a set of evaluation guidelines that affirm the essential process of determining mental capacity had to be developed. This task has been tackled - in chronological order - by myself and Thomae - not acting in concert, but alternating (Thomae & Mathey, 1983; Thomae & Schmidt, 1967; Undeutsch, 1957, 1974).

A set of relatively easily definable, easily identifiable, semiobjective, descriptive evaluation criteria has been developed. Applying those criteria that occur in differently pronounced manifestations rather than signifying a given mental disease or defect, represents a shift from a nominal to an ordinal state of assessment development. The same criteria are applicable if the issue of partial mental responsibility is raised. In a case in which a premeditated design to kill, a specific intent, or knowledge of a particular fact is an essential element of the offense charged, an abnormal mental condition that, although not amounting to lack of mental responsibility, may negate mental capacity to entertain the required premeditation, specific intent, or knowledge.

In 1954, The German Parliament initiated a complete revision of the Criminal Code and for this purpose set up a task force of many members. This task force in turn requested the positions of scientific societies to specific questions. As far as the rules for lack of, or diminished, criminal responsibility were concerned, opinions and proposals were collected both from the German Psychiatric Association and from the German Psychological Association. I submitted a statement on behalf of the German Psychological Association.

My first and most fundamental proposal was to abolish the causal level in the irresponsibility test, that is, the enumeration of certain mental disorders that might cause a substantial impairment of the capacity to appreciate the criminality of the conduct or to conform the conduct to the requirements of the law. Because, once the probability of a substantial impairment of capacity is established, for the purpose of assessing criminal responsibility the lack of substantial impairment of capacity in itself is the decisive finding, whereas what might have caused this total lack or substantial impairment is rather irrelevant. In the event that the legislature would not agree to this - admittedly radical, though not without precedents - proposal, my next concern was to ensure that the list of mental conditions potentially causing lack of criminal responsibility continue to comprise the condition termed "consciousness disorder" as a residual diagnostic class, broad enough in scope to also encompass states of very high emotional arousal. Without being pathological in nature, these states would be capable of causing a substantial impairment of either the capacity to appreciate the criminality of the conduct in progress or the capacity to conform the conduct to the requirements of law (Undeutsch, 1956). The German Psychiatric Association, in contrast, strongly suggested a phrasing of this condition that was very restrictive and confined this condition to states of mind that were similar in nature to a mental disease. As a consequence, a longstanding hot-tempered discussion arose in which again also Thomae was engaged on the part of the psychologists. Details of this discussion before the task force for the revision of the Criminal Code are reported in Undeutsch (1974, 94-98). Eventually, the position advanced by the representatives of the German Psychological Association prevailed. The task force of the Ministry of Justice defined the condition termed "consciousness disorder" as discrete mental disorders, not attributable to a clinical mental condition, not caused by a pathological physical condition nor a psychoactive substance. They are episodic in nature, as they can occur in otherwise mentally normal people in reaction to psychologically distressing events that are outside the range of common human experiences. Practically, they approximate an emotional wildfire of the rage or passion type (Schwalm, 1970, p. 493). In terms of the DSM-III-R classification, the condition under consideration refers to the class of "unspecified mental disorder (nonpsychotic)," code 300.90, perhaps in combination with other disorders like "other interpersonal problems" (V 62.81).

One of the consequences of this broadening of the concept "consciousness disorder" was the reversal of the rank order of the two steps in the lack of responsibility test; no longer was the diagnosis of a mental disorder the threshold for the defense of lack of responsibility, but the procedure is rather reversed: The lack or substantial impairment of the capacity to appreciate the criminality of the conduct or the capacity to conform the conduct to the requirements of the law is indicative of a severe - permanent or temporary - mental dysfunction (Krümpelmann, 1987, p. 192, n 4). This, in fact, comes very close to an abolition of a preceding diagnosis of a mental disorder as a prerequisite for any lack of mental responsibility defense. In retrospect, it can be stated that the forthcoming "crack in the dam" predicted by forensic psychiatrists, as a consequence of this new definition of this condition, did not materialize.

In the following decades, these developments in the psychology of eyewitness testimony and in the assessment of cognitive and volitional capacity of the accused at the time of the crime had considerable impact. Calling psychological experts into certain categories of criminal cases has become more and more a routine practice in the adjudication of crimes to the end that the truth may be ascertained and proceedings justly determined.

References

Binet, A. (1900). *La suggestibilité* [Suggestibility]. Paris: Schleicher.
Boor, W. de (1966). *Bewußtsein und Bewußtseinsstörungen*. [Consciousness and consciousness disorders]. Berlin: Springer.
Ferrari, C. (1908). Editorial note to C.G. Jung: New aspects of criminal psychology. *Rivista di psicologia applicata, IV*, 285.
Galton, F. (1897). Psychometric experiments. *Brain, 2*, 149-162.
Jung, C.G. (1905). Zur psychologischen Tatbestandsdiagnostik. [On the psychological diagnosis of facts]. *Zentralblatt für Nervenheilkunde und Psychiatrie, 28*, 813-815. English translation in C.G. Jung (1972), Collected works. Vol. I: Psychiatric studies (pp. 219-221), (edited by H. Read, M. Fordham, G. Adler, & W. McGuire). London: Routledge & Kegan Paul.
Jung, C.G. (1910). The association method. *American Journal of Psychology, 21*. Republished in C.G. Jung (1973), Collected works. Vol. II: Experimental researchers (pp. 439-465), (edited by H. Read, M. Fordham, G. Adler, & W. McGuire). London: Routledge & Kegan Paul.
Jung, C.G. (1937). Zur psychologischen Tatbestandsdiagnostik. *[On the psychological diagnosis of facts]*. Archiv für Kriminologie, C, 123-130. English translation in C.G. Jung (1973), Collected works. Vol. II: Experimental researches (pp. 605-614), (ed. by H. Read, M. Fordham, G. Adler, & W. McGuire). London: Routledge & Kegan Paul.
Krümpelmann, J. (1987). Schuldzurechnung unter Affekt und alkoholisch bedingte Schuldunfähigkeit. [Culpability when acting in a state of high emotional arousal or severe alcohol intoxication].*Zeitschrift für die gesamte Strafrechtswissenschaft, 99*, 191-227.
Schwalm, G. (1970). Schuld und Schuldfähigkeit im Lichte der Strafrechtsreformgesetze vom 25.VI. und 4. VII. 1969, des Grundgesetzes und der Rechtsprechung des Bundesgerichtshofes. [Culpability and criminal responsibility in light of the reform of criminal law from June 25 and July 4, 1969, the constitution and the jurisdiction of the supreme court of Germany]. *Juristenzeitung, 25*, 287-495.
Stern, W. (1902). Zur Psychologie der Aussage. [On the psychology of statements]. *Zeitschrift für die gesamte Strafrechtswissenschaft, 22*, 315-370.
Stern, W. (Ed.). (1903 - 1906). *Beiträge zur Psychologie der Aussage*. [Contributions to the psychology of eyewitness testimony]. Leipzig: Barth.
Thomae, H., & Mathey, F.J. (1983). Psychologische Beurteilung der Schuldfähigkeit [Psychological assessment of criminal responsibility]. In F. Lösel (Ed.), *Kriminalpsychologie* (pp. 180-190). Weinheim: Beltz.
Thomae, H., & Schmidt, H.D. (1967). Psychologische Aspekte der Schuldfähigkeit [Psychological aspects of criminal responsibility]. In U. Undeutsch (Ed.), *Handwörterbuch der Psychologie*, Vol. 2 (pp. 326-396). Göttingen: Hogrefe.
Trankell, A. (Ed.). (1982). *Reconstructing the past*. Deventer, The Netherlands: Kluwer.
Undeutsch, U. (1953). Die Entwicklung der gerichtspsychologischen Gutachtertätigkeit. [The development of the professional activities of forensic psychological experts]. In A. Welleck (Ed.), *Bericht über den XIV. Kongress der Deutschen Gesellschaft für Psychologie* (pp. 132-154). Göttingen: Verlag für Psychologie.
Undeutsch, U. (1956). Stellungnahme der Deutschen Gesellschaft für Psychologie zu Fragenkreis I: Zurechnungsfähigkeit. [Statement on behalf of the German Psychological Association on criminal responsibility]. In Bundesministerium der Justiz (Ed.), *Gutachten und Stellungnahmen zu Fragen der Strafrechtsreform mit ärztlichem Einschlag*. Umdruck M 15. Bonn: Bundesministerium der Justiz.

Undeutsch, U. (1957) Zurechnungsfähigkeit bei Bewußtseinsstörung [Criminal responsibility in states of conscious disorder]. In A. Ponsold (Ed.), *Lehrbuch der gerichtlichen Medizin*, 2nd ed. (pp. 130-145). Stuttgart: Thieme.

Undeutsch, U. (1967). Beurteilung der Glaubhaftigkeit von Zeugenaussagen. [Assessing the credibility of testimonial statements]. In U. Undeutsch (Ed.), *Handbuch der Psychologie: Vol. 11. Forensische Psychologie* (pp. 26-181). Göttingen: Verlag für Psychologie.

Undeutsch, U. (1974). Schuldfähigkeit unter psychologischem Aspekt. [Criminal responsibility from the psychological aspect]. In G. Eisen (Ed.), *Handwörterbuch der Rechtsmedizin*, Vol. II (pp. 91-115). Stuttgart: Enke.

Undeutsch, U. (1989). The development of statement reality analysis. In J.C. Yuille (Ed.), *Credibility assessment*, (pp. 101-120). Dordrecht: Kluwer.

Wertheimer, M., & Klein, J. (1904). Psychologische Tatbestandsdiagnostik. [The psychological diagnosis of facts]. *Archiv für Kriminologie, 15*, 72-113.

Wigmore, J.H. (1909). Professor Munsterberg and the psychology of evidence. *Illinois Law Review, 3*, 399-445.

Wigmore, J.H. (1978). *Evidence* (revised by J.H. Chadbourne). Boston: Little & Brown.

On the Development of Psychologically Oriented Legal Thinking in German Speaking Countries

Raimund Jakob

Introduction

Legal Psychology is a field in which two sciences with different perceptional interests enter a discourse with each other. It is divided into a more theoretical and legal branch (Psychology of Law) and a more empirical and psychological branch (Psychology in Law). The nucleus of the more legal branch can be described as "research on the essence and meaning of law and justice as psychological phenomena" (Jakob, 1987, pp. 14-15). With regard to the primary object of perception, namely of justice as a feeling and an idea, it undoubtedly belongs to legal science, and its designation as "psychological legal theory" seems correct.

As far as the more psychological branch is concerned, its description as "psychology in the service of law" is adequate. In contrast to the afore-mentioned notion, it is a field of applied psychology. Especially social psychology of the law system and the psychology of legal procedure can be regarded as a field in which the more legal and the more psychological branch intersect. From a juridical point of view, the term "psychological theory of the application of law" is useful.

Psychological legal theory and psychological theory of application of law are the objects of our research, whereas psychology in the service of law is not our subject. Although legal psychology, which is to be dealt with here, has its position in the sphere of legal philosophy and legal theory, it can also be found in the field of legal sociology in connection with problems of legal consciousness and research on judicature.

A historical survey serves manifold purposes: It should summarily remind us who were the first scholars in this field of research in the first decades. Especially it should prove that the psychology of law and the psychological theory of application of law make their appearance approximately at the same time as scientific psychology begins to develop. It is a widespread opinion that this only happened toward the end of the 1960s. Finally we shall deal with the present instrumentarium of jurists in this sphere and with its importance.

Beginnings and First Climax

In the second half of the 19th century and at the turn of the present century a decisive change developed in the conception of man. These new conceptions stemmed from the natural sciences: Empiricism became dominant. At first Darwin's theory on the origin of species assigned man to the world of animals, and later Freud declared him to be a being influenced by drives. These innovations also found their expression in legal thinking in German-speaking countries. From the end of the 1880s till the early 1930s a multitude of theories and currents of psychologically oriented legal thinking developed at the same time, mostly independently of each other. Representatives of this development were not only jurists but also natural scientists, who had an own interest in the cultural product "law" and who made it the subject of psychological research.

As far as legal methodology is concerned, two movements are important for our deliberations, namely psychological legal theories, as represented by the jurists E.R. Bierling (1894-1917) and Arthur Baumgarten (1939), and, at the same time, the "Freirechtsschule" (see Fikentscher, 1976), which attributes a central role to legal consciousness. Bierling reduces law to psychological facts of volition and of recognition. Norms are an expression of will, which expects its execution of others. The speciality of legal norms consists in the fact that they are reciprocally recognized by persons living in a society. The recognition is psychologically understood as the habitual, lasting respect for certain norms. Norms are valid as long as one is conscious of them (cf. Larenz, 1991). It would be worth examining which relations exist between Bierling's theory and the theory of the Pole Petrazycki (1907), which later met with a special response in Anglo-American legal thinking. As far as A. Baumgarten is concerned, we shall mention him later in connection with developments in Switzerland.

In connection with the codification of civil law in Germany and its scientific treatment, the "Begriffsjurisprudenz" reached a new peak. This meant an exegesis of notions for legal dogmatics and literal obedience by the courts. This development was rigorously contested by the Freirechtsschule in both theory and practice. The Freirechtsschule called for closeness to life and more justice in individual cases and demanded the substitution of so-called legal logic by sociological and psychological arguments. In order to investigate legal consciousness and other phenomena of psychic of origin, the representatives of the Freirechtsschule, all of them jurists, made empirical investigations in order to gain not only insights but also better conditions for judicature and legislation.

For Hermann Isay, one of their last and most outstanding representatives, judicial decision is founded on intuition based on legal sense. Only later are decisions compared with law and argued on its basis. This comparison primarily has a control function in addition it should prove the decision to be universally valid. As a proof for his opinion, Isay (1929) referred to extensive material from judicial practice's experience.

But it was not only jurists who were developing psychological legal theories at this time. Thus Wilhelm Wundt, who is regarded by many as the founder of a scientific psychology, maintained that jurisprudence can never do without psychological motivation, although it usually prefers other aspects of interpretation. He himself devoted the ninth volume of his "Völkerpsychologie" in 1918 to his efforts to decode the phenomenon of law. According to Wundt, law is derived from an ethical universal will. Law has not only to secure the society's conditions of life; it also has moreover to further individual and social development. The psychiatrist Sigmund Kornfeld devoted a great work to the psychology of legal sense (under the title "Rechtsgefühl") and investigated into its importance in relation to the legal-philosophical history of dogmatics (1914, 1917 - 1919). For this work, Kornfeld received the Kant prize. 1933 Freud published an article on the roots of and the needs for law.

In this connection, the depth-psychological efforts in criminology and in the theory and practice of criminal law deserve special mention. Criminal law with its specific problems, such as freedom of will, guilt, atonement, prevention, and so forth somehow offered itself as a field for psychological investigations. At the turn of the century - Freud's "Interpretation of Dreams" (original title "Traumdeutung") was published in 1900 - as far as the unconscious is concerned, psychology found an additional and adequate ally in psycho-analysis. It was in connection with criminal law (cf. Freund, 1915) that some of Freud's students and other scholars made their creditable appearance in public: such men as Theodor Reik (1929) who published a work on the compulsion to confess and the need to be punished and Franz Alexander who together with the lawyer Hugo Staub, published a work on criminals and their judges (1929). 1931 Erich Fromm wrote on the psychology of the criminal and punitive society. Already in 1905, C. G. Jung wrote a 40-page article on the psychological diagnosis of facts for the "Schweizerische Zeitschrift für Strafrecht". In 1909 he - as well as Sigmund Freud - received an honorary doctorate of Law from Clark University, Worcester (Mass.) in the United States. Apart from criminal law, the jurists Hans Kelsen und Max Rheinstein devoted themselves to problems of public law. Thus Kelsen dealt in 1922 and 1927 with the notion of the state in psychoanalysis, and Rheinstein published a theory on the justification of state and democracy in 1928.

In the fifth edition of the Staatslexikon of the Görres-Gesellschaft (published since 1926) we find a first lengthy article dealing with legal psychology (1931), its authors were a jurist (Franz Sommer) and a psychologist (Kurt Huber). It is divided into two parts: (1) legal psychology in a narrower sense: the psyche in jurisprudence and (2) legal psychology in a wider sense: psychological auxiliary disciplines of jurisprudence. Assuming that these kinds of scientific encyclopedia and lexicon reflect the knowledge of their time, it would seem that legal psychology had acquired such importance in the social sciences that it could no longer be ignored.

On the other hand, the status of psychological legal theories and that of the Freirechtschule had become problematic; the peak of their influence on legal thinking was already past. As the reason for this, two circumstances may be mentioned: Empiricism had called the neo-Kantians to the scene as a counter-reaction, who reproached the empiricists for having caused the loss of a "material" order of values and who called its representatives "subjectivists." As for the rest, the neo-Kantians maintained a strict separation of Is and Ought. As far as the representatives of the Freirechtsschule were concerned, they had not succeeded in propagating a psychologically and sociologically determined legal thinking in view of the paramount codification of civil law. If one takes into account the influence of codification in France, which had lead to a lasting predominance of the école de exégèse, nearly 100 years, the lost battle of the representatives of the Freirechtsschule appears in a mellow light (cf. Fikentscher, 1976, pp. 366-367).

After the national socialists seized power, the efforts to establish a psychological orientation in legal thinking over the previous 40 years came to an end in Germany and later on in Austria. No wonder, since nearly all well-known representatives of the Freirechtsschule were of Jewish origin; more or less the same was true for the representatives of psycho-analysis, which was declared a "Jewish" discipline. The example of Isay, a representative of the Freirechtsschule, may illustrate the situation. Isay was a public notary and lawyer, and, from 1925 on, associate professor at the Technical University in Berlin. In 1933, he was dismissed as a notary; and in 1934, he lost his professorship. For three years, he then worked as a lawyer in Berlin before committing suicide in 1937.

Switzerland

During the same period, Arthur Baumgarten wrote his "Fundamentals of a Juristic Methodology" (original title "Grundzüge der juristischen Methodenlehre", Bern 1939) in Switzerland, which in its nucleus comprises a psychological legal theory. For him jurisprudence is an empirical science. He declares himself an empiricist. According to him law serves a universal purpose to secure human society. The rules necessary to fulfill this universal aim have to be known and willed by the subjects of law. Consequently mentally sick people can have no legal duties. "Only with the help of the psychology of the unconscious, will empiricism reach its due position" (Baumgarten, 1939, p. 180). Baumgarten points out that methodology needs a philosophical basis. However, he himself sketches his own philosophical standpoint only in rough lines. The conclusion from Is to Ought cannot convince him, mainly because the transgression from Is to Ought can be used to realize ideas that sanction force. At the same time, the psychologist Franziska Baumgarten-Tramer, a Pole, published a number of articles on the problem of democracy (Baumgarten-Tramer, 1944).

During the war, there was nothing additional to be reported from Switzerland; in the 1950s some directive publications appeared there. All those papers were based on the "complex psychology" of C. G. Jung. They represented an attempt to inquire into the symbolic sense and meaning of legal and state institutions using depth psychology to investigate their "Archaic inheritance." On this basis Swiss jurists achieved important results in the years from 1954 to 1959: Hans Fehr in the field of legal comparison (1954), Max Imboden in theory of state (1959), and Hans Marti in regard of the confederate constitution (1958). They are followed by Eduard Naegeli (1965), who published a longer article on criminal law. At present Martin Usteri (for instance 1987) is the represantative of this branch of research.

Postwar and Present Times

By the end of the war, legal naturalism had got into disrepute. This was not only true for its vitalistic but also for its psychological trend. This happened in spite of the fact that its representatives were especially affected by the measures of the national socialist regime. Jurists' legal psychology had ceased to exist, the designation as legal psychologist was reserved *de facto* for those psychologists who worked for the police and judicature, that means, those who worked in the service of the administration of law. In the 6th edition (beginning with the year 1957) of the Staatslexikon of the Görres-Gesellschaft, we find no entry on legal psychology. In the 7th edition (beginning with the year 1985), we can read on the study of psychology at German Universities: "In some places studies on legal psychology are also offered."

Three men prepared the ground so that legal thinking in former West Germany became again a topic for psychological investigations. These were Erwin Riezler, C. A. Emge, and Erich Fechner. In 1946 Riezler prepared a new edition of his work "The Legal Sense" (original title "Das Rechtsgefühl") which had already been published before the war. Emge (1954) wrote a small work stressing the importance of psychology for legal innovation. Fechner (1962) devoted himself to this subject in his textbook on legal philosophy. Here he detects the reason for all law in the "archetypes" (prototypes): Thus law is in this way enclosed in human nature, but at the same time it is also entrusted to man to shape it.

In connection with the so-called "Critical Jurisprudence" (Kritische Jurisprudenz) we see a stronger activation of psychologically orientated thinking in law. The opportunity was seized to make use of American legal-psychological realism in a comparative manner. These works concern themselves especially with the judge and his or her decision. The most important work in this field during this period was done by Robert Weimar (1969).

Albert A. Ehrenzweig's important and directive "Psychoanalytic Jurisprudence" whose German edition was published in Berlin in 1973, may be regarded as the first peak and new starting point of legal-psychological investigation after the war. At least its importance is proved by its controversiality. That in Germany and Austria one is prepared at all to devote oneself more intensively - even skeptically - to legal-psychological thinking is perhaps due to a legal philosophy that finds itself in a dilemma between an absolutely conceived natural law and "pure legal thinking" with which one tries to cope by renouncing absolute insights and communication on positions and scopes capable of consensus. In this connection, attention is drawn to the prerequisites, criteria, and facts of the realization of law.

Since Ehrenzweig's book, depth psychology, especially psychoanalytic theory, has become the preferred instrument for a psychologically oriented legal thinking. An explanation might be found in the fact that the more than two and a half millennia lasting history of occidental legal thinking has for the first time an instrument at hand, that enables it to approach the unconscious and thus offers new possibilities of solution. That law and justice are phenomena, that can be grasped only conditionally by considerations of a traditional kind becomes clear through the fact that both of them are easier to experience than to define.

Apart from the psychoanalytical theory of Sigmund Freud, the theories of C. G. Jung and Alfred Adler have been reflected in literature as a source of knowledge for legal thinking and as an instrument of interpretation. On the latter's approach the work of Max Rheinstein (1928) and Manfred Rehbinder (for instance 1987) are based. At the same time, information from other disciplines is used for such investigations, such as, behavioral research or cultural anthropology.

Apart from criminal law the legal psychology of jurists has led to comprehensive results only in the last decades. Thus it cannot be expected at the moment to meet with a coherent system, not to talk of a complete and refined one. Nevertheless, the structures and the central focuses of research can clearly be detected. Besides a number of more or less developed theories on criminal law and theories on judicial decisions, different elements on a general legal theory, a theory of constitution, and a theory of civil law have been elaborated (References to current literature and the authors see Jakob & Rehbinder, 1987).

In the faculties of law, legal psychology (in the sense of: psychological legal theory and psychological theory of application of law) until now has no standing as an autonomous discipline. Only psychology for jurists has succeeded in establishing itself at German-speaking faculties of law. On the occasion of the reform of studies in 1978 in Austria, psychology for jurists was integrated into the curriculum of legal studies as an alternative field of studies having the same position as legal philosophy and political science. If legal psychology has reached a certain standard in German-speaking countries, this is not due to the respective governments but to regional quasi-private initiatives. Such initiatives, as to my knowledge, can be found especially in Zurich (where in near future a private research institute will be found), also in Bielefeld (Wolfgang Schild), and, if I am allowed to say so, also in Salzburg.

On the Importance of Depth Psychology for Legal Psychology

A special advantage of depth psychology as an instrument of legal psychology can be seen in the fact that psychologists and jurists have equal access to it. For psycho-analysis' point of view, psychoanalytical theory (not without good reason also called meta-psychology) in regard of psychology contains the fundamental assumption, which enables it to avail itself of the function which before was the realm of metaphysics as the theory of the inexperiencable. From this point of view, psychoanalytical theory is a quasi-philosophical discipline, whose results, however, are clinically, and insofar empirically, to a great extent provable. This makes it and its human image equally highly interesting for jurisprudence. Thus psychoanalytical theory enables jurists and psychologists to enter into a discussion.

Like every other social science, jurisprudence tries to base its findings on a theory on human nature. Such theories always contain two elements: One can be seen in certain speculative universalization of human qualities, thus being an uncritical pre-runner of psychology. The other element can be seen in evaluations connected with it. The inadequacy of some legal philosophies, founded on speculations on human reason, can be found here. Theories on criminal law of bygone times are especially apt to prove this. The use of depth-psychological results can in this way only be of advantage for psychological legal theory. The results reached in German-speaking countries up to now justify such expectations.

Let us consider now the psychological theory of application of law. At first it seems that depth psychology used as an instrument of interpretation must fail because of its limited operationalization or quantificability. On closer inspection it turns out that empirical data alone do not suffice. In other words, a narrowly understood psychology cannot adequately grasp phenomena of a certain complexity, let alone judge them. This is true, for instance, for the problem, of how far it is possible to realize justice or a feeling of justice for the citizens in a legal procedure. Every attempt to use empirical measures exclusively here will necessarily lead to unsatisfactory trivialities.

We have arrived here at a point where one cannot dispense with cooperation of jurisprudence and psychology in order to reach reasonable results. It is a point where satisfactory answers can be found only by the interplay of soft and hard data, of well-founded legal-theoretical considerations and empirical knowledge. Depth psychology may offer a great chance for the approximation of these disciplines. As long as problems cannot be formulated adequately empirically acquired data also cannot convince.

References

Alexander, F., & Staub, H. (1929, repr. 1971). Der Verbrecher und seine Richter. In T. Moser (Ed.), *Psychoanalyse und Justiz* (pp. 209-411). Frankfurt a.M.: Suhrkamp.
Baumgarten, A. (1939). *Grundlagen der juristischen Methodenlehre*. Bern: Huber.

Baumgarten-Tramer, F. (1944). *Demokratie und Charakter.* München: Kindler.
Bierling, E.R. (1894-1917, repr. 1961). *Juristische Prinzipienlehre,* 5 Vols. Aalen: Scientia.
Ehrenzweig, A.A. (1971, German transl. 1973). *Psychoanalytische Rechtswissenschaft.* Berlin: Duncker & Humblot.
Emge, C.A. (1954, repr. 1987). Recht und Psychologie. In R. Jakob & M. Rehbinder (Eds.), *Beiträge zur Rechtspsychologie* (pp. 114-124). Berlin: Duncker & Humblot.
Fechner, E. (1962). *Rechtsphilosophie,* 2nd ed. Tübingen: J.C.B. Mohr
Fehr, H. (1954). Primitives und Germanisches Recht. *Archiv für Rechts- und Sozialphilosophie,* XLI, 37-48.
Fikentscher, W. (1976). *Methoden des Rechts,* Vol. 3 (pp. 362-373). München: J.C.B. Mohr.
Freud, S. (1900, repr. 1976). Die Traumdeutung In. A. Freud (Ed.), *Gesammelte Werke, 6th ed, Vol. 2-3.* Frankfurt a.M.: Fischer.
Freud, S. (1915, repr. 1976). Die Verbrecher aus Schuldbewußtsein. In A. Freud (Ed.), *Gesammelte Werke, 6th ed., Vol. 10.* Frankfurt a.M.: Fischer.
Freud, S. (1933). Über Recht, Gewalt und ihre Triebgrundlage. *Psychoanalytische Bewegung,* V, 207-216.
Fromm, E. (1931, repr. 1971). Zur Psychologie des Verbrechers und der strafenden Gesellschaft. In E. Fromm (Ed.), *Analytische Sozialpsychologie und Gesellschaftstheorie,* 6th ed. (pp. 115-144). Frankfurt a.M.: Suhrkamp.
Imboden, M. (1959, repr. 1964). *Die Staatsformen. Versuch einer psychologischen Deutung staatsrechtlicher Dogmen,* Basel: Helbing & Lichtenhahn.
Isay, H. (1929, repr. 1970). *Rechtsnorm und Entscheidung.* Aalen, Scientia.
Jakob, R. (1987). Rechtspsychologie. Einführende Gedanken, Instrumentarium und Problemstellungen. In R. Jakob, & M. Rehbinder (Eds.), *Beiträge zur Rechtspsychologie* (pp. 9-23). Berlin: Duncker & Humblot.
Jakob, R., & Rehbinder, M. (Eds.) (1987). Bibliographie der deutschsprachigen Rechtspsychologie. In R. Jakob, & M. Rehbinder (Eds.), *Beiträge zur Rechtspsychologie* (pp. 215-225). Berlin: Duncker & Humblot.
Jung, C.G. (1905). Die psychologische Diagnose des Tatbestandes. *Schweizerische Zeitschrift für Strafrecht, 18,* 368-408.
Kelsen, H. (1922). Der Begriff des Staates und die Sozialpsychologie. Mit besonderer Berücksichtigung von Freuds Theorie der Masse. *Imago, 8,* 97-141.
Kelsen, H. (1927). Der Staatsbegriff der Psychoanalyse. *Almanach für das Jahr 1927* (pp. 135-141). Wien: Internationaler Psychoanalytischer Verlag.
Kornfeld, S. (1914, 1917-1919). Das Rechtsgefühl. *Zeitschrift für Rechtsphilosophie in Lehre und Praxis, 1,* 135-187, 2, 28-100.
Larenz, C.K. (1991). *Methodenlehre der Rechtswissenschaft,* 6th ed. (pp. 39-43). Berlin: Springer.
Marti, H. (1958). *Urbild und Verfassung. Eine Studie zum hintergründigen Gehalt einer Verfassung.* Bern: Huber.
Naegeli, E. (1965). Das Böse und das Strafrecht. In Festgabe zum Schweizerischen Juristentag 1965 in St. Gallen (pp. 263-305). Bern: Stämpfli.
Petrazycki, L. (1907). *Über die Motive des Handelns und über das Wesen der Moral und des Rechts.* Berlin: H.W. Müller.
Rehbinder, M. (1987). Rechtsgefühl als Gemeinschaftsgefühl. In R. Jakob & M. Rehbinder (Eds.), *Beiträge zur Rechtspsychologie* (pp. 183-196). Berlin: Duncker & Humblot.
Reik, Th. (1929, repr. 1971). Geständniszwang und Strafbedürfnis. In T. Moser (Ed.), *Psychoanalyse und Justiz* (pp. 9-201). Frankfurt a.M.: Suhrkamp.
Rheinstein, M. (1928). Individualpsychologie und Staatsauffassung. *Internationale Zeitschrift für Individualpsychologie,* 6, 172-182.
Riezler, E. (1946). *Das Rechtsgefühl,* 2nd ed. München: Beck.
Sommer, F., & Huber, K. (1931). Rechtspsychologie. In *Staatslexikon der Görres-Gesellschaft,* 5th ed., Vol. 4, cols. 645-654.
Usteri, M. (1987). Beiträge der Tiefenpsychologie zur Ordnung von Eigentum und Raumgestaltung. In *Festgabe für Alois Troller zum 80. Geburtstag* (pp. 417-424). Berlin: Duncker & Humblot.
Weimar, R. (1969). *Psychologische Strukturen richterlicher Entscheidung.* Basel: Helbing & Lichtenhahn.
Wundt, W. (1918) *Völkerpsychologie, Vol. 9, Das Recht.* Leipzig: Alfred Kröner.

Psychology and Law in Spain

Vicente Garrido and Santiago Redondo

Introduction

The aim of writing a paper about the state of the art of legal psychology in Spain was a harder task only 10 years ago. Even though Emilio Mira y López wrote his Manual de Psicología Jurídica (Handbook of Legal Psychology) in 1932, with very interesting facts and suggestions, most of the things we are talking about here are the results of efforts that were born or have had their full development in the 1980s. One of the reasons is that psychology has been introduced into the legal area with more difficulties than in other areas of society; so, the number of legal practitioners coming from psychology is still very small, although it is growing. Another reason is the lack of interest in this subject shown by the universities that are more traditionally oriented toward clinical, educational and organizational topics.

Although, legal psychology in Spain is now in rapid expansion, it is still in its origins. This developmental process is the result of internal as well as external forces, that is to say, coming from the intrinsic development of psychology and from social and institutional demands. In the same way, some obstacles to the development of legal psychology have appeared from both of the sources. This matter is explained in the next section.

The Developmental Process of Legal Psychology in Spain

Among the advances deriving from the intrinsic development of psychology, the constitution of the Psychologists' Official Board in 1980 is the most important. This opened a dialog between legal institutions (courts, boards of lawyers, etc.) and psychology, this latter as an autonomous and differentiated knowledge. On the other hand, the Official Board, especially its Madrid and Barcelona delegations, has contributed notably to spreading interest in legal psychology, organizing conferences, courses, and meetings. One sign of this has been the creation of the Legal Division in Madrid's delegation of the Official Board, in 1987 (Clemente, 1989). Another important fact was the work done by some early professors and researchers of the 1970s that paved the way for the experimental developments in the 1980s. We are especially talking about Ramón Bayés and Muñoz Sabaté (1980), whose collection of papers (appeared earlier) under the title of Introducción a la Psicología Jurídica (Introduction to Legal Psychology), had a marked influence on legal psychologists of the time, mainly for the excellent reflections the papers introduced about the psychological practice applied to the law (Muñoz Sabaté, Bayés, & Munné, 1980).

The third influence coming from psychology was the catalytic effect of prison psychology on the rest of psycholegal topics. There is no doubt that prison psychologists, who started work in the 1970s, were the first to attract the attention of the universities and other social institutions toward the role psychologists might play in legal areas; this interest in prison psychology was also provoked by the explosive situation of Spanish prisons in the period known as "democratic transition" (1975-1982), as well as the prison regulations delivered in 1979, which gave a particularly important role to psychologists in the rehabilitation of offenders. On the other hand, as soon as psychologists were introduced in the legal mechanism, they were requested to participate in the assessment of indicted people (see Garayoa & Arozarena, 1990; Romero, 1990).

As mentioned above, the development of legal psychology was also helped by some factors outside of psychology itself. The 1980s have seen increased public interest in the employment of psychology, mainly among young people and families, not only in justice administration but also in the social services. The social services took over services to juveniles in a decentralized way after Spain was constituted as a "state of autonomias" (something like a federal state), with each province being responsible for several political and social domains. At the same time, there were psychologists working as managers in politics or administration who helped to introduce psychology into social and criminological areas.

However, there were also many difficulties. With respect to psychology as an academic discipline, the universities have not been very interested in legal psychology. For example, we do not have any subject carrying this label in our universities. Perhaps one reason is that the more prestigious professors, who were responsible for creating the faculties of psychology in the 1970s, also came from other areas of psychology. On the other hand, the Institutes of Criminology, which were mostly established in the same period, have not been able to fill this vacuum, because of their precarious institutional situation (see Garrido, 1990a).

Outside of psychology, there were two lines of obstacles: First, the rigidity of the legal mechanism, only very recently altered, and always with very little money. As an example, the 1983 Proposed Spanish Penal Code suggested the "criminological sentence," compulsory, but not binding, which ought to be solicited when the judge had to decide on such important issues as suspension of sentence, parole, enforcement of certain "behavior norms", and the like (García de Pablos, 1988). Currently there are few possibilities for this innovation to become law. The same can be said for the introduction of juries, probation, the programs of victim restitution and mediation, and other alternative measures to the penal code. Second, the critical movement (to Taylor, Walton, & Young's critical criminological way, 1973, 1975) has been stronger in Spain than the positivistic influence (see Funes, 1984), and, as we know, this means more ideological disputes and less reflection about practical issues. It seems that empirical works only recently becoming more prominent perhaps because the public organizations that ask for participation of psychologists are being more exigent in outcome evaluation (Albarrán, 1990; Garrido, 1990; Vázquez, 1990). It is also true that legal psychologists are now less ashamed of carrying out a work that is mainly technical instead of "critical" or "ideological."

The Practice of Legal Psychology in Spain

In the following pages we will show briefly the main lines of applied legal psychology in our country in the areas of criminological research, police psychology, court psychology, minors, and victims (prison psychology is not included here).

Until recently, what little criminological research was made in Spain was performed at the universities. In the last years, however, practitioners have taken part in the investigation of their daily work. The result is that it is now possible to distinguish a small research group of legal psychologists. Even though today universities are carrying out most research, with two exceptions, both of them located in Barcelona: the Rehabilitation Service of the Justice Department, in Catalonia, and the Studies and Formation Centre, in the same Department. The former has been making important contributions to program evaluation and psychological studies of immates during the five last years (see Redondo, Roca, Perez, Sanchez, & Deumal, in press). The latter promotes research on the origins and development of social deviation in Catalonia, as well as evaluative works, especially in the juvenile area.

Other research topics are: personality variables, and, in particular, the studies by Eysenck (Garrido, Nuñez, & Gil, 1990; Pérez, 1987); socialization scales (Silva et al., 1987); sensation seeking (Pérez et al., 1987); cognitive variables, like time orientation (Salcedo & Luengo, 1987), values (Luengo, 1982), role-taking and problem-solving skills (Garrido, Huertas, & Sánchez, 1990; Guillén et al., 1989); the female offender (Clemente, 1985); environment and social interaction variables (Mirón, Otero, & Luengo, 1988; Rouanet, Vallés, & Garrido, 1988).

Criminological research in Spain has two characteristics: On the one hand, there are no centers of investigation specifically devoted to crime research, with the exception of the Barcelona center mentioned above, and almost all work is left to some professors in faculties of psychology and education. On the other hand, there is a lack long-term research program with large samples that are so important in current criminology (Ohlin, Tonry, & Farrington, 1989).

With respect to police psychology, it is now in its very beginning, thanks mainly to the creation of the School of Police Studies and the Police Training Division: With the help of these institutions, there have been improvements in gearing civil servants' skills specifically toward police work, including neighborhood relations for adopting strategies of crime prevention. However, most of this kind of work is carried out by police psychologists, who have almost no links with academic psychology (Clemente, 1989).

Victimology is currently one of the more popular areas, as in many other countries. Child abuse, in particular, has provoked the attention of goverment and local authorities; it is estimated that abuse is present in about 5 to 10% of families. Besides interesting work on this phenomenon (see De Paúl, 1988, on risk factors), societies have been created for its study and prevention, like the Asociación Catalana para la Infancia Maltrada (Catalonian Society for Child Abuse). Similar interest has been raised by cases of wife abuse. A senate task force established in 1988 clearly showed the seriousness of its incidence and effects (see the Official State Report, no. 313, May 12, 1989). Unfortunately, psychological attention in terms of prevention and treatment for the woman abused is very scarce, because there are no psychologists working in the refuges or offices for helping victims). Actually, there is no public psychological help at all for any kind of victim, with the exception of abused children who are under the care of the social services.

In the area of victimology research, we have to point out the recent compilation of crime surveys, both in collaboration with international projects (see van Dijk, Mayhew, & Killias, 1990) and in Spain (Berenguer, Garrido, & Montoro, 1990; Lahosa, 1989).

The participation of psychologists is more extended in courts, through their work in juvenile and family courts and in medical and forensic clinics. In juvenile courts, psychologists, alongside social workers, advise the judge when he or she has to take a measure with juvenile delinquents. Since their establishment in September 1989, 36 psychologists work in these courts. Their current challenges are to go beyond diagnostic advise for the judge's sentence, and achieve a broader responsibility for the supervision, planning, and evaluation of the intervention measures carried out by the social services (Urra, 1990). Psychologists also have an important role in the family court established in 1981; their job involves advising the judge on decisions related to assigning custodes of the child/children to one of the parents applying for divorce, as well as planning the visit regime and assessing parents in cases of adoption. As in the juvenile courts, psychologists want to extend their range of action; in detail, they want to stress the role of mediator, intervening in a preventive way, so the couple can achieve general agreement on divorce conditions and thus avoid the problems inherent in this kind of legal conflict, especially for the children (Ibañez, 1990).

The introduction of psychology in the medical-forensic clinics since January 1988 is very significant for the future of legal psychology in Spain although only three jobs currently exist. Their job involves assessing the people designated by the judge, generally in terms of psychopathology, personality, intelligence, and mental impairment. Psychologists, with social workers, are the only nonmedical professionals who work in the clinic (Vázquez, 1990); although their job involves both the penal and the civil courts, the former is clearly predominant (82% vs. 12%, in Madrid and Barcelona statistics for 1988). Psychological advances in this kind of service will require tests adapted to the population involved, the formulation of theories about people at risk (both victims and offenders), and the dissemination and consolidation of psychologists' work among judges and lawyers (Vázquez, 1990).

We must not forget certain studies carried out by academic psychologists in the phase of the court trial that are assessing the competence of juries (simulated) (Garzón, 1986; Sobral, Arce, & Fariña, 1990) and evaluating witness testimony (Mira & Diges, 1990).

The spread of psychologists in the social services has been impressive in the last ten years, both in management and in technical jobs. There are psychologists in almost every kind of open, semiresidential and residential facility for convicted delinquents or those on demand, as well as in the diagnostic centers that have to study the child to assign him/her to the best resource that fits his/her personal and social deficits. There are also some psychologists working in nongovernmental agencies collaborating in this kind of service. All of them are now in a delicate position, from the point of view of the technical work they have to do, because they are moving from a medical model to a more psychoeducatively oriented model; so they have to achieve a coordination - always difficult - with other professionals and - still more difficult - with other private and public resources (Garrido, 1990). Another current challenge is to involve the families of delinquents in treatment programs; something that has not been tried by the social services in any formal and systematic way.

Main Issues of Legal Psychology in Spain

In this section, we present the main issues of legal psychology in Spain, from three perspectives: as a profession, as a scientific discipline, and as an applied practice.

With respect to the first point, it is true that legal psychologists are obtaining a high status. In the recent 2nd Conference of the Official Board of Psychologists (April 1990), the legal section was one of the most successful in terms of attendance, and the debates were of high quality. There is promising evidence that lawyers, judges, and other law professionals are increasingly requesting the assistance of psychologists in dealing with the topics described in the previous pages. On the other hand, there are good ties among all psychologists working in these fields (perhaps because there are, as yet, so few of them?). Their salary is similar to that of other professionals in the administration of justice.

In the conference mentioned above a fact was observed that is significative for the development of legal psychology as a discipline and helped confirm previous evidence; we mean a growing ability to modify theoretical and action models when empirical evidence supports such change. In fact, this point was already suggested when we pointed out the shift from the medical model to a psychoeducational one in the work of youth welfare psychologists, but it is also obvious in the search for more preventive and ecological models among court (youth and family) psychologists. In a similar way, this innovation can be observed among prison psychologists, especially in Catalonia, where both the medical/clinical model and classical regime/treatment prisons are being replaced by environmental, educational and organizational models (Redondo, Garrido, & Pérez, 1988).

However, there is another point that, at the same time, has defined the practice of a large number of legal psychologists in the last 10 years: a certain lack of confidence in their own strength and performance. Without doubt, this has been partially the result of the lack of tradition in the discipline, but it also reflects the permanent struggle that legal psychologists have had with other professional groups, especially with social workers in prisons and social services and with forensic doctors and psychiatrists in the courts (this has been a common fact in all the countries, given the traditional bonding between psychiatry and law, see Foucault, 1973).

Generally speaking, we can say, that legal psychology in Spain is currently both an art and a science, although with a clear tendency toward science. By using the word "art," we do not wish to deny the "art" involved in good professional practice; we only wanted to use this word to mean practice based mainly on improvisation, selfishness, and the utilization of models that, again and again, do not work.

Now, there is no doubt that legal psychology is still far from the "scientific" stage. Research is one of the more urgent needs to be satisfied, in order to nourish the debate about methods and practice in the several areas of legal administration. In our opinion, despite the great number of conferences and meeting about criminological matters in Spain in the last years (especially in comparison with the past), a good level of discussion, involving the consideration of the latest empirical knowledge, has yet to be accomplished. We have already mentioned the lack of research centers and academic subjects dealing with criminology and psycholegal studies. Accordingly very few journals disseminate this kind of information. It is worth mentioning the pioneering Anuario de Sociología y Psicología Jurídicas (Legal Sociology and Psychology Annual), created by Barcelona's Law School, and the new (1989) journal Delincuencia/Delinquency, the first social sciences interdisciplinary journal ever published in Spain, devoted to every kind of criminological research and practice.

One of the main problems is that criminal policy and penal law are scarcely based on criminological investigation. A symptom of this is that Spain has not witnessed a debate like that in Germany (see Dünkel, 1988) and other countries (see Currie, 1985, for the USA) about the distribution of research tasks together with the basic points to be taken into account in the elaboration of matters pertaining to research. According to Dünkel (1988), this discussion dealt with the division between what is known as "State Criminology," characteristic of administration, removed from theory, but closely related to practice, and university criminology, this being highly critical and closely connected with theory. It is indeed difficult for a discussion of this nature to be held at the moment in Spain. On the one hand, there is as yet no such thing as "Spanish state criminology" (even though one can read, in the introduction of a recent law that updates the penal code, that the main aim is to fit the principle of *minimum intervention*; see Official State Report, no. 148, June 22nd, 1989), while, on the other hand, university criminologists are still a long way from forming a common cause of any appreciable weight (perhaps with the exception of the academic lawyers who have chosen a *critical* orientation). We also have to say that there is no way for us to know whether the government is confident in the use of certain legal, social, and political responses as strategies to reduce crime, even if we look at the daily activities of the justice administration. And the attitude of Spanish criminologists in general cannot really be considered belligerent with regard to the present goverment. Some of the most dissenting voices are directed toward the state of juvenile justice in Spain (which, as in other countries is in urgent need of reform, as well as updating existing social services). The ideal of rehabilitation in prisons also comes in for a great deal of criticism. However, in this country there is no solid core of criminological analysis that presses, advices, or influences state administration or regional governments in any tangible way.

Another issue of the "art"-defined situation involves the absence of a solid technology, of a research tradition on which rapid progress could be built. Almost as a conclusion to the deficiencies mentioned, we can say that it is not yet possible to write a handbook on legal psychology in Spain, presenting the most prominent work techniques and a progressive evaluation of them. Ross and Sales (1985) make a similar statement in their review of the forensic legal programs approved by the American Psychological Association:

> Yet interest alone is not sufficient. If psychologists are to work effectively in activities which overlap with the law, they must be adequately trained in its special demands ... during graduate school most psychologists are not exposed to legal issues involved in the practice of psychology, or at least not sufficiently exposed to make them competent in this area of their work. (p. 87)

Conclusions

The low development of certain areas of legal psychology in Spain is also the product of current legal practices, which do not permit the intervention of psychologists in a legal way. For example, the prediction of violent behavior in delinquents and adult offenders is something strongly regulated by law, and, in practical terms, even if the psychologist shows a good predictive ability, this could not be employed in a useful way. The same can be said of the prediction and assessment of probationers and prisoners on parole. On the one hand, the regime criteria - established by law - are the determinants of probation or a parole order and not the psychological ones. On the other hand, the absence of intervention programs in the community to which these people are assigned does not allow the psychologist to extend his or her work over this part of the sentence. And we find again the same situation in psychology applied to police, where all work is carried out by people who are both psychologists and police officers. Finally, it is obvious that certain areas of research cannot go beyond simulation, because our laws do not provide the legal basis that would allow real experimentation (e.g., assessing the competence of juries and evaluating eyewitness testimony).

Returning to the present, and with respect to the things we can improve from the present, it would be best to summarize by saying that legal psychology is still at a stage of "art" because: (a) we do not yet have adequate theoretical frameworks to guide the different activities in the different legal psychology issues; (b) material and human sources are scarce; (c) there are no empirically oriented criminological research centers; (d) we are only beginning to develop applied technology and legal psychology; (e) we need comprehensive and coordinated social and institutional programs.

We must develop more intensive and common work in the near future, trying to establish some common criteria to be followed by all legal psychologists; these criteria should be established by expert commissions and the Psychologist's Official Board. Some of the basic points to be answered would be the following:

1. Have we sufficient knowledge and technology to carry out every kind of request we receive?

2. In what cases and how does the psychologist have to collaborate with those professionals who work in ways that meet his or her disapproval (e.g., psychiatrists, judges)?

3. In what way could collaboration with psychologists improve work in the social service system?

4. How could psychologists become more involved in the decision points of the legal system, so that their work can have a deeper and more longterm impact?

In our opinion, we need to stress adequate training for legal psychologists. Universities can no longer remain blind to this reality. A well-trained legal psychologist would have the following characteristics: (he/she) (a) knows the law very well; (b) understands the limits of psychology and therefore behaves prudently, but without being skeptical or showing a lack of self-confidence; (c) collaborates easily with other professionals, and prefers work well done rather than fighting for corporate interests; (d) even if critical of the system, he or she does not have prejudices about it or certain subjects; (e) knows the basic frameworks that give structure to his or her work, as well as the most important technology to be applied in every situation; (f) knows the peculiarities of the system in which he or she works, and tries to modify it in order to improve it; (g) believes in the concept of "action research".

On the other hand, we must not forget the important progress made by legal psycholgy in the last 10 years, both in terms of social recognition and the number of jobs occupied. This is the reason by legal psychology is one of the most promising field in current Spanish psychology.

References

Albarrán, A. (1990). Futuro de la psicología forense. *Comunicaciones al II Congreso del C.O.P. Area Psicología Jurídica* (pp. 138-141). Madrid: C.O.P.

Berenguer, M., Garrido, V., & Montoro, L. (1990). Factores psicosociales del miedo al delito. *Comunicaciones al II Congreso del C.O.P. Area Psicología Jurídica* (pp. 1-9). Madrid: C.O.P.

Clemente, M. (1985). Delincuencia en la mujer. In J. de Miguel, & V. Sancha (Eds.), *El tratamiento penitenciario: Su práctica* (pp. 149-158). Madrid: Ministerio de Justicia.

Clemente, M. (1989). La psicología jurídica. *Papeles del psicólogo, 36/37,* 99.

Currie, E. (1985). *Confronting crime.* New York: Phanteon Books.

De Paúl, J. (1988). *Maltrato y abandono infantil: Identificación de factores de riesgo.* Vitoria: S.C. de Publicaciones del Gobierno Vasco.

Dünkel, F. (1988). Tendencias de la investigación criminológica en la R.F.A. *Papers dÉstudis i Formació,* no.4, 165-184.

Foucault, M. (1973). *Moi, Pierre Riviere, ayant égorgé ma mere, ma soeur et mon frere...* Paris: Gallimard.

Funes, J. (1984). *La nueva delincuencia infantil y juvenil.* Barcelona:Paidós.

Garayoa, B., & Arozarena, M.J. (1990). El peritaje psicológico en el ámbito de lo penal. *Communicaciones al II Congreso del C.O.P. Area Psicología Jurídica* (pp. 62-65). Madrid: C.O.P.

García de Pablos, A. (1988). *Manual de criminología.* Madrid: Espasa.

Garrido, V. (1990a). Criminology in present day in Spain (in press).

Garrido, V. (1990b). *Pedagogía de la delincuencia.* Barcelona: CEAC.

Garrido, V., Gil, C., & Nuñez, J. (1990). Análisis de las variables extraversión y neuroticismo de Eysenck en relación con otros factores criminológicos. *Comunicaciones al II Congreso del C.O.P. Area Psicología* (pp. 238-242). Madrid: C.O.P.

Garrido, V., Huertas, E., & Sánchez, F. (1990). Presentación de la adaptación española del test de role-taking de Chandler. *Comunicaciones al II Congreso del C.O.P. Area Diagnóstica y Evaluación Psicológica* (pp. 138-242). Madrid: C.O.P.

Garzón, A. (1986). Psicología social y tribunales de justicia. In J. Burillo, & M. Clemente (Eds.). *Psicología social y sistema penal* (pp. 135-158). Madrid: Alintia.

Guillén, A., Maydeu, A., Pons, J., & Vigil, A. (1989). *Resolución de problemas y delincuencia: Un estudio comparativa* Tarragona: Dpto. Educación y psicología (unpublished manuscript).

Ibañez, V. (1990). Los psicólogos en los juzgados de familia. *Comunicaciones al II Congreso del C.O.P. Area Psicología Jurídica* (pp. 126-130). Marid: C.O.P.

Lahosa, J.M. (1989). La encuesta de victimización de 1988 en Barcelona. *Prevenció,* 3, 51-68.

Luengo, A. (1982). *Sistema de valores, personalidad y delincuencia juvenil.* Doctoral thesis. Universidad de Santiago de Compostela.

Mira y López, E. (1932). *Manual de Psicología Jurídica.* Barcelona: Salvat.

Mira, J., & Diges, M. (1990). Teorías del sentido común sobre el testimonio de testigos. *Communicaciones al II Congreso del C.O.P. Area Psicología Jurídica* (pp. 16-20). Madrid: C.O.P.

Miron, L., Otero, J.M., & Luengo, A. (1988). Un estudio de la influencia de las interacciones familiares sobre los distintos tipos de conducta desviada de los adolescentes varones. *Análisis y Modificación de Conducta,* 14, 5-23.

Muñoz Sabaté, L., Bayés, R., & Munné, F. (1980). *Introducción a la psicología jurídica.* México: Trillas.

Ohlin, L., Tonry, M., & Farrington, D. (1989). *Program on human development and criminal behavior*. University of Cambridge. Unpublished manuscript.

Pérez, J. (1987). La delincuencia como conducta multicausal. In J. Pérez (Ed.), *Bases psicológicas de la delincuencia y de la conducta antisocial* (pp. 205-220). Barcelona: PPU.

Pérez, J., Ortet, G., Plá, S., & Simó, S. (1987). Escala de búsqueda de sensaciones para niños y adolescentes (EBS-J). *Evaluación Psicológica/Psychological assessment, 3*, 283-290.

Redondo, S., Roca, M., Perez, E:, Sanchez, A., & Deumal, E. (in press). Diseño ambiental de una prisión de jóvenes: Cinco años de evaluación.

Redondo, S., Garrido, V., & Pérez, E. (1988). Entorno penitenciario y competencia psicosocial. *Papers DÉstudies i Formació*, no. 4, 9-21.

Romero, J. (1990). Psicología Jurídica: La perical penal en navarra 1984-1990. *Communicaciones al II Congreso del C.O.P. Area Psicología Jurídica* (pp. 66-69). Madrid: C.O.P.

Ross, M., & Sales, B., (1985). Legal/forensic training in clinical psychology. In D.P. Farrington & J. Gunn (Eds.), *Reactions to crime: The public, the police, courts, and prisons.* (pp. 87-111). Chichester: Wiley.

Rouanet, A., Vallés, Y., & Garrido, V. (1988). *Aspectos ecológicos y psicosociales de la delincuencia juvenil en Valencia.* Valencia: Generalitat Valenciana. Consellería de Treball i Seguretat Social.

Salcedo, M.C., & Luengo, A. (1987). Un análisis de la perspectiva de tiempo futuro en delincuentes institucionalizados y no institucionalizados. *Análisis y Modificación de Conducta, 13*, 331-365.

Silva, F., Martorell, C., & Clemente, A. (1987). El cuestionare 16 (Junior). Adaptación española. *Evaluación Psicológica/Psychological Assessment, 3*, 55-78

Sobral, J., Arce, R., & Fariña, F. (1990). Grupos ideológicamente sesgados: Toma de decisiones judiciales. Análisis de la interacción. *Comunicaciones al II Congreso del C.O.P. Area Psicología Jurídica.* (pp. 111-117). Madrid: C.O.P.

Taylor, I., Walton, P., & Young, J. (1973). *The new Criminology.* London: Routledge & Kegan Paul.

Taylor, I., Walton, P., & Young, J. (1975). *The critical Criminology.* London: Routledge & Kegan Paul.

Urra, J. (1990). El psicólogo en los juzgados de menores. *Comunicaciones al II Congreso del C.O.P. Area Psicología Jurídica.* (pp. 134-138). Madrid: C.O.P.

Van Dijk, J., Mayhew, P., & Killias, M. (1990). *Experiences of crime across the world.* Deventer, The Netherlands: Kluwer.

Vázquez, B. (1990). Los psicólogos en las clínicas médico-forenses. *Comunicaciones al II Congreso del C.O.P. Area Psicología Jurídica* (pp. 130-133). Madrid: C.O.P.

Law and Psychology in Italy

Giovanni B. Traverso and Paola Manna

Introduction

The goal of the present paper is to draw a historical overview on the development of the relationships between psychology and law in Italy from the beginning of the 20th century up to the present. This covers the following issues: (1) the development of psychological approaches to an explanation of criminal behavior; in this area, we will focus on the contributions of some of the most famous Italian scholars to the development of a clinical-psychological approach to the study of crime; (2) the development of legal-forensic psychology; in this area, we will outline the contributions of clinical psychology within the Italian criminal justice system. We will skip, for reasons of space, the development of the so-called "judiciary psychology" strictu sensu, which, as everyone knows, is specifically devoted to research on all actors who, in various roles (judges, witnesses, lawyers, defendants, victims), participate in the criminal trial (Gulotta, 1987).

The Development of the Psychological Approach to Criminal Behavior

The psychological approach to an explanation of criminal behavior (in traditional Italian terms: "Criminal Psychology") has an ancient tradition in Italy that arises mainly through the demand, coming from lawyers and jurists, for a greater use of the scientific knowledge that had been accumulating within the field of general psychology, a new science making rapid progress at the beginning of the 20th century. The theoretical frame of reference, represented by so-called "criminal dynamic theory", already stated in its very primitive nucleus by outstanding jurists like Romagnosi (1833) and Carmignani (1831) was defined by Longo (1906), professor of penal procedural law at the Royal University of Naples, in his treatise "Psicologia Criminale": He defined the scientific subject matter of such a discipline as "the set of laws that governs the mental formations of the crime phenomenon", and its tasks not only in the "attempt to analyze the crime phenomenon in its subjective perspective", but also

> in the purpose of coping with both the justice and prison systems; and of countering the criminal's dangerous intrapsychic functioning with some remedy at hand, without violating the demand for justice, the specific force of Society.

Longo's (1906) conceptualization must not surprise us; we need only to recall, in fact, that sciences like criminal sociology and criminal anthropology had already been consolidated by the work of Lombroso (1876), Ferri (1892), and Garofalo (1885). Such sciences had the specific goal of applying experimental (i.e., inductive) methods to the study of crime and penal sanctions, and they considered the psychological study of offenders, although embedded within a biological frame of reference (the so-called "criminal biology"), of the greatest importance (Angiolella, undated). A direct follower of Lombroso, and the founder of the School of Criminal Anthropology at Rome, Benigno Di Tullio (1945) stated his original theory of "criminal constitution" - an approach very close to Pende's (1939) biotypology - as the specific condition of predisposition to crime. Within Di Tullio's theoretical frame of reference, the psychological study of offenders and knowledge of their personality represent the means by which

> we can come to reconstruct the course of the criminal action itself, and to establish how and why the idea of the crime arose; how and why it could develop and persist in the individual consciousness; finally, how and why it could translate into criminal acting out.

Next to Di Tullio's perspective, we can quote that of a very famous Italian jurist, Enrico Altavilla (1949, 1950, 1953) who, especially in his treatise "La dinamica del delitto" (translated into several foreign languages), offers the reader an exhaustive piece of work about contemporary scientific knowledge and theoretical guidelines in the field of psychology and psychopathology applied to the study of criminals.

Agostino Gemelli (1946), in open conflict with the dogmas of the positive school of criminology, with the guidelines of criminal anthropology, and finally with Di Tullio's theory (he upbrided Di Tullio overall for his too rigid deterministic position with its consequent absolute negation of any free choice on the part of the criminal), faces the problem of studying criminals with the methods of psychology (especially differential psychology),

> in order not to build a typology of the various kind of criminals, as the positive school of criminology attempted to do, but in order to pick up, in human personality, in its development, and in its reacting to the social environment, the psychological process by means of which the criminal action reveals itself.

Given that crime is a specific and unique manifestation of a certain individual, we need to perform the so-called "clinic of crime", which consists in the reconstruction of the process through which a given subject has come to commit a crime. By recognizing that psychoanalysis and individual psychology had opened such a path in the field of abnormal offenders, showing the psychogenesis of those criminal acts that are expressions or equivalents of a neurosis, Gemelli proposed transfering this method to the "normal" field, and envisaged that this would make it possible to build that differential psychology of crime for which criminal sociology and criminal anthropology had uselessly attempted to draw the fundamental principles.

Giacomo Canepa (1953, 1974), founder of the School of Criminal Anthropology at Genoa, outstanding forensic medical doctor and criminologist, and currently president of the International Society for Criminology, has dedicated all his scientific life to the analysis of the concept of personality. "The only personality that the research worker can define" - he says -

> is the set of data coming to the surface by a complete examination of a specific individual, studied by all the more recent and useful means that science can supply, in order for him or her to be able to differentiate one person from another. (Canepa, 1974)

By analyzing the relationships between personality theories and criminological research, with special regard to juvenile delinquency, Canepa works out some original ideas starting from the studies of Pinatel (1963) on the "central nucleus of criminal personality" and of Mailloux (1962), psychotherapist at the Boscoville Center in Montreal (Canada). As he states: (a) Crime in general, particularly juvenile delinquency, recognizes a common causal factor in immaturity, which comes to the observation of the clinician under the shape of many psychological traits (like aggressiveness, egocentrism, lability, inconstancy, sense of opposition); these traits are also responsible for tendency to recidivism. (b) In order to understand criminal development we need to set up the mechanisms through which we arrive at frustration from immaturity and at other symptoms of antisocial behavior from frustration. (c) The personality traits must be interpreted in a dynamic sense and, then, must be considered not as an inherited and stable endowment of the individual, but rather the result of peculiar interpersonal processes. In Canepa's view, we need to consider the problem at the individual level according to a phenomenological and psychodynamic perspective: For the author, it is an anthropological perspective in criminology that constitutes the very genuine and concrete ground of modern criminal anthropology ("clinical criminology"). Later on, Canepa elaborated a new definition and conceptualization of criminology, which he defines as an "interdisciplinary science that studies antisocial behavior in order to ascertain its causes and to realize adequate programs of prevention and correction" (Canepa, 1982). In this perspective, human sciences and social sciences converge in the study of crime and offenders, but such convergence does not mean a simple matching of the two sciences, that is, a simple sum of knowledge coming from different approaches (multidisciplinary approach), but a concrete and effective collaboration between sciences, with reciprocal permeation and cultural and methodological interchange (interdisciplinary approach).

A very strong supporter of an integrated approach to the scientific study of criminal personality, criminal behavior, and corrections, Franco Ferracuti (1966), eclectic figure of medical physician, psychologist, and criminologist, with a very deep background in sociology acquired during long years spent in the United States of America in strict contact with the cultural and sociological education of U.S. scholars, elaborates in his monograph "The Subculture of Violence. Toward an Integrated Theory in Criminology", written together with M. E. Wolfgang, one of the most valid attempts to construct an integrated criminological theory. For Ferracuti and Wolfgang, integration in criminology means

> bringing together empirical data relative to the same phenomenon that have been collected by independent disciplines and interpreted within their limited parameters of orientation so that an analytical synthesis becomes minimally the combination of the parts and maximally a new perspective. (Ferracuti & Wolfgang, 1966)

Through this method the authors set up the theory of the "subculture of violence", an approach that offers the advantage of combining psychological and sociological elements in an attempt to explain the concentration of violent behavior in certain socioeconomic groups and certain specific ecological areas.

Many other important Italian scholars embrace an integrated approach in criminology, and independently elaborate original theoretical perspectives in the field of criminology and more specifically in the field of criminal psychology and psychopathology (e.g., Carrieri,

1987; De Vincentiis, Callieri, & Castellani, 1972; Fornari, 1989; Franchini & Introna, 1972; Nivoli & Sanna, 1982; Ponti, 1990; Portigliatti Barbos & Marini, 1964).

More recently, the development of criminal psychology in Italy has received much support from scholars in studying the field of juvenile delinquency. Tullio Bandini and Uberto Gatti (1972) in their first monograph "Family dynamics and juvenile delinquency," were the first in Italy to set up the basis of a psychosocial interpretation of juvenile delinquency. On one hand, they analyze the relationships between family members' attitudes (especially parents') toward children and delinquent behavior, taking into account the different processes through which family members induce individual socialization and, by favoring failure of socialization itself, eventually produce deviant behavior in children. On the other hand, they emphasize - with reference to G.H. Mead's (1934) "symbolic interactionism", - the labeling approach (e.g., Becker, 1966; Goffman, 1961) and, finally, research on undetected crime rates (e.g., Ennis, 1967; Wallerstein & Wyle, 1947). The social processes of labeling and stigmatization favor the internalization of a "negative identity" in adolescents (a concept borrowed from Mailloux, even though interpreted in a much broader sense) that in turn compels them to choose delinquent and criminal behavior as a permanent life-style. This interpretation of juvenile delinquecy is further developed in a second monograph (e.g., Bandini & Gatti, 1974), in which the authors come to an original approach "in search of a new clinical criminology," by utilizing the work of Debuyst (1975), who suggests the overcoming of the concept of personality for the explanation of criminal acting out, and proposes employment at the notion of "meaning" attributed by the agent to his or her deviant behavior. As suggested, in criminal psychology, we must not limit ourselves to the study of overt delinquent and criminal behavior, but we have to study all problematic behavior. In order to understand problematic behavior the concept of identity becomes crucial; a concept that allows the clinical criminologist to get rid of the individualistic approach in the study of crime and delinquency, and to face the problems of the relationships between the single individual and the social environment, defined as the location of potentially criminogenic interactions.

Like Bandini and Gatti, Gaetano De Leo (e.g. De Leo & Cuomo, 1983), professor of criminology at the University of Rome, also analyzes the social world from a psychosocial perspective by studying the social perception of crime and delinquency with particular reference to juvenile delinquency. According to De Leo, criminality is not a fact that stands objectively, that is given ontologically, and thus can be studied, treated, and eliminated. "What we can study, treat, attempt to eliminate," De Leo states, "is not a given fact but only its social meaning, the type of problem it represents for society." Moreover, De Leo attempts to demonstrate a more specific thesis according to which "the quality of actual perceptions and reactions to criminality influences the characteristics of the criminal phenomenon itself." On the basis of such theoretical premises, De Leo proposes to test new hypotheses for the further investigation of common sense, mass media, and intelligentsia attitudes toward young delinquents, their typical forms of deviance, and institutions of social control. Relationships among social perception, institutional control, and the phenomenon of juvenile delinquency are ideally represented by the author in an equilateral triangle with these three variables at its points, none of which is per se original and independent, given that each of them defines its own characteristics in relation to the other two, in a circular way.

In the interactionistic perspective, we can quote also the work of Alessandro Salvini (1982), professor of theories of personality at Padua. Salvini, borrowing the anthropomorphic model elaborated by Harrè and Secord (1972), states that

> deviant behavior is not the simple and automatic by-product of given sociopsychological conditions and causes, but also represents a choice on the part of the individual who plans his or her own actions, defines situations, and gives himself or herself reasons and justifications in view of a given goal. (Salvini, 1982)

For Salvini, human actions have a specific meaning that other events of the natural world do not have. As a consequence, regularities (or irregularities) that we can observe in human behavior cannot be considered as derived from "laws" and, hence, cannot be explained in the same terms as those which apply in the natural world. Such regularities or irregularities are the very by-product of frames of meaning (historically mutable, institutionally objectified and legitimated) that take the name of social reality. On the basis of such premises, Salvini discloses the epistemological mistake of clinical psychology, as well as of psychiatry and criminal anthropology: In fact, such sciences have often confused the level of prescriptive (situational) norms with that of the biological individual.

Finally we want to quote the work of one of the present authors, Giovanni B. Traverso, professor of criminology at the University of Siena. In his studies in the field of general criminology and legal psychology/psychiatry, Traverso emphasizes empirical research and the utilization of quantitative methods and contributes to the development of scientific knowledge especially about issues like the relationships between mental disease and crime (e.g., Traverso, 1977), some patterns of criminal behavior (e.g., Bandini, Gatti, & Traverso, 1983; Traverso, Manna, & Marugo 1989), the role of the expert in the criminal justice system (e.g., Canepa, Bandini, & Traverso, 1973; Traverso, Manna, & Marzi, 1988), and finally sentencing in the juvenile justice system (e.g., Traverso & Manna, 1988). Traverso is also well-known in Italy also for writing the first monograph appearing in our country that critically evaluates so-called "critical" or "marxist" criminology (e.g., Traverso & Verde, 1981).

As we can note, the development of theoretical perspectives in the field of criminal psychology has been enormous, so that the latest approaches that we have just considered appear to be very far away from the first ones. The rapid shift of theoretical reference (from biological constitutionalism to symbolic interactionism and naturalism) did not occur in a sociopolitical vacuum but can be explained through the radical socio-political changes witnessed by our country during the last century, dominated for a long period by fascism and its idealistic philosophy, and only since the late 1960s (years, as we know, characterised by trade-union and student struggles, the strengthening of the Left, and the challenge of some age-old correctional and social control institutions, starting with the mental hospital) becoming permeated by more progressive perspectives, which led Italian scholars in the field of human sciences to embrace radical positions, more and more anchored to a view of the individual human as provided with high degrees of consciousness, rationality, and freedom.

The Development of Legal-Forensic Psychology

As a consequence of the shift of interest of criminology from the study of crime to the study of the individual criminal, from the study of the act to the potential danger of the individual, from the punishment of the offender to the protection of the social system, psychology and psychiatry began to extend their interest to problems of crime and justice, replying to the demands of the new penal systems that, through confinement in prison, hard labor, and isolation, no longer only wish to punish individuals for the perpetration of crime but also want to transform the criminal's personality, habits, and motivations (e.g., Foucault, 1981). Since the beginning of the 19th century, the traditional penal system in Europe began to be supported by a technical apparatus within which medical sciences gained more and more importance. Paradoxically, in Italy, owing to either the radicalism of Ferri's theses (Ferri wanted to eliminate from penal law the concepts of criminal responsibility and of penal sanctions) or the opposition to the implications of the positive school of criminology by the Catholic Church and the fascist regime, we witnessed the failure both of progress in criminological studies and of the preliminary project of a new penal code, based on the concept of "dangerousness," presented by Ferri to the Italian Parliament in 1921 (e.g., Radzinovicz, 1964). As a consequence, a new penal model (the so-called technical-juridical method) set up by Rocco was successful, so that Rocco himself in 1930 made Italy adopt the new code, in which the unique residue of Ferri's concepts of "dangerousness" and "legal responsibility" was represented by the bipartition: penal sanctions-security measures. However, the general ideology of the system was essentially classically retributive. In such a system, characterized by a deep distrust of human sciences in general, particularly psychology, the possibility of a psychological evaluation of the defendant's personality by the expert was excluded (art. 314, Rocco's penal procedural code). Thus, in Rocco's code, the psychological evaluation of the defendant's personality was left to the judge, who had to consider while enforcing penal sanctions, that is within his or her own discretionary power, a whole series of indexes, either objective (the seriousness of the offense) or subjective and therefore of an overt psychological matrix (the so-called "capacity to commit crimes" - art. 133, Rocco's penal code). The only possibility for scientifically investigating on the defendant by the expert was left to those cases in which doubts about the presence of a psychopathological imbalance in the individual were raised. In these cases, and only in these cases, a psychiatrist was entrusted with performing a "psychiatric expertise" with the twofold goal of (a) assessing the defendant's "imputability" (i.e., his/her capacity for understanding and free will at the time of the crime) and (b) evaluating the defendant's "social dangerousness" (which refers to the probability that the defendant will commit new crimes in the future). The prohibition of the criminological (psychological) expertise was severely criticized, mainly during the 1950, by jurists and, more recently, by criminologists and psychologists (e.g., Battaglini, 1955; Canepa, 1987; De Roberto, 1980; Gulotta, 1979; Rossi, 1949;). Indeed, those criticisms had a great impact on the legislator who, by passing the law 3/4/1974 n. 108, reavired the Italian Government to issue a new penal procedural law with, among others, the specific goal of

> reassessing the expertise, with particular reference to medico-legal, psychiatric, and criminological expertise, ensuring at the same time the greatest technical and scientific competence by the expert. (art. 3 n. 10)

However, because of various political vicissitudes, the new project (1978) was never enforced into law. Again, a new project was formulated, which only recently became law (October 24th 1989). The new legislative act, however, returns to the old ideology and, strongly shaped by the criteria of due process of law, excludes once again the possibility of carrying out, during the trial, a criminological (psychological) expertise, which in the meantime had been criticized - with an absolute reversal of the past ideological positions - either by jurists (e.g. Amodio, 1989) or by a large number of criminologists (e.g., Bandini & Gatti, 1982; Ponti, 1989; Traverso, 1978), who were worried about the danger of submitting the defendant to a psychological expertise in a trial phase in which his responsibility for the crime has not yet been assessed (so violating, without a valid justification, the right to privacy), and believed that psychological expertise, utilizing elements which, by their very nature, lack any proof value, must be considered alien from the logic of the new penal procedural code.

Unlike the adult system, in the Italian juvenile justice system, the partnership between penal law and psychological sciences found a concrete exemplification in the institution in 1930 of the Juvenile Court and of a new legislative arrangement that provided juvenile justice with a whole series of correctional interventions. In such a new normative system, experts were introduced whose function within the "observation centers" consists "in carrying out the scientific examination of the juvenile, determining his/her personality and indicating the most adequate means for ensuring resocialization" (art. 8 R.D.L. 20/7/1934 n. 10404). In 1956, by approval a reform law, human sciences reached their greatest expansion within the Italian juvenile criminal justice system through the strong success of a correctional, therapeutic ideology that availed itself of diversified rehabilitative facilities that should have matched old total institutions (asylums). The various dispositions of the new reform law aimed to magnify, on the basis of a positivistic frame of reference, a close relationship between personality traits and causes of deviant behavior, in the perspective of an approach to deviance inspired by the criteria of the medical model. Within the scheme of such model, the law enforced in 1956 exalts particularly a diagnostic model in which the activity of the psychologist is directed to the evaluation of the capacity for understanding and free will in the juvenile, that is, the evaluation of so-called imputability, in order to mitigate the harshness of penal sanctions. This evaluation, beyond any reference to psychopathological parameters, is tied up to a chronological element and, then, to the assessment by the expert of the different phases of individual development and the different levels of individual biological, psychological, and social maturation. The above-mentioned model flourished for many years up to the late 1960s, when in the light of either new theoretical theories (like symbolic interactionism or naturalism) or the results of international evaluative research, both clinical and statistical (e.g., Ash, 1949; Danet, 1964; Lipton, Martinson, & Wilks, 1975; Stoller & Geertsma, 1965), it began to be seriously criticized. Criticisms particularly attacked correctional total institutions, by recognizing that their real function had been that of reinforcing and strengthening the action of labeling performed by police and the judiciary, thus favoring a persistent criminal life-style for stigmatized juveniles. Scientists and social workers realized that personality observation was of little utility, since it could not be followed by effective therapeutic proposals (e.g., La Greca, 1966; Vella, 1965). As a consequence, the activity of the expert (either psychologist or psychiatrist) was judged totally useless, empirical research having demonstrated that the major part of the technician's energies were not aimed at obtaining real benefits for the juvenile under examination but at justifying the presence of the technician in that area (e.g., Canepa, Bandini, & Traverso, 1973). That tremendous criticisms to the correctional system for juveniles gave rise to the request for further reform, matched by the demand placed on technicians and social scientists of setting up adequate instruments to reduce juvenile delinquency, instruments more and more far removed from a clinical and therapeutic approach, and increasingly centered upon the deterrent effect of penal sanctions. Thus, recently, neoclassical approach has reemerged that has reconsidered the whole problem of imputability and responsibility in juveniles and has reexamined the meaning of penal sanctions within the criminal justice system (e.g., De Leo, 1982). In such a conflictual context, the position of psychologists is a difficult one, and their possible choices do not appear easy to take. It is difficult for psychologists or clinical criminologists to accept the neoclassical approach, which emphasizes the positive role of penal sanctions. In fact, on one hand, clinicians clearly perceive the justified risk of falling back, once more, into a more repressive, punitive system; on the other hand, clinicians are well aware of the damages caused by the old correctional system and of the risks of continuing to use the traditional therapeutic, correctional model in the field of juvenile justice. To solve such a conflictual, double-sided situation, a new set of dispositions became law in 1977 (D.P.R. n. 616/1977) which devolved upon local authorities responsibility for social intervention. Whilst, before 1977, in all cases, the juvenile court entrusted minors to services with hierarchical and functional dependence on central government (Ministry of Justice); since 1977, minors involved in civil or administrative dispositions (where no crimes had been committed but the juvenile was considered to have a behavior or character problem) have been entrusted to local authority social services. As Gatti (1986) points out, in recent years, by following this innovative legislative instrument, much was done at the local level to remove juveniles from the penal system, in an attempt to separate, as much as possible, punitive from therapeutic intervention (characteristically these two types of intervention were mixed up in the old correctional, rehabilitative system) and to provide young offenders with the very same community programs used for all juveniles in need of help for any reason. During the same period, the number of juvenile in prison fell markedly and a considerable process of de facto depenalization developed. In light of such new models, technicians would no longer have the task of performing a direct intervention on a given juvenile, but they would provide a function of mediation and negotiation between those who run social services and the juveniles themselves. Paradoxically, the recent approval of the new penal procedural law, and particularly the dispositions of its special section dedicated to juveniles, seem to run strongly counter to the attainment of the above-mentioned goals, rebuilding within the system a whole series of measures stressing the ambiguous mixture of therapy and punishment (e.g., Gatti & Verde, in press; Traverso & Manna, 1989). It is too early to formulate a correct prognostic assessment of what will happen in the future; only concrete, future experiences will clarify the actual most alarming questions.

References

Altavilla, E. (1949). *Il delinquente. Trattato di psicologia criminale*. Napoli: Morano.
Altavilla, E. (1950). *Elementi di antropologia criminale*. Napoli: Morano.
Altavilla, E. (1953). *Psicologia giudiziaria*. Torino: Unione Tipografico-Editrice Torinese.
Amodio, E. (1989). Perizia e consulenza tecnica nel quadro probatorio del nuovo processo penale. In F. De Fazio, & G. Beduschi (Eds.), *La medicina legale ed il nuovo codice di procedura penale* (pp. 113-121). Milano: Giuffrè.
Angiolella, G. (undated). *Manuale di antropologia criminale*. Milano: F. Vallardi.
Ash, P. (1949). The reliability of psychiatric diagnoses. *Journal of Abnormal and Social Psychology, 44,* 272-280.
Bandini, T., & Gatti, U. (1972). *Dinamica familiare e delinquenza giovanile*. Milano: Giuffrè.
Bandini, T., & Gatti, U. (1974). *Delinquenza giovanile. Analisi di un processo di stigmatizzazione e di esclusione*. Milano: Giuffrè.
Bandini, T., & Gatti, U. (1982). Perizia psichiatrica e perizia criminologica: Riflessioni sul ruolo del perito nell'ambito del processo penale. *Rivista Italiana di Medicina Legale, 2,* 321-336.
Bandini, T., Gatti, U., & Traverso, G.B. (1983). *Omicidio e controllo sociale. I risultati di una ricerca*. Milano: Franco Angeli.
Battaglini, E. (1955). L'indagine sulla personalità del soggetto attivo del reato nel processo penale. *La Scuola Positiva, 62,* 495-510.
Becker, H.S. (1966). *Outsiders*. New York: The Free Press.
Canepa, G. (1953). *Il concetto di personalità nei suoi aspetti filosofici, biologici e medico-legali*. Roma: Edizioni dell'Ateneo.
Canepa, G. (1974). *Personalità e delinquenza. Problemi di antropologia criminale e di criminologia clinica*. Milano: Giuffrè.
Canepa, G. (1981). La perizia sulla personalità dell'imputato. Problemi criminologici e medico-legali. *Rassegna di Criminologia, 12,* 23-37.
Canepa, G. (1982). L'attività di insegnamento e di ricerca della criminologia in Italia. Considerazioni preliminari. In G. Canepa, & P. Paradiso (Eds.), *La criminologia Italiana. Insegnamento e ricerca* (pp. 11-26). Siracusa: I.S.I.S.C.
Canepa, G. (1987). La perizia sulla personalità dell'imputato. Problemi criminologici e medico-legali. In G.B. Traverso (Ed.), *Crimonologia e psichiatria forense. Momenti di riflessione dottrinale e applicativa* (pp. 385-397). Milano: Giuffrè.
Canepa, G., Bandini, T., & Traverso, G.B. (1973). La rieducazione in istituto e in libertà. Ricerca longitudinale su un gruppo di 155 minori antisociali. *Rassegna di Criminologia, 4,* 5-53.
Carmignani, G. (1831). *Teoria delle leggi della sicurezza sociale*. Pisa: Nistri.
Carrieri, F. (1987). *Elementi di criminologia clinica e psicopatologia forense*. Bari: Adriatica editrice.
Danet, B.N. (1964). Prediction of mental illness in college students on the basis of "non psychiatric" MMPI profiles. *Journal of Consulting Psychology, 68,* 136-144.
Debuyst, C. (1975). Les nouveax courants dans la criminologie contemporaine. La mise en cause de la psychologie criminelle et de son object. *Revue de Droit Penal et de Criminologie, 10,* 845-862.
De Leo, G. (1982). Oltre la prescrizione di maturità-immaturità. In M.P. Cuomo, G. La Greca, & L. Viggiani (Eds.), *Giudici, psicologici e delinquenza giovanile* (pp. 85-91). Milano: Giuffrè.
De Leo, G., & Cuomo, M.P. (1983). *La delinquenza minorile come rappresentazione sociale. Ipotesi interpretative e di ricerca*. Venezia: Marsilio.
De Roberto, G. (1980). Il rilievo del momento psicologico nel giudizio penale. In C. Serra (Ed.), *Psicologia e giustizia* (pp. 347-362). Milano: Giuffrè.
De Vincentiis, G., Callieri, B., & Castellani, A. (1972). *Trattato di psicopatologia e psichiatria forense*. Roma: Il pensiero scientifico.
Di Tullio, B. (1945). *Trattato di antropologia criminale*. Roma: Criminalia.
Ennis, P. (1967). *Criminal victimization in the United States. Field Survey II*. The President's Commission on Law Enforcement and Administration of Justice. Washington, DC.: U.S. Government Printing Office.

Ferracuti, F., & Wolfgang, M.E. (1966). *Il comportamento violento. Moderni aspetti criminologici.* Milano: Giuffrè.
Ferri, E. (1892). *Sociologia criminale.* Torino: Fratelli Bocca.
Fornari, U. (1989). *Psicopatologia e psichiatria forense.* Torino: Unione Tipografico-Editrice Torinese.
Foucault, M. (1981). L'évolution de la notion d'"individu dangereux" dans la psychiatrie légale. *Déviance et Sociétè, 5,* 403-422.
Franchini, A., & Introna, F. (1972). *Delinquenza minorile.* Padova: Cedam.
Garofalo, R. (1885). *La criminologia.* Torino: Fratelli Bocca.
Gatti, U. (1986). La prevenzione della delinquenza giovanile a Genova. Analisi di un'esperienza. *Rassegna di Criminologia, 17,* 225-251.
Gatti, U., & Verde, A. (in press). The dividing line between punishment and help: New questions, old answers. Observations on the new juvenile penal procedural code in Italy.
Gemelli, A. (1946). *La personalità del delinquente nei suoi fondamenti biologici e psicologici.* Milano: Giuffrè.
Goffman, E. (1961). *Asylums. Essays on the social situation of mental patients and other inmates.* New York: Doubleday & Co.
Gulotta, G. (1979). La psicologia giuridica: Un'introduzione. *Ricerche di psicologia, 3,* 11-22.
Gulotta, G., (Ed.)(1987). *Trattato di psicologia giudiziaria nel sistema penale.* Milano: Giuffrè.
Harrè, R., & Secord, P.F. (1972). *The explanation of social behaviour.* Oxford: Basil Blackwell.
La Greca, G. (1966). Per una migliore utilizzazione dei pensionati di semi-libertà. *Esperienze di Rieducazione, 10,* 6-18.
Lipton, D., Martinson, R., & Wilks, J. (1975). *The effectiveness of correctional treatment: A survey of treatment evaluation studies.* New York: Praeger.
Lombroso, C. (1876). *L'uomo delinquente.* Milano: Hoepli
Longo, M. (1906). *Psicologia criminale.* Torino: Fratelli Bocca.
Mailloux, N. (1962). Genèse et signification de la conduite "antisociale". *Revue Canadienne de Criminologie, 4,* 103-115.
Mead, G.H. (1934). *Mind, self and society.* Chicago: The University of Chicago Press.
Nivoli, G.C., & Sanna, N. (1982). Riflessioni sulle attuali linee di sviluppo delle teorie e delle scuole criminologiche. In G. Canepa, & P. Paradiso (Eds.), *La criminologia italiana. Insegnamento e ricerca* (pp.59-81). Siracusa: I.S.I.S.C.
Pende, N. (1939). *Trattato di biotipologia umana.* Milano: Vallardi.
Pinatel, J. (1963). *Criminologie (Traitè de Droit Pènal et de Criminologie, by P. Bouzat & J. Pinatel, tome III).* Paris: Dalloz.
Ponti, G.L. (1989). Il contributo della criminologia al nuovo processo penale. In F. De Fazio, & G. Beduschi (Eds.), *La medicina legale ed il nuovo codice di procedura penale* (pp. 285-295). Milano: Giuffrè.
Ponti, G.L. (1990). *Compendio di criminologia.* Milano: Raffaello Cortina.
Portigliatti Barbos, M., & Marini, G. (1964). *La capacità di intendere e di volere nel sistema penale italiano.* Milano: Giuffrè.
Radzinovicz, L. (1964). *Alla ricerca della criminologia.* Milano: Giuffrè.
Romagnosi, G.D. (1833). *Genesi del diritto penale.* Prato: Giusti.
Rossi, P. (1949). *Parere sul progetto del codice penale.* Genova: L'Italica.
Salvini, A. (1982). La psicologia nei suoi rapporti con la giustizia penale: appunti per un cambiamento paradigmatico. In M.P. Cuomo, G. La Greca, & L. Viggiani (Eds.), *Giudici, psicologici e delinquenza giovanile* (pp. 5-21). Milano: Giuffrè.
Stoller, R.J., & Geertsma, R.H. (1965). The consistency of psychiatrists' clinical judgments. *Journal of Nervous and Mental Disease, 137,* 58-63.
Traverso, G.B. (1977). Relazioni tra malattia mentale e delinquenza. Risultati di una ricerca su 325 ex degenti. *Neuropsichiatria, 33,* 127-154.
Traverso, G.B. (1978). Devianza, ideologia del trattamento criminologico, limiti della programmazione socio-sanitaria. *Neuropsichitria, 34,* 259-269.
Traverso, G.B., & Verde, A. (1981). *Criminologia critica. Delinquenza e controllo sociale nel modo di produzione capitalistico.* Padova: Cedam.

Traverso, G.B., & Manna, P. (1988). La risposta istituzionale ai minori autori di reato: I risultati di una ricerca sul territorio di competenza della Corte di Appello di Genova. *Rassegna di Criminologia, 19*, 277-308.

Traverso, G.B., Manna, P., & Marzi A. (1988). La perizia psichiatrica nei processi per omicidio. *Rassegna di Criminologia, 19*, 309-332.

Traverso, G.B., & Manna, P. (1989). Note critiche a margine del nuovo codice di procedura penale nei procedimenti a carico di imputati minorenni. In F. De Fazio, & G. Beduschi (Eds.), *La medicina legale ed il nuovo codice di procedura penale* (pp. 413-426). Milano: Giuffrè.

Traverso, G.B., Manna, P., & Marugo, M.I. (1989). *La violenza carnale in Italia. Autori e vittime a confronto con una difficile giustizia.* Padova: Cedam.

Vella, G. (1965). Cultura e metodo degli psichiatri e degli psicologi. *Esperienze di Rieducazione, 12*, 28-35.

Wallerstein, J., & Wyle, C. (1947). Our law-abiding law-breakers. *Probation, 25*, 107-125.

Psychology and Law in Poland

Jan M. Stanik

Introduction

Because of the wide range of problems addressed, the individual topics in this chapter can only be treated in a most summary way. This is unavoidable, because I want to present all the different directions and spheres of application of psychology to law that have appeared in Poland and that are beginning to form a regular entity.

It must first be stressed that in Poland, as in many other countries, numerous names have emerged for this field of psychology that has moved toward cooperation with law. As these variations in nomenclature have not been accompanied by orderly definitions, there has been much terminological chaos. The same subjects of study have received various names, or, in contrast, the same name (in most cases, forensic psychology) has been given to many areas of applied psychology (Stanik, 1985).

When reviewing the literature from both Central and Eastern Europe as well as the West, I concluded that there was much inconsistency, much interference, and fragmentation in the attempts to label the study and application of psychology to law (i.e., most frequently through the incorrect use of the term "forensic psychology"). This results from the failure to apply qualification criteria that are appropriate for legislation, and it has led to a widening, mosaic-like pattern of psychological notions and a lack of terminological order.

Therefore I decided to use legislative criteria to relate various directions of psychological study to law (see Table 1). Table 1 presents only applied functions of psychology and names them appropriately. In each case, I have omitted stressing the research functions of psychology at particular levels.

The Level of Law Formulation and the Social Functioning of Legal Rules

The theoretical and legislative field

In brief, the theoretical and legislative level is related to the process and stages of creating law, that is, formulating definitions to be used by law, elaborating the principles according to which these definitions are interpreted on the basis of law, and - in the legislation process - to specific regulations in particular branches of law, that is, to the creation of a system of legal rules assigning legal relationships between the subjects of law in order to regulate the activities of both institutions and private individuals.

Changes within the sphere of legal doctrines and legal rules are very, very slow. Alongside earlier philosophical, religious, political, and sociological influences on the historical process of change, the influence of psychology can be seen especially since the 19th century: for example, the evolution of views and legal rulings concerning the credibility of witness testimony, regulations on testimony methods for children and the elderly (Stanik, 1985), and the whole set of legal regulations on the criminal responsibility of minors and adolescents (Stanik & Przbyla, 1981). Another group of examples concerns the evaluation of regulations dealing with crimes committed under states of strong emotional arousal or while acting in a state of limited or nonexistent accountability and so forth.

Table 1: Links Between Psychology and Law.

Level of law	Function of psychology	Branch of psychology
Formulation of laws and social functioning of legal rules a) Theoretical-legislative field	Ideocreative	Psychology of law
b) Social psychological filed in which legal rules function	Research	Social psychology/psychology of law
Prosecution and jurisdiction (in criminal and civil law) a) Legal-professional field	Reform	Forensic psychology
b) Field of knowledge and special skillsd	Expertise	Clinical-forensic psychology
Executive law	Correction	Clinical-prison psychology Resocialization Psychotherapy
Preventive law	Prevention	Community psychology

A proper, scientifically valid analysis of the evolution of legal regulations accompanying the development and assimilation of psychological findings would require a very broad approach. This chapter can only stress some research directions and name some examples.

Within the given context, the characteristic function of psychology on the theoretical and legislative level of law is to generate ideas. This ideocreative function is seen in (a) its influence upon the evolution of and changes in the elements of defined doctrines (theory) of law and (b) along with other determinants, in the form of concrete rule solutions (codex) that link the views, findings, and conclusions of psychology to the contents of formulated legal rules.

The social-psychological field in which legal rules function

The social-psychological field in which legal rules function is very closely connected to the field discussed above. As created legal rules are an instrument for regulating social relationships and concrete patterns of human behavior, they have to act through human consciousness and people's various psychological mechanisms. However, in legal science, they are presented in a very abbreviated form or in anachronstic language that has no counterparts in contemporary psychology (Gierowski, 1984; Stanik, 1984).

For the individual, a legal rule is an external controller of behavior, and it can only develop into an internal regulative standard through the processes of socialization and internalization. The differences in the extent to which persons obey legal rules are the result of many highly complex, psychological, sociological, and political mechanisms that would require a separate broader chapter in their own right (see, e.g., Poznaniak, 1982; Reykowski, 1984; Seve, 1975; Stanik, 1980). However, it is worth mentioning here that compliance with legal rules is a measure of the effectiveness of law. This is an important problem for legislation, and psychology plays a major role in the scientific solution of this problem.

Apart from legalistic attitudes toward obeying the law, there are conformist, and opportunistic attitudes that have known psychological mechanisms (Borucka-Arctowa, 1973).

Hence, on the level of the social-psychological functioning of legal rules, psychology and its subdisciplines, namely, psychology of law and social psychology, fulfill important explanatory and investigative functions related to the effectiveness of law. Within this area, many authors (e.g., Kosewski, 1984; Poznaniak, 1982; Stanik, 1980; Wosinska, 1989) have worked on theoretical models and research strategies that may well be used to study the effectiveness of law on this level of interaction between psychology and law. The problem is to elicit interest in the results of these studies among the lawyers cooperating with psychologists, as they are the main addressees and "consumers" of the knowledge gained in this field by psychologists.

The Level of Prosecution and Jurisdiction (in Criminal and Civil Law)

The legal-professional field

This level covers a very wide sphere of activities performed by specialized state-controlled organs involved in the application of law. Basically, the application of law, that is, identifying and defining legal relations among subjects of law, is dealt with by the law courts. However, in order to define and investigate some given legal relation (e.g., an individual's felony, or regulating divorce for parents of minors), law courts must gather the information (or evidence) on which to base their judgment.

Evidence is gathered by various workers and not psychologists (e.g., police officers, public prosecutors, social workers). These workers should receive psychological training so that they can gather reliable information effectively and without making psychological mistakes (e.g., when interrogating witnesses: minors, adults, elderly; detecting lies, etc.; interrogating suspects: confrontation, identification, etc.).

Other problems on this level include: psychological characteristics of the work of judges; the expected personal advantages of judges; psychological analysis of law court sessions (Greer, 1971); and psychological factors influencing judgments.

The psychological problems encountered at this level of legal practice are themselves a separate field of psychological study that should be called forensic psychology. The results of these studies, gathered and canonized in the form of a separate body of psychological knowledge function to improve the effectiveness of law. Its contribution is that lawyers and other officers will use psychology in their daily routines with consequent improvements in legal practice and legal culture in the activities of prosecution agencies, law courts, attorneys, police, and other officials who apply law. Like teachers and managers (who are not psychologists), these persons can be taught psychology and learn to apply this knowledge in their professional activities and thus improve the effectiveness of their work.

Understood in this way, forensic psychology has to fulfill three purposes: (a) research, (b) education (teaching this branch of psychology to future lawyers and legislators), and (c) application (using the knowledge of forensic psychology in legal practice).

The field of knowledge and special skills

From a psychological perspective, this field in the practice of prosecution and jurisdiction is connected with the use of psychology as a specialized science for developing expertise for use in the investigative phase in courts of law (for criminal and civil processes) or other institutions (e.g., prosecutors' offices).

Accordingly, regulations of both civil and penal law are required that specify how the court of justice should ask an expert whether the circumstances influencing judgment require "specialist," for example, psychological knowledge.

Expertises given by psychologists predominantly (but not exclusively) concern their knowledge of clinical psychology (Haward, 1979; Stanik, 1984; Taylor, 1979). This is because many of the psychological problems in court proceedings are connected with problems in the well-documented sphere of abnormal psychology that relate to the widely studied field of clinical psychology among adults and children in Poland. The kinds of task that a psychologist meets in judicial practice vary, making it scarcely possible to provide a complete register of all possible variations. This is even more the case as psychology and clinical psychology in particular, is still extending its sphere of application (Bernstein & Nietzel, 1980; Stanik, 1984).

However, a study of the general and specific tasks shows that psychologists' activities can be classified according to specific processes. This provides the following areas of application in clinical and forensic psychology (in criminal and civil proceedings and before industrial tribunals where the role of the psychologist is clearly defined):

1. Defining and evaluating dimensions of antisocial behavior in juvenile delinquents and formulating recommendations for their resocialization and predictions of their social development.

2. Determining (together with psychiatrists) character and dimensions of personality disorder in adult offenders.

3. Determining the psychological conditions underlying the credibility of eyewitness testimony: For children and the elderly, persons with some mental disorder or retardation (innate or involutionary) or persons who have suffered psychological harm, such as victims of aggression.

4. Determining in divorce processes involving minors the degree of damage to a marriage and the ways of regulating custody and childrearing after divorce.

5. Determining psychological factors arising in custody cases, such as permission for under-18-year-olds to marry, child adoption, or appointing custodians for minors.

6. Determining (together with physicians) the degree of mental health impairment in cases involving pension or compensation claims resulting from vocational diseases or accidents.

7. In cases of alcoholism and drug addiction, determining (together with psychiatrists) the chronicity of the disease and the method of treatment.

8. In other legal situations: (a) In cases in which doubt exists as to the ability of an individual to participate in proceedings, there are two types of expertise: In the first, the problem is to evaluate whether persons are able to control their activities because their mental retardation or other psychological disturbances do not constitute a psychological disorder (or whether they can control their activities with the cooperation of a psychiatrist if they do have a psychlogical disorder). In the second type, the problem is to to evaluate the psychological state of a deceased person; for example (independently or together with psychiatrists), evaluating the psychological background (mental and motivational) of a testator in disputed cases. (b) In criminal proceedings, an example of a psychological expertise is the analysis of the work of persons who have committed suicide (their letters, diaries, etc.), when public or private prosecutors suspect that other persons have influenced the death. (c) A third type of situation is cases in which a person appears before judicial bodies claiming to have committed an offense, and doubt is expressed about the truth of this claim.

When compiling an expertise in relation to the problems listed above, a psycholgist may work alone or in cooperation with other psychologists or specialists from other spheres, such as psychiatrists, neurologists, pediatricians, educational scientists, or sociologists, depending on the kind of expertise required by authorities.

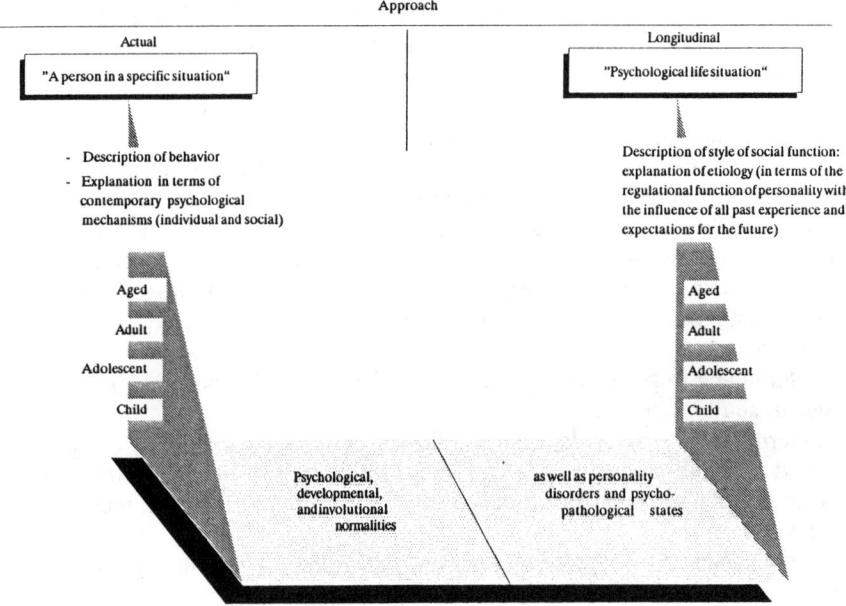

Figure 1: The Analysis of Human Behavior from the Perspective of Clinical Forensic Psychology.

Figure 1 presents a general model of the way psychologists approach these problems in their expertises. It must be stated here that the "Actual" approach is related to "in tempore criminis," while the "Longitudinal" approach (life-span-developmental) is linked to deeper and wider psychological diagnosis depicting the whole personality together with its etiology.

The Executive Level of Law

The executive level of law concerns the application of educational and corrective measures ordained by a court of law, in particular, penalties involving restricted liberty and deprivation of liberty (incarceration). The purpose of all these measures is resocialization. Resocialization is attempted through various educational and psychological programs (within the framework of existing law) such as labor, general and vocational instruction, sports, cultural activities, and so forth. Various forms of individual and group psychological treatment are also applied: psychodrama, psychotherapy, art therapy, and so forth. Last of all, certain persons (e.g., with language deficits or emotional disturbances) receive additional therapeutic and corrective measures mostly taken from the field of special education.

From a psychological perspective, the assumptions underlying the process of resocialization are directed toward rectifying antisocial personality and not just toward modifying behavior related to a narrowly conceived range of criminal acts. This is because psychology views criminal acts as being only one concrete expression of an underlying antisocial personality (of course, this only refers to intentional acts).

The measures imposed by a court of law (educational, corrective, punishment) are implemented either under ambulant conditions (supervision by a probation officer) or in closed institutions (corrective or penitentiary). Particularly in closed institutional conditions, many highly complex social-psychological problems arise that can seriously impede the organized process of resocialization and, in some cases, even cancel out its effects. These can include such phenomena as the existence of a criminal subculture with specific, dehumanizing stratification into "strong men" and "fools;" many cases of aggression and self-injury; sexual deviance; tattooing; the use of criminal slang; and so forth. Studies of these problems in Poland have produced a rich literature. The knowledge gathered through these studies constitutes a separate subdiscipline within the framework of clinical psychology known as clinical-prison psychology or resocialization psychology. It corresponds with the views expressed by leading American psychologists like D. A. Bernstein and M. T. Nietzel (1980). As this brief presentation shows, it can clearly be concluded that psychology on the executive level of law performs corrective functions directed toward persons who have been sentenced to defined legal (penitentiary or corrective) measures.

The Level of Preventive Law

This sphere is connected to symptoms of social functioning in groups and individuals that indicate a risk of creating or deepening various forms of antisocial behavior in adults and juveniles. From the very narrow viewpoint of law, this level may be limited only to those risk factors that lead directly to the commitment of offenses. However, this would only be a formal and artifical limitation. For many years, numerous concepts in psychology, criminology, and many other sciences have pointed out that the backgrounds to crime have much deeper and wider social and individual roots than the sphere of human phenomena and acts that directly precede an offense. This is particularly true when the offense is connected to the functioning of a family or a local community.

From a psychological perspective, antisocial behavior is not just viewed as behavior bearing a criminal label but also as a much wider range of so-called disturbed behavior or behavior from the sphere of social pathology. For example, activities such as alcohol abuse, drug addiction, aggressiveness, or prostitution, which are, in themselves, not offenses in many countries, are both a focus of study and a goal of therapeutic and preventive treatment for psychology.

With reference to the above-mentioned view and the breadth of social backgrounds and reasons for criminality, this particularly concerns those antisocial behaviors, sometimes of a paracriminal nature, that are the direct source of future or present crime. Apart from treating them as causes of criminality, such behaviors are themselves symptoms of social pathology. This is because they lead to the degradation of the human personality and popularize socially harmful patterns of activity that are part of the epidemiology of social deviance in a broader sense.

Hence, on the one hand, we are dealing with certain sections of human behavior that are regulated by law (the tip of the iceberg), while, on the other hand, we are concerned with a very wide range of behaviors that are not crimes in the strict sense but are cases of antisocial behavior from the perspective of society (the rest of the iceberg).

These considerations lead to the conclusion that psychology should contribute to the identification of these risk factors and their liquidation from the sphere of social pathology, and, hence, simultaneously help to block any increase in the probability of criminal behavior. Such applied programs and research projects are already being implemented by community psychologists in the USA and Europe, including Poland. This context clearly reveals the preventive role of psychology in its relationship to law.

References

Bernstein, D. A., & Nietzel, M. T. (1980). *Introduction to clinical psychology.* New York: McGraw-Hill.

Borucka Arctowa, M. (1973). O spolecznym dzialaniu prawa [On social influence of law]. In A. Lopatka (Ed.), *Metody badania prawa.* Wroclaw-Warszawa: Ossolineum.

Gierowski, J.K. (1984). Diagnoza procesów motywacyjnych jako przedmiot opinii sadowo-psychologicznej [Motivation process diagnosis as the subject matter of psychological opinion for the court of law]. In J.M. Stanik (Ed.) *Problemy psychologiczno-psychiatryczne w ekspertyzack sadowych*(pp. 55-174). Katowice: University Press.

Greer, D.S. (1971). Anything but the truth? The reliability of testimony in criminal trials. *British Journal of Criminology, 11,* 131 - 154.

Haward, L.R.C. (1979). The psychologist as expert witness. In D.P. Farrington (Ed.), *Psychology, law and legal process* (pp. 67-82). Oxford: SSRC.

Kosewski, M. (1984). *Agresywni przestepcy [The aggressive offenders].* Warszawa: Wiedza Powszechna.

Poznaniak, W. (1982). *Zaburzenia w uspolescznieniu przestpców [Disturbances in offenders' socialization process].* Poznan: Univiversity Press.

Reykowski J. (1984). *Logika walki [The logic of struggle].* Warszawa: Ksiazka i Wiedza.

Sevé L. (1975). *Marksizm a teoria osobowosci [Marxism and theory of personality].* Warszawa: Ksiazka i Wiedza.

Stanik, J.M. (1980). *Asocjalnosc nieletnich przestepcow jako przedmi psychologicznej diagnozy klinicznej [Asociality of juvenile delinquences: A diagnosis in the terms of clinical psychology].* Warszawa: Wydawnictwo Prawnicze.

Stanik, J.M. (1984). Wspolpraca psychologiczno-psychiatryczna w ekspertyzach sadowych [Psychological-psychiatric co-operation in court of law expertises]. In J.M. Stanik (Ed.), *Problemy psychologiczno-psychiatryczne w ekspertyzach sadowych* (pp. 8-21). Katowice: University Press.

Stanik, J.M. (1985). Zwiazki psychologii z prawem [Connections of Psychology with Law]. *Przeglad Psychologiczny, 4*, 973-1001.

Stanik, J.M., & Przybyla H. (1981). *Opinia bieglo psychologa w sprawach karnych nieletnicht [The opinion of an expert psychologist in juvenile delinquente criminal cases]*. Katowice: Univ. Press

Taylor, A.J.W. (1979). Forensic psychology: Principles, practice and training. In W.A.M. Black, & A.J.W. Taylor (Eds.), *Deviant behaviour - New Zealand studies* (pp. 4-42). Heinemann Educational Books.

Wosinska W. (1989). *Niesprawiedliwosc w stosunkach interpersonalnych [Injustice in interpersonal relationships]*. Katowice: University Press.

Subject Index

Amplification method 502-504
Archetypes 501-504
Archival studies 268-270
Attribution style 424-434, 436-439

Chaos theory 55-60
Child abuse
  case study 356-357
  in Canada 399-402
  in Germany 379-384
  in Israel 385-390
  in Norway 393-398
  in the United Kingdom 365-373
  in the USA 404-409
  interview techniques 361-362
  conceptual frameworks 345-350
  social denial 345-350
Child protection
  decisions 352-355
  errors 352-359
  in Israel 385-390
Child witnesses 360-363
  in Canada 399-402
  in Germany 379-384
  in Israel 385-390
  in Norway 393-398
  in the United Kingdom 365
  in the USA 404-409
Child's testimony 335-342
  content analysis 335-342
  credibility 345-350
  reliability/validity 335
  statement analysis 362
Children's legal position 467-472
Civil law 546
  child's position 467-471
  expert evidence 473-475
Cognitive interview 302-304
Competency criteria for liability 477-489
Content analyses 328-332, 335-342
Conviction 261-262
Correctional treatment 131-142
  effectiveness 133-142, 163-170

Credibility 219-232, 237-239
Crime prevention 193-201
Crimes of passion 55
Criminal behavior 22-33, 535-540
  and drug use 105-110
  explanation 27-30, 37-41, 55-57, 76-85
  prediction 37-42
Criminal law 546-552
Criminal statistics 193-196, 376-378
Criminal suspects 212-218, 228-232, 253-261

Decision-making
  juridical 413-420, 424-433, 435-438
Delictual capabilities 477-489
Delinquency
  juvenile 62-73, 144-160
  officially registered 193-195
  self-reported 195-197
  treatment 163-172
Donation of organs 491-499
Drug therapy 175-181
Drug use 105-110, 175-181

Economic situation 76-85
Evaluation research 26-27, 131-143, 144-160, 163-173, 175-181
Expert evidence 447-462
Expert witnesses 376, 396-397, 447
  in British courts 447-462
  in German courts 379-384
Expertise 451-462, 473-476
Eyewitness report 321-326, 335-342
  accuracy 324-325
  confidence 290-300, 418-419
  content analysis 328-332, 335-342
Eyewitness research 207-208, 265-273
Eyewitness testimony
  accuracy 282, 309-315, 418-419
  confidence 290-300, 418-419
  methodological review 265-272
  race/gender effects 312-315
  reliability 312-315

Eyewitness testimony
   single case studies 270-272
   time of day effect 317-320

Facial recognition 309-315
Field studies 267-268
Fire-setting 477-489
Fitness to stand trial 184-185, 440-445
Forensic assessment 111-119, 182-190, 440-445, 509-518, 535-540

GAL programs in the USA 404-410
Gestures 245-248

Harm-doing 95-104

Identification of suspect 278, 286-291
Interview behavior 212-218, 240-252
Interview techniques 303
   child abuse cases 361-362
Interviewing strategies 218, 362

Judges'
   attribution style 424-433, 436-438
   decision-making 424-433
   profiles 436-438
   responsibility 424-433
Jung's psychology 501-504
Juridical decision-making 413-422, 424-433, 435-439
Juvenile delinquency 62-73, 144-160
   treatment 131-142, 144-160

Law breaking 95-104
Legal decision-making 413-422, 424-433, 435-439
   methodological issues 413-422
Legal position of children 467-472
Legal procedures
   in British courts 365-373
   in Canadian courts 399-403
   in German courts 374-384
   in Israelian courts 385-390
   in the USA 404-410
Legal psychology
   development 3-10, 509-518, 519-524, 526-533, 535-542
   experimental simulations 415-421
   in Germany 509-542
   in Italy 535-542
   in Poland 546-552
   in Spain 526-533
   perspectives 11-18

Legal psychology
   research strategies 413-422
   systemization 10-11
Legal systems for organ donation 495-497
Liability
   competency criteria 477
Lineups
   many-person 286-291
   one-person/many-person 275-284
   target-absent/-present 276-284
Living standard 76-85

Memory
   accuracy 287-289, 293-300, 324-325, 328-332
   arousal effects 317-320
   enhancement 302-308
   performance 319-320
   time of day 317-320
Meta-analysis 133-142, 163-172
Minors's delictual capabilities 477-489
Misinformation effect 292-300
Mock juries 435-438
Modified test 294-300

Offenders 35-49, 111-120
   incarcerated 105-107, 121-127
   juvenile 144-160
   mentally disordered 182-191, 440-445
   substance abuse 105-109
Offending
   prevention and treatment 42-50, 193-200
Organ donation 491-499

Perception differences 321-326
Photographic presentation 287-291
Police 205-210
   interrogation 219-232, 240-251, 255-261
   interview techniques 212-218, 234-238
   officers 234-238
   training 206
Post event information 292-300
Prediction of criminal behavior 37-42
Prevention
   general 193-201
Prosecution 261, 546-551
Protective factors 63-75
Psycho-analysis 519-525
Psychological diagnosis 111-119, 473-476
Psychological research 4-7, 22-30, 47-51, 207-211, 526-529
Psychological tests 111-119

Subject Index

Psychometrical diagnoses 111-119, 440-446, 477-489

Rape 121-127, 219-232, 234-239
Reality
   analysis 328-332
   criteria 336
   monitoring 328-332
Reckless driving 86-93
Recompense 477-489
Resilience 62-73
Right to silence 253-261
Risk factors 62-65
Road traffic incidents 86
Rule violation 76

Self-reported harm-doing 95-104
Sentencing behavior 424-433, 435-438
Sexual abuse
   historical review 345-350
   legal procedures 360-363
Sexual abuse cases
   characteristics 379-382
   current practice in Norway 393-398
   German statistics 376-378
   in Canada 399-402
   in Israel 385-390
   investigation practice 395-398
   in the United Kingdom 365-373

Sexual offenders 121-128
Simulations
   experimental 292-301, 413-422
Smiling 240-251
Social adjustment 122-123
Statement analysis 362
Stress 56-61, 62-73
   child witnesses 366-369
   reduction model 370
Substance abuse 105-110
Suspect identification 275-284, 286-291

Tailgating 86
Traffic offender 86-93
Treatment 175-181, 182-190
   effectiveness 42-48, 134-142, 144-160, 163-173
   modality 136-138

Willingness for organ donation 493
Witness recall 302-308
   accuracy 319-320
   confidence 290-300, 418-419
Witness suggestibility 292-300
Witness testimony
   research strategies 265-274, 418-419

Youth interrogator 386-387